D1327715

THE DEVELOPMENT OF LANGUAGE

The Development of Language

edited by

Martyn Barrett
University of Surrey, UK

Psychology Press
a member of the Taylor & Francis group

Copyright © 1999 by Psychology Press Ltd, a member of the Taylor & Francis group
All rights reserved. No part of this publication may be reproduced, stored in a
retrieval system, or transmitted in any form or by any means, electronic,
mechanical, photocopying, recording or otherwise, without permission in writing
from the publisher.

Psychology Press Ltd, Publishers
27 Church Road
Hove
East Sussex
BN3 2FA
UK

British Library Cataloguing-in-Publication Data

A catalogue record for this book is available from the British Library

ISBN: 0-86377-846-1 (hbk)

ISSN: 1368-2563

Typeset by Graphicraft Limited, Hong Kong
Printed and bound in the UK by Biddles Ltd, Guildford and King's Lynn, UK.

Dedication

In loving memory of my dear mother,
always a wonderful source of inspiration

Contents

12. Language development in atypical children   311

13. Specific language impairment   349

14. Towards a biological science of language development   373

List of contributors

Martyn Barrett, Department of Psychology, University of Surrey, Guildford, Surrey GU2 5XH, UK.

John D. Bonvillian, Department of Psychology, Gilmer Hall, University of Virginia, Charlottesville, VA 22903-2477, USA.

Patricia J. Brooks, The College of Staten Island, City University of New York, 2800 Victory Blvd., Staten Island, NY 10314, USA.

Esther Dromi, School of Education, Tel Aviv University, P.O. Box 39040, Ramat-Aviv, Tel Aviv 69978, Israel.

Paul Fletcher, Department of Speech and Hearing Sciences, University of Hong Kong, Prince Philip Dental Hospital, 34 Hospital Road, Hong Kong, China.

David Ingram, Department of Speech and Hearing Science, P.O. Box 870102, Arizona State University, Tempe, AZ 85287-0102, USA.

Stan A. Kuczaj II, Department of Psychology, University of Southern Mississippi, Box 5025, Hattiesburg, MS 39406-5025, USA.

John L. Locke, Department of Human Communication Sciences, University of Sheffield, 18 Claremont Crescent, Sheffield S10 2TA, UK.

Michael Maratsos, Institute of Child Development, University of Minnesota, 51 East River Road, Minneapolis, MN 55455-0345, USA.

Barbara A. Pan, Harvard Graduate School of Education, Roy E. Larsen Hall, Appian Way, Cambridge, MA 02138, USA.

Kim Plunkett, Department of Experimental Psychology, University of Oxford, South Parks Road, Oxford OX1 3UD, UK.

Vasudevi Reddy, Department of Psychology, University of Portsmouth, King Henry Building, King Henry I Street, Portsmouth PO1 2DY, UK.

Suzanne Romaine, Merton College, University of Oxford, Oxford OX1 4JD, UK.

Graham Schafer, Department of Psychology, University of Reading, Earley Gate, Reading RG6 6AL, UK.

Catherine E. Snow, Harvard Graduate School of Education, Roy E. Larsen Hall, Appian Way, Cambridge, MA 02138, USA.

Helen Tager-Flusberg, Center for Research on Developmental Disorders, Eunice Kennedy Shriver Center, 200 Trapelo Road, Waltham, MA 02452, USA.

Michael Tomasello, Max Planck Institute for Evolutionary Anthropology, Inselstrasse 22, D-04103 Leipzig, Germany.

Studies in Developmental Psychology
Published Titles

Series Editor
Charles Hulme, University of York, UK

The Development of Intelligence
  Mike Anderson (Ed.)
The Development of Language
  Martyn Barrett (Ed.)
The Social Child
  Anne Campbell & Steven Muncer (Eds)
The Development of Memory in Childhood
  Nelson Cowan (Ed.)
The Development of Mathematical Skills
  Chris Donlan (Ed.)
The Development of Social Cognition
  Suzanne Hala (Ed.)
Perceptual Development: Visual, Auditory, and Speech Perception in Infancy
  Alan Slater (Ed.)

CHAPTER ONE

An introduction to the nature of language and to the central themes and issues in the study of language development

Martyn Barrett
University of Surrey, Guildford, UK

This book is about the development of language in children. At first glance, it may be unclear why an entire book is required to cover this topic. After all, children appear to acquire language with considerable ease, with little or no explicit teaching, and relatively few children seem to experience any noticeable difficulties in doing so. However, it is very easy to underestimate the nature of the language acquisition process, and the sheer complexity of the developmental task in which the language-learning child is engaged. In order to appreciate just how complex this task is, we first need to appreciate something about the nature of language itself.

THE NATURE OF LANGUAGE

Spoken language can be characterised as a code in which spoken sound is used in order to encode meaning (Fig. 1.1).

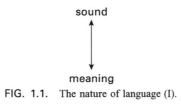

sound

meaning

FIG. 1.1.   The nature of language (I).

1

The level of meaning: Some basic distinctions

To start at the level of meaning, linguists use the term **semantics** to refer to the study of meaning (Lyons, 1977). Meaning may be expressed not only through spoken sounds but also through pictures, conventional signs, objects, etc. (Barthes, 1967; Giraud, 1975). However, because the present book is concerned with language rather than with any of these other symbolic systems, the term "semantics" is generally used throughout this book in the more restricted sense to denote the study of the meanings which are encoded in language.

There are various components in any given sentence which contribute to the meaning of that sentence. Firstly and most obviously, the words which make up the sentence contribute to its meaning. Therefore, if a word in a sentence is changed, the meaning of the sentence changes:

1. *The boys played soccer.*
2. *The boys played cricket.*

In fact, from a semantic point of view, the word itself is not always the smallest unit of meaning in a sentence. For example, in the above sentences, the word *boys* actually contains two meaning units, *boy* and *-s*, where the *-s* contributes the meaning that more than one boy played the game. Similarly, the word *played* consists of two meaning units, *play* and *-ed*.

These smallest units which contribute to the meaning of the sentence are called **morphemes** rather than words. Some morphemes, such as *boy*, *play*, etc. can be used on their own; these are called free morphemes. Other morphemes, such as *-s* and *-ed*, cannot be used on their own; these are called bound morphemes. Sometimes, several bound morphemes can be attached simultaneously to a single free morpheme; for example, the word *untimeliness* contains four morphemes (cf. *time*, *timely*, *untimely*, *untimeliness*). The study of morphemes, and of how morphemes are combined with one another to form larger word structures, is called **morphology** (Matthews, 1974).

However, not all words that contain multiple meaning components can be decomposed into individual morphemes as simply as the above examples suggest. For example, the word *ran* is related to the word *run*, and this relationship is similar to that between *played* and *play*, but *ran* cannot be decomposed into two morphemes in the same way as *played*.

The situation is further complicated by the fact that the term "word" itself is actually ambiguous. Thus, we can say that the words *found* and *find* are two different words, but at the same time we can say that they are both different forms of the same underlying word. In order to overcome the problems which can be caused by this ambiguity of the term "word", linguists sometimes call the underlying vocabulary items **lexemes** or **lexical items**, and they call the sound patterns **word-forms** (Kempson, 1977; Lyons, 1977). Notice that different word-forms can be based upon the same lexeme (as in the case of *found* and *find*), and the same word-form can be based upon different lexemes. For example, the word-forms *ran* in the following two sentences are based upon two different lexemes which have different meanings:

3. *He ran the 100 metres in 10.9 seconds.*
4. *He ran the office for 17 months.*

There is an enormous number of lexemes which make up any given language which the speakers of that language can draw upon in order to construct sentences. The total set of lexemes which make up any given language is called the **lexicon** of that language.

However, words are not the only things that contribute to the meaning of a sentence:

5. *Jack kicked Jill.*
6. *Jill kicked Jack.*

Both of these two sentences contain exactly the same morphemes, word-forms and lexemes, yet these two sentences express different meanings. This difference in meaning arises not from the meaning units themselves but from the different sequencing of these units in the two sentences. The study of the word sequences within sentences, and of the rules which govern such sequences, is called **syntax**.

Sometimes, the use of a particular sequence of words in a sentence requires the obligatory use of certain morphemes in order to make the sentence grammatically correct. For example, in the following two sentences, the different sequences of words require the use of different morphemes:

7. *Jack is kissing Jill.*
8. *Jill is being kissed by Jack.*

Because of this interdependence, the syntax and the morphology of a language are often studied together (Lyons, 1968). The term **grammar** refers to this combined enterprise, which encompasses the study of both word structures (morphology) and word sequences (syntax). Thus, grammar is the study of the rules which determine the permissible sequences of morphemes in the sentences that make up any given language. These grammatical rules dictate how the words and morphemes in that language can be combined, organised, and sequenced to produce well-formed and comprehensible sentences in order to encode particular meanings.

Consequently, our diagram summarising the nature of language can be expanded as in Fig. 1.2.

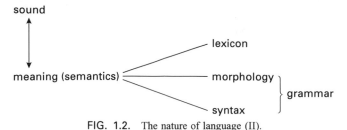

FIG. 1.2.   The nature of language (II).

The level of sound: Some basic distinctions

Turning now to the other principal component of language, linguists use the term **phonetics** to refer to the study of the physical speech sounds which are transmitted from speaker to hearer. These physical speech sounds can be studied from two different perspectives, articulatory phonetics and acoustic phonetics.

Articulatory phonetics focuses upon the movements of the larynx, pharynx, palate, jaw, tongue and lips which the speaker uses to produce a particular sound or sequence of sounds. A fundamental distinction here is that between vowels and consonants (Gimson, 1970). Vowels are sounds which are produced when there is no blockage or partial blockage in the vocal tract and the air escapes from the mouth or nose in a relatively unimpeded way; the different vowels are produced by changing the position and shape of the tongue, the position of the soft palate, and the shape of the lips. By contrast, consonants are sounds which involve either a complete blockage of the vocal tract, or a partial blockage such that the air makes an audible sound when it passes through the partial blockage; the different consonants are produced by varying the place of the blockage in the vocal tract, the type of blockage, the position of the soft palate, by whether the vocal cords are vibrating or not, etc.

The second way of examining the physical sound wave is in terms of its acoustic properties. In **acoustic phonetics**, the physical properties of the acoustic signal (in terms of frequency, amplitude, intensity, and duration) are investigated (Garman, 1990). Two important discoveries which have been made here are: (1) that there is no simple one-to-one mapping between the physical properties of the acoustic signal and individual speech sounds; and (2) that breaks between words in a sentence are not signalled by breaks in the acoustic signal. For these reasons, the difficulties facing the language-learning child, in segmenting and extracting information about the units of speech from the variable and continuous acoustic signal, are considerable.

In addition to articulatory and acoustic phonetics, the sounds which are used to encode meaning in language can be examined from a third perspective which takes the phoneme as the fundamental unit of analysis. A **phoneme** is the smallest unit of sound which functions to differentiate words from one another in a language. For example, in English, *pat*, *pet*, *pit*, *pot*, and *put* all vary in just one phoneme (the central vowel sound), and a change to this one phoneme changes the word into a different word which has a different meaning. Similarly, *chin*, *din*, *gin*, *shin*, and *thin* all vary in just one phoneme (the initial consonant sound: Note that phonemes do not correspond in a simple one-to-one fashion to the individual letters of the alphabet).

An individual phoneme may actually be articulated and encoded in the acoustic signal in a variety of ways. For example, the /p/ phoneme in the words *pin*, *spin*, and *nip* is articulated differently in each case, and the acoustic signal which encodes this phoneme also differs in each case. However, these articulatory and acoustic differences do not function in the English language to distinguish words from one other (thus, pronouncing the /p/ in *spin* in the same way as it is pronounced in *pin* does not change the word into another word with another meaning). Hence, these different sounds do not function as different phonemes, but as variants of the same phoneme; that is, these variations in pronunciation are functionally irrelevant.

Phonology is the study of the set of phonemes which make up any given language, and of how these phonemes may be combined, organised, and structured into syllables, morphemes, and words (Hyman, 1975). Phonology also studies how individual phonemes can change depending upon the other phonemes with which they are combined in a given word (e.g. in the English language, the phoneme /s/ in the word *house* becomes /z/ in the plural form *houses*).

Thus, whereas phonetics is the study of the full range of different sounds which are made using the human vocal apparatus, phonology is the study of just those particular categories of sound which are used in any given language in order to signal differences in meaning. Any individual language only uses a very small number of phonemes compared with the total number of different sounds which can be made. For example, the version of British English which is called Received Pronunciation contains just 24 consonant and 20 vowel phonemes (Gimson, 1970). Different languages (and different dialects of the same language) utilise different sets of phonemes. However, the total number of phonemes used in any one language represents only a minute fraction of the enormous number of different sounds which are actually produced through the vocal tract.

Our diagram summarising the nature of language can therefore now be expanded still further (Fig. 1.3).

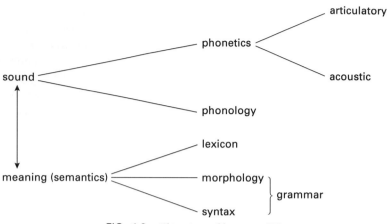

FIG. 1.3. The nature of language (III).

The level of context: Some basic distinctions

So far, we have considered language at the level of meaning and at the level of sound. However, language is never used in a vacuum but always in a particular behavioural, social, or linguistic context. And this context can affect the meaning which is derived from a sentence by a listener, it can affect the choices concerning semantic content which are made by the speaker, and it can affect the lexical, grammatical, and phonetic forms which are chosen by the speaker in order to express that semantic content. The study of this complex relationship between language and the contexts in which it is used is called **pragmatics** (Levinson, 1983).

The fact that context can influence the meaning which is derived by a listener from a sentence is clear from the following example:

9. *Can you open a window?*

This sentence could be produced by someone in a hot, stuffy room, addressed to another person who is close to a window. In this context, the sentence would be interpreted as a request for the person to open the window. However, exactly the same sentence might be produced by a medical practitioner asking a series of questions about the range of everyday actions which a physically disabled person can or cannot perform. In this context, the sentence would be interpreted as an interrogative yes/no question, which requires a verbal response instead. The meaning which is derived from this sentence is thus not only dependent upon its constituent morphemes and its grammatical structure. It is also dependent upon the context in which the sentence has been produced, with the context influencing the communicative function which is attributed to the sentence by the listener.

One of the core concerns of pragmatics is the description of the different **communicative functions** which language can serve in different contexts, and the linguistic means by which these functions are achieved. For example, language can be used to request an action, to request information, to give information, to assert something, to make a promise, to express emotion, etc. (Searle, 1969). And depending upon the context, different linguistic means may be used to achieve a particular communicative function.

Pragmatics also examines how the features of different contexts constrain or influence the content of what we say. Context can clearly constrain our choice of semantic content. For example, one would not normally start telling jokes at a funeral, or utter obscenities in the middle of a lecture. Context can also influence our choice of lexical, grammatical, and phonetic forms. For example, depending upon whether we are in a socially relaxed, informal context (such as a party) or a more formal context (such as a job interview), the words, grammatical structures, and pronunciations which we use can vary. Our choice of language can also be affected by the nature of our relationship with the person to whom we are speaking. For example, we can ask a person to do something for us in any one of a range of different ways, depending upon our relationship with that person:

10. *Close the door!*
11. *Close the door please.*
12. *Could you please close the door?*
13. *I'd be very grateful if you could close the door.*
14. *Would you mind awfully if I were to ask you to close the door?*

Furthermore, in some languages the degree of intimacy between speaker and listener can have an effect upon the choice of individual word-forms (for example, the use of *tu* and *vous* in French).

A great deal of language, of course, is produced either in the context of conversational exchanges with other people, or in the context of more extended stretches of discourse in which just one person speaks for a relatively long period of time (for example, when describing an event, telling a joke, giving an explanation, etc.). Conversation and discourse both require a variety of skills. For example, **conversation** requires individuals to take successive turns in adopting the roles of speaker and listener, to intermesh these roles appropriately and smoothly with one another, to adapt what is said to what the other person has just said, to adapt what is said to the type of relationship which exists between the participants in the conversation, etc. **Discourse** requires the speaker to link successive sentences appropriately and coherently, to take the listeners' perspective into account, to adapt the language that is used to the function of the communication, etc. Conversational analysis and discourse analysis are those sub-branches of pragmatics which are concerned with how coherence, relevance, sequential organisation, and adaptation are achieved by the speakers of a language during conversation and discourse.

Thus, our diagram summarising the nature of language finally takes on the form shown in Fig. 1.4.

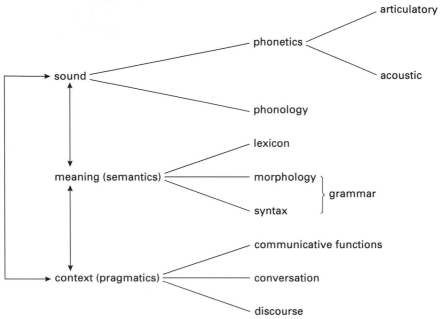

FIG. 1.4.   The nature of language (IV).

THE TASK FACING THE LANGUAGE-
LEARNING CHILD

From this account, it should be clear that language is an immensely complicated communicative system. And in order to master this system, the language-learning child has to: analyse and segment the acoustic signal of speech as it is produced by other people, and identify within that speech stream the units of the language which is being spoken at the multiple levels of phonemes, morphemes, words, and sentences; master all of the complexities of the intricate articulatory patterns necessary for producing individual phonemes and sequences of phonemes; master the set of phonological rules which govern how phonemes may be combined together to form syllables, morphemes, and words; acquire the enormous number of individual lexemes which constitute the lexicon of the language which is being learnt, and map all of these lexemes individually onto their appropriate meanings and word-forms; acquire the complex set of morphological and syntactic rules which dictate how the morphemes and words of the language can be combined, organised, and sequenced into grammatically well-formed sentences that encode particular meanings; master the various communicative functions of language, and how each one of these functions should be linguistically realised in different contexts; master the skills which are necessary for participation in a successful conversation, including turn-taking, topic-continuation, adaptation to the other, etc.; and master the skills which are necessary for producing discourse, including those required for coherence, appropriate sequential organisation, adaptation to the listener, etc. It is perhaps not surprising, then, that the language acquisition process is a very extended process which lasts for several years from infancy right through into early adolescence and beyond.

THE TOPICS COVERED BY THE CHAPTERS IN THIS BOOK

The remaining 13 chapters in this book provide detailed discussions and analyses of all of these various aspects of the language development process in children. Most of the chapters in this book discuss language development as it occurs in normally developing children. However, three chapters focus instead on particular groups of atypical children. As will be seen in these chapters, the developmental process as it occurs in these children can provide a unique opportunity for psychologists and linguists to explore empirically some of the theoretical claims that have been made about the language development process.

In the first of the chapters that follow, Vasudevi Reddy focuses on prelinguistic communication. The child's first words are not usually produced until about 12 months of age on average (Barrett, 1995; Dromi, this volume). In her chapter, Reddy examines how infants communicate with other people prior to this linguistic landmark. She reviews the different theoretical positions that exist on whether the prelinguistic communications of infants are or are not intentional, and she explores what it could be that drives human infants to communicate with other people. She also provides a comprehensive overview of the principal landmarks in the development of prelinguistic communication during infancy. In this overview, she examines neonatal preferences and imitative abilities, the communication of affects at 2–3 months, the emergence of action routines and games which occurs by about 6 months of age, the means which infants use between 8 and 12 months of age to manipulate the attention of others (including giving objects, showing-off, and teasing), and finally the emergence of proto-language, especially proto-imperatives (that is, the use of other people as a means to obtaining desired objects) and proto-declaratives (that is, the use of objects as a means of obtaining other people's attention). Reddy argues that there are numerous continuities which underlie these various developmental changes (for example, continuities in intentionality, and in the motivation to engage with other people's emotional states). She also argues that these continuities are important not just for explaining the origins of language, but also for explaining the nature and origins of human sociality itself.

One of the interesting points to emerge from Reddy's review is that several of the communicative functions for which language is later used (e.g. expressing affects to other people, getting people to do things, directing other people's focus of attention, etc.) are already in place and being fulfilled through non-linguistic means in infancy, prior to the acquisition of language itself. However, the subsequent acquisition of language provides the child with a much more complex and elaborated system for fulfilling these communicative functions. In addition, there are several further communicative functions which are not yet in place by the end of infancy, and which, by virtue of their inherently linguistic nature, cannot be fulfilled except through language (e.g. asserting propositions, making promises, etc.). These further pragmatic developments which occur beyond the end of infancy are discussed in a later chapter by Pan and Snow.

Whereas Reddy's chapter explores how infants communicate with other people before they begin to use language, Chapter 3 by Kim Plunkett and Graham Schafer examines how prelinguistic infants analyse and segment the acoustic stream of speech to identify the phonemes, syllables, and words of the language in their environment. They review the evidence which has now been collected on these matters from a variety of sources, including experimental studies, brain imaging studies, and computational studies. This evidence suggests that pre-linguistic infants are remarkably adept at detecting both phonemes and word boundaries in the acoustic signal. Plunkett and Schafer also examine how infants first begin to map the word-forms which they identify in the speech stream onto meanings. How words are mapped onto meanings, and how this process changes as the child gets older, is discussed further in later chapters by Dromi and Kuczaj.

Chapter 4 by David Ingram also examines language at the level of sound, but the focus of his chapter is upon the young child's ability to produce phonemes rather than to perceive them. Ingram explores the phonological structure of children's first words, and how this early phonological system subsequently develops. The first words which are produced by children have a simple syllabic structure and are based upon a small inventory of vowels and consonants. Ingram argues that children begin their phonological acquisition at this early point in their development, and that they do so using some of the basic properties of the phonological system of the adult language which is being learnt (the alternative view is that children simply learn their earliest words from the speech input as unanalysed holistic phonetic sequences of sound). Ingram argues that subsequent development consists of the further elaboration of this initial phonological system. This view is consistent with the findings reviewed by Plunkett and Schafer in the preceding chapter, which show that infants are remarkably adept at perceiving and extracting phonological information from the speech stream prior to the time when the first words are produced.

Chapters 5 and 6 focus on the lexical development of the child. In Chapter 5, Esther Dromi examines the development of the lexicon during what is called the "one-word" or "single-word" period of language development. This period begins with the appearance of the first words and lasts until the emergence of multi-word speech (which typically happens round about 18–24 months of age; Peters, 1995; Tomasello and Brooks, this volume). Dromi provides a comprehensive overview of the literature on: the size of the early lexicon and the rate at which children acquire new words; the types of words which children acquire during this period, and the typical meanings of these early words; the processes which are involved in acquiring the meanings of words, particularly as indicated by the types of errors which children make in their early use of words; and the role of context and linguistic input in the establishment of early word meanings. In addition, Dromi reviews three different models of early word meaning acquisition which highlight different theoretical assumptions about how children might acquire the meanings of words: the multi-route model (Barrett, 1986), which attempts to explain lexical-developmental changes in terms of the changes which occur to the child's underlying semantic representations; the syntactic bootstrapping model (Gleitman, 1990), which proposes that children use syntactic cues in order to construct semantic representations for words; and the lexical principles framework (Golinkoff, Mervis, & Hirsh-Pasek, 1994), which postulates that children use sets of cognitive processing strategies or principles to assist them in constructing word meanings.

Chapter 6 by Stan Kuczaj continues the discussion of lexical development, focusing more upon the phenomena characterising the child's later lexical development. As Kuczaj points out, word meaning acquisition can continue throughout the lifespan, and even young adults have vocabularies well in excess of 100,000 words (Aitchison, 1987; Seashore & Eckerson, 1940). This is a phenomenal achievement (to acquire 100,000 words by 20 years of age means that the individual has to acquire an average of 13 new words every single day throughout childhood and adolescence). One of the core tasks facing the researcher in this area is to explain how this rate of word learning is achieved.

In his chapter, Kuczaj first provides an analysis of all the different kinds of information about each individual word which the child has to acquire (which includes its phonological, morphological, syntactic, and pragmatic properties, as well as information about the denotation, reference, and sense of the word), and he shows how the errors which children sometimes make in the production and comprehension of words can reveal useful information about children's mental representation of word meaning. Kuczaj then addresses the issue of the sheer number of words and meanings which children acquire. He examines in detail one particular proposal that has been made in the literature, which postulates that children are such prodigious and efficient word learners because there are innately specified ways of interpreting and organising lexical information which radically constrain and simplify the task of word meaning acquisition. Kuczaj analyses the arguments and evidence which have been used in the debate about whether such innate constraints exist. He concludes that the evidence is not convincing, and that the sorts of constraints which have been proposed in the literature are more likely to consist of information processing biases and strategies that children might or might not use, depending upon individual differences and context. Kuczaj concludes his chapter by reviewing children's acquisition of paradigmatic relations (such as synonymy, antonymy, hyponymy, etc.) and syntagmatic relations (which concern how different words can or cannot be used together in individual sentences). He argues that the child's discovery of these paradigmatic and syntagmatic relations is probably the most important factor in driving the pace of later lexical development.

Chapters 7 and 8 explore syntactic and morphological development in children. In Chapter 7, Michael Tomasello and Patricia Brooks examine early grammatical development. They provide an overview of four major steps which occur in early grammatical development: the use of holophrases, where a single word or linguistic unit is used on its own to express the child's communicative intentions (this characterises the one-word period of language development, from about 12 months of age onwards); the use of word combinations, where two or more words are used together in a single utterance to encode two different aspects of the communicative situation (this type of simple multi-word speech usually commences somewhere between 18 and 24 months of age); the use of verb island constructions, where grammatical features such as word order or morphology are used to explicitly mark the different roles of the various sentence constituents, but the child does this independently for different sentences on a verb-specific basis (this type of speech occurs from about 24 months of age onwards); and the use of adult-like syntax and morphology, where word order and grammatical morphemes are used in a generalised and consistent manner across entire classes of sentences to mark the various grammatical roles of the sentence constituents (this occurs from about 36 months of age onwards).

Tomasello and Brooks argue that it is only between about 3 and 5 years of age that children move beyond a linguistic system in which verb-specific islands of organisation exist in an otherwise disorganised system, to a more organised linguistic system which is based upon abstract linguistic categories and generalised grammatical roles and relations. Their view is that children gradually construct their grammatical knowledge, by first acquiring a number of individual words and limited linguistic structures, and by then extracting from these structures the more abstract grammatical roles and relations, using their general cognitive processing abilities to do so. This view stands in marked contrast to the alternative view put forward, for example, by Chomsky (1986) and Pinker (1989), which postulates that children are biologically pre-equipped for the acquisition of grammar through the possession of innate grammatical knowledge.

This alternative nativist view is explored in some detail by Michael Maratsos in Chapter 8. He begins his chapter by carefully disentangling various meanings of the term "innate", in order to clarify some of the theoretical claims that have been made in this area. Later on in the chapter, he also explains and clarifies the

Chomskyan argument about "the poverty of the stimulus", that is, the argument that the linguistic input does not contain sufficient information in itself to permit the induction of grammatical categories, roles and relations from it (this is one of the primary motivations for postulating that at least some grammatical knowledge must be innate: If the child cannot acquire such knowledge from the linguistic input, then it must be available to the child from some other source). The main body of Maratsos's chapter is then taken up with a detailed consideration of three specific problem areas: (1) the acquisition of agent-action-patient structures; (2) the acquisition of grammatical categories (such as verb, noun, subject of sentence, etc.); and (3) the acquisition of wh- questions.

He begins by exploring the encoding of agent-action-patient structures (e.g. *Adam kissed the girl*, *Alex kicked his brother*, etc.) in English, Turkish, and Georgian. The purpose of examining languages such as Turkish and Georgian is to correct any mistaken preconceptions which the English-speaking reader might have about the simplicity of the language acquisition process (due to the relative transparency of the English language in encoding roles such as agent, action, and patient), and to reveal the sheer complexity of the grammatical system which many language-learning children have to acquire. Yet these highly complex systems for encoding agent-action-patient sequences appear to be mastered by Turkish and Georgian children by two years of age (although it is unclear whether this mastery is only at the level of verb island constructions, or at the level of the productive adult grammar). From these examples, Maratsos draws various developmental conclusions, and highlights problems with the proposal that children extract these sorts of grammatical regularities through some kind of inductive process from the language input which they receive.

Maratsos then goes on to consider the nature of the formal grammatical categories of verbs, nouns, grammatical subjects, etc. He reviews the various attempts which have been made to explain how children acquire their knowledge of these categories. These attempts have usually been based on the assumption that these formal categories can be constructed by the child either from semantic concepts (e.g. verb from "action", noun from "object", subject from "agent", etc.), or from the way in which grammatical morphemes and/or word orders flag these formal categories in the linguistic input to the child (e.g. the way *-ing* and *-ed* on the ends of words flag the category of verb, etc.). However, Maratsos again shows the problems with these explanations, drawing once again upon the cross-linguistic evidence to emphasise the sheer complexity of the linguistic system that has to be acquired by the child, and questioning whether either type of explanation is really adequate.

Finally, Maratsos turns his attention to a third and even more complex aspect of grammar, namely the construction of wh- questions (i.e. questions which in the English language begin with a wh- word such as *what, who, where, why, when*, etc.). The acquisitional problem here seems to be even more serious than in the case of agent-action-patient constructions and formal categories. Maratsos himself offers no simple solutions to either this or any of the other problems which he highlights in his chapter. Instead, this chapter serves to problematise the entire area of grammatical development in children, and cautions the reader about accepting models of grammatical development which underestimate the sheer complexity of what children have to achieve during the course of their development in this domain.

In Chapter 9, by Barbara Pan and Catherine Snow, the focus shifts to children's pragmatic development. Pan and Snow begin by exploring the development of children's conversational skills, including turn-taking and the expression of different communicative functions, locating the roots of both of these in the prelinguistic period. Thus, this chapter picks up several of the themes from Reddy's chapter. Pan and Snow show how turn-taking develops after the end of the prelinguistic period, and how the range of communicative functions is expanded once the child has begun to acquire linguistic means for realising these functions. They also explore how children respond to other people's conversational initiations, maintain conversational topics, repair conversations when they break down, and convey referential information to others. Pan and Snow then review the development of discourse skills in children. They examine how children take a listener's perspective, express their own perspective, take alternative stances, and master different genres in their discourse. Pan and Snow argue that participating in conversations and producing extended discourse are highly complex tasks requiring a wide range of cognitive, linguistic, and social processing skills which are only gradually acquired during the course of childhood.

Chapter 10 by Suzanne Romaine addresses a very important issue which is not addressed in any of the preceding chapters. As she points out at the start of her chapter, most of the research which has been conducted on language development in children has been concerned with the developmental process as it occurs in children who are acquiring just a single language. However, it has been estimated that at least half of the world's population is bilingual rather than monolingual. Furthermore, it is by no means clear that conclusions about the developmental process in monolingual children extrapolate to bilingual children.

Consequently, in her chapter, Romaine provides a comprehensive overview of our current knowledge about bilingual language development. She examines the various types of childhood bilingualism that exist, identifying six different types in total which are differentiated by the relationship between the parental language(s) and the language(s) of the wider community in which the child is growing up, and by the strategy that is adopted by the parents in order to teach the languages to the child. Romaine then provides a systematic review of what is currently known about the language development of bilingual children, focusing in turn upon the development of the lexicon, phonology, syntax, and morphology. Finally, she examines how linguistic input, interactional style, and attitudes can affect the rate and order of bilingual acquisition, and she considers whether there may be some cognitive advantages to bilingualism.

Whereas all of the chapters up to this point in the book concentrate upon language development in normally developing children, the next three chapters, by Bonvillian, Tager-Flusberg, and Fletcher, focus attention on various groups of atypically developing children. In Chapter 11, John Bonvillian explores the development of sign language in deaf children. Sign languages differ from spoken languages in that they use visual signs rather than spoken sounds to encode meaning. Nevertheless, sign languages such as American Sign Language (ASL) and British Sign Language (BSL) do have a phonology. The signs which make up these languages are constructed from more basic elements that are defined by hand configuration, place of articulation, movement, and hand arrangement; as in the case of phonemes, these elements themselves do not encode meaning, but they are combined in rule-governed ways to produce an enormous set of different signs analogous to words, each of which encodes a particular meaning. In addition to having a phonology and a lexicon, sign languages such as ASL and BSL also have a morphology and a syntax. In other words, sign languages are full languages with a structure which is entirely analogous to that of spoken languages.

In his chapter, Bonvillian explores the ways in which early sign language acquisition is similar to and different from spoken language development. His review focuses upon early sign production, the acquisition of referential language, the types of words which make up sign-learning children's early vocabularies, the development of syntax and morphology after infancy, and phonological development in sign language acquisition. Bonvillian concludes that, despite the difference in language modality, children learning sign language and children learning spoken language acquire many aspects of their language systems in much the same way. In the course of his chapter, Bonvillian also explores several further issues, including how deaf children who do not have a language model can nevertheless develop their own gestural communicative systems, and how deaf children in a community can create an entirely new sign language over a relatively short period of time.

Chapter 12, by Helen Tager-Flusberg, provides a comprehensive review of our current knowledge about language development in several different groups of atypical children: children with Down syndrome, children with Williams syndrome, children with autism, children with fragile X syndrome, children with Prader-Willi syndrome, and children with hydrocephalus. For each group in turn, Tager-Flusberg systematically reviews what is known about these children's vocal and phonological development, their communicative and pragmatic development, their lexical development, and their morphological and syntactic development.

Tager-Flusberg's review is based upon an explicit model of the language acquisition process which she outlines at the beginning of her chapter. This model postulates that there are three different systems involved in processing language information: a computational system which processes phonological and grammatical information; a theory of mind system, which processes pragmatic and social information; and a general cognitive system which builds the conceptual-semantic structures underlying the lexicon. These systems are effectively integrated in the language development of normally developing children; however, each system can be differentially impaired in children affected by different developmental disorders. Thus, Tager-Flusberg argues that by studying the language development of these children, it is possible to tease out the contributions which each of the three systems makes to the overall process of language development. In the course of her review, she shows that these various groups of children do indeed exhibit different profiles, and that the pattern of profiles which emerges is consistent with this three-system model of language processing.

Chapter 13, by Paul Fletcher, examines language development in another important group of atypically developing children, namely children who exhibit specific language impairment (SLI). Such children have impaired language development but do not appear to have any other identifiable physical or psychological impairment. They are an extremely important group of children in the study of language development due to the fact that numerous theorists have hypothesised that language acquisition is only achievable because the child has a modular cognitive system. Modules are domain-specific information processing systems (that is, a module can only process information about one specific kind of input, e.g. linguistic information, spatial information, mathematical information, etc.), and each module automatically processes its own information relatively independently of the other modules in the cognitive system. Modules are assisted in their operation by containing innately specified principles and structures that are relevant to processing information in that particular domain (Chomsky is in fact one of the most prominent modularity theorists: see Maratsos, Chapter 8). Now, if this modular account is correct, and if information processing in each domain does indeed occur relatively independently of processing in other domains, then it is possible that some children could have an impairment in just the language module alone, without exhibiting any other cognitive impairments. (Notice that this argument is akin to Tager-Flusberg's argument that there can be a deficit in just one of the three sub-systems for processing language, leaving the other two systems relatively intact; indeed, some authors in the field of SLI argue that the deficit in children with SLI is located specifically in the computational sub-system described by Tager-Flusberg which processes phonological and grammatical information.) In addition, if modules contain innately specified information about a domain, and if they are a part of the child's biological endowment, then it is possible that a language-specific impairment could be inherited by children from their parents, and therefore run in families. Hence the interest in children with SLI.

In his chapter, Fletcher reviews the available evidence on children with SLI. This includes evidence about their problems with morphology, and their problems with verb argument structures. He considers whether these children have a language delay or a language deficit; whether their problems stem from a deviant grammatical competence or from impaired performance in the on-line processing of language (in which grammatical morphemes would be particularly vulnerable); whether they experience auditory temporal processing deficits; and whether these children have a phonological short-term memory problem. He also examines the evidence from studies by Gopnik and her colleagues (e.g. Gopnik, 1990; Ullman & Gopnik, 1994), who claim to have identified a family in which SLI has been passed down through three generations; however, Fletcher points out that the members of this family have other inherited disabilities including severe pronunciation difficulties and problems with non-verbal voluntary movements of lips, jaw, and tongue, suggesting an underlying neurological problem. Fletcher concludes that we do not yet have any clear answers to the core questions which are posed by children with SLI, but that the work which is currently being conducted pursuing these various possibilities may begin to yield some interesting answers in the very near future.

The final chapter in the book, Chapter 14 by John Locke, is rather different from the other chapters, in that it takes one step back from the actual research findings and asks a more over-arching question: What type of theoretical explanation is required in order to explain the facts of language acquisition? Locke takes a backward glance at many of the topics which have been covered in the book, including the social predispositions of the infant, the perception and segmentation of the speech stream, the acquisition of words and of longer stretches of speech, the analysis of longer stretches of language to identify recurring patterns and rules, the nativist interpretation of language development, the phenomenon of specific language impairment, etc. Through the course of his review, Locke articulates his own answer to the question concerning the type of explanation that is required to account for the development of language. This answer is an evolutionary-biological one: Locke argues that children develop language because they possess various mechanisms and capabilities which were originally evolved for other individual purposes, but which together coalesce to generate the developmental path that leads to language.

RECURRENT THEMES AND ISSUES IN THE STUDY OF CHILDREN'S LANGUAGE DEVELOPMENT

Nativist vs. developmental theories of language development

From the preceding outline of the contents of this book, it should be apparent that there are several themes which keep recurring through the various chapters. One such theme is nativism, that is, the view that at least some aspects of language are innate and are a consequence of the child's biological endowment, rather than being a product of learning or being acquired during the course of development. For example, in Chapter 2, Reddy reviews the proposal that infants are born with intentions to communicate with other people; in Chapter 3, Plunkett and Schafer review studies into the perceptual abilities of very young infants which suggest that infants have an innate ability to perceive and discriminate phonemes; in Chapter 6, Kuczaj reviews the proposal that the speed and accuracy of word learning during lexical development would be impossible without innate constraints to guide the word learning process; and Tomasello and Brooks in Chapter 7, and Maratsos in Chapter 8, review the proposal that, if children did not have any innate grammatical knowledge, it would be impossible for them to acquire grammar from the language input which they receive. Thus, nativist accounts have been advanced in all of the different areas of language development, including pragmatic, phonological, lexical, and grammatical development.

However, there are also other alternative theoretical positions that have been put forward in each of these areas, arguing that the child's linguistic capacities and knowledge are not innate but are acquired during the course of development. Thus, Reddy also reviews the proposal that intentional communication is not present at birth but only emerges at about 9 or 10 months of age when developments in the infant's understanding of means-ends relationships lead to its emergence. And although few would dispute that newborn infants have very impressive phoneme discrimination abilities, Plunkett and Schafer also review the evidence that these abilities nevertheless undergo significant developmental changes during the second half of the first year of life as a consequence of exposure to a particular language. In the field of lexical learning, several authors (including Kuczaj himself, as well as Nelson, 1988) have argued that what some theorists have interpreted as innate constraints are more properly viewed as word processing biases and strategies which are acquired during the course of development. And in the field of grammatical development, Tomasello and Brooks are themselves prominent advocates (as are Kuczaj, 1982; and Bates & MacWhinney, 1987) of the position that grammatical knowledge is not innate but is instead acquired by the child during the course of development.

As Maratsos makes clear in Chapter 8, the term "innate" is in fact a very complex term which carries many meanings and is open to many possible misinterpretations. Thus, it should not be assumed that all nativist claims that have been made in the different areas of pragmatics, phonology, the lexicon, and grammar are equivalent to one another, either in terms of the types of capacities, skills or knowledge that are argued to be innate, or in terms of the reasons that particular authors have for postulating these to be innate. Something can be said to be "innate" for any one of a large number of different reasons. These include: because it is a product of evolution and natural selection; because it is species-specific; because it is inherited from one or both parents; because it is present in newborn infants; because it is universal in all humans; because it results from an interaction between the genome and the typical environment inhabited by the species; because it is a product of purely endogenous processes that are entirely internal to the organism; because it is hard-wired in the neurological circuitry of the individual; because it is a product of an information-processing system which is a biological given, where the nature of the system itself constrains or determines what input can or cannot be received, how that input can be processed, and what type of output can be generated; because there is a biological-maturational timetable governing neurological growth, plasticity, or decay, which can prevent an acquisition from occurring before a particular point in development, or prevent it from occurring after a particular point in development; etc. Elman, Bates, Johnson, Karmiloff-Smith, Parisi, and Plunkett (1996) provide an excellent discussion of many of these different possible meanings of the term "innate", most of which have been applied by one theorist or another at some time to the field of language development.

Thus, great care needs to be taken in evaluating, on its own grounds, each of the nativist claims reviewed in the various chapters of this book. And it is important not to assume that, just because one aspect of linguistic ability (e.g. phoneme perception) may have an innate substrate, other aspects (e.g. lexical learning, the acquisition of grammar, etc.) must therefore also have innate substrates as well. Or, if all of these different aspects of language development do indeed have innate substrates, it is important not to assume that the evidence which is used to support this conclusion is the same in each case. Comparable considerations apply, of course, to the evaluation of the various theoretical claims that have been made about the different aspects of language acquisition from a developmental perspective.

Domain-specific vs. domain-general theories of language development

A second major theme which also recurs in many of the chapters of this book is whether language development is dependent upon domain-specific or domain-general processes or representations. Precisely what is meant by the term "domain-specific" varies considerably from theorist to theorist, but one common element underlying most current uses of this term is the idea that cognitive processes are specialised and confined to handling just one specific type of information (for example, either linguistic, spatial, or mathematical information, etc.). Domain-general processes, by contrast, are cognitive processes which are applicable to information in many different knowledge domains.

Several of the chapters in this book review theoretical positions which postulate that language development depends upon domain-specific processes or representations. For example, the innate constraints on word learning postulated by Markman (1990) are domain-specific in that they are applicable only to the processing of lexical information (see Kuczaj, Chapter 6). Similarly, the innate grammatical knowledge postulated by Chomsky (1986) and Pinker (1989) is also only applicable to the processing of linguistic information; furthermore, this processing is hypothesised to be executed by a language module which operates relatively independently of the other modules in the child's cognitive system (see Maratsos, Chapter 8). Tager-Flusberg, in Chapter 12, postulates that, in addition to the general cognitive system which builds the conceptual-semantic structures underlying the lexicon, there are two more specialised systems involved in the acquisition of language: the computational system for processing phonological and grammatical information, and the theory of mind system for processing pragmatic and social information. These are domain-specific information-processing systems; because of this, it is possible for a child to have an impairment in just one of the three systems, leaving the other two systems relatively intact. And similarly, Fletcher in Chapter 13 reviews the claim that SLI occurs because language development depends upon domain-specific processes, with the consequence that it is possible for a child to exhibit impaired language development while showing no other psychological or cognitive impairments.

However, the alternative possibility, that language development is dependent upon domain-general processes or representations, also frequently reappears in the different chapters of this book. For example, as we have seen already, Reddy in Chapter 2 reviews the proposal that intentional communication only emerges at 9–10 months of age when developmental changes in the infant's understanding of means-ends relationships occur, changes which simultaneously affect the infant's functioning in a range of different domains, including not just prelinguistic communication but also problem solving, tool use, etc. Similarly, Dromi in Chapter 5 reviews proposals that various aspects of lexical development in the second year of life depend upon changes in the child's representations of concepts, categories, and scripts, representations which are domain-general. And Tomasello and Brooks in Chapter 8 argue that syntactic development is dependent upon the child's abilities to understand and partition scenes into events, states and participants, and to extract commonalities across linguistic constructions, using the same sorts of cognitive processes that are used in other domains to construct schemas, categories, and scripts. All of these proposals are similar in that they suggest that the child's development in the domain of language is in some way dependent upon domain-general cognitive processes or representations.

The core idea underlying the concept of domain-specificity is the notion that cognitive information-processing systems are specialised, with each one handling just one specific type of information. Over and above this core idea, however, different theorists who have postulated domain-specificity in children's cognitive development have stressed different additional notions. For example, some theorists have emphasised that the child's development in a particular domain consists of the acquisition of a specialised body of knowledge, concepts, and relations which are unique to that particular domain, which results in the child acquiring a domain-specific expertise (Chi & Glaser, 1980); others have emphasised the idea that cognitive development consists of the acquisition and elaboration of naive theories (which contain hypothetical constructs, explain and predict empirical phenomena, and mediate the acquisition of new information), these theories being specialised for the different types of conceptual content which characterise different knowledge domains (Wellman & Gelman, 1992); other theorists have stressed the notion that domains are sets of representations sustaining specific areas of knowledge, which may be subject to their own distinctive modes of processing but which only emerge during the course of the child's development (Karmiloff-Smith, 1992); while still other theorists have emphasised the idea that domains are based upon cognitive modules, which can only receive one specific type of input, automatically process that input independently of other modules, and contain innately specified principles and structures to facilitate the processing of the information in that domain (Chomsky, 1986; Fodor, 1983). In addition, it is also worth noting that there is little consensus among domain-specificity theorists concerning the level at which domains exist; for example, whether there is just a single domain of language, or whether language processing is performed by several, more specific, sub-systems which operate relatively independently of each other (cf. Tager-Flusberg, this volume).

Thus, once again, it is important not to confuse the different claims that have been made by different authors about the domain-specificity of language. Different theorists can be making very different claims when they argue that language development is dependent upon domain-specific processes or representations. And different theorists may also be drawing upon very different arguments and lines of evidence in order to support their diverse claims. The same, of course, also applies to the various theorists who postulate that language development is based upon domain-general processes or representations.

The principal theoretical stances on the development of language

These two sets of substantive theoretical differences (nativism vs. developmentalism, and domain-specificity vs. domain-generality) have generated many of the fundamental theoretical disagreements which are reviewed in the various chapters of this book. These two sets of theoretical differences can be used as a framework to categorise the different theoretical stances which have been adopted by different researchers on the development of language. In the diagram which follows, the vertical axis represents the disagreement between nativists and developmentalists, while the horizontal axis represents the disagreement between theorists postulating domain-specificity and theorists postulating domain-generality. This yields four different theoretical stances which can be taken on the development of language (see Fig. 1.5).

Researchers who adopt Stance A argue that language development is dependent upon **domain-specific** processes which involve some kind of **innate** capacities, skills, or knowledge. Thus, this position is exemplified by Chomsky

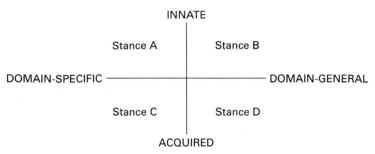

FIG. 1.5.   Four theoretical stances on the development of language.

(1986) and Pinker (1989) who postulate that grammatical development is possible only because the child possesses innate grammatical knowledge, and by Markman (1990) who postulates that lexical development is only possible because the child possesses innate constraints on the types of hypotheses which the child can entertain about the meaning of words. Stance A is also exemplified by those who argue that children are born with a specific ability to perceive and discriminate phonemes (e.g. Eimas, 1975), and those who postulate that the development of the ability to produce phonemes in the first six months of life is dependent upon the specialised neurological and anatomical maturation of the vocal tract (Locke, 1983; Oller, 1980).

Stance B is occupied by researchers who argue that language development is dependent upon the child's possession of **innate** but **domain-general** capacities, skills, or knowledge. This position is exemplified by those theorists who either implicitly or explicitly postulate that the child acquires language using a domain-general information-processing system, where the structure of this system is a biological given (with the system containing, for example, perceptual and attentional mechanisms, a working memory system, a long-term memory store, etc.). This position has been explicitly advocated by Kuczaj (1982) in order to explain children's syntactic and morphological development, and it is also possible to interpret Tomasello and Brooks' account of grammatical development (see Chapter 7) as exemplifying this position as well. Of course, although the information-processing system itself is postulated to be a part of the innate biological endowment of the child, these theorists argue that there is no grammatical knowledge built into this system from the outset, and that all such knowledge is acquired during the course of development via the operation of the system.

Researchers who adopt Stance C postulate that language development depends upon **domain-specific** processes or representations, but that these domain-specific processes or representations are **acquired** or emerge during the course of development, rather than being innately prespecified. This position is exemplified by Karmiloff-Smith (1992), who argues that the child's representations are domain-specific, but also argues that these domains are not biologically prespecified but instead emerge during the course of development via a process of modularisation. Other theorists who exemplify Stance C are Nelson (1988) and Kuczaj (on lexical development, this volume), who argue that the so-called "innate constraints" on lexical learning are really domain-specific processing strategies and biases which are acquired during the course of the child's lexical development (see Chapter 6).

Finally, Stance D is occupied by those researchers who argue that the development of language is dependent upon **domain-general** processes or representations, but that these domain-general processes or representations are **acquired** during the course of development. This position is exemplified by Piagetian and neo-Piagetian theorists who argue that domain-general cognitive representations are constructed by the child during the course of development, and that these representations underpin the child's cognitive functioning in a number of different problem-solving domains (of which language is just one). For example, those who postulate that the onset of intentional communication at the age of 9 or 10 months results from underlying changes in domain-general means-ends understanding (Bates, Benigni, Bretherton, Camaioni, & Volterra, 1979) exemplify this position. This position is also exemplified by those theorists who postulate that early lexical development is dependent upon changes in the child's underlying semantic representations (Barrett, 1986; Gopnik & Meltzoff, 1986); these representations consist of concepts, categories, and scripts, which are domain-general representations that are acquired during the course of the child's cognitive development.

It can be seen that there are many different theoretical positions which currently exist on the development of language. However, beneath the surface of this welter of theoretical positions, there are certain basic recurring themes and issues. As yet, there is no sign of any emerging consensus in the field. In the chapters that follow, the diverse theoretical positions which exist on all the various aspects of the child's language development, including the child's pragmatic, phonological, lexical, morphological, and syntactic development, are examined in detail.

REFERENCES

Aitchison, J. (1987). *Words in the mind: An introduction to the mental lexicon.* Oxford, UK: Blackwell.

Barrett, M. (1986). Early semantic representations and early word usage. In S.A. Kuczaj & M. Barrett (Eds.), *The development of word meaning* (pp. 39–67). New York: Springer Verlag.

Barrett, M. (1995). Early lexical development. In P. Fletcher & B. MacWhinney (Eds.), *The handbook of child language* (pp. 362–392). Oxford, UK: Blackwell.

Barthes, R. (1967). *Elements of semiology.* London: Jonathan Cape.

Bates, E., Benigni, L., Bretherton, I., Camaioni, L., & Volterra, V. (1979). *The emergence of symbols: Cognition and communication in infancy.* New York: Academic Press.

Bates, E., & MacWhinney, B. (1987). Competition, variation, and language learning. In B. MacWhinney (Ed.), *Mechanisms of language acquisition* (pp. 157–193). Hillsdale, NJ: Lawrence Erlbaum Associates Inc.

Chi, M.T.H., & Glaser, R. (1980). The measurement of expertise: Analysis of the development of knowledge and skill as a basis for assessing achievement. In E.L. Baker & E.S. Quellmalz (Eds.), *Educational testing and evaluation: Design, analysis and policy* (pp. 37–47). Beverly Hills, CA: Sage.

Chomsky, N. (1986). *Knowledge of language: Its nature, origins and use.* New York: Praeger.

Eimas, P.D. (1975). Speech perception in early infancy. In L.B. Cohen & P. Salapatek (Eds.), *Infant perception: From sensation to cognition* (pp. 193–231). New York: Academic Press.

Elman, J.L., Bates, E.A., Johnson, M.H., Karmiloff-Smith, A., Parisi, D., & Plunkett, K. (1996). *Rethinking innateness: A connectionist perspective on development.* Cambridge, MA: MIT Press.

Fodor, J.A. (1983). *The modularity of mind.* Cambridge, MA: MIT Press.

Garman, M. (1990). *Psycholinguistics.* Cambridge, UK: Cambridge University Press.

Gimson, A.C. (1970). *An introduction to the pronunciation of English.* London: Edward Arnold.

Giraud, P. (1975). *Semiology.* London: Routledge & Kegan Paul.

Gleitman, L. (1990). The structural sources of verb meaning. *Language Acquisition, 1,* 3–55.

Golinkoff, R.M., Mervis, C.B., & Hirsh-Pasek, K. (1994). Early object labels: The case for a developmental lexical principles framework. *Journal of Child Language, 21,* 125–155.

Gopnik, A., & Meltzoff, A.N. (1986). Words, plans, things and locations: Interactions between semantic and cognitive development in the one-word stage. In S.A. Kuczaj & M. Barrett (Eds.), *The development of word meaning* (pp. 199–223). New York: Springer Verlag.

Gopnik, M. (1990). Feature-blind grammar and dysphasia. *Nature, 344,* 317.

Hyman, L.M. (1975). *Phonology: Theory and analysis.* New York: Holt, Rinehart & Winston.

Karmiloff-Smith, A. (1992). *Beyond modularity: A developmental perspective on cognitive science.* Cambridge, MA: MIT Press.

Kempson, R.M. (1977). *Semantic theory.* Cambridge: Cambridge University Press.

Kuczaj, S.A. (1982). On the nature of syntactic development. In S.A. Kuczaj (Ed.), *Language development: Vol. 1. Syntax and semantics* (pp. 37–71). Hillsdale, NJ: Lawrence Erlbaum Associates Inc.

Levinson, S.C. (1983). *Pragmatics.* Cambridge, UK: Cambridge University Press.

Locke, J.L. (1983). *Phonological acquisition and change.* New York: Academic Press.

Lyons, J. (1968). *Introduction to theoretical linguistics.* Cambridge, UK: Cambridge University Press.

Lyons, J. (1977). *Semantics (Vols. 1 and 2).* Cambridge, UK: Cambridge University Press.

Markman, E.M. (1990). Constraints children place on word meanings. *Cognitive Science, 14,* 57–77.

Matthews, P.H. (1974). *Morphology: An introduction to the theory of word-structure.* Cambridge, UK: Cambridge University Press.

Nelson, K. (1988). Constraints on word learning? *Cognitive Development, 3,* 221–246.

Oller, D.K. (1980). The emergence of speech sounds in infancy. In G. Yeni-Komshian, J. Kavanaugh, & C. Ferguson (Eds.), *Child phonology: Vol. 1. Production* (pp. 93–112). New York: Academic Press.

Peters, A.M. (1995). Strategies in the acquisition of syntax. In P. Fletcher & B. MacWhinney (Eds.), *The handbook of child language* (pp. 462–482). Oxford, UK: Blackwell.

Pinker, S. (1989). *Learnability and cognition: The acquisition of argument structure.* Cambridge, MA: MIT Press.

Searle, J.R. (1969). *Speech acts: An essay in the philosophy of language.* Cambridge, UK: Cambridge University Press.

Seashore, R.H., & Eckerson, L.D. (1940). The measurement of individual differences in general English vocabularies. *Journal of Educational Psychology, 31,* 14–38.

Ullman, M., & Gopnik, M. (1994). The production of inflectional morphology in hereditary specific language impairment. In J. Matthews (Ed.), *Linguistic aspects of familial language impairment. McGill Working Papers in Linguistics, 10*(1 and 2), 81–118.

Wellman, H.M., & Gelman, S.A. (1992). Cognitive development: Foundational theories of core domains. *Annual Review of Psychology, 43,* 337–375.

CHAPTER TWO

Prelinguistic communication

Vasudevi Reddy
University of Portsmouth, UK

HOW DO WE LOOK FOR THE PRELINGUISTIC?

In trying to trace the origins of a phenomenon (e.g. communication), we seem to
have two choices facing us: Either we start from the "developed" phenomenon and
work backwards in age until we cannot see it anymore, or we start at an early age
and work forwards, looking for something like the phenomenon and watching
how it develops. The first strategy is the one most often used in cognitive-
developmental psychology. However, it has several problems. First, working
from the baseline of a "developed" phenomenon encourages and reifies the use
of adult or "developed" criteria in the investigation. Looking backwards through
the filter of advanced criteria keeps us closely tied to the forms we started with;
it does not take long for us to stop seeing the phenomenon and abandon further
investigation. In effect, we search for the wrong things. Second, the task of looking backwards demands that we look for difference and deficiency, and third, the
search for origins becomes hijacked by an unprofitable search for age of onset.
The second strategy starts the search for origins in another way, i.e. from the
"beginning". The characteristic of this strategy is that we do not have a clear idea
of exactly what we are looking for. This might appear to be a disadvantage. But
in fact it is the strategy's advantage. The investigator is more open to phenomena
which are significant and evident at a prelinguistic age, and can uncover data per-
taining to changes and developments with, paradoxically, less adultomorphism![1]

---

[1] The term adultomorphic (from anthropomorphic) is usually used to refer to the attribution of
adult-like qualities and abilities to children. The term could more appropriately refer to the imposi-
tion of adult forms and criteria on the study of young children's behaviour.

The achievements and developments of each age tend, within this forward-looking strategy, to have the impact that they have in normal development, i.e. of being perceived on their own terms. Looking forwards demands that we look out for similiarity rather than difference—this enables a better study of continuity and change.

As we will see in the communicative phenomena and changes described in this chapter, it is not easy to find the point at which initiative or communicative intentions or communication "about" things begins. The question has to be asked: Should we be so interested in fixing times to beginnings if they are hard to make sense of? Where does it leave us, for instance, to say that the soul has entered the body at 23 weeks of gestation, or that "true" communication begins at 12 or 14 months? Drawing cut-off lines is of pragmatic rather than theoretical value to the scientist and prevents an understanding of change. Perhaps the questions guiding investigations into the origins of phenomena should focus: (1) on processes of development rather than times of emergence of developmental products; and (2) on similarities and continuities rather than on differences and deficiencies. For *pre*linguistic communication the central questions should be "How does prelinguistic communication develop?" and "How does it develop into linguistic communication?" rather than "How does it differ from linguistic communication?" or "How is it deficient relative to linguistic communication?"

The study of prelinguistic communication is important not just for illuminating the origins of language but also for understanding the nature and origins of human sociality itself; both these threads will recur throughout this chapter. I will discuss four general and interconnected issues concerning prelinguistic communication. These are: (1) its intentionality; (2) reasons for its emergence; (3) continuities between prelinguistic and linguistic communication; and (4) its embodiment in the interactive process. I will introduce different theoretical positions on these interconnected questions, describe some of the main landmarks in the development of early communication in the light of these theoretical issues, and conclude with suggestions for a coherent theoretical approach to communicative development.

INTENTIONALITY IN COMMUNICATION

A central problem in attempting to define communication with a view to understanding its origins is the issue of intentionality. Papers on animal communication attempt to distinguish between organisms which appear driven to convey information to conspecifics—or indeed to predators—and those which may be less reflexive and more subtle in their information-conveying behaviour. Much of the debate in the 1970s (Newson, 1979; Schaffer, 1977; Trevarthen, 1977), after psychologists' "discovery" of mother–infant communication, centred around the question of whether the infant was playing any intentional part at all in the interactions and therefore whether these interactions should qualify as communication in the first place. The question of the intentionality of communication is unavoidable. We need to take a standpoint of some sort on the definition of intentional communication even if we wish to reach a simple descriptive account of early communicative development.

There are three main theoretical approaches currently available for defining and pinpointing intentionality in communication (see Zeedyk, 1996, for a discussion of approaches to intentionality).

Position 1: The cognitivist approach

This may be described simply in the following way: Communication is defined as the intentional transfer of information from one agent to another, where agent 1 is aware of the information she wishes to "send", and is aware that agent 2 can both receive and understand the information and can understand agent 1's intention to send it (Camaioni, 1993). This approach to unpacking communicative intentions is consistent with a Piagetian approach to the analysis of intentionality which defines intentionality as goal-directedness. This requires the individual's consciousness of (and therefore a mental representation of) a goal as separate from the means to achieve the goal before an intention can be demonstrated (Bates, Benigni, Bretherton, Camaioni, & Volterra, 1979; Fryc, 1991; Piaget, 1952). Thus, communicative intentions, like any other intentions, are *individual* and *mental* conceptions or representations of specific goals.

Position 2: The social constructionist approach

Early communication is seen as a process of interaction from which intentionality emerges. One partner may be acting to communicate unintentionally, but these acts are received and treated as intentional by the other partner and it is this process of social attribution and construction of meaningfulness which creates intentional communication. In other words, intentional communication emerges from a complex social support system of attribution of intentionality (Kaye, 1982; Lock, 1993). In adulthood we are often aware of situations where intentions are created or transformed in the process of interaction. We may be uncertain e.g. about the "real" intention underlying our smile until the other's response treats it as playful, and then our smile becomes "really" playful. With regard to infant communication the situation is slightly more complex. This approach assumes that initially the infant is not acting towards others with *any* intentionality. The actions are driven by other forces. It is the adult's assumption of intentional other directedness which transforms the infant's acts into intentionally communicative acts; that is, during the "precommunication stage (0–9 months)" there is only "communication in the eye of the beholder" until the adult inducts "the infant into a set of meaningful social episodes . . . that provide a structure within which the infant can discover the meanings its activities are being accorded" (Lock, 1993, p. 279). This approach is different from the cognitivist approach in that it does not posit as a prerequisite for intentional communication a conscious awareness of the information to be transferred or of the other's capacity to receive the communication as intended. However, this approach can be used by the cognitivist approach as a first step in communication from which true intentional communication eventually emerges (Camaioni, 1993).

Position 3: The nativist approach

This approach assumes that human infants are born with intentions for a variety of actions, one of which is to communicate with others (Trevarthen, 1982). It argues that from the start of human life, infant actions which are directed towards others are directed intentionally as simple attempts to engage with the emotional expressions and actions of others. The ability to communicate develops in complexity, including the complexity of the intentions, but communicative intentionality itself is a given. This approach therefore contradicts the social constructionist approach on the issue of the origins of communicative intentionality, but not necessarily on the issue of the developing complexity of communicative intentions. Like the social constructionist approach, however, this approach eschews the cognitivism of the first approach which requires conscious cognitions about information and about others' mental states in response to the information. There are two current variants of the nativist position. Trevarthen (1982) prefers to use the term motives for innate communicativeness and the term intentions for the elaboration of the motives on the basis of experience. The communicative motive is seen as one of seeking companionship and communicative engagement rather than other-directed acts which seek comfort or the alleviation of hunger, etc. Vedeler (1991), writing from a similar conviction about early communicative intentions, tackles the issue of the nature of intentionality. He defines intentions as object-directed (i.e. directed towards the object) rather than goal-directed actions (i.e. directed towards a desired outcome in relation to the object). Vedeler adopts Merleau-Ponty's argument that intentionality must precede mental representations (Merleau-Ponty, 1962) and that communicative intentions do not require mental representations of goals, merely organismic directedness towards objects. Both of these definitions of communicative intentionality, i.e. as motives or as object rather than goal directedness, assume that the capacity for intentional communication is innate and present early in life and that this does not require mental representations of goals and means. Therefore, both assume that communicative motives or intentions are present in the act rather than necessarily in the prior plan to act.

So which of these approaches should one adopt? The cognitivist position assumes both an internalist and overly complex approach to communicative intentions; the rather complex goals and means of communication are seen as individual mental representations or plans. This position fails to adequately explain early infant communication or indeed to see it as relevant to changes in communicative actions. Social constructionism seems to assume that intentionality emerges from an earlier mechanistic state which is devoid of intentionality, an assumption that is empirically contradicted by recent findings of intentional actions in neonates (Butterworth & Hopkins 1988; van der Meer, van der Weel, & Lee 1995). Standard nativism is in danger of assuming internalism too, that is, of simply assuming that communicative goals as mental representations are innate. The alternative preferred here is a variant of the standard nativist position which assumes that there is innate other-directedness, but argues that the realisation of specific communicative intentions must happen in the act of engagement rather than prior to it. In other words, it is assumed here that the other directed actions of many organisms are not prompted by simple mechanical causes; rather there is inherent interest in and motivation for engaging with others' emotionality and expressiveness. The precise nature of the engagement and of the actions directed towards others depends, however, on a responsive and appropriate other and develops with experience.

REASONS FOR THE EMERGENCE OF COMMUNICATION

Why do organisms communicate? Why does the human infant begin to communicate with others? Obviously communication achieves some sort of goal for the communicating organism, but it is the nature of this goal that is debated. Two broad positions can be identified on this question: the tool-use argument, which sees the emergence of communication as driven by the *ability to use tools to obtain desired ends*, and the intersubjectivity argument, which sees communication as driven by a *desire to share thoughts and feelings with others*.

The tool-use hypothesis

This argument is based primarily on Piaget's view that language is a kind of tool like any other, and that it emerges as a result of a primary change in sensorimotor intelligence. The ability to separate means from ends and the development of intentionality allows the infant to tolerate diversions en route to achieving an end. This means that different sorts of tools can be used to achieve a goal; e.g. instead of struggling towards a ball that has rolled out of reach under a sofa, the infant can turn aside, take a stick lying nearby and then obtain the ball with it. This ability to use object A to obtain object B extends not just to balls and sticks, but also to people. Once the basic ability is in place, infants can use person A to obtain object B, e.g. by waving an empty cup at an adult as a request for a drink or use object A to obtain person B, e.g. by pointing to a flying airplane to obtain the adult's attention.

This Piagetian approach posits language to be a reflection of changes in thought and is contrary to other approaches, which argue for some degree of autonomy in the emergence of language, e.g. the Chomskyan approach or even the Vygotskyan approach. Chomsky argued for the independence of language from other psychological functions, seeing it as emerging from an innately driven grammatical function. Vygotsky saw language as initially independent of thought, but then merging with thought at the end of infancy into a mutually influencing system where language was not merely a tool which reflected thoughts or changes in it, but also shaped thought. Interestingly, many non-cognitivist writers (including Vygotsky) also focused on the instrumental function of language— i.e. to achieve practical results rather than to express the contents of thought. Wittgenstein emphasised the *uses* of words and the development of language through its use and interchange in language games. This non-cognitive branch of the tool use metaphor (sometimes called "social behaviourism"; Bloom, 1993) is strikingly avant garde in its situatedness and contextualism: The emphasis is on *meaning in action*, on the *observability of thought* and sociality, and on language as a *process* rather than as a product.

Piaget's position, however, still remains the most accessible for translation into the terminology of today's developmental psychology. His view that language was another kind of tool which emerged as a result of the ability to use tools (the "tool use hypothesis") has been widely adopted in explaining the origins of prelinguistic communication at the end of the first year. Bates et al. (1979) for instance, in the first major and still influential longitudinal study of the emergence of prelinguistic communication, supported the idea with data showing the simultaneous emergence of simple object-based tool use (using one object to obtain another), proto-imperatives (using people to obtain objects), and proto-declaratives (using objects to obtain people's attention). To put it in a nutshell, this view suggests that infants' ability to engage in early forms of communication comes from their new effectiveness with tools in general.

The intersubjectivity hypothesis

In contrast to the tool use hypothesis several recent writers have argued that communication has a different motivational function from the use of tools in general, and possibly a separate cognitive basis as well. Camaioni (1993) argues that tool use cannot be a sufficient explanation of the development of language. She pinpoints proto-declaratives as showing the first clear evidence of a desire to share the experiences of the self with others, and as revealing rather more complex cognitions, e.g. about the nature of others' minds, than is evident in or necessary for tool use or proto-imperatives. She uses evidence from studies showing the ontogenetic and phylogenetic dissociation between proto-declaratives and proto-imperatives in support of the idea that only proto-declaratives provide evidence of genuine communicative intentions. Camaioni says little about motives but contrasts what she sees as the social function of proto-communication with the tool use hypothesis. Bloom (1993) similarly argues for an expressive rather than an instrumental function for the development of language, but is interestingly more explicit and coherent about the driving motive. It is a desire to express themselves which drives infants towards language. Infants are motivated to share the contents of their experiences in ways which go beyond displays of affect alone: ". . . the motivation for sharing is in the need they have to sustain intersubjectivity with other persons and thereby locate themselves in a social world" (Bloom, 1993, p. 5). These positions are consistent to some extent with the nativist positions such as Trevarthen's described above which imply that an independent motive for sharing with others (a motive for companionship) is what drives infant communicative development (Trevarthen, 1982) and to some extent with social constructionist positions which also argue for social predispositions and for the role of the social network in drawing the infant into communication. The differences between these various positions on intersubjectivity lie in the extent to which they postulate communicative motives as a primary versus as a derivative aspect of human development. Trevarthen (1982) and Bloom (1993) see intersubjective motives as primary; Camaioni (1993) sees them as deriving from advances in mental representation and from attributions of intersubjectivity from others.

CONTINUITIES IN COMMUNICATIVE DEVELOPMENT

The question of continuities concerns prelinguistic communication in two ways: (1) the nature of its (possible) link with linguistic communication; and (2) the possible connectedness of developments within the prelinguistic phase, especially communication before and after proto-language. It might be fruitful to think of continuities and discontinuities in three different aspects of communication: in causal processes, in motives driving communication, and in the structure and content of the communication.

Prelinguistic and linguistic communication

Both "tool-use" and "intersubjectivist" approaches posit an essential continuity in the causal processes and motives of both types of communication. In the Piagetian model the capacity to use tools is the causal process as well as the motive explaining the occurrence of both prelinguistic and linguistic communication. In intersubjectivist approaches "motives for sharing" run through and explain both. However, the capacity for verbal language has been seen over the centuries as qualitatively different from non-verbal communication and as the single most important distinguishing feature of "man". This is attested to by the uproar over the phenomenon of ape language (Terrace, Petito, Sanders, & Bever, 1979). Prelinguistic communication is not simply replaced, however, by linguistic communication (Bates et al., 1979; Dobrich & Scarborough, 1984); pointing often emerges *after* single word speech is established and gestural communication continues throughout life parallel to linguistic communication and often supplementing it. This evidence has been used by some cognitive-developmental approaches to suggest that gestures and language belong to separate systems, with social rather than cognitive factors linking them (Desrochers, Morisette, & Ricard, 1995; Dobrich & Scarborough 1984). The idea of continuity gives way here to an idea of parallel processes, both being held together by the social responses they elicit.

Is prelinguistic communication qualitatively different from linguistic communication? Some may argue so, suggesting that language reveals a quantum leap in communication, allowing the transfer of otherwise private (mental state) information to others. However, while language may have a special place in sharing the contents of mind, it is clearly not a unique place. Nonverbal actions already embody and reveal not only emotional states, intentions, interests, and thoughts (e.g. surprise or puzzlement) but also their targets. Further, these nonverbal acts can be consciously used to convey such information to others. However, affect expressions are limited in many ways in comparison to the power of language ". . . all that they [one-year-old infants] now know . . . cannot be expressed, much less articulated by displays of affect alone. Language is the preeminent mode of expression provided in a society to embody and make public what is otherwise internal and private to the individual—the beliefs, desires and feelings we have that are our intentional states. Language makes these contents of mind public, in an expression, so that other persons can know them" (Bloom, 1993, pp. 3–4). The prelinguistic infant, then, is limited but not qualitatively different from the linguistic infant in being able to share thoughts and feelings with others.

Furthermore, the process through which language itself arises requires that in order for words to be meaningful to more than one person, the things they refer to must already be mutually available. If the public accessibility of thoughts and feelings were not prior to their linguistic expression, language itself would remain private to each individual. Wittgenstein argues that language emerges as a substitute for existing expressions. Thus, the verbal expression "My leg hurts", admittedly a simple feeling, is not saying anything more than the original "ouch". It is not revealing the ouch, it is merely substituting for (though not replacing) it. The theory could apply to more complex contents of mind too. Even something as complex as a false belief, e.g. that it is warm outside just because the sun is shining into the house, is manifest in people's actions of dressing and of showing surprise and sudden cold. These contextual actions must be mutually understood in order for any expression such as "You thought it was warm" to make sense. Language is a structural, motivational, and processual expansion of prelinguistic communication, rather than a fundamental change.

Before and after proto-language

With the development of proto-language, cognitivist explanations see a major shift in causal processes, motives, and structures. Social or biological processes such as desire for emotional well-being, comfort, etc. are seen to give way to mental processes representing others' attentional states. Early communication is depicted as driven by the same social biological motives that many animals might share, while proto-language is depicted as being driven by a desire to transmit information to an other. Similarly, the structure and content of early communication is devoid of an "object" or target, while that of proto-language is by definition centred around an "object".

Nativist intersubjectivist explanations (Trevarthen, 1977) also note a discontinuity in the structure and content of communication after proto-language, seeing a shift from dyadic communications (i.e. infant and other) or a communication of affects, to triadic ones (infant and other and object) or a communication about motives and intentions involving the external world. The changes are seen to be caused by maturing and shifting interests in the infant. However, these explanations see a fundamental continuity in the causal processes and motives of both types of communication. Both before and after proto-language the infant is motivated to share and seek companionship (as are relevant others) and the communication occurs through similar biological and social processes such as dynamic sensitivity to affects, motives, and intentions in both infant and others.

Social constructionist accounts may posit a continuity in both motivational and causal processes—i.e. by arguing that it is the interactive processes which create meaning both before and after proto-language. However, the sharp distinction that is sometimes made within these accounts (Lock, 1993) between the precommunication stage (0–9 months) of communication-by-default and the later stage where the infant has been enabled to grasp the meanings which his activities have been accorded suggests that the nature of communication changes fundamentally, i.e. from non-communication to communication.

EMBODIMENT IN COMMUNICATION

One issue which emerges from all of the above debates is that of the nature of communication itself. To what extent is communication to be seen as a process which occurs more or less independently of the actions involved in it? Is communication a process of purely mental contact? Nadel and Camaioni (1993) contrast the "telegraphic metaphor" in the traditional approach to communication with what they term an "orchestra metaphor" in some modern approaches.

Telegraphs, orchestras, and jazz groups

For a telegraph to work what is required is an agent A sending information X to agent B along some particular channel Z, knowing that agent B can receive it and understand the information. If this is what human communication is like then we must assume that each agent is a separate individual; that there is a clear item of information; that agent A has the separately formed intention to send information X to agent B; and that agent A has some mental model of agent B's understanding of it. In terms of the models of intentionality it is clear that the cognitivist approach adopts this metaphor; the social constructionist approach clearly does not; and the nativist approach may adopt it in some variants. But is this what communication is really like? Is it such a clean-cut process of exchange of information between individual agents?

In two important respects the orchestra metaphor varies from that of the telegraph. First, there is *no individual performer*—various people play their parts, but not as isolated elements which can be taken apart. Second, the resulting music *is inseparable from the process of playing*. There is a third important feature of communication which even an orchestra cannot represent but jazz groups could; and that is that there may *not be a predetermined score* that is being transmitted from one person to another (Fogel, 1993). The music is a joint rather than an individual achievement; it does not exist outside of the players and their playing; and it emerges in the process of playing. Extended to communication, this metaphor suggests that communication is done jointly; that communication does not exist as a mental process outside actions; and communication emerges and is not scripted (Vedeler, 1991). This implies that our conceptualisation of infant communication as an essentially individual process of transmission of mental information is wrong—it must be studied as a mutual, relational process. It also implies that developments in communication cannot occur in the realm of cognitive or linguistic change independent of the actions and interactions taking place, as it were, on the ground. It rejects two sets of divides that are inherent in the telegraphic metaphor: one, a divide between communicating individuals, and two, a divide between the process of communicative action and the presumed disembodied intentions to communicate. An embodied approach to communication thus argues that to understand communication we must consider it as action (and interaction)—i.e. the bodily actions of the individuals involved; literally, communication is not something that goes on in the head, it occurs inseparable from the body. This is not a trivial point; to consider communication as interaction is to transfer it from the realm of pure mentality (if there is such a thing) to the realm of observable action with all its concomitant influences and effects. Approaching communication as an embodied rather than as a "purely mental" process offers the best chance we have of addressing issues of continuity, both between prelinguistic and linguistic communication and between animal and human communication.

Cognitivist approaches to communication adopt something very like a telegraphic metaphor, focusing on the sender's planned message. All other approaches focus on what infants and others *do* in communication, thus treating communication as an embodied process, adopting a jazz group metaphor. However, nativist approaches acknowledge the importance of the jazz players' predispositions as setting a theme for the performance, while social constructionist approaches give these less emphasis.

LANDMARKS IN THE CHANGING NATURE OF PRELINGUISTIC COMMUNICATION

The emphasis in the following descriptive account of the development of prelinguistic communication in human infancy is on what infants *do* with others' communicative attention, intentions, and acts. The period of prelinguistic communication will be divided here into five phases on the basis primarily of available clusters of research. These are: the neonatal phase, 2–3 months, the middle of the first year, 8–12 months, and 12–15 months. There are substantial amounts of research in the first two and last phases, but relatively little about developments in communication between 5 and 11 months. However, if we are not to accept an all or none approach to the events happening around the end of the first year, it is important to consider what little evidence there is of phenomena during this period and see how they actually present a picture of continuity in prelinguistic development rather than discontinuity as would appear to be the case from a stark focus on isolated developments.

Neonates

Two sorts of evidence are relevant to an answer to the question of communication in neonates: (1) evidence of interest in things to do with human communication, namely, faces, voices, and speech; and (2) evidence of neonates' acts in relation to communicative aspects of persons.

Why are neonatal preferences for human faces and voices important for an understanding of communication? Findings that human infants are already predisposed at birth to be interested in people and in particular in those aspects of people which are central to communication, i.e. faces and voices, offer strong support for the idea of some kind of innate predisposition towards communication in humans. Evidence from a variety of sources shows that human neonates are interested in people and in the specific features distinguishing people from other "objects". They show preferences for human voices over other sounds of similar pitch and intensity (Friedlander, 1970) and for sounds within the human voice range to sounds outside the human voice range (Eisenberg, 1975), to female voices over male and to their mother's voice over other female voices (De Casper & Fifer, 1980). They show preferences for human faces and representations of human faces at birth and will work harder to maintain sight of human face and voice by tracking or sucking than they will for other stimuli (Dziurawiec & Ellis, 1986; Goren, Sarty, & Wu, 1975; Johnson, Dziurawiec, Ellis, & Morton, 1991). Their interest is expressed through an intense knit brow expression or a softening and "opening" of the face (Brazelton, 1986). Further, newborn infants show a sensitivity to human speech sounds over non-speech sounds and an ability to discriminate subtle speech sound variations such as between /p/ and /b/ (Eimas & Friesen, 1971; Mehler, 1993) and between different vowel sounds (Clarkson & Berg, 1983). The finding that these discriminations are of a categorical nature suggest that human infants (and also some birds and mammals) are innately disposed to perceive sounds in a directed way, i.e. directed towards preferential perception of those sounds which are selectively discriminated in human speech (Bloom, 1993; Plunkett and Schafer, this volume).

These predispositional preferences are more than simple devices enabling feature recognition; the neonate is also adapted to *act* appropriately to human communicative attention. The most striking evidence of human neonates' adaptedness to communication comes from studies showing that within minutes of birth neonates can imitate a variety of facial gestures and some sounds (Field, Woodson, Greenberg, & Cohen, 1982; Kugiumutzakis, 1985, 1993; Maratos, 1973, 1982; Meltzoff & Moore, 1977, 1983, 1992). The phenomenon of neonatal imitation is probably the most controversial infant behaviour in developmental psychology. Its significance for an understanding of communication is multifold. It appears to imply a degree of representational skill in neonates that most cognitive-developmental theories cannot easily accommodate. It implies an ability to recognise the similarity between self and other at a time when theories find it hard to conceptualise the ability to even differentiate between self and other. Moreover, it suggests that the human neonate is precociously able to engage in appropriate interaction with people, and particularly in those sorts of interactions which enhance connectedness between people. To those who have tried to engage in interaction with animals or with people who don't share the same language, the value of highlighting those of their acts which can be "understood" through imitation is obvious. Current debates centre not around the existence of the phenomenon but around its representational and communicative significance.

Some authors argue that imitations such as of tongue protrusion are reflexive behaviours since they can be produced by non-human stimuli simulating tongue protrusion such as a pencil poking out of a matchbox (Jacobson, 1979). However the value of such simulations as evidence of the neonate's ability to be tricked by a "mere stimulus" is inevitably limited by the quality of the simulation itself. To be "tricked" by a simulation shows nothing more than that; it does not necessarily demonstrate that the imitation itself is a reflex. Other authors have provided evidence which argue against the reflex hypothesis. The neonate's imitative capacities are not limited to one particular act, i.e. tongue protrusions. They have reliably been shown to imitate mouth opening, eye blinking, and certain sounds (Kugiumutzakis, 1985, 1993), and occasionally to imitate hand waving and expressions such as happy face and surprise face (Field et al., 1982). This variety seems to call for an explanation in terms of a general capacity to recognise the similarity between self and other rather than a specific localised reflex to an innate releasing mechanism. Further, the imitations are not rapid all or none phenomena. They occur after a time lag spent watching the model, and are produced with some bodily effort (Kugiumutzakis, 1993) and show self-corrective changes in the imitation of the model's actions (Meltzoff, 1994). An imitation can be re-elicited by the reappearance of the appropriate partner even after several hours (Meltzoff & Moore, 1992). Further, imitations are easier to elicit in experimental situations where the model is already engaging in affective interaction with the neonate, and are harder to elicit in non-interactive situations where only the experimental stimuli are offered to the infant (Kugiumutzakis, 1993). This suggests that there is something about the communicative situation which boosts the neonate's ability to produce experimentally significant discriminant imitations.

The communication of affects at 2–3 months

Despite the neonate's evident interest in faces and voices, there is often very little that parents observe as active communication. Imitative behaviour is difficult to be certain about outside controlled situations, and the most obvious of them—tongue protrusion—isn't something parents would normally try to elicit unless they discover it by accident or have some prior knowledge of the capacity. Both in terms of responses to adult communicative behaviour and in terms of attempts to initiate communication the neonate is not very forthcoming. Within the next four to six weeks, however, there is a slow but very marked change. Not only does the infant's repertoire of communicative behaviours increase, but the coherence of responses and initiations is visible.

The effect of the beginning of social smiling (between 4 and 8 weeks) on caregivers is often dramatic—it is seen to signal the start of real pleasure in others and of personhood. By the third month the infant is not only showing evidence of coherent initiations and responses which involve the whole body— limbs, vocalisations, gaze, and facial expressions, but is doing so *within* communicative exchanges. These exchanges have been called proto-conversations (Bateson, 1979; Snow, 1977; Trevarthen, 1977) because of their similarity to the dynamic nature of paralinguistic aspects of adult conversations (for a fuller description see Reddy et al., 1997; Trevarthen, 1977). There are some features of these proto-conversations worth repeating here. First, the communicative behaviours which the infant displays are not isolated acts in either an intra-individual or inter-individual sense. Unlike neonatal smiles and other expressions they do not occur out of context in terms of the infant's own bodily expressions and interests, or in terms of the partner's acts towards the infant. The smile, for example, does not stand alone. It occurs in a coordinated pattern of other expressions (gaze, arm gestures, vocalisations) within the infant and in coordination with the adult's gaze, vocalisations, and smiles. Second, the infant is not simply imitating the adult. The adult is much more imitative of the infant (Trevarthen, 1977), and the infant's expressiveness is not always cued in by the adult—the infant shows clear initiatives towards inactive or unresponsive partners (Stern, 1974; Trevarthen, 1977, 1979). Third, the exchanges at this age show very clearly an attunement of affect and attention (Stern, 1985). They involve a communication of affects, not of information—whether about affects or about anything else. This does not simply mean that these engagements consist of displays of affect from both partners; the attunement involves not just a sensitivity to others' affects and some ability to match them, but also a much more dynamic reciprocity between the affects of both. Trevarthen (1993) has shown that increases in boldness and a teasing quality in one partner are responded to by a decrease in boldness by the other, and that this dynamically rises and falls reciprocally rather than synchronously on both sides. Fourth, the infant can not only successfully seek and maintain such communicative interactions, she can also equally successfully avoid them. Avoidance of gaze and interaction intiatives can be active rather than simply a passive and uncontrolled reaction. It can happen with a neutral expression, with the infant repeatedly turning away from unwanted interaction, rather than driven by overwhelming distress.

Perturbation studies of these early communications provide the strongest evidence to date of just how mutual the interactions are and of just how active is the infant's role within them. In response to a sudden blank face from an active partner the infant does not just cease interacting, she makes several attempts to re-engage the partner's participation before withdrawing attention and becoming distressed (Tronick et al., 1978). However, the blank face could be taken as a negative cue in itself to which the infant is reacting negatively. The most interesting perturbation data come from studies by Murray and Trevarthen (1985; and supported by further research by Nadel & Tremblay-Leveau, in press) where the infant and mother were interacting happily via closed circuit television and then were exposed to a slightly de-synchronised re-play of happy interaction. Both mother and infant were disturbed even though there was no negative behaviour by the other. The mothers were unaware that it was a re-play, could not understand why the infant was not responding to them and gradually ended up by reducing their motherese and speaking in more of an adult tone to the infant. The infant responded by confusion and eventual avoidance. Such evidence argues strongly against the interpretation of such interactions that the infant and mother are independently engaging in expressions, that it is particular expressions in the other that each likes to experience, or that it is the filling-in-the-slots behaviour of the mother which gives the impression of genuine engagement. Further, Murray (1980) found that when interruptions (rather than perturbations) to interaction occur, for example when the mother turns to speak to someone else, the infant shows neither confusion, withdrawal, and distress nor active attempts to re-engage the mother; instead the infant ceases active engagement and quietly watches the mother or other person until the mother returns to the infant. This suggests that infants' distress at disruptions are not due to simple withdrawal of engagement, but to inappropriate engagement.

There is little doubt that the affective proto-conversations at 2 and 3 months are mutual and show the infant to be an active participant. Psychologists would still argue, nevertheless, about whether they constitute intentional communication. There are three reasons for supposing that such communication is not

genuinely intentional. One, there is no information being intentionally conveyed other than the affects of the people involved. As we saw earlier in the discussion of intentionality and the telegraphic metaphor, the cognitivist position requires that for communication to be intentional, it must be "about" something rather than be a mere expression of feelings (Camaioni, 1993). Two, and also from a cognitivist position, there is no evidence that the infant understands that the other understands the infant's communicative behaviour. Three, from a social constructionist position, it has been argued that intentions to communicate cannot be innate but must emerge from the attribution of intentions by the adult (Kaye, 1982; Lock, 1993; Newson, 1977). However, none of these positions can adequately explain the complex sensitivity of both partners in such early communication. The problem is very much one of defining intentionality. Fogel (1993), implicitly demonstrating the jazz group metaphor described above, provides evidence of complex micro influences, such as the co-regulation of intentions, during the process of communication. Communication is generally driven not by static pre-defined goals, but by the continual elaboration of actions and intentions in response to the other's actions. From such a perspective it would appear that communicative intentions (in infants as in adults) are constantly being re-formed within rather than prior to the communicative process. This position does not address the argument about whether or not the 2-month-old infant is capable of communicative intentions: It discards it as a false one. We need to study communicative intentions as a dyadic (but not attributionist) process, and we cannot separate the 2-month-old's communication from the 12-month-old's on the grounds of lack of intentionality in the former.

Enjoying regularity and surprise: The middle of the first year

After the intense one-to-one affective interchanges at 2 and 3 months, infants start becoming more interested in their environment, often turning away from familiar partners to watch distant corners of the room, lights, fans, etc. (Trevarthen, 1977). This changing interest coupled with the infant's (and partner's) greater confidence in face to face interactions often serves to raise the nature and level of boisterousness in the interactions. In order to gain or regain the infant's attention and interest in communication, the partner often resorts to rhythmic vocalisations and acts with abrupt changes or endings, using a theme and variation format (Stern, 1985). Interestingly, it is precisely such abruptness within a routine which has been found to elicit most laughter in infants (Sroufe & Wunsch, 1972), whether the "routine" involves a vocalisation, a visual approach, or a tactile stimulus. It appears to be the need to go beyond the gentle interactions of the first few months in order to maintain the infant's interest which gives rise to the development of many early baby songs and action routines. It is interesting that it is the element of controlled surprise which adult partners are manipulating

LIVERPOOL
JOHN MOORES UNIVERSITY
AVRIL ROBARTS LRC
TEL. 0151 231 4022

in order to interact with infants in the middle of the first year. Whatever the reasons for their origin, songs, action routines, and games involving abruptness with babies of this age appear to be a universal phenomenon. Infants react with enthusiasm to rhythmic routines and this responsiveness is used by parents in many ways which appear to both challenge the infant's initiatives and match them in affect (Stern, Hofer, Haft, & Dore, 1985). These early routines and games have been linked by many writers to the acquisition of social and gram-matical rules (Bruner & Sherwood, 1976; Dore, 1983; Ratner & Bruner, 1978).

The infant's role in these games and routines is initially one of simple enjoy-ment, but gradually changes through the middle of the first year. They more and more actively seek out and prompt the desired routines, and gradually, in the last quarter of the first year, start to take on lead roles in the games. This can be seen for example when the infant inclines her head to prompt the next move in a "let's throw the towel over your head" game, or where the infant is not just laughingly anticipating the other's reappearance in a "peepbo" game, but is herself doing the hiding. Perhaps most interesting after about 8 months of age, is the development of infant initiated novel games, where the infant uses the adult's responsiveness and reactions to particular acts and sequences to create novel forms of play. Accidental reactions of adults to events which the infant can repeat are enjoyed and repeatedly invoked in what quickly become short-lived family games; e.g. the infant accidentally gets nappy cream on his foot, the adult protests, the infant repeats with laughter; or the infant accidentally blocks the television, the adult protests and the infant repeats with enjoyment (Reddy, 1991). These are interesting because they make it clear that it is not simply the adult's routines which the infant adopts and learns the dramatic rules of. It is the idea of dramatic exchange itself which has developed, and is inspired by the continuing interest in others' emotional responses and a need to play with and manipulate them.

Playing with attention and emotion: 8–12 months

The infant's understanding of others' attention has recently assumed major significance because it is seen as the earliest manner in which the infant can understand that minds have "objects" (or, to use philosophers' jargon, that minds are "intentional" or have "aboutness"). Attention, like thoughts but unlike feelings, is always 'about' some 'object' or target. It has become standard within devel-opmental psychology to adopt a single criterion, the onset of proto-declarative pointing, to establish the age at which infants achieve an understanding of atten-tion. However, the infant is capable of a number of behaviours much earlier which suggest a continuity in the development of such understanding, and fur-ther that the nature of the understanding is not in the form of a "discovery" about minds, but in the form of an elaboration of existing understanding. This section describes some of these behaviours.

From 2 or 3 months the infant soon becomes able to "call" the attention of inattentive others to herself initially by responding to mutual gaze and positive attention with smiles and pre-speech, then by vocal "calling" which gradually becomes clear and distinguishable. However, the infant seems limited in its manipulation of others' attention to either sustaining, avoiding, or seeking it in relation to *herself alone*. Just as the content of early communication consists solely of the affects of the two participants, so the attention of others seems relevant to the infant only in so far as it is present or absent from herself. This changes, however, with the onset of games as we saw in the last section. The *activity* of the interaction becomes the focus of interest. There are a number of other actions through which it becomes apparent that the infant's interest in the attention of the other soon extends even further. A few of these are worth considering in some detail: giving, clowning and showing-off, gaze following, and social and attentional referencing.

Giving.   Somewhere between 8 and 11 months of age infants become interested in the exchange of objects with others. To adults, this developing interest and ability provides a new source of games and routines (Bruner, 1975). Infants soon start to hold out objects to attract others' attention to them, and to offer them to others. Even when they are initially unable to completely release an object into the open palms of others, it is clear that the offered object has entered the communication as a topic. Even though the infant makes no comment "about" the object, it nonetheless appears to be something outside of herself which the infant is now seeking to involve others with (Wellman, 1993).

Clowning and showing-off.   Another kind of topic which adds to a simple conversation of affects is actions by the self. As Bates et al. (1979) noted, from around 8 months of age infants start to deliberately produce actions which attract attention. They also deliberately repeat actions which they know from past experience will produce positive attention or laughter in others. The actions may be standard "clever" actions like waving or clapping, or they may be non-conventional ones like shaking the head or making funny faces or loud shrieks (Reddy, 1991). The point in relation to the ability to direct others' attention is this: Even though it is unclear whether the infant's primary purpose is to use the actions to obtain attention to self or to direct attention to the act itself, nonetheless, the other's attention is now clearly relevant to more than the infant's affects. The fact that the infant can link the attention of others to discrete actions and not just to direct communicative expressions shows that others are perceived as possessing some degree of general attentiveness to other than the infant alone.

Following others' gaze.   From at least around 6 months of age infants are able to follow others' gaze when they look at other things (Butterworth, 1991; Butterworth & Jarrett, 1991; Scaife & Bruner, 1975). Butterworth has shown that during the second half of the first year this ability becomes more refined and the accuracy of the following increases such that not just simple direction of gaze but also distance can be perceived from watching others' faces. It is still not known, however, just how much, or when, infants do use such gaze-following in everyday interaction. Nonetheless it would appear from the evidence that they spontaneously follow gaze in experimental situations, that they are at the very least interested in looking towards the targets of others' visual perception from remarkably early in life. This is evidence of a third kind that in the second half of the first year others' attention is of relevance to the infant not just in relation to the self, but also in relation to other "objects". Corkum and Moore (1995) criticise this interpretation by showing that infants can be conditioned to turn the head and eyes in the direction of another person's head turn and suggesting that the fact of conditionability detracts from the interpretation that infants of 9 months understand others' gaze as directed to an external target. However, the fact of conditionability does not necessarily imply that that is how infants normally come to follow others' gaze.

Social and attentional referencing.   The clearest evidence that the 9-month-old infant perceives others as attentive to external "topics" comes from studies of social referencing (Sorce, Emde, Campos, & Klinnert, 1985). These studies show that others' expressions are taken as some sort of comment upon ambiguous situations, objects, or persons, which the infant may use to guide her further action. This interpretation is challenged by Perner (1991) who argues that the mother's fearful look may simply evoke fear in the infant or may be remembered as usually preceding negative events. However, even non-ambiguous events are often responded to by infants with gaze to others' faces. For instance, an infant hears a toy make a sudden funny sound and turns to smile at her nearby mother. Others' attention to a target may thus be assumed by the infant, such that the infant does not actually direct the other's attention to it (perhaps even if it is necessary). Alternatively it may be that infants turn to look and smile following an event simply because they need to express their feeling.

Teasing.   During this period infants also show a developing sense of mischief and provocativeness which is expressed in explicit violations of routines and "norms" (Reddy, 1991). Three clear forms of provocativeness are common, usually occurring within positive interactions and responses. These are: provocative non-compliance, cheeky offer-and-withdrawal of objects, and cheeky disruption of others' actions. Such teasing varies in level depending on the nature of the violation, the knowledge of the "norm", and the history of the particular teasing game. These behaviours show that not only is the infant able to understand others' attentional and emotional reactions enough to repeat the acts they are directed to, but is motivated to attempt to further explore others' intentions and emotional reactions by contradictory and provocative initiatives. This is the age at which infants begin to cooperate with commands and prohibitions (Stayton, Hogan, & Ainsworth, 1971). Through cooperation as well as through teasing the infant is arguably demonstrating a developing understanding of others' intentions-for-the-infant.

Proto-language: 12–15 months

With the onset of proto-communicative pointing the infant's attempts to direct attention to targets becomes clearer. Two sorts of pointing are discussed in the literature—proto-imperative pointing and proto-declarative pointing. In both, the infant points to a target and turns back to look at the partner's face presumably to check that the other is attending to the gesture and to the target that is being pointed at. The difference is one of motivation: In proto-imperative pointing the infant seeks to obtain a desired object or help while in proto-declarative pointing the infant seeks to direct the other's attention (for its own sake) to the object. There is some disagreement about the age of onset of these activities. Some would place the onset of pointing on an average at 14 months (Franco & Butterworth, 1988), while some would place it at an average age of 12 months (Perucchini & Camaioni, 1993). Franco and Butterworth (1988) show that while on average pointing with gaze checking emerges at 14 months, it is not until 15 months that infants check gaze prior to pointing. This suggests that there is a slight delay before infants realise that if the adult is not even attending to them in the first place, there is no point in pointing.

There is some evidence that these two kinds of pointing do not in fact emerge simultaneously, but that proto-imperative pointing emerges at least a month or two before proto-declarative pointing (Perucchini & Camaioni, 1993). Further evidence of a dissociation between these two kinds of communication comes from Baron-Cohen's finding that children with autism both produce and understand proto-imperatives but neither produce nor understand proto-declaratives (Baron-Cohen, 1989, 1991). Similarly among the human reared great apes proto-declarative communication is non-existent or rare while proto-imperative communication is evidently present (Gomez, Sarria, & Tamarit, 1993). Such evidence of dissociation between proto-imperatives and proto-declaratives challenges the tool use hypothesis (i.e. that both kinds of communication derive from the same cognitive advance). The reason for the dissociation, however, is not entirely clear. Baron-Cohen (1991) and Camaioni (1993) argue that proto-declaratives are cognitively more complex than proto-imperatives—in order for the infant to show somebody an object, the infant needs to be able to understand (represent) that the other can perceive (represent) objects of attention. A complex (meta)representational skill is argued to be necessary for producing or understanding proto-declaratives. On the other hand, a simple understanding of means-ends relations (without any mind knowledge) is argued to be sufficient for producing and understanding proto-imperatives—e.g. when I point to the biscuit Mother gives it to me.

However, this argument of differential cognitive complexity is problematic on three grounds. First, the dissociation may be due to motivation rather than difficulty. It could be argued that in the case of autistic children and in the case of the apes the motivation to share objects of attention with others is not strong. However, it is not clear why normal infants should be motivated to produce proto-imperative points before proto-declarative points. Second, even proto-imperatives may show evidence of mind-knowledge (Gomez, 1991; Gomez, Sarria, & Tamarit, 1993). Most non-human primates do not engage in any kind of proto-declarative communication but are proficient in proto-imperative communication. Gomez argues that if one looks closer at the ontogenetic development of proto-imperatives in apes one sees that the process is gradual and phased in a number of steps. His critical finding is that while early proto-imperatives occur without gaze to the face of the recipient, and often manipulate the recipient's body in an object-like fashion, later proto-imperatives are more restrained and involve gaze to the recipient's face. Gaze to face is used here as an index of some recognition that attention, understanding, and intentions to act are visible not just in gross motor acts, but also in facial expression. Third, one could argue that neither proto-imperatives nor proto-declaratives need show any understanding of the other's mind. Perner (1991) challenges the general assumption that infant proto-declaratives are motivated by a desire to share objects of attention with others. He argues that it is quite possible that infants are performing some sort of experiment upon the adult's eyes by pointing and turning to check for an effect. In other words, proto-declaratives could be another form of imperative, both requiring nothing more than simple means-ends knowledge and the desire for a particular effect.

Why *do* infants produce proto-declaratives? There is surprisingly little literature in answer to this question. A naturalistic study of one infant's proto-declaratives at 14 months showed that proto-declaratives appear to be motivated by a variety of different motives (Reddy, submitted). The motives range from surprise at an event, perception of a favourite target, family routines about particular targets, to ritualistic ice-breaking gestures with strangers. Most proto-declaratives occur immediately after the infant has newly perceived the target. This suggests that it is the perception of a target of interest rather than a desire to experiment that prompts most declaratives. Further, declaratives are not always accompanied by gaze checking especially if the other is previously in close contact with the infant. Nor are declaratives repeated once a simple appropriate response is obtained. This suggests that neither the other's eyes nor their responses are the goal of the declarative acts.

Understanding the establishment of joint attention between the infant, an other and a target is of significance not just for resolving debates about the tool use hypothesis and about the infant's knowledge of attention in others. It is vital for an understanding of lexical development. One view of how children learn names for things is that faced with a variety of possible referents when an adult offers a name such as "car" while looking at area "X" is that despite the infinite number of possible hypotheses the child's hypotheses are constrained to take a particular form, that of assuming the name refers to a whole object (Quine, 1960). It could be argued, however, that reference is not infinitely open or inherently indeterminate; the "constraints" upon referential focus may lie as much in a history of shared actions upon the world, as in ideal forms within the infant. Indeed by the time the infant understands names for things, the adult and infant have already established a history of shared meanings and joint attentional focus. Baldwin (1993) shows that by 18 months of age infants are proficient in identifying the adult's referential intent even when the infant is looking at a different object from the adult. The infant of 12 and 18 months is not only sensitive to others' gaze as a reflection of their attention and intent, but also uses gaze checking strategically for directing their attention. Attention to targets is assumed if the adult and infant are in close proximity or prior joint attention has been established (Reddy, submitted; Reddy & Simone, 1995). From the above review of developments in joint attention it is clear that, even prior to the emergence of clear proto communication, infants and adults are engaged in joint activities where external targets whether they are games, infant actions, objects of adult gaze, or events of interest and fear, are important features of communication. Shared meanings about other than affects are already being established from the second half of the first year. The emergence of words expands and elaborates these shared meanings and shared objects of attention.

UNDERSTANDING PRELINGUISTIC COMMUNICATION: CONTINUITY AND EMBODIMENT

From the above description of developments *several kinds of continuity* are evident: In intentionality, in actions with others' attention, with others' communicative intentions, and with others' emotional reactions. The infant's *understanding of others' emotionality* changes from a simple interest in expression at birth to a sensitivity to the reciprocity of emotions at 2 months to a more complex management of affects at 6 months and then at 9 months, to a more pronounced interest in exploring specific emotional reactions and relating them to their targets. Proto-declarative communication is seen to mark the onset of intentional communication, of understanding of others' attentionality and of understanding of others' communicative intentions. It is often argued that only with proto-declarative pointing is a clear mental message or mental "object" evident, separate from the tangible "messages" in giving, showing-off, etc. However, it is clear that an *understanding of others' attention* is gradually developing through the first year well before proto-declarative pointing: first understanding others' attention to self, then understanding attention to joint activities, and then understanding attention to the activities of the self. It is also clear that *communicative intentions* are changing and developing through the first year; the simple intiatives of the 2-month-old, the boisterous enjoyment of the 6-month-old, and the mischief of the 9-month-old all precede proto-declarative pointing. Similarly an *understanding of others' communicative intentions* is changing from a recognition of communicativeness and its absence or inappropriateness at 2 months, to a recognition of invitations to games at 6 months, and a recognition of commands and prohibitions at 9 months. Therefore, to abandon communication up to 12 months as non-intentional simply because some arbitrary criteria have not been met is tantamount to neglecting the very activities which can help us to understand the nature of communication.

Such continuities provide powerful evidence that in order to understand the development of communication we need to study it in action and as an embodied process. Focusing on communication first and foremost as a disembodied mental process that is presumed to direct action has caused a distortion of even a description of communicative developments, and does not offer any explanation of the processes of change. This tendency to focus on the representational processes presumed to lead to behaviour rather than on behaviour itself is common to most of psychology, and is born of a dualism between mind and behaviour. This dualism is shared as much by behaviourism as by cognitivism (Coulter, 1979). In the cognitivist's agenda it is the mind which may direct the behaviour which is of interest, while for the behaviourist it is the behaviour itself without concern for mind. The solution is to recognise the mentality *of* behaviour, not to separate mind and behaviour and prioritise the one above the other.

Within a dualist model of communication it is logically impossible to prove the existence of mental "objects" from tangible ones evidenced as behavioural reactions. Even proto-declarative pointing could simply be interpreted as a testing of behavioural reactions (Perner, 1991) or as conditioned behaviour (Corkum & Moore, 1995). The 14-month-old who corrects his mother's misunderstanding by repeating his action until the mother shows she understands (Golinkoff, 1983, 1993) could simply be waiting for a particular response or object and not have any understanding of the mother's misunderstanding (Shatz & O'Reilly, 1990). Evidence of purely mental "objects" or understanding—i.e. without contamination through behavioural contingencies—is actually impossible to obtain. If the intentionality of communication is not evident in the infant's behaviour, but must be inferred from presumed representations of mental objects, then we have a problem. No amount of inference is going to allow us access to these representations. The intentionality of communication then becomes logically unprovable. If we view communication as a disembodied mental process we have in fact no evidence at all, not even in adults, that it is ever taking place.

Why *do* we search for criterial points in development to signal onsets of new kinds of understanding? Why are we not content with describing continuous change? Partly, discontinuity is pragmatic—it provides a useful shorthand for talking about change. Partly, discontinuity provides theoretical simplicity. Change as a process is much more difficult to explain than change as a leap or a product. However, discontinuous descriptions invite representational explanations—they allow us to ignore the relevance of all that goes in between as irrelevant behavioural noise. Arbitrary cut-off points are also useful in portraying development as an advance—we are reassured by clear leaps forward which differentiate the juvenile from the mature. Midgley (1980) describes a similar problem in comparative studies; we have been compelled by such a desire to establish man's superiority over beast that the search, lured by oversimplicity, has been for single differentia and unique features. The failure to find simplistic differences does not make man identical to beast: "We can do justice to the miracle of the trunk without pretending that nobody else has a nose . . . People . . . need not act as if they were threatened every time something that has been supposed an exclusively human attribute is detected in other creatures" (pp. 206–7). The search for single (and simple) differentia is both absurd and not especially flattering to any species since it obscures its truly characteristic richness and versatility. "What is special about each creature is not a single, unique quality but a rich and complex arrangement of powers and qualities, some of which it will certainly share with its neighbours" (p. 207). Similarly it could be argued that to mark the adult communicator as fundamentally different from the infant serves to obscure the emotionality and complexity of all communication.

REFERENCES

Baldwin, D. (1993). Early referential understanding: Infants' ability to recognise referential acts for what they are. *Developmental Psychology, 29*, 832–843.

Baron-Cohen, S. (1989). Perceptual role-taking and protodeclarative pointing in autism. *British Journal of Developmental Psychology, 7*, 113–127.

Baron-Cohen, S. (1991). Precursors to a theory of mind: Understanding attention in others. In A. Whiten (Ed.), *Natural theories of mind* (pp. 233–251). Oxford, UK: Blackwell.

Bates, E., Benigni, L., Bretherton, I., Camaioni, L., & Volterra, V. (1979). *The emergence of symbols: Cognition and communication in infancy.* New York: Academic Press.

Bateson, M.C. (1979). The epigenesis of conversational interaction: A personal account of research development. In M. Bullowa (Ed.), *Before speech: The beginning of human communication* (pp. 63–77). London: Cambridge University Press.

Bloom, L. (1993). *The transition from infancy to language: Acquiring the power of expression.* Cambridge, UK: Cambridge University Press.

Brazelton, T.B. (1986). Development of newborn behaviour. In F. Faulkner & J.M. Tanner (Eds.), *Human growth: A comprehensive treatise* (pp. 519–540). New York: Plenum Press.

Bruner, J.S. (1975). The ontogenesis of speech acts. *Journal of Child Language, 2*, 1–19.

Bruner, J.S., & Sherwood, V. (1976). Early rule structure: The case of "peekaboo". In R. Harre (Ed.), *Life sentences: Aspects of the social role of language* (pp. 277–285). New York: Wiley.

Butterworth, G.E. (1991). The ontogeny and phylogeny of joint visual attention. In A. Whiten (Ed.), *Natural theories of mind* (pp. 223–232). Oxford, UK: Blackwell.

Butterworth, G., & Jarrett, N. (1991). What minds have in common is space: Spatial mechanisms serving joint visual attention in infancy. *British Journal of Developmental Psychology, 9*, 55–72.

Butterworth, G., & Hopkins, B. (1988). Hand-mouth coordination in the new-born baby. *British Journal of Developmental Psychology, 6*, 303–314.

Camaioni, L. (1993). The development of intentional communication: A re-analysis. In J. Nadel & L. Camaioni (Eds.), *New perspectives in early communicative development* (pp. 82–96). London: Routledge.

Clarkson, M., & Berg, K. (1983). Cardiac orienting and vowel discrimination in newborns: Crucial stimulus parameters. *Child Development, 54*, 162–171.

Corkum, V., & Moore, C. (1995). Development of joint visual attention in infants. In C. Moore & P. Dunham (Eds.), *Joint attention: Its origins and role in development* (pp. 61–83). Hillsdale, NJ: Lawrence Erlbaum Associates Inc.

Coulter, J. (1979). *The social construction of mind.* London: Macmillan.

DeCasper, A.J., & Fifer, W.P. (1980). Of human bonding: Newborns prefer their mothers' voices. *Science, 208*, 1174–1176.

Desrochers, S., Morisette, P., & Ricard, M. (1995). Two perspectives on pointing in infancy. In C. Moore & P.J. Dunham (Eds.), *Joint attention: Its origins and role in development* (pp. 85–101). Hillsdale, NJ: Lawrence Erlbaum Associates Inc.

Dobrich, W., & Scarborough, H.S. (1984). Form and function in early communication: Language and pointing gestures. *Journal of Experimental Child Psychology, 38*, 475–490.

Dore, J. (1983). Feeling, form and intention in the baby's transition to language. In R. Golinkoff (Ed.), *The transition from prelinguistic communication.* Hillsdale, NJ: Lawrence Erlbaum Associates Inc.

Dziurawiec, S., & Ellis, H.D. (1986). *Neonates' attention to face-like stimuli: Goren, Sarty, & Wu (1975) revisited.* Paper presented at the annual conference of the Developmental Psychology Section of the British Psychological Society, Exeter, UK.

Eimas, P., & Friesen, W. (1971). Speech perception in infants. *Science, 171*, 303–306.

Eisenberg, R.B. (1975). *Auditory competence in early life: The roots of communicative behaviour.* Baltimore: University Park Press.

Field, T., Woodson, R., Greenberg, R., & Cohen, D. (1982). Discrimination and imitation of facial expressions by neonates. *Science, 218*, 179–181.

Fogel, A. (1993). Two principles of communication: Co-regulation and framing. In J. Nadel & L. Camaioni (Eds.), *New perspectives in early communicative development* (pp. 9–22). London: Routledge.

Franco, F., & Butterworth, G. (1988). *The social origins of pointing in human infancy.* Paper presented at the annual conference of the BPS Developmental Section, Coleg Harlech, Wales.

Friedlander, B. (1970). Receptive language development in infancy. *Merrill Palmer Quarterly, 16*, 7–51.

Frye, D. (1991). The origins of intention in infancy. In D. Frye & C. Moore (Eds.), *Children's theories of mind: Mental states and social understanding* (pp. 15–38). Hillsdale, NJ: Lawrence Erlbaum Associates Inc.

Golinkoff, R.M. (1983). Infant social cognition: Self, people and objects. In L. Liben (Ed.), *Piaget and the foundations of knowledge* (pp. 57–78). Hillsdale, NJ: Lawrence Erlbaum Associates Inc.

Golinkoff, R.M. (1993). When is communication a "meeting of minds"? *Journal of Child Language, 20*, 199–207.

Gomez, J.C. (1991). Visual behaviour as a window for reading the mind of others in primates. In A. Whiten (Ed.), *Natural theories of mind* (pp. 195–207). Oxford, UK: Blackwell.

Gomez, J.C., Sarria, E., & Tamarit, J. (1993). The comparative study of early communication and theories of mind: Ontogeny, phylogeny and pathology. In S. Baron-Cohen, H. Tager-Flusberg, & D. Cohen (Eds.), *Understanding other minds: Perspectives on the theory of mind hypothesis of autism* (pp. 397–426). Oxford, UK: Oxford University Press.

Goren, C.G., Sarty, M., & Wu, P.Y.K. (1975). Visual following and pattern discrimination of face-like stimuli by newborn infants. *Paediatrics, 56*, 544–549.

Jacobson, S.W. (1979). Matching behaviour in the young infant. *Child Development, 50*, 853–860.

Johnson, M.H., Dziurawiec, S., Ellis, H., & Morton, J. (1991). The tracking of face-like stimuli by newborn infants and its subsequent decline. *Cognition, 40*, 1–21.

Kaye, K. (1982). *The mental and social life of babies: How parents create persons.* London: Harvester Press.

Kugiumutzakis, G. (1985). The origin, development and function of early infant imitation. *Acta Universitatis Upsaliensis, 35* (Uppsala, Sweden).

Kugiumutzakis, G. (1993). Intersubjective vocal imitation in early mother-infant imitation. In J. Nadel & L. Camaioni (Eds.), *New perspectives in early communicative development* (pp. 23–47). London: Routledge.

Lock, A. (1993). Human language development and object manipulation: Their relation in ontogeny and its possible relevance for phylogenetic questions. In K.R. Gibson & T. Ingold (Eds.), *Tools, language and cognition in human evolution* (pp. 279–299). Cambridge, UK: Cambridge University Press.

Maratos, O. (1973). *The origin and development of imitation in the first six months of life.* Doctoral dissertation, University of Geneva, Switzerland.

Maratos, O. (1982). Trends in development of imitation in early infancy. In T.G. Bever (Ed.), *Regressions in mental development: Basic phenomena and theories* (pp. 81–101). Hillsdale, NJ: Lawrence Erlbaum Associates Inc.

Mehler, J. (1993). *What infants know.* Oxford, UK: Blackwell.

Meltzoff, A.N., & Moore, M.K. (1977). Imitation of facial and manual gestures by human neonates. *Science, 198,* 75–78.

Meltzoff, A.N., & Moore M.K. (1983). Newborn infants imitate adult facial gestures. *Child Development, 54,* 702–709.

Meltzoff, A.N., & Moore, M.K. (1992). Early imitation within a functional framework: The importance of personal identity, movement and development. *Infant Behavior and Development, 15,* 479–505.

Meltzoff, A. (1994). *Foundations for the notion of self.* Paper presented in symposium on Early Sense of Self, at the 9th international conference on Infant Studies, Paris, 2–5 June, 1994.

Merleau-Ponty, M. (1962). *Phenomenology of perception.* London: Routledge & Kegan Paul.

Midgley, M. (1980). *Beast and man: The roots of human nature.* London: Methuen.

Murray, L. (1980). *The sensitivities and expressive capacities of young infants in communication with their mothers.* Unpublished PhD thesis, University of Edinburgh, UK.

Murray, L., & Trevarthen, C. (1985). Emotional regulation of interactions between two-month-olds and their mothers. In Field, T. (Ed.), *Social perception in infancy.* Norwood, NJ: Ablex.

Nadel, J., & Camaioni, L. (Eds.). (1993). *New perspectives in early communicative development* (pp. 177–197). London: Routledge.

Nadel, J., & Tremblay-Leveau, H. (in press). Early perception of social contingencies and interpersonal intentionality: Dyadic and triadic paradigms. In P. Rochat (Ed.), *Early social cognition.* Mahwah, NJ: Lawrence Erlbaum Associates Inc.

Newson, J. (1979). The growth of shared understandings between infant and caregiver. In M. Bullowa (Ed.), *Before speech: The beginning of human communication* (pp. 207–222). London: Cambridge University Press.

Perner, J. (1991). *Understanding the representational mind.* Harvard: MIT Press.

Perucchini, P., & Camaioni, L. (1993). *Protodeclarative and protoimperative pointing.* Poster presented at the annual conference of the Developmental Section of the British Psychological Society, University of Birmingham, UK.

Piaget, J. (1952). *The origins of intelligence in children.* New York: International Universities Press.

Quine, W. (1960). *Word and object.* Cambridge, MA: MIT Press.

Ratner, N., & Bruner, J.S. (1978). Games, social exchange and the acquisition of language. *Journal of Child Language, 5,* 391–401.

Reddy, V. (1991). Playing with others' expectations: Teasing and mucking about in the first year. In A. Whiten (Ed.), *Natural theories of mind* (pp. 143–158). Oxford, UK: Blackwell.

Reddy, V. (submitted). The point of pointing: Sharing perceptions or manipulating behaviour? *Journal of Child Language.*

Reddy, V., & Simone, L. (1995). *Acting on attention: Towards an understanding of knowing in infancy*. Paper presented at the annual conference of the Developmental Section of the British Psychological Society, Strathclyde, Glasgow, September.

Reddy, V., Hay, D., Murray, L., & Trevarthen, C. (1997). Communication in infancy: Mutual regulation of affect and attention. In G.J. Bremner, A. Slater, & G. Butterworth (Eds.), *Infant development: Recent advances* (pp. 247–273). Hove, UK: Psychology Press.

Scaife, M., & Bruner, J.S. (1975). The capacity for joint visual attention in the human infant. *Nature, 253,* 265–266.

Schaffer, H.R. (Ed.). (1977). *Studies in mother-infant interaction*. London: Academic Press.

Shatz, M., & O'Reilly, A.M. (1990). Conversational or communicative skill? A reassessment of two year-olds' behaviour in miscommunication episodes. *Journal of Child Language, 17,* 131–146.

Sorce, J.F., Emde, R.N., Campos, J.J., & Klinnert, M.D. (1985). Maternal emotional signaling: Its effects on the visual cliff behaviour of 1-year-olds. *Developmental Psychology, 21,* 195–200.

Sroufe, L.A., & Wunsch, J.C. (1972). The development of laughter in the first year of life. *Child Development, 43,* 1326–1344.

Snow, C.E. (1977). The development of conversation between mothers and babies. *Journal of Child Language, 4,* 1–22.

Stayton, D.J., Hogan, R., & Ainsworth, M.D.S. (1971). Infant obedience and maternal behaviour: The origins of socialisation re-considered. *Child Development, 42,* 1057–1070.

Stern, D.N. (1974). Mother and infant at play: The dyadic interaction involving facial, vocal and gaze behaviours. In M. Lewis & L. Rosenblum (Eds.), *The effect of the infant on its caregiver*. New York: John Wiley.

Stern, D. (1985). *The interpersonal world of the infant*. New York: Basic Books.

Stern, D.N., Hofer, L., Haft, W., & Dore, J. (1985). Affect attunement: The sharing of feeling states between mother and infant by means of inter-modal fluency. In T. Field (Ed.), *Social perception in infancy* (pp. 249–268). Norwood, NJ: Ablex.

Terrace, H.S., Petito, L.A., Sanders, R.J., & Bever, T.G. (1979). Can an ape create a sentence? *Science, 206,* 891–902.

Trevarthen, C. (1977). Descriptive studies in infant behaviour. In H.R. Schaffer (Ed.), *Studies in mother-infant interaction* (pp. 227–270). London: Academic Press.

Trevarthen, C. (1979). Communication and cooperation in early infancy: A description of primary intersubjectivity. In M. Bullowa (Ed.), *Before speech: The beginning of human communication* (pp. 321–347). London: Cambridge University Press.

Trevarthen, C. (1982). The primary motives for cooperative understanding. In G. Butterworth & P. Light (Eds.), *Social cognition: Studies of the development of understanding* (pp. 77–109). Brighton, UK: Harvester Press.

Trevarthen, C. (1993). The function of emotions in early infant communication and development. In J. Nadel & L. Camaioni (Eds.), *New perspectives in early communicative development* (pp. 48–81). London: Routledge.

Tronick, E., Als, H., Adamson, L., Wise, S., & Brazelton, T.B. (1978). The infant's response to entrapment between contradictory messages in face-to-face interaction. *Journal of American Academy of Child Psychiatry, 17,* 1–13.

Van der Meer, A., van der Weel, F.R., & Lee, D.N. (1995). The functional significance of arm movements in neonates. *Science, 267,* 693–695.

Vedeler, D. (1991). Infant intentionality as object directedness: An alternative to representational-ism. *Journal for the Theory of Social Behaviour, 21,* 431–448.

Wellman, H.M. (1993). Early understanding of mind: The normal case. In S. Baron-Cohen, H. Tager-Flusberg, & D. Cohen (Eds.), *Understanding other minds: Perspectives from autism* (pp. 10–39). Oxford, UK: Oxford University Press.

Zeedyk, M.S. (1996). Developmental accounts of intentionality: Toward integration. *Developmental Review, 16,* 416–461.

CHAPTER THREE

Early speech perception and word learning

Kim Plunkett
University of Oxford, UK

Graham Schafer
University of Reading, UK

INTRODUCTION

In this chapter, we divide early language acquisition into three phases: early speech perception, word detection, and word learning. For each of these phases, we consider recent behavioural, brain imaging, and computational studies. Of course, neither these phases of language acquisition, nor the methodologies used to study them, are truly distinct. Processes overlap; so do methodologies. Our goal is to demonstrate, through an interdisciplinary approach to each of these three phases, how linguistic development may be driven by the interaction between general learning mechanisms and a richly structured environment.

EARLY SPEECH PERCEPTION

Experimental studies of speech sound discriminations

Long before they are capable of understanding or producing speech, infants appear capable of making judgements about speech sounds which resemble the judgements made by mature speakers. One important finding relates to their ability to perceive speech sounds as organised into a system of categories. For example, the sounds /ba/ and /pa/ are distinguished by the delay between the release of air from between the lips, and the onset of vocal fold vibration. This delay is termed voice onset time, or VOT. The longer the delay between the release of the plosive and the onset of voicing, the more likely that adult subjects will judge the sound that they hear to be a "p" rather than a "b". Using a speech synthesiser, it is possible to create artificial speech stimuli which differ from one another in fixed amounts of VOT. Pairs of stimuli can be presented, and subjects asked whether they can discriminate between them. How does one ask 4-month-old babies to discriminate between two stimuli? Eimas, Siqueland, Jusczyk, and Vigorito (1971) employed a technique called high-amplitude sucking. In this technique, infants are trained to suck at an artificial nipple, and rewarded by repeated presentation of a sound. The more they suck, the more they hear the sound. Infants soon become bored by this repetition, and reduce their rate of sucking. However, if they detect a difference in the sound presented, their sucking rate will increase. Eimas et al. showed that, like adults, 1–4-month-old infants can detect a change from /pa/ to /ba/, but fail to detect an equally-sized difference in VOT between two exemplars of /pa/ or /ba/. This phenomenon is called categorical perception. Categorical perception by 2–6-month-old infants has been demonstrated for many different category boundaries and in many different types of syllable (Eimas, 1975; Jusczyk, 1977; Jusczyk & Thompson, 1978).

The presence of categories for speech sounds can also be inferred from conditioned head turn experiments. In this paradigm, infants are conditioned to look at an interesting toy when they hear a particular sound. The extent to which this learning transfers to new stimuli can be used to assess whether or not subjects treat the new stimuli as equivalent to the training stimuli. Kuhl has used this technique to investigate infants' responses to acoustically different tokens drawn from the same phonetic category. Such differences may arise for example from changes in intonation or in speaker identity. Six-month-old infants treat acoustically different tokens of the same phoneme as equivalent (Kuhl, 1983).

During the first six months or so of life, infants actually outperform adults in a variety of tasks that tap into sensitivity for speech contrasts. Languages may be described in terms of phonemes. These in turn are composed of features. To take an example from English, the initial phonemes of the two words "lip" and "rip" are different. This contrast relies on the different featural make-up of the two phonemes /l/ and /r/, which differ by a single phonological feature. To produce the sound /l/, the tip of the tongue is placed against the alveolar ridge, behind the top teeth. To make /r/, the tip of the tongue is moved upwards and back towards the hard palate. This contrast conveys meaning in English. Phonemes are language-specific, however: The words "lip" and "rip" do not differ phonemically in Japanese, and therefore do not convey any difference in meaning.

Adults have difficulty discriminating between pairs of similar sounds which do not form phonetic contrasts in their own language. Infants between the ages of 6 and 10 months, on the other hand, have little difficulty making such discriminations. It appears that the infant is a sort of "universal phonetician", capable of making judgements about speech drawn from any of the world's human languages. For example, 6–8-month-old infants from an English-speaking background are able to distinguish the glottalised velar/uvular stop contrast /k'i/–

/q'i/ in Nthlakapmx (a North American language) and the Hindi retroflex/dental contrast /T/–/t/, neither of which is exploited in English (Werker & Tees, 1984). At around the age of one year, however, this ability to discriminate between pairs of sounds drawn from any of the world's languages disappears (Kuhl, 1993; Werker & Tees, 1984). Older infants appear to be sensitive only to speech contrasts present in their own language. An interesting aspect of this selective sensitivity appears to be that contrasts which are acoustically and phonologically very distinct from those of the native language can still be perceived (Best, McRoberts, & Sithole, 1988). Best et al. (1988) showed that infants of 7, 9, and 13 months of age were all able to discriminate between the lateral and the apical click contrast in Zulu. Werker and Pegg (1992) suggest that discriminability may depend upon the extent to which the contrast in question is assimilable within the subject's native phonology. The implication is that because Zulu click phonology is distant from English phonology, it is not processed by the speech sound system in learners of English.

What kind of representations underlie infants' performance in the first 6 months of life? Jusczyk and coworkers have addressed this question using a modified version of the high-amplitude sucking procedure described above (Bertoncini, Bijeljac-Babic, Jusczyk, Kennedy, & Mehler, 1988; Jusczyk, 1985; Jusczyk & Derrah, 1987). Instead of hearing repeated versions of a single stimulus during the preshift phase, subjects hear a number of different stimuli presented in a random order. In the postshift phase, a new stimulus is added to the original set of stimuli. For example, the subject is habituated to /bi/ /si/ /li/ /mi/. In postshift, the subject hears /bi/ /si/ /li/ /mi/ /di/ (all in random order, of course). Because the sounds in the preshift set already differ from one another in various ways, detection of a new item in the group depends upon the subject having already encoded a certain amount of information about the relations between group members. Using this technique it has been shown that 2-month-old infants encode information about both vowels and consonants, whereas 4-day-olds appeared to detect vowel shifts only, remaining relatively insensitive to consonantal changes (Bertoncini et al., 1988). Furthermore, comparison between groups allows experimenters to draw conclusions about the structure of the underlying representations. It can be argued that the data point to a holistic encoding of the syllabic stimuli, rather than an encoding based upon knowledge of phonetic category class. Subjects could have succeeded in Bertoncini et al.'s discrimination experiment by forming a separate representation for each syllable. Representations at the phonemic level are not necessary. This interpretation is supported by evidence which questions the status of the phoneme as a psychological entity, at least in older children. For example, Bruce (1964) asked preschoolers to imagine what a word would sound like if a particular sound were removed from it. Even five-year-olds found the task extremely difficult. Liberman, Shankweiler, Fischer, and Carter (1974) gave preschoolers learning tasks in which they had to tap out either the number of syllables in a word, or the number of phonemes. The phoneme task was a great deal harder. By analogy, it may be that babies are sensitive to features which distinguish amongst syllables, rather than features within syllables. In this context, discrimination judgements in young infants can be ascribed to an increasingly complex knowledge of syllabic structure, rather than truly phonetic representations. This is consistent with evidence that the discriminatory capacity for speech sounds is not the exclusive preserve of the human species (see Kuhl, 1986).

Brain imaging studies of speech sound discriminations

Very soon after birth the brain's left hemisphere shows a preference for speech sounds over non-speech. This is evident from electrophysiological studies such as those reported by Molfese (1977). Such findings should not be taken as evidence of hardwiring however. Children who are born deaf will sign with the same facility that hearing infants speak. In these infants the left hemisphere shows a preference for sign (Neville, 1985). Although in right-handed adults the left hemisphere is usually dominant for language, that dominance need not reflect a neural substrate specialised for language. Recent findings regarding the plasticity of the infant brain show that in certain circumstances, the right hemisphere will do the job equally well (Bates, Thal, Turner, Fenson, Aram, & Eisele, 1997).

The mechanisms by which the newly born infant can discriminate all human speech sounds, and the process by which the child becomes attuned to the parental language are not well understood. Dehaene-Lambertz and Dehaene (1994) have shown that auditory Event Related Potentials (ERPs) can be used to unravel the temporal and spatial organisation of the neuronal processes underlying phoneme discrimination. A light mesh of electrodes encased in saline-soaked sponges is placed over the infant's head and the infant is played synthesised speech stimuli, such as /ba/ and /ga/. Dehaene-Lambertz and Dehaene played 2-month-old infants synthesised speech stimuli as groups of five syllables (e.g. /ba/, /ba/, /ba/, /ba/, /ga/) where the first four syllables were identical (the standard) and the fifth was either identical or phonetically different (deviant). A significant difference in auditory ERPs between standard and deviant stimuli showed that the infant could discriminate the deviant stimuli. These differences were reflected in two peaks in scalp potentials occurring 220 ms and 390 ms after presentation of the stimulus, suggesting two stages in speech processing. Both peaks have been localised to the temporal lobes. Christophe and Morton (1994) suggest that this technique might be used to study the developmental profile of responses to native and non-native contrasts. This might shed light on whether the brain is still sensitive to non-native speech contrasts but ignores the information, or whether the ability to discriminate non-native speech contrasts is truly lost.

Computational studies of speech sound discriminations

Experimental work can tell us about infants' discriminatory powers. Auditory ERPs enable investigation of the spatial and temporal sensitivity of the brain to language-specific features in the acoustic stimulus. Neither approach, however, is likely to tell us how the brain responds to the demands of the tasks performed. One way to understand the organisation and operation of the neural systems underlying speech perception is to build a working computational model. Nakisa and Plunkett (1998) have developed a neural network model of early phonological development. This genetic connectionist model implements Jusczyk and Bertoncini's (1988) proposal that the development of speech perception should be viewed as innately guided learning. Speech contrasts of the native language are learned rapidly because the system is innately structured to be sensitive to correlations of certain distributional properties in speech and not others.

In the model, neurons are allowed to grow synapses under the control of genes for trophic factors. Other genes then control the way in which synapses are modified by experience. A population of these neural networks is generated and allowed to breed, with a selective pressure for networks that are able to classify spectral sounds into the phonemes of English. The fitness function that controls selection favours networks that represent occurrences of the same phoneme as similarly as possible and different phonemes as differently as possible. (In this, it differs from such models of phoneme recognition as that of Waibel, 1989, which tend to learn to associate a given set of sounds with a given phoneme, and hence provide no insight into the development of the ability to classify speech sounds.) After many generations of this evolutionary process one of these neural networks is exposed to test speech. This speech may be a sample drawn from any of 14 natural languages (English, Cantonese, Swahili, Farsi, Czech, Hindi, Hungarian, Korean, Polish, Russian, Slovak, Spanish, Ukranian, and Urdu). After its "birth", the network rapidly modifies its connections in response to the sounds in its environment. The representations it forms are generally the same regardless of the language to which it has been exposed. To see whether any sounds could be used for training, the network was trained on white noise. This resulted in slower learning and a lower final fitness. An even worse impediment to learning was to train on low-pass filtered human speech. The network behaves like the "universal phonetician".

When tested with contrastive stimuli from "non-native" languages—of the sort that 6-month-olds discriminate but adults do not—categorical boundaries are observed. For example, the network was tested on a series of 11 spectra which formed a linear continuum from the pure /sh/ to a pure /s/. Each of the 11 spectra in the continuum were individually fed into a network that had been trained on 30 sentences of continuous speech in English. The output feature responses were stored for each spectrum in the continuum. The distances of these feature vectors from the pure /sh/ and pure /s/ indicated the categorical nature of the network's internal representations of the speech spectra as shown in Fig. 3.1.

The advantages of innately guided learning over other self-organising networks are that it is much faster and is *less* dependent on the correct environmental statistics, offering an account of how infants from different linguistic environments can display similar sensitivities to speech contrasts soon after birth. In this sense, innately guided learning as implemented in this model shows how genes and the environment could interact to ensure rapid development of a featural representation of speech on which further linguistic development depends. In terms of the taxonomy of "ways to be innate" offered by Elman, Bates, Johnson, Karmiloff-Smith, Parisi, and Plunkett (1996), this model is lacking in any form of representational innateness—there is no hard-wiring of the micro-circuitry of the network. On the other hand, the model exemplifies what Elman et al. call "architectural/computational innateness"—innate processing biases in the network make it ideally suited to extracting structural information from speech input when the opportunity presents itself.

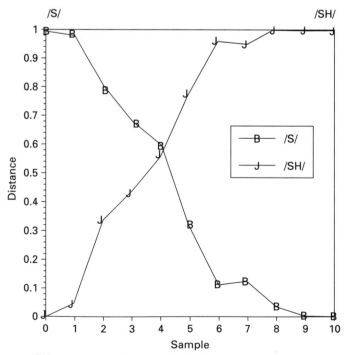

FIG. 3.1.   Categorical perception in the /s/ → /sh/ continuum.

WORD DETECTION

How does a child recognise that a word is present in a stream of speech? Are the capacities for speech sound discrimination discussed in the previous sections sufficient for this task? Word-finding constitutes a more difficult task than speech sound discrimination. The latter task may be accomplished using a "same" vs. "different" judgement. The task demands of word detection are higher than those of mere discrimination. Same–different judgements are insufficient for the detection of a word in the speech stream. Instead, the task is one of *recognition*. The infant must compare a stream of input with a set of stored representations. These representations must be of sufficient richness to encode the various patterns of words in the native language. In this section, we consider evidence of infants' ability to find words in the input stream. Specifically, we consider *segmental cues* and *correlation detection*.

Experimental studies

Within a few days of birth, infants are already sensitive to the structure of their native language, preferring to listen to it rather than a non-native language (Mehler, Jusczyk, Lambertz, Halsted, Bertoncini, & Amiel-Tison, 1988). This may well result from *in utero* exposure to the language environment. Griffiths, Brown, Gerhardt, and Abrams (1994) have demonstrated that the foetus is exposed to a great deal of high-quality speech during the third trimester of pregnancy. But what kind of word-finding information is the neonate sensitive to?

Using the high-amplitude sucking technique, it has been shown that 3-day-old infants can detect the difference between speech tokens containing word boundaries, and speech tokens which do not (Christophe, Dupoux, Bertoncini, & Mehler, 1994). Two sets of tokens were selected from speech samples. Both sets contained the same phonemic content, but in one set the phoneme string bridged a boundary between two words. Strings used were /mati/, taken for instance from the utterances "mathé*mati*cien", or from "pyja*ma ti*ssé". Infants were able to detect the switch. The authors argue that this is evidence of an ability to detect "prelexical cues" for word boundaries. However, it is possible that the subjects were simply responding to acoustic differences between the two stimuli sets, or that newborns have some knowledge of the rhythmic structure of their native language. Whether the infants are using acoustic or rhythmic information to perform this discrimination, or another representation entirely, cannot be established from a single experiment. This is particularly true in the case of an experiment such as this one where the same phoneme string is used repeatedly (/mati/). It would be more convincing if the experimenters had used two stimulus sets, each containing several strings of phonemes, and the sets had been distinguished only by whether or not they included a word boundary.

That an experimenter can provide an analytic description of a set of stimuli is not sufficient grounds to conclude that that description is the one that is being used in performing the task (Kemler Nelson, 1984). Converging evidence from several overlapping experiments may strengthen such an inference however. Whatever explanation turns out to be behind this result, as the authors point out, it should be regarded as "pre-lexical". Not because of the age of the subjects, but because the task itself is a same–different one.

In the second half of their first year, infants add to the knowledge enabling them to identify words and other linguistic units in speech. For example, Jusczyk, Cutler, and Redanz (1993) suggest that prelinguistic infants have identified a regularity of English wherein disyllabic words tend to adhere to a trochaic (strong–weak) stress pattern, and that they can use that knowledge to segment words from the main speech stream. Cutler and Carter (1987) suggest that perceptual or attentional biases, such as the tendency to attend to stressed and word-final syllables, may assist the infants in identifying word-level units in speech. Fernald, McRoberts, and Herrera (1996), using a preferential looking task, have shown that infants are more likely to recognise familiar words in utterance-initial or final position than when the word occurs in the middle of the utterance.

Saffran, Aslin, and Newport (1996) focused on the ability of young children to acquire linguistic structure via statistical cues. They point out that one potentially useful type of information for infant word segmentation is the statistical properties of multisyllabic words. Over a corpus of speech sounds, there are measurable regularities that distinguish those recurring sound sequences which comprise words from the more accidental sound sequences which occur across word boundaries. Saffran et al. used the familiarisation–preferential looking procedure developed by Jusczyk and Aslin (1995) and depicted in Fig. 3.2. In this procedure, infants are exposed to auditory material that serves as a potential learning experience. They are subsequently presented with two types of test stimuli: (1) items that were contained within the familiarisation material, and (2) items that are highly similar but were not contained within the familiarisation

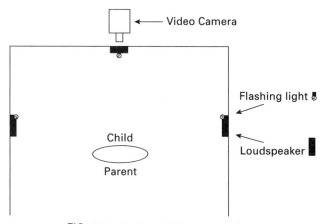

FIG. 3.2.   Preferential listening paradigm.

material. During a series of test trials that immediately follows familiarisation, infants control the duration of each test-trial by their sustained visual fixation of a blinking light. If infants have extracted the crucial information about the familiarisation items, they may show differential durations of fixation (listening) during the two types of test trials.

Saffran et al. (1996) showed that 8-month-old infants are able to perform the necessary statistical computations. Following a 2 minute exposure to a synthetic speech stream containing only statistical cues to word boundaries, the infants' listening preferences demonstrated that they had extracted and remembered serial order information about the familiarisation items. They distinguished "words" (recurrent syllable sequences) from syllable strings spanning word boundaries. This preferential behaviour indicates that the infants computed the co-occurrence frequencies for pairs of sounds across the familiarisation corpus. Saffran et al.'s (1996) findings suggest that infants have access to a powerful mechanism for the computation of statistical properties of the language input even from very brief exposures. They argue that infants may be far better at deriving structure from statistical information than has often been assumed in the acquisition literature. In particular, certain aspects of language which are argued to be unlearnable and thus innately specified may be discoverable by appropriately constrained statistical learning mechanisms.

This statistical ability may well underlie infants' success in tasks which tap sensitivity to phonotactic properties of stimuli. Phonotactic properties are those statistical properties of a language which determine which sounds can be followed by which other sounds. Jusczyk, Friederici, Wessels, and Svenkerud (1993) tested English- and Dutch-learning infants of 6 and 9 months on their preference for native over non-native word lists. Subjects were presented with lists of unfamiliar words in English and Dutch. The younger group showed no preference, but the older children preferred the native word list. This preference disappeared when the lists were low-pass filtered to preserve prosody but abolish phonetic information. To check that subjects were using phonotactics to make the discrimination, the experimenters removed from the lists all words containing non-native phones. The 9-month-olds still preferred the native list in this condition, where the only difference between the two lists was in distribution of sound sequences. Friederici and Wessels (1993) examined infants' sensitivity to phonotactics at 4.5, 6, and 9 months. Only the oldest group showed a preference for phonotactically legal over phonotactically illegal strings embedded in short sequences of continuous speech. Once more, this preference was abolished by low-pass filtering.

So far, we have seen that 8-month-old infants can detect statistical regularity in the linguistic environment, and detect the regularity of their own language. Can they put this ability to use in word finding? Jusczyk and Aslin (1995) have shown that they can. Infants are familiarised to two monosyllabic words. At the age of 7.5 months, infants show a preference for a continuous stream of speech which includes these words, over one which does not. Younger infants, of 6 months, cannot. Evidence suggesting that subjects perform this segmentation by using relatively detailed phonetic information comes from the intriguing finding that subjects fail if the target word differs from the familiarisation word by a single phoneme.

Brain imaging of word finding

We know of no published study of a neural correlate of the processing of phonotactics in infants.

Computational studies

Elman (1990) discusses a neural network that discovers word boundaries in a continuous stream of phonemes. Elman's network attempts to simulate the young toddler's task of identifying words from a continuous sequence of input phonemes. The network is fed one phoneme at a time and has to predict the next input state, i.e. the next phoneme in the sequence. The difference between the predicted state (the computed output) and the correct subsequent state (the target output) is used by a learning algorithm to adjust the weights in the network at every time step. In this fashion, the network improves its accuracy in predicting the subsequent state—the next phoneme. A context layer is a special subset of inputs that receive no external input, but feed the result of previous processing back into the network's internal representations. In this way, at time 2, the hidden layer processes both the input of time 2 and, from the context layer, the results of its processing at time 1. And so on recursively. It is in this way that the network captures the sequential nature of the input. These architectural constraints—particularly appropriate for sequential input—are built into the network—see Fig. 3.3. By contrast, network hypotheses concerning phonotactic constraints are not. They emerge from the processing, as we see later.

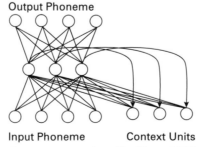

FIG. 3.3.   The type of simple recurrent network used by Elman (1990) to predict the next phoneme in a string of phonemes. The input to the network represents the current phoneme. The output represents the network's best guess as to the next phoneme in the sequence. The context units provide the network with a dynamic memory to encode sequence information.

The input corpus consists of sentence-like strings made up of a sequence of phonemes. The phonemes themselves go together to make up English words and the words make up sentences. In attempting to predict the next phoneme in the sequence, the network must exploit the statistical regularities implicit in the phonotactics of the language. It is not given any explicit information about the structure of the language.

Figure 3.4 depicts the root mean squared error for predicting individual letters in the string:

Manyyearsagoaboyandgirlllivedbytheseatheyplayedhappily.

Notice how the error tends to be high at the beginning of a word and decreases until the word boundary is reached. The error level for any phoneme can be interpreted as a measure of the level of confidence with which the network is making its prediction. Before it is exposed to the first phoneme in the word, it is unsure what is to follow. However, the identity of the first two phonemes is usually enough to enable the network to predict with a high level of confidence subsequent phonemes in the word. The time course of this processing is akin to Marslen-Wilson's proposal for a cohort model of word recognition (Marslen-Wilson, 1973; Marslen-Wilson & Welsh, 1978). Of course, when the input string reaches the end of the word the network cannot be certain which word is to follow so it cannot confidently predict the next phoneme. Consequently, the error curve for the phoneme prediction task has a saw-tooth shape with words falling into the teeth. The increased error at the beginning of a word (the start of the next tooth) shows that the network has discovered the word boundary.

Sometimes the network makes segmentation errors. For example, in Fig. 3.4 the string of phonemes "aboy" is treated as a single chunk by the network—the

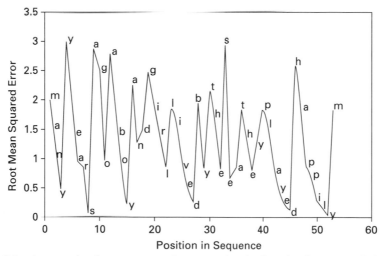

FIG. 3.4.   An example of an error curve for a network trained on the phoneme prediction task (after Elman, 1990). Error is high at the beginning of a word and decreases as the word is processed.

error continues to decline across the word boundary. This prediction is simply a consequence of the distributional characteristics of the article "a" and the noun "boy" in the language—they often occur together just like phonemes within a word occur together. In fact, there is considerable evidence in the child language literature that children make this type of mistake too. Peters (1983) and Hickey (1993) document the use of formulaic expressions in early first language acquisition. Similarly, Plunkett (1993) shows how two Danish children produce overshooting solutions to the problem of lexical segmentation. For example, young children often say "the nelephant" having missegmented the indefinite article and the noun ("an elephant"). Plunkett also identifies undershooting solutions in which children seem to postulate lexical units which are in fact shorter than the target words in the adult language. A typical equivalent in English would be "dult" instead of "adult" or the "ife" from missegmenting a "knife".

Elman's network also produces these undershooting segmentation errors (this time based on orthographic missegmentation). For example, notice in Fig. 3.4 that the error curve for the sequence "they" rises after the "e" at the 39th position. The network recognises the sequence "the" as a legal sequence and leaves the "y" stranded, unattached to any word. The "aboy" chunk produced at the 13th position constitutes an example of an overshooting segmentation error.

The network can learn to rectify some of these segmentation errors. On exposure to further training examples where the indefinite article "a" combines with a wider range of nouns, it will eventually learn to split "aboy" into two separate words. In contrast, the network will continue to have difficulty deciding whether "the" should be continued into "they" since the former is a legal unit itself. In order to solve this problem, the network would require higher order information as to whether to expect a pronoun ("they") or an article ("the"). Since sentences can begin with either, there will be some contexts where it can never decide. Within a sentence, however, the network might eventually be able to make a better guess.

More recent connectionist and statistical analyses (Brent & Cartwright, 1996; Christiansen, Allen, & Seidenberg, 1998; Redington & Chater, 1998) of the properties of real language corpora have contributed further to the view that the distributional information in the input may be of considerable utility to the language-learning child. For example, Christiansen et al. (1998) trained a simple recurrent network on a phoneme prediction task (just like Elman's model above). The model was explicitly provided with information about phonemes, relative lexical stress, and boundaries between utterances. Individually, these sources of information provide relatively unreliable cues to word boundaries and no direct evidence about actual word boundaries. After training on a large corpus of child directed speech, the model was able to use these cues to reliably identify word boundaries. Christiansen et al.'s model again shows that aspects of linguistic structure that are not overtly marked in the input can be derived by efficiently combining multiple probabilistic cues.

WORD LEARNING

Behavioural studies of word learning

One of the most dramatic events in children's early language development is the vocabulary spurt that occurs during the second half of the child's second year. Figure 3.5 depicts a typical profile of development in the size of a child's productive vocabulary during the second year. A relatively slow period of development (the plateau stage) is followed by a marked acceleration in rate of growth (the vocabulary spurt). Goldfield and Reznick (1992) have also argued that a similar accelerated rate of growth can often be observed in children's receptive vocabularies, though prior to the onset of their productive vocabulary spurts. There are three main families of theories about the mechanism under-lying the vocabulary spurt. These are linguistic development (Dore, 1978; Lock, 1980; Plunkett, 1993), conceptual development (Corrigan, 1978; Gopnik & Meltzoff, 1987), and the development of constraints on word learning (Clark, 1993; Golinkoff, Hirsh-Pasek, Bailey, & Wenger, 1992; Markman, 1991). All of these theories postulate the triggering of a new principle of organisation into the child's understanding of the object/label relationship. Woodward, Markman, and Fitzsimmons (1994; p. 554) argue that these explanations imply that learning a new word prior to the vocabulary spurt is likely to be a time-consuming process, requiring considerable exposure to a new word:

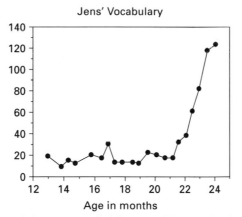

FIG. 3.5.   Profile of vocabulary scores typical for many children during their second year—taken from Plunkett (1993). Each data point indicates the number of different words used by the child during a recording session. It is usually assumed that the "bumps" in the curve are due to sampling error, though temporary regressions in vocabulary growth cannot be ruled out. The vocabulary spurt that occurs around 22 months is observed in many children (Bates, Bretherton, & Snyder, 1988). It usually consists of an increased rate of acquisition of nominals—specifically names for objects (McShane, 1979). Reprinted by permission of Cambridge University Press.

[. . .] these explanations imply that before the naming explosion and the insights or cognitive milestones that lead to it, learning a single new word would be a time-consuming process, requiring much exposure to the new word. [. . .] At the time of the naming explosion, it is argued, children become efficient word learners, capable of learning new words after only limited exposure to them.

There is growing evidence, however, that the young (pre-vocabulary spurt) child may not be as hampered in learning new words as was previously thought. Woodward et al. report that 13-month-olds can, under favourable circumstances, learn novel words from as few as nine presentations of a novel word token. In their experiment, subjects played with a pair of unfamiliar objects, both of which were brought to their attention, but only one of which was named; the new label was "toma". Each of the two objects was brought to the child's attention nine times. In *new label* trials, subjects were presented with two objects and asked for the "toma". In *familiar label* trials, subject's ability to understand the task was confirmed by asking them to choose between two objects whose names they knew. Subjects (32 13-month-olds) chose the target 64% of the time on the new label trials—a result significantly above chance. However, the experiment is open to criticism. As the authors themselves acknowledge, the visual distractors have never been named. Hence, the target may have been selected only because it had previously been named whereas Baldwin and Markman (1989) have shown that infants prefer to look at an object if it has been repeatedly named. Preferential looking at the target during testing might therefore have been caused by increased interest in the target object because it had previously been named, rather than because subjects knew that the label "toma" went with that object. The only sure way to avoid the effects of differential repetition is to equate the number of times that the distractor is named during training with the number of times that the target is named during training.

Schafer and Plunkett (1998) have succeeded in replicating Woodward et al.'s results under tightly controlled conditions which do not require the presence of an instructor, suggesting that the pre-vocabulary spurt child is already equipped with a powerful learning mechanism for forming object-label associations. Twelve- to sixteen-month-old infants were taught *two* novel words for two images of novel objects. Learning took place by pairing presentations of novel auditory label with presentations of the novel image. This was followed by a period of testing using the *preferential looking task* in which the subject was presented with the pair of novel images, and an auditory stimulus. Infants took longer looks at an image if it matched the auditory stimulus than if the auditory stimulus matched the other image, or matched neither image. The design of the experiment controlled for a variety of possible confounds including pragmatic factors, contrastivity, naming effects, object and word familiarity, visual salience, side preference, and auditory and phonological features of the stimulus. Subjects showed some learning after six presentations of the auditory label, and learned to distinguish between the two labels after 12 presentations. These results support the view that rapid word learning can occur prior to the vocabulary spurt. Nevertheless, it remains unclear whether the nature of the object/label relationship learnt in these experimental settings has the same linguistic status as words learnt after the vocabulary spurt.

Imaging early vocabulary development

Event-related potentials have been used to examine the neural correlates of word recognition in normal children. Mills, Coffey-Corina, and Neville (1997) examined the changes in the organisation of brain activity linked to comprehension of single words in 13–20-month-old infants. ERPs were recorded as children listened to a series of words whose meanings they did or did not understand, as well as to backwards words. The ERPs differed as a function of word comprehension within 200 ms after word onset. At 13–17 months comprehension-related differences were bilateral and broadly distributed over anterior and posterior cortex. In contrast, at 20 months these effects were limited to temporal and parietal regions of the left scalp.

Molfese, Morse, and Peters (1990) compared ERPs in 14-month-old infants who had been trained by their parents to associate each of two novel objects with two novel CVCV sequences ("gibu" and "bidu"). Subjects were trained by their parents for 20 minutes per day over five days. The infants were subjected to electrophysiological recording sessions both before, and after, training. The first session recorded the subjects' responses to the auditory stimuli "gibu" and "bidu". In the second session subjects heard the auditory stimuli, whilst looking at the objects. In half of the trials there was a match between the object and the auditory stimulus. In the other half of trials, there was a mismatch: The auditory stimulus matched the alternative object. The results indicated that responses of two brain areas discriminated a match from a mismatch: an early, bilateral, frontal response and a later, left hemisphere response.

These results indicate that the neural organisation for word comprehension shifts precisely during the period of development when language acquisition is most pronounced. The implication is that plasticity and reorganisation may be a natural property of the developing system, that is not restricted to compensatory changes in damaged brains. Mills et al. (1997) suggest that aspects of their ERP findings are linked to changes in early lexical development that typically occur between 13 and 20 months. Still unclear, however, is whether the ERP changes reflect qualitative changes in the underlying language processing of lexical items or a consolidation of existing lexical representations. Schafer and Plunkett (1998) have developed a technique based on the preferential-looking task for training infants on novel words. Combining novel-word learning with ERP measures offers an opportunity to evaluate whether the observed hemispheric specialisation for lexical processing arises from prolonged experience with words or from the development of new cognitive processing strategies.

Computational studies of word learning

Recent work in connectionist modelling has demonstrated that small and gradual changes in a network, not involving the maturation of new systems, can lead to dramatic non-linearities in its behaviour. For example, Plunkett, Sinha, Møller, and Strandsby (1992) trained a neural network to associate object labels with distinguishable images. The images form natural (though overlapping) categories so that images that look similar tend to have similar labels. The network was constructed so that it was possible to interrogate it about the name of an object when only given its image (call this production) or the type of image when only given its name (call this comprehension)—see Fig. 3.6.

Network performance during training resembled children's vocabulary development during their second year. During the early stages of training, the network was unable to produce the correct names for objects—it got a few right but improvement was slow. However, with no apparent warning, production of correct names suddenly increased until all the objects in the network's training environment were correctly labelled. In other words, the network went through a vocabulary spurt. The network showed a similar improvement of performance for comprehension, except that the vocabulary spurt for comprehension preceded the productive vocabulary spurt. Last but not least, the network made a series of under- and over-extension errors en route to masterful performance—again, a phenomenon observed in young children using new words (Barrett, 1995; Dromi, this volume).

There are several important issues that this model highlights. First, the pattern of behaviour exhibited by the model is highly non-linear despite the fact that the network architecture and the training environment remain constant throughout

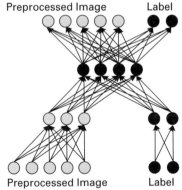

FIG. 3.6.   Simplified version of the network architecture used in Plunkett et al. (1992). The image is filtered through a retinal pre-processor prior to presentation to the network. Labels and images are fed into the network through distinct "sensory" channels. The network is trained to reproduce the input patterns at the output—a process known as auto-association. Production corresponds to producing a label at the output when an image is presented at the input. Comprehension corresponds to producing an image at the output when a label is presented at the input. Reprinted with permission.

learning. The only changes that occur in the network are small increments in the connections that strengthen the association between an image and its corresponding label. No new mechanisms are needed to explain the vocabulary spurt. Gradual changes within a single learning device are, in principle, capable of explaining this profile of development.

Second, the model predicts that comprehension precedes production. This in itself is not a particularly radical prediction to make. However, it is an emergent property of the network that was not "designed in" before the model was built. More important is the network's prediction that there should be a non-linearity in the receptive direction, i.e. a vocabulary spurt in comprehension. When the model was first built, there was no indication in the literature as to the precision of this prediction. The prediction has since been shown to be correct (Goldfield & Reznick, 1992). This model provides a good example of how a computational model can be used not only to evaluate hypotheses about the nature of the mechanisms underlying some behaviour but also to generate predictions about the behaviour itself. The ability to generate novel predictions about behaviour is important in simulation work as it offers a way to evaluate the generality of the network model for understanding human performance.

The behavioural characteristics of the model are a direct outcome of the interaction of the linguistic and visual representations that are used as inputs to the network. The non-linear profile of development is a direct consequence of the learning process that sets up the link between the linguistic and visual inputs and the asymmetries in production and comprehension can be traced back to the types of representation used for the two types of input. The essence of the interactive nature of the learning process is underscored by the finding that the network learns less quickly when only required to perform the production task. Learning to comprehend object labels at the same time as learning to label objects enables the model to learn the labels faster.

It is important to keep in mind that this simulation is a considerable simplification of the task that the child has to learn in acquiring a lexicon. Words are not always presented with their referents and even when they are it is not always obvious (for a child who does not know the meaning of the word) what the word refers to. Nevertheless, this modelling work suggests that the results observed in children with focal lesions and in ERP studies of word comprehension need not necessarily imply pre-wired, dedicated, modules. The results are entirely consistent with the non-linear onset of overt behaviours linked to gradual experience-driven learning processes and coordination of multiple representations in the underlying neural system.

SUMMARY

In this chapter, we have offered a selective review of some of the landmark phenomena exhibited by infants acquiring language during the first 18 months of life. From a methodological perspective, our approach has been decidedly eclectic, including evidence from empirical studies, computational modelling, and neuro-imaging. However, our selection of phenomena has not been neutral from a theoretical perspective. In each case, we have attempted to demonstrate how relatively general learning mechanisms might be capable of driving the acquisition of domain specific representations that underly speech perception, word recognition, and word learning. These general learning mechanisms need to be sufficiently powerful to extract the correct information from the environment. This implies that the mechanisms of language acquisition in some sense "know" what they are doing and that the information in the environment is there to be extracted. We do not suppose, however, that the mechanisms already possess the structures they are supposed to represent. The representations are not innate, just the computational resources necessary to build them (Elman et al., 1996). The studies we have reviewed indicate that these constructivist assumptions are not implausible. From the very beginning of language acquisition, or at least from when the neonate emerges from the womb, we suppose that powerful domain-general learning mechanisms are available to support the construction of linguistic representations.

Of course, it might be argued that our selective review has ignored some of the big questions of language acquisition. For example, we have not attempted to address the difficult problems associated with the acquisition of morphosyntax. This is clearly an important area of enquiry for any coherent theory of language acquisition—even though it is beyond the scope of this chapter. However, we suppose that the type of learning mechanisms postulated in this chapter are equally applicable to the construction of linguistic representations associated with later stages of acquisition (see Elman, 1993; Plunkett & Marchman, 1993). Few would make the mistake of underestimating the linguistic achievements of the 18-month-old child and the relevance of these achievements for further linguistic development. Likewise, it would be a mistake to underestimate the power of learning systems that can offer insights into how the infant might construct the foundations for further development.

REFERENCES

Baldwin, D.A., & Markman, E.M. (1989). Establishing word-object relations: A first step. *Child Development, 60*, 381–398.

Barrett, M. (1995). Early lexical development. In P. Fletcher & B. MacWhinney (Eds.), *The handbook of child language* (pp. 362–392). Oxford, UK: Blackwell.

Bates, E., Bretherton, I., & Snyder, L. (1988). *From first words to grammar: Individual differences and dissociable mechanisms.* New York: Cambridge University Press.

Bates, E., Thal, D., Turner, D., Fenson, J., Aram, D., & Eisele, J. (1997). From first words to grammar in children with focal brain injury. *Developmental Neuropsychology, 13*, 275–343.

Bertoncini, J., Bijeljac-Babic, R., Jusczyk, P.W., Kennedy, L.J., & Mehler, J. (1988). An investigation of young infants' perceptual representations of speech sounds. *Journal of Experimental Psychology: General, 117*, 21–33.

Best, C.W., McRoberts, G.W., & Sithole, N.N. (1988). The phonological basis of perceptual loss for non-native contrasts: Maintenance of discrimination among Zulu clicks by English-speaking adults and infants. *Journal of Experimental Psychology: Human Perception and Performance, 14*, 345–360.

Brent, M.R., & Cartwright, T.A. (1996). Distributional regularity and phonotactic constraints are useful for segmentation. *Cognition, 61*, 93–125.

Bruce, D.J. (1964). The analysis of word sounds. *British Journal of Educational Psychology, 34*, 158–170.

Christiansen, M.H., Allen, J., & Seidenberg, M.S. (1998). Learning to segment speech using multiple cues: A connectionist model. *Language and Cognitive Processes, 13*, 221–268.

Christophe, A., Dupoux, E., Bertoncini, J., & Mehler, J. (1994). Do infants perceive word boundaries? An empirical study of the bootstrapping of lexical acquisition. *Journal of the Acoustical Society of America, 95*, 1570–1580.

Christophe, A., & Morton, J. (1994). Comprehending baby-think. *Nature, 370*, 250–251.

Clark, E.V. (1993). *The lexicon in acquisition.* Cambridge, UK: Cambridge University Press.

Corrigan, R. (1978). Language development as related to stage 6 object permanence development. *Journal of Child Language, 5*, 173–189.

Cutler, A., & Carter, D.M. (1987). The predominance of strong initial syllables in the English vocabulary. *Computer Speech and Language, 2*, 133–142.

Dehaene-Lambertz, G., & Dehaene, S. (1994). Speed and cerebral correlates of syllable discrimination in infants. *Nature, 370*, 292–295.

Dore, J. (1978). Conditions for the acquisition of speech acts. In I. Markova (Ed.), *The social context of language* (pp. 87–111). New York: Wiley.

Eimas, P.D. (1975). Speech perception in early infancy. In L.B. Cohen & P. Salapatek (Eds.), *Infant perception: From sensation to cognition* (pp. 193–231). New York: Academic Press.

Eimas, P.D., Siqueland, E.R., Jusczyk, P., & Vigorito, J. (1971). Speech perception in infants. *Science, 171*, 303–306.

Elman, J.L. (1990). Finding structure in time. *Cognitive Science, 14*, 179–211.

Elman, J.L. (1993). Learning and development in neural networks: The importance of starting small. *Cognition, 48*, 71–99.

Elman, J.L., Bates, E., Johnson, M.S., Karmiloff-Smith, A., Parisi, D., & Plunkett, K. (1996). *Rethinking innateness: A connectionist perspective on development.* Cambridge, MA: MIT Press.

Fernald, A., McRoberts, G.W., & Herrera, C. (1996). *Effects of prosody and word position on infants' ability to recognize words in fluent speech.* Unpublished manuscript.

Friederici, A.D., & Wessels, J.M.I. (1993). Phonotactic knowledge of word boundaries and its use in infant speech perception. *Perception and Psychophysics, 54*, 287–295.

Goldfield, B., & Reznick, J.S. (1992). Rapid change in lexical development in comprehension and production. *Developmental Psychology, 28*, 406–413.

Golinkoff, R.M., Hirsh-Pasek, K., Bailey, L.M., & Wenger, N.R. (1992). Young children use lexical principles to learn new nouns. *Developmental Psychology, 28*, 99–108.

Gopnik, A., & Meltzoff, A. (1987). The development of categorization in the second year and its relation to the other cognitive and linguistic developments. *Child Development, 58*, 1523–1531.

Griffiths, S.K., Brown, W.S., Gerhardt, K.J., & Abrams, R.J. (1994). The perception of speech sounds recorded within the uterus of a pregnant sheep. *Journal of the Acoustical Society of America, 96*, 2055–2063.

Hickey, T. (1993). Identifying formulas in first language acquisition. *Journal of Child Language, 20*, 27–42.

Jusczyk, P.W. (1977). Perception of syllable-final stop consonants by 2-month-old infants. *Perception and Psychophysics, 215*, 450–454.

Jusczyk, P.W. (1985). The high amplitude sucking procedure as a methodological procedure in speech perception research. In G. Gottlieb & N.A. Krasnegor (Eds.), *Measurement of audition and vision in the first year of postnatal life: A methodological overview* (pp. 195–222). Norwood, NJ: Ablex.

Jusczyk, P.W., & Aslin, R.N. (1995). Infants' detection of the sound patterns of words in fluent speech. *Cognitive Psychology, 29,* 1–23.

Jusczyk, P.W., & Bertoncini, J. (1988). Viewing the development of speech perception as an innately guided process. *Language and Speech, 31,* 217–238.

Jusczyk, P.W., Cutler, A., & Redanz, N. (1993). Preference for the predominant stress patterns of English. *Child Development, 64,* 675–687.

Jusczyk, P.W., & Derrah, C. (1987). Representation of speech sounds by young infants. *Developmental Psychology, 23,* 648–654.

Jusczyk, P.W., Friederici, A.D., Wessels, J.M.I., & Svenkerud, V.Y. (1993). Infants' sensitivity to the sound patterns of native language words. *Journal of Memory and Language, 32,* 402–420.

Jusczyk, P.W., & Thompson, E. (1978). Perception of a phonetic contrast in multisyllabic utterances by 2-month-old infants. *Perception and Psychophysics, 232,* 105–109.

Kemler Nelson, D.G. (1984). The effect of intention on what concepts are acquired. *Journal of Verbal Learning and Verbal Behavior, 23,* 734–759.

Kuhl, P.K. (1983). Perception of auditory equivalence classes for speech in early infancy. *Infant Behavior and Development, 6,* 263–285.

Kuhl, P.K. (1986). Infants' perception of speech: Constraints on the characterization of the initial state. In B. Lindblom & R. Zetterstrom (Eds.), *Precursors of early speech* (pp. 219–244). Basingstoke, UK: Macmillan.

Kuhl, P.K. (1993). Early linguistic development and phonetic perception: Implications for theories of developmental speech perception. *Journal of Phonetics, 21*(1–2), 125–139.

Liberman, I.Y., Shankweiler, D., Fischer, F.W., & Carter, B. (1974). Explicit syllable and phoneme segmentation in the young child. *Journal of Experimental Child Psychology, 18,* 201–212.

Lock, A. (1980). *The guided reinvention of language.* London: Academic Press.

Markman, E.M. (1991). The whole object, taxonomic and mutual exclusivity assumptions as initial constraints on word meanings. In J.P. Byrnes & S.A. Gelman (Eds.), *Perspectives on language and thought: Interrelations and development* (pp. 72–106). Cambridge, UK: Cambridge University Press.

Marslen-Wilson, W.D. (1973). Linguistic structure and speech shadowing at very short latencies. *Nature, 244,* 522–523.

Marslen-Wilson, W.D., & Welsh, A. (1978). Processing interactions and lexical access during word recognition in continuous speech. *Cognitive Psychology, 10,* 29–63.

McShane, J. (1979). The development of naming. *Linguistics, 17,* 879–905.

Mehler, J., Jusczyk, P.W., Lambertz, G., Halsted, N., Bertoncini, J., & Amiel-Tison, C. (1988). A precursor of language acquisition in young infants. *Cognition, 29,* 143–178.

Mills, D.L., Coffey-Corina, S.A., & Neville, H.J. (1997). Language comprehension and cerebral specialization from 13 months to 20 months. *Developmental Neuropsychology, 13,* 397–445.

Molfese, D.L. (1977). Infant cerebral asymmetry. In S.J. Segalowitz & F.A. Gruber (Eds.), *Language development and neurological theory* (pp. 21–35). New York: Academic Press.

Molfese, D.L., Morse, P.A., & Peters, C.J. (1990). Auditory evoked responses to names for different objects: Cross-modal processing as a basis for infant language acquisition. *Developmental Psychology, 26,* 780–795.

Nakisa, R.C., & Plunkett, K. (1998). Evolution of a rapidly learned representation for speech. *Language and Cognitive Processes, 13,* 105–127.

Neville, H.J. (1985). Effects of early sensory and language experience on the development of the human brain. In J. Mehler & R. Fox (Eds.), *Neonate cognition* (pp. 349–363). Hillsdale, NJ: Lawrence Erlbaum Associates Inc.

Peters, A.M. (1983). *The units of language acquisition.* New York: Cambridge University Press.

Plunkett, K. (1993). Lexical segmentation and vocabulary growth in early language acquisition. *Journal of Child Language, 20,* 43–60.

Plunkett, K., & Marchman, V.A. (1993). From rote learning to system building: Acquiring verb morphology in children and connectionist nets. *Cognition, 48,* 21–69.

Plunkett, K., Sinha, C., Møller, M.F., & Strandsby, O. (1992). Symbol grounding or the emergence of symbols? Vocabulary growth in children and a connectionist net. *Connection Science, 4,* 293–312.

Redington, M., & Chater, N. (1998). Connectionist and statistical approaches to language acquisition: A distributional perspective. *Language and Cognitive Processes, 13,* 129–191.

Saffran, J.R., Aslin, R.N., & Newport, E.L. (1996). Statistical learning by 8-month-old infants. *Science, 274,* 1926–1928.

Schafer, G., & Plunkett, K. (1998). Rapid word learning by 15-month-olds under tightly controlled conditions. *Child Development, 69,* 309–320.

Waibel, A. (1989). Modular construction of time-delay neural networks for speech recognition. *Neural Computation, 1,* 39–46.

Werker, J.F., & Pegg, J.E. (1992). Infant speech perception and phonological acquisition. In C. Ferguson, L. Menn, & C. Stoel-Gammon (Eds.), *Phonological development: Models, research and implications.* Timonium, MD: York Press.

Werker, J.F., & Tees, R.C. (1984). Cross language speech perception: Evidence for perceptual reorganisation during the first year of life. *Infant Behavior and Development, 7,* 49–63.

Woodward, A.L., Markman, E.M., & Fitzsimmons, C.M. (1994). Rapid word learning in 13- and 18-month-olds. *Developmental Psychology, 30,* 553–566.

CHAPTER FOUR

Phonological acquisition

David Ingram
Arizona State University, Tempe, USA

INTRODUCTION

It is well established that children begin producing words typically around the end of the first year. This is followed by a relatively slow period of word acquisition up to approximately 18 months when, with a vocabulary in and around 50 words, they undergo a word spurt (a sudden increase in vocabulary acquisition). Subsequent development involves the onset and development of a grammatical system, and the refinement of the phonological system to a point when their speech is by and large intelligible.

The developmental facts about the acquisition of phonology have been reasonably assessed and reported in many places (Ingram, 1989; Vihman, 1991a, 1991b). A brief summary is as follows. The first 50 words or so have a simple syllable structure, e.g. CV, CVC, and reduplicated CVCV, and a small inventory of vowels and consonants. Development after the word spurt involves an elaboration of all of these, with a period of systematic errors, e.g. fricatives and affricates may be made into stops, unstressed syllables tend to be left out, velar and alveopalatal sounds are replaced with alveolars, consonant clusters are reduced to single consonants. Speech becomes more or less intelligible by age 3, with further need to acquire more elaborate words and possibly acquire a few of the more difficult sounds, such as English dental fricatives.

What has not been established, however, is how to interpret these facts. It is the issue of interpretation that will be the focus of the present chapter. That is, what is the nature of the young child's phonological system?

A PHONOLOGICAL CASE STUDY: THE DATA

Table 4.1 presents the first words of a young girl named Alice at 16 months, from Vihman and McCune (1994). The data are typical in many ways of the samples of first words that researchers use to determine the nature of phonological development. Some words are frequent and used in a range of contexts, while others are more restricted. The fundamental question here is the nature of the phonological system that underlies these words. The answer to such a question involves both theoretical assumptions about the form of children's phonological systems, and methodological questions about how data are analysed. Central theoretical questions include whether or not a child at this level even has a phonological system and if so, what is its nature. Is it developed with the same building blocks as the adult language being acquired, or do children have phonological systems that are qualitatively distinct? Methodological questions focus on what a phonological analysis involves. What data do we extract from Table 4.1 to make judgements about Alice's system, e.g. consonants, vowels, syllable positions, syllable structure, segmental interactions, phonological features, phonemes?

TABLE 4.1
The First Words from Alice, Taken from Vihman and McCune (1994)

apple (4) [ʔæ]	egg (8) [ʔeɪ]	milk (1) [m̩mæ̃]
baby (7) [beibi]	elephant* (4) [ãːɪjʌ]	mommy** (10) [maːn̩i]
bang* (1) [pãi]	eye (4) [ʔaɪ]	no (1) [næ]
belly (1) [vei]	flower (3) [p'adi]	nose* (1) [n̩ːæ]
blanket (1) [k'ɛt]	Grandpa** (3) [p'a]	Oscar (= puppet) (6) [ʔaʔ]
bottle (14) [baḍi]	hat (2) [ʔa]	plate (4) [p'ɛɪ]
bunny (3) [bʌn̩n̩ːi]	hello (1) [loʊ]	shiny (3) [taːji]
bye (1) [bai]	iron (2) [ʔãɪji]	shoe (1) [çi]
clean* (2) [tiːni]	key (1) [çi]	tea (1) [t̪iː]
daddy (2) [daːdi]	lady (4) [jɛːji]	up* (2) [ʔʌːp]
down (2) [dãʊ]	man (1) [mæ̃ː]	
duck (1) [tæʔ]	meat (1) [miʔ]	

The number of times each word was observed is entered within parentheses. Those marked with * were words with a "limited" range of use, i.e. restricted contexts. Those with ** were specific nominals, i.e. names for specific individuals.

THEORETICAL ISSUES

Before presenting an analysis of Alice's data, it is necessary to make some theoretical assumptions about early phonological acquisition, and present a phonological model to be used in the analysis. The theoretical assumptions involve when children begin phonological acquisition and the nature of their early phonological systems. The theoretical model that will be used is the current phonological theory generally known as non-linear phonology (see Kenstowicz, 1994 for a comprehensive overview).

The onset of phonological acquisition

In order to talk about a child's phonological abilities, we need at the onset to determine when in fact phonological acquisition begins. One possibility is that children begin acquiring words as unanalysed units without any phonological form whatsoever. The child's system in such a case would involve the simple mapping of phonetic sequences onto word meanings. This position was suggested by Schvachkin (1973), and has been proposed more recently in Macken (1978), Locke (1983), and Vihman (1991a). Locke (1983) suggests this is the case at least up to the 50th word in production. If this were true, it would be of little use to do phonological analyses on data like those from Alice who has only acquired 34 words at this point in her acquisition. We can call this perspective a Discontinuity View on phonological acquisition.

An alternative to discontinuity is to argue that children begin phonological acquisition from the very onset of word acquisition. Further, this acquisition will involve the use of properties of the adult phonological system. This position involves a claim that there is continuity in phonological acquisition rather than discontinuity. This Continuity View can also be found supported in the research literature in Demuth and Fee (1995), Dinnsen (1996), and Macken (1987).

How than are we to decide between these two perspectives? My assessment of the arguments for both sides falls in favour of the Continuity View (Ingram, 1992, pp. 434–5). There are both logical and empirical arguments that can be given to support continuity. The logical argument is one taken from Pinker (1984) who proposes that continuity is the default assumption in language acquisition. Without evidence to the contrary, the initial assumption is that children are using the same mechanisms to acquire language as the adult has. In the area of syntactic acquisition, continuity has been widely assumed since Pinker's discussion. This has not been the case, however, in phonological acquisition where it remains a central point of contention.

There is no one empirical finding that leads one to decide this issue, but there are a series of points that together support continuity. Here we will just consider three of these. First, there is a substantial research literature on the development of speech perception in infants. These results show that infants are remarkably good at perceiving speech, and that they are becoming aware of language specific properties of their linguistic input before they begin word acquisition. Such results indicate that infants at least have the perceptual abilities needed to extract relevant acoustic information from the speech signal for phonological analyses. Second, we know that children's receptive vocabularies are much larger than their expressive ones. Based on data in Benedict (1979), for example, a child who is producing 50 words may have a receptive vocabulary in the neighbourhood of 250 words. The question then becomes how children are storing these receptive word forms. It is a reasonable expectation that a vocabulary of that size would trigger the child's innate phonological abilities for their representations.

Third, the claim that children store holistic, unanalysed representations implies that their word forms should not show the consistent phonological patterns of children's words at a later time. Analyses of the first 50 words, however, as we will see in our analysis of Alice's data, do show consistent patterns similar to later development.

The nature of children's early representations

A central assumption in all current work in phonological theory is that there is a distinction between the surface (phonetic form) of a word, and an underlying (more abstract) representation. Further, the underlying form is one that consists of prosodic information about syllable structure and distinctive features. The acquisition issue is how much of this information is in place at the onset of phonological acquisition. We will begin with a discussion of the nature of the first syllables, then turn to the acquisition of distinctive features.

Syllable structure.   If we assume continuity, it follows that the young child will be using the more basic phonological structures available from the innate system that allows phonological knowledge to be developed; then they will build up more complex structures over time. Regarding the nature of the child's first syllables, Demuth and Fee (1995) have offered a continuity model which claims that children follow several stages in the acquisition of syllable structure (see also Fikkert, 1994). Underlying their approach is the assumption that syllables have the universal structural properties shown in Fig. 4.1. Syllables consist of an optional coda consonant and a rhyme. The rhyme has a nuclear vowel, and an optional coda, which can be either a consonant or another vowel. The individual parts that form the rhyme are each a "mora" (a unit of time). For example, whether the rhyme is a VC or a VV, it will contain two moras.

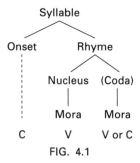

FIG. 4.1

Given that the structure in Fig. 4.1 is the building block of phonological systems, Demuth and Fee attempt to account for how a child might develop both this and more complex syllables through several stages. Here we will look at the first two stages that they propose. The first stage (or Stage 1) is the *Core Syllable*

Stage. The child begins with a core syllable CV, a syllable consisting of a single consonant onset and a nucleus, e.g. [dɑ]. This core syllable contains just one element in its rhyme and therefore it consists of just a single mora. The first words, therefore, will not have final consonants nor any complex vowels such as diphthongs or long vowels.

The second stage follows shortly after the very first words and will cover many of the first 50 words or so. This is the *Minimal Word Stage* where a minimal word consists of the syllable structure in Fig. 4.1 with one additional aspect: Syllables form feet, and feet are bimoraic. This allows the two foot structures in Fig. 4.2, and results in three possible syllable structures: CVCV, CVC, and CVV, e.g. [badi], [kit], and [ki:]. It is at this stage that final consonants emerge, as well as more complex vowels. It is also of importance that the model predicts that these new additions to the system will only be found in single syllable words. Words which contain two syllables such as reduplications will only consist of core syllables.

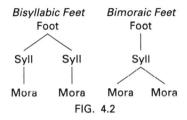

FIG. 4.2

Later, we will apply these stages to the analysis of Alice's data. For now, we finish the presentation with an example of how this model can account for variations in word acquisition. Stemberger (1992), reported that his daughter had the following variations in her early words. A word with a final consonant would sometimes be pronounced with a final consonant, and sometimes it would be deleted. When it was deleted, however, she would change the vowel to a diphthong, otherwise it was a simple vowel. Some examples are *bite* [bɑj] & [bɑt], and *grape* [dɑj] & [dɑp]. These variations can be explained by the Demuth and Fee model by saying that this child was at the Minimal Word Stage, and that her word needed to consist of two moras. When the final consonant was included, the vowel was simplified to meet this requirement. When the consonant was omitted, however, then the bimoraic diphthong could surface.

Feature representations.   Feature representation refers to the extent to which the child has acquired the distinctive features that underlie his consonants and vowels. For example, consider a child who has acquired a phonological contrast between /p/ and /t/, as in words such as *pop* [pɑ] vs. *top* [tɑ]. The representations for [p] and [t] would contain one or more distinctive features. Let us assume further that this was the only phonological contrast that this child had acquired.

Such a situation is typical, as noted years ago by the Russian linguist Roman Jakobson (Jakobson, 1968) who is in many people's minds the founder of phonological acquisition research. Jakobson suggested that the feature distinction acquired was labial vs. dental.

In more recent years, researchers have become more concerned about the exact form of such feature representations. There are two fundamental questions involved: (1) what features are represented, and (2) how they are represented. Continuing with our simple example, we have several choices for which features are selected, e.g. [labial], [dental], [coronal]. If we select [labial], we can say that [p] is [+labial] and [t] is [−labial]. Other features would be filled in by redundancy rules, i.e. rules that state the predictable. One such rule would be that any sound not specified for manner of articulation is a stop consonant. A sound that is [−labial] with no other place feature is redundantly [+coronal].

Concerning how features are represented, there are in general two ways that are currently being discussed in the phonological literature. One of these is known as radical underspecification (RU). RU proposes that only marked features are shown underlyingly; other features are supplied by redundancy rules. In our example, we could claim that [labial] is a marked feature, and that [coronal] is unmarked. [p] in this case would be underlyingly [+labial], and [t] would have no representation of a distinctive feature. Since [t] has no features, it is filled in by redundancy rules as [t], i.e. the least marked consonant. A further development of RU is to propose that features are not binary, i.e. plus or minus, but unary, i.e. the feature either exists or not. This makes the [p] simply [labial] underlyingly. An alternative to RU is contrastive specification (CS). Contrastive specification maintains the notion of binary features, and proposes that all distinctive features are marked underlyingly. This approach then would represent both [p] and [t] with a feature, e.g. [+labial] for [p] and [−labial] for [t].

Current research is actively involved in trying to determine which features should be represented and how. An interesting proposal in this regard is that found in Rice and Avery (1995). Central to the Rice and Avery proposal is an attempt to capture that variation in feature acquisition that occurs between children. Jakobson (1968) first suggested that features are acquired in an invariant sequence, e.g. first nasal vs. oral, then labial vs. dental. This predicts that the first consonants for all children with be /p/, /t/, /m/, /n/. Subsequent research has shown that this is too rigid, and that children vary quite a bit in their first features (Ferguson & Farwell, 1975).

Rice and Avery propose a system whereby children have choices concerning where they may start feature acquisition. Figure 4.3 provides a simplified version of their model. Root marks the beginning point of a tree-like structure containing features that are hierarchically arranged. At the next level down, there are four major types of features. Laryngeal represents features that concern the activity of the vocal cords so that voicing and aspiration are under this node (we will ignore the specifics of these features for now). Air Flow and Place are self-evident. SV is an abbreviation for Sonorant Voice, and deals at the first level below with nasal vs. oral articulations. This is a feature proposed and defended in Rice (1993) and its status is somewhat controversial. All features are unary, i.e. they either exist or not. Further, unmarked features are shown within parentheses.

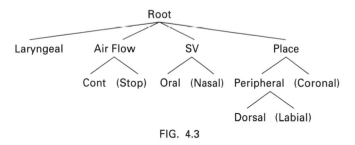

FIG. 4.3

This system would be applied to our simple example in the following manner. First, our child has a choice of starting acquisition at any one of the four nodes. In our case the child has decided to start at the Place node, i.e. to acquire a place distinction. [t] would need only to be represented as having Place, since (coronal) is the predictable feature for a sound unmarked for any Place features. [p], however, is represented as Place, Peripheral. The unmarked (or redundant) feature for Peripheral is Labial, so it does not need to be marked. The details of this system need to be developed and applied to a range of data. Later we will do so for our data from Alice.

The limited research to date on how children represent features supports the RU approach. Rice (1995) has argued that underspecifying features accounts for patterns of variability in children's words. It has been known for some time that children consistently produce some sounds, yet show variable pronunciations for others. For example, Amahl Smith (Smith, 1973) at one point had acquired the word initial stops as [b], [d], and [g]. He did not yet, however, have any features for the Laryngeal node where [voice] occurs. As a result his pronunciation of these stops varied at time between voiced and voiceless sounds. Rice suggests that variable pronunciations will be just in those cases where the variable sounds involve non-specified features.

Rice also proposes that the underspecification of features predicts the range of substitutions that a child will use. Using Amahl as an example again, she points out that Amahl used the consonant [w] for the adult consonants /f/, /v/, and /w/. In the Rice and Avery system, his features for [w] are Place [Labial], and Continuant. Since /f/, /v/, and /w/ all share these features, words with these sounds are pronounced as [w].

Evidence for underspecification of the feature [coronal] can be found in Stemberger and Stoel-Gammon (1991). Stemberger and Stoel-Gammon examined consonant harmony in 51 children acquiring English. Consonant harmony involved instances where one consonant in a word harmonises with or becomes like another consonant within the same word. For example, a word like *duck* might be pronounced as "guck" where the coronal [d] has assimilated to the velar point of articulation of the final [k]. RU predicts that assimilations of this kind are always predictable: Marked features will spread to segments that are unmarked for those features. In our example, the marked feature Dorsal on the [k] has spread to the underspecified Place feature of the [d]. Stemberger and Stoel-Gammon predicted that children's assimilations should be in one direction, i.e. alveolar (or Coronal) sounds becoming labial or dorsal, rather than the reverse. Their results confirmed this, as approximately 95% of the assimilations were in the predicted direction.

Support for the RU model for children's representations can also be found in Dinnsen (1996). Dinnsen, however, argues for a modification to RU, which he refers to as context-sensitive RU. This approach argues for the specification of marked features, but allows for marked features to vary according to syllable position. Dinnsen shows this in the patterns of acquisition of voiced and voiceless stops in English. In syllable initial position, voiced and voiceless stops become voiced, indicating that [+voiced] is the unmarked feature (and therefore is not specified), and [−voiced] is the marked one. When syllable initial voiceless stops are acquired, they become specified as [−voiced]. This situation is reversed in syllable final position, however, where voiced and voiceless stops are first produced as voiceless. For this position, therefore, the unmarked feature is [−voiced] and the marked one is [+voiced].

Besides acquiring features and their specifications, a theory of phonological acquisition also needs some constraints on how features are acquired over time. Take, for example, a case where a child produces [ga] for *duck*. We could propose that the representation for [g] is Place [Dorsal] since it is pronounced with a dorsal (velar) consonant. The problem with this account is that the [d] in the adult word does not contain a Dorsal feature. The child will need to restructure its underlying form in order to reach the adult form, which would constitute a violation of continuity. Another example of a different kind is a child who produces non-low vowels (let us say /i/, /e/, /o/, /u/) as [u], and all low vowels (/æ/, /ɔ/, /a/) as [a]. What feature underlies this contrast? Without any constraints on possible features, it could be + or − [round], [low], or [high].

Ingram (1991, 1995) proposed the Distinctive Feature Hypothesis (DFH) to constrain the possible features that a child may select. The DFH states: "Children phonologically analyse and represent their first words in distinctive features selected from the set of available phonetic features in the fully specified phonetic representation" (p. 431). The gist of this proposal is that children do not assign a feature to a segment unless that segment contains that feature in the adult word. In our [ga] for *duck* example, the child cannot assign an underlying Dorsal to [g] in its word because the adult word *duck* does not have a Dorsal consonant in syllable initial position. This constraint leads us to an alternative account. An analysis that meets the DFH is to claim that the child has the underlying form CVC, and the Dorsal feature is part of the underlying representation of the final /g/. This feature than spreads to the initial [d] (as predicted above because the [d] is unmarked for Place), with the subsequent deletion of the final consonant. In the vowel example, the features [+high] or [+round] are ruled out for /u/ because the target sounds /i/, /e/, /o/, /u/ are not uniformly either one. The only feature that works for all the substitutions is [low], because /a/ can be specified as [+low] and the other vowels /i/, /e/, /o/, /u/ are [−low].

PHONOLOGICAL ANALYSIS

Let us now return to the data for Alice and see if we can account for her phonological system using the theoretical approaches presented above. The data were part of a study on word identification done by Vihman and McCune (1994) on 20 children. This is of importance because they were not given as part of a study on phonological acquisition and thus in defence of any particular phonological theory on acquisition. The study did, however, follow a set of criteria for word identification, and carefully transcribed each word. Therefore, the data can be considered an objective set of word forms from a child in the early stage of phonological development. The sample from Alice was selected simply because it was one with a large enough number of words for detailed analysis.

General observations

Before presenting a detailed analysis of these data, it is important to examine the individual words and reach certain decisions about how the data will be analysed. First and foremost is the issue of *frequency*. How often does a pattern need to occur in a set of data for it to be considered part of the child's system? Certain patterns will be lexical, meaning that they will only be found in individual words. Take, for example, the two words *no* [næ] and *nose* [nːæ]. Here we find a minimal pair which differs only in the length of the initial consonants. *No* has a single consonant while *nose* has a geminate (i.e. long consonant). One could argue that this child has acquired a phonological contrast between long and short consonants in the onset position. This would be a peculiar thing for the child to do, however, given that English does not have geminate consonants of this kind. A simpler explanation, however, is that this was an idiosyncratic pattern attributable to the single transcription of a single word *nose*. Ingram (1981) has argued that such lexical patterns should be kept distinct in a phonological analysis from those ones that meet a frequency criterion, and we will do so in the present analysis.

An examination of the words in Table 4.1 indicates several aspects of the data that merit a closer examination. Certain phonological properties are standardly examined, such as syllable structure and the nature of the child's consonants and vowels. Alice is using a small set of consonants, and her vowels are clearly not yet acquired (e.g. *duck* [tæʔ], *flower* [p'adi]). There also are certain unique properties to her language. One of these is the role of nasal consonants and nasalisation of vowels. For example, we have words like *bang* [pãi] with a nasal vowel, and others like *bunny* [bʌn̩n̩ːi], which has nasal consonants but no nasalisation. There should be pattern to when nasals do and do not appear. Another striking feature is the extensive use of diminutive forms, i.e. words ending in "y" [i]. Some are simply cases of modelling the input word, e.g. *belly*, *bunny*, but others are not so simply explained, e.g. *bottle*, *clean*. Still another pattern is Alice's use of a word medial [j] in words such as *elephant*, *iron*, *lady*, and *shiny*. The subsequent sections will look at each of the areas identified above in more detail.

Syllable structure

Table 4.2 presents a breakdown of the syllable types found in Alice's 34 word forms. There are eight forms that have a simple CV structure, the form predicted by Demuth and Fee to occur as the canonical syllable. (We will ignore here the idiosyncratic occurrence of long consonantal onsets as discussed above.) If these are canonical syllables, these words should be among the first that Alice acquired. Unfortunately, the data does not date the ages at which these words were acquired so this prediction cannot be tested. Also, six or the eight forms involve the use of a low vowel (either [ɑ] or [æ]. We could refine the Demuth and Fee model based on such data to propose that canonical syllables will typically involve low vowels. This fits our data and conforms to the claims made in Jakobson about the first syllables. The remaining two forms involve the vowel [i] which could be interpreted as a tense (bimoraic vowel) and thus moved into the CVV column.

The rest of the syllable types can be interpreted with some qualifications as comprising minimal words. We have 5 CVC forms, with just one form [ʔʌːp] showing a complex rhyme which is not predicted by the minimal word stage, i.e. there are three moras. This use may fall into the idiosyncratic usage category. A more frequent monosyllabic pattern is CVV, which consists of 10 words. These forms support the minimal word stage which requires the vocalic nucleus to

TABLE 4.2
Distribution of Syllable Structures in Alice's 34 Word Forms

CV	CVV	CVC	CVCV	Other
apple [ʔæ]	bang [pãi]	blanket [k'ɛt]	baby [beibi]	bunny [bʌn̩n̩ːi]
Grandpa [p'a]	belly [vei]	duck [tæʔ]	bottle [baḍi]	elephant [ãːıjʌ]
hat [ʔa]	bye [bai]	meat [miʔ]	clean [tiːni]	
key [çi]	down [dãʊ]	Oscar [ʔaʔ]	daddy [daːdi]	
milk [m̩mæ]	egg [ʔeı]	up [ʔʌːp]	flower [p'adi]	
no [næ]	eye [ʔaı]		iron [ʔãıji]	
nose [nːæ]	hello [loʊ]		lady [jɛːji]	
shoe [çi]	man [mæ̃ː]		mommy [maːn̩i]	
	plate [p'ɛı]		shiny [taːji]	
	tea [tiː]			

consist of two moras. The CVCV or bisyllabic forms show the dominance of the diminutive pattern; all these forms end in the vowel [i]. The striking pattern in this list of 10 forms is the use of a bimoraic vowel in the first syllable for 8 of the 10, with one showing a VC nucleus. This requires at least for these data a refinement to the definition of the minimal word for bisyllabic forms. Instead of the structure on the left side of Fig. 4.2, we need to replace or have as an alternative the structure in Fig. 4.4 where the first syllable is also bimoraic.

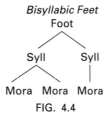

FIG. 4.4

Given that Alice is still acquiring her first words, it does not seem likely that she has passed from the bisyllabic stage as proposed in Demuth and Fee. Data from individual subjects such as this one demonstrate how hypotheses on phonological acquisition can be examined and developed.

In summary, the data from Alice indicate support for the first stages of prosodic structure in Demuth and Fee with a few adjustments to account for these particular data. Alice's syllables showed the following patterns: (1) words with canonical syllables where canonical syllables are CVs with a vocalic nucleus consisting of a low vowel; (2) words with minimal word structures, CVV, CVC, and CVVCV where the first syllable must be bimoraic. These patterns capture approximately 82% of the word forms in the data.

Vowels

Vowel acquisition has been studied much less than other aspects such as consonants. One reason is that the early results on vowels suggested that they are acquired earlier than consonants (Templin, 1957). Because of this early acquisition, data on children's early vocabularies often show relatively accurate vowel productions. Other factors are that there are dialect variations involved, and vowel transcriptions are not always as easy to do as consonantal ones. Nonetheless, as pointed out by Stoel-Gammon and Harrington (1990) for English and Fee (1991) for Spanish and Hungarian, children acquire vowels over time and will at the earlier stages show developmental errors.

The earliest proposal on the order of acquisition is found in Jakobson (1968). He suggested that children have two choices they may follow in their development of vowels. One is that they may be acquired on the height dimension, so that one early system would be i, e, a. The alternative is to acquire the basic vowel triangle, i.e. i, a, u. More recently, Fee (1991) has observed that the sequence of vowel acquisition may also be sensitive to language specific patterns of development. Fee found, for example, that Spanish children are more apt to acquire the mid vowels earlier than the high ones. Similar findings on consonant acquisition have also been noted (Pye, Ingram, & List, 1987).

Alice provides useful data for the study of vowels in that she has a limited set of vowels at this time and shows errors in her usage. We have already seen in Table 4.2 that she uses only the vowel [i] in the second syllable of her bisyllabic forms. The analysis here, therefore will examine only the vowels in monosyllables or in the first syllable of bisyllabic forms. We also set a frequency criterion of two, i.e. any vowel has to occur at least twice in her production (we will alter this in a moment). The frequencies of Alice's vowels are shown in Fig. 4.5 in the form of a phonetic chart, along with those target vowels they represent. Frequencies for both Alice's productions and the English phonemes they represent are given in parentheses.

[i]   (4):   /i/ (3), /u/ (1)
[eɪ]   (4):   /eɪ/ (3), /ɛ/ (1)
[æ]   (6):   /æ/ (2), /oʊ/ (2), /ʌ/ (1), /ʌ/ (1)   [ʌ]   (2):   /ʌ/ (2)
[ɑɪ]   (3):   /ɑɪ/ (3)   [ɑ]   (8):   /ɑ/ (4), /æ/ (2), /ɑɪ/ (1), /ɑʊ/ (1)

FIG. 4.5

It is at this point in a phonological analysis that issues around the interpretation of the data become critical. Some target sounds are produced both correctly and incorrectly, e.g. /æ/ which is produced twice correctly, but also twice as [ɑ]. Ingram (1989) suggests a simple frequency criterion for such data: Interpret a target phoneme as acquired (or at least produced correctly), if it is correct over 50% of the time. By this criterion, Alice has acquired the following vowels: /i/ (100%), /eɪ/ (100%), /ɑ/ (100%), /ʌ/ (67%), and /ɑɪ/ (75%). If we were to raise our frequency criterion to at least three words correctly produced, this would eliminate /ʌ/ from the acquired list. Such decisions can be justified on the grounds that the stiffer the criterion the more apt we are to identify the established system.

When we impose the stronger criterion, Alice is following the first of the two paths that Jakobson suggested, that is, she is acquiring her consonants from the top to the bottom of the vocalic chart, with a concentration of front consonants. This front vowel tendency can also be used to explain several patterns in the data. The high vowel [i] is used once for the phoneme /u/ *shoe*. This pattern follows from an analysis in which the distinctive feature is [high], since both [i] and [u] are [+high]. A redundancy rule states that the unmarked high vowel is [i]. It also captures the use of variability that we see within the low vowels. The acquisition of the vowels /i/ and /ɑ/ can also be used to explain the early and accurate use of the diphthong which is a combination of these two vowels. The determination of the vowel features actually acquired would require examination of current systems and how they are represented. Here we will simply suggest that features used to distinguish height would be the relevant ones.

Word initial consonants

Consonant acquisition has been much more extensively studied than vowels. They are a larger set of speech sounds which are also acquired over a longer period of time. Since Ferguson and Farwell (1975), word initial consonants have received particular attention since they are more frequent than consonants in other positions so constitute a more robust set of data for the examination of the child's phonological development.

The first predictions by Jakobson (1968) on consonant acquisition were that the first system children acquire across languages was universally m, n, p, t. We have noted that this was a proposal that was too rigid, and that individual children will show their own orders requiring the flexibility of the Rice and Avery feature system (Fig. 4.3). At the same time, grouped data from children indicate that there are basic inventories of consonants that all children in a linguistic environment acquire (Ingram, 1992). They may show variant individual orders of acquisition but collectively tend to acquire specific groups of consonants before others. Support for this proposal comes from combining the more frequent consonants by groups of individual children and seeing the consonantal inventory that results. These inventories tend to be different across languages.

Table 4.3 presents some examples of consonantal inventories for English, K'iche' (a Guatemalan language), Turkish, and Dutch. The English data on word initial consonants are taken from Ingram (1981) based on 15 children between the ages of 17 and 26 months (mean age 21 months). Similar results can also be found in Stoel-Gammon (1985) with the addition of /j/ which did not meet the frequency criterion in the Ingram (1981) study. The K'iche' data represent the frequent word initial consonants in five children between 19 months and 3 years (mean age 27 months) as reported in Pye et al. (1987). The Turkish data are based on 22 children observed longitudinally (2 subjects), and cross-sectionally

TABLE 4.3
Consonants Acquired and Not Acquired by English, K'iche',
Dutch, and Turkish Children

Acquired

English	*K'iche'*	*Turkish*	*Dutch*
m n	m n	m n	m n
b d g		b d	
p t k	p t ʧ k ?	p t ʧ k	p t k
f s h	x		f s h
w	w l	j	w j

Not Acquired
English: ʧ, dʒ, θ, ʃ, ð, z, j, r, l
K'iche': ts, q, b', t', ts', ʧ', k', q', s, ʃ, r
Turkish: dʒ, g, f, s, h, v, z, ʒ, ɣ, r, l
Dutch: x, b, d, l, r.

(20 subjects) as reported in Topbas (1992). The inventory for Turkish consists of those consonants acquired by 21 months, combining data across all syllable positions. (Topbas does not break down the data by syllable position.) The Dutch data are based on my analysis of the cross-sectional data on syllable initial consonants used by 10 children between 27 and 29 months in Beers (1995). A sound was considered acquired if six or more children used the sound correctly in at least 75% of instances.

A comparison of these inventories reveals how different the acquisition order can be from language to language. English, for example, has both /l/ and /ʧ/, yet they are not part of the basic inventory of 2-year-olds. They are, however, part of the early K'iche' inventory, and actually constitute two of the most frequently used consonants. English and Turkish both have /f/, /s/, /ʃ/, and /ʧ/ but their acquisition order is quite different. English children acquire /f/ and /s/ first, while Turkish children acquire the affricate /ʧ/ first. The subsequent acquisition of these is /ʃ/ (2 years), /s/ (29 months), and /f/ (34 months). Pye et al. (1987) suggest that these differences result from the different distribution or functional load of consonants in the word types in the language. For example, /ʧ/ in K'iche' is the most frequent sound used in children's words but it is only 13th most frequent in English. Such results indicate that children's articulatory skills are sufficiently developed by the time of the first words that their speech will reflect the characteristics of the particular linguistic system being acquired.

Inventories such as those in Table 4.3 are useful for comparisons of the consonantal systems of individual children. To analyse Alice's consonants, again we need to raise the issue of frequency. As mentioned before, one needs to be cautious in using single instances of words. Since they are only recorded once, they are more apt to be the result of either an atypical production by the child, or a transcription error by the experimenter. Table 4.4 provides an analysis of Alice's word initial consonants for those words that were used at least twice

TABLE 4.4
Word Initial Consonants in Alice's First Words*

English phoneme	Words and Consonants Used	Frequency
/b/	[b]baby, [b]bottle, [b]bunny	[b] 3/3
/p/	[p]plate, (Grand)[p]pa	[p] 2/2
/d/	[d]daddy, [da]down	[d] 2/2
/k/	[t]clean	[t] 1/1
/f/	[p]flower	[p] 1/1
/h/	[ʔ]hat	[ʔ] 1/1
/l/	[j]lady	[j] 1/1
/m/	[m]mommy	[m] 1/1
/ʃ/	[t]shiny	[t] 1/1
/ʔ/	[ʔ]apple, [ʔ]egg, [ø]elephant, [ʔ]eye, [ʔ]Oscar, [ʔ]iron, [ʔ]up	[ʔ] 6/7, [ø] 1/7

*[ø] indicates a missing consonant.

in Table 4.1. This decision eliminates the following words from the analysis: *bang, belly, blanket, bye, duck, hello, key, man, meat, milk, no, nose, shoe, tea*. A glance at these forms will show that these are also among the most unusual looking forms. Later we will discuss the effect this decision has on the analysis.

The data in Table 4.4 are just the first step in the organisation of data for an analysis. We need to decide on the basis of such information the nature of the child's system. Frequency again becomes an issue. Do we want to include the consonants that occur only once, i.e. the data for /k/, /f/, /h/, /l/, /m/, and /ʃ/? For demonstration purposes we will do so. Another decision involves variant forms. In these data, we have only one such case for vowel initial forms. Six of the seven words begin with a glottal stop, and one has no consonant. Ingram (1989) suggests that we take the majority occurrence in such cases. Here we will do so since the one form, the glottal stop, is much more frequent.

A summary of the data in Table 4.4 is given in Fig. 4.6. Cases where there was only a single instance of a pattern are placed within parentheses. The data have been divided into two general groups. The sounds occurring in more than one instance have been named *productive*. Those with only one instance are *lexical*, meaning that they can only be verified in a single word.

Productive
[b] /b/   [d] /d/
[p] /p/, (/f/)   [t] (/ʃ/, /k/)   [ʔ] /vowels/, (/h/)

Lexical
([m] /m/)   ([j] /l/)

FIG. 4.6

Before doing a final analysis, we can ask how the data would have looked if we had included the words excluded by the frequency criterion. Their inclusion would result in two differences. First, the inclusion of *man, meat*, and *milk* raise the status of [m] to a productive pattern. Second, the inclusion of *no* and *nose* would introduce [n] as a productive pattern. The inclusion of the [m] data would appear to be a reasonable one. Three separate instances of a sound also in the more restricted data suggests the child has [m]. The inclusion of [n], however, is more problematic. Recall that *no* and *nose* are odd forms; they involve an odd vowel substitution and are virtually the same form except for the odd gemination of the initial consonant. Technically we are dealing with two consonants, [n] and [nː], so their inclusion would only put them into the lexical category.

Another decision involves the status of [t]. It occurs for two target consonants, yet only once for each. We could include another frequency criteria which states that the child's sound has to occur twice, but it also has to be used for at least two target sounds. If so, [t] would be eliminated. We can see then that these various decisions about what data to include will vary to a degree the claims we make about the child's knowledge. Fig. 4.7 summarises these variant forms and their subsequent analyses.

a. Exclude words with single tokens, and consonants with single targets:
   productive: [b]/b/, [p]/d/, [d]/d/, [ʔ]/vowels/
   lexical: [m]/m/, [j]/l/
b. Exclude words with single token:
   productive: [b]/b/, [p]/d/, [d]/d/, [t]/t/, [ʔ]/vowels/
   lexical: [m]/m/, [j]/l/
c. Include single instances:
   productive: [m]/m/, [b]/b/, [p]/d/, [d]/d/, [t]/t/, [ʔ]/vowels/
   lexical: [n]/n/, [n:]/n/, [j]/l/

FIG. 4.7

We have now reached the point where a phonological analysis can be done of the patterns that have been extracted from the primary data. We will do this for the productive patterns in Fig. 4.7. A first issue to address is the nature of the glottal stop that occurs before words beginning with vowels and /h/. It is well known that there is phonetically a glottal stop before these words in English. This is normally treated as a low level phonetic process, and that the underlying forms consist of a vowel. There is less consensus, however, on how to treat the nature of the underlying forms in either the adult language or child language data such as the above. There is also a lack of agreement on how to treat /h/ in terms of its features and relation to vocalic onsets and the predictable glottal stop. Descriptively we can say that Alice is using a difference between onsets that have supralaryngeal features and those that do not. We will treat these cases as words which have an onset that is empty versus those that are filled. Empty onsets are redundantly filled with a glottal stop.

All three productive patterns in Fig. 4.7 require a feature that distinguishes labials from alveolars, and a voice feature. Figure 4.7(c) also requires a nasal feature. We can then say that Alice has at least acquired a difference between labials and coronals, voiced and voiceless stops, and possibly nasal vs. oral stops. The main differences between the three analyses is whether nasal vs. oral is acquired, and the extent to which the other two features are represented in the system.

We can represent these analyses more formally within the Rice and Avery system of features. Rice and Avery do not discuss [voice], but Rice (1995) suggests that [−voice] is unmarked, and that [+voice] or simply [voice] is marked, at least for obstruents, under the Laryngeal node. Table 4.5 presents the representations of Alice's word initial consonants in the Rice and Avery system with the adjustments discussed for the three possible analyses in Fig. 4.7.

There is an interesting problem for the analysis of the [m] in Fig. 4.7(c). To get the labial feature we need to specify it, otherwise the redundancy rules will produce an [n]. By specifying it, however, there is the implication that a contrast exists between labial and coronal nasals. This problem is resolved, of course, if we include [n] as productive, and there is at least a case to be made that it should be.

This analysis is based on Radical Underspecification (RU). An analysis from the perspective of Contrastive Specification (CS) would use binary features and fill in those contrasts which were minimally contrastive, i.e. just differ by one

TABLE 4.5
A Radical Underspecification Analysis of Alice's Word Initial Consonants

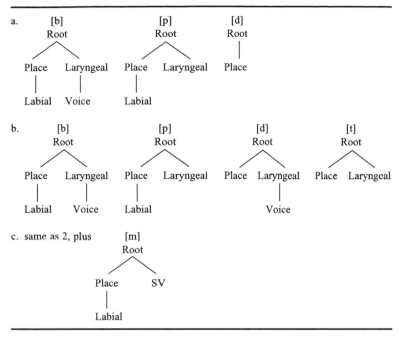

c. same as 2, plus

b. Place   Laryngeal   Place   Laryngeal   Place   Laryngeal   Place   Laryngeal

TABLE 4.6
A Contrastive Specification Analysis of Alice's Consonants

A.

	/b/ [b]	/p/ [p]	/d/ [d]
voice	+	−	
labial	+		−

B.

	/b/ [b]	/p/ [p]	/f/ [p]	/d/ [d]	/ʃ/ [t]	/k/ [t]
voice	+	−	−	+	−	−
labial	+	+	+	−	−	−

C.

	/b/ [b]	/p/ [p]	/f/ [p]	/d/ [d]	/ʃ/ [t]	/k/ [t]	/m/ [m]
voice	+	−	−	+	−	−	
labial	+	+	+	−	−	−	
nasal	−						+

feature (Goad & Ingram, 1988). For example, the minimal contrasts in Fig. 4.7(c) would be b:m [+/−nasal], b:d & p:t [+/−labial], b:p & d:t [+/−voice]. CS analyses are provided in Table 4.6. The CS approach has the advantage of showing more directly the contrasts that a child has acquired, and provides the opportunity to count features. For example, we could view the three analyses as three stages of development of a hypothetical child. We see the addition of a feature over these stages and the spread of features across adult targets. There are two features acquired at stages A and B, but the number of contrasts has expanded greatly at B. [voice] is specified only twice at stage A, but six times at B.

Nasalisation

The concentration on word initial consonants in the previous section does not mean that there are no other consonantal patterns in a child's data. This and the next section will look at other consonants in Alice's words. We know from Table 4.2 that Alice does not have much in the way of final consonants. There is a [t] in *blanket*, and a [p] in *up*, and a few glottal stops in other words. With any frequency criteria applied, it would lead to an analysis concluding that she has not yet begun final consonant acquisition. More formally, we would say that she has not yet acquired coda consonants, i.e. consonants that fill a moraic position within a Rhyme. While that is superficially true, we will examine in this section Alice's use of nasal vowels and consonants which leads to a somewhat different conclusion.

We begin by looking at all the words in the sample which contain a nasalised vowel. These words are shown in Fig. 4.8.

bang [pãi]	*iron* [ʔãɪji]
down [dãʊ]	*man* [mæ̃ː]
elephant [ãːljʌ]	*milk* [m̩mæ̃]

FIG. 4.8

The first issue to resolve is the source of nasal vowel. English does not have a phonemic difference between nasal and oral vowels, but it does have phonetic instances of nasalised vowels adjacent to nasal consonants, as in *can't* [kæ̃nt]. An initial hypothesis is that Alice is using these nasal vowels in contexts where she hears them. This will be called the Nasal Vowel analysis. An examination of the words in Fig. 4.8 shows that six of the eight words are words which contain a nasal consonant in the coda position in the adult word, supporting this analysis.

There are other words, however, which bring the Nasal Vowel analysis into question. First, there is the word for *milk* which has a nasal vowel without a nasal coda consonant. This raises the possibility that she is also nasalising vowels if the onset contains a nasal. This is true for *man*, but this word also has a final nasal which can be accounted for by the Nasal Vowel analysis. Other words with nasal onsets, however, i.e. *meat*, *mommy*, *no*, and *nose*, do not have nasal vowels. It appears then that *milk* is an isolated example of a nasal vowel without a nasal coda consonant in the English target word. The form for *milk*, in fact, contains a syllabic nasal consonant, suggesting the word was produced with a great deal of nasality to begin with, possibly requesting milk.

More problematic for the Nasal Vowel analysis is the word *elephant*. If we assume that Alice is producing three vowels corresponding to the vowels in the word, her mapping would be roughly as in Fig. 4.9. The first vowel is long, fitting the bimoraic requirement discussed earlier, while the second is a lax vowel corresponding to the unstressed medial vowel.

FIG. 4.9

The adult pronunciation of *elephant* would not normally contain a nasalised first vowel since it is not adjacent to the nasal coda consonant. An alternative to the Nasal Vowel hypothesis is one which claims that Alice's nasal vowels are not just reflexes of the vowels she is hearing, but the result of her phonological system's marking of underlying nasal consonants. This alternative analysis claims that she has acquired nasal consonants in coda position, but has an output constraint on producing them (Kiparsky & Menn, 1977). The output constraint is the general one already mentioned that prohibits her at this stage of her development from producing syllable final consonants. Since they are part of her underlying system, however, she finds a way to mark them phonetically. Using the rule system proposed in Fee (1995), her rules informally are: (1) Nasal Spread: spread [+nasal] to the first vowel in a word; (2) Coda Delink: delink (delete) the features to coda consonants. For reference purposes this alternative will be called the Nasal Coda analysis.

Since the Nasal Coda analysis is based so far on a single word, it suffers from the problems raised earlier about the use of single lexical items to support one analysis over another. Support of the Nasal Coda analysis, however, shows up in other places in Alice's words. One important place is her word *clean* [ti:ni] which occurred twice in the data. The Nasal Vowel analysis would predict this word to be pronounced [tĩ] since the vowel is adjacent to a nasal consonant. Alice, however, adds an [i] to the word, which allows the nasal coda consonant to surface in an onset position. (Note also that the expansion of the word initial consonant analysis above to word internal onsets provides additional evidence for the existence of [n] in Alice's phonology.) Alice has two means to provide phonetic evidence for her underlying nasal codas, either vowel nasalisation or resyllabification of the nasal. Importantly, if she resyllabifies then the vowel nasalisation does not take place. This pattern requires that the Nasal Spread rule be restricted to nasal features in the coda position at the time of the rule application. It also requires two additional rules to precede the Nasal Spread, a rule which insert the vowel [i] at the end of the word, and a rule which resyllabifies the prosodic structure. The motivation for these rules will be discussed in the next section.

Consonantal templates

It is necessary to look at Alice's word medial consonants in more depth to understand her nasalisation process more fully. Of central interest is the fact that some of the underlying nasal consonant codas surface phonetically and others do not. For example, we get *bunny* [bʌn̩n̩ːi] and *clean* [tiːni], but we also get *iron* [ʔãɪji] and *shiny* [taːji]. The occurrence of a medial [j] also happens in cases which do not involve nasal consonants, i.e. *lady* [jɛːji].

The pattern of medial consonants can be explained by looking at their co-occurrence with initial consonants. Figure 4.10 shows the combinations of word initial and word medial consonants.

Set 1				Set 2	
b b *baby*		d d *daddy*		ʔ j	*iron*
b d *bottle*		p d *flower*		ø j	*elephant*
b n *bunny*		m n *mommy*		j j	*lady*
t n *clean*				t j	*shiny*

FIG. 4.10

In Set 1, a medial consonant is a stop consonant when the word initial consonant is a stop as well. It is here where we see the appearance of the [n] as a medial onset. In Set 2, [j] is used when the word initial consonant is not a stop consonant. This condition is on the underlying consonant, i.e. the consonant in the adult model form. For example, *shiny* has a process whereby the initial /ʃ/ is changed into a stop [t]. This is a common change in children's early words which is commonly referred to as Stopping, i.e. more broadly changing fricatives into stops. It is also occurs in *flower* as well where the /f/ becomes a [p]. If Alice's pattern of [j] insertion were determined by her output form, then *shiny* should contain an [n] since the word initial consonant is [t]. The appearance of [j], however, indicates that the pattern is determined at a more abstract level where *shiny* has a /ʃ/ represented.

It has been observed for a long time (Waterson, 1970) that children's early words fall into patterns or templates like this (see also Vihman, 1991a for a comprehensive discussion of these forms). More recently, phonological research has found that there are adult languages such as Hebrew and Arabic that can be best seen as consisting of templates as well (McCarthy & Prince, 1986). Children acquiring English in this fashion, therefore, are not following some idiosyncratic path, but applying what may be an initial hypothesis about the nature of phonological structure. Figure 4.11 provides an informal description of the two templates that Alice is using in her bisyllabic words.

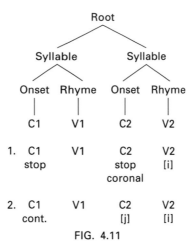

1. C1   V1   C2   V2
    stop   stop   [i]
                        coronal

2. C1   V1   C2   V2
    cont.   [j]   [i]

FIG. 4.11

As discussed in Kiparsky and Menn (1977), templates such as these operate as an output constraint on the wellformedness of children's words. That is, they are not part of the words underlying representation, but they influence the mapping from the child's underlying form to their phonetic output. We can see this in Alice's words in the pair *iron* [ʔãɪji] and *shiny* [taːji]. If the templates in Fig. 4.11 were part of the underlying form of these words, we would not expect nasalisation in the vowel in *iron*. The templates do, however, trigger or otherwise are the cause for certain rules to operate. For example, Template 1 requires a rules which changes any medial stop into an alveolar (or coronal) consonant as in *mommy* [maːṇi] and *flower* [p'adi]. (*Baby* [beibi] is the only exception to this.) Both templates require the insertion of the [i] vowel in the rhyme of the second syllable.

We can now complete the discussion of Alice's consonants by combining the rule patterns that capture both her nasalisation and consonant harmony. Alice's rule of Nasal Spread operates differently for Template 1 versus Template 2 words. In *clean* [tiːni], either Nasal Spread does not apply, or else it applies but the vowel later undergoes denasalisation. In either case, the vowel does not need to be nasalised since the nasal consonant surfaces phonetically. In *iron* [ʔãɪji], however, it applies because the nasality of the coda consonant will otherwise be lost. It doesn't apply in *shiny*, however, because there is no nasal coda consonant in the underlying form.

SUMMARY

The focus of this chapter has been on the onset of phonological acquisition and the nature of the child's early phonological system. It has been argued that children begin phonological acquisition at the onset of their word acquisition between the ages of one and two years, when they acquire their first 50 words.

When they do so, they begin using properties of phonological organisation that are part of those that underlie the adult language. This position is one of continuity, that is, that children and adults have phonological systems of the same type. The characteristics of the child's phonological system, however, will lack the more complex properties of the adult language. The child builds up structure, using the basic or simplest of the mechanisms available.

If the above were not so, we would have much less to say about phonological acquisition than we do. For example, we could propose that children begin acquisition around age two or so when their vocabularies are relatively larger, say between 50 and 100 words. At that point, however, they show relatively complex ·syllable structures and segmental inventories. The development is sufficiently advanced that only the most general statements could be made about the course of acquisition. Phonological analyses on the child's first words, however, can be done with careful transcriptions and the judicious use of frequency criteria. When such is the case, we see developmental continuities from the first words through to the later ones.

While research is still ongoing into the nature of this system, it has been able to reach some fruitful hypotheses about it. We have presented here some of these hypotheses and have applied them to data from a young girl named Alice. Regarding syllable structure, children begin with simple CVs or core syllables, then develop minimal words. The minimal words proposed are the structures CVC, CVV, and CVCV where onsets can be optional. Alice's data fit this proposal reasonably well, with a need to adjust the structure of bisyllabic forms to CVVCV, i.e. with a bimoraic initial syllable. The data also show how empirical work in language acquisition proceeds with a constant interaction between theory and data.

Regarding the development of segments, it has been known for some time that children do not follow an invariant sequence of development, despite trends. (We saw that Alice's vowel system was a top-down system in contrast to a triangular one that some children first use.) This fact requires a theory of features in which children have some choice in the features they acquire. One possible solution is a feature system which allows for some choice, but which also constrains development. We examined one such system for consonants which allows children to choose between nodes marking Laryngeal, Air Flow, Sonorant Voice, and Place features. Within each node, however, certain features are predictable or unspecified so that they can be filled in by redundancy statements.

The study of feature acquisition also requires a theoretical stance on the way in which children represent them in their underlying representations. If we assume continuity, then the child will do this the same way as adults. We briefly reviewed two approaches within current phonological theory, radical underspecification and contrastive specification. It was noted that both have been applied to phonological acquisition, and we showed both kinds of analyses for Alice's word initial consonants. It was also concluded that research to date has indicated radical underspecification has been particularly accurate in accounting for the pattern of children's substitutions. At the same time, we pointed out that contrastive specification more overtly shows the expansion of the feature system over time. The assignment of features to children's underlying forms also requires restrictions on the range of the features that the child may select. The Distinctive Feature Hypothesis does just this: It proposes that children can only assign features to a phoneme that are present in that phoneme in the adult word. The adult model words were also argued to have another influence on the child's phonemes, this being the functional load of the phonemes in the target language. The more a sound is used in the native vocabulary, the more likely it is to occur in the child's early words. We saw, for example, that [ʧ] is an earlier acquired sound in Turkish and K'iche' than it is in English.

In examining Alice's initial consonants, it was shown that analysis will be influenced by the criteria that are applied to the data. Her system ranged from a potential analysis with three phonemes (/b/, /p/, /d/), to one that contained six (/b/, /p/, /d/, /t/, /m/, /n/). It was also suggested, however, that the range of analyses were similar in many ways and mostly differed in whether a feature was productive or lexical, and the number of phonemes that a feature represented.

A significant claim was made that children not only have phonological systems, but that these systems are abstract in ways that are parallel to adult languages. This was demonstrated in the analysis of Alice's process of nasalisation. Alice often nasalised vowels and deleted nasal consonants. It was seen that she would nasalise vowels just in those cases where the target word contained a final nasal consonant, and the nasal consonant did not surface as a word internal onset. These patterns reflected that she had acquired nasal coda consonants, but has a surface constraint against their use. Alice compensated for this constraint by either vowel nasalisation or resyllabification. She showed other surface constraints in the form of templates, i.e. restrictions on the possible surface form of CVCV sequences. Such templates have also been proposed as part of the phonological systems of adult languages.

REFERENCES

Beers, M. (1995). *The phonology of normally developing and language-impaired children*. Studies in Language and Language Use 20. IFOTT, University of Amsterdam.

Benedict, H. (1979). Early lexical development: Comprehension and production. *Journal of Child Language, 6*, 183–200.

Demuth, K., & Fee, E.J. (1995). *Minimal words in early phonological development*. Unpublished paper, Brown University & Dalhousie University, Canada.

Dinnsen, D. (1996). Context-sensitive underspecification and the acquisition of phonemic contrasts. *Journal of Child Language, 23*, 57–79.

Fee, E.J. (1991). *Underspecification, parameters, and the acquisition of vowels*. PhD thesis, University of British Columbia, Canada.

Fee, E.J. (1995). Segments and syllables in early language acquisition. In J. Archibald (Ed.), *Phonological acquisition and phonological theory* (pp. 43–61). Hillsdale, NJ: Lawrence Erlbaum Associates Inc.

Ferguson, C.A., & Farwell, C.B. (1975). Words and sounds in early language acquisition. *Language, 51*, 419–439.

Fikkert, P. (1994). *On the acquisition of prosodic structure*. PhD thesis, University of Leiden, The Netherlands.

Goad, H., & Ingram, D. (1988). Individual variation and its relevance to a theory of phonological acquisition. *Journal of Child Language, 14*, 419–432.

Ingram, D. (1981). *Procedures for the phonological analysis of children's language*. Baltimore, MD: University Park Press.

Ingram, D. (1989). *First language acquisition: Method, description, and explanation*. Cambridge, UK: Cambridge University Press.

Ingram, D. (1991). Toward a theory of phonological acquisition. In J. Miller (Ed.), *Research on child language disorders: A decade of progress* (pp. 55–72). Austin, TX: Pro-ed.

Ingram, D. (1992). Early phonological acquisition: A crosslinguistic perspective. In C.A. Ferguson, L. Menn, & C. Stoel-Gammon (Eds.), *Phonological development: Models, research, implications* (pp. 147–158). Parkton, MD: York Press.

Ingram, D. (1995). The acquisition of negative constraints, the OCP, and underspecified representations. In J. Archibald (Ed.), *Phonological acquisition and phonological theory* (pp. 63–79). Hillsdale, NJ: Lawrence Erlbaum Associates Inc.

Jakobson, R. (1968). *Child language, aphasia, and phonological universals* (A. Keiler, Trans.). The Hague, The Netherlands: Mouton. (Original work published in 1941)

Kenstowicz, M. (1994). *Phonology in generative grammar*. Cambridge, MA: Blackwell.

Kiparsky, P., & Menn, L. (1977). On the acquisition of phonology. In J. Macnamara (Ed.), *Language learning and thought* (pp. 47–78). New York: Academic Press.

Locke, J.L. (1983). *Phonological acquisition and change*. New York: Academic Press.

Macken, M.A. (1978). Developmental reorganization of phonology: A hierarchy of basic units of acquisition. *Lingua, 49*, 11–49.

Macken, M.A. (1987). Representation, rules and overgeneralization in phonology. In B. MacWhinney (Ed.), *Mechanisms of language acquisition* (pp. 367–397). Hillsdale, NJ: Lawrence Erlbaum Associates Inc.

McCarthy, J., & Prince, A. (1986). *Prosodic morphology*. Unpublished paper, Brandeis University, Waltham, MA.

Pinker, S. (1984). *Language learnability and language development*. Cambridge, MA: MIT Press.

Pye, C., Ingram, D., & List, H. (1987). A comparison of initial consonant acquisition in English and Quiche. In K.E. Nelson & A. van Kleeck (Eds.), *Children's language* (Vol. 6; pp. 175–190). Hillsdale, NJ: Lawrence Erlbaum Associates Inc.

Rice, K. (1993). A reexamination of the feature [sonorant]: The status of sonorant obstuents. *Language, 69*, 308–344.

Rice, K. (1995). Aspects of variability in child language acquisition. In B. Bernhardt, D. Ingram, & J. Gilbert (Eds.), *Proceedings of the UBC international conference on phonological acquisition* (pp. 1–14). Somerville, MA: Cascadilla Press.

Rice, K., & Avery, P. (1995). Variability in a deterministic model of language acquisition: A theory of segmental elaboration. In J. Archibald (Ed.), *Phonological acquisition and phonological theory* (pp. 23–42). Hillsdale, NJ: Lawrence Erlbaum Associates Inc.

Schvachkin, N. (1973). The development of phonemic speech perception in early childhood. In C.A. Ferguson & D.I. Slobin (Eds.), *Studies of child language development* (pp. 91–127). New York: Holt, Rineholt & Winston. (Original work published in 1948)

Smith, N.V. (1973). *The acquisition of phonology: A case study*. Cambridge, UK: Cambridge University Press.

Stemberger, J. (1992). A performance constraint on compensatory lengthening in child phonology. *Language and Speech, 35,* 207–218.

Stemberger, J., & Stoel-Gammon, C. (1991). The underspecification of coronals: Evidence from language acquisition and performance errors. In C. Paradis & J.-F. Prunet (Eds.), *Phonetics and Phonology: Vol. 2. The special status of coronals: Internal and external evidence* (pp. 181–199). New York: Academic Press.

Stoel-Gammon, C. (1985). Phonetic inventories, 15–24 months: A longitudinal study. *Journal of Speech and Hearing Research, 28,* 505–512.

Stoel-Gammon, C., & Harrington, P. (1990). Vowel systems of normally developing and phonologically disordered children. *Clinical Linguistics and Phonetics, 4,* 145–160.

Templin, M. (1957). *Certain language skills in children.* Minneapolis, MN: University of Minnesota Press.

Topbas, C. (1992). *A pilot study of phonological acquisition for Turkish children and its implications for phonological disorders.* Paper presented at the 6th international conference on Turkish Linguistics, Anadolu University, Turkey.

Vihman, M.M. (1991a). Early phonological development. In J.E. Bernthal & N.W. Bankson (Eds.), *Articulation and phonological disorders* (pp. 60–109). Englewood Cliffs, NJ: Prentice Hall.

Vihman, M.M. (1991b). Later phonological development. In J.E. Bernthal & N.W. Bankson (Eds.), *Articulation and phonological disorders* (pp. 110–144). Englewood Cliffs, NJ: Prentice Hall.

Vihman, M.M., & McCune, L. (1994). When is a word a word? *Journal of Child Language, 21,* 517–542.

Waterson, N. (1970). Some speech forms of an English child: A phonological study. *Transactions of the Philological Society, 1,* 1–24.

CHAPTER FIVE

Early lexical development

Esther Dromi
*Tel Aviv University, Israel, and The University of Texas
at Dallas, USA*

There are three principal means of acquiring knowledge: observation of nature, reflection, and experimentation. Observation collects facts, reflection combines them, experimentation verifies the results of that combination. Our observation must be diligent, our reflection profound, and our experiments exact.

Denis Diderot (1713–1784; *On the interpretation of nature*)

INTRODUCTION

Only two decades ago, the mere possibility of carrying out scientific linguistic investigations with one-word stage subjects was seriously doubted by Brown (1973, pp. 152–3). Theoretical as well as methodological concerns about how researchers could elicit, record, transcribe, and analyse single-word utterances, that are highly contextual and often idiosyncratic, led Brown to his explicitly stated doubts. In the last 20 years, however, we have witnessed considerable progress in the utilisation of complementary empirical means (observational as well as experimental) for the investigation of the period that precedes the emergence of syntax. These advances in methodology have yielded interesting results which have led to the construction of theoretical models that help us better understand the different factors that determine the course of early lexical growth. The goal of the present chapter is to review the rich empirical findings on children's lexical behaviours throughout the one-word stage, and to present the major theoretical arguments that so far have been suggested in the literature.

During the one-word stage children's utterances are constrained to "one word at a time" (Bloom, 1973). Prior to the emergence of first words, children utilise gestures, facial expressions, intonation patterns, and non-systematic vocalisations for communicating their basic pragmatic intentions (Carter, 1979; Dromi, 1993a; Harding, 1983; see also Reddy, this volume). The beginning of the one-word stage is marked by the emergence of systematic, repeated productions of phonetically consistent forms. Early words (which phonologically are different from adult conventional words) are produced by the child in expected contexts, and hence are recognised by a familiar listener as linguistic units that convey meanings (Bloom, 1993; Dore, 1974; Dromi, 1987, p. 70;[1] Veneziano, 1981, 1988; Vihman & McCune, 1994). The one-word stage ends with the emergence of productive multi-word combinations that constitute the majority of recorded utterances in a language sample (Greenfield & Smith, 1976; see also Tomasello & Brookes, this volume). During the one-word stage children might occasionally produce multi-word combinations that do not yet reflect productive syntactic abilities. Such expressions often directly derive from the input to the child, and are, in fact, unanalysed speech routines (e.g. "what's this" or "daddy went to work").

A distinction should be made between "comprehensible" words, which are phonetically consistent forms that caregivers understand, but do not yet convey adult conventional meanings, and "meaningful" words that are symbolic, arbitrary, and conventional terms of reference. Throughout the one-word stage, children gradually modify the overt phonetic forms of their words as well as their underlying meanings. At the end of the one-word stage, nearly all the words that are included in the child's productive lexicon convey conventional meanings. The major developmental achievement that is attained during the one-word stage, therefore, is the ability to use words as symbolic means for representing discrete contents, independently of the extra-linguistic contexts of the utterance or its pragmatic function (Dromi, 1987, 1993a).

This chapter is devoted to the study of lexical development prior to the emergence of syntax. The chapter is divided into two major parts. In the opening sections of the chapter I examine empirical results on early lexical development throughout the one-word stage. The review of observational and experimental cross-linguistic research findings is focused on changes over time in lexical behaviours. Special reference is made to the underlying linguistic and cognitive processes that interactively operate in the construction of a productive lexicon. In the second part of the chapter, three theoretical models that have been recently proposed to account for how children might identify the underlying meanings of early words are presented. These models provide important insights on how word-reference relationships might be established by the young child. The review of the theoretical models is aimed to highlight the various contributing factors that are related to early lexical behaviours in general, and to word meaning acquisition in particular. The timing of word acquisition throughout the stage, the child's level of cognitive functioning, the relationship between

---

[1] A second printing of Dromi (1987) is Dromi (1996). See the reference list of this chapter.

linguistic input and extra-linguistic conditions for word modelling, and the role of syntax in conjecturing word meanings are invoked as important variables to consider. The theoretical section of the chapter is concluded with new and as yet unanswered questions that will be the challenge for future active research in this area.

THE SIZE OF THE ONE-WORD LEXICON AND THE RATE OF ACCUMULATING NEW WORDS

Typically developing children begin to produce their first comprehensible words around the first birthday, and continue to utter single words throughout a period of several months and sometimes up to a whole year (Barrett, 1995; Benedict, 1979; Dromi, 1987; Fenson, Dale, Reznick, Bates, Thal, & Phethick, 1994). A number of intensive diary investigations of individual subjects revealed that during the one-word stage, large productive lexicons of several hundred different words are constructed. My daughter Keren, who was 10(12)[2] when I recorded her first comprehensible word, and 17(23) when she started to produce novel word combinations, learned 337 different Hebrew words throughout the one-word stage. Her vocabulary size approximated counts of other diarists (Braunwald, 1978; Gillis, 1986; Mervis, Mervis, Johnson, & Bertrand, 1992).

Evaluations of the vocabulary size in larger groups of subjects have confirmed that during the second year of life some children indeed establish very large vocabularies of several hundred words. The computation of the number of different words used in recorded speech samples indicated, however, that not all children establish large single-word vocabularies. Remarkable individual differences were identified in a sample of 15 Italian middle-upper class children whose lexical behaviours were measured at 16 and 20 months, respectively. The subjects varied with respect to the rate of lexical learning as well as to the total number of words in their productive lexicons at these two measurement times (Camaioni & Longobardi, 1995).

In the large-scale standardisation project of the MCDI,[3] Fenson and his collaborators assessed verbal production in a sample of 1803 English speaking subjects ranging in age from 8 to 30 months old. The Toddler form of the MCDI (ages 16 to 30 months) consists of a checklist of 680 different words. The analysis of the parents' reports revealed that vocabulary learning during the second year of life exhibits a great range of variation (Bates, Marchman, Thal, Fenson, Dale, Reznick, Reilly, & Hartung, 1994; Fenson et al., 1994). The

---

[2] Throughout this chapter, child's ages are given in months and days; hence 10(12) is to be read as 10 months and 12 days.

[3] MacArthur Communicative Development Inventories (MCDI) is a parent questionnaire that was constructed in order to assess communicative and lexical behaviours in young children. The instrument was published by Fenson, Dale, Reznick, Thal, Bates, Hartung, Phethick, & Reilly (1993).

LIVERPOOL
JOHN MOORES UNIVERSITY
AVRIL ROBARTS LRC
TEL. 0151 231 4022

observed median score for vocabulary production at 16 months of age was 44 different words. The range of words used was substantial: Subjects at the tenth percentile produced only few words, and subjects at the ninetieth percentile produced over 120 different words. Throughout the second year of life the vocabulary growth curves for all the subjects showed a steady increase in the number of different words produced. At the age of 23 months the median score of different words was 300, the tenth percentile was only 50 words, and the ninetieth percentile was 550. The great variability observed in the carefully selected, huge sample of Fenson et al. clearly indicates that age is not a good indicator of lexicon size.

The rate at which children accumulate new words is unsteady throughout the stage.[4] During the first few weeks of production, new words are learned very slowly, and during the last few months of the one-word stage, a significant change in the rate of learning new words is noted. Several researchers have documented the lexical spurt phenomenon which is characterised by a sudden change in the rate of learning new words (Bloom, 1973, 1993; Bloom, Tinker, & Margulis, 1993; Corrigan, 1978; Dromi, 1987; McShane, 1980; Mervis & Bertrand, 1995). Researchers disagree with regards to exactly when during the stage the spurt is observed, and whether it is a universal phenomenon that is documented for all children. Some researchers claim that the spurt is noted at approximately the level of 50 different words (Goldfield & Reznick, 1990), and others suggest that the spurt occurs much later in the stage, only a few weeks before syntax emerges (Dromi, 1987; McShane, 1980; Mervis & Bertrand, 1995).

Goldfield and Reznick (1990) examined the lexical growth of 18 English-speaking children. They assessed the vocabulary size of their subjects at intervals of two and a half weeks. When a child demonstrated an increase of at least 10 words between two successive measurements, they concluded that this was an evidence for the lexical spurt. In this sample, a lexical spurt was never identified for 5 out of the 18 subjects. On the basis of this finding, the researchers concluded that some children do not manifest a lexical spurt at all (see a similar claim in Fenson et al., 1994, p. 43). The possibility that methodological inadequacies rather than individual differences account for Goldfield and Reznick's finding was raised by Mervis and Bertrand (1995). In a longitudinal

---

[4] Carey (1978) estimated the rate of acquiring new words during the first years of life to be at about 8 to 10 new words a day. This figure is extensively cited in the word-meaning literature, yet most writers today fail to acknowledge the fact that this figure was intended to be only an estimate based on Templin's (1957; cf. Carey, 1978) proposal that by the age of six the average American child enters school responding in comprehension to 14,000 different English words including derived and inflected forms. My exact count of the rate of learning new words throughout the one-word stage was significantly lower than Carey's estimate. Even during the most hectic week of word learning, Keren accumulated only 44 new Hebrew words in her productive lexicon. As is shown in this chapter, the rate of learning words is not constant across the stage, and therefore the notion of average lexical learning per day is extremely misleading.

study that they conducted, three subjects who had not evidenced a lexical spurt at the beginning of the follow-up, eventually demonstrated the spurt at much higher lexical levels. Mervis and Bertrand claim that individual differences in the timing of the lexical spurt are attributed to differences in the rate of cognitive development. The spurt, according to this proposal, is a reflection of the child's cognitive attainment of spontaneous exhaustive sorting of objects (see also Gopnik & Meltzoff, 1987). The ability to sort objects exhaustively coincides with the onset of fast mapping which explains the sudden change in the rate of learning new words. Mervis and Bertrand conclude that "all normally developing children eventually evidence a vocabulary spurt" (1995, p. 467).

Clark (1993), who compared the rate of lexical learning of her son, Damon, with that of my daughter, Keren, argued that the two children followed different paths of lexical accumulation. Damon, unlike Keren, started to produce multiword combinations only eight weeks after his first word was recorded. He demonstrated a steady increase in the rate of learning new words (and in the rate of producing novel combinations) throughout the 41 weeks of study. Clark reported that she had not noticed a sudden spurt in Damon's rate of learning words. The curve of Damon's vocabulary growth clearly indicates, however, that during the last five months of the diary study, he added new words at a much higher rate than during the earlier phases of production (1993, pp. 24–26).

Figure 5.1 compares the cumulative vocabulary curves of three subjects throughout the one-word stage. Keren and Or acquired Hebrew as their first and only language. Their lexical development throughout the one-word stage was recorded by me. The third subject, Maarten, acquired Dutch as his first language. His lexical development was closely recorded by his uncle (Gillis, 1986).

Regardless of the differences inherent in the linguistic structure of the two target languages, a similar overall shape of the lexical growth curve is observed for the three subjects. The time that elapsed between the recording of the first and the tenth comprehensible word in each subject was different. It is remarkable to note that in all three subjects, five months separated the establishment of the ten-word lexicon and the emergence of syntax.

Differences in research methodologies, as well as individual differences in cognitive abilities and early linguistic experiences, might explain conflicting results. Thus, for example, information that was gathered in detailed case studies (Clark, 1993; Dromi, 1987; Mervis et al., 1992; Tomasello, 1992) is radically different from information obtained through periodic audio-recordings (Bloom, Tinker, & Margulis, 1993; Camaioni & Longobardi, 1995; Greenfield & Smith, 1976; McShane, 1980), and is also different from results that are gathered via interviews with mothers (Bates et al., 1994; Goldfield & Reznick, 1990). The findings reported in this section strongly suggest that lexical acquisition is not a simple additive process. In-depth analyses of early lexical behaviours help us to better understand the underlying complex interactions among various factors that determine the efficiency of word learning.

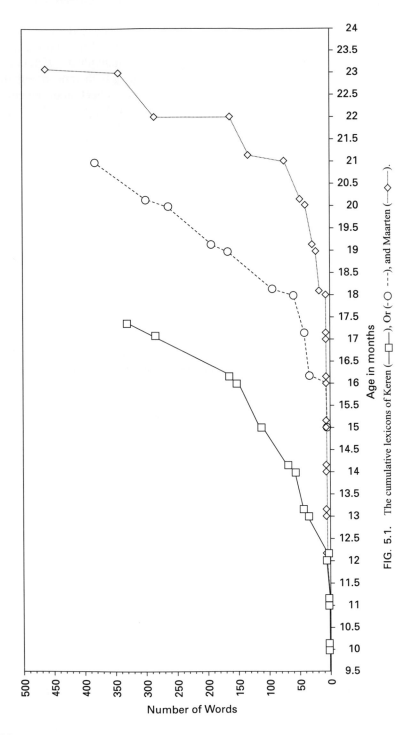

FIG. 5.1. The cumulative lexicons of Keren (——□——), Or (-○ - - -), and Maarten (——◇······).

THE DISTRIBUTION OF EARLY WORDS IN VARIOUS WORD-CLASSES

Adults use words to talk about various entities: people, objects, places, properties, different states of being, activities, and relations among entities. Without words, syntactic categories at the word level (i.e. noun, verb, adjective, and adverb), or at the phrase level (i.e. noun phrase, verb phrase) could not be determined (Barrett, 1995; Clark, 1993; Dromi, 1987). The question of how and when children learn which aspect of reality is denoted by a given word form, is of major theoretical and empirical significance.

The goal of determining the category membership of an early word is two-fold. On the theoretical level, classification systems may reveal the existence of psychologically real categories that are functional in the child's cognitive and linguistic systems (Tomasello, 1992). On the practical level, classification systems can serve as instruments for discerning regularities in the data (Braunwald, 1995; Gentner, 1982).

In a paper entitled "A 'door' to verbs", Griffiths and Atkinson (1978) illustrated the difficulty of classifying early words. Their 12(10) subject used the English word "door" both as a noun and as a verb. When he wanted the door to be opened he said "door, door, please", and when he pointed to the door he said "a door". Similar examples of verbs or nouns in adult language which were used by children across different part-of-speech categories are described by Bowerman (1980), Braunwald (1995), Dromi (1987), Gentner (1982), and Tomasello (1992).

Nelson (1973) was the first researcher who grouped early words into different word classes, and based a strong theoretical argument on this analysis. In Nelson's study, each of the first 50 words that were used by her 18 English-speaking subjects was assigned to one of five mutually exclusive classes: objects (specific and general), actions, attributes, social, and functional words. Nelson used mothers' reports on a child's first usage of each word in order to assign it to one of the five word classes. She found that children in her sample followed one of two styles in early lexical learning: the referential and the expressive. Nelson's referential subjects had 50% object words in their 50-word vocabularies. Her expressive subjects used more social words relatively to referential subjects. Nelson's classification system was used by other researchers (Bates et al., 1994; Benedict, 1979; Bonvillian, Orlanski, & Novack, 1983), who replicated her findings. Her distinction between the referential and expressive styles was modified and is now seen as a continuum along which children may vary. Camaioni and Longobardi (1995), for example, found that in a sample of 15 Italian one-word stage speakers, most children showed a balanced distribution of referential (object words) and expressive (social words) terms, and only a few children exhibited a distinct style similar to the one originally proposed by Nelson (1973).

Bloom's (1973) prominent argument that the one-word stage consists of two developmental phases was based on her distinction between two classes of words that are dramatically different in their underlying cognitive underpinnings. According to Bloom, functional words (such as "here", "more", "no", and "allgone") express relations among different objects, and originate from repeated experiences of the child with a variety of referents. Bloom argued that during the first phase of the one-word stage, functional words constitute the dominant class of words and show a high mortality rate. Substantive terms that refer to objects (such as, "chair", "cookie", "sit") enter the child's lexicon later, following the cognitive achievement of object permanence (Piaget, 1952). In Bloom's earlier accounts, which she herself questioned later (Bloom, 1993), only during the second half of the one-word stage do children attain the cognitive skill of object permanence that affects the general efficiency in learning new words. During this later phase, not only are substantive words learnt fast, but also their uses become more consistent. Bloom's early claim that children start to learn words with a strong non-nominal bias was recently reopened (Bloom, 1993; Bloom et al., 1993). In a longitudinal study of 14 infants aged 9 months old to 2 years old, Bloom and her colleagues compared the prevalence of object terms against that of all the other word classes. They report that object names made up less than 40% on average of the new words learned by their subjects between the emergence of the first word and the documentation of the lexical spurt. Bloom argues that words other than common nouns predominate in children's early vocabularies, and therefore the theoretical proposal that lexical principles that focus on learning object words can explain how young children learn to talk is refutable (see more on that claim in the next sections).

Bloom's (1973) claim about the relationship between the cognitive attainment of object permanence and early uses of words did not stand empirical testing (Corrigan, 1978; Gopnik & Meltzoff, 1986). Her suggestion, however, to investigate the relationships between cognition and language led other researchers to reveal more specific relationships between cognitive skills and early lexical behaviours. In a number of studies by Gopnik and Meltzoff (1986, 1987, 1992), a strong and causal association between children's non-linguistic ability to form categories of objects and the acquisition of specific words was identified. It has recently been argued that a strong cognitive and linguistic link (i.e. especially between the exhaustive sorting of objects and the lexical spurt) explains the speed and efficiency by which object terms are mapped onto real-world concepts during the later months of the one-word stage (Dromi, 1993b; Mervis & Bertrand, 1994).

I classified Keren's complete one-word stage lexicon according to the different classes of words she used by examining repeated uses of the same word over time in different non-linguistic contexts (i.e. categories of reference in Dromi, 1987). My analysis was based on the child's linguistic utilisation of every term regardless of its assignment to part of speech category in adult speech (Dromi, 1987). Keren's complete lexicon included: Words for objects (59%), Indeterminant words (16%), Words for actions (14%), Social words (7%), and Modifiers (4%).

The category of Indeterminant words consisted of words which were used ambiguously for both action and object (e.g. "ham" for *food* and *to eat*), or for action and modifier (e.g. "xam" (hot) for *heaters*, *ovens*, and as an attribute, e.g. for *a frozen pitta bread*). Bowerman (1980), Gentner (1982), Gillis (1986), Griffiths and Atkinson (1978), Nelson and Lucariello (1985), and Tomasello (1992) have all reported on similar instances of early indeterminant uses of the same words to refer either to an object or to an activity that is typically associated with that object, or to both.

The distribution of early words in various word classes is especially interesting when considering cross-linguistic data. Complex theoretical questions related to universal versus language-specific patterns of early language growth can be best tested with such evidence (Choi & Bowerman, 1997; Slobin, 1985; Tardif, Shatz, & Naigles, 1997). Gentner's (1982) analysis of children's early lexicons exemplifies the strength of such an approach. On the basis of comparisons between the relative frequency of nouns and verbs in five languages (English, Japanese, German, Kaluli, and Turkish), she asserted that the distribution of words into various grammatical classes is universal. In all languages that she studied, nouns comprised the largest and the earliest group of words learned, and the acquisition of verbs (which constituted a much smaller category) lagged behind that of nouns. Gentner argued that infants acquiring typologically different languages show a "noun bias" which is explained by the relative ease by which young children perceive concepts for objects versus concepts for actions. She rejected the possibility that language-specific structural characteristics such as frequency in input, morphological transparency, or relative position in the utterance dictate the order of word acquisition.

Several in-depth studies of English (Bates et al., 1994; Goldfield, 1993; Shatz, 1994; Tomasello, 1992), Italian (Caselli, Bates, Casadio, Fenson, Fenson, Sanderl, & Weir, 1995), Spanish (Jackson-Maldonado, Thal, Marchman, Bates, & Gutierrez Clellen, 1993), and Hebrew (Dromi, 1987; Maital, Dromi, Sagi, & Bornstein, submitted), based on diverse methodologies such as diary studies, observational studies, and checklist investigations, support Gentner's generalisation that words for objects constitute the largest group of words learned by young children during the one-word stage.

The cognitive explanation of why nouns are easier to learn than verbs has not been accepted by all researchers. Gillis and Verlinden (1988), who studied Dutch child-directed speech, Goldfield (1993), who examined English child-directed speech, and Tardif (1996), who examined early lexical composition in Mandarin Chinese as well as child-directed speech of Chinese mothers, argued that positional preferences, frequency of use, morphological transparency, and pragmatics of language use (i.e. differential distribution of free nouns and verbs in the input to the child, or different focus of interest in adult–child conversations) explain why nouns override verbs in some languages but not in all. These researchers claimed that the "noun bias" is recorded only in those languages in which nouns usually appear at salient positions in the utterance, nouns are morphologically simpler than verbs, and nouns are used more frequently in adult–child interchanges as single words. Along the same line of argument, it has been proposed that languages that favour verb-initial constructions demonstrate a higher proportion of verbs, which morphologically are as simple as nouns, and in cultures that do not highlight objects as topics of interest, verbs will be acquired early and predominate early vocabularies (Tardif, 1996; Tardif et al., 1997). Gillis and his collaborators demonstrated that in Dutch child-directed speech the rate of nouns increase while the rate of verbs is kept constant. They argue that this distributional fact explains why early vocabularies of Dutch speaking children consist mainly of object terms. Similarly, Tardif (1996) and Tardif et al. (1997) reported that in Mandarin Chinese child-directed speech is different from in English and Italian in ways that are consistent with patterns observed in early child speech.

The hypothesis that structural linguistic variables rather than cognitive factors explain cross-linguistic differences with regards to the composition of early vocabularies was also raised by Gopnik and Choi (1990, 1995). These authors replicated with Korean- and French-speaking babies a study on the use of a few vocabulary terms by English-speaking children and its relationship with the attainments of specific cognitive skills (Gopnik & Meltzoff, 1986, 1987). A very small sample of only five Korean- and three French-speaking children participated in the study. Korean-speaking children, whose target language resembles Mandarin with regards to the relative frequency, perceptual salience, and the relative semantic significance of verbs, demonstrated a much later naming spurt than the English or the French subjects (Gopnik & Choi, 1990). On the basis of this finding, the researchers proposed that differences in linguistic input lead to differences in cognitive focus, and therefore it is mistaken to entertain the idea that nouns are easier to learn than verbs in all languages.

Caselli et al. (1995) compared the results of the Italian MCDI (Infant version) with that of the English MCDI, and found that the structure of early vocabularies in the two languages was strikingly similar. Italian and English are radically different with respect to their syntactic structure. Italian, as a pro-drop language, has a clear bias towards a much more salient and marked semantic and morphological significance of verbs. Caselli et al. reported that, as in English, the earliest words in Italian were Indeterminant terms that were neither nouns nor verbs and often referred to both objects and actions. At the developmental window of 50 to 100 first words, the overwhelming majority of words in Italian were nominals; verbs were extremely rare at this developmental level. These findings led to the conclusion that "the underrepresentation of verbs in very young children reflects a fundamental developmental fact: lexical verbs do not develop until common nouns are a well-established component of the emerging lexicon" (1995, p. 180). A striking similarity between the early vocabulary composition in English and Hebrew was reported recently by Maital et al. (submitted). The comparison between Hebrew CDI data on 253 Israeli toddlers, and the original sample of Fenson et al. (1994) for English, indicated that the relation between vocabulary size and age as well as the shape of the growth curves for nouns, predicate terms, and closed class words relative to size of lexicon were almost identical. On the basis of their checklist data, Maital et al. concluded that the cross-linguistic similarities among typologically different languages such as Hebrew and English support the claim that early lexical development follows widely generalisable patterns that are explained primarily by robust developmental processes.

In his monograph on the early acquisition of verbs by his daughter Travis, Tomasello (1992) examined in a very careful way the order and the different contexts in which early verbs were uttered. His analysis was based on the assumption that the different nature of object concepts and action concepts explain why verbs emerge later than nouns. In his view "while object concepts evidence the child's emerging ability to package her cognition into 'permanent' entities, action and change of state concepts package process containing a temporal dimension" (1992, p. 211). The conceptual operation of packaging that is involved in the representation of actions is complex, and this fact explains why the acquisition of the symbolic means for encoding such concepts (i.e verbs and adjectives) are recorded late in the one-word stage and towards the emergence of grammar. The packaging of actions and changes of state involve a higher level of intersubjectivity and a more matured understanding of situations, and therefore verbs constitute a small category of words in the one-word stage.

The acquisition of non-nominal linguistic terms is the focus of intensive current discussion (see a recent edited volume by Tomasello & Merriman, 1995). Most researchers agree that in most languages studied so far, verbs emerge later than nouns. Observations of toddlers learning Korean and Mandarin indicate that they use more verbs than nouns in early speech. This finding contradicts the earlier reports on vocabulary composition in English, Italian, Spanish, and Hebrew. However, it is noteworthy that Au, Dapretto, and Song (1994) reported on the basis of checklist data that even Korean children acquire more nouns than verbs and learn object words faster than action words just as English-speaking toddlers do. These researchers suggest that the discrepancy between the checklist findings and those reported by Gopnik and Choi (1990, 1995) are related to differences in methodology. Although diverse measures may converge on a single unitary vocabulary construct (Bornstein, Haynes, & Painter, 1998), Pine, Lieven, and Rowland (1996) provide evidence that different methods of data collection point up different outcomes with respect to relative and absolute proportions of particular kinds of words in children's early vocabularies. These discrepancies call for further comparisons based on parallel-standardised measures with additional contrasting languages and cultures.

THE CONTENT OF EARLY WORDS

The contents that one-word stage speakers choose to lexicalise are remarkably similar. This appears to be true for children acquiring the same language, and also for those acquiring different languages. Content analyses of early vocabularies reveal that initially children acquire terms which label objects and actions that are commonly encountered in the immediate and familiar environment (e.g. "car", "daddy", "walk", "give"), and words which are very frequently modelled to the child in repeated contexts of everyday routines (Nelson, 1985). Words which are acquired later are more generic in the sense that they encode classes of equivalent instances or kinds of objects and actions (e.g. "stone", "box", "tree", "draw", "bring") (Dromi, 1993b).

In her 1973 study, Nelson reported that, initially, children tend to use words for movable objects, or small objects that the child himself can manipulate. Nelson's finding was replicated by other researchers who studied early lexical development by English-speaking children (Benedict, 1979), other spoken languages (Gentner, 1982), and American Sign Language (Bonvillian et al., 1983).

A content analysis of the various semantic classes and their differentiation over time in four one-word stage Hebrew speakers, revealed very similar patterns of vocabulary accumulation (Dromi & Fishelzon, 1986). During the first three months of the stage, a trend was observed in all subjects to learn semantically unrelated words belonging to different semantic fields in adult language. The following contents were lexicalised by the subjects during the first few months of production: animals and the sounds they make; foods, drinks, and eating; toys; clothes, jewellery, and small object accessories; furniture and other household accessories; social words; words for motion; and words for locations, and change of locations. Dromi and Fishelzon termed the trend of learning a few representatives in different unrelated semantic fields of adult speech a "horizontal" pattern of lexical accumulation. During the second phase of the stage, the rate of learning new words considerably accelerated in all subjects, and in a short period of time, they started to use semantically related terms that conveyed closely related meanings in adult speech. Consider, for example, Keren's differentiation of the category of clothing during three days during the 26th week of study. During this short interval of time Keren added the following lexical items to her productive lexicon: "a zipper", "to take off", "to put on", "undershirt", "underpants", "pants", "pantyhose", and "socks" (Dromi, 1987, p. 175).

The learning of words belonging to the same semantic field was termed by Dromi and Fishelzon (1986) a "vertical" pattern of lexical accumulation. This pattern is characterised by the growing differentiation of related meanings. We hypothesised that the growing ability of the child to encode more subtle semantic contrasts (Clark, 1993) is related to the improving cognitive ability of the child to form cognitive categories on the basis of the identification of similarity relations. The rapid and accurate learning of semantically related meanings requires that the child succeed in differentiating between members of the same and different categories, and also entertain the idea that each category in the world has a name (Anglin, 1983; Golinkoff, Mervis, & Hirsh-Pasek, 1994; Markman, 1993; Mervis & Bertrand, 1994).

SEMANTIC PROCESSES IN THE ACQUISITION OF EARLY WORD MEANINGS

How children map new words onto their adult conventional meanings is a question that has attracted philosophers, linguists, and psychologists. Several questions are related to this issue. Do children first generate non-linguistic concepts and only then label these concepts with words? Are new words initially associated with individual referents and only later generalised across several instances that comprise a concept in adult language? When and to what extent do children realise that words convey conventional meanings? Do all the words that are acquired throughout the one-word stage show a similar route of meaning acquisition? Do meanings of new words become more and more generalised with time, or more and more specific? What is the relationship between chronological age, cognitive abilities, and meaning acquisition? To what extent do the characteristics of the input directed to the child shape mapping of word meanings? Emerging answers to the above questions are given below.

A number of models can be utilised to abstractly represent lexical meanings (for a review see Lyons, 1977). In my own research on word meaning acquisition, I adopted a distinction that was originally proposed by Frege (1892). Frege's original proposal was to distinguish between reference and sense in the representation of word meaning. Anglin (1977, 1983) integrated Frege's distinction into the study of early language development, and provided an explanation of why the meanings of children's words ought to be represented in two distinct levels: the level of extension and the level of intension.

"The extension of a term of reference includes all the objects which an individual is willing to denote with that term of reference" whereas "the intension of a term of reference is the set of properties which an individual believes to be true of the instances of the category denoted by that term" (Anglin, 1977, p. 27). According to this definition the extension of the word "animal", for example, is: cow, dog, cat, elephant, crocodile, penguin, mink . . . etc. and its intension is: it lives, it digests, it reproduces itself, it is capable of spontaneous motion, etc. (Anglin, 1983). Conceptual word meaning representations include both the extensional and the intensional aspects of a category of objects or events which are denoted by a word in the individual's language. It is logical to assume, then, that the extension and the intension of a word are intrinsically tied and are concurrently constructed in the mental lexicon.

It is extremely difficult to demonstrate empirically the implicit relationship between extension scope and the intension properties in very young subjects.

This is primarily because children who are younger than 3 years old can hardly cooperate in experimental manipulations and therefore the underlying meaning of their terms can only be indirectly inferred from habituation research paradigms or repeated uses of words in various non-linguistic contexts (Anglin, 1977; Dromi, 1987; Gelman & Markman, 1986; Golinkoff & Hirsh-Pasek, 1995). As I argue below, it is feasible to utilise the logical distinction between extension and intension when analysing repeated spontaneous productions of one-word stage subjects.

In my own research, I examined words' extensions as a heuristic for: (1) documenting changes over time in the ways a particular word was used by the child throughout the one-word stage, and (2) comparing the child's extensions with those of adults' for the same lexical items. This was a powerful means of testing the extent to which the child's uses of words resembled conventional adult uses. The relationships between the child's and the adult's extension of the same word might take one of the following five logical forms: identity, partial overlap, mismatch, underextension, or overextension (Anglin, 1977, 1983; Clark, 1983a; Reich, 1976).

In the earlier literature on the acquisition of word meanings, the most commonly discussed extension type was overextension. Overextension is the use of a word for a class of referents, some of which fall outside of the corresponding adult category for the same word (e.g. "doggie" for all four-legged animals). The neglect of the phenomenon of underextension was noted by Anglin (1977) and Kay and Anglin (1982), who claimed that while overextensions are more noticeable in spontaneous speech productions, they are not necessarily more prevalent than underextension in early speech. Anglin reported that some early words are initially used by the child very restrictively for a single referent only or for very limited subsets of instances of the corresponding adult category for the same word (e.g. "elephant" to one blue elephant toy only). The difficulty in identifying underextension of early words lies in the fact that underextensions are in fact conventional uses of words. Underextensions cannot be identified unless all the instances for using a word are compared with the instances where the word should have been produced, but did not occur.

Four categories of extension exhibit themselves in early speech: regular extension, underextension, overextension, and unclassified. Regular extension is defined as a flexible use of a word for a number of different referents all belonging to the corresponding adult category for the same word. Such a use indicates that the child has attached the word with an underlying category. Unclassified extension is defined as an ambiguous use of a word that does not allow a clear identification of a consistent relationship between the word and a referent or a class of referents (see Dromi, 1987, pp. 95–105 for operational definitions with a set of examples). In Table 5.1 a few examples of each category are given.

Throughout the one-word stage, words change their extension behaviours. This is particularly true in cases where a word's initial extension was different

TABLE 5.1
Examples of the Four Categories of Extensions in Early Speech

A. Regular Extension

Word	Referents	Source
oto "car"	daddy's car, noise of a car, toy cars, pictures of cars in books, in response to the question: "what do we drive?"	Dromi, 1987, 1996
ball	while the child looks at, plays with, or requests: tennis balls, large colourful play balls, a beach ball	Barrett, 1986, 1995
open	as a request by the child for: a door to be opened, a jar of jelly to be opened, a box of cookies to be opened, her mother's hand to be opened	Tomasello, 1992

B. Underextension

Word	Referents	Source
bottle	plastic baby bottles only	Anglin, 1983
pil "an elephant"	a blue toy elephant only	Dromi, 1987, 1966
halax "walked"	while walking in mother's shoes only	Dromi, 1987, 1966

C. Overextension

Word	Referents	Source
dog	dogs, lambs, cats, wolves, cows	Anglin, 1983
peca "wound"	cuts, wounds, Scotch-tape, dark spots on fabrics and balloons	Dromi, 1987, 1966
kick	kicking of balls, cartoon turtles doing can-can, pushing a chest against the mirror or a sink, while observing a fluttering moth	Bowerman, 1978
tik "a handbag"	folders, nylon bags, plastic sacks, boxes, a hat upside down, pockets	Dromi, 1987, 1966

D. Unclassified

Word	Referents	Source
niyar "a paper"	pencils, pens, pieces of paper, a painting, an appliqué of two birds on a pillow cover, an arrow painted in chalk on the sidewalk, a sticker on a container of food, newspapers, a request that mommy will draw a picture	Dromi, 1987, 1966
dod "an uncle"	strangers we met in the street, any loud noises, barking of dogs, hitting of objects, unfamiliar faces on TV, visitors at the house	Dromi, 1987, 1966
bow-wow	sound of barking, birds chirping, car and airplane engines, sight of dogs, sight of cars	Braunwald, 1978

from the adult's. Underextension is a relatively short-lived phenomenon that is recorded early in the case history of a word. Overextension is documented (in most cases) subsequent to a period of regular extension or underextension. I recorded many more overextensions of new words during the second half of the one-word stage, when the rate of learning new words was accelerated. Regular extension was the most prevalent pattern of extension that I recorded during

Keren's one-word stage. One third of Keren's words demonstrated unclassified extension patterns. This relatively high proportion of non-conventional word use demonstrates that the phenomenon of unclassified extension is not an artifact of measurement.

By looking at changes over time in the extension of a single word, its extension profile is obtained. I identified as many as 58 different profiles of extension for Keren's 337 words. On the basis of this great variability, I concluded that different words take various routes as their meanings develop. My analysis revealed a close link between the timing of acquisition and the extension profile that was demonstrated by the majority of the words. During the first few months of study, the extension of a new word was highly associated with the conditions of its modelling to the child by the adult. Words that were modelled in opaque non-linguistic contexts were initially used by the child in an ambiguous way. Early words demonstrated many more changes over time in their extension behaviours than later acquired words. Words which were learned during and subsequent to the lexical spurt period showed more regular behaviours even from the beginning of their use. These words were less malleable with respect to input conditions and tended to indicate conventional meaning from their very first applications.

The relationship between the timing of the lexical spurt and the efficiency and accuracy in the mapping of new words was recently demonstrated by Mervis and Bertrand (1994). Thirty-two subjects ranging in age from 15 to 20 months participated in the study. Each subject was given a fast mapping task, a categorisation task, and an object permanence task, along with a general assessment of the size of his/her productive vocabulary. The results indicated that only those subjects who had large productive lexicons (and whose mothers affirmed that they had recently learned many new words) were found to successfully fast map novel words. The relationship in timing between the occurrence of a lexical spurt and the ability to fast map was further confirmed in a longitudinal follow up of those 16 subjects who in the first study exhibited inefficiency in fast mapping. When the vocabulary spurt was documented in these subjects, they demonstrated fast mapping as well as exhaustive sorting of objects. The interrelationships among timing, representational abilities, and input characteristics are further explored in the following section.

THE ROLE OF CONTEXT AND EXPERIENCE IN THE ACQUISITION OF WORD MEANINGS

As we have seen, not all early words show regular extension from their outset, some words are initially produced only in very specific contexts. Barrett (1986, 1995) examined early context-bound productions, and claimed that they are related to actions, to social routines, or to perceptually salient events which occur frequently in the everyday experiences of the young child. Barrett's most famous example of a context-bound word is "duck" which was initially uttered by Adam only while hitting a specific toy duck off the edge of the bath. As the child's lexical development proceeds, context-bound words are decontextualised from the original context in which they were learned. A word that was initially produced in just one situation is now uttered in a much wider range of contexts until it becomes completely context free. According to Barrett, "the reference of the word after decontextualisation seems to derive from one of the core aspects of the event which previously elicited context bound use of the word" (1995, p. 371). Thus, the process of decontextualisation in Adam's use of the word "duck" involved the following steps: playing with the same toy duck in other situations than bathing, answering the question "what is this?" in reference to any toy duck, looking at a toy duck on the floor, referring to a real duck and pictures of ducks (Barrett, 1986, 1995). As is seen in this example, subtle changes are documented in the uses of the same word over time. With time, the child extends the range of agents that can perform the action with the object, extends the range of objects which could appear in the eliciting context, or both.

Harris, Barrett, Jones, and Brookes (1988) documented the contexts in which the first 10 words were used by four English-speaking subjects. They found that more than 50% of the 40 words studied were initially used in a context-bound manner. Barrett, Harris, and Chasin (1991) and Harris (1992) reported that by the age of two, all but three of the initially recorded context-bound words showed referential meaning. A pivotal finding in this research programme addresses the relationship between the characteristics of mothers' modelling practices and the extension of the same words. The analysis of longitudinal speech samples indicated that children's initial productions resembled the most frequent context in which the words were modelled by the mothers. Mothers' modelling behaviours were significantly correlated with the initial extension of the word by the child. The relationship between mothers' input practices and subsequent uses of the same words by the children was dramatically weaker. Later productions of the same words were not tied to the non-linguistic characteristics of the input. On the basis of these correlational results, Barrett et al. (1991), and Harris (1992) concluded that the effects of maternal input characteristics decline with time and are much less pronounced once the child has established a sizeable productive lexicon.

Explanations for non-referential use of early words were provided by a number of researchers who postulated, often independently of each other, that such words lack categorical properties and are initially connected to non-differentiated representations of a situation, a scene, or an event. It was argued that context-related productions might be triggered by the identification of a single component of an event, as well as by the activation of a script representation (Barrett, 1986; Dromi, 1982, 1987, 1993a; Gillis, 1986; Nelson, 1985; Nelson & Lucariello, 1985; Schanck & Abelson, 1977; Tomasello, 1992). I speculated that Keren's unclassified extensions reflected the fact that some of her early words were produced in appropriate contexts before she carried out a detailed analysis of their categorical meanings. I termed those productions "situational" words, and argued that they were elicited as a result of a "word-context production strategy" and were used as cover terms for unanalysed representations of habitual situations.

Early non-referential uses of words provide strong empirical support for Mandler's theoretical assumption that schematic and categorical representations co-exist in human cognition. Mandler (1979, 1983) explained the distinction between categorical and schematic cognitive representations. She claimed that a scheme is a structure which is organised around contiguities of space and time, unlike categories which are based on similarity relationships among the members of a class. During the early phases of the one-word stage, when children fail to correctly map a word onto a single component of a situation (i.e. an agent, an object, or an action), the word is embedded in the schematic representation of the context in which it was modelled to the child.

Several intrinsic factors which are related to the child's cognitive functioning and the growing experience with language throughout the one-word stage, as well as more extrinsic factors that are related to input conditions, have been invoked to account for why some early words convey categorical meanings and others are initially used in a context-bound fashion. While reviewing recent theoretical models on word meaning acquisition I further discuss these factors.

THEORETICAL MODELS ON WORD MEANING ACQUISITION

Rich empirical findings were presented in the earlier sections of this chapter. These findings should be considered together with recent theories on word meaning acquisition. Three models of word meaning acquisition[5] which highlight theoretical assumptions on how young children might learn what words in adult language mean are summarised here. The models were formulated within different theoretical perspectives, and hence differ with respect to the factors they examine. Barrett's model emphasises the interaction among the timing of acquisition during the one-word stage, the child's linguistic experience, and the cognitive representational abilities of the child. Gleitman examines the role of syntax in conjecturing word meanings. Her model was formulated within a formal linguistic theory, and provides a set of interesting hypotheses that grant the basis for experimental efforts especially in word comprehension. Golinkoff, Mervis, and Hirsh-Pasek's model emerged from the constraint theoretical approach. This model introduces initial and later hypotheses that children entertain when they learn their first words. Unlike earlier accounts on the origin and scope

---

[5] A review of the early models of word meaning acquisition which were based on a strong categorical perspective is beyond the scope of this chapter (see a review in Dromi, 1987: chapter 5; Barrett, 1995, pp. 375–382; Clark, 1983a, 1983b, 1993, pp. 43–108).

of linguistic constraints (which were strongly embedded within nativistic views), the model proposed by Golinkoff et al. highlights the role of development, and closely examines factors that are related to changes over time in cognitive functioning as well as the growing linguistic experiences of the child.

The multi-route model of early lexical development—Barrett (1986)

Barrett's multi-route model was formulated to account for the diversity of findings on early words' extensions and their subsequent changes throughout the one-word stage. Barrett proposes to distinguish between two classes of early words: (1) context-bound and social pragmatic words, and (2) referential words. In his opinion, these two classes of words follow different routes to adult conventional meaning. While context-bound and social pragmatic words are initially mapped onto holistic event representations, referential words are initially mapped onto mental representations of categories that are organised around prototypes (Bowerman, 1978). As lexical learning proceeds, the words in the two sub-groups undergo semantic differentiation that results in their conventional, symbolic, and contrastive application.

The multi-route model postulates five hypothetical levels in the process of meaning acquisition. Words differ with regards to their entry level, and not all words will demonstrate a transition through all of the five levels in their developmental projection. Level A is characterised by either an initial mapping of a new word onto an event representation or its attachment to the representation of the prototype of a category. At level B, the event representation is modified. Changes may include the addition of several actors or possible objects who participate in the represented event. At level C, a single constituent in the event representation is disembedded and subsequently used by the child as the prototypical referent for the word. At level D, words that initially presented context-bound behaviours, and words which exhibited referential use from their outset, expand their referential scope. This expansion is related to the identification of the principal features that characterise the prototype of the category. At level D the child is aware of the underlying category which is attached to the word, and hence might now overextend a word for a referent which is similar to the prototype. At Level E, the refinement of the underlying semantic representation of words take place. Words are now organised in semantic fields, recession of overextension is noted, and contraction of referential scope is observed. The refinement of word meaning results from the identification of the contrastive features which differentiate among different prototypes of semantically related words.

The five hypothetical levels that are included in the model capture the ontogenesis of single words, but can also be viewed as reflecting the changing cognitive and linguistic levels of the child throughout the one-word stage. At the beginning of the one-word stage children sometimes attach words to event representations which are non-categorical, but towards the end of the stage lexical learning is differentiated and words are only attached to categorical representations. The multi-route developmental model was strongly influenced by Nelson's (1985) argument that during late infancy children build up holistic mental representations of the frequently occurring events that take place in their life. It also incorporates Nelson's idea that event representations are gradually analysed into their constituent components of people, objects, actions, and relations and thus become categorical. Bowerman's (1978) prototype model of word meaning, which was based on Rosch and her colleagues (Rosch, 1975, 1977; Rosch & Mervis, 1975), is also incorporated into Barrett's multi-route model. In this model, categories are assumed to be centred around one member which is the prototype or the "best exemplar" of that category. The prototype is the core of the category and it is surrounded by other members which are not as representative for the category. The members in a given category share attributes with the best exemplar. The degree of membership in a category (which is not a matter of all-or-none) is determined by the sum of attributes that an entity shares with the prototype. The prototype model predicts that children will initially attach new words to the abstracted underlying representation of the "best" exemplar and only subsequently will extend the word to other exemplars that share principal features with it.

The multi-route model explains well the diverse findings on initial mapping of new words, the decontextualisation process, and the gradual refinement of the meaning relations among different words in the child's lexicon. It explains why some words show consistent patterns of word extension from their outset, while others generalise or refine their referential scope over time.

The syntactic bootstrapping hypothesis— Gleitman (1989)

The idea that young children utilise syntactic cues as means for gathering word meanings is not new. In his experimental article that was published over 30 years ago, Brown (1957) demonstrated how preschoolers who are shown a picture and at the same time are presented with sentences which contrast syntactically infer on the basis of syntactic cues the meanings of novel target words. In Brown's original word-meaning experiment, three groups of subjects were presented with the same picture which depicted a novel action done to a novel substance with a novel instrument. At the time of picture presentation, each group was presented with a different sentence in which the root "sib" was incorporated. The first group heard: "in this picture you see sibbing", the second group heard "in this picture you can see a sib", and the third group heard "in this picture you can see sib". When later the subjects were asked: "what is sib?" the subjects in the first group inferred that sib is an action, the subjects in the second group inferred that sib is an object, and the subjects in the third group inferred that sib meant a substance.

Children's capacity to infer word meanings from syntactic cues was termed by Gleitman (1989, 1990) "syntactic bootstrapping". Gleitman proposed that in the structural information provided by the linguistic code, children can find resourceful evidence for constructing semantic representations. According to this view, children attend to the regularities in the input from a young age, and are sensitive to syntactic and semantic correspondences that exist in the linguistic design. In light of earlier proposals by Bowerman (1974, 1977) and by Pinker (1984) that children make syntactic conjectures on the basis of semantic information, Gleitman postulated the reverse procedure. In this procedure, children are assumed to utilise the constructional facts about verbs as an evidence for their semantic interpretations. Gleitman (1989, 1990) holds the view that extra-linguistic contingencies for using verbs are not sufficient for generating meaning representations. Some verbs encode meanings that cannot be observed (e.g. mental verbs); there is evidence that blind children use verbs and other words quite similarly to sighted children (Landau & Gleitman, 1985); and the same scene in the world can be linguistically described in many optional ways (just as the same linguistic form can be produced in quite different extra-linguistic contexts). For this reason, there is impetus to seek for procedures that will provide children with information about the semantics of verbs.

Gleitman and her colleagues carried out several studies in order to test the hypothesis that young children are capable of extracting meanings of verbs from syntactic cues. In one study, 27-month-old infants were shown two competing videos (Hirsh-Pasek, Gleitman, Gleitman, Golinkoff, & Naigles, 1988). In one video, Big Bird and Cookie Monster similarly rotated next to each other; in the second video, Big Bird rotated Cookie Monster. As the subjects were viewing the tapes, they were exposed to two corresponding sentences each including a novel verb. The first sentence was: "Big Bird is gorping with Cookie Monster", and the second was: "Big Bird is gorping Cookie Monster". Laboratory measurements of the looking behaviours of the subjects indicated that when hearing the intransitive verb form, subjects tended to look more at the video in which the two puppets performed the same action. Similarly when hearing the transitive verb form, the subjects looked more at the video which depicted the scene of one puppet performing an action on another (see Golinkoff & Hirsh-Pasek, 1995, for a description of the preferential looking research paradigm).

In a series of experiments, Naigles, Gleitman, and Gleitman (1993) elicited children's and adult's interpretations of transitive and intransitive verbs in different syntactic frames. The subjects were asked to act out grammatical sentences in which the verb meaning and the syntactic frame corresponded, and ungrammatical sentences containing the verbs which were embedded in syntactic frames that led to contradicting interpretations (i.e. transitive verbs appearing in intransitive frames, or intransitive verbs appearing in transitive frames). In acting out the ungrammatical sentences 2-, 3-, and 4-year-olds showed a strong tendency of frame compliance. This was particularly true for intransitive verbs appearing in transitive frames (e.g. "*The elephant comes the giraffe towards the arch"). A slightly less significant result was obtained for transitive verbs in intransitive frames (e.g. "*The zebra brings"). The frame compliance tendency was significantly smaller in adult subjects. In a case of conflict adults followed verb semantics rather than the syntax of the frame. These results led the researchers to the conclusion that while adults who are entitled to firm convictions about verb meanings tend to bring the syntactic frame in alignment with the verb semantics, young children bring the verb meaning into alignment with the syntactic frame.

In several publications Gleitman and her colleagues highlighted the view that syntactic bootstrapping co-exists with other sources of evidence about word meanings. They invoked the claim that in order to recover the meaning of a verb the child has to examine a wide range of syntactic frames in which this verb appears. The process of word meaning acquisition is viewed in this framework as a task of gathering probabilistic evidence from several imperfect databases while seeking the simplest fit among them (e.g. Naigles et al., 1993, p. 138).

When do children start to utilise a syntactic source of information to construct word meanings? Do children utilise syntactic cues at the one-word stage, even before they show evidence for productive syntactic abilities? My analysis on Keren's data indicated that as soon as her first verb forms were used (during the fifth month of study), they were extended regularly and consistently for actions only. I speculated that linguistic rather than cognitive factors determined the relative ease by which verb meanings were mapped by Keren. Most of the verbs that she initially produced took infinitive or imperative morphological forms. I hypothesised that these forms were selected partly because they were consistently modelled in the input to the child embedded in syntactic frames (e.g. "do you want to eat/to drink/to go outside" etc.). To what extent changes in the speed and accuracy of mapping new words towards the end of the one-word stage are related to the child's increasing sensitivity to syntactic information is a very timely research question that cries out for future experimental research.

Another direction for future research is to test the universality of the syntax–semantics correspondences in different languages. If such correspondences are true only for English, the scope of Gleitman's arguments will be narrowed (P. Bloom, 1994). To what level of semantic specificity syntactic bootstrapping might lead the child, is a question that requires further experimentation. P. Bloom (1994) raised the argument that at best syntax can provide a clue for the broad grammatical category of a word (i.e. a kind of individual, a property, or an activity). Syntactic evidence, however, cannot lead the child to the generation of a complete semantic representation for a new word. In order to explain how children might solve the puzzle of the infinity of possible hypotheses that are consistent with a set of exposures to a new word, much more specific principles that might direct word meaning acquisition should be invoked. This idea was developed by constraint theorists and is discussed next.

The developmental lexical principles framework— Golinkoff et al. (1994)[6]

Several researchers have postulated that in acquiring the meanings of words children utilise built-in assumptions, biases, or strategies that direct word mapping. It is argued that the existence of such constraints explain the accelerated speed by which new words are accumulated (Carey, 1993; Clark, 1983a, 1983b, 1988, 1993; Markman, 1989, 1992, 1993; Markman & Hutchinson, 1984; Markman & Wachtel, 1988; Merriman & Bowman, 1989; Merriman, Marazita, & Jarvis, 1995; Soja, Carey, & Spelke, 1991). Constraint theorists have tried to explain how the logical problem of generating limitless numbers of possible hypotheses about the meaning of a new word might be solved by learners. The problem of correct mapping was asked by Quine (1960). He asked how is it that when one hears a new term, one knows to which aspect of the situation this term refers. Carey demonstrated the correct mapping problem with the following example: "Suppose a child hears 'that's a cup' when the speaker is indicating a brown plastic cup half filled with coffee. Suppose also that the child does not know any word which refers to any aspect of this situation. . . . 'Cup' could refer to cups, tableware, brown, plastic, coffee, being half full, the front side of the cup and the table, the handle, any undetached part of a cup, a temporal stage of the cup (that is the particular cup at some particular time), the number one, the cup shape, and so on for an infinitude of possibilities" (Carey, 1993, p. 88).

The Taxonomic and the Whole-Object constraints, and the constraint of Mutual Exclusivity, were articulated by Markman (1989, 1992, 1993). Markman attempted to explain: how the induction of word meanings can be correct; how the meanings of new words are learned so quickly by young children; and what the mechanism is that motivates young children to learn terms other than object words (e.g. labels for properties, parts of objects, and categories of objects). Markman postulated that when children are exposed to a new word in the presence of a novel object, they assume that: (1) the new word labels the whole object, rather than its parts, substance, or other properties; and (2) the new word labels a class of objects of similar kind rather than objects that are thematically related. When children hear a new word applied to an object for which they already have a name, they assume that the new word cannot be a second name for the same object, and hence the new word is linked to some property of that object or one of its salient parts (see also Carey, 1993). In a series of well-planned experimental word-training studies, Markman and her colleagues have

---

[6] Since the manuscript of the present chapter was submitted to press, "the developmental lexical principle framework" has been slightly revised and further experimentally tested. As the major theoretical arguments have been so elegantly presented by Golinkoff and her coauthors in their original (1994) publication, I decided not to incorporate some new ideas in this section. I however wish to direct the attention of interested readers to Hirsh-Pasek and Golinkoff (1996) for further analyses and a discussion of the early emerging lexical principles and their development over time.

demonstrated that under controlled conditions, 3–5-year-old subjects seem to follow the Taxonomic and the Whole-Object constraint, and the constraint of Mutual Exclusivity (Markman, 1989, 1992, 1993; Markman & Hutchinson, 1984; Markman & Wachtel, 1988).

Clark (1988, 1990) has also proposed that lexical principles (which act very similarly to constraints) are utilised by children in the course of establishing lexical knowledge. Clark discussed the fundamental role of the two linguistic principles of "conventionality" and "contrast". According to Clark, from a very young age, and even before children start to produce their first words, children arrive at some primitive form of these two important linguistic notions that: (1) every word in the language has a conventional meaning which is shared by all speakers in the same language community; and (2) any word in the lexicon contrasts in meaning with any other word. Clark summarises empirical evidence to support her claim that lexical principles pre-empt the use of two words which are synonymous, and that new words and innovative lexical forms are used by children to fill in lexical gaps (Clark, 1993, chapter 4).

Objections to the idea of linguistic constraints was raised in the literature (Gathercole, 1987, 1989; Nelson, 1988). Nelson, for example, questioned the proposal that such constraints exist from the beginning of the one-word stage. She invoked descriptions of early complexive uses of words (Bowerman, 1978) and of highly contextual use of early words (Barrett, 1986) as support for her argument that early meanings are not yet categorical. Nelson questioned the scope of the constraints account by arguing that it is relevant to object words only (P. Bloom, 1994). Finally, she objected to the all-or-none sense of constraints which imply a limitation on which information an individual may be able to learn. If constraints are innate and universal, Nelson argued, they would not allow for individual differences. Gathercole (1987, 1989) presented a strong set of arguments against Clark's position that lexical meanings always contrast. She cited a rich set of examples for non-contrastive use of words by young children and adults. Gathercole argued that it is important to consider pragmatic principles, and to study mothers' input practices in order to better understand how children construct their lexical knowledge.

In the light of earlier criticisms on the all-or-none interpretation of lexical constraint, Golinkoff et al. (1994) adopted the use of the term lexical principles. Within their conceptual framework, lexical principles are intelligent strategies that young children adopt to increase the likelihood of forming certain word-meaning hypotheses over others. In this account, lexical principles are the product of cognitive and linguistic developments, and they operate in concert to produce skilful vocabulary learning by restricting the search space.

Golinkoff and her collaborators proposed a set of six lexical principles which are organised in two developmental tiers. Unlike other theorists, who hypothesised that the same lexical constraints guide word learning from its beginning, the present account makes a clear distinction between early and late lexical principles. The first tier of simple principles is operating at the beginning of vocabulary learning. The second tier of more advanced principles is constructed by the child on the basis of active experience with language. Late-emerging principles are closely linked to the child's cognitive ability to exhaustively categorise objects. Their construction is related to the child's ability to utilise linguistic input and to gather cues from social interaction. The clustering of principles into two developmental tiers serves to explain the distinction between pre-spurt and post-spurt mapping abilities.

The first tier consists of the following three principles: the principle of reference, the principle of extendibility, and the principle of object scope. The principle of reference states that words are mapped onto the child's representation of objects, actions, events, or attributes. Mapping refers to the symbolic relationship between the word and the real-world aspect it represents. When children start to produce words, they know that words "stand for" or "go with" real-world referents. The principle of extendibility states that a word is used to name various referents, and not only the exemplar with which it was modelled to the child. From the outset of production, children know that words do not name unique objects. The criteria for initial extension of a new word might be based on the identification of perceptual similarity, or by the identification of thematic relations among objects (e.g. associative relations or relations in time and space). Similarity of appearance seems to be a primary basis for initial extension, and it can not serve as an evidence for a word's full categorical scope. The principle of object scope states that words name whole objects rather than parts or attributes. This principle is close to Markman's whole object constraint. Its origin is assumed to be related to infants' predisposition to attend to objects rather than to actions when a label is provided. The observation that nouns in adult speech override verbs in the early lexicons of one-word stage subjects is seen as empirical evidence for the operation of this principle. Golinkoff et al. do not assume that syntactic cues play a central role in learning the first words. Syntactic knowledge, they argue, becomes beneficial for children only at the second phase of the one-word stage.

The second tier of principles include: the principle of categorical scope, the novel name-nameless category principle (N3C), and the principle of conventionality. The principle of categorical scope states that the extension of novel words occurs on the basis of the same basic level category (Mervis, 1987). At this level, categorical judgements will dictate the extension of a new word. The inclusion of a new referent in a given basic level category will be based on decisions of "the same kind", and categorical judgements will override perceptual similarities (see also Carey, 1993; Gelman & Markman, 1986).

The novel name-nameless category principle (N3C) states that a novel word will be mapped with an object for which the child does not yet have a name. This principle explains the rapid and efficient learning of new words which characterise the second phase of the one-word stage. It also captures the lexical spurt phenomena. After the appearance of this principle, word learning becomes highly economical, rapid, and much less effortful than before. A single hearing of a new word, even without an ostensive definition (e.g. pointing to the referent or showing it), will be sufficient for a correct mapping. The N3C lexical principle is different from Markman's mutual exclusivity constraint, or Clark's contrast-and-fill-in-the-gap principle in quite a fundamental way. Mervis, Golinkoff, and Bertrand (1994) do not assume that children reject the possibility of learning more than one word for one referent. On the contrary, they cite compelling evidence from a comprehension study, that even 2-year-old subjects are willing to link a second label to an already named object (e.g. "truck" and "lorry" for the same vehicle).

In experimental studies by Mervis and Bertrand (1994), the hypothesis that the appearance of N3C is closely associated with underlying changes in the child's cognitive non-verbal categorisation abilities was tested. Their results showed that children who can categorise objects exhaustively, manifest fast mapping, and are utilising the N3C principle. Longitudinal results on 16 children, who were non-users of N3C at the beginning of the study, revealed that when the lexical spurt was recorded N3C was already in place.

The suggestion that the emergence of N3C is associated with conceptual underlying changes is interesting. It concords with the claim that the one-word stage is divided into two qualitative different phases with regards to the child's linguistic as well as cognitive functioning (Bloom, 1973; Dromi, 1987, 1993b). It explains why during the later phases of the one-word stage children are not as dependent on the nature of the input as they were earlier in the stage (Harris et al., 1988). In the second phase of the one-word stage, children's lexical learning is much more directed by internal cognitive organisational abilities than by environmental factors.

The principle of conventionality is the third included in the second tier. This principle was first described by Clark (1983a, 1983b, 1993). It states that children expect meanings to be expressed by conventional forms. The principle of conventionality accounts for the child's increasing attempts, during the second phase of the stage, to adopt adult forms; to apply words with generalised meanings; to correct irregular extension patterns; to pre-empt idiosyncratic forms; and to modify "childish" phonological forms.

The developmental lexical principle model attributes significance to the role of input and experience in the construction of linguistic knowledge. This perspective is reminiscent of Schlesinger's (1982) Word-Referent Pairing Model. Two major arguments that were made by Schlesinger reappear in the present framework. The first is that initially children match words with single referents on the basis of a simple one-to-one mapping strategy. The second is that early words are not labels for pre-defined concepts, but rather they facilitate the gradual construction of underlying concepts. Schlesinger holds the view that the formulation of cognitive categories that underlie words (i.e. protoverbal elements in

Schlesinger's terminology) is gradual. He contends that category formation is dependent on interactional linguistic experiences between the child and the adult, and is also based on the child's growing cognitive abilities (i.e. the child's ability to attend to non-verbal cues, to match words with non-linguistic referents, and to form categories on the basis of accumulating positive and negative cues). According to Schlesinger, covert but active processes, by which the child compares his assumptions on a word's meaning to linguistic evidence he gathers from the linguistic input, bring the child to appreciate the categorical nature of words. This process explains why during the initial phase of the one-word stage new words are accumulated so slowly, and the characteristics of input seem to be so crucial.

EPILOGUE

My goal in this chapter was to review the empirical data on early lexical development that have been collected over the last 20 years. The summary of the empirical findings was followed by a condensed presentation of theories that provide explanations of the observed findings, as well as create the basis for new predictions. It was my intention to show that complex interactions among various factors determine the course of early lexical development.

Past research has indicated that distinctive qualitative differences exist between the course of lexical learning during the first and the second phases of the one-word stage. During the first few months of production—the preparatory phase—the child learns each word as a special case in a slow rate. Idiosyncratic patterns of word extension are noticed during this phase, and the initial extension of a new word is highly dependent on the characteristics of input and the conditions of modelling. The second phase of the stage is characterised by a much more efficient word learning. It is marked by the lexical spurt phenomenon during which a clear indication for consistent, categorical, and conventional use of new words is documented. During the second phase, words are immediately attached to underlying concepts, and the child shows context-free uses of words. It is assumed that the child's utilisation of syntactic cues is much greater in the second phase of the stage then it was in the first phase. Following the lexical spurt, the child's linguistic behaviours are much more directed by internal, cognitive organisation of experiences, rather than by the immediate non-linguistic contexts in which new words are modelled.

How universal is the above characterisation? Do all children go through the two phases in production? When does the transition between the early and late phases of lexical production occur? How vast are individual differences in quantitative and qualitative aspects of early lexical development? In a commentary on the complexity associated with the exploration of all factors that dictate the course of early lexical development, Snow (1988) likens lexical development to a rope which consists of several strands that mature at independent rates.

Snow says that "not until all [strands] are present can the rope itself be woven" (1988, p. 343). The rope metaphor nicely captures the idea that covert interactions among different variables dictate the rate of lexical development.

The goal of future research is to further explore how child-related variables interact with environmental factors. It is necessary to better understand how the child's perceptual and phonological abilities, cognitive representational abilities, as well as social and communicative skills relate to the nature of the input, and the effectiveness of mother–child bi-directional interactions. Additional experimental as well as observational data are needed in order to further test the predictions of the theories on word-meaning acquisition. How efficient are the proposed lexical principles in predicting the learning of different classes of words (e.g. action words, attributes, social words)? To what extent do different modelling conditions (e.g. ostensive definition in laboratory condition, vs. naturalistic learning situations in which words are embedded in various syntactic frames) determine when a word will be learned and how it will initially be mapped? Is the list of lexical principles suggested so far in the literature inclusive? These questions will be the focus of future investigations in this area.

ACKNOWLEDGEMENTS

This chapter was written during my stay as a visiting scientist at the University of Texas at Dallas. I wish to acknowledge the input I received from my colleagues Sandy Friel-Patti and Gloria Olness at the Callier Center for Communication Disorders; their comments helped me to better formulate my ideas in words. Thanks are also extended to Jerry Anglin, Martyn Barrett, and Roberta Golinkoff for very careful reading and detailed feedback on an earlier draft of this chapter. I wish to also thank my graduate students at the School of Human Development of UTD, Jeannie Sutton, Aire Skowronska, and Ilse Wambacq who assisted in the preparation of this manuscript.

REFERENCES

Anglin, J.M. (1977). *Word object and conceptual development*. New York: Norton.

Anglin, J.M. (1983). Extensional aspects of the preschool child's word concepts. In T. Seiler & W. Wannenmacher (Eds.), *Concept development and the development of word meaning* (pp. 247–266). New York: Springer-Verlag.

Au, T.K., Dapretto, M., & Song, Y.K. (1994). Input versus constraints: Early word acquisition in Korean and English. *Journal of Memory and Language, 33*, 567–582.

Barrett, M.D. (1986). Early semantic representations and early word usage. In S.A. Kuczaj & M.D. Barret (Eds.), *The development of word meaning* (pp. 39–67). New York: Springer.

Barrett, M.D. (1995). Early lexical development. In P. Fletcher & B. MacWhinney (Eds.), *The handbook of child language* (pp. 362–392). Oxford, UK: Blackwell.

Barrett, M.D., & Harris, M. (1989). *Children's first words and their relation to maternal speech.* Proceedings of the 1989 Child Language Seminar, Hatford Polytechnic, UK.

Barrett, M.D., Harris, M., & Chasin, J. (1991). Early lexical development and maternal speech: A comparison of children's initial and subsequent uses of words. *Journal of Child Language, 18*, 21–40.

Bates, E., Marchman, V., Thal, D., Fenson, L., Dale, P., Reznick, J.S., Reilly, J., & Hartung, J. (1994). Developmental and stylistic variation in the composition of early vocabulary. *Journal of Child Language, 21*, 85–123.

Benedict, H. (1979). Early lexical development: Comprehension and production. *Journal of Child Language, 6*, 183–201.

Bloom, L. (1973). *One word at a time*. The Hague, The Netherlands: Mouton.

Bloom, L. (1993). *The transition from infancy to language: Acquiring the power of expression*. Cambridge, UK: Cambridge University Press.

Bloom, L., Tinker, E., & Margulis, C. (1993). The words children learn: Evidence against a noun bias in early vocabularies. *Cognitive Psychology, 8*, 431–450.

Bloom, P. (1994). Overview: Controversies in language acquisition. In P. Bloom (Ed.), *Language acquisition: Core readings* (pp. 5–48). Cambridge, MA: MIT Press.

Bonvillian, J.D., Orlansky, M.D., & Novack, L.L. (1983). Developmental milestones: Sign language acquisition and motor development. *Child Development, 54*, 1435–1445.

Bornstein, M.H., Haynes, O.M., & Painter, K.M. (1998). Sources of child vocabulary campetence: A multivariate model. *Journal of Child Language, 25*, 367–393.

Bowerman, M. (1974). Learning the structure of causative verbs: A study in the relationship of cognitive, semantic, and syntactic development. *Papers and Reports on Child Language Development, 8*, 142–179.

Bowerman, M. (1977). The acquisition of rules governing "possible lexical items": Evidence from spontaneous speech errors. *Papers and Reports on Child Language Development, 13*, 148–156.

Bowerman, M. (1978). The acquisition of word meaning: An investigation into some current conflicts. In N. Waterson & C. Snow (Eds.), *Development of communication* (pp. 263–287). New York: John Wiley.

Bowerman, M. (1980). The structure and origin of semantic categories in the language learning child. In M. Foster & S. Brandes (Eds.), *Symbol as sense* (pp. 277–299). New York: Academic Press.

Braunwald, S.R. (1978). Context, word and meaning: Toward a communicational analysis of lexical acquisition. In A. Lock (Ed.), *Action, gesture and symbol: The emergence of language* (pp. 485–527). London: Academic Press.

Braunwald, S.R. (1995). Differences in the acquisition of early verbs: Evidence from diary data from sisters. In M. Tomasello & W.E. Merriman (Eds.), *Beyond names for things: Young children acquisition of verbs* (pp. 81–111). Hillsdale, NJ: Lawrence Erlbaum Associates Inc.

Brown, R. (1957). Linguistic determinism and the part of speech. *Journal of Abnormal and Social Psychology, 55*, 1–5.

Brown, R. (1973). *A first language: The early stages*. Cambridge, MA: Harvard University Press.

Camaioni, L., & Longobardi, E. (1995). Nature and stability of individual differences in early lexical development of Italian-speaking children. *First Language, 15*, 203–218.

Carey, S. (1978). The child as a word learner. In M. Halle, J. Bresnan, & G. Miller (Eds.), *Linguistic theory and psychological reality* (pp. 264–293). Cambridge, MA: MIT Press.

Carey, S. (1993). Ontology and meaning: Two contrasting views. In E. Dromi (Ed.), *Language and cognition: A developmental perspective* (pp. 88–103). Norwood, NJ: Ablex.

Carter, A.L. (1979). Prespeech meaning relations: An outline of one infant's sensorimotor morpheme development. In P. Fletcher & M. Garman (Eds.), *Language acquisition: Studies in first language development* (pp. 71–92). Cambridge, UK: Cambridge University Press.

Caselli, C.M., Bates, E., Casadio, P., Fenson, J., Fenson, L., Sanderl, L., & Weir, J. (1995). A cross-linguistic study of early lexical development. *Cognitive Development, 10*, 159–199.

Choi, S., & Bowerman, M. (1997). *Semantic categorization of spatial words: A crosslinguistic developmental study of English and Korean*. A presentation given at the SRCD meeting in Washington, DC.

Clark, E.V. (1983a). Meanings and concepts. In P.H. Mussen (Ed.), *Handbook of child psychology: Vol. III. Cognitive development* (pp. 787–840). New York: John Wiley.

Clark, E.V. (1983b). Convention and contrast in acquiring the lexicon. In B. Seiler & W. Wannenmacher (Eds.), *Concept development and the development of word meaning* (pp. 67–89). Berlin, Germany: Springer-Verlag.

Clark, E.V. (1988). On the logic of contrast. *Journal of Child Language, 15*, 317–335.

Clark, E.V. (1990). The pragmatics of contrast. *Journal of Child Language, 17*, 417–431.

Clark, E.V. (1993). *The lexicon in acquisition.* Cambridge, UK: Cambridge University Press.

Clark, E.V., & Sengul, C.J. (1978). Strategies in the acquisition of deixis. *Journal of Child Language, 5*, 457–475.

Corrigan, R.L. (1978). Language development as related to stage 6 object permanence development. *Journal of Child Language, 5*, 173–89.

Dore, J. (1974). A pragmatic description of early language development. *Journal of Psycholinguistic Research, 3*, 343–50.

Dromi, E. (1982). *In pursuit of meaningful words: A case study analysis of early lexical development.* Unpublished doctoral dissertation. The University of Kansas, TX.

Dromi, E. (1987). *Early lexical Development.* Cambridge, UK: Cambridge University Press.

Dromi, E. (1993a). The development of pre-linguistic communication: Implications for language evaluation. In N.J. Anastasiow & S. Harel, (Eds.), *At risk infants: Interventions, families, and research* (pp. 13–18). Baltimore: Paul H. Brookes.

Dromi, E. (1993b). The mysteries of early lexical development. In E. Dromi (Ed.), *Language and cognition: A developmental perspective* (pp. 32–60). Norwood, NJ: Ablex.

Dromi, E. (1996). *Early lexical development* (2nd ed.). San Diego, CA: Singular Publishing Group.

Dromi, E., & Fishelzon, G. (1986). Similarity, specificity and contrast: A study of early semantic categories. *Papers and Reports on Child Language Development, 25*, 25–32.

Fenson, L., Dale, P.S., Reznick, J.S., Bates, E., Thal, E., & Phethick, J.P. (1994). Variability in early communicative development. *Monographs of the Society for Research in Child Development*, Serial no. 242, vol. *59*(5).

Fenson, L., Dale, P.S., Reznick, J.S., Thal, D., Bates, E., Hartung, J., Phethick, J.P., & Reilly, J. (1993). *MacArthur communicative development inventories: User guide and technical manual.* San Diego, CA: Singular Publishing Group.

Frege, G. (1892). Uber sinn und bedeutung [On sense and reference]. *Zeitschr. F. Philosophie und philosoph. Kritik, 100*, 25–50. (Reprinted in F. Zabeeh, E.D. Klemke, & A. Jacobson (1974). *Readings in semantics.* Urbana, IL: University of Illinois Press.)

Gathercole, V.C. (1987). The contrastive hypothesis for the acquisition of word meaning: A reconsideration of the theory. *Journal of Child Language, 14*, 493–531.

Gathercole, V.C. (1989). Contrast: A semantic constraint? *Journal of Child Language, 16*, 685–702.

Gelman, S.A., & Markman, E.M. (1986). Understanding naturalkind terms: A developmental comparison. *Papers and Reports on Child Language Development, 25*, 41–48.

Gentner, D. (1982). Why nouns are learned before verbs: Linguistic relativity versus natural partitioning. In S. Kuczaj (Ed.), *Language development: Language, culture, and cognition* (pp. 301–332). Hillsdale, NJ: Lawrence Erlbaum Associates Inc.

Gillis, S. (1986). This child's "Nominal Insight" is actually a process: The plateau-stage and the vocabulary spurt in early lexical development. *Antwerp Papers in Linguistics*, No. 45. University of Antwerp, Belgium.

Gillis, S., & Verlinden, A. (1988). Nouns and verbs in early lexical development: Effects on input frequency? *Antwerp Papers in Linguistics*, No. 54. University of Antwerp, Belgium.

Gleitman, L. (1989). The structural sources of verb meaning. *Papers and Reports on Child Language Development, 28*, 1–48.

Gleitman, L. (1990). The structural sources of verb meaning. *Language Acquisition, 1*, 3–55.

Goldfield, B.A. (1993). Noun bias to maternal speech to one-year olds. *Journal of Child Language, 20*, 85–99.

Goldfield, B.A., & Reznick, J.S. (1990). Early lexical acquisition: Rate, content, and the vocabulary spurt. *Journal of Child Language, 17*, 171–183.

Golinkoff, R.M., & Hirsh-Pasek, K. (1995). Reinterpreting children's sentence comprehension: Toward a new framework. In P. Fletcher, & B. MacWhinney (Eds.), *The handbook of child language* (pp. 430–461). Oxford, UK: Blackwell.

Golinkoff, R.M., Mervis, C.B., & Hirsh-Pasek, K. (1994). Early object labels: The case for a developmental lexical principles framework. *Journal of Child Language, 21*, 125–155.

Gopnik, A., & Choi, S. (1990). Do linguistic differences lead to cognitive differences? A cross-linguistic study of semantic and cognitive development. *First Language, 10*, 199–215.

Gopnik, A., & Choi, S. (1995). Names, relational words, and cognitive development in English and Korean-speakers: Nouns are not always learned before verbs. In M. Tomasello & W. Merriman (Eds.), *Beyond names for things: Young children's acquisition of verbs* (pp. 63–80). Hillsdale, NJ: Lawrence Erlbaum Associates Inc.

Gopnik, A., & Meltzoff, A.N. (1986). Relations between semantic and cognitive development in the one word stage: The specific hypothesis. *Child Development, 57*, 1040–1053.

Gopnik, A., & Meltzoff, A.N. (1987). The development of categorization in the second year of life and its relation to other cognitive and linguistic developments. *Child Development, 58*, 1523–1531.

Gopnik, A., & Meltzoff, A.N. (1992). Categorization and naming: Basic level sorting in eighteen-month-olds and its relation to language. *Child Development, 63*, 1091–1103.

Greenfield, P.M. & Smith, J.H. (1976). *The structure of communication in early language development*. New York: Academic Press.

Griffiths, P., & Atkinson, M. (1978). A "door" to verbs. In N. Waterson & C. Snow (Eds.), *The development of communication* (pp. 311–319). New York: John Wiley.

Harding, C.G. (1983). Setting the stage for language acquisition: Communication in the first year. In R.L. Golinkoff (Ed.), *The transition from prelinguistic to linguistic communication* (pp. 93–113). Hillsdale, NJ: Lawrence Erlbaum Associates Inc.

Harris, M. (1992). *Language experience and early language development: From input to uptake.* Hillsdale, NJ: Lawrence Erlbaum Associates Inc.

Harris, M., Barrett, M.D., Jones, D., & Brookes, S. (1988). Linguistic input and early word meaning. *Journal of Child Language, 15*, 77–94.

Hirsh-Pasek, K., Gleitman, H., Gleitman, L.R., Golinkoff, R.M., & Naigles, L.G. (1988). *Syntactic bootstrapping: Evidence from comprehension.* Paper presented at Boston Language Conference, Boston.

Hirsh-Pasek, K., & Golinkoff, R.M. (1996). *The origins of grammar: Evidence from early language comprehension.* Cambridge, MA: MIT Press.

Jackson-Maldonado, D., Thal, D., Marchman, V., Bates, E., & Gutierrez-Clellen, V. (1993). Early lexical development in Spanish-speaking infants and toddlers. *Journal of Child Language, 20*, 523–549.

Kay, D.A., & Anglin, J.M. (1982). Overextension and underextension in the child's expressive and receptive speech. *Journal of Child Language, 9*, 83–98. •

Landau, B., & Gleitman, L. (1985). *Language and experience: Evidence from the blind child.* Cambridge, MA: Harvard University Press.

Lyons, J. (1977). *Semantics* (Vol. 1). Cambridge, UK: Cambridge University Press.

Maital, S., Dromi, E., Sagi, A., & Bornstein, M. (submitted). The Hebrew CDI: Language specific properties and cross-linguistic generalizations. *Journal of Child Language.*

Mandler, J.M. (1979). Categorical and schematic organization in memory. In C.R. Puff (Ed.), *Memory organization and structure* (pp. 259–299). New York: Academic Press.

Mandler, J.M. (1983). Representation. In J.H. Flavell & E.M. Markman (Eds.), Cognitive development, Vol. 3 of P. Mussen (Ed.), *Manual of child psychology* (pp. 420–494). New York: John Wiley.

Markman, E.M. (1989). *Categorization and naming in children: Problems of induction.* Cambridge, MA: MIT Press.

Markman, E.M. (1992). The whole object, taxonomic, and mutual exclusivity assumptions as initial constraints on word meanings. In J.P. Byrnes & S.A. Gelman (Eds.), *Perspectives on language and thought: Interrelations in development* (pp. 72–106). Cambridge, UK: Cambridge University Press.

Markman, E.M. (1993). Ways in which children constrain word meanings. In E. Dromi (Ed.), *Language and cognition: A developmental perspective* (pp. 61–87). Norwood, NJ: Ablex.

Markman, E.M., & Hutchinson, J.E. (1984). Children's sensitivity to constraints in word meaning: Taxonomic vs thematic relations. *Cognitive Psychology, 16,* 1–27.

Markman, E.M., & Wachtel, G.F. (1988). Children's use of mutual exclusivity to constrain the meanings of words. *Cognitive Psychology, 20,* 121–157.

McShane, J. (1980). *Learning to talk.* Cambridge, UK: Cambridge University Press.

Merriman, W.E., & Bowman, L.L. (1989). The mutual exclusivity bias in children's word learning. *Monographs of the Society for Research in Child Development,* Serial no. 220.

Merriman, W.E., Marazita, J., & Jarvis, L. (1995). Children's disposition to map new words. In M. Tomasello & W.E. Merriman (Eds.), *Beyond names for things.* Hillsdale, NJ: Lawrence Erlbaum Associates Inc.

Mervis, C.B. (1987). Child-basic object categories and early lexical development. In U. Neisser (Ed.), *Concepts and conceptual development: Ecological and intellectual factors in categorization* (pp. 201–233). Cambridge, UK: Cambridge University Press.

Mervis, C.B., & Bertrand, J. (1994). Acquisition of the novel name-nameless category (NC3) principle. *Child Development, 65,* 1646–1662.

Mervis, C.B., & Bertrand, J. (1995). Early lexical acquisition and the vocabulary spurt: A response to Goldfield & Reznick. *Journal of Child Language, 22,* 461–468.

Mervis, C.B., Golinkoff, R.M., & Bertrand, J. (1994). Two-years-olds readily learn multiple labels for the same basic-level category. *Child Development, 65,* 1163–1177.

Mervis, C.B., Mervis, C.A., Johnson, K., & Bertrand, J. (1992). Early lexical development: The value of the diary method. In C. Rovee-Collier & L. Lipsett (Eds.), *Advances in infancy research* (pp. 291–378). Norwood, NJ: Ablex.

Naigles, L.G., Gleitman, H., & Gleitman, L.R. (1993). Children acquire word meaning components from syntactic evidence. In E. Dromi (Ed.), *Language and cognition: A developmental perspective* (pp. 104–140). Norwood, NJ: Ablex.

Nelson, K. (1973). Structure and strategy in learning to talk. *Monograph of the Society for Research in Child Development, 38* (1–2, Serial no. 149).

Nelson, K. (1985). *Making sense: The acquisition of shared meaning.* New York: Academic Press.

Nelson, K. (1988). Constraints on word learning? *Cognitive Development, 3,* 221–246.

Nelson, K., & Lucariello, J. (1985). The development of meaning in first words. In M.D. Barrett (Ed.), *Children's single-word speech.* New York: John Wiley & Sons.

Piaget, J. (1952). *The origins of intelligence in children.* New York: Norton.

Pine, J.M., Lieven, E.V.M., & Rowland, C. (1996). Observational and checklist measures of vocabulary composition: What do they mean? *Journal of Child Language, 23,* 573–589.

Pinker, S. (1984). *Language learnability and language development.* Cambridge, MA: Harvard University Press.

Quine, W.V.O. (1960). *Word and object.* Cambridge, MA: MIT Press.

Reich, P.A. (1976). The early acquisition of word meaning. *Journal of Child Language, 3,* 117–123.

Rosch, E. (1975). Cognitive representations of semantic categories. *Journal of Experimental Psychology, 104,* 192–233.

Rosch, E. (1977). Human categorization. In N. Warren (Ed.), *Studies in cross-cultural psychology* (Vol. I). New York: Academic Press.

Rosch, E., & Mervis, C.B. (1975). Family resemblances: Studies in the internal structure of categories. *Cognitive Psychology, 7,* 573–605.

Schank, R.C., & Abelson, R.P. (1977). *Scripts, plans, goals and understanding: An inquiry into human knowledge structures*. Hillsdale, NJ: Lawrence Erlbaum Associates Inc.

Schlesinger, I.M. (1982). *Steps to language*. Hillsdale, NJ: Lawrence Erlbaum Associates Inc.

Shatz, M. (1994). *A toddler's life*. New York: Oxford University Press.

Slobin, D.I. (1985). Introduction: Why study acquisition crosslinguistically? In D.I. Slobin (Ed.), *The crosslinguistic study of language acquisition* (Vol. 1, pp. 3–23). Hillsdale, NJ: Lawrence Erlbaum Associates Inc.

Snow, C.E. (1988). The last word: Questions about the emerging lexicon. In M.D. Smith & J.L. Locke (Eds.), *The emergent lexicon* (pp. 341–353). New York: Academic Press.

Soja, N.N., Carey, S., & Spelke, E.S. (1991). Ontological categories guide young children's inductions of word meaning: Object terms and substance terms. *Cognition, 38*, 179–211.

Tardif, T. (1996). Nouns are not always learned before verbs: Evidence from Mandarin speakers' early vocabularies. *Developmental Psychology, 32*, 492–504.

Tardif, T., Shatz, M., & Naigles, L. (1997). Caregiver speech and children's use of nouns versus verbs: A comparison of English, Italian, and Mandarin. *Journal of Child Language, 24*, 535–565.

Templin, M. (1957). Certain language skills in children: Their development and interrelationships. *Institute of Child Welfare Monograph, No. 26*. Minneapolis, MN: University of Minnesota Press.

Tomasello, M. (1992). *First verbs: A case study of early grammatical development*. Cambridge, UK: Cambridge University Press.

Tomasello, M., & Merriman, W.E. (1995). *Beyond names for things: Young children's acquisition of verbs*. Hillsdale, NJ: Lawrence Erlbaum Associates Inc.

Veneziano, E. (1981). Early language and nonverbal representation: A reassessment. *Journal of Child Language, 8*, 541–563.

Veneziano, E. (1988). Vocal-verbal interaction and the construction of early lexical knowledge. In M. Smith & J. Locke, (Eds.), *The emergent lexicon* (pp. 110–147). New York: Academic Press.

Verlinden, A., & Gillis, S. (1987). *Nouns and verbs in the input: Gentner (1982) reconsidered*. Unpublished manuscript, University of Antwerp, Belgium.

Vihman, M.M., & McCune, L. (1994). When is a word a word? *Journal of Child Language, 21*, 517–542.

CHAPTER SIX

The world of words: Thoughts on the development of a lexicon

Stan A. Kuczaj II
University of Southern Mississippi, Hattiesburg, USA

As you read this book, you will undoubtedly be impressed by the wealth of information that children must perceive, process, interpret, organise, and store in order to acquire their first language. The information with which a language-learning child must contend includes: (1) the sounds of the language, particularly the categories into which such sounds fall, and the manner in which these categories can be combined to produce words; (2) the words of the language; (3) the ways in which *bound morphemes* (e.g. the English past tense *-ed*) may be added to words to alter their meanings (e.g. adding *-ed* to *walk* results in *walked*, the past tense form of *walk*), information that requires attention to both the correct uses of such forms and the exceptions to such uses (e.g. English requires the use of *ate* rather than *eated*); (4) the combination of words and bound morphemes to produce sentences; and (5) the manner in which speakers of a language use language to communicate with one another. Clearly, children acquiring their first language face a formidable task, a task in which the acquisition of words plays a central role.

The typical 2-year-old child uses between 50 and 600 words, and adds an average of 10 words *per day* to her vocabulary, resulting in a vocabulary of approximately 14,000 words by the age of six years (Carey, 1978; Smith, 1926; Templin, 1957). Once children enter school, they are exposed to 10,000 or more new words each year, and annually add 3000 or so of these words to their vocabulary (Nagy & Anderson, 1984; Nagy & Herman, 1987). By the time an individual has graduated from high school, she is likely to know more than 50,000 words. The acquisition of words need not end during an individual's lifetime, so that an adult may easily have a vocabulary in excess of 100,000 words. Of course, not all of the words in a child's or adult's vocabulary are equally well known. Certain words are likely to be very well known and understood, such as the word *toy* to the typical 3-year-old child or the word *money* to the parents of an undergraduate university student. Other words may be less well known and understood, and still others might be understood only in context. Word counts of vocabulary, then, can be misleading to the extent that they imply that all the words that an individual knows are known to the same degree.

Given that word meaning acquisition continues (or at least can continue if one has an active intellectual life) throughout the lifespan, word meaning acquisition differs from all other aspects of language development. The ability to perceive sound categories (*phonemes*) is thought to be determined in the first year or two of life (Eimas, 1985; Plunkett and Schafer, this volume; Werker, 1989). Much of the ability to produce speech sounds and their permissible combinations has been acquired by the time children enter first grade (Ingram, 1989; and this volume). Children learn the rules governing the regular use of most bound morphemes before the age of 5 years, although learning the exceptions to some of the rules may take years (Kuczaj, 1977). Similarly, the acquisition of syntax is largely complete by the age of 5 years (Maratsos, 1983; and this volume). The discovery that language may be used to communicate and that there are implicit rules of conversation also occurs in the first years of life (Bornstein, 1996; Ingram, 1989; Pan & Snow, this volume). Although aspects of the sound, communicative, morphological, and syntactic systems continue to develop after the age of 5 years, the acquisition of words exhibits the most significant improvements after the preschool years. If the language development of an individual was mysteriously halted at the age of 5 years, this individual would possess most of the sound, morphological, syntactic, and communicative systems of her native language. However, her vocabulary, *at best*, would be 25% of that of a normal adult. The unique characteristic of word meaning development is that much of it occurs after other aspects of language development are more or less completed.

Although adults learn many words, I will typically use the term "child" to refer to the word learning individual. This reflects the primary concern of this chapter, the acquisition of words after the age of 2 years, and the fact that precious little work has been done on vocabulary development in adults.

THE WORD AS UNIT

In order to acquire a word, the child must recognise that the word is a meaningful unit of language. In the early phases of word meaning development, the child may hear words used as single units, as when a mother points to an animal and says "dog". Later on, children may be exposed to words as individual units in school. For example, a teacher may introduce biology by presenting and defining terms such as *cell*, *nucleus*, and *mitosis*. Of course, as children read, they experience words as isolated units on a page (even though there may be many such units on the page). In such situations, children are provided with words as independent units. In normal speech, however, words are part of the speech stream, and so must be separated by one another by the listener. For adults, this process is effortless (unless the speaker is mumbling or some such thing), and so is taken for granted. To illustrate the complexity of this phenomenon, imagine that you are listening to two individuals converse in a language that you do not know. Obviously, you will not understand what is being said. In fact, you will most likely not be able to distinguish one word from another. Consider the following example, written without any word boundaries (from Slobin, 1979):

wheredidyougowithgrandpa

Using your knowledge of English and reading, you most likely interpreted this uninterrupted string with ease. Now try the following example:

dedenlenereyegittinsen

This is the Turkish equivalent of the English example given above. Unless you are a Turkish speaker, even learning the meaning is of little help in segmenting and interpreting the string of sounds. The Turkish string is segmented in the following way:

dede n le ne re ye git t in sen

Young children are faced with the task of separating the spoken speech stream into words, a task that they begin when they have little knowledge of their native language. This challenge may be aided by children's willingness to listen to human speech. Human infants prefer to listen to human speech rather than to other sounds in their environment (Gibson & Spelke, 1983), a predisposition that may help them to determine sound categories and word boundaries. Nonetheless, the infant's preference for human speech sounds over other sounds does not explain the processes by which children are able to segment the speech stream in the early phases of language development. In fact, given the importance of the ability to extract individual words from the speech stream, we know very little about the development of this skill (although see Plunkett and Schafer, this volume, for some discussion of this topic).

We cannot explain how children extract individual words from the speech stream, but we know they can do so. Otherwise, they could not learn so many words so quickly. It is possible that children are born with the ability to pluck words from speech. However, simply stating that a phenomenon is innate is not an explanation unless one can specify exactly what is innate and how the innate ability allows the child to parse words from any of the thousands of languages to which she might be exposed as her native tongue. It is also possible that children are not born with the ability to choose words from the speech they hear, but are instead constrained to develop to hear words as units by some factor that has evolved with our capacity to acquire language. In order for this possibility to be an explanation, it would be necessary to specify the nature of the constraint and to demonstrate that it operates for all language-learning children. If we decided to abandon all notions of innate predispositions, it would then be necessary to specify the manner in which the environment leads children to distinguish one word from another. These sorts of explanations (innate ability, innate constraints, and experiential) are common in attempts to account for various aspects of language development, including word meaning acquisition. Consequently, the above qualifications concerning standards for explanations of the ability to perceive words as separate units also hold for explanations of word meaning acquisition (and other aspects of language development).

WHAT'S IN A WORD?

Given that children are somehow able to extract individual words from the speech they hear, what else is involved in word meaning acquisition? In order to learn a word, the child must learn at least four things: (1) the pronunciation of the word; (2) the syntactic properties of the word; (3) the meaning of the word; and (4) how the word is used to communicate one's intended message. This information is stored in the *lexicon*, which might be thought of as a mental dictionary. Although a consideration of how children learn the pronunciations and syntactic and communicative properties of words is beyond the scope of this chapter, the fact that such information is part of the lexicon means that any explanation of the development of the lexicon is incomplete unless it also accounts for pronunciations and syntactic and communicative properties.

THE REPRESENTATION OF MEANING

In order to acquire words, children must be able to mentally represent the relevant information about words. The mental lexicon consists of these representations. Given that meaning is an important aspect of the lexicon, determining the nature of the representation of meaning would seem to be an important first step in attempts to explain word meaning acquisition. Disappointingly, despite numerous attempts, philosophers, linguists, and psychologists have all failed to specify the manner in which meaning is represented in the human mind. Nonetheless, attempts to characterise *meaning* itself have produced some important insights that have implications for the study of word meaning acquisition.

It is not possible in this chapter to examine all of the types of meaning that are contained in the lexicon. For example, some words have both denotative and connotative meaning (Leech, 1974). Denotative meaning is the type of meaning involved when words are used to refer to something, be it an object, some property of an object, some action, or a hypothetical idea. Thus, the denotative meaning of *dog* has to do with dogs, the denotative meaning of *furry* has to do with the hairy properties of certain objects, the denotative meaning of *walk* has to do with an activity that certain objects perform, and the denotative meaning of *unicorn* has to do with certain fantasy objects. The connotative meaning of these words has to do with the emotional associations that words conjure up in the minds of speakers and listeners. For example, the use of the word *dog* to refer to one's pet has a different connotation than does the use of the word *dog* to insult another human being. Although the development of connotative meaning is an important part of the development of the lexicon (Livingston, 1982), I will limit my discussion in this chapter to denotative meaning, reference, and sense.

The distinction between *denotation*, *reference*, and *sense* was made by Lyons (1977). As noted above, denotation describes the relation between a word and that to which it is used to refer. In Lyon's view, reference is an act performed by speakers, not an inherent property of words. In Lyon's words, it is "the person who refers who invests the [word] with reference by the act of referring" (Lyons, 1977, p. 177). Although this sounds like double talk, the point is in fact a very important one. Scholars interested in word meaning and word meaning acquisition err when they say that words refer to things. Words *do not* refer to things. Speakers of a language *use* words to refer to things.

Despite their differences, denotation and reference share one basic characteristic. They relate words to other things. Denotation concerns the relation of words to objects, events, ideas, etc. Reference concerns the relation of words to speakers, listeners, and things. Sense differs from denotation and reference in that sense does not relate words to entities (objects, events, speakers, listeners, etc.) that are outside of the mental dictionary. Instead, sense describes the ways in which words are related to one another in the lexicon. In his discussion of these sorts of semantic relations, Lyons distinguished syntagmatic relations and paradigmatic relations.

Syntagmatic relations concern the ways in which words can and cannot be used together. For example, one can say *the chicken flew the coop,* but it makes no sense to say *the chicken drove the coop* (unless the coop is actually a coupe and the chicken has more ability than the average fowl). Simply put, not all words make sense if put together.

Paradigmatic relations are those relations that hold among the meanings of words. For example, some words are lexical opposites: *male-female, hot-cold,* and *come-go.* Although there are many types of lexical opposites (Kuczaj, 1982a; Lyons, 1977), all lexical opposition occurs along some dimension of similarity. In order for a pair of words to be opposites, they must bear some crucial semantic similarity as well as some crucial semantic difference. In his discussion of lexical opposites, Lyons notes that most antonyms in English and other languages are morphologically unrelated (*hot-cold, good-bad*) rather than morphologically related (*happy-unhappy,* which in fact has a morphologically unrelated counterpart, *happy-sad*). He goes (p. 277) on to suggest that:

> Antonymy reflects or determines what appears to be a general human tendency
> to categorize experience in terms of dichotomous contrasts . . . lexicalization of

polarity in two morphologically unrelated [forms] enhances . . . the distinctiveness of the two [opposite] poles.

Other types of paradigmatic relations include hyponymy, part-whole, synonymy, and semantic sets. Hyponymy is the relation between a subordinate term (e.g. *cow*) and a superordinate term (e.g. *mammal*). The part-whole relation is one that exists between an entity and its parts. For example, a *finger* is part of a *hand*, and a *star* is part of the *cosmos*. Synonymy occurs when more than one word may express a given meaning.

Semantic sets are word groups that contain more than two members. Serially ordered semantic sets contain two outermost members, the remaining words being ordered between the two extremes. For example, the group of temporal adverbs *always*, *usually*, *sometimes*, *seldom*, and *never* is a serially ordered semantic set. *Always* and *never* comprise the outer limits, with *usually*, *sometimes*, and *seldom* ordered relative to the two extremes and one another. Cyclically ordered semantic sets are those in which each word is ordered between two others. Words for days of the week comprise one such set.

The distinctions between reference, denotation, and sense provide a framework for the study of word meaning acquisition (Dockrell & Campbell, 1986). In the following sections, I will examine the developmental significance of each of these aspects of the lexicon.

REFERENCE

Words are arbitrary conventional symbols. They are arbitrary because there is no inherent relation between a particular sound pattern (word) and its meaning. For example, the sound pattern *elephant* bears no necessary relation to the pachyderms associated with the term. This is true for all words in all languages. The relation between words and meanings is a function of the evolution of specific languages, not a function of the physical properties of the words themselves. Speakers of English could just as easily refer to the creatures we call dogs as *gorts* or *zatels*. If there were some necessary relation between words and meanings, all languages would use the same words. Instead, different languages use different sound combinations to refer to the same meaning. The English *dog* is *hund* in German, *perro* in Spanish, and *chien* in French.

Words are conventional because the relation between words and meanings is implicitly agreed upon by the speakers of a language. Although the relation between *elephant* and its meaning is arbitrary, speakers of English agree about the relation. It is this agreement that makes words conventional symbols, and makes communication possible.

Words are symbols because they represent meanings. The word *elephant* represents elephants, but the word *elephant* is not itself an elephant. The word is a conventional symbol, not an instance of the object it symbolises. Regardless of their meaning(s), all words are symbols (Harnad, 1996).

Before the young child can begin to acquire words and meanings, she must understand that a word is a meaningful sound that can be used to represent something else. (This knowledge need not be conscious, and is in fact likely to be tacit, that is, not at the level of conscious awareness.) In other words, the child must have a capacity for reference (Bever, 1970; Kuczaj, 1975).

To what extent, though, are children's early words arbitrary conventional symbols? Such words certainly have symbolic status, although it is not clear exactly *how* symbolic early words are. They represent aspects of the child's world, but we certainly do not know the nature or limits of these representations (see Barrett, 1982, 1986; Greenberg & Kuczaj, 1982; Kuczaj, 1986; Dromi, this volume, for discussions of this issue). But are words actually representational for children? Piaget (1929) suggested that young children believe that a word is either an integral part of a word or the same thing as the object which it represents. Piaget referred to this misconception as *nominal realism*.

This supposed confusion on the part of children is troublesome, for how do children use words as symbols for something if they actually believe that the word *is* the thing? For example, does the young child actually believe that the word *dog* is in fact a dog? The word *dog* is not furry, does not bark or wag its tail, and is certainly not man's best friend. Most scholars of word meaning acquisition assume that, even for young children, words are symbols that stand for (i.e. represent) something. Young children may err in what they believe a word represents, but most of us assume that they know (perhaps tacitly) that the word *dog* and the object dog are qualitatively different. The word represents the object, but it is not the object.

Is there a way to reconcile these two disparate notions? Could children believe that words and objects are the same and at the same time use the words symbolically to represent the objects? This is unlikely, since it is difficult to imagine a scenario in which something is both an object and a symbol of itself. So either children do not treat words as symbols or nominal realism does not really exist. In an earlier paper, I have argued that children recognise the difference between words and objects from the very beginning of the word meaning acquisition process (Kuczaj, 1988). In this view, children never equate words and objects, for they know from the beginning that words are used to label things.

If this is correct, what are we to make of the research that has suggested an inability on the part of young children to distinguish words and objects? It is true that some children exhibit behaviour consistent with the notion of nominal realism. However, the incidence of nominal realism depends on the particular task used (Kuczaj, 1988; Rosenblum & Pinker, 1983). When children do seem to exhibit nominal realism, it is most likely that they do not understand the question and respond in terms of their bias toward thinking and talking about objects rather than words. Children probably find using language to talk about language a novel experience. Thus, they may reasonably assume that the conversation is about objects, not realising that words are being used to refer to words as well as objects.

In most studies of nominal realism, children are asked to consider hypothetical situations in which objects mysteriously vanish or a word is mysteriously taken from the lexicon of the child's language. Although young children can and do refer to hypothetical events, they also find it more difficult to successfully engage in hypothetical reference when the hypothetical situation is proposed to them than when they initiate the hypothetical context (Kuczaj, 1981; Kuczaj & Daly, 1979). Given this and the strangeness of being asked to think about words as objects, it is not surprising that some children confuse words and objects in their answers. This confusion does not mean that they equate words and objects, but instead reflects the confusion caused by the task.

Although nominal realism seems best viewed as an epiphenomenon, the fact that children distinguish words and referents does not mean that children acquire all aspects of a word's use and meaning at once. Children's early words and gestures seem to have limited communicative value (see the chapters by Dromi and Reddy in this volume for discussions of this phenomenon). However, by the time children have acquired their first 100 words (and remember that this is just the proverbial drop in the bucket, given the number of words that children will acquire), words seem to have acquired a more conventional status. It seems likely that the desire to acquire additional conventional forms with which to communicate and the desire to make more sense of the world are primary motivating factors that underlie word meaning acquisition.

To sum up our discussion of reference, children seem to acquire the capacity for reference sometime around their first birthday (see the chapters by Dromi and Reddy in this volume for detailed considerations of this topic). This capacity does not emerge in full bloom, but is instead initially highly contextually dependent. In the next few years, the capacity for reference blossoms to the extent that children can use words to represent and refer to real, possible, and imaginary aspects of their world. Thus, the toddler who uses the word *ball* only when a parent is rolling a ball on the floor becomes a 3-year-old who can use words to express complex thoughts such as *I don't want to go to sleep and dream the dream I dreamed last night* (Kuczaj, 1982b).

DENOTATION

Word meaning acquisition is a comprehension-based process. Children will not learn words that they have not heard. However, children need not immediately produce a word they have just heard in order to learn it. They can store the information in memory for later use (Kuczaj, 1987). No matter when children first produce words that they hear, they must determine the denotation of each word that they learn. How do children decide exactly what particular words denote? Certainly, children must depend on contextual information to interpret words. The manner in which a child interprets a recently discovered word depends on the child's existing lexicon, knowledge of the world, and cognitive skills (Kuczaj, 1975, 1982a).

The child's interpretation and memory of the situation in which the word was first encountered will determine the child's initial guess about the word's denotation. If the word has a concrete referent, it is possible that the object might be pointed to or shown to the child. In such cases, the child is likely to infer that the word has something to do with the object, even though the child may not immediately determine the exact nature of the word-object relationship. Regardless of whether or not a new word has a concrete referent, children may make a quick guess about a word's denotation, oftentimes on the basis of limited experience, a phenomenon that has come to be called "fast mapping" (Carey, 1978; Dockrell & Campbell, 1986; Heibeck & Markman, 1987). For example, if a child is first exposed to the word *beige* in the context of the instruction "bring me the beige one, not the blue one", the child might conclude that *beige* is a colour term and that it is a colour other than blue (assuming that the child knows the denotation of the word *blue*; Carey & Bartlett, 1978).

Although neither the extent to which children engage in fast mapping nor the nature of the circumstances that increase (or decrease) the likelihood of fast mapping have been reliably determined, the phenomenon itself has been fairly well documented. Heibeck and Markman (1987) reported that 2-year-old children are capable of making reasonable guesses about a novel word's denotation based on fast mapping (see also Merriman & Bowman, 1989). However, the extent to which children engage in fast mapping depends on their previous knowledge and the type of novel word to which they are exposed. Mervis and Bertrand (1994) found that 15–20-month-old children were more likely to employ fast mapping if they had relatively large productive vocabularies. In fact, the vocabulary "spurt" of young children seems to be correlated with the incidence of fast mapping decisions that children make (see Dromi, this volume, for further consideration of this possibility). The successful use of fast mapping by older children also seems to be affected by the type of novel word being considered by the child. Three- and four-year-old children make more accurate guesses with their fast mapping attempts when faced with a novel animal word rather than a novel colour word (Dockrell & Campbell, 1986).

As the child gains additional experience with a word and its uses, she must compare the information gleaned from these experiences with that already stored in the lexicon. Such comparisons will result in the child eventually determining the conventional denotation for the word. Even though many words do not have concrete referents, the basic processes of word meaning acquisition are the same. The child encounters all words in situations, which she interprets with respect to her current knowledge, and this interpretation determines the denotation initially granted to words. Subsequent experiences and interpretations must be compared to earlier ones in order for these initial guesses to be sharpened and shaped into the conventional denotations of the language the child is learning. This requires the child to be a prodigious information processor. She must interpret, organise, store, and retrieve vast amounts of information about words and all possible worlds (physical, mental, spiritual, imaginary—anything that words denote).

ARE OBJECT WORDS BASIC?

Words that denote objects have received the greatest amount of attention from scholars of word meaning acquisition. One reason for this concerns the relative ease with which one can assess the denotation that a child has granted an object word. If a child uses words like *bird, dinosaur, dream,* and *know,* it is easier to determine the objects that the child is willing to count as instances of the category represented by *bird* and the objects that the child views as types of *dinosaurs* than it is to figure out exactly what the child thinks is denoted by *dream* and *know.* Another reason that object words have garnered so much attention has to do with their perceived importance in the early phases of the development of the lexicon (see Tomasello & Merriman, 1995; Dromi, this volume, for other discussions of this topic).

It has been suggested that, regardless of the language they are learning, young children's vocabularies are likely to contain more words for objects than words for actions (Gentner, 1982; Gentner & Boroditsky, in press). One possible explanation for this developmental pattern relies on the differences between the denotations of nouns and verbs. At least some nouns denote concrete objects that can be touched, pointed to, and seen. Verbs tend to denote relations among nouns. For example, *the deer ate the grass, the girl knows the answer,* and *the kite is flapping in the wind* contain verbs that describe relations among nouns. Although one might argue that it is possible to witness the act of eating and the act of flapping, it is difficult to imagine how one might observe an act of knowing (by the same token, it is difficult to observe the wind as an entity—not all nouns are readily observable). The basic idea is that young children find it easier to learn words and their denotations if the words have concrete referents, i.e. are object words. However, Bloom, Tinker, and Margulis (1993) and Gopnik and Choi (1995) have suggested that it is not true that young children are more likely to learn nouns than verbs. Bloom et al. noted that when words like *off* and *up* and children's words for specific actions (e.g. *peek-a-boo, upsy-daisy*) are counted as verbs, the discrepancy between nouns and verbs in early vocabularies diminishes. These actions are ones that the child can observe (or perform, once they have learned the actions), and so do not refute the notion that children's early words are most likely to reflect aspects of their world that can be directly perceived.

Gopnik and Choi found that children who are learning languages such as Korean and Japanese are more likely to acquire verbs than are children who are learning English. Verbs in Korean and Japanese tend to occur at the end of sentences, which may make it easier for children to segment them from the speech stream. Children are more likely to learn bound morphemes that occur at the end of words and words that occur at the end of sentences (Kuczaj, 1979; Slobin, 1973), so the use of verbs at the end of sentences may be one reason that young children learning Korean and Japanese are more likely to acquire verbs than are children learning English. Gopnik and Choi also point out that English verbs do not denote the kinds of actions and relations that young children are most likely to express. Korean and Japanese verbs do, and so children learning these languages have another advantage over their counterparts who are attempting to learn English verbs. The verbs children learning Japanese and Korean hear are more likely to be used to refer to aspects of the world in which children are interested.

To further complicate matters, Nelson (1995; see also Dromi, this volume) noted that young children may use a word as a noun and as a verb, so even the distinction between words that denote objects and those that denote actions (or states) is not always an easy one to justify in young children's speech. Rather than arguing about whether young children find it easier to learn nouns or verbs, it seems more important to remember that young children's early words are based on aspects of the world that they can directly experience, regardless of whether the words are nouns, verbs, or adjectives.

THE DENOTATION OF EARLY OBJECT WORDS

The early phases of word meaning acquisition demonstrate that children's initial guesses about the denotation of words are often incomplete. A child may attach an overly broad denotation to a word, and so may use a word like *dog* to denote dogs, cows, sheep, and bears. Such a mistake is called an overextension error. Or a child may attach too narrow a denotation to a word, and so restrict a word like *man* to only her father. This type of mistake is called an underextension error.

These sorts of errors illustrate the fact that children must continually refine the meanings that they attach to words until they determine the appropriate conventional meaning. In Kuczaj (1986), I suggested that young children might learn object words in the following sequence: (1) the word is underextended; (2) the word is underextended and overextended (e.g. only some dogs are called *dog*, but some non-dogs are also called *dog*); (3) the word is overextended; (4) the word is used correctly. The data reported in Kuczaj (1986) demonstrated that the first and third steps need not occur in the acquisition of every early object word, but that if the steps did occur, the sequence outlined above was upheld.

If underextension and overextension errors reflect the denotation that children have granted words, then such errors should occur in both comprehension and production. Thomson and Chapman (1977) studied a group of children who produced overextension errors, e.g. instances of both sheep and dogs might be labelled *dog*. However, when shown a picture of a dog and a picture of a sheep, and asked to point to a *dog*, the children tended to point to the dog. These results suggested that children's overextension errors in production may not reflect the denotation that children have granted words, but instead a communicative strategy in which children are pointing out the similarity of two objects. If this is true, the child who calls a sheep a *dog* is not actually equating dogs and sheep, but is instead using a word she knows to point out the similarity of the novel object (the sheep) to a familiar category (dogs).

A different interpretation has been offered by Kuczaj (1982c). For each word that the young children had overextended in production, a set of six objects was constructed. This set consisted of two appropriate objects, two objects to which the child had overextended the word in production, and two clearly inappropriate objects. For example, a child who had overextended the term *doggie* in production was shown two dogs (the two appropriate objects), a bear and a lion (two of the objects to which the word had been overextended), and a car and a tree (the two inappropriate objects). When the child was shown the array, she was asked to give the experimenter a *doggie*. After she had chosen an object, she was asked to give the experimenter another *doggie*. This procedure was repeated until the child indicated that there were no more doggies to be given. Children tended to first choose appropriate objects, consistent with the findings of Thomson and Chapman (1977) and Fremgen and Fay (1980). However, the children also tended to next choose the objects to which the words had been overextended in production. Children rarely chose an inappropriate object, suggesting that they were not simply choosing objects at random. Similar results have been reported by Mervis and Canada (1983) and Kuczaj (1986). All in all, these data demonstrate that overextension errors occur in comprehension as well as in production, suggest that overextension errors may reflect the denotation of words for children, and have implications for theories about how the denotation of object words may be represented in the minds of young children.

During the past 20 years, various attempts have been made to explain object word meaning acquisition in terms of prototype-based denotation (Anglin, 1977; Barrett, 1982, 1986; Greenberg and Kuczaj, 1982; Kuczaj, 1982c, 1986; Tager-Flusberg, 1986). The basic idea of a prototype is that some instances of object categories are better examples of the category than are other instances (Rosch, 1978). In other words, instances of a category differ in terms of their status as instances. Simply being a member of a category does not entail equal status with other instances of the category. Prototypes are the central examples of a category. The status of other instances depends on their similarity to the prototypic instances. If a child thinks that sparrows are the prototypical bird, then creatures that resemble sparrows will be more likely to be considered to be birds. Birds like penguins, ostriches, and condors are not very similar to sparrows, and as a result might be considered as peripheral examples of birds (once the child understood that they were in fact birds despite their glaring differences from sparrows).

In the comprehension task used by Kuczaj (1982c), children tended to first choose appropriate objects before they chose objects to which they had overextended the words in production. This pattern suggests that children's choices may have been governed by prototype-based denotations. If one assumes that the appropriate objects are more prototypic than are the objects to which the word is overextended, then the data demonstrate that children choose more prototypic objects before less prototypic objects. Additional support comes from Kuczaj (1986), in which children's comprehension was assessed on two different occasions. In both testing sessions, children were more likely to choose appropriate objects before objects to which words had been overextended (as in Kuczaj, 1982c). Appropriate objects that were chosen first for underextended terms in the first testing session were also usually chosen first in the second testing session, even in those instances in which the word was no longer underextended. This pattern suggests that the objects to which children apply an underextended word may become the prototypes for the word as the child broadens the word's denotation.

Even though the notion of some prototype-based representational system for object word denotation seems justified by the data (see Barrett, 1982, 1986; Tager-Flusberg, 1986, for additional data and supporting arguments; also see Clark, 1993, for a discussion of the possibility that the denotation of some verbs may involve prototype-based representations), we are not yet able to specify the precise nature of the prototype-based representational system. Adherence to the notion of prototype-based object representation does not entail acceptance of one particular view of prototype-based concepts (Rosch, 1978). Two of the more plausible possibilities (at least according to my prototype of prototype theories) are the "holistic" and the "family resemblance" models. The holistic model assumes that children and adults store and use holistic information about instances of objects (Brooks, 1978; Greenberg & Kuczaj, 1982). The family resemblance model assumes that information about objects is based on bundles of non-criterial features (Mervis & Canada, 1983; Rosch & Mervis, 1975; Smith & Medin, 1981; Tversky & Hemenway, 1984). A complete explanation of the manner in which prototypes are involved in object word denotation requires the determination of the precise nature of prototype-based categories, and so will have to wait until such knowledge is gained.

THE PROBLEM OF TOO MANY POSSIBILITIES

To this point, my consideration of the acquisition of the denotation of object words has focused on young children who have less than 500 words in their productive vocabularies. As mentioned earlier, children are prodigious word learners. The 24-month-old child with a productive vocabulary between 50 and 600 words will easily quadruple or quintuple her vocabulary in the next year, and then add between 3000 and 4000 words per year to her productive vocabulary until she graduates from high school. If our hypothetical individual pursues a college education, and/or remains intellectually active, her vocabulary will continue to increase throughout her life.

The sheer number of words and meanings that children acquire is phenomenal. Any viable theory of word meaning development must account for the manner in which children attach meanings to individual words and the impressive number of words and meanings that children acquire. Remember that words do not have meaning in and of themselves, so the word learner must discover the conventional denotation associated with each word that is acquired. To further complicate matters, there is rarely a one-to-one correspondence between words and denotations. The same object may be referred to by a variety of words and linguistic forms. For example, the same creature might be called *Spot, dog, mutt, cur, nice doggy, man's best friend*, etc. depending on the speaker and the context. In addition, some categories are part of larger categories. For example, a dog might be a Bouvier (a breed of the larger category "dog"), but is also a mammal (a category which includes dogs), an animal (a category that includes mammals), and a terrestrial (a category that includes mammals). A given object, then, can have more than one label. And as even a casual perusal of a dictionary reveals, many words have more than one denotation.

Despite the potential for confusion that the multiple relations between words and denotations creates, children somehow construct a lexicon. Perhaps children begin the construction of a lexicon with the creation of one-to-one correspondences between words and objects, and only later begin to build the multifaceted links between words and objects. Although this possibility seems plausible (Clark, 1993; Kuczaj, 1982a), the child's task remains formidable. As stated earlier, word meaning development is a comprehension-based process, in which the child must make some guess about a newly encountered word from the context in which the word occurred. Consider a situation in which a child is shown a horse pulling a carriage and told to "look at the horse". Prior to this, the child has never heard the word *horse* nor seen a horse. We will assume that the child can segment the word *horse* from the rest of the sentence. Even so, the possibilities for the denotation of *horse* are numerous. The child might guess that *horse* means "horse and carriage", "wheel", "mane", "hoof", "tail", "long big nose", "rolling buggy", "animal pulling a machine", and so on. As noted by Quine (1960) and Goodman (1983), there are many possible interpretations for every situation such as our example. Given this, how does the child make her initial guesses about the denotation of words? Moreover, how does she do this for the thousands of words she will experience and add to her lexicon?

IS CHILDREN'S ACQUISITION OF WORD MEANING CONSTRAINED?

In the earlier discussion of the ability to differentiate words in the speech stream, three types of possible explanations were mentioned. One type of possible explanation relied on the notion of constraints, the basic idea being that during the course of evolution, innately specified ways of interpreting and organising information have come to determine the manner in which children acquire language. This type of explanation has become popular in recent accounts of word meaning development. In this section, I shall examine the theoretical under-pinnings of the notion of constraints and the evidence for and against constraints of word meaning acquisition.

As we have seen, the task that children face in the construction of a lexicon is a formidable one. They must deal with an abundance of information, and somehow sort out individual words, their pronunciations, meanings, permissible combinations, and communicative status. Given the complexity of the task faced by children and the many interpretations possible when one is exposed to a new word, it has been suggested that children manage to acquire words and meanings as quickly as they do because children's choices are constrained. In other words, acquiring a lexicon is thought to be less difficult than one might suppose be-cause children neither need to consider the wealth of information available to them nor to be bothered by an overwhelming array of possibilities. Instead, both the information to be considered and the possible interpretations of the informa-tion are thought to be limited by innately specified constraints.

Constraints for word meaning acquisition?

In her recent book, Clark (1993) has suggested that the following constraints might ease the burden of the young child who might otherwise be in the throes of word meaning acquisition.

Whole object constraint.   Children believe that speakers use words to refer to whole objects, not just a property or a part of the object. If true, the child who hears an adult say *horse* while pointing to a horse and carriage will not assume that the adult is referring to part of the horse or part of the carriage. Of course, this constraint does not preclude the child from incorrectly guessing that *horse* denotes the horse and the carriage as a single whole object.

Object type constraint.   Children believe that speakers use words to denote types of objects rather that individual instances. If true, the child who hears *dog* used to refer to an animal will suppose that *dog* is used to label the category of objects of which the particular dog is an instance. The child will not assume that *dog* is a proper name that is used to refer to a single object.

Basic level constraint.   Children believe that speakers use words to describe basic-level categories. If true, the child who hears *dog* used to refer to an object assumes that the word denotes a category that is neither too broad (e.g. *mammal*) nor too narrow (e.g. *Bouvier*), but somewhere between these two extremes. Because the mid-level categories are not extreme, they are called basic level categories.

Equal detail constraint.   Children believe that speakers use words to refer to equally detailed instances of object categories within a single domain. If true, the child who has learned the denotation of *dog* before being exposed to the word *cat* will assume that *cat* denotes a category of creatures at the same level of categorisation as does *dog*. Thus, instead of thinking that *cat* refers to a specific type of cat, the child will assume that *cat* denotes a category of objects at the same level as *dog*. This constraint overlaps with the basic level constraint, but is not subsumed by it. Children do learn many categories that are not basic level categories, and this hypothesised constraint is intended to account for the manner in which children acquire words to refer to basic level categories and categories that are less specific and categories that are more specific than basic level categories. Note that if there were not different levels of categories, then the equal detail constraint and the notion of basic level categories would be superfluous. All categories would all be at the same level of abstraction.

Taxonomic constraint.   Children assume that speakers use words to denote coherent categories of objects. If true, the child that hears *elephant* assumes that the word has something to do with a type of object category in which all instances share some similarity. Thus, the category denoted by *elephant* would not include swimming pools, kangaroos, or pavements. This hypothesised constraint overlaps with the object type constraint, and might best be considered as an elaboration of that constraint.

The above hypothesised constraints are intended to account for the relative ease with which children learn words that denote objects. Clark has suggested that the same types of constraints might affect the acquisition of words that denote actions (see Golinkoff, Hirsh-Pasek, Mervis, Frawley, & Parillo, 1995, for another discussion of the way in which constraints for words that denote objects might also apply to the acquisition of words that denote actions).

Whole action constraint.   Children believe that speakers use words to denote whole actions rather than parts of actions.

Action type constraint.   Children believe that speakers use words to denote types of actions.

Basic level constraint.   Children believe that speakers use words to refer to basic level action categories.

Equal detail constraint.   Children assume that speakers use words to refer to equally detailed instances of action categories.

Clark also supposes that children are constrained in the types of relations they assume words have to one another. Although these constraints are more apropos for the sections on paradigmatic and syntagmatic relations, I will list them here in order to keep all of the hypothesised constraints we will consider in one place.

Single level constraint.   Children assume that speakers use words at a single level of the lexicon. If true, children do not realise that words may denote categories at different levels of specificity. Thus, children would assume that *bird, duck,* and *sparrow* denote categories at the same level, rather than realising that *bird* denotes a class that includes those denoted by *duck* and *sparrow.*

No level constraint.   Children assume that the denotation of words does not overlap. If true, children believe that the denotations of words are mutually exclusive. Thus, the child would not believe that the denotations of *ball, football, baseball,* and *basketball* overlapped, but would grant each term its own denotation that excludes the others.

The above list of constraints is not meant to be exhaustive, but does represent the types of constraints that have been purported to make word meaning acquisition possible (Clark, 1993; Golinkoff, Shuff-Bailey, Olguin, & Ruan, 1995; Markman, 1990; Soja, Carey, & Spelke, 1991). However, not all theorists have accepted the notion that the child is equipped with innate constraints that guide the construction of the lexicon (Kuczaj, 1990; Nelson, 1988).

What counts as a constraint?

Nelson (1988) contrasted the notion of "constraint" with that of "bias". For Nelson, a constraint implies some sort of restriction that should result in uniform developmental patterns. In contrast, a bias implies some sort of preference rather than an absolute predisposition, and would result in "trends that fall short of universally consistent response patterns" (Nelson, 1988, p. 288). Nelson's view of constraints fits well with those suggested by Chomsky (1988) for syntactic development.

According to Chomsky, children are equipped at birth with a universal grammar. The parameters of universal grammar are not set at birth, but instead restrict the number of choices available to children. In this view, parameters are like switches, their eventual settings being determined by the language children hear. The settings are either-or decisions, and help to determine the characteristics of the grammar children acquire (see Kuczaj, 1990, for a discussion of word meaning acquisition constraints in terms of Chomsky's proposed parameters). In my consideration of the role constraints might play in word meaning acquisition, I will follow the lead of Nelson (1988), Chomsky (1988), and Kuczaj (1990) and assume that the notion of constraints implies absolute predispositions.

Are constraints necessary for word meaning acquisition?

If constraints are absolute predispositions, there is no evidence to suggest that constraints for word meaning acquisition exist (Kuczaj, 1990; Nelson, 1988). Despite valiant attempts to demonstrate the validity of constraints, not one of the hypothesised constraints has been shown to be an absolute predisposition

(Behrend, 1995; Bloom, 1994; Bloom & Kelemen, 1995; Golinkoff et al., 1995; Merriman, Marazita, & Jarvis, 1995). In addition, many of the constraints that have been suggested are at odds with what children actually acquire (Bloom, 1994; Bloom & Keleman, 1995; Clark, 1993, 1995a, 1995b; Kuczaj, 1982a). For example, if the whole object and whole action constraints do guide children's acquisition of word meaning, why and how do children acquire so many words that denote parts of objects and actions? Similarly, if children are constrained to believe that word meanings are mutually exclusive, how do they ever learn that a *dog* is also a *mammal*, an *animal*, and may also be a *Bouvier*? The following attempt to salvage the notion of constraints illustrates the problems of this theoretical approach (Markman, 1991, p. 102):

> Much of the evidence against (this constraint) is in fact evidence that quite young children have the capacity to override mutual exclusivity when given enough information. Just as mutual exclusivity helps children overcome the limitations of the whole-object assumption, other kinds of evidence help them overcome the limitations of mutual exclusivity. These constraints can be overridden when they conflict with other constraints or when enough evidence is provided in the input that contradicts the bias.

Although Markman attempts to explain away the data that contradict certain proposed word-learning constraints, she instead weakens the notion of constraints such that the constraints operate only in the absence of contradictory evidence. Essentially, this means that constraints rarely operate, given the overwhelming array of evidence that contradicts them. At best, the proposed constraints might be biases or strategies that children use when trying to sort out the plethora of information available to them, along the lines of the strategies initially suggested by Kuczaj (1982a). If children do exhibit biases in their acquisition of word meaning, the biases are not absolute, but instead reflect information processing strategies that children *might* use (rather than *must* use), such use depending on individual differences and context (Kuczaj, 1982a).

Although this discussion has focused on proposed constraints for the acquisition of single words, the same problems and conclusions are warranted for constraints that were purported to influence the development of paradigmatic relations (see also Clark, 1995a, 1995b).

THE ACQUISITION OF PARADIGMATIC RELATIONS

In the earlier discussion of the types of meaning that comprise the lexicon, paradigmatic relations such as lexical opposites, hyponymy, and semantic sets were mentioned. These sorts of relations provide one type of structure for the lexicon. Consequently, the manner in which children learn such relations has important implications for the development of the lexicon (Carey, 1985; Clark, 1993; Kuczaj, 1975, 1982a).

Just as children may experience difficulty in determining the correct denotation of a word, they may have trouble ascertaining which semantic relation is the relevant one for words they are trying to relate. For example, a child studied by Kuczaj (1982a) initially treated the words *hot* and *cold* as if they denoted absolute differences in temperature, and only later learned the relative nature of the terms and their intermediaries *cool* and *warm*. Even after the child had learned that *hot* and *cold* expressed end points on a relative dimension, he did not understand how to best express movement up and down the dimension. For some time the child used *cool off* only to refer to changes from one cool state to another cool state and *warm up* only to refer to changes from one warm state to another. For example, on an occasion when the child was tasting his hot chocolate, he exclaimed "Too hot! I'm gonna let it warm up", meaning that he intended to let the hot chocolate change from a hot state to a warm one.

When children learn semantic sets like *hot, warm, cool, cold* and *always, usually, sometimes, seldom, never*, they acquire the words for the end of the dimension (*hot-cold, always-never*) before they learn the words that are arranged between the two extremes (Kuczaj, 1975, 1982a). This developmental pattern suggests that the extremes of semantic dimensions are more salient to young children than are points between the two extremes. These findings support Lyons' (1977) assumption that polar opposites are important components of both the lexicon and human thought.

As children expand their lexicon, they learn more and more semantic relations. As a result, children are continually refining the nature and structure of their semantic sets and fields (Clark, 1993; Dromi, 1987; Dromi & Fishelzon, 1986; Kuczaj, 1975). Part of this process involves the refinement and elaboration of earlier acquired semantic relations. For example, children first learn the general dimensional size pair *big-small*, next learn *tall-short* and *long-short*, followed by *high-low*, then *thick-thin*, and finally *wide-narrow* and *deep-shallow* (Clark & Clark, 1977).

Of course, in addition to learning lexical opposition, children must discover a number of paradigmatic relations in order to correctly structure their lexicon. For example, children must learn that objects can be referred to by more than one word (a fact which even young children can learn; Mervis, Golinkoff, & Bertrand, 1994). A dog might be called *Spot, dog, mutt, canine, cur, mammal, animal*, and so on. The child must also determine how these words relate to one another, and discover how words can be used to create metaphor (as in *that boy is a dog*; Winner, 1988). As the child discovers these sorts of relations, it is likely that word meaning development begins in earnest. The child becomes better able to organise her blossoming lexicon (Kuczaj, 1982a), and may also become aware of gaps in her lexicon (Clark, 1993). For example, the child who knows that arms end in hands and hands end in fingers may also know that legs end in feet, and wonder what one calls those things at the end of one's feet.

I suspect that the acquisition of paradigmatic relations is more responsible for word meaning development than any of the supposed constraints/biases that are so popular today. Although the manner in which children learn semantic relations is still a mystery, it is the acquisition of paradigmatic and syntagmatic relations that allows the child to structure her lexicon in meaningful ways.

SYNTAGMATIC RELATIONS

Although I have devoted little space to the significance of syntagmatic relations in the child's construction of a lexicon, it is likely that such relations play a crucial role in word meaning acquisition. Since syntagmatic relations concern the manner in which words may and may not appear together, such information is undoubtedly important in the construction of a lexicon. Moreover, the child's understanding of sentences is based on paradigmatic and syntagmatic relations as well as the meaning of individual words and the syntax of her language. Consider the following types of semantic interpretations:

1. Anomaly: The sentence "the orange dream ate a cloudy intention" is anomalous.
2. Self-contradiction: The sentence "my bachelor brother is married to his third wife" is self-contradictory.
3. Ambiguity: The sentence "the shooting of the hunters was terrible" is ambiguous.
4. Synonymy: The sentence "the rope is too short" is synonymous with the sentence "the rope is not long enough".
5. Entailment: The sentence "Keith is a widower" entails that "one of Keith's wives is dead".

The above semantic relations illustrate the importance of paradigmatic and syntagmatic relations in the production and comprehension of sentence meaning. The information that dreams are not coloured and do not eat is represented in the lexicon via such relations, as is the fact that intentions are not edible. Similarly, the lexicon represents the fact that bachelors are not married, that *too short* and *not long enough* express the same meaning, and that being a widower requires a minimum of one dead wife. Finally, the information that allows two interpretations of the "terrible shooting of the hunters" is also contained in the lexicon. These examples suffice to illustrate the importance of paradigmatic and syntagmatic relations.

Syntagmatic information may also influence children's word meaning acquisition in a more direct fashion. Children use information about syntactic cues to hazard guesses about the denotation of words. This process has been called "syntactic bootstrapping" (Gleitman, 1990), and emphasises the point that word meaning acquisition does not take place in a vacuum, but instead occurs in a larger context, one context being the sentences in which children initially hear novel words (Bloom, 1994; Bloom & Keleman, 1995; Lederer, Gleitman,

& Gleitman, 1995; McShane, Whittaker, & Dockrell, 1986; Naigles & Hoff-Gingsberg, 1995). Given the complexity of word meaning acquisition, it seems likely that children use whatever information will help to narrow the available possibilities. The information provided by syntactic bootstrapping is important in at least two respects. It provides hints about the possible denotation of words, hints that may be especially important for words that lack concrete referents. By definition, this information also helps to delineate the syntagmatic relations of words. These relations allow children to generalise from one type of form class to another, as when a child uses a noun as a verb. Kuczaj (1978) reported a number of such generalisations, including *why is it weathering?* (referring to thunder and lightning) and *you're gunning him* (shooting with a gun).

Perhaps the most important component of the syntactic bootstrapping hypothesis is the recognition that aspects of language acquisition do not occur in isolation. Instead, word meaning development and syntactic development occur side by side, and developments in one area impact developments in the other.

THE INTERACTION OF LANGUAGE AND COGNITIVE DEVELOPMENT

As the child constructs her lexicon, she is building a rich and complex representational system. Although this representational system is not necessary for thought, it does influence thought. For example, hearing a novel word used to label novel objects facilitates children's ability to categorise the novel objects (Kuczaj, 1989; Waxman & Gelman, 1986). In the process of acquiring a lexicon, the child is also acquiring a world view that is shaped at least in part by the language she hears (Anglin, 1995; Bowerman, 1989; Gellatly, 1995; Gopnik & Choi, 1995; Hunt & Agnoli, 1991; Kuczaj, 1975, 1982a; Kuczaj, Borys, & Jones, 1989; Nelson, 1996). In other words, language acquisition influences the representational nature of thought by virtue of the manner in which language dissects and organises the world.

This does not mean that language determines or is necessary for thought (see Sapir, 1931, and Whorf, 1956, for discussions of the view that language determines thought). Before children begin to acquire words, they have formed concepts of the world. This existing conceptual framework affects the initial development of the lexicon (Bowerman, 1981; Clark, 1973; Mervis, 1987) rather than vice versa. However, it is also likely that the early development of the lexicon results in changes in children's conceptual systems. Following Cassirer (1955), Werner and Kaplan (1963), Slobin (1973), and Kuczaj (1982d), two strategies were suggested by Kuczaj (1982a) as guides that children might use when faced with gaps in their lexicon and/or conceptual system. These strategies are meant to reflect the notion that language development and cognitive development are intertwined rather than isolated or related in such a manner that one invariably influences the other.

Strategy 1: When acquiring a new word, search known concepts in case the word denotes a previously acquired concept. If no existing concept seems appropriate, attempt to construct a new one.

Strategy 2: When acquiring a new concept, attempt to attach a known word to it. If no word seems appropriate, look for one.

The above strategies are relevant for the acquisition of all types of words— words that denote objects, words that denote actions, words that denote states, words that denote possibilities, words that denote impossibilities, words that denote anything and everything. It is possible that being exposed to a new word that denotes a hypothetical construct, an unobservable entity or a mental state is necessary for the acquisition of the concepts that represent the hypothetical construct, the unobservable entity, or the mental state. The words that denote such concepts may be the best clues for the existence of the non-concrete refer- ents, and so may play crucial roles in directing the child's efforts to comprehend abstract properties of her world.

It also seems likely that the distinction between the representational system that underlies the lexicon and the representational system that underlies the non-linguistic conceptual system becomes fuzzier as children build their lexicon. As children attempt to fill in lexical gaps and make sense of words that they have encountered, they structure not only their lexicon, but also their knowledge of their world. Adults, like children, find it easier to form concepts and solve tasks when they are able to use language as a guide (Cabrera & Billman, 1996; Hunt & Agnoli, 1991; Simons, 1996).

The influence of language on cognition is not unlimited, and may depend on the type of information to be processed. For example, Simons found that adults' memory for objects was facilitated by verbal labelling, but that memory for the spatial configuration of objects was excellent even when verbal labelling was prohibited.

Once more is known about the ways in which language can influence thought and the ways in which it cannot, we will be "able to determine the significance of language in the ontogenesis of that remarkable container and creator of human experience—the human mind" (Kuczaj, Borys, & Jones, 1989, p. 186).

CONCLUSIONS

The development of the lexicon consists of the acquisition of information about thousands of individual words and the semantic relations that provide structure for this universe of words. The words that children acquire denote all aspects of the world—physical objects, ideas, values, relations, activities, possibilities, fantasies, etc. Explanations of the development of the lexicon must account for the acquisition of all possible words and meanings, not just those that concern concrete objects, actions, or properties.

The child must also learn the pronunciation, syntactic characteristics, and communicative uses of each word. Newly acquired information must be related to that already stored for the target word and other words. Consequently, the acquisition of the lexicon requires considerable interpretation, organisation, storage, and retrieval of information.

The child's task may be made easier by certain strategies that help her to sort through the morass of information and possible interpretations. These strategies are not absolutes, and so do not count as constraints, at least not in the sense that the notion of constraint is used in this chapter. The child's discovery of syntagmatic and paradigmatic relations probably propels the child's construction of the lexicon more so than do children's early strategies. If they do in fact exist, many proposed strategies would need to be abandoned relatively early in the development of a lexicon since the strategies are at odds with much of what has to be acquired. Thus, the strategies would be more of a hindrance than a help. In contrast, the semantic relations provide a firm and continuous foundation upon which to build a lexicon, a representational system which continues to grow throughout one's life.

The emerging lexicon influences cognitive development in ways that we are only beginning to understand. Language provides cues about the ways in which our cultures characterise the world, and so plays a crucial role in socialisation as well as conceptual development. As we learn more about the interaction of language and cognitive development, we will be in a better position to determine how children make sense of the world of words, a rich world indeed.

REFERENCES

Anglin, J.M. (1977). *Word, object, and conceptual development*. New York: Norton.

Anglin, J.M. (1995). Classifying the world through language: Functional relevance, cultural significance, and category name learning. *International Journal of Intercultural Relations, 19*, 161–181.

Barrett, M.D. (1982). Distinguishing between prototypes: The early acquisition of the meaning of object names. In S.A. Kuczaj II (Ed.), *Language development: Vol. 1. Syntax and semantics* (pp. 313–334). Hillsdale, NJ: Lawrence Erlbaum Associates Inc.

Barrett, M.D. (1986). Early semantic representations and early word-usage. In S.A. Kuczaj II & M.D. Barrett (Eds.), *The development of word meaning* (pp. 39–67). New York: Springer-Verlag.

Behrend, D.A. (1995). Processes involved in the initial mapping of verb meanings. In M. Tomasello & W. Merriman (Eds.), *Beyond names for things* (pp. 251–273). Hillsdale, NJ: Lawrence Erlbaum Associates Inc.

Bever, T. (1970). The cognitive basis for linguistic structures. In J. Hayes (Ed.), *Cognition and the development of language* (pp. 279–352). New York: Wiley.

Bloom, L., Tinker, E., & Margulis, C. (1993). The words children learn: Evidence against a noun bias in early vocabularies. *Cognitive Development, 8*, 431–450.

Bloom, P. (1994). Possible names: The role of syntax-semantic mappings in the acquisition of nominals. In L. Gleitman & B. Landau (Eds.), *The acquisition of the lexicon* (pp. 297–329). Cambridge, MA: MIT Press.

Bloom, P., & Kelemen, D. (1995). Syntactic cues in the acquisition of collective nouns. *Cognition, 56*, 1–30.

Bornstein, M.H. (1996). Origins of communication in infancy. In B.M. Velichkovsky & D.M. Rumbaugh (Eds.), *Communicating meaning* (pp. 139–172). Hillsdale, NJ: Lawrence Erlbaum Associates Inc.

Bowerman, M. (1981). Cross-cultural perspectives on language development. In H.C. Triandis & A. Heron (Eds.), *Handbook of cross-cultural psychology* (Vol. 4, pp. 93–185). Boston: Allyn & Bacon.

Bowerman, M. (1989). Learning a semantic system: What role do cognitive dispositions play? In M. Rice & R.L. Schiefelbusch (Eds.), *The teachability of language* (pp. 133–169). Hillsdale, NJ: Lawrence Erlbaum Associates Inc.

Brooks, L. (1978). Nonanalytic concept formation and memory for instances. In E. Rosch & B. Lloyd (Eds.), *Cognition and categorization* (pp. 169–211). Hillsdale, NJ: Lawrence Erlbaum Associates Inc.

Cabrera, A., & Billman, D. (1996). Language-driven concept learning: Deciphering *Jabberwocky*. *Journal of Experimental Psychology: Learning, Memory, and Cognition, 22*, 539–555.

Carey, S. (1978). The child as word learner. In M. Halle, J. Bresnan, & G. Miller (Eds.), *Linguistic theory and psychological reality* (pp. 264–293). Cambridge, MA: MIT Press.

Carey, S. (1985). *Conceptual change in childhood*. Cambridge, MA: MIT Press.

Carey, S., & Bartlett, E. (1978). Acquiring a single new word. *Papers and Reports on Child Language Development, 15*, 17–29.

Cassirer, E. (1955). *The philosophy of symbolic forms*. New Haven, CT: Yale University Press.

Chomsky, N. (1988). *Language and problems of knowledge: The Nicaraguan lectures*. Cambridge, MA: MIT Press.

Clark, E.V. (1973). What's in a word? On the child's acquisition of semantics in his first language. In T.E. Moore (Ed.), *Cognitive development and the acquisition of language* (pp. 65–110). New York: Academic Press.

Clark, E.V. (1993). *The lexicon in acquisition*. Cambridge, UK: Cambridge University Press.

Clark, E.V. (1995a). Language acquisition: The lexicon and syntax. In J. Miller & P. Eimas (Eds.), *Speech, language, and communication* (pp. 303–337). New York: Academic Press.

Clark, E.V. (1995b). Later lexical development and word formation. In P. Fletcher & B. MacWhinney (Eds.), *The handbook of child language* (pp. 393–412). Oxford, UK: Blackwell.

Clark, H.H., & Clark, E.V. (1977). *Psychology and language*. New York: Harcourt Brace Jovanovich.

Dockrell, J., & Campbell, R. (1986). Lexical acquisition strategies in the preschool child. In S.A. Kuczaj II & M.D. Barrett (Eds.), *The development of word meaning* (pp. 121–154). New York: Springer-Verlag.

Dromi, E. (1987). *Early lexical development*. Cambridge, UK: Cambridge University Press.

Dromi, E., & Fishelzon, G. (1986). Similarity, specificity and contrast: A study of early semantic categories. *Papers and Reports on Child Language Development, 25*, 25–32.

Eimas, P. (1985). The perception of speech in early infancy. *Scientific American, 252*, 46–61.

Fremgen, A., & Fay, D. (1980). Overextensions in production and comprehension: A methodological clarification. *Journal of Child Language, 7*, 205–211.

Gellatly, A. (1995). Colourful Whorfian ideas: Linguistic and cultural influences on the perception and cognition of colour, and on the investigation of them. *Mind and Language, 10*, 199–225.

Gentner, D. (1982). Why nouns are learned before verbs: Linguistic relativity versus natural partitioning. In S.A. Kuczaj II (Ed.), *Language development: Vol. 2. Language, culture, and cognition* (pp. 301–334). Hillsdale, NJ: Lawrence Erlbaum Associates Inc.

Gentner, D., & Boroditsky, L. (in press). Individuation, relativity and early word meaning. In M. Bowerman & S. Levinson (Eds.), *Language acquisition and conceptual development*. Cambridge, UK: Cambridge University Press.

Gibson, E., & Spelke, E. (1983). The development of perception. In P.H. Mussen, J.H. Flavell, & E.M. Markman (Eds.), *Handbook of child psychology: Vol. 3. Cognitive development* (pp. 1–76). New York: Wiley.

Gleitman, L.R. (1990). The structural sources of verb meanings. *Language Acquisition, 1,* 3–55.

Golinkoff, R.M., Hirsh-Pasek, K., Mervis, C., Frawley, W., & Parillo, M. (1995). Lexical principles can be extended to the acquisition of verbs. In M. Tomasello & W. Merriman (Eds.), *Beyond names for things* (pp. 185–221). Hillsdale, NJ: Lawrence Erlbaum Associates Inc.

Golinkoff, R.M., Shuff-Bailey, M., Olguin, R., & Ruan, W. (1995). Young children extend novel words at the basic level: Evidence for the principle of categorical scope. *Developmental Psychology, 31,* 494–507.

Goodman, N. (1983). *Fact, fiction, and forecast.* Cambridge, MA: Harvard University Press.

Gopnik, A., & Choi, S. (1995). Names, relational words, and cognitive development in English and Korean speakers: Nouns are not always learned before verbs. In M. Tomasello & W.E. Merriman (Eds.), *Beyond names for things: Young children's acquisition of verbs* (pp. 63–80). Hillsdale, NJ: Lawrence Erlbaum Associates Inc.

Greenberg, J., & Kuczaj, S.A. II (1982). Toward a theory of substantive word meaning acquisition. In S.A. Kuczaj II (Ed.), *Language development: Vol. 1. Syntax and semantics* (pp. 275–311). Hillsdale, NJ: Lawrence Erlbaum Associates Inc.

Harnad, S. (1996). The origins of words: A psychophysical hypothesis. In B.M. Velichkovsky & D.M. Rumbaugh (Eds.), *Communicating meaning* (pp. 27–44). Hillsdale, NJ: Lawrence Erlbaum Associates Inc.

Heibeck, T.H., & Markman, E.M. (1987). Word learning in children: An examination of fast mapping. *Child Development, 58,* 1021–1034.

Hunt, E., & Agnoli, F. (1991). The Whorfian hypothesis: A cognitive psychology perspective. *Psychological Review, 98,* 377–389.

Ingram, D. (1989). *First language acquisition.* Cambridge, UK: Cambridge University Press.

Kuczaj, S.A., II (1975). On the acquisition of a semantic system. *Journal of Verbal Learning and Verbal Behavior, 16,* 589–600.

Kuczaj, S.A., II (1977). The acquisition of regular and irregular past tense forms. *Journal of Verbal Learning and Verbal Behavior, 16,* 589–600.

Kuczaj, S.A., II (1978). Why do children fail to overgeneralize the progressive inflection? *Journal of Child Language, 5,* 167–171.

Kuczaj, S.A., II (1979). Evidence for a language learning strategy: On the relative ease of acquisition of prefixes and suffixes. *Child Development, 50,* 1–13.

Kuczaj, S.A., II (1981). Factors influencing children's hypothetical reference. *Journal of Child Language, 8,* 131–138.

Kuczaj, S.A., II (1982a). The acquisition of word meaning in the context of the development of the semantic system. In C. Brainerd & M. Presley (Eds.), *Verbal processes in children* (pp. 95–123). New York: Springer-Verlag.

Kuczaj, S.A., II (1982b). On the nature of syntactic development. In S.A. Kuczaj II (Eds.), *Language development: Vol. 1. Syntax and semantics* (pp. 37–71). Hillsdale, NJ: Lawrence Erlbaum Associates Inc.

Kuczaj, S.A., II (1983c). Children's overextensions in comprehension and production: Support for a prototype theory of object word meaning acquisition. *First Language, 3,* 93–105.

Kuczaj, S.A., II (1982d). Old and new forms, old and new meanings: The form-function hypotheses revisited. *First Language, 3,* 55–61.

Kuczaj, S.A., II (1986). Thoughts on the intensional basis of early object word extension: Evidence from comprehension and production. In S.A. Kuczaj II & M.D. Barrett (Eds.), *The development of word meaning* (pp. 99–120). New York: Springer-Verlag.

Kuczaj, S.A., II (1987). Deferred imitation and the acquisition of novel lexical items. *First Language, 7,* 177–182.

Kuczaj, S.A., II (1988). The symbolic nature of words in young children. In R.L. Schiefelbusch & L.L. Lloyd (Eds.), *Language perspectives: Acquisition, retardation, and intervention* (pp. 23–34). Austin, TX: Pro-Ed.

Kuczaj, S.A., II (1989). On the search for universals of language acquisition. *First Language, 9*, 39–44.

Kuczaj, S.A., II (1990). Constraining constraint theories. *Cognitive Development, 5*, 341–344.

Kuczaj, S.A., II, Borys, R.H., & Jones, M. (1989). On the interaction of language and thought: Some thoughts and developmental data. In A. Gellatly, D. Rogers, & J. Slobada (Eds.), *Cognition and social worlds* (pp. 168–189). Oxford, UK: Oxford University Press.

Kuczaj, S.A., II, & Daly, M. (1979). The development of hypothetical reference in the speech of young children. *Journal of Child Language, 6*, 563–580.

Lederer, A., Gleitman, H., & Gleitman, L. (1995). Verbs of a feather flock together: Semantic information in the structure of maternal speech. In M. Tomasello & W. Merriman (Eds.), *Beyond names for things* (pp. 277–297). Hillsdale, NJ: Lawrence Erlbaum Associates Inc.

Leech, G. (1974). *Semantics*. Baltimore: Penguin Books.

Livingston, K. (1982). Beyond the definition given: On the growth of connotation. In S.A. Kuczaj II (Ed.), *Language development: Vol. 1. Syntax and semantics* (pp. 429–444). Hillsdale, NJ: Lawrence Erlbaum Associates Inc.

Lyons, J. (1977). *Semantics* (Vol. 1). Cambridge, UK: Cambridge University Press.

Maratsos, M.P. (1983). Some current issues in the study of the acquisition of grammar. In J. Flavell & E. Markman (Eds.), *Handbook of child psychology: Cognitive development* (pp. 707–786). New York: Wiley.

Markman, E.M. (1990). Constraints children place on word meanings. *Cognitive Science, 14*, 57–77.

Markman, E.M. (1991). The whole-object, taxonomic, and mutual exclusivity assumptions as initial constraints on word meanings. In S. Gelman & J. Byrnes (Eds.), *Perspectives on language and thought* (pp. 72–106). New York: Cambridge University Press.

McShane, J., Whittaker, S., & Dockrell, J. (1986). Verbs and time. In S.A. Kuczaj II & M.D. Barrett (Eds.), *The development of word meaning* (pp. 275–302). New York: Springer-Verlag.

Merriman, W., & Bowman, L. (1989). The mutual exclusivity bias in children's word learning. *Monographs of the Society for Research in Child Development*, No. 220.

Merriman, W., Marazita, J., & Jarvis, L. (1995). Children's disposition to map new words onto new referents. In M. Tomasello & W. Merriman (Eds.), *Beyond names for things* (pp. 147–183). Hillsdale, NJ: Lawrence Erlbaum Associates Inc.

Mervis, C.B. (1987). Child-based object categories and early lexical development. In U. Neisser (Ed.), *Concepts and conceptual development* (pp. 201–233). Cambridge, UK: Cambridge University Press.

Mervis, C.B., & Bertrand, J. (1994). Acquisition of the novel name-nameless category (NC3) principle. *Child Development, 65*, 1646–1662.

Mervis, C.B., & Canada, K. (1983). On the existence of competence errors in early comprehension: A reply to Fremgen and Fay and Chapman and Thompson. *Journal of Child Language, 10*, 431–440.

Mervis, C.B., Golinkoff, R.M., & Bertrand, J. (1994). Two-year-olds readily learn multiple labels for the same category. *Child Development, 65*, 1163–1177.

Nagy, W.E., & Anderson, R.C. (1984). The number of words in printed school English. *Reading Research Quarterly, 19*, 304–330.

Nagy, W.E., & Herman, P.A. (1987). Breadth and depth of vocabulary knowledge: Implications for acquisition and instruction. In M. McKeown & M. Curtis (Eds.), *The nature of vocabulary acquisition* (pp. 19–35). Hillsdale, NJ: Lawrence Erlbaum Associates Inc.

Naigles, L.R., & Hoff-Ginsberg, E. (1995). Input to verb learning: Evidence for the plausibilty of syntactic bootstrapping. *Developmental Psychology, 31*, 827–837.

Nelson, K. (1988). Constraints on word learning? *Cognitive Development, 3*, 221–246.

Nelson, K. (1995). The dual category problem in lexical acquisition. In M. Tomasello & W. Merriman (Eds.), *Beyond names for things* (pp. 223–249). Hillsdale, NJ: Lawrence Erlbaum Associates Inc.

Nelson, K. (1996). *Language in cognitive development*. New York: Cambridge University Press.

Piaget, J. (1929). *The child's conception of the world*. New York: Harcourt Brace.

Quine, W.V. (1960). *Word and object*. Cambridge, MA: MIT Press.

Rosch, E. (1978). Principles of categorization. In E. Rosch & B.B. Lloyd (Eds.), *Cognition and categorization* (pp. 27–48). Hillsdale, NJ: Lawrence Erlbaum Associates Inc.

Rosch, E., & Mervis, C.B. (1975). Family resemblances: Studies in the internal structure of categories. *Cognitive Psychology, 7,* 573–605.

Rosenblum, T., & Pinker, S. (1983). Word magic revisited: Monolingual and bilingual children's understanding of the word-referent relationship. *Child Development, 54,* 773–780.

Sapir, E. (1931). Conceptual categories in primitive categories. *Science, 74,* 578–579.

Simons, D.J. (1996). In sight, out of mind: When object representations fail. *Psychological Science, 7,* 301–305.

Smith, M. (1926). An investigation of the development of the sentence and the extent of vocabulary in young children. *University of Iowa Studies in Child Welfare, 3*(5).

Soja, N.N., Carey, S., & Spelke, E.S. (1991). Ontological categories guide young children's inductions of word meaning: Object terms and substance terms. *Cognition, 38,* 179–211.

Slobin, D.I. (1973). Cognitive prerequisites for the acquisition of grammar. In C.A. Ferguson & D.I. Slobin (Eds.), *Studies of child language development* (pp. 175–208). New York: Holt, Rinehart, & Winston.

Slobin, D.I. (1979). *Psycholinguistics*. Dallas, TX: Scott, Foresman.

Smith, E., & Medin, D.L. (1981). *Categories and concepts*. Cambridge, MA: Harvard University Press.

Tager-Flusberg, H. (1986). Constraints on the representation of word meaning: Evidence from autistic and mentally retarded children. In S.A. Kuczaj II & M.D. Barrett (Eds.), *The development of word meaning* (pp. 69–81). New York: Springer-Verlag.

Templin, M.C. (1957). *Certain language skills in children: Their development and interrelationships*. Minneapolis, MN: University of Minnesota Press.

Thomson, J.R., & Chapman, R.S. (1977). Who is "Daddy" revisited? The status of two-year-olds' over-extended words in use and comprehension. *Journal of Child Language, 4,* 359–375.

Tomasello, M. (1995). Pragmatic contexts for early verb learning. In M. Tomasello & W. Merriman (Eds.), *Beyond names for things* (pp. 115–146). Hillsdale, NJ: Lawrence Erlbaum Associates Inc.

Tomasello, M., & Merriman, W. (Eds.). (1995). *Beyond names for things*. Hillsdale, NJ: Lawrence Erlbaum Associates Inc.

Tversky, B., & Hemenway, K. (1984). Objects, parts, and categories. *Journal of Experimental Psychology: General, 113,* 169–191.

Waxman, S.R., & Gelman, R. (1986). Preschoolers' use of superordinate relations in classification. *Cognitive Development, 1,* 139–156.

Werker, J. (1989). Becoming a native listener. *American Scientist, 77,* 54–59.

Werner, H., & Kaplan, B. (1963). *Symbol formation*. New York: Wiley.

Whorf, B.L. (1956). *Language, thought, and reality*. Cambridge, MA: MIT Press.

Winner, E. (1988). *The point of words*. Cambridge, MA: Harvard University Press.

CHAPTER SEVEN

Early syntactic development: A Construction Grammar approach

Michael Tomasello
Max Planck Institute for Evolutionary Anthropology, Leipzig, Germany

Patricia J. Brooks
The College of Staten Island, City University of New York, USA

In this chapter we adopt a constructivist perspective on children's early syntactic development, concentrating mostly on the acquisition of English. In the constructivist perspective children acquire linguistic competence in the particular language they are learning only gradually, beginning with more concrete linguistic structures based on particular words and morphemes, and then building up to more abstract and productive structures based on various types of linguistic categories, schemas, and constructions. This process involves children's most basic skills of cognition and social interaction (Bates & MacWhinney, 1989; Bloom, 1991; Bowerman, 1982; Braine, 1987; Budwig, 1995; Slobin, 1985; Tomasello, 1992; Van Valin, 1991).

Our account will be cognitively grounded in children's understanding of the various "scenes" that make up their lives, including both dynamic events and relatively static states of affairs. Scenes are the appropriate unit of analysis for identifying the cognition involved in complex linguistic expressions because scenes contain, all in one conceptual package, multiple participants related to one another in clearly differentiated ways (Fillmore, 1977; Langacker, 1987). By the time children begin to acquire language at one year of age they already conceptualise any number of specific scenes from their daily lives, many of which are "manipulative activity scenes" such as someone pushing, pulling, or breaking an object, and many of which are "figure-ground scenes" such as objects moving up, down, or into a container (Slobin, 1985). As development proceeds children come to (1) partition these specific scenes into their various component elements, with different linguistic symbols indicating different components, and (2) use syntactic symbols such as word order and case marking to identify the role these different components are playing in the scene as a whole. At some later point still they come to categorise or schematise these specific scenes into various categories of scenes that allow similar patterns of linguistic partitioning and marking.

Our account will be socially grounded in children's communicative goals, including both the speech acts they perform and the different perspectives they take on scenes in different communicative circumstances (Lambrecht, 1994). First, on different occasions children may have different communicative goals with respect to the same basic scene and so on one occasion ask a question about it, on another request that someone make it happen, on another simply report on its existence, and on another socially mark its occurrence with some kind of performative. For example, for the scene of someone leaving, the child might comment "Go-away", request that they "Go-away!", ask them "Where-go?", or tell them "Bye-bye"—depending on his or her communicative purposes. Second, children at some point come to understand that in different communicative circumstances scenes are most appropriately described from different points of view, depending on such things as the discourse topic previously established. For example, an event such as Daddy's breaking of the clock may be approached from the point of view of Daddy, as in "Daddy broke the clock", or from the point of view of the clock, as in "The clock got broken" (see Clark, 1990, on the role of perspective in language acquisition and use).

The linguistic counterparts to scenes are the various types of grammatical constructions that make up a language. Although some theorists use the term construction to refer to linguistic structures on all levels of analysis, for current purposes a linguistic construction is a complete and coherent verbal expression associated in a relatively routinised manner with a complete and coherent communicative function (see van Valin, 1993, on syntactic templates; Langacker, 1987, on sentence schemas; and Fillmore, Kay, & O'Conner, 1988, and Goldberg, 1995, on grammatical constructions). At the simplest level of analysis, all linguistic constructions are composed of one or more of four types of symbolic element: words, markers on words, word order, and intonation (Bates & MacWhinney, 1989). A simple construction might consist of one word functioning as an entire speech act (e.g. *Hello!*—perhaps with a special intonation contour), whereas more complex constructions may include any number of elements in complex combination. Independent of complexity, constructions also vary in abstractness. Thus, *A penny for your thoughts* is a highly concrete construction (despite its complexity) defined by a particular constellation of particular words. *Where's ___?* is a partially concrete and partially abstract construction, since it is defined by particular words, a particular intonation, and an abstract slot for the entity being sought. The English ditransitive construction—defined as NP + V + NP + NP and instantiated in sentences such as *He gave me a book*—is almost totally abstract since no particular words or morphemes are involved. The basic point is that linguistic constructions, at whatever levels of complexity or abstraction, provide language-learning children with pre-constituted semantic-pragmatic packages that allow them to talk about the scenes they experience from various discourse perspectives and for various communicative purposes. In cognitively and functionally based approaches to linguistic structure, human languages are comprised totally of inventories of linguistic symbols at several different levels of complexity including at least words, phrases, and constructions—each at various levels of abstraction (Langacker, 1987, 1991).

Our account of early syntactic development will centre on children's mastery of linguistic constructions. This focus is somewhat novel since the majority of research on children's syntactic development has focused on their acquisition of lexically and phrasally based categories such as nouns and verbs, subjects and objects. However, the language that children experience consists entirely of particular instantiations of whole linguistic constructions (or some reduced form appropriate to the discourse situation), and so this is what they attempt to learn and reproduce from the very first steps of development—with various levels of success and at various levels of abstraction. As they become more skilful with linguistic constructions over time, and as they acquire the productive use of more and more abstract constructions, children begin to identify the lexically based and phrasally based syntactic categories that are common among them. In this chapter we attempt to give an account of this process. In the first section we attempt to identify the major steps in children's early syntactic development, and the second section we attempt to identify the ontogenetic processes that might be responsible for this developmental sequence.

MAJOR STEPS IN EARLY SYNTACTIC DEVELOPMENT

There are four major steps in children's developing competence with the linguistic constructions of English: (1) holophrases, in which they use a single linguistic symbol (often with a specific intonational contour) to communicate their intentions about an entire scene; (2) word combinations, in which they use multiple words to express their communicative intention, thus partitioning the scene into at least two component parts; (3) verb island constructions, in which they use syntactic marking such as word order or grammatical morphology to indicate explicitly some participant roles in a scene, but they learn to do this independently for different scenes; and (4) adult-like constructions, in which they express their communicative intentions through specific instantiations of relatively abstract and adult-like linguistic constructions that syntactically mark

TABLE 7.1
Summary of Construction Types Constituting Children's Early Syntactic
Development and the Characteristics in Terms of Which They are Defined

	Lexical Partitioning of Scenes	Syntactic Marking of Participant Roles in Scenes	Categorisation of Specific Scenes
Holophrases (12 months)	−	−	−
Word Combinations (18 months)	+	−	−
Verb Island Constructions (24 months)	+	+	−
Adult-like Constructions (36 + months)	+	+	+

participants for whole classes of scenes. Table 7.1 provides an overview of these steps in children's early syntactic development and the characteristics in terms of which the construction types are defined.

At each of these ontogenetic steps, a central issue is children's productivity. It is a central issue because producing creative utterances—utterances that have never before been heard—implies that the children themselves have constructed some kind of abstract categories, schemas, or constructions from the specific utterances they have heard emanating from mature language users. Children may be productive with their language in different ways at different points in development, however, and so the challenge is to document and explain the various types of productivity evident at particular points in ontogeny.

Holophrases

By the time children begin acquiring the linguistic conventions of their communities at around one year of age, they have already been communicating with others gesturally and vocally for some months—both imperatively to request things of others and declaratively to point things out to them (Bates, Benigni, Bretherton, Camaioni, & Volterra, 1979). Children's first linguistic expressions are learned and used in the context of these prior forms of non-linguistic communication (Bruner, 1983). Thus, when they begin using language at some point after their first birthdays, young children of all cultures do so both declaratively and imperatively, and they soon learn to ask things interrogatively as well. Each of these types of speech act is accomplished with a distinctive intonational pattern. Across all the languages of the world the scenes children most often talk about with their initial speech acts are such things as: the existence-nonexistence-recurrence of people and objects, the exchange-possession of objects, the movement-location of people and objects, various states and changes of states of objects, and the physical and mental activities of people (Brown, 1973).

When these communicative goals and conceptual scenes are combined we find that young children of all linguistic communities tend to use their early language, typically one word at a time, to do such things as: (1) request or indicate the existence of objects (e.g. by naming them with a requestive or neutral intonation); (2) request or describe the recurrence of objects or events (e.g. *More, Again, Another*); (3) request or describe dynamic events involving objects (e.g. as described by *Up, Down, On, Off, In, Out, Open, Close*); (4) request or describe the actions of people (e.g. *Eat, Kick, Ride, Draw*); (5) comment on the location of objects and people (e.g. *Here, Outside*); (6) ask some basic questions such as *Whats-that?* or *Where-go?*; (7) attribute a property to an object (e.g. *Pretty* or *Wet*); and (8) use performatives to mark specific social events and situations (e.g. *Hi, Bye, Thank You*, and *No*). At this early age the communicative functions of children's early single-word constructions are an integral aspect of their reality for the child, and initially these functions may not be well-differentiated from their associated linguistic forms (Ninio, 1992, 1993). That is to say, children's early one-word utterances may be thought of as "holophrases" that convey an undifferentiated communicative intention composed of both a semantic and pragmatic dimension (Barrett, 1982).

An important issue for later language development is what parts of adult expressions children choose for their initial holophrases. The answer presumably lies in the specific language they are learning and the kinds of discourse in which they participate with adults. Thus, in English, most beginning language learners acquire a number of so-called relational words such as *more, gone, up, down, on*, and *off*, presumably because adults use these words in salient ways to talk about salient events (Bloom, Tinker, & Margolis, 1993; McCune, 1992). Many of these words are verb particles in adult English, and so the child at some point must learn to talk about the same events with phrasal verbs such as *pick up, get down, put on, take off*, and so forth. In Korean and Mandarin Chinese, on the other hand, children learn fully adult verbs from the onset of language development because this is what is most salient in adult speech to them (Choi & Gopnik, 1996; Gopnik & Choi, 1995; Tardiff, 1997). When they begin with a relational word or verb as a holophrase, children must then at some point learn, at least for some discourse purposes, to fill in linguistically the nominal participants involved in the scene (e.g. "Shirt off!"). Children also learn object labels for some events, for example, "Bike!" as a request to ride a bicycle, which means that they still need to learn to linguistically express the activity involved (e.g. "Ride bike!"). The point is that children may begin talking about different scenes in different ways initially, and these ontogenetic starting points frame the subsequent task in particular ways.

In addition, most children begin language acquisition by learning some unparsed adult expressions as holophrases—such things as "I-wanna-do-it", "Lemme-see", and "Where-the-bottle". In these cases there is different syntactic work to do to isolate the linguistic elements involved so that they can be used in other utterances (Peters, 1983). The prevalence of this pattern in the early combinatorial speech of English-speaking children has been documented by Pine and Lieven (1993), who found that almost all children have at least some of these so-called "frozen phrases" in their early speech. This is especially true of some children (especially laterborn children who observe siblings; Barton & Tomasello, 1994; Bates, Bretherton, & Snyder, 1988), and it may be that for some types of lexical items this is the predominant pattern of learning for all children (e.g. extracting unstressed prepositions such as *of* from such phrases as "piece-of-ice" and "scared-of-that"). This aspect of early syntactic development has not been sufficiently studied to see how such individual differences manifest themselves in different languages, but in languages that are less isolating than English (e.g. agglutinative languages such as many Eskimo languages) the phrase-to-elements pattern of acquisition is required routinely. In any case, the general principle is that young children come equipped to move in either direction—part to whole or whole to parts—in learning to partition scenes and indicate their constituents with different linguistic elements in syntactic constructions. All children probably use both processes to some extent in different aspects of language acquisition.

Overall, then, the situation is this: Infants come to language acquisition at around their first birthdays with an understanding of various real-life scenes and some prelinguistic ways of communicating about them. They soon learn to talk about these scenes using conventional linguistic expressions taken from the relatively fully formed adult constructions they hear used for these scenes. Which aspect of the adult construction the child acquires depends on many factors including the salience of particular words in the adult construction and the like (Slobin, 1985). Functionally speaking, children's early one-unit utterances are entire semantic-pragmatic packages—holophrastic constructions—that express a relatively specific communicative intention. Because children begin by talking about events holistically with single words, or unparsed adult expressions, the linguistic task ahead is to "fill in" the description of the event by learning to indicate more than one of its elements within the boundaries of a single utterance, or to break down the expression into elements. Why children begin with only one-unit expressions—either individual words or single holistic expressions—is not known, but it is presumably the case that in many instances they initially only attend to limited parts of adult utterances, or can only process one linguistic unit at a time. The degree to which children productively control communicative functions as expressed by intonations separately from linguistic forms—so that they could hear an expression used for one function with one intonation but use it themselves for another function with another intonation—is also unknown.

Word combinations

Some of the holophrases that young children use correspond to adult constructions from the outset, for example, "Hello" and "Thank-You". But most of what
they hear are utterances consisting of multiple word constructions, and so they
soon come to use multi-word utterances as well. Children's earliest word combinations are used to talk about the same basic types of scenes as their holophrases—
existence-nonexistence-recurrence, exchange-possession, movement-location,
and identification. Across many different types of languages, children's first productive word combinations typically have three salient linguistic characteristics
(Braine, 1976): (1) different words are used to indicate different components of
the scene (e.g. "More juice", indicating both the event and the object involved);
(2) one event-word is used with a wide variety of object labels (e.g. "More
milk", "More grapes", "More juice"); and (3) there is a consistent ordering
pattern of event-word and participant-word (e.g. "More ___"). These kinds of
combinations begin appearing in the spontaneous speech of many children learning many different languages at around 18 months of age.

With regard to the first characteristic, using multiple words to partition an
event into multiple constituents is true of word combinations by definition. How
children learn to do this is not entirely clear, however. Some of the most interesting ideas have to do with so-called vertical discourse structures (Scollon,
1973). Vertical structures occur in discourse when the child lexicalises one
aspect of the event and then the adult gives a reply that lexicalises another aspect
of the event (or vice versa). For example, the child might say "More!" and the
adult reply "You want some *grapes*?". Or the adult might say "Do you want
your *shoes*?" and the child replies "On!". The multi-word structure thus only
exists across the discourse turns of the two interlocutors. Also important may be
so-called replacement sequences in which the adult expands the child's utterance, for example, the child says "More!" and the adult says "Do you want *more
grapes*?". And indeed Tomasello, Akhtar, Dodson, and Rekau (1997) found that
discourse with others is necessary for children to know how to partition specific
scenes linguistically at all. That is, when taught a novel verb as a single-word
utterance (e.g. "Look! Meeking!") 22-month-old children were not then able to
talk about the event in a more differentiated way that included reference to a
participant in the event based on some generalised knowledge of how other
events are partitioned in the English language (e.g. they did not say "Ernie
meeking!"). They needed to hear adult discourse highlighting both the event
and participant in a particular scene in order to produce multi-word utterances
about that scene.

The second characteristic of early word combinations is that they are often
produced by a formula in which there is one constant element (usually an event
or relational word of some type) and one variable slot (usually filled by an object
label or proper name). This general pattern is what was first referred to as "pivot

grammar" (Braine, 1963), and later as simply the "pivot-look" (Brown, 1973). That this is a widespread strategy across many of the world's languages was demonstrated by Braine (1976) who found the pivot-look in many of the combinatorial formulae used by children of five different language communities, sometimes including productive utterances never before heard from adults, for example, "Allgone sticky" (Braine, 1971). Tomasello et al. (1997) demonstrated more systematically that these pivot-type constructions are indeed productive in this way. They found that the same children who did not know how to combine novel verbs with any other words knew immediately how to combine novel nouns with other words. That is, when taught a novel object label as a single word utterance (e.g. "Look! A wug!"), 22-month-olds were able to use that new object label in combination with pivot-type words already in their vocabularies (e.g. "Wug gone" or "More wug"). This productivity suggests that young children possess some kind of paradigmatic category of "noun" or "noun phrase" (perhaps confined to people and concrete objects) corresponding to the types of linguistic items that can play particular roles in specific pivot-type constructions. They do not possess this same type of productivity in categorising the various pivot-type constructions themselves, however; the partitioning of each scene described by a particular pivot word must be dealt with separately at this early stage of development.

With regard to the third characteristic, it has been found that pivot-type constructions often, though not always, have consistent ordering patterns associated with them (Braine, 1963, 1976). However, a consistent ordering pattern is not the same thing as a productive syntactic symbol used contrastively to indicate what role a word is playing in a larger combinatorial structure. Thus, if "Gone juice" does not mean something different from "Juice gone", then the word order is not doing any significant syntactic work. The consistent ordering patterns used by children are very likely direct reproductions of the ordering patterns they have heard in adult speech, not productive syntactic symbols. This means that although young children are partitioning events with different words in their early word combinations, they are not using syntactic symbols to indicate the different roles being played by each participant in the event. Nor is their evidence for this ability in children of this age learning other types of languages. To cite just one example, Berman and Armon-Lotem (1995) found that young Hebrew-speaking children, who must learn different morphological patterns with verbs in order to syntactically mark the different participants involved, do not use their verb morphology in their early word combinations productively, that is, in ways that they have not heard it used by adults.

To summarise: Children's early word combinations for talking about a specific scene follow closely the way adults have talked about that scene. At this stage young children do not know how to linguistically partition scenes on a generalised basis; they must hear adult discourse about each scene individually and follow the linguistic model for that scene. Their early word combinations are productive, however, in the sense that a given participant role in an already partitioned scene can be filled by many different entities (e.g. *More ___*). This pattern of learning and use indicates that children of this age are beginning to form some kind of abstract category of "noun" or "noun phrase" to linguistically indicate participants in scenes on a generalised basis, but as yet have no abstract categories or schemas for the scenes themselves. Said another way: The vast majority of children's early word combinations are produced as they combine individual words with one another or with some member of the category of "noun" or "noun phrase" (see Maratsos, 1990, for a discussion of reasons for the privileged status of nouns in early syntax). However, there are no productive syntactic symbols in these early word combinations to symbolically indicate specific participant roles, presumably because children at this age have yet to discern the function of these special symbols in the adult language they hear.

Verb island constructions

One hypothesis that gained widespread acceptance early in the modern study of child language acquisition was that children's early language was underlain by some basic categories of sensory-motor cognition that resembled the categories of Case Grammar (Fillmore, 1968). For example, Brown (1973) proposed that such things as "agent", "possessor", "location", "patient", and so forth, were responsible for the fact that most children, no matter what language they spoke, talked about the same kinds of events. In addition to semantic content, these categories were thought to provide some basis for syntax as well. That is, the idea was that children had cognitively semantically based formulae for produc-ing syntactic phrases involving such things as Agent+Patient, or Possessor+ Possessed, or Object+Location. Theoretically, this meant that if a child were to learn some new words he or she could produce novel utterances with those words that would match the semantically based formulae.

This approach, sometimes called the semantic relations approach, was critic-ised by Howe (1976), who pointed out a number of empirical inadequacies of the proposal. Most telling, it seemed that different researchers looking at the same corpus of child speech tended to come up with different semantic cat-egories. Howe argued that the semantic relations that various researchers posited were researcher categories rather than child categories. Noting some of the same problems, Braine (1976) proposed that what children were learning during early development were "limited scope formulae" tied to individual words that the child had acquired, especially to relational words and verbs. Thus, if a child produced an utterance such as "Ball gone" it was on the basis of knowledge of those two words, not on the basis of any general semantic categories. This proposal had the merit that it allowed children learning different languages to be aimed from the outset at acquiring the specific semantic and syntactic categories of their specific languages (see Pine, 1995, for an interesting discussion). One implication of this view is that children first learn syntactic symbols, indicating the role being played by various participants in particular scenes, on a word-specific basis; for example, they learn that in English the "thrower" goes in the pre-verbal position and the "thing thrown" goes in the post-verbal position (as opposed to learning about participant roles defined more generally such as agent and patient).

This pattern is illustrated in a study by Tomasello (1992), who found that almost all of his daughter's early multi-word utterances during her second year of life revolved around the specific verbs or predicative terms involved. This was referred to as the Verb Island hypothesis since each verb seemed like its own island of organisation in an otherwise unorganised language system. The lexically specific pattern of this phase of combinatorial speech was evident both in the patterns of participant roles with which individual verbs were used as well as in the way similar participant roles were syntactically marked or not marked across verbs. Thus, during exactly the same developmental period some verbs were used in only one type of sentence frame and that frame was quite simple (e.g. "Cut ___"), whereas other verbs were used in more complex frames of several different types (e.g. "Draw ___", "Draw ___ on ___", "Draw ___ for ___", "___ draw on ___"). The general explanation of such specificity would seem to be that for some scenes, the child was exposed to and attended to rich discourse involving multiple participant types and pragmatic functions for the associated verb, while for other activities she either was not exposed to or did not attend to talk about multiple participants and functions. This same pattern of verb-specific organisation characterised this child's early use of syntactic symbols; for example, the instruments of some verbs were marked with the preposition *by*, while the instruments of other verbs were not. What this means is that the child did not have a general semantic or syntactic category of "instrument", but rather she possessed something more verb-specific such as "thing to draw with". And the same would be true of her other syntagmatic categories involving what adults would call agents, patients, recipients, locations, and so forth, which from the child's point of view were actually such scene-specific things as "kisser", "person kissed", "breaker", "thing broken", and so forth.

The one place where this kind of analysis led to some ambiguities in Tomasello's study was in the marking of what adults would call agents and patients of transitive verbs. The problem is that the child used canonical English word order patterns (agent preverbal, patient postverbal) for a number of different transitive verbs, but it was impossible to tell whether this ordering pattern was due to some generalisation on the child's part or to the fact that each of these verbs was observed and learned independently from adult discourse in which the canonical ordering pattern was used. To test this hypothesis experimentally, Olguin and Tomasello (1993) taught 25-month-old children four novel transitive verbs over a month-long period, each taught in a different combinatorial configuration: with both participants expressed, agent only, patient only, or neither argument expressed. When given the opportunity to use their newly learned verbs in new ways, children almost always reproduced the same exact combinatorial pattern they had heard (possibly substituting a novel object label). When they did try to express an argument not present in the model for a given verb, they did not know how to mark it in canonical English fashion (e.g. when they wanted to talk about the agent they were equally likely to place it before or after the verb). The conclusion was that while children of this age may use newly learned verbs in novel word combinations (they now know how to partition events in a generalised way), they do not know how to syntactically mark participant roles in generalised ways. Akhtar and Tomasello (1997) found similar results for children up to 3 years of age, even when subjects were pre-trained in the use of the transitive construction with another novel verb and learning was assessed via comprehension tests. In contrast to these findings with newly learned verbs, Tomasello and Olguin (1993) found that when children in this same age range were taught novel nouns in specific participant roles (e.g. they heard them only as agents), they used them productively in a number of ways (e.g. as patients)—indicating some general category of "noun" or "noun phrase" independent of particular participant roles.

In apparent contrast to these studies are studies of sentence comprehension that seem to show an earlier understanding of word order by English-speaking children. For example, Roberts (1983) observed that children under 2 years of age could act out reversible sentences with familiar verbs differentially depending on word order (e.g. "The cow kicks the horse" versus "The horse kicks the cow"), although other studies have found later acquisition (Slobin & Bever, 1982). Similar findings for children in the middle of their second year of life were reported by Hirsh-Pasek and Golinkoff (1991) using a preferential looking paradigm. However, in both of these studies familiar verbs were used. These findings thus suggest that children of this age have learned how to syntactically mark the participant roles of the individual verbs they hear adults using but the findings do not speak to the issue of how children might generalise this syntactic marking to novel verbs without specific linguistic evidence of how that verb is used. The one preferential looking study that did use a novel verb was that of Naigles (1990), but that study compared the two sentences "Big Bird is glorping Cookie Monster" and "Big Bird and Cookie Monster are glorping", which does not address the issue of whether children can use word order to ascertain the different participant roles involved (Pinker, 1994).

It is possible that the relatively late mastery of the syntactic marking of agents and patients may be peculiar to English. Word order languages such as English may pose special challenges for children relative to case-marking languages due to differences in the accessibility/perceptibility of the marking devices employed. Slobin and Bever (1982) observed that children learning Turkish, which has extremely regular case marking and free word order, typically use the accusative case marker associated with transitive sentences appropriately and regularly prior to their second birthdays. Other case marking systems, however, are more difficult for children to master. For example, Slobin and Bever reported that Serbo-Croatian children were delayed in acquiring canonical transitive marking relative to children learning Turkish. This finding was attributed to the complexity of the Serbo-Croatian inflectional system in which case-marking is neutralised in some noun sub-classes. The problem is that no studies with novel verbs have been done with children learning these languages to test the productivity of these case markers.

To summarise, during their second year of life English-speaking children begin to elaborate on their holophrases and word combinations of a few months before by talking more fully about events and the participants involved in them, sometimes from different discourse perspectives. In addition they learn to use syntactic symbols such as morphology, adpositions, and word order to syntactically mark the roles participants are playing in these events. They have something like a category of noun that allows them to create new sentences by simply substituting object labels (and perhaps proper names and more abstract nominals) for one another. Children also have some other sentence construction operations involving the juxtaposing of already constructed elements, for example, combining a verb island construction that previously had been used with single nouns only (e.g. *See* ___) with an already learned attributive such as "Daddy's car" to create "See Daddy's car". But all of this constructing is done on a verb-specific basis, that is, the child does not generalise across scenes to syntactically mark similar participant roles in similar ways without having heard those participants used and marked in adult discourse for each verb specifically. This means that the syntagmatic categories with which the child is working at this period—and that underlie their productivity—are not such verb-general things as agent, patient, and instrument, but rather are verb-specific things such as "hitter", "thing hit", "thing hit with", and so forth. This limited generality is presumably due to the difficulty of categorising or schematising entire scenes, including both the events and the participant roles involved, into a more abstract construction.

Adult-like constructions

The acquisition of an inventory of verb island constructions enables children to talk about more and more scenes in increasingly differentiated ways during their second and third years of life. Many adult constructions revolve around particular words, of course, and so children continue to learn and use some word-specific constructions, which may also have various "slots" of a more abstract nature. However, it is only when they begin to extract canonical patterns of argument marking across verbs that children's linguistic productivity truly flourishes (Bowerman, 1982, 1990). Overall, the evidence seems to indicate that it is during the preschool years (ages 3 to 5) that children learning all types of languages clearly move beyond verb island constructions and show evidence of possessing more abstract linguistic constructions. Again it must be stressed that from an early age children produce utterances that appear to be instances of adult-like constructions, but in many cases this simply reflects the learning of specific word patterns as heard in adult speech (with some substitution of nominals). The best sources of evidence that children possess more abstract linguistic structures, therefore, are "overgeneralisations" in spontaneous speech (presumably reflecting sentences the child has never before heard) and the production of novel utterances in experimental contexts in which children's exposure to particular verbs and constructions is carefully controlled.

English-speaking preschoolers gradually master a variety of abstract linguistic constructions and use them in a seemingly productive manner, as evidenced both by overgeneralisations and by performance with novel verbs in experimental contexts. The most common constructions to show such evidence of early productivity for children learning English are: simple transitives, locatives, datives, resultatives, and passives. The primary function of these abstract linguistic constructions is to focus attention on a coherent portion of an event while backgrounding other aspects. Thus, Fisher, Gleitman, and Gleitman (1991) say that constructions serve as a "zoom lens" which the speaker uses to direct the listener's attention to a particular perspective on a scene; Pinker (1994) emphasises that certain verb-argument structures indicate event perspectives in a way that is relatively independent of the verb's core meaning; and Talmy (1996) describes the use of linguistic constructions to highlight certain aspects of a scene, at the expense of other aspects, as the "windowing of attention". The age at which children master particular linguistic constructions will be a function of both the cognitive and social-cognitive skills involved in understanding the semantic-pragmatic function of the construction, as well as basic processing requirements of the construction involved (length and complexity, saliency and consistency of key syntactic markers in the speech stream, and so forth). We give a very brief account of the most abstract English constructions for which there is the most solid evidence for early productivity.

Simple transitives.   The simple transitive construction in English (NP–Verb–NP) is used for depicting scenes that differ greatly in their semantics—for example, "Nancy broke the vase", "Jessie received the package", "Dave entered the room", "Ingrid liked the roses", and "The car cost 4000 dollars"—whose only commonality is a general focal asymmetry among the main participants. English-speaking children typically produce sentences of this type in their spontaneous speech early in language development. It is not clear, however, the extent to which the child understands these as exemplars of the same syntactic construction. Akhtar and Tomasello (1997) found that it was not until 3.5 years of age that children began to use new verbs modelled for them as one word utterances to produce and comprehend novel transitive sentences with appropriate word order marking. Similar ages for productivity with this construction were reported by Braine and Brooks (1995), Ingham (1993/94), and Maratsos, Gudeman, Gerard-Ngo, and DeHart (1987). (The study by Braine, Brody, Fisch, Weisberger, and Blum, 1990 is the only one to test 2-year-olds for this skill and they did not report the data for this age separately from that of older children.) It was also at around this age that Bowerman's children spontaneously said things such as "He falled me down", overgeneralising the transitive construction to intransitive verbs. Children learning case marking languages may learn the simple transitive construction at a younger age (Slobin & Bever, 1982), although, as noted above, no studies using novel verbs have yet been conducted with these languages.

Locatives. Beginning with their first words and word combinations, English-speaking children use a variety of locative words to express spatial relationships. These include prepositions such as *up, down, in, out, on, off, over,* and *under,* and verb+particle constructions such as *pick up, wipe off,* and *get down.* Once children start producing more complex sentences designating events with two or more participants, two-argument locative constructions are common. For Tomasello's (1992) daughter these included such utterances as "Draw star on me" and "Peoples on there boat" which were produced at 20 months of age. By three years of age most children have sufficient flexibility with their acquired sentence schemas to talk explicitly about locative events with three participants. The acquisition of three-argument locative constructions has been of major interest because a wide range of verbs occur in two distinct types of locative constructions that are associated with differentiated event perspectives (Brinkmann, 1995; Gropen, Pinker, Hollander, & Goldberg, 1991a, 1991b; Levin & Rappaport Hovav, 1991; Rappaport & Levin, 1988).

The "content as object" locatives are of the form "Melissa cleared the dishes off the table" or "Ken loaded hay onto the wagon" (NP_x–Verb–NP_y–Locative–NP_z). The "location as object" constructions are of the form "Melissa cleared the table of dishes" or "Ken loaded the wagon with hay" (NP_x–Verb–NP_z–Loc–NP_y). The "content as object" constructions serve the discourse function of focusing attention on the participant that is changing location (dishes and hay) whereas the "location as object" constructions highlight the resultant change of state (the now-clean table or now-loaded wagon). Bowerman's work (1978, 1982, 1988) has amply documented that preschool age children overgeneralise usage of these three-argument locative constructions by producing such novel utterances as "I spilled it of orange juice" and "She's gonna pinch it on my foot". On the experimental side, the work of Gropen and colleagues (1991a) has shown that 3- to 4-year-olds will use novel verbs in both "content as object" and "location as object" constructions, and they show some sensitivity to the different discourse perspectives involved (i.e. focus on the moving participant or the change of state).

Datives.   The dative alternation concerns primarily events of transfer and is associated with two distinct constructions: The ditransitive form NP_x–Verb–NP_y–NP_z, as in "John gave Jack a book", requires that NP_y be construed as a recipient. The prepositional form NP_x–Verb–NP_z–to–NP_y, as in "Jack sent a package to Minneapolis", does not have this same restriction. Many verbs occur in both constructions (e.g. *give*, *bring*, *offer*), with the choice of which construction to use jointly affected by the semantic and discourse status of the participants (Erteschik-Shir, 1979). Most clearly, the prepositional form is most appropriate when the recipient is new information and what is being transferred is known (compare "Jody sent it to Julie" with "Jody sent Julie it"). However, the selection of a construction is only partially determined by discourse because a great many English verbs occur only in the prepositional form (e.g. *choose*, *donate*) and a few occur only in the ditransitive (e.g. *cost*, *deny*, *fine*).

Most English-speaking children produce both ditransitive and prepositional forms of the dative in their spontaneous speech from fairly early in development (Bowerman, 1990; Gropen, Pinker, Hollander, Goldberg, & Wilson, 1989). By 3 years of age children are at least occasionally using dative constructions in clearly innovative ways (e.g. "I'll brush him his hair", "You put me just bread and butter"; Bowerman, 1978, 1988, 1990; Mazurkewich & White, 1984). With regard to experimental studies, Gropen et al. (1989) found that usage of dative constructions with novel verbs could readily be elicited in children at age 5 to 6 years. A major finding was that the children tested were rather conservative in that they preferred to use each novel verb in the construction they heard the verb modelled with. Nonetheless, children of this age seem to know some of the specific semantic-pragmatic implications of the ditransitive and prepositional dative constructions and obey broad constraints on their usage. Accounting for the child's mastery of the subtle semantic-pragmatic features influencing usage of these two constructions, and the verbs that may be used in each, has proven to be a major challenge (Bowerman, 1988; Mazurkewich & White, 1984; Pinker, 1989).

Resultatives.   The resultative construction is of the form NP_x–Verb–NP_y–Adj, as in "Betty wiped the table clean". Although no experimental studies of the resultative construction have yet been conducted with novel verbs, the occurrence of novel resultatives in spontaneous speech attests to the productivity of the construction. In Bowerman's (1982) study of her two daughters' early language the following developmental progression was observed. At around 2 years of age the two children learned various combinations of "causing verb + resulting effect" such as *pull+up* and *eat+all gone*. For the next year or so, each child accumulated an assortment of these forms which were used in an apparently adult-like manner. Subsequently each child, at some point after her third birthday, seemed to reorganise her knowledge of the independently learned patterns and extracted a more abstract schema. Evidence for this reorganisation came from each child's production of a number of novel resultative utterances such as "And the monster would eat you in pieces" and "I'll capture his whole head off".

Passives.   The English passive construction consists of a family of related constructions that remove the primary focus of attention from the agent of a transitive action (relative to active voice constructions), placing the primary focus on the patient and what happened to it. Thus, "Bill was shot by John" focuses on Bill and what happened to him, rather than on John's act of shooting (with the truncated passive "Bill was shot" serving to strengthen this perspective further). In addition to this general function of the passive, Budwig (1990) has shown that the "get" and "be" forms of the passive are themselves associated with distinct discourse perspectives. Thus, the prototypical "get" passive in "Spot got hit by a car" or "Jim got sick from the food" tends to be used when there is a negative consequence which occurs when an animate patient is adversely affected by an inanimate entity or a non-agent source. In contrast, the "be" passive construction in "The soup was heated on the stove" is used when there is a neutral outcome of an inanimate entity undergoing a change of state where the agent causing the change of state is unknown or irrelevant.

English-speaking children typically do not produce full passives in their spontaneous speech until 4 or 5 years of age, although they occasionally produce truncated passives (often with *get*) and adjectival passives a year or two earlier (e.g. "He got dunked" or "He was hurt"). Although passive sentences are infrequent in English-speaking children's spontaneous speech, a number of researchers have observed that preschoolers occasionally create truncated passives with verbs that in adult English do not passivise, e.g. "It was bandaided", "He will be died and I won't have a brother anymore", indicating some productivity with the construction (Bowerman, 1982, 1988; Clark, 1982). With regard to experimental studies, Pinker, Lebeaux, and Frost (1987) showed that with training 3- to 4-year-old English-speaking children were able to produce passive sentences with novel verbs; however, it was not reported whether any of the utterances Pinker et al.'s subjects generated were full passives.

It is important to note that children acquiring certain non-Indo-European languages typically produce passive sentences quite early on. This result has been obtained for children learning Inuktitut (Allen & Crago, 1996), K'iche' Mayan (Pye & Quixtan Poz, 1988), Sesotho (Demuth, 1989, 1990), and Zulu (Suzman, 1985). Allen and Crago (1996) report that a child at age 24–33 months (as well as two slightly older children) produced both truncated and full passives quite regularly. Although a majority of these were with familiar actional verbs, also present were passives with experiential predicates and several clearly innovative forms with verbs that do not passivise in adult Inuktitut. The reasons for this precocity relative to English-speaking children are hypothesised to include the facts that: (1) Inuktitut passives are very common in child-directed speech; and

(2) passive utterances are actually simpler than active voice constructions in Inuktitut because the passivised verb has to agree only with the Subject, whereas the transitive verb has to agree with both Subject and Object. Thus, passive sentences may be especially difficult for children learning English because of the complexity of the grammatical marking involving auxiliary selection, generation of the verbal past participle and the by-phrase, as well as the low frequency of exposure to the construction.

Summary.   It is important to recognise the possibility that children may have active control of any one of these constructions prior to the time it has been tested for in experiments and prior to the time when they overgeneralise these constructions in their spontaneous speech; not enough research has been done to know this for sure. On the other hand, Bowerman's work (1978, 1982, 1988) on construction "errors" attests to the fact that young children's spontaneous utterances which seem to be adult-like may often be underlain by a different understanding of the particular semantic-pragmatic requirements of the construction in adult language. To learn the adult pattern children must make appropriate generalisations about the verbs that may occur in particular constructions and those that may not, coping with various idiosyncrasies along the way. What the actual constraints on constructions are, and how children acquire them, is not well understood at this time and has been the topic of considerable debate (see Bowerman, 1988; Braine, 1971; Braine & Brooks, 1995; Brinkmann, 1995; Goldberg, 1995; Ingham, 1992; and Pinker, 1989). By all indications, however, children are well on their way to school age before they manage to restrict their usage of many productive constructions in adult-like ways and so avoid making overgeneralisation errors.

PROCESSES OF DEVELOPMENT

In attempting to account for this developmental progression, there are three sets of processes of special importance: (1) those by which early constructions are made more complex; (2) those by which early constructions are made more abstract; and (3) those responsible for the formation of abstract linguistic categories inside constructions (i.e. syntagmatic categories, paradigmatic categories, and word classes).

Complexity of constructions

Throughout our account of early syntactic development we have emphasised the role of discourse in providing children with linguistic models that help them to go from their initially quite simple constructions (e.g. holophrases and word combinations) to more adult-like constructions. When children produce an instantiation of a simple and concrete construction, adults often reply with an utterance that helps to "fill in the gaps" relative to the adult version of that construction (Farrar, 1990; Nelson, 1986). Adults also address children with utterances more complex than their productions. Children's subsequent utterances then come to look more adult-like as they follow the adult model in terms of such things as what kinds of participants go with which verbs and how these might be syntactically marked (irrespective of the level of abstraction at which they comprehend the linguistic structures involved).

Another sort of process that we have not emphasised is children's ability to simply combine words, schemas, and constructions on their own—perhaps in some cases without the aid of an explicit adult model. For example, it is possible that if a child learned how to talk about "Throw ball" in one context and about putting things "In basket" in another context, on an appropriate occasion she might create for herself, without any directly relevant adult discourse, the utterance "Throw ball in basket"—just as children create novel mental combinations of sensory-motor actions from around of the middle of the second year of life (Piaget, 1952). Relatedly, the child might know how to say "Mommy throw" and "Throw toy" as word combinations and then, possibly without hearing an adult model, make the mental combination to "Mommy throw toy". This same process is presumably at work even later in development as children learn to fill the argument slots of certain verbs with entire verb island constructions. An example of this from Tomasello's (1992) diary study was his daughter's early "Look at Pete eating a bone" (she had previously used constructions of the *Look at* __ variety and of the *Pete eating* __ variety). The work of Bloom, Tackeff, and Lahey (1984) and Bloom, Rispoli, Gartner, and Hafitz (1989) on 2- to 3-year-old children's acquisition of complex sentences—including both *wh-* complementation and *to* complementation—provides many other examples of similar constructions.

All of these types of sentence construction operations were observed in the Tomasello diary study in which it was possible to trace in detail virtually all of the uses of particular words over time (although not all of the necessary details of adult discourse were available). Interestingly, there was some indication in this study that the pieces put together in all three of these ways must each have been used as independent and fully formed speech acts (constructions) before the novel combination could be made (i.e. it did not seem that this child took a prepositional phrase used only in conjunction with one verb, never alone, and extracted it for use with another verb). It is also notable that in almost all cases of combinations of constructions such as these, there was a simple juxtaposition of constructions with no reordering of elements. Experimental confirmation of these observations (in which all of the discourse the child experiences is carefully controlled) is sorely needed.

As children progress linguistically, and perhaps cognitively, they become able to learn more complex constructions as wholes from the beginning (perhaps initially at a concrete level only). Thus, Tomasello's (1992) subject had several two- and three-argument constructions that she learned as whole utterances late in her second year of life without ever having used the verbs in simpler constructions. For example, her first utterance with the verb *left* was "Left my coat in Schaufele's house", and her first utterance with the verb *gave* was "Aunt Lulu gave me boots" (with no help from the present tense forms of these verbs either). In these cases the child's utterance was presumably taken from adult discourse directly, as a whole, with perhaps some generalisation across noun phrases.

Overall, then, children's progress toward adult-like constructions is mostly driven by the adult language they hear, either as independent models of utterances or as discourse replies to their child-like utterances. Although we do not have the data needed to make a definite determination, it also seems likely that before their second birthdays children also create some novel mental combinations with their constructions as well. These most likely involve filling a participant slot with a construction previously used as an independent speech act, or else adding some ancillary participant or setting information that again had been used as an independent construction previously. In the early stages, what are being learned and/or creatively combined in these ways are all linguistic constructions defined in terms of specific words and, perhaps, some kind of category of "noun".

Abstractness of constructions

As children learn an ever-increasing number of complex constructions they are also extracting commonalities among these structures and so moving toward a more abstract form of linguistic competence. They presumably do this in the same way that they form schemas, scripts, and categories in other cognitive domains, that is, by extracting commonalities of both form and function. As reviewed earlier under "Adult-like constructions", the best evidence that children have formed some type of abstract, adult-like constructions is their overgeneralisations of constructions to novel, often inappropriate, verbs—either spontaneously or in experimental settings.

The best known theory of this process is in fact not a constructivist theory at all, but rather the nativist theory of Pinker (1989). Pinker posits that children innately possess basic syntactic categories such as sentence subject and object, as well as innate linking rules, so that children learning different languages can link the language they are learning to these innate categories (e.g. that the agent of an action as cognitively determined will initially be linked to sentence subject). Innate linking rules are posited to enable the child to recognise the innate syntactic categories in whatever linguistic input is available. The problem is that in order to properly link the arguments of a verb with the relevant syntactic categories, the child must discover the syntactically relevant semantic features of the verb (which, for instance distinguish the English verb *give* which may appear in a ditransitive dative construction from the semantically similar verb *donate* which may not). Until children have acquired the conventional semantic representation for each of their verbs they will have a tendency to be over-productive. Pinker claims that children deal with this problem by gradually constructing narrow range conflation classes of verbs that do and do not parti-cipate in particular constructions.

Currently Pinker's theory has no empirical support. First, Bowerman (1990) derived a number of predictions from the model of innate linking rules (e.g. verbs with prototypical agents should be appropriately linked to sentence sub-ject earlier in development), and when she compared them to her diary data found clear disconfirmations. Bowerman also pointed out that almost all of the sentence-level overgeneralisation errors are made by children at ages 3 to 4 years and older, whereas nativist theories would expect there to be even more overproductivity earlier—since children have not yet had time to construct all the narrow range conflation classes necessary. Second, Ingham (1992) points out that there is basically no evidence in any of Pinker's analyses or experiments that children construct narrow range conflation classes at the ages at which they begin to be overproductive (all of his evidence concerns more broad range classes of verbs which do not provide adequate constraints on sentence produc-tivity). And finally, in a thorough analysis of children acquiring many different languages, complemented by an analysis of the historical development of some important linguistic structures, Slobin (1998) concluded that there can be no innate linking rules that are invariably reliable in indicating to all children, learning all of the world's languages, at all historical periods, how the meanings they need to understand and convey are linked to some innate set of abstract syntactic structures. There is just too much variability across languages and across different forms of the same language over historical time.

Constructivist approaches to this problem have focused mainly on children's acquisition of syntactic categories below the level of constructions (see next section). But, as we have argued throughout this chapter, the construction level is psychologically primary in the sense that it is at the level of entire speech acts that children must endeavour to understand and produce language if they are to become effective communicators. There are two steps that need to be explicated: (1) children's acquisition of abstract, adult-like constructions that sometimes produce overgeneralisations, and (2) their fine-tuning of those constructions to fit adult-like usage. First, as we have documented, children use a variety of verb island constructions correctly for an extended period of time prior to formulating any more general constructions. But at some point in the preschool years they begin to use adult-like constructions productively. There is no precise model at this point for how they do this, but to begin to construct abstract constructions such as the transitive construction children presumably must notice that many of their verb-specific constructions are similar in both form and function, for example, the participant "causing" the action or state is in the preverbal position and the participant being affected is in the immediately postverbal position. It takes some time for children to make these abstractions because verb island constructions are complex objects to categorise, and because it takes some time for them to master enough of these constructions to possess the critical mass necessary for categorisation. It is possible that the most appropriate model to describe the developmental process is some kind of prototype model in which some verb island constructions are seen as more central members of an abstract construction than others, for example, *give* as the prototype for the ditransitive construction (see Taylor, 1996, for an interesting discussion).

It is important to note that as children begin constructing more abstract and adult-like constructions these sentence-level schemas begin to take on a meaning of their own. Some nativistic theorists have claimed that the meaning of the construction is entirely predictable given a complete lexical specification of a verb's meaning and innate linking rules (Levin, 1993; Levin & Rappaport Hovav, 1991; Pinker, 1989). The motivation for this theoretical stance is that it enables nativistic theory to retain a highly abstract innate syntactic module, with a lexicon containing all of the semantic information necessary for interpretation. Goldberg (1995) has argued that this view of the lexicon is untenable because it requires an enormous number of verb meanings, some quite implausible. For example, the normally intransitive verb *sneeze* would have to be given an additional transitive meaning to account for such utterances as "Jill sneezed the napkin off the table", and even a ditransitive meaning to account for such creative utterances as "Jill sneezed Harry the napkin". The explosion of verb meanings would be at the expense of failing to note the regularities in semantic interpretation that follow immediately from an analysis of constructions as independently meaningful linguistic structures. This view also implies that constructions may provide children with important top-down clues to the meanings of verbs used in them (see Gleitman, 1990, on syntactic bootstrapping).

All of this still leaves the constructivist theory with the problem of how children learn to cut back on the kinds of construction-level overgeneralisation errors that Bowerman and others have documented. The age at which these arise is different for different constructions, but in general they do not occur at the early periods of word combinations or verb island constructions; they mostly occur after age 3 or 4. The most detailed theory of how this might take place is outlined by Braine and Brooks (1995). Initially children form constructions on the basis of exposure to many exemplars of similar utterances from which they extract commonalities of both form and function. This is a straightforward process of categorisation or schema formation. Children's overgeneralisations, going beyond the particular verb-construction combinations to which they have been exposed, are primarily one-shot innovations created under discourse pressure to focus attention on particular participant roles (e.g. "What did Bert do to Ernie?" tends to pull for an answer using a transitive sentence). Under these conditions children sometimes resort to using a novel verb-construction combination as they attempt to resolve the competition between their semantic intention as manifest in the verb and the discourse perspective they are being pressured to take as manifest in the construction (leading to, e.g. "He disappeared him"). Note that these can only occur after the age at which children have begun constructing abstract constructions—which seems to fit with the evidence.

In the Braine and Brooks model overgeneralisations are eliminated by means of two further learning processes that are also relatively straightforward. First, as children hear a particular verb used in one or more constructions repeatedly— and they do not hear it in other constructions—they begin to infer that these are the only constructions in which that verb may conventionally participate. This is a straightforward notion of strengthening or entrenchment (complemented by some noticing of non-occurrences). Second, if children hear a verb used in a linguistic construction that serves the same communicative function that is served by a second construction, they infer that the one not heard is not conventional. For example, if children hear "She made the bunny disappear", they may infer that "She disappeared the bunny" is not usual for English speakers. This is the notion of pre-emption, as elaborated by any number of theorists interested in this problem (it is especially compatible with the competition model of Bates & MacWhinney, 1989). The prediction that results from this account but which has yet to be tested is that, all other things being equal (especially discourse pressure), children will be most prone to overgeneralisation errors with less entrenched verbs, using constructions that have not been pre-empted for that verb with other constructions in the child's experience.

Categories inside constructions

Traditionally, most constructivistic theories of syntactic development have focused on children's acquisition of the syntactic categories of which many constructions are composed, rather than on constructions as holistic entities. We have argued here, however, that the level of constructions is the level at which children seek to understand and produce meaningful communicative acts—and so we are left with the problem of how these smaller scope categories are formed. Our basic thesis is simply that as they are communicating with particular utterances used as speech acts, children are constructing abstract linguistic entities at multiple levels of analysis simultaneously. Our model of categorisation is that people primarily understand categories on the basis of function— what in common its exemplars **do**. Function is of course highly correlated with form, and so form may be used to identify exemplars of the category once it has been constructed on the basis of function (Mandler, 1997).

Previous approaches to the problem of grammatical category formation have focused on several different kinds of grammatical categories. One kind is syntagmatic or relational categories, both at the level of case roles (agent, patient) and at the level of grammatical relations (subject, object). One theory of this process is Schlesinger's (1982, 1988) theory of semantic assimilation in which children start with relational (syntagmatic) categories that are extremely narrow in scope and are likely verb specific. These relational categories are then generalised more widely to become such things as (actor) + (action) on the basis of similarities of both form and function; for example, in English, words that refer to animate objects and occur in pre-verbal position are typically actors of some type. Eventually these categories turn into adult-like syntactic categories, such as subject, again through a process of semantic assimilation based on both form and function across instances. Bates and MacWhinney (1982, 1987, 1989) have proposed a somewhat analogous theory (the competition model) in which the child's task is viewed as one of inducing the structure of the language she is learning through a complex of various cues, each of which has its own issues of reliability and validity. The categories so induced have prototypical structure and so grow and change gradually as new language is experienced during ontogeny (see Rispoli, 1991, 1994, for a related but different view of relational category formation based on a "mosaic", rather than a prototype, model of category formation). These are both eminently reasonable theories, and our only quarrel is that function has been conceived mostly as a form's semantic correspondence to particular types of entities, whereas in a construction grammar approach function can also be conceived in terms of the role the form plays in the speech act as a whole. The form on the basis of which these categories are recognised are syntactic markers such as case markers and word order.

A second type of category is paradigmatic categories. This term has been used to refer both to categories of items that behave similarly syntactically and to items that receive similar morphological treatment. On the syntactic level, the noun phrase is a paradigmatic category since different instances of noun phrases behave similarly syntactically (though not identically—it is likely that this category has prototypical structure as well) in being able to instantiate different syntagmatic categories such as agent or subject. Paradigmatic categories have most often been characterised in terms of their distributional-combinatorial properties, for example, many noun phrases contain some form of determiner (excepting mainly proper names and sometimes mass or abstract nouns) and verb phrases in English are always marked for tense. In the view of Langacker (1991) these small-scale grammatical markers serve, in all languages, to ground the referential entity and event in the current speech context (i.e. in the case of nominals so that the referent entity can be located by the listener in space, and in the case of predicates so that the referent process can be located by the listener in time). This analysis thus provides the functional basis by means of which these paradigmatic categories cohere, while the grammatical morphemes provide a basis for identification (note that neither nouns as a class nor verbs as a class have any commonalities of form other than these small-scale markers).

Paradigmatic categories in the sense of word classes such as nouns and verbs have also been investigated, mostly in terms of their necessity for processes of morphology. The major reason for this is that membership in some paradigmatic word classes is essentially semantically arbitrary, for instance, many noun subclasses, such as those characterised as "gender" sub-classes, have semantic correlates among only a small subset of class members. We view the function of "gender" sub-classes of nouns as providing additional cues which help to identify participant roles (e.g. in Russian the verb agrees in gender with the subject NP). These categories appear to cohere on the basis of overlapping phonological similarities among subsets of class members, perhaps in the form of prototypical or family resemblance structure (Karmiloff-Smith, 1978; Zubin & Kopcke, 1981). Maratsos and Chalkley (1980) suggested that children construct formal word classes, such as nouns, verbs, adjectives, and prepositions, by analysing distributional regularities, that is, the patterns of occurrence and non-occurrence of lexical items with respect to closed-class morphemes, without recourse to the semantic significance of the items being categorised (although the class of nouns may be special in several respects cross-linguistically; Maratsos, 1990). The capacities of children to conduct distributional analyses of this sort have been experimentally verified through the use of artificial languages (Braine, Brody, Brooks, Sudhalter, Ross, Catalano, & Fisch, 1990; Brooks, Braine, Catalano, Brody, & Sudhalter, 1993).

We thus believe that a construction centred view of language acquisition is a necessary complement to the constructivist focus on individual grammatical categories. Indeed, we believe that for speakers of a language, including children learning a language, it is the whole communicative act as embodied in a linuistic construction that is primary. The decomposition of the speech act into individual lexical items and categories is accomplished as language users "slice and dice" various events and constructions to abstract elements from these wholes by noting similarities in the way particular items function in various speech acts (see Morris, 1996, for an interesting proposal). It is very likely that the category on which researchers of all types have lavished most attention, sentence subject, is a generalisation across a variety of adult-like constructions in which one participant, for one reason or another and despite its semantic role, is the focal participant in the scene designated by the verb (Langacker, 1991). As demonstrated by Braine, Brooks, Cowan, Samuels, and Tamis-LeMonda (1993), construction-general syntactic categories such as these may actually be very late developing, which is consistent with the view of subject as a generalisation across a number of adult-like constructions.

CONCLUSION

The major problem for constructivist theories has always been to explain how children can begin with utterances containing only words and end up with productive grammatical constructions based on abstract lexical and relational categories. Some theorists have thought the problem so serious that only theories that posit the abstract structures as innate can ever be sufficient (Gleitman & Wanner, 1982). But constructivist theories are able to account for development, at least in principle if not yet in full detail, if the endpoint is characterised not in terms of the mathematics of formal grammars, but rather in terms of an inventory of linguistic symbols, categories, schemas, and constructions—as in the work of Cognitive and Functional linguists such as Langacker, Fillmore, and Goldberg. In the constructivist view as we have presented it—centred on the level of constructions as primary and phrasal and lexical categories as derivative—the view is that children learn the linguistic constructions they are exposed to first on the level of individual words (perhaps using some kind of category of concrete noun) and then come to schematise more abstract constructions. The process of abstraction sometimes leads to overgeneralisations, especially under certain kinds of discourse pressure, which children must learn to eliminate. They do this on the basis of both positive evidence, entrenchment of the construction, and indirect negative evidence involving the non-occurrence of some forms and the pre-emption of others. In this process children also parse out smaller level constituents (words, word classes, phrases, phrase classes) and their functions, categorising those on the basis of form and function as well. In general, the relative contributions of adult discourse and the child's own generalisations across verbs in creating constructions is a central question in the study of children's syntactic development.

At this point, to continue research along the lines we have outlined, three things are needed. First, more investigations of children's understanding and use of individual constructions are needed, especially experimental studies so that children's productivity can be evaluated precisely at different ages. Second, competing theories to account for children's productivity at the construction level, and how they constrain this productivity, are needed, and these theories need to be experimentally compared. Third, the various psychological processes involved in early syntactic development (i.e. mainly cognitive and social cognitive processes) need to be identified and characterised. These include most importantly: (1) children's early understanding of scenes and their ability to partition them conceptually into the designated event or state and its various participants; (2) children's early skills of perspective-taking, which allow for the ability to view the same event from different discourse-pragmatic perspectives as required by many linguistic constructions; and (3) children's early skills to categorise not only isolated bits of language into item-based categories, but also their skills at categorising larger linguistic units into the various syntactic schemas and constructions that underlie much of the productivity of human language. Research on these three sets of cognitive processes as they are manifest in language acquisition and use is essential if we are to create a psychologically realistic account of children's early syntactic development.

ACKNOWLEDGEMENTS

The authors thank Nameera Akhtar, Martyn Barrett, Gina Conti-Ramsden, and Kelly Dodson for helpful comments on an earlier version of the manuscript.

REFERENCES

Allen, S.E.M., & Crago, M.B. (1996). Early passive acquisition in Inuktitut. *Journal of Child Language, 23*, 129–156.

Akhtar, N., & Tomasello, M. (1997). Young children's productivity with word order and verb morphology. *Developmental Psychology, 33*, 952–965.

Barrett, M. (1982). The holophrastic hypothesis: Conceptual and empirical issues. *Cognition, 11*, 47–76.

Barton, M., & Tomasello, M. (1994). The rest of the family: The role of fathers and siblings in early language development. In C. Galloway & B. Richards (Eds.), *Language addressed of children* (pp. 109–134). Cambridge, UK: Cambridge University Press.

Bates, E., Benigni, L., Bretherton, I., Camaioni, L., & Volterra, V. (1979). *The emergence of symbols: Cognition and communication in infancy*. New York: Academic Press.

Bates, E., Bretherton, I., & Snyder, L. (1988). *From first words to grammar: Individual differences and dissociable mechanisms*. New York: Cambridge University Press.

Bates, E., & MacWhinney, B. (1982). Functionalist approaches to grammar. In E. Wanner & L.R. Gleitman (Eds.), *Language acquisition: The state of the art* (pp. 173–218). New York: Cambridge University Press.

Bates, E., & MacWhinney, B. (1987). Competition, variation, and language learning. In B. MacWhinney (Ed.), *Mechanisms of language acquisition* (pp. 157–194). Hillsdale, NJ: Lawrence Erlbaum Associates Inc.

Bates, E., & MacWhinney, B. (1989). Functionalism and the competition model. In B. MacWhinney & E. Bates (Eds.), *The crosslinguistic study of sentence processing* (pp. 1–53). New York: Cambridge University Press.

Berman, R.A., & Armon-Lotem, S. (1995). *How grammatical are early verbs?* Paper presented at the Colloque International de Besancon sur l'Acquisition de la Syntaxe. Besancon, France: November.

Bloom, L. (1991). *Language development from two to three*. New York: Cambridge University Press.

Bloom, L., Rispoli, M., Gartner, B., & Hafitz, J. (1989). Acquisition of complementation. *Journal of Child Language, 16*, 101–120.

Bloom, L., Tackeff, J., & Lahey, M. (1984). Learning *to* in complement constructions. *Journal of Child Language, 11*, 391–406.

Bloom, L., Tinker, E., & Margulis, C. (1993). The words children learn: Evidence for a verb bias in early vocabularies. *Cognitive Development, 8*, 431–450.

Bowerman, M. (1978). Systematizing semantic knowledge: Changes over time in the child's organization of word meaning. *Child Development, 49*, 977–987.

Bowerman, M. (1982). Reorganizational processes in lexical and syntactic development. In E. Wanner & L.R. Gleitman (Eds.), *Language acquisition: The state of the art* (pp. 319–346). New York: Cambridge University Press.

Bowerman, M. (1988). The "no negative evidence" problem: How do children avoid constructing an overgeneral grammar? In J.A. Hawkins (Ed.), *Explaining language universals* (pp. 73–101). Oxford, UK: Blackwell.

Bowerman, M. (1990). Mapping thematic roles onto syntactic functions: Are children helped by innate linking rules? *Linguistics, 28*, 1253–1289.

Braine, M.D.S. (1963). The ontogeny of English phrase structure. *Language, 39*, 1–14.

Braine, M.D.S. (1971). On two types of models of the internalization of grammars. In D.I. Slobin (Ed.), *The ontogenesis of grammar* (pp. 153–186). New York: Academic Press.

Braine, M.D.S. (1976). Children's first word combinations. *Monographs of the Society for Research in Child Development, 41* (Serial No. 164).

Braine, M.D.S. (1987). What is learned in acquiring word classes—A step toward an acquisition theory. In B. MacWhinney (Ed.), *Mechanisms of language acquisition* (pp. 65–87). Hillsdale, NJ: Lawrence Erlbaum Associates Inc.

Braine, M.D.S., Brody, R.E., Brooks, P.J., Sudhalter, V., Ross, J.A., Catalano, L., & Fisch, S.M. (1990). Exploring language acquisition in children with a miniature artificial language: Effects of item and pattern frequency, arbitrary subclasses, and correction. *Journal of Memory and Language, 29,* 591–610.

Braine, M.D.S., Brody, R.E., Fisch, S.M., Weisberger, M.J., & Blum, M. (1990). Can children use a verb without exposure to its argument structure? *Journal of Child Language, 17,* 313–342.

Braine, M.D.S., & Brooks, P.J. (1995). Verb argument structure and the problem of avoiding an overgeneral grammar. In M. Tomasello & W.E. Merriman (Eds.), *Beyond names for things: Young children's acquisition of verbs* (pp. 353–376). Hillsdale, NJ: Lawrence Erlbaum Associates Inc.

Braine, M.D.S., Brooks, P., Cowan, N., Samuels, M., & Tamis-LeMonda, C. (1993). The development of categories at the semantic/syntax interface. *Cognitive Development, 8,* 465–494.

Brinkmann, U. (1995). *The locative alternation: Its structure and acquisition.* Nijmegen, The Netherlands: Thesis Katholieke Universiteit Nijmegen.

Brooks, P.J., Braine, M.D.S., Catalano, L., Brody, R.E., & Sudhalter, V. (1993). Acquisition of gender-like noun subclasses in an artificial language: The contribution of phonological markers to learning. *Journal of Memory and Language, 32,* 76–95.

Brown, R. (1973). *A first language: The early stages.* Cambridge, MA: Harvard University Press.

Bruner, J. (1983). *Child's talk.* New York: Norton.

Budwig, N. (1990). The linguistic marking of nonprototypical agency: An exploration into children's use of passives. *Linguistics, 28,* 1221–1252.

Budwig, N. (1995). *A developmental-functionalist approach to child language.* Hillsdale, NJ: Lawrence Erlbaum Associates Inc.

Choi, S., & Gopnik, A. (1996). Early acquisition of verbs in Korean: A cross-linguistic study. *Journal of Child Language, 22,* 497–530.

Clark. E.V. (1982). The young word maker: A case study of innovation in the child's lexicon. In E. Wanner & L.R. Gleitman (Eds.), *Language acquisition: The state of the art* (pp. 390–425). New York: Cambridge University Press.

Clark, E. (1990). Speaker perspective in language acquisition. *Linguistics, 28,* 1201–1220.

Demuth, K. (1989). Maturation and the acquisition of the Sesotho passive. *Language, 65,* 56–80.

Demuth, K. (1990). Subject, topic, and Sesotho passive. *Journal of Child Language, 17,* 67–84.

Erteschik-Shir, M. (1979). Discourse constraints on dative movement. In T. Givon (Ed.), *Syntax and semantics: Vol. 12. Discourse and syntax* (pp. 441–467). New York: Academic Press.

Farrar, J. (1990). Discourse and the acquisition of grammatical morphemes. *Journal of Child Language, 17,* 607–624.

Fillmore, C.J. (1968). The case for case. In E. Bach & R.T. Harms (Eds.), *Universals in linguistic theory* (pp. 1–88). New York: Holt, Rinehart, & Winston.

Fillmore, C.J. (1977). Topics in lexical semantics. In R. Cole (Ed.), *Current issues in linguistic theory* (pp. 189–214). Bloomington, IN: University of Indiana Press.

Fillmore, C.J., Kay, P., & O'Conner, M.C. (1988). Regularity and idiomaticity in grammatical constructions: The case of *let alone. Language, 64,* 501–538.

Fisher, C., Gleitmann, H., & Gleitmann, L.R. (1991). On the semantic content of subcategorization frames. *Cognitive Psychology, 23,* 331–392.

Gleitman, L. (1990). The structural sources of verb meaning. *Language Acquisition, 1,* 3–55.

Gleitman, L.R., & Wanner, E. (1982). Language acquisition: The state of the art. In E. Wanner & L.R. Gleitman (Eds.), *Language acquisition: The state of the art* (pp. 3–50). New York: Cambridge University Press.

Goldberg, A.E. (1995). *Constructions: A construction grammar approach to argument structure.* Chicago: University of Chicago Press.

Gopnik, A., & Choi, S. (1995). Names, relational words, and cognitive development in English and Korean speakers: Nouns are not always learned before verbs. In M. Tomasello & W.E. Merriman (Eds.), *Beyond names for things: Young children's acquisition of verbs* (pp. 63–80). Hillsdale, NJ: Lawrence Erlbaum Associates Inc.

Gropen, J., Pinker, S., Hollander, M., Goldberg, R., & Wilson, R. (1989). The learnability and acquisition of the dative alternation in English. *Language, 65,* 203–257.

Gropen, J., Pinker, S., Hollander, M., & Goldberg, R. (1991a). Affectedness and direct objects: The role of lexical semantics in the acquisition of verb argument structure. *Cognition, 41,* 153–195.

Gropen, J., Pinker, S., Hollander, M., & Goldberg, R. (1991b). Syntax and semantics in the acquisition of locative verbs. *Journal of Child Language, 18,* 115–151.

Hirsh-Pasek, K., & Golinkoff, R.M. (1991). Language comprehension: A new look at some old themes. In N. Krasnegor, D. Rumbaugh, M. Studdert-Kennedy, & R. Schiefelbusch (Eds.), *Biological and behavioral aspects of language acquisition* (pp. 301–320). Hillsdale, NJ: Lawrence Erlbaum Associates Inc.

Howe, C. (1976). The meaning of two-word utterances in the speech of young children. *Journal of Child Language, 3,* 29–48.

Ingham, R. (1992). Review of S. Pinker, Learnability and cognition: The acquisition of argument structure. *Journal of Child Language, 19,* 205–211.

Ingham, R. (1993/94). Input and learnability: Direct-object omissibility in English. *Language Acquisition, 3,* 95–120.

Karmiloff-Smith, A. (1978). The interplay between syntax, semantics, and phonology in language acquisition. In R. Campbell & P. Smith (Eds.), *Recent advances in the psychology of language* (pp. 110–141). New York: Plenum.

Lambrecht, K. (1994). *Information structure and sentence form.* Cambridge, UK: Cambridge University Press.

Langacker, R. (1987). *Foundations of cognitive grammar* (Vol. 1). Stanford, CA: Stanford University Press.

Langacker, R. (1991). *Foundations of cognitive grammar* (Vol. 2). Stanford, CA: Stanford University Press.

Levin, B. (1993). *English verb classes and alternations.* Chicago: University of Chicago Press.

Levin, B., & Rappaport Hovav, M. (1991). Wiping the slate clean: A lexical semantic exploration. *Cognition, 41,* 123–151.

Mandler, J. (1997). Representation. In D. Kuhn & R. Siegler (Eds.), *Handbook of child psychology: Vol. 2. Cognition, perception, and language* (pp. 911–959). New York: Wiley.

Maratsos, M. (1990). Are actions to verbs as objects are to nouns? On the differential semantic bases of form, class, category. *Linguistics, 28,* 1351–1379.

Maratsos, M., & Chalkley, M. (1980). The internal knowledge of children's syntax: The ontogenesis and representation of syntactic categories. In K.E. Nelson (Ed.), *Children's language* (Vol. 2, pp. 98–135). New York: Gardner Press.

Maratsos, M., Gudeman, R., Gerard-Ngo, P., & DeHart, G. (1987). A study in novel word learning: The productivity of the causative. In B. MacWhinney (Ed.), *Mechanisms of language acquisition* (pp. 89–114). Hillsdale, NJ: Lawrence Erlbaum Associates Inc.

Mazurkewich, I., & White, L. (1984). The acquisition of the dative alternation: Unlearning overgeneralizations. *Cognition, 16,* 261–283.

McCune, L. (1992). First words: A dynamic systems view. In C. Ferguson, L. Menn, & C. Stoel-Gammon (Eds.), *Phonological development: Models, research, and implications* (pp. 211–238). Parkton, MD: York Press.

Morris, W. (1996). *Emergent grammatical relations: An indictive learning system.* Unpublished manuscript.

Naigles, L. (1990). Children use syntax to learn verb meanings. *Journal of Child Language, 17*, 357–374.

Nelson, K.E. (1986). A rare event cognitive comparison theory of language acquisition. In K.E. Nelson & A. van Kleeck (Eds.), *Children's language* (Vol. 6, pp. 289–324). Hillsdale, NJ: Lawrence Erlbaum Associates Inc.

Ninio, A. (1992). The relation of children's single word utterances to single word utterances in the input. *Journal of Child Language, 19*, 87–110.

Ninio, A. (1993). On the fringes of the system: Children's acquisition of syntactically isolated forms at the onset of speech. *First Language, 13*, 291–314.

Olguin, R., & Tomasello, M. (1993). Two-year-olds do not have a grammatical category of verb. *Cognitive Development, 8*, 245–272.

Peters, A.M. (1983). *The units of language acquisition.* New York: Cambridge University Press.

Piaget, J. (1952). *The origins of intelligence in children.* New York: Basic Books.

Pine, J. (1995). First verbs and what they tell us. *First Language, 15*, 77–102.

Pine, J.M., & Lieven, E.V.M. (1993). Reanalysing rote-learned phrases: Individual differences in the transition to multi-word speech. *Journal of Child Language, 20*, 551–571.

Pinker, S. (1989). *Learnability and cognition: The acquisition of argument structure.* Cambridge, MA: MIT Press.

Pinker, S. (1994). How could a child use verb syntax to learn verb semantics? *Lingua, 92*, 377–410.

Pinker, S., Lebeaux, D.S., & Frost, L.A. (1987). Productivity and constraints in the acquisition of the passive. *Cognition, 26*, 195–267.

Pye. C., & Quixtan Poz, P. (1988). Precocious passives and antipassives in Quiche Mayan. *Papers and Reports on Child Language Development, 27*, 71–80.

Rappaport, M., & Levin, B. (1988). What to do with theta-roles. In W. Wilkins (Ed.), *Syntax and semantics: Vol. 21. Thematic relations* (pp. 7–36). New York: Academic Press.

Rispoli, M. (1991). The mosaic acquisition of grammatical relations. *Journal of Child Language, 18*, 517–551.

Rispoli, M. (1994). Structural dependency and the acquisition of grammatical relations. In Y. Levy (Ed.), *Other children, other languages: Issues in the theory of language acquisition* (pp. 265–301). Hillsdale, NJ: Lawrence Erlbaum Associates Inc.

Roberts, K. (1983). Comprehension and production of word order in stage 1. *Child Development, 54*, 443–449.

Schlesinger, I.M. (1982). *Steps to language: Toward a theory of language acquisition.* Hillsdale, NJ: Lawrence Erlbaum Associates Inc.

Schlesinger, I.M. (1988). The origin of relational categories. In Y. Levy, I.M. Schlesinger, & M.D.S. Braine (Eds.), *Categories and processes in language acquisition* (pp. 121–178). Hillsdale, NJ: Lawrence Erlbaum Associates Inc.

Scollon, R. (1973). *Conversations with a one year old.* Honolulu, Hawaii: University of Hawaii Press.

Slobin, D.I. (1985). Crosslinguistic evidence for the language-making capacity. In D.I. Slobin (Ed.), *The crosslinguistic study of language acquisition: Vol. 2. Theoretical issues* (pp. 1157–1256). Hillsdale, NJ: Lawrence Erlbaum Associates Inc.

Slobin, D.I. (1998). Why are grammaticizable notions special?—A reanalysis and a challenge to learning theory. In M. Bowerman & S. Levinson (Eds.), *Language acquisition and conceptual development* (pp. 1–42). New York: Cambridge University Press.

Slobin, D.I., & Bever, T. (1982). Children use canonical sentence schemas: A crosslinguistic study of word order and inflections. *Cognition, 12*, 229–265.

Suzman, S.M. (1985). Learning the passive in Zulu. *Papers and Reports on Child Language Development, 24*, 131–137.

Talmy, L. (1996). The windowing of attention in language. In M. Shibatani & S. Thompson (Eds.), *Grammatical constructions* (pp. 235–288). Oxford, UK: Oxford University Press.

Tardiff, T. (1997). Nouns are not *always* learned before verbs, but why? Evidence for a verb bias in Mandarin speakers' early vocabularies. *Developmental Psychology, 33*, 54–72.

Taylor, J. (1996). *Linguistic categorization* (2nd edn.). Oxford, UK: Oxford University Press.

Tomasello, M. (1992). *First verbs: A case study of early grammatical development.* Cambridge, UK: Cambridge University Press.

Tomasello, M., Akhtar, N., Dodson, K., Rekau, L. (1997). Differential productivity in young children's use of nouns and verbs. *Journal of Child Language, 24*, 373–387.

Tomasello, M., & Olguin, R. (1993). Twenty-three-month-old children have a grammatical category of noun. *Cognitive Development, 8*, 451–464.

Van Valin, R.D. (1991). Functionalist theory and language acquisition. *First Language, 31*, 7–40.

Van Valin, R.D. (1993). *Advances in role and reference grammar.* Amsterdam: John Benjamins.

Zubin D.A., & Kopcke, K.M. (1981). Gender: A less than arbitrary grammatical category. In R.A. Hendrick, C.S. Masek, & M.F. Miller (Eds.), *Papers from the 7th regional meeting of the Chicago Linguistics Society* (pp. 143–166). Chicago: University of Chicago Press.

CHAPTER EIGHT

Some aspects of innateness and complexity in grammatical acquisition

Michael Maratsos
University of Minnesota, Minneapolis, USA

INTRODUCTION: SOME BASIC IDEAS ABOUT COMPLEXITY, INNATENESS, AND HETEROGENEITY

Grammar is rarely one of anyone's better-loved school subjects. Yet grammatical acquisition probably currently constitutes the central aspect of language acquisition. As is often the case in scientific work, this is not because of its intrinsic interest. It is because certain general issues here arise most sharply and receive the most focused treatments.

In particular, we probably know more about human grammar than we do about any other complex mental function. It is not clear why this is so. Maybe there is something more clearly analysable about sentence structure than other mental functions. Or maybe it is just a matter of luck, really.

In any case, this knowledge, and the nativist views of Chomsky, the most influential linguist of our time, have made two issues central in grammatical acquisition: first, the very great complexity of much that is acquired; and second, the possibility that children can only carry out this complex acquisition, untaught, under a wide variety of circumstances, because they have a great deal of faculty-specific innate equipment and knowledge ready to focus on the task. These two problems, along with one other—conceptual heterogeneity vs. homogeneity—form the natural foci of this chapter. Each of these deserves some preliminary discussion, before we get into more focused analyses of grammar-particular problems.

Heterogeneity of domain

First of all, at a very general level, we need to be cautious of a general human tendency in thinking of any complex problem or domain. Basically, the mind naturally takes a given thought-domain or problem to be *homogeneous* in nature. As a result, unless aided by much prior knowledge, it is easy to take particular aspects or facts to be *representative* of the whole (a problem much discussed in modern cognitive psychology; see Dawes, 1988, for summary).

In fact, for a few domains, like puddings, one can indeed assume a sample anywhere is as good as a sample elsewhere. But in complex systems, this is not true. For example, suppose someone wanted to study the human body, and got a "sample" consisting of bone, and concluded the human body is solid throughout. Or just as misleading, he might get a sample of muscle, or brain tissue. Worse still, for a complicated, highly organised and configured domain, even very general-looking facts can be misleading. For example, it is a general fact that the human body is 86% water. But from this, it would turn out to be foolish to make inferences such as "the body is 86% water; water is chemically simple; so the body is basically chemically simple". Or even more sadly, to infer "since the body is mostly water, I will spend a lifetime studying water, and thereby understand the body very well when I am through". Such inferences and strategies are of course obviously wrong when one knows the falsifying counter-information in advance. But when one has very little knowledge of the domain, they are commonly recruited.

In fact, we shall assume here that grammar is, like the body, a heterogeneous system. Thus, "facts" about one aspect of it do not necessarily generalise to other aspects. This reduces, of course, the utility, and drama, of individual findings. Finding that one aspect of grammar, for example, clearly looks grounded in general cognition and perception, does not prove that *all* of grammar works this way. Nor does finding that some aspect is very odd, prove that grammar is odd in every aspect.

Second, we can profitably apply this awareness of conceptual heterogeneity to our other core concepts: complexity and innateness. As to complexity in grammar, the main sections of the chapter will exemplify the variety in the kinds of complexity to be found in different grammatical acquisition problems. But innateness is worth particular discussion, because "innateness" provides the central conceptual motive for grammatical studies; yet it is typically either unexplicated, or worse, misunderstood and oversimplified.

Some heterogeneous aspects of "innateness"

Different "specificity levels" of innateness. In speaking of "innateness," it is useful to distinguish three different kinds: (1) innate features common to many species; (2) species-specific innate features of humans in particular; (3) faculty-specific innate features of grammar acquisition. As an example of (1),

Eimas, Siqueland, and Vigorito (1971) found that young human infants categor-
ically perceive certain voiced-voiceless perceptual boundaries innately. These
boundaries discriminate various phoneme pairs like /p/–/b/, /t/–/d/, /k/–/g/, and
the discriminations also figure in some grammatical operations. But as Kuhl and
Miller (1975) found, chinchillas make the same innate auditory discriminations;
rhesus monkeys and minks do likewise. So this discrimination is indeed used for
language acquisition, and is indeed innate. But it is innate to many mammals; it
is specific to neither humans nor language.

There are also human-specific abilities that no doubt contribute to language
acquisition. Humans are probably especially good at remembering and representing information about sequences of sound and behaviour. This no doubt
feeds grammatical analysis, and may be requisite for learning human languages,
but is not an ability specific to grammar. Ardent anti-Chomskyans like Bates
and MacWhinney (1989) and O'Grady (1987) specifically state they are sure
that language acquisition requires human-specific innate abilities; but this is not
equivalent to faculty-specific innate abilities, that is, abilities adapted specifically for grammar.

Finally, Chomsky of course holds that human language acquisition requires
grammar-specific innate knowledge and abilities. Such knowledge might include
grammar-specific basic properties like innate knowledge that languages have nouns
and verbs, or innate knowledge of sentence structural relations like subjacency.
It can also include specifications of *which* properties from non-language systems
can enter into grammatical acquisitional systems (Pinker, 1984).

None of the above kinds of innateness are mutually exclusive. Grammar
could well be acquired using a combination of all three kinds. The central
argument in grammatical acquisition studies really revolve not around whether
human language requires innate abilities—nearly all researchers believe that
human-specific abilities are minimally required, for example—but whether there
is faculty-specific innate adaptation, and the degree to which innate knowledge
"preknows" the end product of acquisition.

"Modularity" and grammar acquisition.   It is claimed above that generally
speaking, innate, human-specific, and faculty-specific abilities are not mutually
exclusive. Yet the impression is common that Chomsky specifically believes
that language acquisition is a qualitatively unique, "encapsulated", isolated
ability that has no relation to other abilities. This can be shown to be false by
an analysis of his actual linguistic theories; but it is easier to quote Chomsky
himself (1994, personal communication), responding to a direct query on this
issue:

> the idea that language is completely isolated from other cognitive and perceptual
> functions cannot have been proposed by anyone. What could that possibly mean?
> That language is not perceived? that it doesn't enter into thought? I've come across

LIVERPOOL
JOHN MOORES UNIVERSITY
AVRIL ROBARTS LRC
TEL. 0151 231 4022

arguments of that sort, but rarely comment on them . . . Life's too short . . . As far as is known, there are properties of language that are specific to it . . . But from that fact, it plainly does not follow that every aspect of language is language-specific, or that language is completely isolated from other functions. The inference is utterly irrational.

Again, there are methodological consequences to this rejection of complete "encapsulatedness". For example, suppose we show that some aspect of grammatical acquisition rests on more general conceptual development (Bloom, 1970, Slobin, 1973); such a finding does *not* particularly address the general Chomskyan thesis. It does address the thesis that grammar acquisition is *completely* encapsulated; but this strong view has never actually been a thesis of the chief protagonist (Chomsky) in these arguments, though rhetorical style can make it seem so.

Animal work, innateness, and "privileged" learning. In fact, no child can know the grammar of her native language in advance. Languages do not differ infinitely in grammatical structure, but they do differ. So the child has to "learn" something particular to her own grammatical system.

Chomsky himself believes that for certain "core" aspects of grammar (not for all grammar—Chomsky, 1992), the child does innately know the possible language-variations so well, that induction of the right language-particular structure is a relatively trivial task. In fact, his views here very much resemble the "fixed reaction patterns", with their "innate releasers" of classic ethological studies (Tinbergen, 1951). In such patterns, the unconscious "knowledge" of how to behave is biologically given. The animal needs only to encounter the right stimulus "trigger" for the behaviour. Thus, the male stickleback fish, during the mating season, automatically attacks any red dot that approaches his nest, whether it is on another fish or not. (In nature, the stickleback males *do* have red dots on the stomach in the mating season.) The animal "knows" what response to give to what stimulus innately, without prior learning.

So Chomsky's views on core grammar acquisition indeed resemble about as closely as possible, "classic" innate behavioural patterns, which we will call here highly *targeted* (the animals' programming has the system at birth, essentially, waiting only for the right input stimulus). Chomsky allows there is language-variation, but holds that ideally, the child's innate targeted knowledge of the right language-variation is "triggered" almost as quickly as fixed reaction patterns.

In fact, however, the animal literature itself has long moved past simple "innate"–"learned" polarities. What has been found is that many animal systems do learn something; but simultaneously, the animal's biology specifies much about *how* it can learn it, or how much can be learned (Gallistel, Brown, Carey, Gelman, & Keil, 1991). For example, the animal may begin by having *part* of the behavioural trigger initially known. The vervet monkey gives a warning call to any long, thin object on the ground; this is a headstart on the adult behaviour of giving such calls to dangerous snakes, and the monkey has this initial trigger-knowledge shaped by further learning. Or in other animal behaviours, the "trigger" itself may be virtually unspecified to start with, but there may be a "sensitive period" for learning it. For example young ducks will socially "imprint" on virtually anything they can follow in the second day after birth, including non-ducks, or even boulders moving on a wagon. Or the product of learning may be highly open, but there may be innate specifications on what data can enter the system, and how they are to be computed. For example, some species of ants wander from their paths in complicated paths, but go back to the nest in a straight line. They apparently store how long they went, and how fast, in each direction, and "sum" up these vectors to give their location. (If one picks up one of these ants, and moves it 30 feet to the right, they go straight back to a point 30 feet to the right of their nest; they can only "tabulate" their own movements.) Rats normally only learn to avoid aversive stimuli that occur right after making a response. But if the response is eating novel-smelling food, and the aversive stimulus is getting sick (even if not from the food), the rat will avoid the novel food even if getting ill occurs *an hour* after eating the food. This is a very long conditioning-interval, unique to the learning of the new-food-illness connection. Gallistel et al. (1991) discuss many such "privileged learning" behaviours, in which there is genuine learning, but in which innate specifications also control some aspect of the learning.

A central fact here is that there is no *homogeneous* innate specification: For one behaviour, there may be innate specification of the life-period for learning (imprinting), but little innate specification of the target stimuli; for other behaviours, the target stimulus may be *partly* innately specified (vervet monkey long-thin object response), with no known critical period for when further learning can take place; or certain stimuli-response pairings may have numerous complex innate conditions (food aversion), but left relatively open in life-period for learning, or possible behavioural triggers. That is, these innate-learning coordinations are *heterogeneous* in nature, often in complex ways. It would be surprising if innateness in grammatical acquisition, a complex system of systems, was not similarly heterogeneous, rather than being "one simple thing". It will be assumed throughout this chapter that faculty-specific innateness for grammatical acquisition includes "Chomskyan targeted innateness" as a particular variety of possible innateness, but not as the *only* meaning of faculty-specific innateness.

Chomsky vs. Skinner.   Finally, we note here that Skinner's psychology, typically taken as the opponent to Chomsky, in fact only represents a now mostly outdated opposition, a view that virtually nothing interesting is innate in any species. The current animal literature already devastates Skinner's adequacy as an opponent; in fact, his influence in grammatical acquisition itself is currently virtually nil. The Chomsky–Skinner "debate" plays no role throughout the rest of this chapter.

THEMATIC RELATION MAPPING IN
ENGLISH AND OTHER LANGUAGES:
MASSIVE COMPLEXITY IN SOME SYSTEMS

Let us now begin the analysis of some actual developmental phenomena. Throughout these discussions, we will be interested in explicating the heterogeneous ways that grammar can be complex, and the heterogeneous ways that "innateness" can be made relevant.

We will start with a discussion of one of the basic properties of grammar: the ways that different languages encode some of the basic general meanings that grammar maps onto form—agent-patient relations, and definite-indefinite relations. As we will see, what is "basic" in other languages can look extremely complicated to an English-speaker; yet, children often do surprisingly well in analysing the relevant meaning-form mapping.

English: Relatively "transparent" agent-patient mapping

One of the basic meaning-conceptual schemas mapped by grammar across many languages is usually called agent-patient relations. These relations apply to a verb that maps a *transitive action*: an action initiated by one being (agent), which changes or moves or has some other concrete impact on some other being or object (patient). It should be noted that not all transitive verbs denote transitive actions. For example, "to resemble" is not an action, nor are emotion predicates like "to need" or "to like". But a typical language vocabulary includes hundreds or even thousands of agent-patient transitive action verbs like "cut" or "eat" or "push", making such verbs a basic part of the language repertory.

These diverse verbs all have a simple general schema in English basic sentences: the agent is encoded before the action, which is encoded before the patient, thus agent+action+patient. English thus uses *constituent order* to encode agent-patient relations. Examples include "Mary—killed—Sam", "the doctor—cured—the patient".

Early English acquisition of agent-patient order.   In early English acquisition, children typically mark various agent-action or action-patient or agent-action-patient relations before the age of 2 (Bloom, 1970; Schlesinger, 1971), using appropriate adult orders. Making this analysis was historically quite important; for before that time, meaning had been given no role in accounting for children's grammar; the agent-action-patient analysis showed that clearly, aspects of the conceptual world were analysed by children to analyse grammar (Brown, 1973), contrary to the Chomskyan implication that meaning played very little part (Chomsky, 1965; McNeill, 1970).

Transparency of agent-action-patient schemas.   As Bruner (1975) pointed out, furthermore, this agent-action-patient schema seems a very "natural" mapping from cognition-perception. In agent-patient events, the agent begins the event, which "ends up" on the patient. Grammar apparently maps natural perception quite transparently.

Such analyses are certainly representative of something languages often do, which is to use various conceptual-meanings to control grammatical properties like constituent order. Indeed, some of grammar may really be not very complicated. But the prevalence of relatively simple constituent-order mappings of certain event-meanings (like agent-patient) can also be highly misleading. One might think that in general, perhaps grammar is not so complicated as has been claimed, after all. Making this inference, of course, rests upon assuming that (1) later acquisition is like early acquisition, and (2) English-like acquisition is like acquisition everywhere, both assumptions being that grammar is really a "homogeneous" rather than "heterogeneous" area.

Case-marking in other languages: Turkish and Georgian

A good way to falsify these assumptions is to look at acquisition of different kinds of agent-patient marking systems. These are languages, very common throughout the world, in which constituent order is not the sole, or even an important, means of expressing agent-patient relations. Rather, in many languages, these relations are expressed by *morphological inflection* on the noun stem, or on some noun-associated word (like the definite-indefinite markers). For example, in Turkish, any of the six possible orderings of "Sam-u", "Ann", and "scratched" would mean "Ann scratched Sam". For the use of /u/ (pronounced "oo") on "Sam", means that Sam is the patient of the scratching action. "Sam-u scratched Ann", "Ann Sam-u scratched", "Scratched Sam-u Ann", and so on, all mean the same as English "Ann scratched Sam". English-speakers tend to think of such languages as "free constituent order". Actually, the constituent order is just being used to express something else. There is a grammatical variable called *Focus*. This means, in Turkish, reference to new information, or a contrastive claim. For example, suppose everyone knew that Sam ate something, but only one person knew what. When this person then says "Sam ate *curried chicken*", "curried chicken" is new information, and so in focus. In Turkish, focused elements must precede the main verb. So in conveying "curried chicken" as new information, the speaker could say "curried chicken ate Sam", or "Sam curried chicken ate", but not "Sam ate curried chicken" (which would say "Sam" as eater was new information).

"Noticing" case marking.   Let us return to the accusative (patient) case-marker. How could a child figure out that "-u" marks patienthood? In general, when people are asked how the child could do this, they tend to think "the child *notices* that '-u' is used on nouns that denote patients of actions". That is, suppose the child has already somehow analysed that "Sam" is the noun stem,

and so analyses that "-u" must mark something meaningful about Sam. The child sees that Sam is being acted on in the current event, and so "guesses" that "-u" marks this acted-on patient relation.

But as Pinker (1984) and Talmy (1980) point out, there is a problem here. Suppose the child does hear "Sam-u scratched Ann", and can tell in context that "Sam" refers to a patient of scratching. Sam also refers to, or might refer to, many other things, all of which can also be marked morphologically in some language or another. Many languages mark shape-information morphologically, and treat humans as long-thin objects (vs. for example, non-long flat objects, or rounded objects). Or "-u" could mark gender (male), humanness, animacy, person (third person), affectionate regard on the part of the speaker, social status, being the end-point of an action in space, and so on. All of these are object-relevant meanings morphologically marked in some language or another. All of them might be true of Sam in the particular situation. So how can the child "guess" correctly just the right meaning for her own language? Or if we say that the "right guess" is a generally salient one (e.g. being acted-on is very conceptually salient), then we need to provide mechanisms to make sure the child can guess the *other* appropriate meanings for other languages.

Property-registers and induction processes.   No one is instructing the child about how all this works. No one says "now Sarah, '-u' added to a noun means 'acted-on'". Nor would a 2- or 3-year-old be amenable to this kind of instruction. So the child must be able to register for herself *at least* any of the properties actually encoded by languages morphologically, to be able to guess the appropriate morphological meaning for her own language. So there must be an initial *property-register* which contains, potentially, all the meanings that might be marked. This register must have a procedure for registering whether a particular property actually matches a particular morphological use; it must have a procedure for evaluating the match and non-matches over a variety of speech situations. For example, suppose the child guesses that "-u" means "male", because "Sam" is a male. This "guess" can then be compared to future situations; in many, of course, males will *not* be marked by "-u", e.g. "Sam ham-u cut" ("Sam cut the ham"), and these non-matches will eventually disconfirm "male" as an hypothesis. (All of this is assumed to be quite unconscious, of course.) In such a *serial* match-nonmatch registration process, properties are tested against the input one at a time, until one is found that works (Pinker, 1984).

There are also *parallel* induction systems (MacWhinney & Chang, 1995). In these, all the register-properties are tested together against the input. Thus, in "Sam-u scratched Ann", "-u" would be marked as having occurred in a situation which was + for all of the following (at least): male, animate, human, acted-on, endpoint of an action in space, third person, long-thin, and (possibly) affectionately regarded, high relative status, and so on. Next time, the child might hear

"-u" used in an utterance "Ann ham-u cut", which would be marked + for acted-on, third person, perhaps + for "affectionately regarded" but would be marked – for the other characteristics on the list. Over time, the right property would emerge as consistently marked *vis-à-vis* "-u".

The actual nature of Turkish: Multiple-property markings.   This looks complicated enough. But in reality, virtually no language that morphologically marks noun case (relations like agent-patient) employs a simple "one meaning→one marker" system. Other properties always interact. In Turkish, in reality, there are four accusative (patient)-markers: /u/, /ü/, /i/, and /ï/. The umlaut signifies pronunciation with rounded lips. These are four meaningfully different sounds in Turkish. So no single marker consistently marks patients; and furthermore, *not all patients* are marked in Turkish anyway—some are left completely unmarked, with no morphological inflection for case.

What is going on? First, in Turkish, only *definite* patients, equivalent to "the dog", or "him" or "Tom" are accusatively marked. Indefinite patients, like "a dog", or "someone", or "something" are left unmarked (as are agents). So the patient-marker is actually the *definite-patient* marker, not the patient-marker.

Second, the definite-patient marker is chosen to match the stem vowel in (1) roundedness of lips and (2) front-back high-point for the tongue. Some vowels have the tongue highest near the front of the mouth (e.g. "ee" or "eh", corresponding to /i/ and /e/); some have it highest towards the back (e.g. "oo", corresponding to /u/, or "oh", corresponding to /o/). So for the unrounded back vowel in "coat", (roughly, /kot/), the definite-patient marker would be back unrounded /u/.

Obviously this makes the induction process more complicated in various ways. First of all, a simple one-property-at-a-time serial process will not work at all. For example, suppose the child luckily guesses "patient" for "-u" after hearing "Ann Sam-u scratched". But most of the time, unrounded /u/ will *not* mark patients. It will not mark indefinite patients, and it will not mark patients denoted by nouns with front vowel stems, or with rounded back vowel stems. Probably the "success-rate" of "patient" *by itself* as a predictor of unrounded /u/ is below 25%. Even though "patient" is a valid *part* of the analysis for /u/, most of the patients will not be marked by /u/. The only thing a "serial processor" could do, is keep a property-morpheme hypothesis, when it approaches some "reasonably substantial" match proportion, which would have to be as low as 5–10% in some languages.

A parallel processor, of course, would just keep registering + and – for all available properties, until a consistently property-cluster emerged, across many utterances. Thus over time, /-u/ would correspond consistently the following four noun-properties: definite reference; acted-on (patient) status; unrounded stem vowel; back stem vowel. But this means the "property-register" must include not just all the possibly morphology-relevant meanings like "definiteness" and "patienthood", but also whatever *phonological* properties of words might play a role in controlling morphological marking across languages. Since the child does not know ahead of time which properties might figure in her own language, the "property register" must potentially be able to inspect them all.

Georgian: An example of "non-local" partial control.   Furthermore, in many languages, aspects of *other* constituents may partly control agent-patient marking. For example, in Georgian, verb-aspect controls part of accusative-case marking on the noun. What is verb-aspect? It refers to whether a process is completed or not at the time of reference. Thus, aspect is *Ongoing* or *progressive* in both "John was singing" or "John will be singing", even though they refer to past vs. future times. Aspect is *Completed* for "ate" and "eat" in "John ate then left", and "John will eat before he leaves", because the sentences refer to completed past and future acts of eating.

In Georgian, when the verb is Ongoing in aspect, sentence agents are marked by "-i" or nothing ("-0"), depending on the noun phonology. But when the verb is Completed aspect, the same "-i" or "-0" markers now mark the *patient* of the action. So obviously, there is *no* consistent agent vs. patient value for "-i" by itself. Only if the aspect of the verb is simultaneously recorded does the "-i" patterning emerge. So for Georgian, the non-local aspect of the *verb*, must be part of the "property-register" for the case-marking of the *noun* case-inflections. Georgian thus requires inducing a property-combination that includes certain noun-stem phonological properties, agent vs. patient status, and incomplete-completed verb process, just to control *one* noun-case-marker correctly).

Acquisition of Turkish and Georgian agent-patient marking.   A colleague of mine showed the Turkish case-marking system to a class in developmental psychology. She asked people in the class (who had no previous background in language development) when they thought Turkish children might master it in their productive speech. Guesses ranged around 8 to 10 years old. This is not surprising, because texts often inform us that preschool children cannot analyse more than one aspect of a situation at once (Cole & Cole, 1992), and obviously this will not do for either Turkish or Georgian case marking. Also, the systems just look very "complicated" to the adult conscious mind. Most people who see Georgian or Turkish systems also naturally guess children would commit many *positive errors* (errors of using a morphological marker incorrectly) in acquiring them. For example, a Georgian-speaking child might have inferred from ongoing aspect sentences that "-i" marks agents. Thus the child would use "-i" to mark agents generally. This procedure would produce errors in completed aspect sentences (where "-i" marks patients, not agents). Or a Turkish-speaking child might have analysed that /u/, /ü/, /i/, and /ï/ mark patients, but not have analysed the vowel harmony or definiteness contingencies, and so use them on indefinite patients, or inappropriate stems.

The developmental findings from these languages are accordingly surprising. Turkish children typically have acquired the complete noun-inflexion paradigms (including a number of other case markings) by age 2 (Slobin, 1982), with *no* case-marking errors along the way. In experimental comprehension tests, furthermore, they can comprehend who did what to whom in all possible sentence-orders as well as, or better than, English-speaking children dealing with one constituent-order (Slobin, 1982). The Georgian results come from detailed diaries of three children (Imedadze & Tuite, 1992). They indicate that the children did not use aspect marking or case marking until about age 3. At this point, aspect marking appeared on verbs, and case marking appeared on nouns, again *without positive error*. So these results are characterised, really, by their *lack* of "interesting" developmental results: no especially late acquisition, no interesting or expectable positive errors.

It should be emphasised that Turkish and Georgian are *not* unusual in combining other factors with agent-patient relations in morphological marking. Indeed, this is probably the rule rather than the exception. The way in which the same marker is used for both agents and patients even in basic Georgian sentences is somewhat unusual; but about 5% of the world's languages commonly require some kind of agent-patient marking "switch", depending on factors like verb-properties, but also on properties like humanness, person, definiteness, of the agent and patient. Acquisition of these languages is, generally speaking, again rather uneventful, considering the apparently great complexity of the systems (Maratsos, 1989; Rispoli, 1991; Slobin, 1992a).

Some developmental conclusions

Properly looked at, these "bland" case-marking findings are very striking indeed. They cannot be used to draw conclusions about all of grammar, because not all of grammar presents similar problems. But they can be used to draw some conclusions about some aspects of grammatical acquisition, and this we now do.

Grinding-through instead of "noticing". First, it is obvious no child could just "notice" how Turkish or Georgian accusative markers work, from a "lucky guess" or "inspiration" from one utterance-situation analysis. This is important, for again, when students are asked how children might figure out morphological markers, they typically say something like the child "notices" the marker is used on a patient. (Personally, I believe this is a projection from conscious problem solving, where one often does seem to "notice" a particular key aspect of the situation.)

Instead, to analyse these complex case-marking contingencies, the child must, clearly, "grind through" or "sift through" a large number of initial possibilities, over a wide number of utterances. Guessing quickly from a single utterance or two, and quickly generalising the guess would typically produce many positive errors, and these are not seen. Besides, it would not work in the long run.

The role of adult input and social interaction.   These findings are relevant to another general issue. Many developmentalists do not like to think of language acquisition as "asocial". They like to stress how sensitive adult interaction with the child, in real-world meaningful situations, could somehow give the child important information that "simplifies" the acquisition task, or points out central analyses to the child (Cole & Cole, 1992; Shaffer, 1996). They also like to stress how "general cognitive development" can contribute.

In fact, no such complete "isolation" or "asocial" nature of grammatical analysis is claimed to be shown here. Basic grammaticised meanings like agency, patienthood, ongoing vs. completed, definite (specific) vs. indefinite, obviously are recruited from the more general conceptual world of the child. Nor is this claimed to be "asocial" development. For example, definiteness, which plays an important role in many case-marking systems, is partly social in nature. Something is only "definite" when it refers to a referent made referentially specific for both the speaker and listener in a particular conversation (Brown, 1973; Maratsos, 1976). Autistic children who do well at many aspects of grammar in fact often have problems with grammatical markers that encode socially-loaded meanings like definiteness (Tager-Flusberg, 1988).

It is also obvious the child must have an interlocutor whose utterances at least match what the child can analyse in the situations. For example, reference to situation-definite referents must match the child's own apprehension of what is situationally established; reference to ongoing vs. completed times in events, must match what the child can understand is being encoded. Presumably, highly insensitive interlocutors could give the child highly confusing meaning-form matches, which would impair or potentially detail grammatical analysis.

Partly asocial induction.   On the other hand, essential parts of the analytic task, it should be obvious, *are* relatively "the child's own business" to conduct. For example, developmentalists commonly hope that somehow, the parent can use utterances in such a way that "makes clear" to the child, situationally, what the marker must be encoding. But really, what could the Georgian-speaker do to make it "situationally clear" to the child in a particular situation that the "-i" noun case-marker is encoding, for nouns with certain stem phonological properties, both the patient status of the noun referent, and the completed aspect status of the verb? What could the Turkish-speaking parent do to make especially clear to the child that the "-u" marker is encoding the definiteness of the noun, the patient status of the noun, and the back-unrounded vowel quality of the noun-stem, as opposed to the noun's possible human status, family status, colour-scheme, shape, and so on? This sort of thing cannot be viewed as any more than hopeful fantasy that somehow someone else can solve the whole language-induction problem for the child.

In reality, as we have seen, the child's own "property-register" must be prepared to "guess" salient and non-salient properties corresponding to all those which might figure across languages. The child must have an "induction process" which furthermore can use information from many situations to "sift out" the right property-combinations. Since more properties are potentially "confirmed" in any single situation than are relevant, the property-analyser must be able to use information from *many* situations, to eliminate such properties.

So to sum up: The interlocutor must use form-meaning matches which at least provide child-readable particular correct examples. The child must have the right social-cognitive-perceptual properties available to start with. But the child must have a property-register which can "see" all the possible right properties for the world's languages herself; the child's own induction mechanisms must themselves "sift out" the right property-combinations. Part of grammar acquisition is indeed social in nature; but some of the very complex parts of it must be largely the child's own doing.

Negative feedback and grammatical acquisition.   It has also been hoped that parents might give highly valuable "negative feedback" that informs the child when utterances have positive errors, or are missing some part; this might crucially "shape" the child's inductive processes (Bohannon, MacWhinney, & Snow, 1990). Contrary to such a hope, Brown and Hanlon (1970) showed that typically, parents do not in fact say things like "yes that's right" or "no that's wrong" in response to the grammaticality of children's utterances; instead, they use such direct feedback to confirm or disconfirm the factual accuracy or inaccuracy of the child's statement, regardless of its grammaticality.

But recently it has been pointed out that sometimes parents partly "imitate" children's utterances, to continue conversations (Bohannon et al., 1990). If the child's utterance is missing some marker, the parent's "imitation" usually supplied it—since parents speak grammatically. Since Turkish- and Georgian-speaking children do sometimes leave out relevant markers, might such "imitations" provide them valuable information that shows the children what to do?

There are two difficulties with this input "solution". First, when parents' "imitations" are different from the child's utterance, about two-thirds of the time they do fill in something missing (e.g. "he going" becoming "yes, he's going") (Bohannon et al., 1990). But about 30% of the time, they also add or change things when the child's utterance was grammatical to start with. The child might say "the dog's eating", and the parent might say "yes, he's eating, isn't he?", where "he" is substituted for "the dog" and "isn't he?" is added. It is thus difficult to see how the child would know whether the parent's "changes" meant she was doing something wrong or not, without already understanding most of what was going on.

Second, suppose the parent does add something that is actually missing, and somehow the child realises this. This does not tell the child what the actual properties are, that determine the right use. For example, suppose the Georgian-speaking child said "eating dog bone", leaving out the incomplete aspect-agent marker on "dog", and the parent said, "yes, eating dog-i bone". This might say that "-i" should have been used: But why? The parent is not saying directly "/-i/ should be added because 'dog' here is an agent of an incomplete aspect verb, and 'dog' is phonologically the kind of noun that takes /-i/". The adult may know this, of course; but the child simply has the parental utterance; the job of figuring out what properties account for the adult's use, vs. her own non-use, is still the child's. This seems to require all the same multiple-property-combination induction as the child simply hearing and analysing normal parental input. I would conclude that hopes for the special "information value" of such imitation-changes, are much inflated.

Innateness and case-marking.   In many ways, the problems discussed above obviously do *not* correspond to classic "Chomskyan" innateness. Acquisition of individual case-markers must be a grinding-through, sifting process, rather than one quickly "triggered" by one or two input stimuli (it is indeed ironical that Chomskyans and many non-Chomskyans both often favour "instant" acquisition). Clearly, the child cannot in any usual meaning of "target" innateness have the right Turkish or Georgian possible property combinations pre-known innately. Or at least, this would be very surprising.

But as was emphasised in the introduction, Chomskyan innateness is only one possible form of faculty-specific innateness. Let us stipulate that there has to be much "grinding-through", sifting induction in these morphological processes. Does this leave no room for faculty-specific innateness anywhere in the process?

This obviously is not true. For example, we saw that in many "privileged learning" animal systems, there were specifications of what input could be registered by the relevant system in the first place. Paradoxically, as the range of possible properties that can figure in morphological marking grows large, it becomes apparent that one cannot have the child register *all* the potentially relevant properties that speech-situations might contain. Should the child worry, for example, about the height of the referent of the noun, or hair-colour, or colour of clothes, or approved moral status, or part of the room in which the referent is found, or whether the referent is an electrical apparatus or not, or edible on social grounds (e.g. humans are edible in some cultures, not in others)? Does the child have to worry about all the potential combinations of all conceivable cognitive-perceptual properties?

In fact, this seems theoretically impossible. In reality, there is a relatively restricted (though still fairly rich) set of perhaps about 30 kinds of semantic-conceptual properties that figure in morphological stem-marking across the world's languages, including properties such as those we have discussed (agent-patient relations, location, goal-endpoint, humanness, singular-plural, ongoing-completed, definite-definite, individuated-mass, affectionately regarded, desired (marked on verbs in some languages), and so on). Some rather likely properties, like colour, artificial vs. natural, or moral goodness, do not seem to be encoded.

Presumably, also, only certain phonological properties of certain constituents can partly control morphology. Talmy (1985) and Pinker (1984) propose that there is a faculty-specific "property-register" list; that not any property can enter the morphological analysis system. Also, not all non-local properties enter into controlling morphology; it is difficult to point to a system in which patient-marking is affected by the definiteness of a location-phrase for the sentence. Thus, there might be specifications on what properties can enter the morphological-analytic system at all, and perhaps on what possible combinations are generally allowable; after that, of course, induction is relatively "open". In theory, of course, perhaps these property-restrictions follow from more general species-specific properties of the human conceptual-symbolic systems (see O'Grady, 1987). But certainly, faculty-specific restrictions on "entry properties" are plausible as well.

Connectionist networks and property-lists. The kind of massive, parallel sifting-over instances described above is something that "connectionist" neural-network systems often do. These systems are typically presented as relatively unbiased, non-nativist general inducers (MacWhinney & Chang, 1995; Plunkett, 1995; Rumelhardt & McClelland, 1986). So this seems to argue that such massive, sifting morphological systems are truly "non-innate" systems.

But in reality, these systems always must have a restricted, carefully specified list of "register properties" which can enter into the induction at all (Karmiloff-Smith, 1992; Lachter & Bever, 1989). This is usually just left implicit, but careful inspection of simulations typically shows very careful choice indeed of the relevant "input-properties". Such input-restrictions are implicitly, and sometimes explicitly, a form of innateness, whether faculty-specific, species-specific, mammal-specific, or combinations of all of these.

FORMAL CATEGORIES:
SOME DEVELOPMENTAL ISSUES

So far we have had to deal with three kinds of "primitive properties" for grammatical analysis: (1) phonological-auditory properties; (2) semantic-conceptual properties, like agent, action, patient, definite-indefinite, ongoing-completed aspect, past-present tense, possessor, negation; and (3) sequencing operations for words, constituents, and inflections defined by the properties of (1) and (2). All these properties, however, can be seen as being "borrowed" from the non-linguistic world, even if the combinations made of them in grammar are indeed peculiar to grammar (e.g. the natural world does not seem to combine patienthood and ongoing vs. completed aspect in the way Georgian grammar does).

In adult grammar, however, there is also reference to what are called *formal* categories like "verb", or "grammatical subject", which seem like basic categories of grammar, but do not seem to correspond directly to any non-linguistic categories. Let us see what is meant here.

There is a well-known task usually called the Berko task (Berko, 1958), which shows such categories at work. Suppose a speaker of English hears a sentence like "today John nisses". He can predict other possible uses of "niss", like "yesterday John _____" (fill in "nissed"), or "does John _____?" (fill in uninflected form of "niss"), and so on. The basic importance of this ability, which preschool children show, is that the new, predicted sequences could not have been heard before. "Niss" is a nonsense-word (nonce-word), which the subject has never heard in sentences before. So the speaker could not be producing "John nissed" from having heard "niss+ed" used before.

How does this productive scheme work? Roughly, it seems to work as follows: In learning English, a speaker has formed a category which we name "verb". The speaker has learned various grammatical properties which verbs have, including marking present tense with "-s" when the subject is third person singular (e.g. "John niss-es"), marking past tense with "-ed" when the sentence is past, marking a past question with "did-subject—verb . . ." marking a negation with subject—{don't, didn't, doesn't}+verb . . ." and so on. So when one hears "John niss-es", one can categorise "niss" as a verb; then one can predict that it has the other grammatical properties that verbs always or typically have.

Now if "verb" meant "action-word", we should simply say that speakers have learned the distinctive grammatical properties of action-words in English; so that "John nisses" cues that "niss" is an action-word, and action-words also take "-ed" past, or forms like "did subject action-word . . ." and so on. But in fact, "verb" does not just mean "action-word". Verbs include meanings like "want", "need", "believe", "trust", "consist", "belong", "resemble", which are not actional meanings; they are, variously, emotion-words, cognition-words, or miscellaneous meanings hard to categorise. In some other languages, meanings that are clearly state-words to English speakers, like "hungry", "thirsty", "wet", "sad", "in danger", "responsible", "sleepy", are often encoded by main verbs.

Besides, if anything, some non-verbs are more actional than some verbs. Some rather actional adjectives include "brave", "quick", "fast", "loud", "obnoxious", "helpful", "polite", words which tend to denote ways of acting. There is an interesting test for whether a predicate (which can include adjectives, verbs, or prepositions) is truly actional. Actions are often controllable. Thus one can reasonably command someone to do them, e.g. "eat your cereal!", "look closely at this!". In contrast, it is odd to try to command someone "know the answer!" or "resemble Tom!", or "need a drink of water!" or "want a dog!" (Fillmore, 1968). For some adjectives, it turns out that one can indeed command someone: "be brave!", "don't be obnoxious" (or "be obnoxious!"), "be polite!", "(don't) be loud!". This implies they indeed denote controllable activities.

So what makes something a verb? Most linguists would say that something is a verb if it shares in the set of verb-grammatical properties. In other words, "want" or "resemble" are verbs just because they take verb-grammatical properties like "-ed" past tensing, "do + subject + verb . . ." question-forms, and so on.

Similarly, consider "grammatical subject". For talking about subjects and direct objects, we need to define what are called predicate-argument relations. Basically, predicates denote a relation between, or a property of, the referents of arguments. So in "John—likes—Sam", the verb "like" is a two-argument predicate, and "John" and "Sam" are its arguments in this sentence. Adjectives are also predicates: "John (is) sad" is a one-argument sentence. ("Is" is just a "helping verb" for adjectives; many languages dispense with any form of "be" in such sentences, and say, in effect, "John sad".)

What are the grammatical properties of subjects vs. direct objects in English? In English basic clauses, we can name three major properties (there are more, of course):

1. The subject usually is the first argument, placed before the major predicate.
2. If the verb or form of *be* is marked for number-person, the subject controls its form (e.g. it is "John eats" because "John" is a third-person-singular subject).
3. There is a set of nominative pronouns, "he", "she", "they", "we", "I", which is used only for subjects; e.g. in "he helped him", "he" is the subject-pronoun, and "him", an objective pronoun.

Again, these properties apply to arguments which include agents ("*he* ate"), but also include non-agents, such as experiencers of emotions ("*the dog*—wants—a bone"), things having their location described ("*she*—is at the store"), and in passives, even patients (e.g. "*he*—was killed by the storm"). So "subject" is not the same as "agent". One might also think "subject" means "what the conversation is about". But this only tends to be true. For example, consider the following: "We had a Ming vase. But our cat broke *it*. We took *it* to a porcelain repairer, but he couldn"t fix *it*." Clearly here the vase is the main conversational topic, yet *it*, which refers to the vase, is a direct object in every sentence after the first.

So "subject" also refers to a key set of grammatical properties. Knowing an argument-role has one of them, we can predict the others. For example, suppose we hear a new, non-agentive predicate, in a context which says the predicate denotes a mixed emotional attitude towards other entities, e.g. "they—glin—dogs". The glinner-role is the subject ("John" is the one that has the feeling). Now we know that we could say "he—glins—dogs", predicting the use of "he", and the third person singular control of "glin-s" by "he". In fact, we can now predict any English-subject use for this glin-role, like "does—the dog—glin cats" (from "does—subject-3-singular—verb . . .").

But we seem to have a paradox. On the one hand, grammatical categories like "verb" and "subject", are used to predict new grammatical properties of words and predicate-roles. But on the other hand, we are claiming they are defined by these grammatical properties in the first place. So how can the child break into this system, and put together the right formal grammatical category–grammatical operation associations?

Semantic-beginnings theories

This problem is in fact too complicated for any complete treatment here. What we will do is put forth a generally popular, fairly simple kind of theory. Then we will inspect this theory in terms of what is known about actual grammatical input to children, and formal categories in a cross-linguistic perspective, to see its strong and weak points.

In this kind of theory, which has both non-Chomskyan (Bates & MacWhinney, 1982; Braine, 1994; Schlesinger, 1982) and Chomskyan (Grimshaw, 1981; Pinker, 1984) forms, the child is viewed as taking advantage (unconsciously, of course) of the partial relations between notional (meaning "semantic") properties like "agent" and "action" and "concrete object", and formal categories like "subject", "verb", and "noun". That is, in English simple clauses, even if not all subjects are agents (e.g. "I" is not an agent in "I want that"), agents are very reliably subjects. Or even if not all verbs are action-words, action-words are typically verbs. Or, again, even if not all nouns are object-words (e.g. "game", "fun"), object-words are always nouns.

Let us call these correspondences—agent-subject, patient-direct object, action-verb, object-noun, state-adjective, the *core* notional-formal correspondences. I will concentrate here on the nativist theory of how these correspondences can be used to analyse formal categories. The theory is quite simple, and illustrates how Chomskyan theories can employ non-grammatical properties. Grimshaw (1981) proposes that the child *does* know innately there are formal subjects, direct objects, verbs, nouns, adjectives, and so on. The child innately initially uses an identification heuristic: an agent constituent is a subject, an action-word is a verb, an object-word is a noun, an object-phrase is a noun phrase, a physical state-word is an adjective. This is not the same as saying that "agent is the same as subject". Rather, it is more like using someone's uniform to identify their underlying nationality; uniforms do not define nationality, but they can cue it very nicely. Similarly, in the Grimshaw-Pinker account, agency cues subjecthood, but does not define it.

So suppose the child hears and understands "he—moved—the hat". "He" denotes an agent, and so is marked as subject; "moved" denotes an action, and so is a verb; "the hat" is an patient-object-phrase, and so is a direct object noun phrase; "hat" itself denotes an object-category, so is a noun.

From this single input, the child can analyse that in English, subjects appear before the verb, which appears before the direct object; further, that verbs can be marked for tense by "-ed", that nouns are marked as definite in English by "the", and so on.

In another language, of course, things would work out differently. For example, a Turkish child might first hear the equivalent of "Tom—moved—hat-u", and so register that the sentence has an initial subject noun phrase, a subsequent verb, and a subsequent direct object noun phrase. But of course, the Turkish child would also hear sentences like "hat-u moved Tom", in which the subject-agent was after the verb, and the direct object-patient, in front. So in Turkish, the child would learn quickly that subjects can have any position *vis-à-vis* the verb, unlike English. The child would also analyse the morphological structure of patient-direct objects, and figure out how rounded and unrounded /u/ and /i/ mark direct objects, regardless of position.

In other words, use of the core notional-formal correspondences gives the child instant identification of many subjects, verbs, direct objects, nouns, noun phrases, adjectives. The child can then analyse the distinctive grammatical properties of these categories that are important in the child's language; these give the child the grammatical properties that characterise the formal categories.

Incorporating non-core notions.   Note here that some sentences would initially go largely unclassified, in formal terms. For example, "he wanted a spoon" has an experiencer as main predicate, one which takes experiencer-experienced arguments. Experiencer-experienced does *not* fit into the "core" innate notional-formal heuristic, and so would be unclassified at first.

As time goes on, two things will happen:

1. The child will be able to use the category-grammatical properties of his language to analyse non-core constituents and words. For example, suppose the Turkish child hears "bed-i likes Tom" ("Tom likes the bed"). Even though "like" is not an action-word, and "bed-i" is not a patient of an action, the distinctive direct object marker "-i" indicates that "bed-i" is a direct object; the unmarked stem "Tom" means that "Tom" is the subject.
2. The child must in fact *switch* away from using the notional properties to give formal membership. The reason for this is that adult grammar includes counter-core uses. For example, in passives like "he was kissed by his mother", the agent-constituent is "his mother", but "he" is the grammatical subject. It is the grammatical subject because it fits the English-grammatical properties for subjects (used before main predicate, controls number-person agreement on "was", nominative pronoun), even though it is semantically a patient. If the child stuck to the core notional-formal heuristic, the child would have to classify "he" as a direct object, and "his mother" as a subject, which gives the wrong analysis. Or to take another case, action-words can indeed be non-verbs, in sentences like "we played a nice *game*", or "the *explosion* was loud". But these words should not be classified as verbs, but as nouns, as their grammatical properties indicate.

Non-Chomskyan semantic-beginnings theories.   Non-Chomskyan notion-first theories are highly similar in nature, except the child does not know she is aiming for grammatical-defined formal categories. The child begins by classifying words and constituents by important semantic properties because this is cognitively natural. The child gradually analyses the grammatical properties of these words and constituents. When non-fitting words and constituents appear, the child uses both semantic properties and grammatical properties to classify them; but as grammatical properties accumulate, they come to predominate as classifying devices. It is not really clear why, in these accounts, the child would so determinedly emphasise the grammatical properties over the notional properties, however; it is not clear why the child switches criteria, in effect. The Chomskyan theories specify this switch as part of the innate programme. I believe myself that in any case, children's determined eventual use of the grammatical properties over the notional ones calls for some kind of species-specific or faculty-specific stipulation.

Problems with the notional beginnings accounts

These accounts are very appealing, especially since speakers typically mostly have conscious access to properties like "agent", and "patient", and not much conscious access to grammatical properties. But in fact, the Notional Beginnings theories in the form above, are both strongly flawed, and cannot cover all formal category formation across languages; one might hope that in languages where they do not work, children would show a great deal of developmental distress; but they do not (Maratsos, 1989; Pinker, 1990; Rispoli, 1991; Slobin, 1992a, 1992b). Pinker himself (1987, 1990), for example, no longer holds to the instant-identification, notional-first theory proposed in Grimshaw (1981) and Pinker (1984).

What could be wrong with such appealing, relatively straightforward theories? This is a complicated problem, but I will try to outline a few answers. First, the early input has to match the core notional-semantic stipulations. For example, suppose the very young child actually did hear and understand action-words that are *not* adult formal verbs? These non-verb action words would have the grammatical properties of some other formal category; but the action=verb heuristic requires the child to classify the word with the emerging verb category; so the grammatical properties of this non-verb would become part of the verb category.

In fact, English-speaking children do hear non-verb action-words. Pinker (1984) found that about 85% of the action-words in early input to Adam and Eve (Brown's subjects) were indeed verbs; but this means that 15% are *not* verbs, and have non-verb grammatical properties. Nelson (1994) shows evidence that some of these words, like "bath" (e.g. "take a bath", where "bath" is a noun), are indeed comprehended and sometimes used early on. But in "take a bath", for example, "bath" is an action-word which takes "a" as indefinite-marker; so classifying "bath" as a verb, has the danger of putting the use of "a" into the *verb* category, which of course is a poor result. Yet we see no disruptive results in children's actual formal-category uses.

To take another case: Early input cannot include passives, for in passives, agents are non-subjects; again a wrong assignment of grammatical properties would occur. English-speaking children probably hear no passives in early input (Pinker, 1984, shows zero rates for Adam and Eve's parents). But Sesotho adults do use passives in speech to young children, and Sesotho children appear to use passives earlier than English-speaking children (Demuth, 1990). So Sesotho children *do* hear agents which are not subjects. Yet again no developmental disruption is known.

Cross-linguistic variation in "core" notional-formal correspondences. Furthermore, some languages fail to show the "basic" core correspondences *even in basic clauses.* In about 5% of the world's languages, agents are not reliably grammatical subjects in basic clauses. In some of these languages, the subject properties reliably fall to the patient. Pinker (1984) and Marantz (1985) propose an innate "parametric variation" known to children, such that they quickly "classify" their language as agent-centred or patient-centred.

But in fact, in most of the 5%, agents and patients actually *trade off* controlling subject properties, depending on complex language-particular contingencies such as definiteness, relative humanness, being more first-person like, and so on. Let me give one such example, from Tagalog (Gonzales, 1984; Schachter & Otanes, 1985). In Tagalog, the main verb appears first, followed by noun phrase arguments in no fixed order. There is a set of noun-markers for the subject, and the verb "agrees" with the subject in aspect-marking (to be discussed). But how is the "subject" chosen in the first place?

Let us take action-verb sentences which have an agent, patient, and recipient, such as "threw—ball—John—(to) Mary". If the patient is semantically definite, it will be the subject. But if the patient is semantically indefinite, it cannot be the subject. Then either one of the agent or recipient can be the subject, if they are semantically definite. The verb is then marked for aspect according to the semantic-grammatical case of the subject. So for patient-as-subject, the completed aspect of "read" is "b-in-asa"; for agent-subject, it would be "b-um-asa"; for recipient-subject, it would be "basa-han". (The verb agreement with subject is a typical subject-property, though agreement with the semantic-grammatical case of the subject is somewhat unusual among the world's languages.)

In other languages, as mentioned above, it might be relative humanness, or person of agent and patient, that are critical for choosing the subject. For example, in some languages, first person nouns get to be subject over second or third person nouns, and so on.

Imagine if a child tried to learn such languages by determinedly trying to use the heuristic that agent=subject. Then agents would have subject-properties some of the time, but would also have non-subject properties a great deal of the time. Again, we might expect enormous developmental disruption, until the child could find a "back-up" analysis. But in fact, developmental data are basically bland: The systems seem to be in place by 2 or 3, little developmental error is found (Maratsos, 1989; Rispoli, 1991; Slobin, 1992; see Rispoli, 1991 for an interesting acquisitional approach to such languages).

Basically, across languages and inputs, the only "core" heuristic that consistently works is that object-words like "table" and "dog" are indeed always nouns. This is because as far as can be told, this heuristic works even for adult grammars across languages (Maratsos, 1992). The other notional-formal heuristics all fail strongly in some input or language situation, yet so far we fail to see acquisitional problems from such failures.

Formal categories with no known "notional core" at all.   Finally, there are formal categories in some languages which are all grammatical property-set, and no notional core. These are categories like formal noun gender, or formal verb conjugations, in languages like Polish, Russian, German, Greek, and others. Let me illustrate one of these briefly, with part of the Polish system (Smoczynska, 1985). Polish uses noun-stem inflections to mark semantic-grammatical case. For some nouns, for example, "-a" marks nominative case (agents, intransitive subjects), and "-e" marks most patients and other direct objects. The inflection "-i" marks the genitive case, which is used to mark possessors (e.g. like "John's" in "John's dog"), but also for patients of negated or non-exhaustive actions; for example, "carrot" in "John didn't eat (the) carrot", or "John ate (some of the) carrot", would be *genitive*, not accusative.

So we have, for some nouns: Nom.: -a; Acc.: -e; Gen.: -i. But there are other nouns which work differently. For these nouns, we have: Nom. -o; Acc.: -o; Gen.: -a. Let us put this chart form (Table 8.1).

TABLE 8.1

	Noun Set I	*Noun Set II*
Nom.	-a	-o
Acc.	-e	-o
Gen.	-i	-a

There are no general reliable notional "cores" to these two noun sets, and no evidence children try to find any. So how can the child form the categories? Apparently, what the child must do is something like the following. The child must analyse, first, individual case-markers for individual nouns. Over time, of course, the evidence will pile up that those nouns which happen to take /-a/ to mark nominative uses, take /-e/ to mark accusative, and /-i/ to mark genitive. Those nouns which happen to take /-o/ for nominative uses, generally take /-o/ for accusative uses, and /-a/ for genitive uses. The noun-sets thus are defined by how one set of words takes a particular set of case-markers, while another set of words takes a different set.

In other words, the child must record which words individually take which grammatical operations. The word-set patterns grow from an internal process which, starting with such individual word-marker sets, analyses how many different words take the same marker-patterns, and comprises a word-category from this combinatorial commonality. This kind of analysis of sets of word-operation patterns is usually called *distributional*.

In fact, children apparently master the Polish case-marking system (which is far more extensive than the fragment summarised above), with no observed error for singular nouns, by the age of 2 (Smoczynska, 1985; Weist, 1990). This freedom from productive error is typical of reports of acquisition of noun-set and verb-set systems in Greek (Katis, 1984; Stephany, 1995), German (Walter, 1975; though see Mills, 1985, for some disagreement), the non-eccentric core of Russian (Maratsos & Chalkley, 1980), and other similar systems. Only when such systems become hopelessly contingent and complex do developmental errors tend to persist strongly (Slobin, 1982, for Serbo-Croatian; Maratsos & Chalkley, 1980, for "eccentric" aspects of Russian).

Distributional analysis applied to major formal categories

In fact, Maratsos and Chalkley (1980) note that this same process will work for the major formal categories, like noun and verb, or, applied to individual predicate-roles, will give subject and direct object. Given that distributional analysis can give both the major and minor formal category-systems in like fashion, and does not have some of the cross-linguistic problems of Semantic Beginnings accounts, it should be the preferred account.

This argument, however, has itself two problems, one highly correctable, and one not. First, as Keil (1981) notes, there must be initial restrictions on what can count as a significant grammatical property for such analyses, because sentences have too many potential grammatical properties for the child to tabulate in the first place. (Pinker, 1984 computes 9,000,000 possible "grammatical properties" for a simple seven-word sentence.) The major categories of the world's languages indeed seem to use certain families of grammatical properties quite frequently as category-properties. For example, how definiteness and quantity are marked frequently serve as key distributional properties of noun formal categories. How tense, aspect, and person-number agreement are marked, frequently comprises central aspects of verb (or verb vs. adjective) delineation. So it is virtually certain that distributional accounts must be restricted in what kinds of grammatical properties can count as input. Indeed, such restrictions must comprise part of any formal category acquisitional account (e.g. Pinker, 1987).

Supplemented in this way, distributional accounts can apparently flexibly encompass the formal category systems of all the world's languages, both major and minor systems. But this, ironically, leads to another difficulty. As Braine

(1994) points out, this process is almost too flexible: It can account for formal categories of *any* shape. But the major formal categories of world's languages really show strong, if not perfect, core-formal tendencies: Agents are subjects in basic clauses in 95% of the world's languages, object-words are nouns in all of them, and so on; whatever causes these correspondences probably plays some role in children's formal category acquisition, though obviously not as clear a one as in the straightforward Semantic Beginnings accounts discussed above.

Mutual acceptance of criticisms

In fact, neither a purely distributional or semantic-based account seems to handle all the facts quite adequately. Many participants in the theoretical discussions have in fact appropriately changed their initial formulations because of such difficulties. For example, Pinker (1987, 1990), a strong supporter of fast-acting semantic-first analyses, accepts that distributional analyses are probably at work from the beginning of the process. Maratsos (1992) maintains that especially for nouns, heavy use of object-meaning as an initial organiser is likely; the paragraph above accepts some use of notional properties as initial category-organisers more widely. While it may seem disappointing to have an apparently clear theoretical dispute emerge with "no winner", it can also represent a constructive recognition of the good arguments of both sides.

Some conclusions and remaining problems

Presently, it is difficult to say that an adequate, thoroughly worked-out account of formal category formation is to be found. The apparently complex, and probably heterogeneous interaction of formal and semantic factors will indeed probably make such an account full of special provisions and property-interactions (Maratsos, 1992). But this does not mean that we cannot draw some preliminary conclusions, while noting problems that remain unresolved.

1. Theories based only on English, and on a somewhat idealised picture of early English, are inadequate; it is not just a matter of getting a good theory for English, then taking in other languages as slight revisions. Problems like agent-patient switches, or non-notional core categories cannot be handled as theoretical footnotes to English.
2. Grammar does achieve some of its own category analysis; "verb" does not correspond to any non-grammatical category directly. Yet some partial semantic-formal correspondences also are important for many formal categories. Indeed, the "object"–noun correspondence works quite well; this particular notion-core correspondence is probably an especially central one.
3. A theory that the child innately knows all formal categories in advance cannot be correct; for the child cannot know the "minor" categories in advance, nor could the child know in advance the complex agent-patient switch systems. Yet these latter, non-pre-knowable categories share much of the same analytic nature as the more familiar "major" ones. This argues that in the most general

theory, the child knows no formal categories in advance, but constructs them all from a limited set of basic properties and procedures.

Yet we cannot even be sure of this last argument. As argued earlier, grammar cannot be expected to be "homogeneous" in nature. Possibly one or more major formal categories are partly pre-known (e.g. nouns, easily cued by object-reference), while the construction of others is left more open. It is clear children must be able to construct at least some non-pre-known formal categories; but this does not preclude of some partial "preformation" for a more limited set of formal categories.

4. Again, despite the obvious complexity of these problems, we see little developmental disruption in actual acquisition. The unconscious processes which somehow juggle the word-set and notional configurational contributions, work with surprisingly little observed difficulty (Maratsos, 1982; Maratsos & Chalkley, 1980; Slobin, 1985a, 1985b; Smoczynska, 1985). It is not obvious from what else is known of the preschool children's general abilities, that children would be so good, for example, at constructing the Polish noun-case-gender system by the age of 2, with so little difficulty. Even if the question of innately pre-known, "targeted" formal category knowledge is quite open, it seems increasingly likely, in a Bayesian sort of way, that language-specific processes of some kind co-operate with some species-specific abilities to produce such surprisingly efficient acquisitional processes.

CHOMSKYAN ACQUISITIONS: FORMAL AND ABSTRUSE PROPERTIES OF GRAMMAR

Key to the Chomskyan programme: "Poverty of the stimulus"

The preceding sections have illustrated something, it is hoped, about the complexity of grammar. But except in passing, we have not really discussed any particularly Chomskyan arguments or ideas. Indeed, little that we have discussed touches at the core of Chomskyan confidence that a good deal of grammatical acquisition must rely upon highly innate, targeted, and faculty-specific abstruse pre-knowledge of how grammar can work.

Before settling down to a more specific discussion of particulars, however, it is appropriate here to give a more general background perspective on the Chomskyan turn of mind. This can be done, in part, through a (relatively brief) discussion of one of Chomsky's key ideas, an idea which he holds constant even as his own particular ideas about linguistic structure change. This idea he usually calls the "poverty of the stimulus".

What Chomsky means by this key idea shifts from context to context. But its most general meaning remains constant: The stimulus situation itself does not have enough information to "tell" the organism the right idea. The organism must interpret this stimulus information the right way. Such interpretation must come from internal, biological structure the organism brings to the situation.

A first illustration: The "similar-different" problem.   In fact, there can be no doubt that Chomsky is quite right in this matter. We can see this by reference to some surprising findings about animal vs. human learning, where animals consistently fail to "see" something in a situation that is obvious to humans. Consider this apparently very simple problem. You are shown pairs of stimuli, in particular the following pairs: 1 1   0 0   0 1   0 0. You are to guess "yes" or "no" for each. If you are right, you will be rewarded somehow.

Let us start: 1 1 ("yes" is right). 1 0 ("no" is right). 0 1 ("no" is right). 0 0 ("yes" is right).

Most people, including children, very quickly catch on. If the two stimuli are the same, the right answer is "yes". If they are different, the right answer is "no". They can quickly generalise what they have figured out here to new pairs, like 2 2, 3 4, and so on. Any adult human would say the problem is "obvious". Yet perfectly intelligent dogs and cats will fail to solve this problem, no matter how many hundreds or thousands of learning trials with feedback they are given. They cannot even "solve" the original set of four stimuli. How could they fail to get it right?

Apparently they always see the "1" and the "0" as being separate stimuli, in separate positions. So they try to solve the problem, apparently, using implicit "guesses" for "yes" like "1 is always on the right", or "the more 1's, the better". They never *see* the problem as one of the similarity-difference between the two slots.

Interestingly, primates typically do solve the problem, but only after hundreds of trials. In this, their performance is much like current connectionist hidden-layer network learning systems, which "solve" the problem without ever having the "insight" that it is a same-different problem.

So the stimulus array by itself does *not* contain the information, even with training and feedback. If the organism does not see or interpret the stimuli the right way, it is not true that the "solution is just there in the stimuli". The solution also has to "be in the organism", in some sense.

The "poverty of the stimulus" applied to language acquisition.   At a basic level, then, Chomsky is absolutely correct. For any problem where knowledge is induced or deduced from stimulus inputs, one cannot say the "answer is just in the stimuli". The organism has to be able to supply the right interpretation of those stimuli.

In his early arguments with Skinner, who proposed a highly stripped-down picture of what the relevant stimuli were for organisms, Chomsky emphasised the *richness* of interpretations that the child has to apply to the stimuli. Stimuli which look highly similar, for example, often have to be given quite different linguistic analyses. For example, "John" in "John is easy to please" means someone who is to be the object of pleasing. "John" in "John is eager to please" means that John is to be the doer of the pleasing. Yet "John is easy to please" and "John is eager to please", in Skinnerian stimulus analyses, would seem much the same kind of stimulus-configuration. Indeed, sometimes one sentence has two major underlying analyses, as shown in "the ducks are ready to eat" or "visiting relatives can be tedious".

So this first "poverty-of-the-stimulus" argument basically refers to how the stimuli are not *rich* enough in themselves to supply all the needed interpretation.

Later, Chomsky became interested in another meaning: There are many possible interpretations of the same stimulus-inputs. If an organism consistently settles on just one of them, this cannot be due to the nature of the inputs themselves. Rather, the organism must be innately structured so as to supply just one possible interpretation. This argument again is, quite simply true. Anytime we look at any set of possible input stimuli, we can always find more than one possible interpretation of it, if we work at it. Ironically, the more Chomsky is correct, the harder it is to believe. For if humans are highly structured to see stimulus situations just one way, they will have a hard time believing there are other ways they could be analysed.

Thus the second "poverty of stimulus" problem is really not that the stimuli are exactly impoverished: If anything, they are too rich, in allowing too many interpretations. What Chomsky means here is that the stimulus information is not sufficient to select just one among the many possible interpretations. Yet judging from how people agree reasonably well on how much grammatical structure works, without direct environmental feedback or instruction (see later discussion), they *must* be seeing the data very selectively, and resolving the inherent ambiguities by use of internal constraints. So the claim is that people's interpretations are also highly selective.

Both of these "poverty of stimulus" properties are illustrated in certain problems central to modern linguistic theory: that is, on the one hand, mature language users have typically settled on solutions that are more "constrained" than the input data really required; on the other hand, the constraining interpretations they read into the data look, at times, very odd and abstruse. This latter property in particular is what Chomskyans point to, as evidence of faculty-specificity: "odd" and "abstruse" typically mean the relevant interpretations seem to involve properties specific to language itself, that could not have come from elsewhere.

Limits on the discussion. In an ideal discussion, it would be possible to look in some detail at the actual proposals made by linguists about linguistic structure. It would then be possible to inspect their likely ramifications for acquisitional theory, and see whether indeed acquisitional data bear out such ramifications.

Our own discussion here, however, must be much more severely limited, for two reasons. First, quite consistent with the claim of how abstruse these matters are, a clear discussion typically requires one or two years of linguistic courses as background. Such background, given the instructional purpose of this volume, is not presupposed here.

Second, it would be foolish, in a way, to tie a general discussion too specifically to a current analysis of linguistic structure. For in reality, linguistic theory often changes in rapid and widespread ways. For example, a basic hope of linguistic theory in the 1980s, was that for a "core" set of grammatical processes, languages would vary in only a very few, well-specified ways, which the child would know in advance. The child's task for each of these variation-dimensions, was to find the right parametric value for his own language, among a very small set of possible variations. This was usually called "setting the parameter" for the particular dimension.

Furthermore, it was hoped that parameter-settings are highly correlated across languages. If this is so, and the child knows this correspondence, then figuring out one significant grammar property for one's own language, would automatically set the parametric values of a number of other dimensions. So a well-prepared child might, in reality, very quickly analyse much of his own language's particular structure, by making just one key analysis.

What would be an example of this multiple parameter-setting process? For example, some languages allow subjects to be dropped relatively freely. In Greek or Italian, one can say, as a complete sentence, the equivalents of "Ate" or "Will sing". Such languages are said to have a + value for Pro-drop. Languages like English do not allow such free omission of subjects, and are said to have −Pro-drop. Thus the + or − value for Pro-drop constitutes a single parametric dimension for grammars.

Now suppose whether or not a language allows pro-drop also predicts the settings for other grammatical processes. For example, Italian allows a wider range of wh- questions than English (see later discussion): One can say things like "what does John wonder who ate?". Rizzi (1982) proposed that such correlated properties might be predictable from Pro-drop. So setting the + Pro-drop parameter, would automatically solve other acquisitional problems (Hyams, 1986).

But in work through the 1980s, cross-parameter settings that seemed to work initially for some sets of languages, typically failed when more languages were investigated (papers in Webelhuth, 1995a, such as Webelhuth, 1995b, Harbert, 1995). It is difficult to say that any convincing proposal for multiple-correlated parameter-settings is currently known. Probably partly in response to such problems, Chomsky (1992) has recently radically revised much of his own theorising (again). Many of the revisions appear to be quite radical. For example, most psychologists have heard of "deep structure" and "surface structure", but they are now no more (Chomsky, 1992). More specifically, problems once handled through parameter-setting are now commonly handled through other means. Writers such as Webelhuth (1995a) believe that the resulting acquisitional theories are much more complex, and this seems to me correct.

Let us take it that the original simplicity of the parameter-setting approaches is no longer uniformly accepted. History further indicates that resultant new approaches are not necessarily going to last very long. Why, then, should we consider any particular problems here in detail?

It is worth doing so for two reasons. First, it is still a good idea to try to give a focused idea of the kind of thinking, at the most general level, that still remains potent in Chomskyan "poverty of the stimulus" approaches. Second, we can hope that if we study an illustrative case at the right level of generality, it will remain a valid case across whatever new perspectives are brought to bear upon it by future linguistic approaches. Indeed, the case we are going to discuss has remained highly resilient as a focal problem for three decades, even as particular linguistic analyses of it have changed.

An "abstruse" problem: Restrictions on wh- question processes

Before beginning the illustration, I further want to be clear about something else: Not *all* the processes in "core grammar" really are very abstruse. For example, one cross-language problem is whether or not a language allows subjects to be omitted freely (in tensed clauses in particular) (referred to as "Pro-drop" above). By itself, this is not an impressively abstruse problem, compared to some of the problems we have already considered which look as though they would have to fall outside "core processes" (e.g. hooking up stem phonology with case-marking in many languages). It is doubtful that Pro-drop has ever been of much interest in itself, as compared to its role in Multiple-Parameter-setting schemes, which, as briefly indicated above, do not currently seem to have a promising future.

So we especially need an example of the kind of "abstruse" problems Chomskyans have as their "home base". That is, we need an example of a problem likely to support faculty-specific abstruse nativism, regardless of the linguistic theory in which it comes to be embedded. One such problem is found in the restrictions on wh- processes (Chomsky, 1986; Ross, 1967). These wh- problems have played a prominent role in linguistic theory since Ross's ground-breaking work.

What is meant by wh- processes?   "Wh- processes" is itself a convenient gloss for processes which play a central role in wh- questions like "what did he see?" but which also play a role in cross-clause comparatives, relative clauses, topicalisations, and a number of other traditional grammatical constructions. For our purposes here, we will confine the discussion to wh- questions, occasionally bringing in relative clause or topicalisation examples.

Wh- questions are not "isolated" grammatical processes. They refer to a particular kind of social information-exchange, and require much social-information analysis. For example, when would someone ask "What did John eat?" He would ask it, typically, if he (the speaker) and his listener(s) already shared information equivalent to "John ate X". Furthermore, he apparently does not know much about "X", but thinks the listener(s) might. So the wh- question is a specific request for information about the identity of a constituent in a proposition, the rest of which is presupposed to be known to listener and speaker. Any acquisitional theory of wh- questions must include the child's ability to analyse the relation between grammatical structure and social intention (DeVilliers, 1995).

But on the other hand, cross-linguistic variation shows that this complex social-cognitive content does not by itself determine any universal grammatical *form* for wh- questions. For example, compare the wh- question equivalents below for Chinese, Welsh, Arabic, and English (I have put in English-like auxiliary verb placement, to allow focus on the placement of the wh- constituent):

1. Mary thinks John made what?—Chinese
2. What-i does Mary think John made it-i?—Welsh, Arabic
3. What-i does Mary think John made _____-i?—English

Chinese leaves the wh- constituent in its "normal" sentence order. In this sentence, the wh-constituent is a request for information about the direct object of 'ate', and that is where it appears—in "normal" direct object position. Welsh and Arabic realise the wh- constituent at the front of the sentence; but they also put in a pronoun, here "it", at the "normal" direct object position; this left-behind pronoun thus also refers to the constituent in its "normal" position. The little "-i" indices are used to show that "What-i" and "it-i" refer to the same referent, and this is signified by giving them the same reference index "-i".

English places the wh- constituent in front; it has no "left-behind" pronoun to mark the normal position, but instead leaves a "gap" behind; this "gap" corresponds to the "normal position" for the relevant constituent. This "gap" is psychologically real. First, the speaker must be careful not to fill in anything there. One must not say, in standard English, "what-i does Mary think that John made it-i?". Second, in comprehending the wh- question, one needs to process where the gap occurs, in order to interpret the grammatical-semantic role of the initial wh- constituent. For example, compare "What-i did John think _____-i destroyed the army?" vs. "What-i did John think the army destroyed_____-i?". Both sentences begin with "What did John think . . ." The information as to whether "what" refers to the destroyed or destroyed entity, requires processing of where there is a gap in the later part of the sentence (Wanner & Maratsos, 1978).

So Chinese, Welsh, and English may differ in whether the wh- constituent is realised overtly in "normal" position or in clause-front position, and in whether there is a left-behind pronoun ("resumptive pronoun") in that normal position, or simply a "gap". Presumably, however, an intelligent symbol-sequence analysing child with a good long-term memory and excellent interpretative and structure-comparison abilities could figure this out, so there is nothing impressively "abstruse" here yet.

Odd restrictions on wh- processes.   But now consider the following range of wh- initial questions:

1. Which diseases-i does John think [doctors can cure _____-i?]
2. Which diseases-i does John think [_____-i cannot be cured?]
3. Which diseases-i does John think [that _____-i cannot be cured?]
4. Which diseases-i does John wonder [who can cure _____-i?]
5. Which diseases-i does John wonder about [the claim [that doctors can cure _____-i]]?
6. Which diseases-i does John admire [any doctor [who can cure _____]]?
7. Which diseases-i does John admire [the well-known doctor [who can cure _____-i]]?

English-speakers generally accept wh- questions of the two types exemplified by (1) and (2), but not those exemplified by (3)–(7). One might venture that (3)–(7) must be "unnatural" for some basic cognitive or social or processing reason. But in fact, Italian-speakers accept the types illustrated in (3)–(4), Swedish-speakers accept the types illustrated by (3)–(7), and Danish and Norwegian speakers fall in between Italian and Swedish speakers.

Obviously there must be properties which differ crucially among English, Italian, Norwegian, Danish, and Swedish, and speakers of these languages have unconsciously analysed these properties during acquisition. Just as obviously, children are not actually overtly instructed in these abstruse-looking differences. Furthermore, as far as we know, it is not the case that children produce errors which are then corrected; besides, even if this happened, the children would still have to figure out what the general properties were that accounted for why some individual sentences were corrected and some were not.

It is important to be clear that one cannot just say that speakers have just "not heard" the odd sentences. Speakers accept many new sentences they have not heard before. Nor can it be some vaguely defined "relative novelty" compared to past wh- questions. For example, suppose you are introduced to a completely novel word "eshem", which is a container for space alien jewellery. Obviously any sentence with "eshem" in it is quite novel. Yet it is easy to produce, or comprehend, new wh- sentences like "which eshem-i did John say Mary needs _____-i for the store", or "What-i did John put _____-i into the eshem?". All these sentences with "eshem" have *something* new about them, compared to previously heard wh- sentences, but these particular "something new" properties are not the particular wh- relevant properties children have been paying attention to. In other words, at a general level, we have to say there is a general "property-register" which contains a particular, restricted set of properties relevant to wh- questions; children automatically analyse which of these selected properties are present in the wh- questions they hear in their own language.

The relevant general restrictions seem to apply to aspects of the context for the left-behind "gap" in the sentence. In fact, some of the relevant gap-context properties are, it turns out, semantic. For example, in English, leaving a wh- gap in a definite noun phrase usually causes some unacceptability. This accounts for the difference between "What faces-i does John like [pictures of _____ -i]?" vs. *"What faces-i does John like [Mary's pictures of _____ -i]?". Definiteness does not play a similar restrictive role in all languages; but it is obviously a property that the child must be attending to in analysing wh- questions, to notice that English wh- gaps do not generally occur in definite noun phrase contexts (while in some other languages, they can indeed occur in such contexts).

Let us call a property which can either restrict or not restrict wh- gap contexts a "wh- gap boundary property". Some wh- gap boundary properties are indeed semantic-conceptual, like definite-indefinite. Across languages, however, only a relatively small set of such semantic-conceptual properties can be wh- boundary-properties, which points to some possible innate restrictions. Furthermore, most linguists believe, however, that at least some wh- boundary-properties refer to relatively abstruse formal grammatical properties, such as differences between types of internal sentence boundary, or whether or not two such boundaries occur right next to each other in the sentence. Again, it is not that wh- gaps can never occur in such conditions in any language; rather, it is that such boundary-properties restrict wh- gaps for some languages, and not others. So the child must have some property-set to register the appropriate ± value for the gaps in her own language.

All this seems, in fact, virtually tautological. It is true that linguists has still not resolved the exact nature of relevant wh- gap boundary-properties that dif-ferentiate languages; but whatever they should turn out to be, the child must be using them automatically and unconsciously to analyse the input, and many of the candidate properties do not seem very "natural" on general grounds.

Thus the wh- restriction problem illustrates both facets of the "poverty-of-the-stimulus" argument. First, some of the boundary-properties seem like highly abstruse ones to focus on as relevant to the input. Second, by having a restricted property-register, the child's possible range of interpretations of the data is implicitly restricted. Both the "rich-abstruse" and "ambiguity" aspects of "poverty-of-stimulus" are thus illustrated.

Alternative descriptions.   Are there any alternatives? Some linguists are indeed pursuing a programme of trying to account for the "unnaturalness" of wh- processes another way. For example, let us take the common influence of definiteness. Definite expressions refer to referents, the identity of which is supposed to be already firmly established in the conversation (see previous discussion). But a wh- constituent indicates that something is not well-identified. So having a wh- gap in a definite expression is, expressively, somewhat self-contradictory. It is saying the referent of the expression is both already presupposed to be clearly known, yet part of it is, importantly, not known, which contradicts the first part. Linguists like Bever (1970), Eretshik-Shir (1982), Kuno (1988), and Van Hoek (1995) have shown how similar such "functional" explanations apply plausibly within languages in a number of cases.

But as Eretshik-Shir notes, if the restrictions of this kind are all completely cognitively and socially "natural", one would expect that they would apply the same ways across all languages.

Or since speakers vary individually in various ways, what is "natural" for one speaker should be "unnatural" for another, exposed to the same language input; thus one would expect individual variation *within* languages to be quite considerable. There is some individual variation among speakers of a language in what they find acceptable, but it is quite minor compared to the strong cross-language differences. So the child must indeed *learn* something, and must have a property-register and induction system to allow this. Nor is it at all clear that functional primitive properties can supply *all* the relevant boundary-properties. Most linguists would currently guess not.

Acquisitional work.   One might hope that acquisitional work would sort out some of these matters. Indeed, we have some important acquisitional facts: children are not specifically instructed in these matters, and make few if any known observed errors. These findings are important; they show that children must have a set of register-properties of the right sort for solving the problems. But they do not choose among alternative proposals for what the boundary-properties might be.

Similarly, work showing that acquisition is surprisingly early for some restrictions (Crain, 1992; DeVilliers, 1995), though apparently slow for others (Wexler & Mancini, 1987), does not resolve such matters. Suppose acquisition is fast. Both "Chomskyans" and "functionalists" alike can say this is because the relevant properties are indeed natural ones for children to register, whether on faculty-specific grounds (Chomskyans) or other grounds (functionalists). Suppose acquisition is relatively slow. It is always possible to claim this is due to some "adjunct" developmental problem, like special memory-processing demands of the construction, or difficulty interpreting the low-level grammatical properties of the relevant words (Wexler & Mancini, 1987) (see Maratsos, in press, for discussion of "adjunct" competence and acquisition).

Basically, the problems here are so abstract, that general acquisitional facts such as fast vs. slow learning, do not really pointedly address them. Perhaps if functional accounts in particular developed more specifically, contrasting developmental accounts could be found for different theories.

This inconclusive summary, however, does not undo a basic conclusion: Whatever the contributing factors, and however they are chosen by the acquisitional systems, a look at the actual restriction-contrasts points up how odd it is that children are consistently paying attention to whatever boundary-properties are relevant to distinguishing the languages. Again, it is difficult not to be impressed by the combined complexity and stability of the process, here likely tied to matters of some considerable abstruseness as well.

SOME GENERAL CONCLUSIONS ABOUT COMPLEX GRAMMATICAL ACQUISITION

Space forbids going back over the conclusions of the previous sections in detail. Instead, I would like to raise another issue. By and large, the pro- and anti-Chomskyan issue has been taken to be faculty-specificity: Does grammatical acquisition require something partly specific to grammar itself, to work? This does not mean that *all* grammar is self-specific, as I hope has been clear; but certainly some aspects of it, either in the restricted borrowing of cognitive-social properties from general development, or the complexity and sometimes abstruseness found in some aspects, generally support the possibility of some faculty-specific features playing acquisitional roles; this seems likely even if we cannot currently say just what these might be (Maratsos, 1989; Slobin, 1985a).

I would like to suggest a more general perspective as well, however. When Chomsky opposed Skinnerian analyses, it was naturally assumed, I think, that he proposed the mind was generally rational, in some generally understandable sense; for Skinner was best known for proposing the opposite view (there is no rational mind at all). Instead, however, Chomsky turned out to be proposing that the mind is not generally "rational". In fact, he was proposing that the mind is somewhat "quirky" from the viewpoint of general conscious cognition (which is assumed to be somewhat rational): that grammar in particular involves very odd mind-properties. He also thought this oddness was put into an architecturally specific grammar-section. So "quirkiness" and "faculty-specificity" became associated.

This association is not necessary. It is also possible that grammatical acquisition is a function of the "whole mind", but the "whole mind" itself is in reality somewhat quirky. From this point of view, faculty-specificity might just be a question of whether the quirkiness is contained architecturally in one "section" of the mind, or more generally scattered throughout its workings (or even highly characteristic of its workings). My own view is that while some aspects of grammar are reasonably "rational" and "transparent" looking (e.g. strictly ordered agent-action-patient schemas), other aspects of it—its various kinds of complexity, apparently not needed for communicative purposes in any straightforward way—simply look "quirky", compared to what we might have expected on general, "rational" grounds. Yet children are obviously very well-suited to deal with these problems which look so complicated and odd to the adult conscious mind. So I think it is fair to conclude that at one general level, we have indeed learned something from studies of grammatical acquisition: The mind is "quirky" a good deal of the time, and not what we might have expected; it is not "rational" according to the standards of what conscious thought would naturally expect. Personally I think that the strong support for this proposition that grammatical acquisition gives, is the currently central contribution of grammatical acquisition to our understanding of the mind.

REFERENCES

Bates, E., & MacWhinney, B. (1982). Functionalist approaches to grammar. In E. Wanner & L. Gleitman (Eds.), *Language development: The state of the art* (pp. 173–218). Cambridge, UK: Cambridge University Press.

Bates, E., & MacWhinney, B. (1989). Functionalism and the competition model. In B. MacWhinney & E. Bates (Eds.), *The cross-linguistic study of sentence processing* (p. 12). New York: Cambridge University Press.

Berko, J. (1958). The child's learning of English morphology. *Word, 14*, 150–177.

Bever, T. (1970). The cognitive basis for linguistic structures. In J.R. Hayes (Ed.), *Cognition and the development of language* (pp. 279–352). New York: Wiley.

Bloom, L. (1970). *Language development: Form and function in emerging grammar.* Cambridge, MA: MIT Press.

Bohannon, J.N., III, MacWhinney, B., & Snow, C. (1990). No negative evidence revisited: Beyond learnability, or who has to prove what to whom. *Developmental Psychology, 26*, 221–226.

Braine, M.D.S. (1994). Is nativism sufficient? *Journal of Child Language, 21*, 1–23.

Brown, R. (1973). *A first language: The early stages.* Cambridge, MA: Harvard University Press.

Brown, R., & Hanlon, C. (1970). Derivational complexity and order of acquisition in child speech. In J.R. Hayes (Ed.), *Cognition and the development of language* (pp. 11–54). New York: Wiley.

Bruner, J. (1975). From communication to language: A psychological perspective. *Cognition, 3*, 255–287.

Chomsky, A.N. (1965). *Aspects of the theory of syntax.* Cambridge, MA: MIT Press.

Chomsky, A.N. (1986). *Barriers.* Cambridge, MA: MIT Press.

Chomsky, A.N. (1992). A minimalist program for linguistic theory. In K. Hale & S. Keyser (Eds.), *The view from building 20: Essays in linguistics in honor of Sylvain Bromberger.* Cambridge, MA: MIT Press.

Cole, M., & Cole, S. (1992). *The development of children* (2nd edn.). San Francisco: Freeman.

Crain, S. (1992). Language acquisition in the absence of experience. *Brain and Behavioural Science, 14*, 597–611.

Dawes, R. (1988). *Rational choice in an uncertain world.* New York: Harcourt Brace Jovanovich.

Demuth, K. (1990). Subject, topic, and Sesotho passive. *Journal of Child Language, 17*, 67–84.

DeVilliers, J. (1995). Empty categories and complex sentences: The case of wh- questions. In P. Fletcher & B. MacWhinney (Eds.), *The handbook of child language* (pp. 508–540). Oxford, UK: Blackwell.

Eimas, P., Siqueland, E.R., & Vigorito, J. (1971). Speech perception in infants. *Science 171*, 303–306.

Eretschik-Shir, E. (1982). Extractibility in Danish and the pragmatic principle of dominance. In E. Engdahl & E. Ejerhed (Eds.), *Readings on unbounded dependencies in Scandinavian languages* (pp. 175–192). Stockholm: Almqvist & Wiksell.

Fillmore, C.J. (1968). The case for case. In E. Bach & R.T. Harms (Eds.), *Universals in linguistic theory* (pp. 1–90). New York: Holt, Rinehart Winston.

Gallistel, C.R., Brown, A.L., Carey, S., Gelman, R., & Keil, F. (1991). Lessons from animal learning for the study of cognitive development. In S. Carey & R. Gelman (Eds.), *The epigenesis of mind: Essays on biology and cognition* (pp. 1–36). Hillsdale, NJ: Lawrence Erlbaum Associates Inc.

Gonzalez, A. (1984). *Acquiring Pilipino as a first language: Two case studies*. Manila, Philippines: Linguistic Society of the Philippines.

Grimshaw, J. (1981). Form, function, and the language acquisition device. In C.L. Baker & J. McCarthy (Eds.), *The logical problem of language acquisition* (pp. 73–102). Cambridge, MA: MIT Press.

Harbert, W. (1995a). Binding theory, control, and pro. In G. Webelhuth (Ed.), *Government and binding theory and the minimalist program* (pp. 177–240). Oxford, UK: Blackwell.

Hyams, N. (1986). *Language acquisition and theory of parameters*. Dordrecht, The Netherlands: D. Reidel.

Imedadze, N., & Tuite, K. (1992). The acquisition of Georgian. In D.I. Slobin (Ed.), *The crosslinguistic study of language acquisition* (pp. 39–110). Hillsdale, NJ: Lawrence Erlbaum Associates Inc.

Karmiloff-Smith, A. (1992). *Beyond modularity: A developmental perspective on cognitive science*. Cambridge, MA: MIT Press.

Katis, D. (1984). *The acquisition of the modern Greek verb*. Unpublished doctoral dissertation, University of Reading.

Keil, F. (1981). Constraints on knowledge and cognitive development. *Psychology Review, 88*, 197–227.

Kuhl, P., & Miller, J.D. (1975). Speech perception by the chinchilla: Voice-voiceless distinction in alveolar plosive consonants. *Science, 190*, 69–72.

Kuno, S. (1988). *Functional syntax*. Chicago: University of Chicago Press.

Lachter, J., & Bever, T.G. (1989). The relation between linguistic structure and associative theories of language learning: A constructive critique of some connectionist learning models. In S. Pinker & J. Mehler (Eds.), *Connections and symbols* (pp. 195–248). Cambridge, MA: MIT Press, Bradford Books.

MacWhinney, B., & Chang, W. (1995). Connectionism and language learning. In C. Nelson (Ed.), *The Minnesota Symposia on child psychology: Vol. 28. Basic and applied perspectives on learning, cognition, and development* (pp. 33–59). Minneapolis, MN: The University of Minnesota Press.

Marantz, A. (1985). *Grammatical relations*. Cambridge, MA: MIT Press.

Maratsos, M. (1976). *The use of definite and indefinite reference in young children: An experimental study of semantic acquisition*. Cambridge, UK: Cambridge University Press.

Maratsos, M. (1982). The child's construction of grammatic categories. In E. Wanner & L. Gleitman (Eds.), *Language acquisition: The state of the art* (pp. 240–266). Cambridge, UK: Cambridge University Press.

Maratsos, M. (1989). Innateness and plasticity in language development. In M. Rice & R. Schiefelbusch (Eds.), *The teachability of language* (pp. 109–125). Baltimore: Brookes.

Maratsos, M. (1992). How the acquisition of nouns may be different from that of verbs. In N. Krasnegor, D. Rumbaugh, R. Schiefelbusch, M. Studdert-Kennedy (Eds.), *Biological and behavioral determinants of language development* (pp. 67–88). Hillsdale, NJ: Lawrence Erlbaum Associates Inc.

Maratsos, M., & Chalkley, M.A. (1980). The internal language of children's syntax. In K. Nelson (Ed.), *Children's language* (pp. 127–213). New York: Gardner.

McNeill, D. (1970). *The acquisition of language: The study of developmental psycholinguistics*. New York: Harper & Row.

Mills, A. (1985). The acquisition of German. In D. Slobin (Ed.), *The crosslinguistic study of language acquisition* (Vol. 1, pp. 157–196). Hillsdale, NJ: Lawrence Erlbaum Associates Inc.

Nelson, K. (1994). The dual category problem in the acquisition of action words. In M. Tomasello & B. Merriman (Eds.), *Beyond words for things: Young children's acquisition of verb meanings* (pp. 57–76). Hillsdale, NJ: Lawrence Erlbaum Associates Inc.

O'Grady, W. (1987). *Principles of grammar and learning.* Chicago: University of Chicago Press.

Pinker, S. (1984). *Language learnability and language development.* Cambridge, MA: Harvard University Press.

Pinker, S. (1987). The bootstrapping problem in language acquisition. In B. MacWhinney (Ed.), *Mechanisms of language acquisition* (pp. 399–441). Hillsdale, NJ: Lawrence Erlbaum Associates Inc.

Pinker, S. (1990). In D. Osherson & H. Lasnik (Eds.), *An invitation to cognitive science* (Vol. 1, pp. 199–243). Cambridge, MA: MIT Press.

Plunkett, K. (1995). Connectionist approaches to language acquisition. In P. Fletcher & B. MacWhinney (Eds.), *The handbook of child language* (pp. 36–72). Oxford, UK: Blackwell.

Rispoli, M. (1991). Mosaic theory of grammatical acquisition. *Journal of Child Language, 18,* 517–551.

Rizzi, L. (1982). *Issues in Italian syntax.* Dordrecht, The Netherlands: Foris.

Ross, J.R. (1967). *Constraints on variables in syntax.* Unpublished MIT dissertation.

Rumelhardt, D.E., & McClelland, J.L. (1986). On learning the past tense of English verbs. In J.L. McClelland, D.E. Rumelhardt, & the PDP Research Group (Eds.), *Parallel distributed processing: Explorations in the micro-structure of cognition: Vol. 2. Psychological and biological models* (pp. 173–209). Cambridge, MA: Bradford Books, MIT Press.

Schlesinger, I.M. (1971). The production of utterances and language acquisition. In D.I. Slobin (Ed.), *The crosslinguistic study of language acquisition* (Vol. 1, pp. 63–102). Hillsdale, NJ: Lawrence Erlbaum Associates Inc.

Schlesinger, I.M. (1982). *Steps to language.* Hillsdale, NJ: Lawrence Erlbaum Associates Inc.

Shaffer, D. (1996). *Developmental psychology: Childhood and adolescence.* Belmont, CA: Brooks & Cole.

Slobin, D.I. (Ed.). (1971). *The ontogenesis of grammar: A theoretical symposium.* New York: Academic Press.

Slobin, D.I. (1973). Cognitive prerequisites for the development of grammar. In C.A. Ferguson & D.I. Slobin (Eds.), *Studies of child language development* (pp. 175–276). New York: Holt, Rinehart & Winston.

Slobin, D.I. (1982). Universal and particular in the acquisition of language. In E. Wanner & L. Gleitman (Eds.), *Language development: The state of the art* (pp. 128–172). Cambridge, UK: Cambridge University Press.

Slobin, D.I. (1985a). Cross linguistic evidence for the language-making capacity. In D.I. Slobin (Ed.), *The crosslinguistic study of language acquisition* (Vol. 1, pp. 1157–1256). Hillsdale, NJ: Lawrence Erlbaum Associates Inc.

Slobin, D.I. (Ed.). (1985b). *The crosslinguistic study of language acquisition* (Vol. 1). Hillsdale, NJ: Lawrence Erlbaum Associates Inc.

Slobin, D.I. (Ed.). (1992a). *The crosslinguistic study of language acquisition* (Vol. 2). Hillsdale, NJ: Lawrence Erlbaum Associates Inc.

Slobin, D.I. (1992b). Introduction. In D.I. Slobin (Ed.), *The crosslinguistic study of language acquisition* (Vol. 2, pp. 1–14). Hillsdale, NJ: Lawrence Erlbaum Associates Inc.

Smoczynska, R. (1985). The acquisition of Polish. In D.I. Slobin (Ed.), *The crosslinguistic study of language acquisition* (Vol. 1, pp. 595–686). Hillsdale, NJ: Lawrence Erlbaum Associates Inc.

Stephany, U. (1995). *The acquisition of Greek.* Arbeitspapier No. 22. Institut fur Sprachwissenschaft, Univeritat zu Koln.

Tager-Flusberg, H. (1988). On the nature of a language acquisition disorder: The example of autism. In F. Kessel (Ed.), *The development of language and language researchers: Essays in honor of Roger Brown* (pp. 249–268). Hillsdale, NJ: Lawrence Erlbaum Associates Inc.

Talmy, L. (1985). Lexicalization patterns: Semantic structure in lexical forms. In T. Shopen (Ed.), *Language typology and syntactic description: Vol. 3. Grammatical categories and the lexicon* (pp. 215–227). Cambridge, UK: Cambridge University Press.

Tinbergen, N. (1951). *The study of instinct.* Oxford, UK: Clarendon Press.

Tomasello, M., & Merriman, B. (Eds.). (1994). *Beyond words for things: Young children's acquisition of verb meanings*. Hillsdale, NJ: Lawrence Erlbaum Associates Inc.

Van Hoek, K. (1995). Conceptual reference points: A cognitive grammar account of pronominal anaphora constraints. *Language, 71*, 310–340.

Walter, S. (1975). *Zur Entwicklung morphologischer Strukturen bei Kinder*. Heidelberg, Germany: Diplomarbeit.

Wanner, E., & Maratsos, M. (1978). An ATN approach to comprehension. In M. Halle, J. Bresnan, & G. Miller (Eds.), *Linguistic theory and psychological reality* (pp. 119–161). Cambridge, MA: MIT Press.

Webelhuth, G. (Ed.). (1995a). *Government and binding theory and the minimalist program*. Oxford, UK: Blackwell.

Webelhuth, G. (1995b). X-bar theory and case theory. In G. Webelhuth (Ed.), *Government and binding theory and the minimalist program* (pp. 17–96). Oxford, UK: Blackwell.

Weist, R.M. (1990). Neutralization and the concept of subject in Polish. *Linguistics, 28*, 1331–1351.

Wexler, K., & Mancini, M. (1987). Parameters and learnability in binding theory. In T. Roeper & E. Williams (Eds.), *Parameter-setting* (pp. 41–89). Dordrecht, The Netherlands: D. Reidel.

CHAPTER NINE

The development of conversational and discourse skills

Barbara A. Pan and Catherine E. Snow
Harvard Graduate School of Education, Cambridge, USA

It is somewhat striking that so much research effort and interest has been focused on trying to understand how children come to learn the sounds, words, and syntax necessary to produce sentences in their native language, given that very little real language use is confined to the sentence level. While it is well within the realm of possibility to programme a computer capable of producing thousands of phonologically and grammatically correct sentences, writing software to enable the computer to engage in unstructured conversation with a native speaker is a much more challenging task. It should perhaps not be surprising, then, that children do not master the skills required for extended conversations, let alone for extended discourse, in a matter of a few years. What are the skills required to engage in small talk, to relate an anecdote, to tell a joke, or to explain how to programme a VCR? How do children come to master those skills? These are abilities that are not explained by formal descriptions of syntax or lexicon, though they presuppose syntactic and lexical knowledge. Rather, they are part of the body of knowledge speakers of a particular speech community acquire about how to use language effectively to achieve communicative goals. As such, they depend on social, as well as cognitive and linguistic skills.

We begin by looking at face-to-face conversation, the first kind of extended discourse in which children engage. The demands of conversation are many: Children must develop control over turn-taking, learn to express their intents, provide the appropriate amount of information (and no more) for their listeners, respond appropriately and build on the conversational moves of their partners, and repair conversational breakdown when it occurs. In the first half of this chapter, we consider each of these demands of face-to-face conversation, concluding with a more challenging situation in which the child and her partner are

229

not face to face, and thus can rely less extensively on shared context. In the second half of the chapter, we move on to consider forms of extended discourse that require new cognitive and linguistic skills, and which children come to produce more autonomously with age.

DEVELOPMENT OF CONVERSATIONAL SKILLS

Turn-taking

At its most basic, conversation requires two participants, each of whom alternates assuming the roles of speaker and listener. Without some alternation of speaker-listener roles, or turn-taking, discourse would be monologic, rather than dialogic, or conversational.

Well before infants begin producing speech in the adult sense, they have rather extensive practice in turn-taking with an adult caregiver. Some researchers have suggested that the roots of turn-taking can be observed in the "gaze coupling" in which infants and their caregivers engage (Jaffe, Stern, & Perry, 1973). Others have noted that sequences of alternating action-inaction are typical of mother–infant interaction during feeding (Kaye, 1977). Patterns of verbal or vocal turn alternation in mother–child dyads are also observable from infancy. Snow (1977), for example, has described how mothers of infants as young as 3 months old treat their children as conversational partners, interpreting burps and vocalisations as child conversational turns:

Child:	[smiles]
Mother:	oh what a nice little smile!
Mother:	yes, isn't that nice?
Mother:	there.
Mother:	there's a nice little smile.
Child:	[burps]
Mother:	what a nice wind as well!
Mother:	yes, that's better, isn't it?
Mother:	yes.
Mother:	yes.
Child:	[vocalises]
Mother:	yes!
Mother:	there's a nice noise.

As infants get older, mothers adopt a stricter interpretation, acknowledging as turns only those child vocalisations that more closely resemble speech. Garvey (1984) has noted that in order to take their turn or pass it back when they don't know what to say, children often use fillers such as *hmm*, or repeat the adult question. Caregivers cooperate in maintaining the conversation by answering their own questions and speaking for the child when necessary (Martinez, 1987).

Turn alternation between mothers and infants is quite smooth, no doubt in part because adults rarely compete with young children for the floor. Within this kind of highly supportive interactional context, infants' turn-taking skills appear quite sophisticated. In conversations with peers and siblings, turn-taking tends not to proceed in such orderly fashion (Ervin-Tripp, 1974). Children's conversations are characterised by longer between-turn gaps and fewer anticipatory overlaps during which the listener chimes in to finish the speaker's thought (Garvey & Berninger, 1981). In addition, children's attempts to enter into conversation with peers are often unsuccessful, resulting in monologic rather than dialogic talk (Schober-Peterson & Johnson, 1991). Thus, interaction with peers, who are less competent and usually less cooperative partners than adults, requires use of more sophisticated conversational skills, such as knowing how and when to interrupt, how to remedy overlaps and interruptions by others, and how to make topic-relevant moves. By about age 4, children show some control over the use of devices like sentence-initial *and* or repetitive *et puis* (and then) as floor holders, signalling that their turn is not yet complete by initiating a new syntactic unit (Jisa, 1985; Peterson & McCabe, 1988). These skills are ones that children begin developing as preschoolers, but continue to work on at least through the early elementary school years.

Expressing intents

Above we noted that mothers of infants seem to structure conversation out of rather minimal production on the infant's part, attributing communicative intent to infant smiles and vocalisations. Although cooperative adults continue to carry the brunt of the conversational burden for quite some time, by 9–10 months of age infants have begun to produce what more objective observers agree is intentful communication. How can one tell that the child indeed intends to communicate, and furthermore, how does one know what the child's specific communicative intent is? Although it is difficult to say with certainty whether a child's vocalisation constitutes intentional communication, many researchers rely on accompanying child behaviours in assessing intentionality. One indication that the child intends to direct the caregiver's attention to an object is visual checking behaviour (looking back and forth between caregiver and the object). Another indication of purposeful communication is the child waiting for a response and persisting in repeating his attempt until the adult acknowledges or acts on it.

Of course, preverbal children's intents are interpretable only in rather global terms. It is often possible, for example, to deduce that the child is calling the adult's attention to himself, or directing the adult's attention to an object. It is much more difficult, if not impossible, to interpret more specific intents such as requests for object labels, or inquiries about a non-present object.

By drawing the adult's attention to an object and vocalising, children are engaging in rudimentary topic initiations; at this stage, topic elaboration is still in the adult's hands. Goldfield (1987, 1990) has shown that the way in which caregivers respond to child object-mediated topic nominations is reflected later in how children themselves initiate and extend topics. Children whose mothers reliably respond with object names come to rely themselves on naming as a conversational strategy. In contrast, children whose mothers tend to respond with expressions such as *nice* or *pretty* are later themselves more "expressive".

By their second birthday, most children express about a dozen different kinds of speech acts (Snow, Pan, Imbens-Bailey, & Herman, 1996). These include requests for action (*catch!*), refusals and agreements to comply with the requests of others (*no*; *okay*), statements of proposition (*that a flower*), and statements of intent (*I sit here*), as well as answers to yes/no and wh- questions posed by others. Most of these speech acts occur in the context of negotiating an ongoing activity or discussing an object in the immediate environment. With age, children not only learn to express other speech acts (e.g. promises, threats), but also to engage in negotiations and discussions about the non-present. These communicative activities involve use of what has been called *decontextualised* language, language that is not tied to the here and now. Increasing participation in discussion of non-present topics provides a crucial context for acquiring control over linguistic structures such as past tense and future aspect.

Conversational maxims

Simply alternating verbal turns, of course, does not constitute conversation. Each speaker's utterances must be related not only temporally, but also substantively, to those of the other speaker. Adults' failure to abide by the conversational maxim of relevance is likely to be interpreted as indicative of extreme rudeness or mental incompetence. Other obligations incumbent upon conversational participants, according to Grice (1975), are the requirements to be truthful, informative, and clear. With the possible exception of truthfulness, children are generally accorded greater latitude than adults in adhering to these conversational maxims. Being informative, for example, means providing sufficient information to meet one's listener's needs, without offering superfluous information. In order to gauge the level of specificity required, the speaker must accurately assess the listener's state of knowledge, taking into account general world knowledge, as well as specific knowledge shared by the two participants. Children are somewhat handicapped in making this kind of calibration both by their own limited world knowledge, as well as by the challenge of appreciating that other people's thoughts and knowledge differ from their own. Failure to provide sufficient information is often remedied in conversation by clarification exchanges, usually initiated by children's adult partners. As we will see later, the extent to which children rely on adults to monitor information level becomes more apparent when one observes their attempts at producing extended discourse independently.

Responding to others' initiations

Some conversational initiations require closure from the other speaker. Requests by one speaker, for example, generally call for a response—agreement, refusal, countersuggestion, or excuse—by the other speaker. Failure to respond to a greeting is considered a social slight. Likewise, non-rhetorical questions posed by one speaker in adult–adult conversation require a response by the other speaker. Despite children's precocity in smooth turn alternation, they initially often fail to uphold their part of the conversational bargain. Our ongoing study of conversational development shows that at 20 months, for example, children answer or acknowledge only a third of the questions posed by their caregivers. By ages 29–36 months, the proportion of appropriate responses to maternal questions has increased to 56.7% (Olsen-Fulero & Conforti, 1983). Children's much lower response to declarative statements by the mother (16.7%) indicates that they understand something of the conversational obligation imposed by questions. Further evidence of this rudimentary understanding is the fact that children in the Olsen-Fulero study were more likely to respond to some kinds of questions, such as repair questions, than to tag questions that are essentially comments (e.g. *That's too many people in there, isn't it?*).

Topic continuation

The conversational moves of 2-year-olds tend to be either initiations that require a response from the other speaker, or responses to the speaker's move. "Turnabouts", in which a speaker both responds to and requires a response from the other speaker, are rare in young children's speech, but very frequent in adult speech to children (Kaye & Charney, 1980, 1981). Adults' turnabouts in conversation with children not only demonstrate the adult's attentiveness to the child's utterance, but also serve to maintain and elaborate the topic. Much of the apparent continuity of topic observed in adult–child conversation can be traced to the support provided by the adult.

When interacting with peers, children often either fail to maintain a topic (Blank & Franklin, 1980) or use relatively primitive devices such as exact or partial imitation to do so (Keenan & Klein, 1975). Garvey (1975) showed that dyads up to age 5 used sound play, as well as repetition and ritualised variations on each others' utterances, to generate conversational cohesion. McTear (1985, pp. 151–152) reports a conversation between two 4-year-olds to illustrate a similar phenomenon that he calls "dialogue play":

Heather:	horrible smell.
	it's not my shoes.
Siobhan:	it's not my shoes.
Heather:	it's not my shoes.
Siobhan:	uh?

Heather:	it's not my shoes.
	it's
Siobhan:	it's not my sandals.
Heather:	they're not my sandals.
Siobhan:	it's not my bottle.
Heather:	it's not my bottle. (both laugh) . . .

This exchange goes on for some time, with each girl taking more than 20 turns at filling the semantic slot in the frame *it's not my . . .*

From age 2 to 5, children come to rely less on sound play, immediate repetition, and recasts of the other's utterance to create and maintain conversational cohesion (Benoit, 1982), though these kinds of interactions continue to figure prominently even in the conversation of elementary school children (Dorval & Eckerman, 1984). In a study of age differences in conversational skill, Dorval and Eckerman found that second graders produced more unrelated conversational turns than older children or adults, and that the second graders' contributions were often related to peers' non-verbal actions, rather than to what was said. Fifth and ninth graders, in contrast, produced a substantial proportion of factually related turns, and frequently engaged in trading personal narratives (e.g. each speaker saying what they had done over the weekend). Conversations among 12th graders and adults increasingly incorporated turns that took into account the perspective of the participants (e.g. comparing attitudes, offering supporting evidence for one's opinion). Linguistic devices such as conjuncts (*for example*, *so*, *anyway*) and "attitudinal" expressions (*really*, *perhaps*) gradually come to be used by children to create cohesion, though even 12-year-olds do not yet employ them with adult-like frequency (Scott, 1984). The development of control over cohesive devices is important not only for maintaining conversation, but also for the independent production of coherent narratives, as we will see later.

A number of researchers have investigated individual differences in children's conversational skills by having children role-play the host of a talk show. In this paradigm, first used by Donahue, Pearl, and Bryan (1980), the child subject is told that he or she is to interview a guest, as if for a television show like Phil Donahue's or Geraldo's. Donahue et al. observed child pairs, but Schley and Snow (1992) used an adult interviewee who was instructed to be politely responsive but not helpful in keeping the conversation going—i.e. to answer questions but not to elaborate on responses. This task is a particularly challenging one for children, precisely because there is no predetermined topic or other task on which the conversational partners are focused. In fact, some children aged 7 to 12 simply could not keep going for the four minutes requested, and adult experimenters could not resist the temptation to help out by asking questions, despite their instructions and training to the contrary. Schley and Snow (1992) found that children who were rated higher as conversational partners in the talk-show task (1) used open-ended questions and questions contingent upon previous utterances, (2) avoided long lapses in conversation, and (3) successfully elicited elaborated responses from their adult partner. Conversational skill was not related, however, to dysfluencies like word choice and grammatical self-corrections, repetitions, interruptions, or vocal hesitations, even though half the children tested were non-native speakers of English with less than native-like oral skills.

Conversational repair

Young children have difficulty understanding much of the speech addressed to them; likewise, their own speech is often unintelligible to their adult conversational partners. Thus, one might expect discussion about unclear utterances to be a frequent activity among adult–child dyads from very early on. On the other hand, the topic of conversation in clarification exchanges is language itself, a topic that cannot be nominated indexically (i.e. by pointing). On these grounds, one might expect clarification exchanges, like other discussions of the non-present, to be later-emerging activities. Examination of interaction between parents and their 14- and 20-month-old children shows that only about two-thirds of parents attempt to discuss verbal clarification with 14-month-olds, despite the very high incidence of unintelligible child talk. Such discussions are much more likely six months later, even though the incidence of unintelligible child utterances has decreased substantially. On the other hand, most parents do attempt to engage children in clarification discussions earlier than they do in other discussions of non-present topics (Pan, Imbens-Bailey, Winner, & Snow 1996; Snow et al., 1996). Thus, parents seem to be responding to their children's increased language sophistication by holding children more accountable for their utterances, and creating contexts in which children have to reflect on language and respond to adult clarification requests.

Requests for clarification posed by adults and children can take several forms. Gallagher (1981) found that with 2-year-olds, adults' most frequent clarification requests were confirmation requests in which adults repeated part or all of the child utterance, using rising intonation. Less common were non-specific requests for repetition (e.g. *what?*, *huh?*) and requests for clarification of specific parts of the message, e.g.

Child: I got fire engine.
Adult: you got what?

The 2-year-olds Gallagher studied were able to respond to requests for confirmation, and tended to do so in the affirmative, e.g.

Child: build something.
Adult: build something?
Child: yeah.

Although only some 2-year-olds were able to respond appropriately to requests for clarification of specific parts of the message, Gallagher's study indicates that even very young children are able to distinguish among different types of clarification requests and respond differentially. These abilities were confirmed in a larger study of children aged 20 to 42 months by Anselmi, Tomasello, and Acunzo (1986), who found that children responded appropriately to adult queries about 85% of the time and were able to differentiate between general and specific queries.

With very young children, most parental requests for clarification focus on remedying unintelligible child utterances. Occasionally, however, clarification requests are used instead to challenge the child's meaning, e.g.

Child: no!
Adult: no?
Child: no.
Adult: yeah.

For their part, children sometimes adopt strategies other than exact repetition, such as revision or elaboration, in responding to non-specific clarification requests (Gallagher, 1981), as in the following exchange between a 32-month-old and his mother:

Child: how they go here?
Adult: hmm?
Child: how they get here?[1]

This kind of experimentation with linguistic forms may reflect children's rudimentary appreciation of the fact that message transmission can fail for more than one reason (McTear, 1985).

Requests for clarification initiated by children themselves are occasionally observed as young as 18 months (Johnson, 1980), though they remain less frequent than adult-initiated requests at least through age 3 (Gallagher, 1981; Ninio & Snow, 1996). During this period, children's clarification requests consist primarily of *huh?*, *what?*, or repetition of some part of the preceding adult utterance, typically the final stressed word. In interaction with peers, as well, young children rarely request clarification (McTear, 1985) and tend to favour non-specific clarification forms (Garvey, 1977).

Referential communication

Much of what we know about young children's ability to convey and understand verbal information, and to deal with communication breakdown, is based on observations of naturally occurring conversations between children and their

---

[1] This example was taken from the New England corpus in the CHILDES Database; see Pan, Imbens-Bailey, Winner, and Snow (1996).

adult or peer interlocutors. Other information comes from research in which children's conversational performance is examined in the context of more structured tasks, called *referential communication* tasks. In this research paradigm, the speaker knows something that needs to be conveyed to a listener. Conversational partners are usually seated on opposite sides of a screen (so that the information to be conveyed is not visually available to the listener), or are talking by telephone. Often the task requires the child in the role of speaker to describe one item from an array of similar items (which differ on features such as colour or size) so that the listener can identify the specified object from an identical array. Alternatively, the speaker may be asked to give route directions in such a way that the listener can navigate his or her way from one location to another on a pictorial map.

Children reveal remarkable and persistent inadequacies in this kind of task throughout most of elementary school. In one study of 7-year-old, 10-year-old, and adult dyads conveying and receiving route information by telephone, Lloyd (1991, 1992) found that not only were many of the messages produced by younger speakers inadequate, such messages frequently went unchallenged by younger listeners. On those occasions when child listeners did detect ambiguity, older children tended to produce more specific clarification requests (e.g. *which one?*), while younger children tended to use simple requests for repetition (*what?*) or solicit confirmation by repeating part of the utterance themselves. In a subsequent study designed to probe the referential communication skills of English and Italian children in this age range, Lloyd, Camaioni, and Ercolani (1995) found that children performed better as speakers than as listeners. Though all children performed quite successfully when presented with unambiguous messages, less than 10% of 6-year-olds and only 20% of 9-year-olds were consistently able to detect message ambiguity without help. These limitations in listening skills may be problematic in one-to-many settings such as classrooms, where children need to monitor their own comprehension and request clarification when necessary messages are ambiguous.

DEVELOPMENT OF DISCOURSE SKILLS

We have seen how children become better conversationalists over the course of development. In addition, they become better autonomous producers of extended discourse. In order to be able to tell stories, make arguments, give explanations, provide definitions, or tell jokes, children need a number of new cognitive and linguistic skills: (1) they must be able to take the listener's perspective into account; (2) they must be able to express their own perspective; (3) they must be able to take and signal alternative stances towards the information to be conveyed; and (4) they must master the conventions of different genres of discourse. We will discuss each of these in turn.

Taking a listener's perspective

There are a number of linguistic indicators that a speaker is taking the listener's perspective into account. Clearly, manipulating deictic terms like *this, that, come, go, you*, and *I* correctly requires differentiating the speaker's from the listener's perspective. A second indicator is the choice between definite and indefinite articles. In English and many other languages, mature speakers generally use indefinite articles such as *a/an* to introduce new referents in discourse and definite articles such as *the*, pronouns, or zero elements to maintain reference thereafter. However, there are many contexts in which definite articles are appropriate for first mention of a referent. For example, one uses definite reference for first mention of a referent that is unambiguous or known to be identifiable by the listener, e.g. *the state capital* or *the movie we saw last night*. Although children by age 5 are able to use definite and indefinite articles to distinguish between new and given information in situations where the information is physically present and visible to their partners (MacWhinney & Bates, 1978), they do not consistently use indefinite articles to introduce referents not visible or known to their listeners until about age 9 (Kail & Hickmann, 1992; Warden, 1981).

The understanding that is required for correct use of definite reference is probably similar to that needed to adequately estimate the listener's need for background information during story telling or referential communication tasks. For example, although 3- and 4-year-olds make some adjustments in the amount of information and referent specificity they provide for naive vs. knowledgeable listeners (Menig-Peterson, 1975; Perner & Leekam, 1986; Sonnenschein, 1986, 1988), they do not consistently exercise control over the relevant linguistic means until some years later (Peterson, 1993). When talking to a strange adult, children as young as 4 will explain the referents of proper nouns, both toy names (*and he came in with a Power Ranger—that's a kind of really neat toy . . .*) and names of people (*and then Sally—she's a kid in my day care . . .*) (Sachs, Anselmi, & McMollam, 1990). However, coordinating provision of information with other communicative and linguistic demands can be very difficult, as illustrated by the following less-than-comprehensible toddler narrative (Peterson & Dodsworth, 1991, pp. 411–412):

Adult:	can you tell me about the barbecue that you had?
Child:	we had a barbecue right over here and I told him to don't put it . . .
Child:	I told Dan what he was doing.
Child:	and . . .
Adult:	you told Dan what he was doing?
Child:	yeah.
Child:	and when I was doing it I turned, pushed him, what I do pushed way up high.
Adult:	you pushed him way up high.
Child:	yes.

Child: but he turned to go.
Adult: but he what?
Child: he turned to go on me.
Child: he didn't come to my house.

Before about age 9, children often produce this type of ambiguous or erroneous reference—nouns that do not match up with subsequent pronouns, or new referents introduced in pronominal rather than nominal form. Referential communication tasks such as those described earlier also reveal persistent deficiencies in the information provided by children under age 10 in their descriptions for a distant listener (Lloyd, 1991).

A third domain in which speakers can signal the adoption of the listener's perspective has to do with acknowledging the listener's likely interpretation or evaluation of an event. A straightforward example is avoidance of vulgar language with certain audiences. More subtle examples include explicitly acknowledging the listener's perspective in arguments, or anticipating the listener's likely response to a request or interpretation of a story or joke. This aspect of taking the listener's perspective is closely related to politeness as conceptualised by Brown and Levinson (1987). Children as young as 3 make some listener-oriented anticipatory adjustments in their request forms, using *please* at greater rates with older and less familiar addressees (Bates, 1976), and 5-year-olds differentiate their responses lexically when asked to produce "nice" versus "bossy" requests (e.g. *please* versus *right now*), whereas 10-year-olds also differentiate these two types of request syntactically (*would you mind* versus *give me*) (Becker, 1986). Other markers indicating anticipation of the listeners' perspective, e.g. selection of address terms as a function of age and status, have not been studied developmentally.

Expressing one's own perspective

It may not be obvious that children need to learn to express their own perspectives—in fact, it might seem that they do so with considerable vigour from quite a young age. Difficulties arise, though, when the child's perspective needs to be articulated in combination with other information, e.g. when the child needs to express a perspective on who was the perpetrator and who the innocent victim in a narrative of a playground transgression, or to indicate what she or he believes in a retelling of an event. The development of the capacity to express one's own perspective has been almost exclusively studied in the domain of narrative, where expression of the narrator's perspective is referred to as *evaluation*. The category of evaluation has been very broadly interpreted within narrative analysis, to include such relatively easy forms as stress, exclamation, repetition, onomatopoeia, and emphatic forms like *very*. More sophisticated evaluative elements include hedges, adverbials like *evidently*, and unusual syntactic structures like left-dislocation (*it was the boy who hit the floor*). Even relatively young narrators use evaluation in personal experience narratives—the 4-year-olds in Peterson and McCabe, 1983, used evaluation in about 13% of their clauses, though they produced, for example, more repetition and fewer inferences than older children, and fewer different sorts of evaluative devices. In retelling a story from a picture book, children did not produce much evaluation until about age 9 (Berman & Slobin, 1994), and even some 9-year-olds focused on the facts rather than the elaboration of those facts. Bamberg (1994) points out that German children telling a story from a picture book use evaluation locally until about age 9, when they start to evince the capacity to express linguistically their perspective on how units of the narrative relate to one another.

One explanation for the relatively late appearance of evaluation in some narrative types has to do with displacement of the narrative perspective from the child's natural perspective. A personal event narrative about a happening in which the narrator was also the main protagonist is easier to evaluate than a personal event narrative in which the narrator was a minor character. In the latter, the child must shift between two stances towards the events, her own and the protagonist's. Evaluating a fictional narrative, like the frog story picture books, requires overcoming even more displacement (Bamberg & Damrad-Frye, 1991).

Taking alternative stances

By taking alternative stances, we mean indicating whether the information being conveyed is meant to be interpreted literally or not, e.g. signalling that one is entering a fantasy world by saying *Let's pretend*, or that one is being ironic or sarcastic by using a certain tone of voice. In the following example, 32-month-old Lindsay and her mother are carrying on a make-believe conversation between two puppets.

Mother:	you want cookies?
Lindsay:	yeah.
Mother:	I don't have any.
Lindsay:	what?
Mother:	I don't have any, Cookie Monster.
Lindsay:	why?
Mother:	I don't know. I must have eaten them all.
Lindsay:	no-o-o!
Mother:	yes I did.
Mother:	I ate them for lunch.
Lindsay:	no, not for lunch for dinner.
Mother:	I ate them for dinner.
Lindsay:	for lunch.
Mother:	and lunch . . . and breakfast.[2]

---

[2] This example was taken from the New England corpus in the CHILDES Database; see Pan, Imbens-Bailey, Winner, and Snow (1996).

Lindsay is able to participate in this fantasy, though in a somewhat rudimentary fashion—she does not initiate the fantasy nor indicate linguistically that she is engaging in fantasy talk. Unlike her mother, she is not yet able to include stylistic components such as falsetto voice to mark shifts in role, or to move the puppet's mouth as she speaks.

By the late preschool years, children not only initiate fantasy autonomously, but also use a variety of means, both linguistic (person, tense, and type of verb) and non-linguistic (gaze, posture, position, intonation) to signal shifts between real-world and fantasy-world talk (Wolf, Moreton, & Camp, 1994). Still later, children learn to signal shifts among genres within fantasy play as well. Hoyle (1994), for example, illustrates how children of 8 or 9 use discourse markers such as *well*, *now*, and *okay* to mark shifts between pretend face-to-face interviews and pretend sportscasting.

A slightly different kind of stance is required in talking about hypothetical, or counterfactual, events. Here the challenge is not to describe purely fantastical events or to assume imaginary roles, but to reflect on a set of possible but not realised events. As with fantasy talk, children's earliest forays into hypothetical discussions are usually initiated by adults, and their own contributions often lack the linguistic markers (conditional *if*, modal auxiliaries, and appropriate tense) used by mature speakers (Kuczaj & Daly, 1979). Even in Spanish, where the subjunctive mood used for marking *irrealis* clauses is extremely frequent, and children use it contrastively by about age 3 in some contexts (Lopez-Ornat, 1994), they do not demonstrate complete control over it until much later (Floyd, 1990), perhaps in part because of the shift in perspective it requires. By the late preschool years, English-speaking children are able to make predictions about possible events (*who do you think would win if they fight?*), as well as reflect on counterfactual situations, as does 5-year-old Adam:

Child: Mummy, only if the refrigerator was out there I could show them how this [magnet] can stick to it.[3]

Through much of elementary school, however, children still have some difficulty in maintaining proper verb tense and mood in extended discourse on hypothetical topics, especially when those events are hypothetical events in the past, rather than potential events in the future (Kuczaj & Daly, 1979).

One non-literal stance that children demonstrate from a very early age involves the use of metaphor. Although some metaphoric renamings produced by young children are perhaps more accurately described as misnamings, or word overextensions, other instances clearly are intentional comments on the similarity of two objects, as when a child calls the wastebasket on his foot a boot

---

[3] This example was drawn from transcripts collected by the Home-School Study of Language and Literacy Development, Harvard Graduate School of Education; see Snow (1991).

(Winner, 1988). Such metaphoric renamings are common in the context of pretend play in the preschool years, and tend to decrease in frequency as children get older. In the school years, children develop the linguistic means to engage in more extended analogies and to use figurative speech in service of other goals, such as providing explanations. Winner gives the example of a 7-year-old who explains that tree roots are like wires because "wires store electricity and let electricity run through them, just like roots which let rain water run through them" (Winner, 1988, p. 108). At the same time, children are also developing the ability to adopt a hyper-literal stance, as evidenced by their appreciation of certain kinds of verbal humour (*Do you know what time it is? Yes*).

Mastering different genres

Genre refers to an organisational structure for information. It is a term borrowed from literary analysis and is used in the study of language development to distinguish, for example, scripts, personal experience stories, and fictional stories in terms of their distinctive content, organisation, and linguistic features (Hudson & Shapiro, 1991).

Scripts are generalised representations of recurrent events, e.g. a recounting of what happens when one goes to a restaurant or when one takes an aeroplane trip. Sometimes narrators include a specific event as illustration, or to contrast with the general event. Very young children can verbally report what happens in familiar events, though in the beginning they require considerable help from adults. Consider the following exchange in which 20-month-old Rachel, with her mother's help, describes what happens in football games:

Rachel:	ball.
Mother:	that's a football ball?
Rachel:	yes.
Mother:	yeah.
Rachel:	people play. [unintelligible] on the tv [unintelligible].
Mother:	people play football on the tv? did you see football on tv Rachel?
Rachel:	yes.
Mother:	what do they do?
Rachel:	play with ball.
Mother:	do they run?
Rachel:	yes.
Mother:	and then what happens?
Rachel:	fell down. (falls down on floor to demonstrate)[4]

With age, children learn to produce scripts more autonomously, and their scripts come to include the features specific to the genre, including timeless

---

[4] This example was taken from the New England corpus in the CHILDES Database; see Pan, Imbens-Bailey, Winner, and Snow (1996).

present tense, the general pronoun *you*, and a timeline that follows real-event chronology (Wolf, Moreton, & Camp, 1994, pp. 292–293):

Adult:	tell me about what happens when you go out on the playground.
Child:	about my school? where I go, the Harrington?
Adult:	yeah, about your school.
Child:	okay . . . when you're all done with recess you go outside to the playground and you can play in the field or on the swings or the jungle gym.
Adult:	what? the what?
Child:	you know, the climbing thing, the jungle gym.
Adult:	oh, okay, the jungle gym.
Child:	ya, then you stay out there until Bissie . . . your teacher . . . rings the bell and says "Everyone to come in".

In contrast to scripts, personal narratives relate a specific rather than a generalised event, although general event knowledge may be presented as background information. The events are usually narrated using past rather than present tense and first person *I*, and typically include orientation (background/setting), complicating actions, a high point (marked by evaluation), and a resolution. Young children's personal narratives that occur spontaneously in conversation are usually more sophisticated than those they produce in response to elicitation in more formal contexts. By age 3, many children produce relatively autonomous, if sketchy, personal stories. Developmental improvements in the later preschool years include provision of a story resolution, and increases in the amount and variety of orientation information and evaluation provided. Five-year-old Evan, for example, dramatically re-enacts fear by means of pretend screaming and stuttering:

Evan:	like um, like um, like um, like um I was dreaming about a tyrannosaurus rex and he saw me and he came after me.
Mother:	yeah?
Evan:	and went and didn't pick me up.
Mother:	oh.
Evan:	that like [screams].
Evan:	I said, "wh- wh- wh- wh- wh- where were we?"[5]

A third genre that children begin to develop control over in the preschool years is fictitious stories. Fictitious stories include initiating events, a problem to be solved, and a resolution. They generally employ past tense and may have stylised beginnings and endings such as *Once upon a time . . .* or *. . . and they*

---

[5] This example was drawn from transcripts collected by the Home-School Study of Language and Literacy Development, Harvard Graduate School of Education; see Snow (1991).

lived happily ever after. Potential sources for fictitious stories include general event knowledge, other stories, and real or imagined personal experience. Pretend play, in which children manipulate play objects and generate plot lines as they go along, and the recollection of dreams provide the context for many child fictitious narratives. With age, children's stories become more complex in content, incorporating sub-plots and psychological elements such as motivation and interpersonal relations, as in Michelle's narration of a scary dream:

Michelle:	it was about when we, when my, when my mother had to go to the grocery store, me and [brother] went with her and then there was um, and then there was some people talking about police that were coming to put people in jail because we didn't, it was all for no reason 'cause we didn't do nothing.
Adult:	and then what'd you do?
Michelle:	and then we had to run, and there was a, and there was a ocean, and we, and we, we didn't know what to do, and we, and so we had to jump in the ocean.
Adult:	and then what happened?
Michelle:	and then we had, and then my mommy and daddy was drowning and me and [brother] had to go under the water to get 'em.
Adult:	oh!
Michelle:	because they didn't know how to swim.
Adult:	did it, did it end up okay?
Michelle:	and then we got out and we went up and we said was they gonna put us in jail.
Michelle:	only the rest of the people.
Adult:	oh my goodness that was a scary dream.[6]

Children's notions of what is required in different genres is highly dependent on their culture. Hicks (1991) compares the performance of two first-grade girls, one an Afro-American and the other a white middle-class American, on three narrative tasks (an eventcast, a news report, and a fictional story). Both girls varied their narratives for the three genres, but in different ways. The Afro-American child organised her eventcast and news report around themes, rather than around temporal sequencing of real events, and included fewer details and much more evaluation in these two genres than did the white middle-class child.

Genres are not limited to narrative sub-types. Non-narrative genres include explanations, definitions, and arguments, as well as some highly stylised genres of mutual insults that have been described among youth groups. Each of these forms has its own structure, and rarely are these structures explicitly taught to children. Not only must children learn how the various genres are organised, but

---

[6] This example was drawn from transcripts collected by the Home-School Study of Language and Literacy Development, Harvard Graduate School of Education; see Snow (1991).

also when each is appropriate—it would be a serious mistake to respond to a teacher's compliment as if it were a ritual insult.

The Aristotelian definition is a genre which has been studied extensively because of its demonstrated relationship to children's school achievement (Litowitz, 1977; Snow, 1990; Watson, 1985). Very young children, when asked for word meanings, are likely to give extrageneric responses, e.g. in the following the 5-year-old offers a narrative to explain the meaning of *cat* rather than a definition. (Watson, 1985, p. 182)

We have a cat named Fluffy and you know what? Fluffy had babies under my bed.

Even with children this young, though, targeted questioning can elicit a superordinate, one of the hallmarks of a formal definition (Watson & Olson, 1987):

Adult: But what *is* a cat?
Child: A cat is an animal.

After children have mastered the basic form of a definition (superordinate term and restrictive relative clause), they still need to acquire an extensive vocabulary of precise superordinates (e.g. *mammal*, *utensil*, *vehicle*) in order to produce sophisticated definitions. They also need to learn how to analyse their knowledge about a word to determine which bits of information are most characteristic, and thus most informative if included in a restrictive relative clause. The following examples of definitions offered by 8-year-olds show how children often underspecify their restrictions:

a hat is something you wear.
a diamond is a rock that is worth a lot of money.
a donkey is an animal that has brown skin and is not very tall.
a knife is something you cut with.[7]

Clearly, these children have control over the syntactic structures needed for formal definitions, but have not adequately analysed their knowledge to identify the information that would properly specify the target word.

CONCLUSION

Conversation and discourse are domains in which development continues well into adulthood, and indeed some adults remain remarkably unskilled throughout their lives. Thus, we have only been able to sketch the emergence and early

---

[7] This example was drawn from transcripts collected by the Home-School Study of Language and Literacy Development, Harvard Graduate School of Education; see Snow (1991).

development of these skills, and we note enormous lacunae in our research-based knowledge of their later development.

We have argued that extended discourse—the maintenance of a topic over several utterances—has two forms, conversational and monologic. Children's abilities to produce extended discourse autonomously emerge after and from their participation in multi-party extended discourse—we see dialogue as the cradle of monologue. Children's early participation in conversation is successful because they enjoy the indulgence of their conversational partners, who offer them many questions and other opportunities to respond, who favour topics of interest to them, and who protect their right to speak. Children's early production of extended discourse is equally supported by adult willingness to interpret unclear utterances, to pose clarification questions, to supply needed background information, and to resonate to children's evaluations.

We have seen as well that children's skills in conversation and producing autonomous extended discourse depend on their understanding of perspective, their own and the listener's, and of how to represent objects, events, and perspectives linguistically. Furthermore, children must learn to differentiate a variety of linguistic stances, genres, and communicative tasks—knowing when literal or non-literal responses are required, knowing whether a narrative or an explanation is called for, knowing whether they are meant to take a brief conversational turn or hold the floor.

A child telling an anecdote during a family dinner table conversation must seize a turn, insert the story into the ongoing conversation in a topic-related way, produce a clear and linguistically coherent account of the events, evaluate those events, and provide a perspective from which to understand the story—all at the same time. Thus, the task of participating appropriately in conversation or of producing effective extended discourse requires the simultaneous, on-line processing of several kinds of information and poses a wide array of cognitive and linguistic challenges.

REFERENCES

Anselmi, D., Tomasello, M., & Acunzo, M. (1986). Young children's responses to neutral and specific contingent queries. *Journal of Child Language, 13*, 135–144.

Bamberg, M. (1994). Development of linguistic forms: German. In R. Berman & D.I. Slobin (Eds.), *Relating events in narrative: A crosslinguistic developmental study* (pp. 189–238). Hillsdale, NJ: Lawrence Erlbaum Associates Inc.

Bamberg, M., & Damrad-Frye, R. (1991). On the ability to provide evaluative comments: Further explorations of children's narrative competencies. *Journal of Child Language, 18*, 689–710.

Bates, E. (1976). *Language and context: The development of pragmatics.* New York: Academic Press.

Becker, J. (1986). Bossy and nice requests: Children's production and interpretation. *Merrill-Palmer Quarterly, 32*, 393–413.

Benoit, P. (1982). Formal coherence production in children's discourse. *First Language, 3*, 161–180.

Berman, R., & Slobin, D.I. (1994). *Relating events in narrative: A crosslinguistic developmental study*. Hillsdale, NJ: Lawrence Erlbaum Associates Inc.

Blank, M., & Franklin, E. (1980). Dialogue with preschoolers—a cognitively-based system of assessment. *Applied Psycholinguistics, 1*, 127–150.

Brown, P., & Levinson, S. (1987). *Politeness: Some universals in language usage*. Cambridge, UK: Cambridge University Press.

Donahue, M., Pearl, R., & Bryan, T. (1980). Conversational competence in learning disabled children: Responses to inadequate messages. *Applied Psycholinguistics, 1*, 387–403.

Dorval, B., & Eckerman, C. (1984). Developmental trends in the quality of conversation achieved by small groups of acquainted peers. *Monograph of the Society for Research in Child Development, 49*(2).

Ervin-Tripp, S. (1974). Children's verbal turn-taking. In E. Ochs & B. Schieffelin (Eds.), *Developmental pragmatics* (pp. 391–414). New York, NY: Academic Press.

Floyd, M. (1990). Development of subjunctive mood in children's Spanish: A review. *Confluencia, 5*, 93–104.

Gallagher, T. (1981). Contingent query sequences within adult-child discourse. *Journal of Child Language, 8*, 51–62.

Garvey, C. (1975). Requests and responses in children's speech. *Journal of Child Language, 2*, 41–63.

Garvey, C. (1977). The contingent query: A dependent act in conversation. In M. Lewis & L. Rosenblum (Eds.), *The origins of behavior: Vol. V. Interaction, conversation, and the development of language* (pp. 63–94). New York: Wiley.

Garvey, C. (1984). *Children's talk*. Cambridge, MA: Harvard University Press.

Garvey, C., & Berninger, G. (1981). Timing and turn taking in children's conversations. *Discourse Processes, 4*, 27–57.

Goldfield, B. (1987). The contributions of child and caregiver to referential and expressive language. *Applied Psycholinguistics, 8*, 267–280.

Goldfield, B. (1990). Pointing, naming, and talk about objects: Referential behavior in children and mothers. *First Language, 10*, 231–242.

Grice, H.P. (1975). Logic and conversation. In P. Cole & J.L. Morgan (Eds.), *Syntax and semantics: Vol. 3. Speech acts* (pp. 41–58). New York: Academic Press.

Hicks, D. (1991). Kinds of narrative: Genre skills among first graders from two communities. In A. McCabe & C. Peterson (Eds.), *Developing narrative structure* (pp. 55–88). Hillsdale, NJ: Lawrence Erlbaum Associates Inc.

Hoyle, S. (1994). Children's use of discourse markers in the creation of imaginary participation frameworks. *Discourse Processes, 17*, 447–464.

Hudson, J., & Shapiro, L. (1991). From knowing to telling: The development of children's scripts, stories, and personal narratives. In A. McCabe & C. Peterson (Eds.), *Developing narrative structure* (pp. 89–136). Hillsdale, NJ: Lawrence Erlbaum Associates Inc.

Jaffe, J., Stern, D., & Perry, C. (1973). "Conversational" coupling of gaze behavior in prelinguistic human development. *Journal of Psycholinguistic Research, 2*, 321–330.

Jisa, H. (1985). French preschoolers' use of *et puis* (*and then*). *First Language, 5*, 169–184.

Johnson, C.E. (1980). Contingent queries: The first chapter. In H. Giles, W. Robinson, & P. Smith (Eds.), *Language: Social psychological perspectives* (pp. 11–19). Oxford, UK: Pergamon.

Kail, M., & Hickmann, M. (1992). Children's ability to introduce referents. *First Language, 12*, 73–94.

Kaye, K. (1977). Towards the origin of dialogue. In H.R. Schaffer (Ed.), *Studies in mother-infant interaction* (pp. 89–117). New York: Academic Press.

Kaye, K., & Charney, R. (1980). How mothers maintain "dialogue" with two-year-olds. In D. Olsen (Ed.), *The social foundations of language and thought: Essays in honor of Jerome S. Bruner* (pp. 211–230). New York: Norton.

Kaye, K., & Charney, R. (1981). Conversational asymmetry between mothers and children. *Journal of Child Language, 8*, 35–50.

Keenan, E., & Klein, E. (1975). Coherence in children's discourse. *Journal of Psycholinguistic Research, 4*, 365–378.

Kuczaj, S., & Daly, M. (1979). The development of hypothetical reference in the speech of young children. *Journal of Child Language, 6*, 563–579.

Litowitz, B. (1977). Learning to make definitions. *Journal of Child Language, 4*, 289–304.

Lloyd, P. (1991). Strategies used to communicate route directions by telephone: A comparison of the performance of 7-year-olds, 10-year-olds, and adults. *Journal of Child Language, 18*, 171–190.

Lloyd, P. (1992). The role of clarification requests in children's communication of route directions by telephone. *Discourse Processes, 15*, 357–374.

Lloyd, P., Camaioni, L., & Ercolani, P. (1995). Assessing referential communication skills in the primary school years: A comparative study. *British Journal of Developmental Psychology, 13*, 13–29.

Lopez-Ornat, S. (1994). *La adquisición de la lengua española*. Madrid, Spain: Siglo Ventiuno.

MacWhinney, B., & Bates, E. (1978). Sentential devices for conveying givenness and newness: A cross-cultural developmental study. *Journal of Verbal Learning and Verbal Behavior, 17*, 539–558.

Martinez, M.A. (1987). Dialogues among children and between children and their mothers. *Child Development, 58*, 1035–1043.

McTear, M. (1985). *Children's conversation*. New York: Basil Blackwell.

Menig-Peterson, C. (1975). The modification of communicative behavior in preschool-aged children as a function of the listener's perspective. *Child Development, 46*, 1015–1018.

Ninio, A., & Snow, C. (1996). *Pragmatic development*. Boulder, CO: Westview.

Olsen-Fulero, L., & Conforti, J. (1983). Child responsiveness to mother questions of varying type and presentation. *Journal of Child Language, 10*, 495–520.

Pan, B.A., Imbens-Bailey, A., Winner, K., & Snow, C. (1996). Communicative intents expressed by parents in interaction with young children. *Merrill-Palmer Quarterly, 42*, 72–90.

Perner, J., & Leekam, S.R. (1986). Belief and quantity: Three-year-olds' adaptation to listener's knowledge. *Journal of Child Language, 13*, 305–315.

Peterson, C. (1993). Identifying referents and linking sentences cohesively in narration. *Discourse Processes, 16*, 507–524.

Peterson, C., & Dodsworth, P. (1991). A longitudinal analysis of young children's cohesion and noun specification in narratives. *Journal of Child Language, 18*, 397–416.

Peterson, C., & McCabe, A. (1983). *Developmental psycholinguistics: Three ways of looking at a child's narrative*. New York: Plenum Press.

Peterson, C., & McCabe, A. (1988). The connective *and. First Language, 8*, 19–28.

Sachs, J., Anselmi, D., & McMollam, K. (1990). *Young children's awareness of presuppositions based on community membership*. Paper presented at the 5th International Congress for the Study of Child Language, Budapest, Hungary, July.

Schober-Peterson, D., & Johnson, C.J. (1991). Non-dialogue speech during preschool interactions. *Journal of Child Language, 18*, 153–170.

Schley, S., & Snow, C. (1992). The conversational skills of school-aged children. *Social Development, 1*, 18–35.

Scott, C. (1984). Adverbial connectivity in conversations of children 6 to 12. *Journal of Child Language, 11*, 423–452.

Snow, C.E. (1977). The development of conversation between mothers and babies. *Journal of Child Language, 4*, 1–22.

Snow, C.E. (1990). The development of definitional skill. *Journal of Child Language, 17*, 697–710.

Snow, C.E. (1991). The theoretical basis for relationships between language and literacy development. *Journal of Research in Childhood Education, 6,* 5–10.

Snow, C.E., Pan, B.A., Imbens-Bailey, A., & Herman, J. (1996). Learning how to say what one means: A longitudinal study of children's speech act use. *Social Development, 5,* 56–84.

Sonnenschein, S. (1986). Development of referential communication skills: How familiarity with listener affects a speaker's production of redundant messages. *Developmental Psychology, 22,* 549–552.

Sonnenschein, S. (1988). The development of referential communication: Speaking to different listeners. *Child Development, 59,* 694–702.

Warden, D. (1981). Learning to identify referents. *British Journal of Psychology, 72,* 92–99.

Watson, R. (1985). Towards a theory of definition. *Journal of Child Language, 12,* 181–197.

Watson, R., & Olson, D. (1987). From meaning to definition: A literate bias on the structure of word meaning. In R. Horowitz & J. Samuels (Eds.), *Comprehending oral and written language* (pp. 329–353). Orlando, FL: Academic Press.

Winner, E. (1988). *The point of words: Children's understanding of metaphor and irony.* Cambridge, MA: Harvard University Press.

Wolf, D., Moreton, J., & Camp, L. (1994). Children's acquisition of different kinds of narrative discourse: Genres and lines of talk. In J. Sokolov & C. Snow (Eds.), *Handbook of research in language development using CHILDES* (pp. 286–323). Hillsdale, NJ: Lawrence Erlbaum Associates Inc.

CHAPTER TEN

Bilingual language development

Suzanne Romaine
University of Oxford, UK

INTRODUCTION

Most of the research on children's language acquisition has been concerned with monolinguals rather than bilinguals, despite the predominance of bilingualism in the world's population. Moreover, most of it deals with the acquisition of English (see however, Slobin, 1985/1992), and is largely biased towards middle class children. In principle, the acquisition of bilingual competence is no different from monolingual acquisition. Nevertheless, given the diversity of the contexts in which children acquire language(s), it is not easy to extrapolate from the available studies, what the "normal" sequence of development might be for a child growing up in very different circumstances from those which have been studied. It is therefore not yet clear what constitutes "delay" or "abnormality" as far as bilingual acquisition is concerned. Investigators face the difficult issue of how to decide whether utterances deviating from adult monolingual norms reflect errors or are simply transitional stages in the normal development of bilingual competence.

The available literature on children's bilingualism is also fraught with methodological problems and does not yet provide a solid basis for answering decisively many of the important questions one would like most to have answers to, e.g. to what extent are the bilingual's two languages differentiated both at the conceptual and linguistic levels; to what extent does bilingual acquisition parallel monolingual acquisition; is it the case that a feature or category acquired from one language acts as a booster to its acquisition in the other; and is there a cognitive advantage to bilingualism?

There are also many practical questions arising from bilingualism among minority populations relating to the educational needs of bilingual children (see

Romaine 1995: chapter 6). Many children have had no choice in becoming bilingual. For them, questions which have motivated most of the scholarly research into childhood bilingualism among relatively privileged populations, for example at what age and in what manner is it best to introduce a second language, are purely academic.

TYPES OF CHILDHOOD BILINGUALISM

Simultaneous vs. consecutive acquisition

There are a number of possible routes involved in bilingual acquisition: For example, children may acquire more than one language more or less simultaneously, or they may acquire one of the languages before the other, i.e. consecutively or successively. In the first instance, Swain (1972) has referred to the acquisition of "bilingualism as a first language" and Meisel (1990) to the idea of "two first languages" or "bilingual first language acquisition". McLaughlin (1978) suggests that acquisition of more than one language up to age 3 should be considered simultaneous, but he readily admits this criterion is arbitrary. Padilla and Lindholm (1984) argue that we should speak of simultaneous acquisition of two languages only when a child has been exposed to two languages from birth onwards. There are two arguments for maintaining such a strict criterion. One is that anything a child learns in one language might have a subsequent effect on the language learned later. The second is to ensure adequate comparisons with monolingual children. Otherwise, we will not be able to disentangle two variables from one another, i.e. age of first exposure and exposure to two languages.

Unfortunately, studies often do not describe their subjects' linguistic history or input and exposure patterns precisely enough to decide whether we are dealing with a strict case of simultaneous acquisition or McLaughlin's looser sense. In this chapter I have taken as my main focus the literature on simultaneous acquisition in both its strict and loose sense in order to give a comprehensive overview. I will have little to say about "consecutive" or "successive" bilingualism since I consider that to belong to the field of second language acquisition.[1] I use the term "bilingual" broadly here to include cases involving the acquisition of two as well as more than two languages.

Some early studies

The earliest systematic studies of childhood bilingualism go back to Ronjat (1913) and Leopold (1939–49), who raised their children bilingually. Now there are even several books available which serve as guides for parents who want to raise bilingual families (Arnberg, 1987; Harding & Riley, 1986; Saunders 1982,

---

[1] This decision is, of course, arbitrary, but the field of second language acquisition has been much written about elsewhere (Gass & Selinker, 1994; Larsen-Freeman & Long, 1991). The age at which acquisition takes place can have consequences for the level and kind of skills that develop.

1988), and a *Bilingual Family Newsletter* published by Multilingual Matters since 1982. It was Ronjat who introduced and endorsed the "one-person-one-language" principle as the most effective method for bringing up a child bilingually in a home where the parents had different mother tongues. Leopold and many others followed the same approach.

There are, however, other possibilities for bringing up children bilingually which have been described in the literature and still others which occur but have not been studied systematically. Following Harding and Riley (1986, pp. 47–8), I have classified the main types of early childhood bilingualism which have been studied into five categories, depending on factors such as the native language of the parents, the language of the community at large and the parents' strategy in speaking to the child.

I have also listed some of the available studies of particular languages to be discussed in the course of this chapter (for a more detailed discussion see Romaine, 1995, chapter 5). I have given each of the five types a brief descriptive name based on some aspect of the strategy employed by the parents. In addition, I have included a sixth type, not mentioned by Harding and Riley, because their aim is mainly to give advice on the most successful methods of raising children bilingually. As will be seen later, the sixth strategy leads (arguably) to more mixing and interference than the other types, but it is nevertheless probably the most frequently occurring context for "natural" bilingual acquisition in multilingual societies. Unfortunately, it has also been the least systematically studied and most researchers treat mixing as a stage in the child's development which must be overcome if the child is to be a "true" bilingual.

Six types of childhood bilingualism

Type 1: "One-person-one-language"

Parents: The parents have different native languages with each having some degree of competence in the other's language.

Community: The language of one of the parents is the dominant language of the community.

Strategy: The parents each speak their own language to the child from birth.

Some studies and the languages in each of mother, father, and the community, respectively: Ronjat (1913; German, French, French); Leopold (1939–49; English, German, English); Taeschner (1983; German, Italian, Italian); De Houwer (1990; English, Dutch, Dutch); Döpke (1992; German, English, English).

Type 2: "Non-dominant home language"/ "one language-one-environment"

Parents: The parents have different native languages.

Community: The language of one of the parents is the dominant language of the community.

Strategy: Both parents speak the non-dominant language to the child, who is fully exposed to the dominant language only when outside the home, and in particular in nursery school.

A study, and the languages of mother, father, and the community, respectively: Fantini (1985; Spanish, English, English).

Type 3: "Non-dominant home language without community support"

Parents: The parents share the same native language.
Community: The dominant language is not that of the parents.
Strategy: The parents speak their own language to the child.
A study, and the languages of mother, father, and the community, respectively: Oksaar (1977; Estonian, Estonian, Swedish/German).

Type 4: "Double non-dominant home language without community support"

Parents: The parents have different native languages.
Community: The dominant language is different from either of the parents' languages.
Strategy: The parents each speak their own language to the child from birth.
A study, and the languages of mother, father, and the community, respectively: Hoffman (1985; German, Spanish, English).

Type 5: "Non-native parents"

Parents: The parents share the same native language.
Community: The dominant language is the same as that of the parents.
Strategy: One of the parents always addresses the child in a language which is not his/her native language.
Some studies and the languages of mother, father, and the community, respectively: Saunders (1982/1988; English, English (German), English); Döpke (1992; English, English (German), English).

Type 6: "Mixed languages"

Parents: The parents are bilingual.
Community: Sectors of community may also be bilingual.
Strategy: Parents code-switch and mix languages.
Some studies, and the languages of mother, father, and the community respectively: Tabouret-Keller (1962; French/German, French/German, French/German); Smith (1935; English, English, Chinese); Burling (1959; English, English, Garo).

Similarities and differences in the types of bilingualism

Each of the types has something in common with the others. For example, in Types 1 and 2, the parents have different languages and the language of one is the dominant language of the community. What distinguishes them is the strategy used to address the child. In Type 1 the child is exposed systematically to both languages at home, while in Type 2, exposure to the community language is generally later and outside the home. In Type 4 the parents also have different native languages, but neither one is the same as the dominant language. Here the child gets exposed to its parents' two languages in the home and introduced to the community language later outside the home. In this case the outcome is a trilingual child. In Types 3 and 5 the parents share the same language, but in one case (3), the language of the parents is not the community language, and in the other, one of the parents addresses the child in a language which is not native to him/her.

Type 6 is perhaps a more common category than it might seem to be on the basis of its representation in the literature. In other words, multilingual communities are in the majority in the world's population so many children grow up in cases where individual and societal multilingualism coincide. There are a number of reasons why this kind of acquisition is not proportionately reflected in the literature on childhood bilingualism. The main one is that a great many of the studies have been done by parents educated as linguists, i.e. middle class professionals, investigating their own children's development.[2] Thus, the majority of detailed longitudinal studies deal with so-called "additive" bilingualism among privileged children, whose acquisition of a second language does not threaten or undermine the development of the other language (see discussion on any cognitive advantages to bilingualism at the end of the chapter).

Strictly speaking, Smith's and Burling's studies probably do not come under the heading of Type 6. Or perhaps Type 6 conflates what are really two different situations. I have included them here, however, because they represent cases where the child is exposed to two languages in the home in an apparently unsystematic fashion. Thus, the notion of "strategy" is misleading in all the Type 6 cases since no deliberate attempt was made to address the child in this fashion. In the case of Smith's study, the child had input in Chinese from nurses and playmates and input from parents in English. In Burling's case there was a Garo-speaking nurse and Burling himself, a native English speaker, reports that he also sometimes spoke in Garo (a Tibeto-Burman language) to his son.

A very common outcome of the "one person-one-language" method was a child who could understand the languages of both parents, but spoke only the language of the community in which they lived. Sociolinguistic studies of

---

[2] This is a well-established research practice in the study of first language acquisition too.

minority languages have shown that it is usually very difficult for children to acquire active command of a minority language, where that language does not receive support from the community. This is especially the case if there is only one parent in the home speaking this language. In such circumstances the child can use the other language, but generally does not. There are, however, some success stories. Saunders (1982/1988), for example, has described in detail how he managed to bring his children up bilingually in German and English in Australia, even though neither he nor his wife are native speakers of German. Similarly, the comparatively greater success of one boy (Keith) out of the six English/German bilingual children whom Döpke (1992) studied in Australia is noteworthy since the father, like Saunders, was not a native speaker and he provided virtually all of Keith's German input. Other successes include those of Kielhöfer and Jonekeit (1983) with French and German in Germany, and Taeschner (1983) with German and Italian in Italy. However, it should be pointed out that in all these cases the minority language was not stigmatised, and the children came from an advantaged background.

As I will argue later, both Saunders' and Döpke's studies underline the fact that quality of input is more important than the amount. Both studies also attest the positive role that fathers can play in their children's language development, particularly in the transmission of a minority language.

In my discussion of some of the studies of these six types of childhood bilingualism, I will highlight only some of the major developments noted by the researchers. Often it is not possible to compare exactly the same phenomena across the different cases due to differences in methods and aims of the studies. Further in this chapter I will take a more detailed look at some of the issues arising from this research, e.g. cross-linguistic influence and code-switching.

There are obviously also many other factors I will discuss later which affect the outcome in each case. Among these are amount and kind of exposure to each language, parents' consistency in language choice, attitudes towards bilingualism on the part of children and parents, and the individual personalities of children and parents.

THEORETICAL ISSUES IN CHILDHOOD BILINGUALISM

Among the issues I will consider here are whether there are discernible stages in bilingual acquisition which parallel those of monolingual acquisition. A number of scenarios are possible:

1. Each language develops independently as it would in a monolingual child.
2. The acquisition of both languages is delayed by comparison to monolingual acquisition.

3. The child prefers or is dominant in one of the languages, and the acquisition of the dominant language determines the development of constructions and categories which are matched in both systems.
4. The two languages develop differently with respect to different types of constructions and categories.

I will examine evidence in the domains of vocabulary, phonology, and syntax. Opinion is currently divided between what has been called the "one or two system theory". While many researchers agree that the child has only one lexical system in the early stages (see, however, Pye, 1986), others have claimed that differentiation is present from the early stages. I will also consider the relevance of the bootstrapping metaphor to bilingual acquisition (see Gawlitzek-Maiwald & Tracy, 1995).

Saunders (1982) proposed a three-stage developmental sequence based on his childrens' acquisition of English and German: a first in which the child has one lexical system; a second in which the lexicon is differentiated; and a third in which both lexicon and syntax are differentiated, but each language is associated with the person using it.

Stage one lasted from the onset of speech until about age 2 years. The majority of the child's utterances consisted of one word until about 18 months. The child went through a two word stage until 2 years old. During this time the child possessed only one lexicon, which contains words from both languages. Saunders (1982, p. 43), for example, says that at 16 months his son Frank knew and responded to both *horse* and its German equivalent *Pferd*, but in his speech used only *Pferd*, regardless of his addressee until he reached the age of 2. The child at this stage treated all items as if they were part of the same linguistic system. Similarly, Vihman (1985) reported that her son Raivio had a single lexicon made up of Estonian and English words until age 18 months. Redlinger and Park (1980) also claimed that a German/Spanish bilingual child had one lexical system consisting of English and German words plus some items which could be considered as belonging to either language.

During the second stage the child might still be using utterances which contain words from both languages, but will increasingly differentiate the languages according to person and context. For example, Saunders' son Thomas at age 26 months said to his grandfather: "Lots of Möwen [seagulls] Granddad!" Thomas knew the corresponding English word and could produce it on request, but for a while he showed a preference for the German word. Saunders (1982, p. 45) also noted that during this same stage a child might repeat an item in both languages, as if aware that there were two words for everything, but not yet sure which to use in which circumstance. For example, at 23 months Frank referred to the gas fire in the lounge by saying: "heiss, hot". One of Taeschner's (1983, p. 28) daughters at age of 16 months had a similar Italian-German "compound" she used when she approached the radiator: "cotta-heiss" [< *scotta* "burns" + *heiss* "hot"]. Grosjean (1982) mentions a French/English bilingual 2-year-old girl who blended French *chaud* "hot" with English *hot* into *shot*. Both Saunders (1982) and Oksaar (1977) noted that their children used the second language to repeat a request that a parent failed to attend to in the other language.

At stage three, the child will have fully differentiated both languages, using them appropriately. Some researchers have claimed that the child is not truly bilingual until this separation occurs.

Is a bilingual the sum of two monolinguals?

There has been a tendency to regard bilingual competence as the sum of the acquisition of monolingual competence in each of the two languages rather than as a unitary system which allows the pooling of resources across two languages. Researchers have often noted that bilingual children lag behind monolinguals in terms of vocabulary development (Doyle, Champagne, & Segalowitz, 1978). In an early study Smith (1949) tested Hawai'i children of Chinese ancestry in both English and Chinese. She found that the scores of these children on vocabulary development were below the monolingual norms. However, when the scores from the two languages were combined, the children compared favourably with monolinguals. Nevertheless, she (1949, p. 309) concluded that it would be unwise to start children in a second language unnecessarily during the preschool years, unless they were of superior linguistic ability.

Another example is Fantini's son Mario, who was first tested in English on the Peabody Picture Vocabulary Test when he was 4 years and 9 months and dominant in Spanish. He ranked only in the 29th percentile according to the established norms for monolingual English speakers. A day or so later he was tested in Spanish and his raw score doubled. However, in subsequent formal testing in English at school Mario compared favourably with his monolingual peers (Fantini 1985, p. 186).

Saunders tested his children's ability in the two languages at various stages. The boys scored well on tests for both German and English vocabulary. At age 5 years and 5 months Frank scored in the 75th percentile and Thomas in the 93rd in English vocabulary. Thomas at age 7 years and 3 months scored in the 98th percentile. Thomas's German was, however, consistently more accurate than Frank's. Saunders reports (1982, p. 162) that at age 5 years and 5 months Frank knew 144 out of 200 items in German and 135 out of 200 in English. At the same age Thomas knew more in both languages (155 in German and 145 in English). In both cases the boys knew slightly more German than English words. Even at 7 years and 3 months Thomas still knew more German than English words, which Saunders says is striking in view of the fact that there was a 3:1 balance in favour of English in the boys' input.

It is more revealing, however, to look at the boys' total vocabulary across the two languages since a bilingual's total vocabulary may exceed that of a monolingual child. This is the case for Thomas and Frank. Frank knew 163 out of 200 items in at least one of the languages. This is a higher score than he obtained in either of the languages tested individually. Thomas knew 169 out of 200 items in at least one language, which is also a higher score than either of the ones for the languages assessed individually.

These results serve to underline a point which is now increasingly made in the study of bilingual proficiency. It does not make much sense to assess bilinguals as if they were two monolinguals since it is unlikely that a bilingual will have the same experiences in both languages. For instance, Thomas at age 5 years and 5 months did not know the English term *soldering*, but knew its German equivalent.

The development of the bilingual lexicon

Most researchers have found that at any particular stage there are more words in a given language without equivalents in the other language than there are with equivalents. Taeschner (1983, p. 29) kept a detailed record of her daughters' production of equivalents for individual lexemes and for grammatical categories (see also Vihman, 1985). The girls began using equivalent vocabulary items around the end of the first year. Between the ages of 2 and 3, roughly one-third of the vocabulary items in the girls' lexicons were equivalents and two-thirds were new acquisitions. She (1983, p. 54) says that it is therefore problematic to compare the bilingual's acquisition of the lexicon with that of the monolingual child. The bilingual child's capacity to produce new words is split between the two languages. The child deals with this by giving priority to new words at the expense of equivalents. Thus, by using the total lexicon available at any given time, she is able to speak both languages and to denote the same number of new concepts as the monolingual child.

Taeschner (1983, p. 23) stresses the importance of bilingual children's acquisition of synonyms. Children learn the German word *Baum* in one context and the word *tree* in another. Words which may function as equivalents for adults do not necessarily do so for children. One of her daughters used German *da* for things that were present and visible, and Italian *là* (both of which mean "there") for things that were not present and not visible. Leopold's daughter Hildegard knew both *please* and *bitte*, but used the English words in formal situations, while the German one was used in familiar contexts.

Bilingual children also face the problem of apparent equivalents in the two languages which have different semantic extensions. Imedadze (1967) found that a bilingual Georgian/Russian child used the Georgian word *ball* to denote a toy, a radish, and stone spheres at the park entrance and then transferred these same denotations to the Russian equivalent.

The fact that bilingual children do not have twice the number of words in their vocabulary as monolinguals does not impair their ability to communicate.

Doyle et al. (1978) came to this conclusion after examining 22 bilingual and 22 monolingual children between the ages of 42 months and five years, seven months. They found that the monolinguals had a greater number of words than the bilinguals did in their dominant language, but that the verbal fluency of the bilinguals was greatly superior to that of the monolinguals. This was measured in terms of ability to tell stories and by the number of concepts expressed by each child per story (see under the final heading of this chapter for further evidence of the superiority of bilinguals).

As with monolingual acquisition, there is considerable variability among children in the rate of vocabulary acquisition. For example, Fantini (1985, p. 142) comments that at the end of his second year Mario used only 21 words compared to Hildegard's 337. By age 3, however, he had a productive lexicon of 503 words.

The development of bilingual phonology

During the first two years, Hildegard evidently did not confuse the sounds of English and German. Leopold said that the deviations from adult norms were not due to interference between the languages, but to more general processes of simplification and substitution that are systematically found in the speech of monolingual children (see also Saunders 1982, p. 201). By comparison, Ronjat (1913) observed that his son Louis had mastered the phonemes of both languages at 3 years and 5 months, which represents a slight lag in terms of the norms for monolingual children. Leopold, however, admits that English and German are too similar to decide which language the child's early vocalisations belong to. It is impossible to tell whether Hildegard had separate phonological systems before the age of two.

Mario's Spanish sound system was the first to be established and accordingly his earliest English words, which were acquired later than Spanish, were given Spanish pronunciations. This phonological interference gradually decreased, although some residual problems remained until the fifth year. By contrast, English phonology exerted practically no influence on Mario's Spanish. Fantini (1985, p. 180) reports that at age 5, Mario's phonemic inventory was normal for both languages.

The development of bilingual syntax

As far as syntactic and morphological development is concerned, there are also conflicting reports on the degree of separateness of the systems being acquired. Saunders (1982, p. 47) found that both his sons tended to keep the syntactic systems separate. Only certain types of syntactic constructions posed some difficulty. Frank, for example, differentiated the word order rules in English and German in his use of the first past tenses he learned. Occasionally, however, he used the English pattern in his German utterances. Leopold's daughter and Taeschner's daughters had some difficulty with word order too. An example of one of these word order "errors" is: *Du hast vergessen das* [You have forgotten that]. The correct German should be: *Du hast das vergessen*, where the (pronominal) object, *das*, occurs between the auxiliary, *hast*, and the past participle, *vergessen*, or is "embraciated" by the two verbal elements. Frank's speech during this stage, however, always showed the correct placement of the verb at the end, when the first verbal element was a modal auxiliary.

Taeschner claims that her two daughters initially developed a single syntactic system which was applied to the lexicons of both Italian and German. Meisel (1989, p. 16) has, however, pointed out that her evidence is not altogether consistent with the three stage hypothesis. It is really only Lisa whose behaviour is consistent with the claim that there is a single syntactic system and Italian was clearly Lisa's dominant language.

Taeschner (1983, p. 164) found that although her girls acquired Italian word order in the same way and order as Italian monolinguals, their development in German was only partially the same as that of monolinguals. They did not immediately use the correct word order for subordinate clauses. Yet their word order strategy was not simply transferred from Italian, but reflected simply the ordering which would have been used if the two clauses had stood on their own.

Meisel's (1986, 1990) data from French/German bilinguals indicated that not all bilingual children use this strategy. He (1986, p. 146) found that children who were acquiring French and German simultaneously used predominantly SVO word order, a pattern which is common to both languages, but not the preferred order for monolingual children acquiring either French or German. Monolingual French children more frequently placed the subject at the end, while German children put the verb in final position (see, however Meisel, 1990, p. 285 for further details). Because the bilingual children learned very early to distinguish the word order regularities of the two languages, Meisel (1986, p. 170) concluded that bilinguals used grammatical means of expression earlier than monolinguals, although they acquire them in the same way. The use of SVO word order may, however, be the outcome of two factors, one of which is the overlap between the two languages with respect to this ordering. The other may be a universal preference for SVO order.

In other cases researchers have reported that the order of acquisition of grammatical categories reflected their difficulty as indicated by factors such as the perceptual salience and regularity of the linguistic means used to mark them. For example, Hungarian/Serbo-Croat bilingual children use locative case relations in Hungarian earlier than in Serbo-Croat (see Mikes, 1967). In Hungarian the locative is encoded by means of a noun inflection. In Serbo-Croat it is marked by both noun inflection and preposition. Monolingual speakers of Serbo-Croat also acquire the locative relatively late (in comparison with Hungarian speakers).

Cross-linguistic influence

While virtually all researchers report some degree of cross-linguistic influence in bilingual acquisition, there is a great deal of variation in the amount reported at various stages, depending on the child's acquisition pattern. Researchers have also used a number of different terms defined in different ways to describe this influence, e.g. mixing, interference, borrowing, and code-switching. Volterra and Taeschner (1978), for example, use the term "mixing" to refer to the application of the same syntactic rules to two lexicons, while Redlinger and Park (1980) apply it to indiscriminate combinations of elements from each language. Genesee (1989), however, defines it as an interaction between the child's developing language systems (see also Genesee et al., 1995). Meisel (1995) proposes that the term "mixing" be restricted to errors in language choice on the part of a child already possessing two grammatical systems and fusion to refer to the inability to separate two grammatical systems. Fusion is the result of insufficient competence. Code-switching (i.e. alternation between two languages) can only occur then, according to Meisel, once there are two distinct grammatical systems in place.

Fantini (1985, pp. 127, 168) prefers to speak of a gradual process of separation rather than interference in cases where the languages appear fused from the beginning. What has been called interference may be a reflection of incomplete acquisition. Thus, in the case of his son Mario, he does not speak of interference until after the stage where the child began to use the languages separately, i.e. at 32 months. Imedadze (1967) found that separation occurred as early as 20 months for a Russian/Georgian bilingual child. Yet, many other researchers suggest that children younger than 3 years of age have not yet differentiated their languages. It would appear that at different stages in the developmental process and depending on various social circumstances, e.g. amount of mixing in the input, various components of the child's linguistic system go through periods of fusion and separation.

Bergman (1976), for example, attributed the use of mixed possessive forms to the child's exposure to a context in which a clear distinction was not maintained between Spanish and English. Although the child, Mary, was able to use correct forms in Spanish and English, she also produced forms like: *es annie's libro* ("it's Annie's book") and *es de papa's* ("It's Papa's"). (Compare Spanish: *es el libro de Annie/es de Papa*). Bergman noticed that the mother of some of Mary's playmates used possessives like these. When Bergman asked her if she had used them often, she said that she had picked them up from her children. Thus, the mother's input was probably reinforcing the children's use of mixed forms, although it is not clear whether the mother was the original model. Bergman attributed interference to input rather than to the child's failure to differentiate the two codes.

It is not clear, however, that this was the only contributing factor. From the earliest stage Mary, unlike, for example, the Taeschner girls, kept the constructions separate in both languages and then went through a period of mixing before finally using each morpheme correctly in its respective language. Other studies of Spanish/English bilingualism in the United States have reported mixing in the child's input, but no evidence of an abnormal rate of linguistic development (see Huerta, 1977; Padilla & Liebmann, 1975).

Gawlitzek-Maiwald and Tracy (1995) observed mixed utterances such as *ich hab gemade you much better* ("I have made you much better") in the speech of Hannah, a German/English bilingual at age 28 months, and *Esther du cutst dein toe* ("Esther you cut your toe") at age 32 months. Taeschner (1983, p. 131) too found instances of word internal mixing. Lisa between 28 months and 36 months, for example, used the German prefix *aus-* with Italian verbs, as in *Giulia hat ausbevuto?* "Has Giulia drunk everything?" (Compare German: *Hat Giulia ausgetrunken?*). Both girls also used the German past participle prefix *ge-* with Italian verbs, as in *Io ho gevinto*, "I have won." [< German *ge-* + Italian *vinto* "won"].

Such examples violate one of the major constraints operative in adult code-switching, namely, the free morpheme constraint proposed by Sankoff and Poplack (1981). This predicts that a switch may not occur between a bound morpheme and a lexical form unless the lexical form has been phonologically integrated into the language of the morpheme. To take an example from Spanish/English bilingual speech, this constraint would predict that *flipeando* "flipping" would be permissible, but that *catcheando* would not be, because *catch* has not been integrated into the phonology of Spanish, and therefore cannot take the Spanish progressive suffix *-eando*.

Petersen (1988), who found word internal mixing of this type in her study of Thea, a Danish/English bilingual child at age 38 months, attributed it to the fact that the girl was English-dominant. She found that Danish lexical morphemes could co-occur with either English or Danish grammatical morphemes, but Danish grammatical morphemes could co-occur only with Danish lexical morphemes. English grammatical morphemes, however, could co-occur with either Danish or English lexical morphemes. Thus, Danish *vask* "wash" could combine with the English suffix *-ing* to produce a mixed verb form *vasking* "washing". Combinations such as *her dukke* "her doll" are also grammatical, but forms like *liver* "lives", which combine English *live* with the Danish present tense verb suffix *-(e)r*, are not. Similarly, *wateret* "the water", which combines an English word with the Danish suffixed definite article *-et*, and *min bed* "my bed", a combination of Danish possessive pronoun and an English noun, are ungrammatical.

This means that of the four logically possible word types shown below which might occur through the free mixing of English and Danish grammatical and lexical morphemes, only the first three are permitted to occur. Petersen (1988, p. 486) found that the second type accounted for just under one-third of her data (28.5%). Half of the child's utterances were in English. Although the lexical morphemes were almost evenly divided between the two languages, there were many more instances of English grammatical morphemes. Over three-quarters of the grammatical categories Petersen examined contained English grammatical morphemes, while only 21% contained Danish ones:

Type 1 monolingual combinations of English grammatical morphemes and lexemes
Type 2 bilingual combinations of English grammatical morphemes plus Danish lexemes
Type 3 monolingual combinations of Danish grammatical morphemes and lexemes
Type 4 bilingual combinations of Danish grammatical morphemes and English lexemes

Lanza's (1992) study of Siri, a bilingual Norwegian/English girl, found a pattern of mixing different from that of Petersen's Thea. Siri used English lexical morphemes with Norwegian grammatical morphemes, e.g. *jeg eat* "I eat" (i.e. Petersen's Type 4), but Norwegian lexical morphemes did not occur with English grammatical morphemes, e.g. **I spiser* (i.e. Petersen's Type 2).

Petersen claims more generally that in utterances containing morpheme level code-switching, the encoding of grammatical morphemes in one of the languages is an indication of that language's dominance. This hypothesis requires testing with a larger sample of bilingual children. Thea represents somewhat of a special case like many of the other children whose development I have discussed in this chapter. She was always addressed in Danish by her parents and was never exposed to individuals who code-switched. Siri, on the other hand, was brought up in Norway with the "one-person-one-language" strategy. Her father spoke to her in Norwegian and her mother, in English. Lanza (1992) notes that the directionality of Siri's mixing, which is the mirror-image of Thea's, indicates Siri's dominance in Norwegian. She relied on Norwegian grammatical structure when communicating in English, but not on English grammatical structure when communicating in Norwegian. Siri also mixed more when speaking with her mother. Her mixing with her father was mainly lexical (discussed later on).

Nevertheless, Petersen's hypothesis would make the wrong prediction in a number of other cases. Burling's (1959) comment that Garo was his son's first language suggests dominance in Garo. Yet he found word level mixing of all four possible types. His son assimilated English vocabulary into Garo and used Garo endings on English words, as in the following example: *mami laitko tunonaha* "Mommy turned on the light". The roots of every word are English, but the suffixes *-ko* "direct object marker", and *-aha* "past tense", word order and phonology are Garo. Later when English sentences appeared, the boy borrowed Garo words into them and gave them English inflections. Petersen's hypothesis would predict that if the child were Garo-dominant, he would not use Garo words with English grammatical morphemes.

Petersen cites Leopold's daughter, Hildegard, as a case which follows her hypothesis, but the extent to which this is true depends on whether Hildegard is to be considered English- or German-dominant at any particular stage. Leopold suggests that his daughter was at least at times German-dominant (particularly after a period of 7 months' residence in Germany at the end of her fourth year) until she went to school in English. If she were German-dominant, we would not expect to find German lexemes with English grammatical morphemes. Leopold, however, reports that at age 4, her language consisted mostly of German vocabulary items inserted into English sentences, including English grammatical endings on German nouns and verbs. It is, of course, possible that Hildegard did not use mixed utterances with monolingual English speakers, but since Leopold did not collect any examples of her speech in this context, we have no way of knowing. Leopold focused his attention on reporting Hildegard's mixed utterances even though in his third volume there are utterances containing non-mixed ones.

Researchers have since recognised the importance of looking at mixed utterances as a separate category. Gawlitzek-Maiwald and Tracy (1995) observed that Hannah's unmixed utterances followed the paths of development observed in monolingual children. That is, she fell within the normal range with respect to MLU for age, types of structures produced, and the sequence of emergence of structures.

Evidence for differentiation or fusion

It is often difficult to decide what counts as evidence for differentiation or fusion, with different studies counting different phenomena. Taeschner (1983), for instance, bases her decision on whether the child makes appropriate sociolinguistic choices. Does she speak the "right" language to the "right" person? This is a distinct issue, however, from whether the child has one or two linguistic systems. Part of the problem is the familiar one of what we can infer about competence from performance. Genesee (1989, p. 189) argues that in order to maintain the one language system hypothesis one would need to show that bilingual children could use items from both languages indiscriminately in all contexts. However, even if a young child at the two or three word stage of development produces mixed utterances, it may mean only that the child is drawing on his or her total communicative repertoire in order to be understood. Some children, such as De Houwer's (1990) Dutch/English bilingual, Kate, showed no significant change over time either in address patterns or in her use of mixed utterances. From the outset, Kate tended to use English with English speakers and Dutch with Dutch speakers. In fact, De Houwer argues that no language dominance can be discerned. Nor in her view can mixed utterances be used to determine whether two languages are separate or fused. The problem in comparing studies is compounded by lack of consistency in defining terms such as switching, mixing, etc. as well as by lack of adequate studies of first language acquisition by monolingual children for comparison.

Some researchers consider the child to be "truly bilingual" only at the stage where there is separation of the two systems (Arnberg & Arnberg, 1985, p. 21). Leopold, for example, says that Hildegard was not really bilingual during the first two years. Some studies have found a reduction in the use of mixed forms after the point at which separation is alleged to have occurred (Redlinger & Park 1980), while others have reported an increase (see Vihman, 1985, p. 316). However, since Redlinger and Park's study followed the children' development for only 9 months between the ages of 2 to 3, the decrease in mixing may reflect simply an increase in the number of lexical equivalents. In some cases it is not clear whether there are two separate languages to be acquired because the adults to whom the child is exposed always use a code-mixed variety. Redlinger and Park found more mixing in the speech of a child who had mixed input from adults. For this reason, language mixing *per se* is not a valid measure for determining whether the child lacks awareness of the two languages. Lexical mixing, in particular, may decline over time as the child's vocabulary increases thus lessening the need for borrowing from one language when speaking the other.

As far as Arnberg and Arnberg (1992) are concerned, awareness of the two languages as distinct plays a crucial role in deciding the issue of differentiation. However, as McLaughlin (1984) points out, the argument that bilingual children separate the languages when they are aware there are two systems is circular unless some criterion is provided for assessing what is meant by awareness other than that children separate the languages. Arnberg and Arnberg asked a sample of bilingual children to name pictures in each of the two languages on separate occasions. They also asked parents to rate their children on a scale of awareness. In addition, they collected a half-hour speech sample from the children to measure the percentage of mixed utterances. On the basis of their performance on the picture naming task, the children were grouped into categories of "aware" and "non-aware". The mean score for language mixing in the aware group was 1.7% and 12.3% for the non-aware group. There were no differences related to age or level of linguistic development as assessed by MLU and other measures.

Arnberg and Arnberg (1992) attribute differences in awareness primarily to social factors, such as patterns of exposure to the two languages and the extent to which parents drew attention to the two languages by offering children prompts such as "Mommy says", "how does Daddy say it?", and translations such as, "in Swedish that's called". Some parents reported they never spoke about the languages in this way, while one family had signs attached to common objects in the home with the words for each object in both languages.

Separate development

Evidence has recently been mounting in favour of the separate development hypothesis, although as yet, this needs more extensive testing with acquisition of languages which are very different typologically. De Houwer (1990), who has argued strongly in favour of separate development from birth, looked at two very similar languages, Dutch and English. Despite the obvious extensive similarities between Dutch and English, there are some clear differences, e.g. Dutch grammatical vs. English "natural" gender, and word order, where Dutch is more like German than English. De Houwer found that in both these areas and indeed with regard to the development of other areas of the grammar, Kate kept the two language systems separate. Her use of both gender systems was language specific from the start. There was also no influence from one language to the other in the verb phrase. De Houwer proposed a principle of morphological language stability, which predicts that when children acquire two languages simultaneously from birth using the one-person-one-language method, bound morphemes belong to the main language of the utterance from the beginning. Morphemes do not travel from one language to another.

INPUT AND SOCIAL CONTEXT AS FACTORS AFFECTING RATE AND ORDER OF ACQUISITION

Quantity of input

More studies need to be done to determine the extent to which differential distribution of a form in the child's input has an effect on the emergence of a structure. A suggestive case can be found by comparing children's acquisition of the ergative in Samoan and Kaluli, a Papua New Guinean language. Kaluli children acquire ergative case marking quite early (i.e. at 26 months) according to Schieffelin (1981), while Samoan children do not learn it until relatively late (i.e. after 4 years) according to Ochs (1982). If linguistic and cognitive factors take precedence over other ones, then we would expect Samoan children to acquire ergative case marking no less early than Kaluli children since the category is encoded in both languages in a transparent and uniform manner. In Ochs's (1982, p. 78) view, however, the reason for "delayed acquisition" is social. Ergative case marking is not distributed equally throughout the Samoan community. It is more typical of men's than women's speech. Furthermore, it rarely appears in the speech of family members within the household, where women and older siblings are the child's primary socialising agents.

Ochs's findings certainly have far-reaching implications for developmental psycholinguistic studies which attempt to explain the order of acquisition of various structures in terms of purely cognitive and innate principles. Many of those who have argued for a link between complexity and order of emergence have not taken account of the fact that social context is an important mediator in this process. In De Houwer's study (1990, p. 234) the use of tense forms cannot be explained in terms of complexity. In English Kate used exclusively the simple past, while in Dutch she used mainly the present perfect, a form which could be said to be more complex than the English past. The simple past is, however, more frequently used in English than in Dutch, so it appears Kate is following the most frequent forms in her input.

Those aspects of language structure which are more specifically determined by or related to aspects of social structure will obviously be affected by exposure to the social contexts in which input for these features is present in sufficient amounts to trigger acquisition. One area in which this can be clearly seen is in the acquisition of the so-called T/V distinction. Languages like German, Spanish and French require the speaker to make socially appropriate choices between the second person singular vs. plural form of the personal pronoun (compare German *Du/Sie*, French *tu/vous*, Spanish *tu/usted*) depending on factors such as the social status of the addressee and the intimacy of the relationship between speaker and addressee. The stage at which these distinctions are acquired varies even for monolingual speakers (see Romaine 1984, p. 142). Rural Hungarian children, for example, learn the system of address later than urban children because the rural child's network includes mainly family members and peers with whom the familiar pronouns are used. The formal pronouns are not used until a later stage (Hollos, 1977).

Similar factors can be seen to work in the case of some of the bilingual children under discussion here. Although Fantini's son Mario showed sensitivity to social distinctions at a very early age, even at age 10 he did not consistently employ the *tu/usted* distinction in Spanish (Fantini 1985, pp. 110–111). Similarly, the Saunders' boys rarely used the more polite German form *Sie*. They scarcely heard it in the speech of others and needed only the more familiar form with their father. In addition, the familiar form is more frequently used in the Australian German-speaking community than in Germany (Saunders 1982, p. 205).

Taeschner unfortunately does not comment on her daughters' acquisition of the pronominal address system, which might be expected to proceed differently for various reasons. For one thing, both German and Italian have similar systems. In the case of the Saunders' children and Mario, however, German and Spanish, which do have such systems, were being acquired along with another language, namely English, which did not. In both cases English was the language of the society at large, and the main language of schooling. Thus, the fact that English did not make such a distinction, coupled with the fact that the distinction did not receive support in the home context, could have had an effect on rate of acquisition.

One would expect that in the case of Taeschner's girls, acquisition of the distinction in German might have been accelerated because the category was matched in Italian and would have been supported outside the home and in school. Thus, its acquisition in Italian might have acted as a pacesetter for its earlier acquisition in German (earlier at least by comparison with say, other bilingual children like the Saunders' boys and possibly even by comparison with Italian and German monolinguals). This would constitute another form of "bootstrapping".

Quality of input

Within the fields of both first and second language acquisition increasing emphasis has been given to the quality of interaction between child and caretaker and nature of input as an important factor in learning (Galloway & Richards 1994). Kielhöfer and Jonekeit (1983, p. 16) observe that the interactive styles of the parents are likely to have an effect on the child's acquisition of two languages. In particular, they claim that the child's language development will reflect the nature of the emotional bond between child and parent. If the child's ties to one parent are stronger, then that language will develop faster and stronger. From the examples given above, it is clear that interaction patterns can affect the development of individual structures.

Döpke's (1992) detailed study of the types of input and interactional strategies employed by parents provides evidence in support of this. While the families she studied were all middle class, there were considerable difference in their individual circumstances which could have accounted for the different outcomes in the children's acquisition. I have already mentioned the greater success of one boy (Keith) as well as one girl (Fiona), who progressed between the time of Döpke's first recording and the second (a period of 6 months) as measured in terms of increase in MLU (mean length of utterance) and auditory comprehension. Three of the children, however, had not progressed and did not want to speak German, while the remaining child had progressed but no longer wanted to speak German. I also noted the particular success of Keith, neither of whose parents were native speakers of German and whose main input came from his father.

Keith's father not only talked more to Keith than did his mother, but his interactions were more child centred and intensive than the mother's, suggesting, contrary to the findings from studies of Welsh language maintenance in mixed marriages, for instance, that fathers can play a positive role in the transmission of the minority language to their children. Quality of input is more important than amount. Döpke's results give rise to both pessimism and optimism for parents wishing to raise their children bilingually. There is reason to be optimistic because it appears that parents can have an impact on their children's bilingualism by providing an environment rich in input. Pessimism, however, arises from the fact that an enormous amount of time and effort must be spent to give the child an enriched environment. Döpke also found that the childrens' English utterances increased in complexity from the first to second recording in most cases too. Moreover, none of the children ever put English grammatical markers on German lexical items or German grammatical markers on English lexical items.

Interactional styles

Other aspects of parents' interactional styles can make a difference too. Parents have differed in the extent to which they have adhered strictly to the one-person-one-language principle. Siri's Norwegian-speaking father, for instance, accepted replies from her in English, while her mother adopted a monolingual English strategy with her. Leopold and Ronjat did not supply vocabulary requested by their children in the other language, while Fantini and Saunders freely gave translations and supplied words when they thought the children needed them.

Döpke's (1992, p. 62) study of the varying degrees of language competence achieved by six German/English bilingual children in Australia stresses the importance of both these points. She concludes that there are two main factors which create a necessity for the child to become bilingual: One is the parents' consistency of choice of language and the other is their insistence that the child respects the "one-parent-one-language" principle. The children who achieved the highest degree of proficiency in German were Keith and Fiona. Both sets of parents were most consistent in their language choice and also most insistent that the child speak German when spoken to by the German-speaking parent. As I noted above, Keith's success was all the more remarkable given that all the odds were against him. Not only did he have a non-native speaking father, but his primary care-giver, his mother, was the non-German speaking parent. Even though Keith's father tried to provide contact with other German-speaking people and a variety of different language media, Fiona had a naturally much richer language environment. She had German-speaking relatives who came for long visits as well as the most contact with German-speaking friends of the family. Fiona also later made several trips to Austria, while Keith never visited a German-speaking country.

Attitudes

Attitudes of the extended family, the school, and society at large are also important. Even children within the same family can react differently to the attitudes of outsiders. One of Saunders' sons, Frank, ignored covert or overt disapproval of German and spoke to his father in that language wherever they were or whoever was present. Thomas, however, was much more sensitive and was reluctant to speak German at certain stages. For example, at 40 months he did not want to speak to his father in German in the environment of the English-speaking kindergarten. Frank, however, showed no such inhibition. When Thomas began primary school, the presence of other bilingual children encouraged him and he aligned himself with them (Saunders, 1982, p. 134). Both boys have expressed the desire to pass German on to their own children. Saunders' daughter Katrina at age 40 months reacted adversely at first when the family went to Hamburg for 6 months. She would not speak German to any adults but her father during the whole of her stay. Although she was able to interact in German with children at kindergarten, she did not speak to the teacher.

Saunders (1982, p. 114) notes that he was warned by a doctor just after Thomas's third birthday that speaking two languages was too great a burden and was inhibiting his acquisition of English. He advised the family to address him only in English. This assessment was made after a 15-minute examination in which Thomas's failure to perform well was attributed to his bilingualism, rather than to shyness or other factors in the testing situation. Similarly, Mario's English pronunciation attracted the attention of a teacher who wanted to send him for speech therapy. She was unaware that he spoke another language at home and was still Spanish-dominant when he entered kindergarten. His parents, however, resisted this attempt at remediation. Only two years later, however, his teacher expressed surprise when she found out that he spoke Spanish at home. His ability in Spanish and English thereafter continued without interruption to the extent that native speakers of Spanish and English never perceived Mario as anything other than a native speaker of their respective languages.

Many professionals such as speech therapists view normal language mixing as harmful and are therefore liable to give advice to parents which is not in keeping with the realities of normal bilingual development in bilingual communities elsewhere. Beliefs about bilingualism causing stuttering and delayed onset of language are also widespread, despite lack of evidence for them. Harding and Riley (1986, p. 126) write bluntly in their advice to parents: "It makes as much sense to ask your doctor for advice about bilingualism as it would to ask him about your car".

IS THERE COGNITIVE ADVANTAGE TO BILINGUALISM?

Contrary to the prevailing view in the first half of this century that bilingualism had a negative effect on children's intellectual development (see Hakuta, 1986 for further discussion), both Ronjat and Leopold believed that bilingualism did not disadvantage their children. Leopold in fact emphasised that there was some positive advantage in bilingualism. He said that Hildegard came to separate word from referent at an early stage and was aware of the arbitrary nature of the relationship through using two languages. Monolingual children are not aware of this until a later stage in their development.

Meisel (1990, pp. 17–18) suggests that bilingual children exhibit less variation than monolinguals in their acquisition. Thus, the task of "cracking" the codes of two different language systems simultaneously enhances the child's awareness of grammatical categories and helps rather than hinders learners. He found, for example, that both bilingual German/French and monolingual German children go through an initial stage in which all inflection is lacking. However, this stage ends earlier for the bilingual than monolingual children. Compare this positive statement with Karniol's (1992) unsubstantiated claim that stuttering is prevalent in bilinguals due to the syntactic overload imposed by processing and producing two languages (see Paradis & Lebrun, 1984 for counter evidence).

The alleged advantages and disadvantages of bilingualism have been generally assessed with reference to their impact on intelligence, itself a controversial concept. Martin-Jones and Romaine (1985) have discussed the ways in which negative and erroneous ideas about bilingual children's language development become "received wisdom" in educational circles and are passed on uncritically.

In a series of studies done by Bialystock (1987, 1991, 1992), bilinguals were more advanced than monolinguals in specific uses of language applied to certain types of problems. She says (1987, p. 138) that bilingual children were notably more advanced when they were required to separate out individual words from meaningful sentences, focus on only the form or meaning of a word under highly distracting conditions, and reassign a familiar name to a different object. Each of these tasks requires selective attention to words or their features and the performance of some operation on that isolated component, e.g. counting the number of words in a sentence. The ability to attend selectively to units of language such as words and their boundaries and to apply specific processes to them is an integral part of using language for advanced and specialised purposes such as literacy. Bialystock says that the seemingly diverse range of tasks on which bilinguals are superior to monolinguals are all dependent on high levels of selective attention, which is a central mechanism of cognitive performance.

These kinds of general abilities to manipulate language as a formal system have sometimes been referred to as "metalinguistic" skills, or in other words, the use of language to talk about or reflect on language. They allow an individual to step back, so to speak, from the comprehension or production of language to analyse its form. Such skills are believed to be helpful in learning how to read and necessary for advanced uses of oral and literate language in school (Bialystock, 1991). Schooling in general increases an awareness of language as an object in and of itself (Romaine, 1984). Metalinguistic problems demand a high level of selective attention, such as when a child is asked what the sun and moon would be called if they switched names. In order to separate the word from its meaning children must attend selectively in an unusual way. Translation is also another example of a metalinguistic task. Many bilingual children are habitual and skilled translators.

Yet bilingualism is still in many quarters seen as a stigma and a hindrance to children's intellectual development, and cited as a reason for children's failure in school. It is no accident that many of the alleged negative consequences emerge in cases where children are socially disadvantaged, e.g. the children of migrant workers in various parts of the European community, or among the Chicano population in California. Most of the studies demonstrating positive advantage have looked at bilinguals who were equally proficient in both languages and given every opportunity to develop that proficiency.

There are many different ways and contexts in which children become bilingual, and not surprisingly, many different outcomes. It is too early to compare with any confidence the outcomes of monolingual and bilingual acquisition.

REFERENCES

Arnberg, L.N. (1987). *Raising children bilingually: The pre-school years.* Clevedon, UK: Multilingual Matters.

Arnberg, L.N., & Arnberg, P.W. (1985). The relation between code differentiation and language mixing in bilingual three to four year old children. *Bilingual Review, 12,* 20–32.

Arnberg, L.N., & Arnberg, P.W. (1992). Language awareness and language separation in the young bilingual child. In R.J. Harris (Ed.), *Cognitive processing in bilinguals* (pp. 475–500). Amsterdam: North-Holland.

Bergman, C.R. (1976). Interference vs. independent development in infant bilingualism. In G. Keller, R. Teschner, & S. Viera (Eds.), *Bilingualism in the bicentennial and beyond* (pp. 86–95). New York: Bilingual Press.

Bialystok, E. (1987). Words as things: Development of word concept by bilingual children. *Studies in Second Language Acquisition, 9,* 133–140.

Bialystock, E. (1991). Metalinguistic dimensions of bilingual language proficiency. In E. Bialystock (Ed.), *Language processing in bilingual children* (pp. 113–140). Cambridge, UK: Cambridge University Press.

Bialystock, E. (1992). Selective attention in cognitive processing: The bilingual edge. In R.J. Harris (Ed.), *Cognitive processing in bilinguals* (pp. 501–513). Amsterdam: North Holland.

Burling, R. (1959). Language development of a Garo and English speaking child. *Word, 15,* 45–68. [Reprinted in: Bar-Adon, A., & Leopold, W. (Eds.). (1971). *Child language: A book of readings* (pp. 170–185). Englewood Cliffs, NJ: Prentice-Hall.

De Houwer, A. (1990). *The acquisition of two languages from birth: A case study.* Cambridge, UK: Cambridge University Press.

Döpke, S. (1992). *One parent, one language: An interactional approach.* Amsterdam: John Benjamins.

Doyle, A., Champagne, M., & Segalowitz, N. (1978). Some issues on the assessment of linguistic consequences of early bilingualism. In M. Paradis (Ed.), *Aspects of bilingualism* (pp. 13–20). Columbia, SC: Hornbeam Press.

Fantini, A. (1985). *Language acquisition of a bilingual child: A sociolinguistic perspective.* San Diego, CA: College Hill Press.

Galloway, C., & Richards, B. (Eds.). (1994). *Input and interaction in language acquisition.* Cambridge, UK: Cambridge University Press.

Gass, S.M., & Selinker, L. (1994). *Second language acquisition: An introductory course.* Hillsdale, NJ: Lawrence Erlbaum Associates Inc.

Gawlitzek-Maiwald, I., & Tracy, R. (1995). Bilingual bootstrapping. *Linguistics, 34,* 901–926.

Genesee, F. (1989). Early bilingual language development: One language or two? *Journal of Child Language, 16,* 161–179.

Genesee, F., Nicoladis, E., & Paradis, J. (1995). Language differentiation in early bilingual development. *Journal of Child Language, 22,* 611–631.

Grosjean, F. (1982). *Life with two languages: An introduction to bilingualism.* Cambridge, MA: Harvard University Press.

Hakuta, K. (1986). *Mirror of language: The debate on bilingualism.* New York: Basic Books.

Harding, E., & Riley, P. (1986). *The bilingual family: A handbook for parents.* Cambridge, UK: Cambridge University Press.

Hoffman, C. (1985). Language acquisition in two trilingual children. *Journal of Multilingual and Multicultural Development, 6,* 479–495.

Hollos, M. (1977). Comprehension and use of social rules in pronoun selection by Hungarian children. In S. Ervin-Tripp & C. Mitchell-Kernan (Eds.), *Child discourse* (pp. 211–223). New York: Academic Press.

Huerta, A. (1977). The acquisition of bilingualism: A code-switching approach. *Sociolinguistic Working Paper, 39,* 1–33.

Imedadze, N.V. (1967). On the psychological nature of child speech formation under conditions of exposure to two languages. *International Journal of Psychology, 2,* 129–132.

Karniol, R. (1992). Stuttering out of bilingualism. *First Language, 12,* 255–283.

Kielhöfer, B., & Jonekeit, S. (1983). *Zweisprachige Kindererziehung.* Tübingen, Germany: Stauffenberg.

Lanza, E. (1992). Can bilingual two year olds switch? *Journal of Child Language, 19,* 633–658.

Larsen-Freeman, D., & Long, M.H. (1991). *An introduction to second language acquisition research.* London: Longman.

Leopold, W. (1939). *Speech development of a bilingual child: A linguist's record: Vol. I. Vocabulary growth in the first two years.* Evanston, IL: Northwestern University Press.

Leopold, W. (1947). *Speech development of a bilingual child: A linguist's record: Vol. II. Sound learning in the first two years.* Evanston, IL: Northwestern University Press.

Leopold, W. (1949a). *Speech development of a bilingual child: A linguist's record: Vol. III. Grammar and general problems.* Evanston, IL: Northwestern University Press.

Leopold, W. (1949b). *Speech development of a bilingual child: A linguist's record: Vol. IV. Diary from age 2.* Evanston, IL: Northwestern University Press.

McLaughlin, B. (1978). *Second-language acquisition in childhood.* Hillsdale, NJ: Lawrence Erlbaum Associates Inc.

McLaughlin, B. (1984). Early bilingualism: Methodological and theoretical issues. In M. Paradis & Y. Lebrun (Eds.), *Early bilingualism and child development* (pp. 19–45). Lisse, The Netherlands: Swets & Zeitlinger B.V.

Martin-Jones, M., & Romaine, S. (1985). Semilingualism: A half-baked theory of communicative competence. *Applied Linguistics, 6,* 105–117.

Meisel, J. (1986). Word order and case marking in early child language. Evidence from simultaneous acquisition of two first languages: French and German. *Linguistics, 24,* 123–183.

Meisel, J. (1989). Early differentiation of languages in bilingual children. In K. Hyltenstam & L. Obler (Eds.), *Bilingualism across the lifespan: Aspects of acquisition, maturity, and loss* (pp. 13–40). Cambridge, UK: Cambridge University Press.

Meisel, J. (1990). Grammatical development in the simultaneous acquisition of two first languages. In J. Meisel (Ed.), *Two first languages: Early grammatical development in bilingual children* (pp. 5–22). Dordrecht, The Netherlands: Foris.

Meisel, J. (1995). Code-switching in young bilingual children: The acquisition of grammatical constraints. *Studies in Second Language Acquisition, 16,* 413–439.

Mikes, M. (1967). Acquisition des catégoires grammaticales dans le langage de l'enfant. *Enfance, 20,* 289–298.

Ochs, E. (1982). Talking to children in Western Samoa. *Language in Society, 11,* 77–105.

Oksaar, E. (1977). On becoming trilingual. In C. Molony (Ed.), *Deutsch im Kontakt mit anderen Sprachen* (pp. 296–306). Kronberg, Germany: Scriptor Verlag.

Padilla, A.M., & Liebman, E. (1975). Language acquisition in the bilingual child. *Bilingual Review, 2,* 34–55.

Padilla, A.M., & Lindholm, K. (1984). Child bilingualism: The same old issues revisited. In J.L. Martinez, Jr. & R.H. Mendoza (Eds.), *Chicano psychology* (pp. 369–408). Orlando, FL: Academic Press.

Paradis, M., & Lebrun, Y. (Eds.). (1984). *Early bilingualism and child development.* Lisse, The Netherlands: Swets & Zeitlinger B.V.

Petersen, J. (1988). Word internal code-switching constraints in a bilingual child's grammar. *Linguistics, 26,* 479–494.

Pye, C. (1986). One lexicon or two?: An alternative interpretation of early bilingual speech. *Journal of Child Language, 13,* 591–593.

Redlinger, W., & Park, T.-Z. (1980). Language mixing in young bilinguals. *Journal of Child Language, 7,* 337–352.

Romaine, S. (1984). *The language of children and adolescents: The acquisition of communicative competence*. Oxford, UK: Blackwell.

Romaine, S. (1995). *Bilingualism* (2nd edn.). Oxford, UK: Blackwell.

Ronjat, J. (1913). *Le développement du langage observé chez un enfant bilingue*. Paris, France: Champion.

Sankoff, D., & Poplack, S. (1981). A formal grammar for code-switching. *Papers in Linguistics*, *14*, 3–46.

Saunders, G. (1982). *Bilingual children: Guidance for the family*. Clevedon, UK: Multilingual Matters.

Saunders, G. (1988). *Bilingual children: From birth to teens*. Clevedon, UK: Multilingual Matters.

Schieffelin, B. (1981). A developmental study of pragmatic appropriateness of word order and case marking in Kaluli. In W. Deutsch (Ed.), *The child's construction of language* (pp. 105–120). New York: Academic Press.

Slobin, D.I. (Ed.). (1985/1992). *The crosslinguistic study of language acquisition* (3 Vols.). Hillsdale, NJ: Lawrence Erlbaum Associates Inc.

Smith, M.E. (1935). A study of the speech of eight bilingual children of the same family. *Child Development*, *6*, 19–25.

Smith, M.E. (1949). Measurement of vocabularies of young bilingual children in both of the languages used. *Journal of Genetic Psychology*, *74*, 305–310.

Swain, M. (1972). *Bilingualism as a first language*. PhD dissertation, University of California, Irvine.

Tabouret-Keller, A. (1962). L'acquisition du langage parlé chez un petit enfant en milieu bilingue. *Problèmes de Psycholinguistique*, *8*, 205–219.

Taeschner, T. (1983). *The sun is feminine: A study on language acquisition in bilingual children*. Berlin, Germany: Springer.

Vihman, M. (1985). Language differentiation by the bilingual infant. *Journal of Child Language*, *12*, 297–324.

Vihman, M. (1986). More on language differentiation. *Journal of Child Language*, *13*, 595–597.

Volterra, V., & Taeschner, T. (1978). The acquisition and development of language by bilingual children. *Journal of Child Language*, *5*, 311–326.

CHAPTER ELEVEN

Sign language development

John D. Bonvillian
University of Virginia, Charlottesville, USA

INTRODUCTION

In recent years, the study of sign language acquisition has emerged as one of the most exciting areas of inquiry in child language research. Three decades ago, virtually no research had been conducted on sign language acquisition. Today, whole sections of major international conferences are devoted to research on this topic. What led to this dramatic upsurge of interest at this particular time? It was not because scholars had recognised for the first time the existence of deaf persons and sign communication. Deaf persons, after all, have learned and used sign languages throughout recorded history (Schein & Stewart, 1995). Nor was it the discovery that sign communication training could benefit non-speaking mentally retarded persons. The efficacy of the use of signs with such individuals had been recognised at least a century and a half ago (Bonvillian & Miller, 1995; Scott, 1847).

A critical reason for this outpouring of sign language research activity was that many scholars became convinced that sign languages were full, genuine languages. Much of the credit for this acceptance of sign languages as full languages must go to William Stokoe. Stokoe, in his pioneering investigations of American Sign Language (ASL),[1] showed that ASL signs had a distinct linguistic structure (Stokoe, 1960; Stokoe, Casterline, & Croneberg, 1965). Prior to Stokoe's research, most scholars viewed sign languages as consisting primarily of pantomimic gestures with little evidence of grammatical structure. In the

---

[1] American Sign Language or ASL is the principal language of the deaf community in the United States. Deaf persons in most countries of the world have their own distinct sign languages.

years following Stokoe's discoveries, evidence quickly accumulated that showed that ASL (and other sign languages) had a large lexicon and that ASL operated according to rule-governed phonological, morphological, and syntactical processes (Klima & Bellugi, 1979; Wilbur, 1987). The acceptance of sign languages as full languages made the study of sign language acquisition a topic worthy of linguistic inquiry.

A second important reason for the enormous growth in volume of research on sign language development was that investigators realised that the systematic study of sign language acquisition provided a way to answer important questions about human language abilities. One question of interest was whether there were effects of language modality on language acquisition. This question sparked a series of investigations to determine how much children's sign language acquisition resembled children's spoken language acquisition. A second question that intrigued investigators was whether the human brain processed sign languages in much the same way as spoken languages. When researchers interested in this topic studied the development of young children, they often focused on the children's hand preference as they signed as an indicator of cerebral hemispheric involvement in sign production. A third question of interest was whether hearing individuals who failed to acquire a spoken language could make progress in acquiring a signed language. If so, then this finding would indicate that signed and spoken languages were not processed identically and might open up a lot of opportunities for speech-limited individuals. A final question of interest to investigators was whether the varying ages and settings in which deaf children learned to sign affected their level of sign language mastery. In answering this question, researchers might be able to gain insights into how much of language development was the product of environmental factors and how much the product of innate mechanisms. Before proceeding to examine the results of investigators' efforts to answer these important questions, it is necessary to set the stage by providing some background information on sign languages and the development of deaf children.

Sign languages and deafness

For most persons who are born deaf or who become deaf early in their lives, sign languages constitute their principal means of communication. In some cases, hearing individuals who lose their ability to speak or who take vows of silence learn to sign or to fingerspell (the spelling of words on the hand or hands using the letters of a manual alphabet). Hearing children of deaf parents also often attain facility in signing. In the vast majority of instances, however, it is the members of the deaf community who have embraced signing and who have been responsible for the transmission of sign languages from one generation to the next. But how this language transmission occurs is varied and complicated. Nevertheless, in order to understand sign language acquisition research, it is important to be aware of the reasons why sign languages often are acquired at ages and in settings quite different from those of spoken language acquisition.

Like most hearing children learning to speak, most deaf children of deaf parents learn to sign at their parents' feet. The parents model the language their children learn and engage their children in developmentally appropriate conversational exchanges. For deaf children as a group, however, such parental language transmission has been the exception rather than the rule. This is because the large majority of deaf children—more than 90%—have hearing parents (Meadow, 1980; Schein & Delk, 1974). Historically, these parents often were advised to refrain from signing to their young children. Instead, these parents typically were urged to make every effort to foster their children's spoken language development. Although a small proportion of these children acquired proficiency in speech through this approach, most did not.

Although some hearing parents make a concerted effort to sign to their deaf children, most deaf children with hearing parents learn to sign in schools for deaf students. The ages at which these deaf students begin learning a sign language, however, may extend from early childhood through adolescence or even into adulthood. Some deaf children with hearing parents may be introduced to sign communication in special preschool programmes. Others may commence their elementary education at a school for deaf students and begin signing at that time. Many deaf students, however, begin their education in classrooms in their neighbourhood elementary schools. There they often are surrounded by normal-hearing peers. Even if various support services are available, a substantial proportion of these deaf students experience educational difficulties and social isolation. They often will transfer to a residential school for deaf students and begin their educations anew. There, many of these students encounter classmates who have deaf parents. These children probably have signed since infancy and are highly fluent signers. It is these children of deaf parents who, together with the fluent signers on the school's staff, often are the first highly fluent signers that deaf students with hearing parents actually encounter.

Needless to say, the wide differences in backgrounds among deaf children make the education of deaf students a formidable task. At the same time, the diversity in language-learning environments experienced by deaf students also provides researchers with a rare opportunity to examine the effects of the environment on language acquisition.

EARLY SIGN LANGUAGE ACQUISITION: SIMILARITIES AND DIFFERENCES WITH SPOKEN LANGUAGE DEVELOPMENT

Soon after scholars began accepting Stokoe's position that American Sign Language was a full and genuine language, they started asking whether the course of language development was the same for both spoken and signed languages. This question was important for several reasons. First, if language acquisition processes were shown to be the same, this would indicate that language was a higher cognitive process that transcended the modality of expression. Second, if the processes were the same, then investigators could study linguistic processes in sign and then extrapolate their findings to languages in general. And, third, if the course of acquisition were found to be different across modalities, then many of the assumptions in linguistic theory about universal processes would need to be changed. Clearly, much was riding on the answer to this question.

After nearly three decades of research, the answer to this question at a general level is "Yes, the course of development across modalities is highly similar". Systematic comparisons between children of deaf parents learning to sign and their hearing counterparts learning to speak have revealed that there are a number of parallels in language acquisition across language modalities (Meier, 1991; Newport & Meier, 1985). Most children, regardless of language modality, first babble, then utter their first recognisable words or signs, and this is followed by their acquisition of referential language—the ability to use names or labels. These early language milestones then typically are followed by a period of substantial vocabulary growth, the emergence of the ability to combine lexical items, and, finally, the formation of short sentences. Although there is widespread agreement among researchers that the general course of language development is quite similar across modalities, there has been considerable debate among investigators over whether language development is "virtually identical" (Petitto, 1996) across modalities or whether there are some important modality differences. To appreciate this debate, it will be necessary to review the evidence for the existence of similarities and differences in language development across modalities.

Early language processing

At least in the very beginning, spoken language processing is advanced relative to that of signed languages. Most 6- to 7-month-old fetuses can hear; there is no comparable intrauterine sign processing, although there is often considerable fetal motor activity. The human fetus responds to voices, in particular to the maternal voice because of its largely internal transmission (Locke, 1993). Shortly after birth, most human babies display an impressive array of speech-processing skills. When neonates are tested, they typically show a distinct preference for their mothers' voice (DeCasper & Fifer, 1980). Very young infants also can discriminate many basic human speech sounds or phonemes (Eimas, Siqueland, Jusczyk, & Vigorito, 1971).

Although speech discrimination skills may have an early headstart, infants soon are making great strides in visuomotor processing. By 4 months of age, hearing infants with no sign language experience are able to discriminate between gestures based on the movement contrasts present in ASL signs (Carroll

& Gibson, 1986). Thus, important language discrimination skills are manifested early in development for both modalities. It should be noted, however, that it is not clear whether the discrimination of language elements in speech and sign actually takes place in the same way. Speech discrimination appears to be mostly a categorical process, whereas visual discriminations may operate more along a continuum.

Babbling

The emergence of babbling is an important milestone in early language development. Vocal babbling is clearly evident in hearing children by 6 to 8 months of age. Deaf children also babble vocally, but the onset of their vocal babbling is quite delayed in comparison with that of hearing children (Oller & Eilers, 1988). The emergence of babbling in the manual mode during the latter half of the first year has been reported as well. Children of deaf parents often have been observed to babble manually (Maestas y Moores, 1980; Meier & Willerman, 1995; Petitto & Marentette, 1991; Prinz & Prinz, 1979). These young sign-learning children produce numerous sign-like gestures prior to making their first recognisable lexical signs.

Although there is widespread agreement among investigators that sign-learning children babble manually, investigators disagree as to the degree this phenomenon occurs in hearing children not exposed to a sign language. Petitto and Marentette found a much higher incidence of manual babbling in deaf children learning to sign than in hearing children learning to speak. They interpreted this finding as strong evidence for a single human language capacity that operated without regard to language modality. This language capacity also was seen as independent of motor development. Meier and Willerman, in contrast, found similar levels of manual babbling in both deaf and hearing infants. Because the hearing infants in their study received no sign input, Meier and Willerman concluded that manual babbling was a developmentally robust phenomenon that occurred regardless of language input modality. They also suggested that neuromotor development and processing may play a substantial role in both vocal and manual babbling. In light of these two studies' wide differences in findings and interpretation, it is clear that additional research will be needed in the future to resolve the role of neuromotor development in both vocal and manual babbling. For the present, we can conclude that there is strong evidence for babbling in both language modes at about the same ages.

Early sign production

Much of the information about early sign production has come from two longitudinal studies of sign language acquisition in children of deaf parents (Bonvillian, Orlansky, & Novack, 1983; Folven & Bonvillian, 1991). In these studies, a total of 22 young children (both deaf and hearing) were followed for periods ranging from 4 months to over 2 years. The sign language development of these children was compared with the spoken language development of 18 hearing children studied by Nelson (1973).

The deaf parents who participated in the two longitudinal investigations reported that their children produced their first recognisable sign at 8.5 months. In contrast, an age range of 11 to 14 months for onset of first spoken word frequently is given in large-scale studies of children's speech development that also relied heavily on parental report (Capute, Palmer, Shapiro, Wachtel, Schmidt, & Ross, 1986; Cattell, 1940; Fenson, Dale, Reznick, Bates, Thal, & Pethick, 1994; Shirley, 1933). There are, however, real difficulties in determining the precise age at which a word is first used. Because of these difficulties, Nelson (1973) decided to use the date at which a child attained a vocabulary of 10 different words as her index of initial vocabulary development. For her 18 children learning to speak, this language milestone was attained at a mean age of 15.1 months. For the 22 children learning to sign, this milestone was reached significantly earlier, at a mean age of 13.3 months. These signing children began combining signs for the first time at a mean age of 16.7 months. Again, this age is somewhat in advance of the age range of 18 to 22 months frequently given for the onset of spoken word combinations (Bowerman, 1973; Cattell, 1940; Fenson et al., 1994; Gesell & Thompson, 1934).

This slightly accelerated acquisition in sign of the first steps of expressive language is in accord with the findings of a number of previous studies. Indeed, an early observation of this modality difference in early language acquisition was made well over a century ago by Whitney (1867). At that time, he observed that the hearing children of teachers of the deaf, exposed to both sign and speech, typically acquired facility in the former first. In recent years, a number of case studies have supported this finding of somewhat more rapid early sign language development by both deaf and hearing children (Holmes & Holmes, 1980; McIntire, 1977; Prinz & Prinz, 1979; Williams, 1976).

Across the two longitudinal investigations of sign language acquisition (Bonvillian et al., 1983; Folven & Bonvillian, 1991), the mean ages at which early language milestones were attained were very similar, but there were very wide individual differences among the children. For age of onset of first recognisable sign, the parents' reports extended from a low of 5.5 months to a high of 11 months. Vocabulary size at one year also varied widely, from a low of 2 to a high of 30 different signs. For the age of acquisition of a lexicon of 10 different signs, the range among the children extended from 11 to 17 months. Similarly, there was a very wide range in the onset ages for two-sign combinations, with one child beginning to combine signs at 12.5 months whereas another child did not make his first combination until he was 22 months old. These findings of quite wide differences among the children in the ages at which they attained various early language milestones in sign are consistent with the findings of wide individual differences in early spoken language development reported by Fenson et al. (1994) and McCarthy (1954). Moreover, the wide individual differences in the ages at which young children achieve early language milestones in sign underlines the importance of collecting early language acquisition data from a number of children.

Although the young children learning to sign varied widely in the ages at which they attained early language milestones, this finding should not be misconstrued as indicating that there was not substantial consistency in the rates of early sign language acquisition across children. Those children who were among the first to produce recognisable signs also tended to attain a 10-sign vocabulary and to combine signs at younger ages. Similarly, those children who attained early language milestones in signs at later ages also typically attained subsequent milestones at later ages. The overall pattern that emerged was that age of attainment of early language milestones in sign highly predicted the age of attainment of subsequent milestones (Bonvillian, Richards, & Saah, 1996).

A second difference between young sign-learning children and children learning to speak was in the rate at which they acquired new vocabulary items. Children acquiring a spoken language typically make relatively slow progress in building a vocabulary in the months following the production of their first expressive word, but then often show very rapid vocabulary growth in the latter half of their second year. Bloom, Lifter, and Broughton (1985, p. 152) wrote of this phenomenon: "One of the most consistent observations in child language is the often precipitous increase in vocabulary and volubility sometime during the last half of the second year." In contrast, the sign-learning children tended to gradually and steadily increase their rate of sign acquisition in the months following their initial production. A sudden spurt in vocabulary size was not common among the sign-learning children.

In discussing these young children's initial sign productions, it should be noted that they often neither formed their signs fully accurately nor used them consistently in an appropriate manner. Many of the children's early signs resembled their parents' versions of the same signs only in part (Bonvillian, Orlansky, Novack, Folven, & Holley-Wilcox, 1985; Siedlecki & Bonvillian, 1993). Children learning to speak similarly only gradually acquire the ability to produce the sounds of their language (Ingram, 1976; Locke, 1983). In addition, young children, regardless of language modality, often do not fully understand the concepts underlying the words or signs they produce. Records and observations of the young children's early signing revealed examples of occasional undergeneralisation (e.g. using the sign DOG[2] only to refer to the family dog) and overgeneralisation (e.g. using the sign MILK to refer to all liquids) of concept boundaries. A similar phenomenon occurs in the early vocabulary development of children learning to speak (Clark, 1973).

---

[2] By convention, English glosses for signs are printed in all capital letters.

Referential language

Those investigators who made claims of slightly accelerated early acquisition of language in the manual mode were not without their critics. The chief criticism was that they ignored the context of the children's sign usage and attributed linguistic status to a sign based entirely on its form. If one focused on the context of much of the early sign production, the critics argued, then many of the signs would be seen as either imitations of caregivers' signs or part of a restricted interactional routine (Petitto, 1988; Volterra & Caselli, 1985). For Volterra and Iverson (1995), the evidence for a sign advantage in vocabulary development did not represent a modality difference in symbol production or linguistic usage. Rather, they maintain, the evidence for an early sign advantage should be seen as a prelinguistic communicative gesture advantage.

Although there is not widespread agreement as to the criteria to be used in deciding when a child starts using language, the emergence of referential language has been advanced as a very important step in the acquisition process. With the onset of referential language, the child is able to use vocabulary items to name new instances of objects or events (Bates, Benigni, Bretherton, Camaioni, & Volterra, 1979; Bates, Camaioni, & Volterra, 1975). This represents an important advance for the young language learner. A child who uses a sign or a word to name a new exemplar of a concept demonstrates an understanding that language can be used to categorise objects, people, and events, that things have names or labels, and that language is not tied to a particular item or context.

The first recognisable signs that were produced by the young children studied by Folven and Bonvillian (1991) were all used non-referentially. Some of these early productions were imitations of others' signs, requests, or parts of gestural routines. Moreover, many of the children's initial sign productions were used rather indiscriminately. With increasing age and feedback, these early signs were employed more and more consistently with the appropriate persons, objects, and actions. For the children as a group, the mean age of their first referential sign was 12.6 months; the range in ages extended from 10.1 to 16.2 months. This age of onset of referential usage in ASL is quite close to the age of 13 months that is reported as typical for the onset of referential spoken word usage (Bates et al., 1975, 1979).

Young children learning to sign often produce recognisable signs somewhat earlier than their speaking counterparts produce recognisable words. Yet when the age at onset of referential language is used in comparisons of the two groups, the two groups do not appear to differ. What would account for this pattern? The explanation advanced (Folven & Bonvillian, 1991) is that recognisable non-referential language production and referential usage may be governed by different constraints. The ability to produce non-referential words and signs may depend primarily on motor abilities. For many children, the motor abilities needed for sign production may emerge earlier than those needed for speech. The ability to use language referentially—to use signs or words to name new instances of things—probably involves a much stronger cognitive component. This cognitive component may well be independent of language modality.

The controversy over whether or not there is a gestural advantage in early symbol acquisition, however, does not appear to be ending any time soon. In recent months, this debate has been renewed. This time the focus of discussion is not findings from studies of sign language and deafness, but new data from a study of the development of hearing children of hearing parents. In this study, half the children received parental speech input designed to assist them in their acquisition of a small lexicon of spoken words. The other half were taught a collection of "baby signs" by their parents. Group comparisons conducted monthly between 12 and 15 months indicated that, at each age, significantly more target gestures (baby signs) had been learned by the sign-trained infants than target words by the verbal-trained infants (Goodwyn & Acredolo, 1998). The investigators attributed the slower development of the verbally trained infants to the difficulties posed by the speech production component at this point in development.

Vocabulary content

Although many sign-learning children were slightly accelerated in their early vocabulary production in comparison with norms for spoken language acquisition, this should not be interpreted as indicating that the children were talking about different things. In fact, the content of the lexicons for children learning to sign and their counterparts learning to speak is quite similar during their first 2 years. In arriving at this conclusion, the English glosses of the sign language vocabularies of young children learning ASL from their deaf parents were compared with the records provided by Nelson (1973) for young children learning to speak English.

The signing children's vocabularies showed considerable overlap with those of children learning to speak both in terms of the distribution of vocabulary items into grammatical and semantic categories as well as in specific lexical entries. Moreover, this conclusion held when analyses were conducted at the 10-item (Folven & Bonvillian, 1991) and 50-item vocabulary levels (Bonvillian et al., 1983). Both the signing and speaking children named many of the same objects, actions, persons, and properties that were common to their environments. Indeed, the same vocabulary items that occurred most often among the sign-learning children (e.g. cookie, Mommy, Daddy, hot, car, no, shoes, milk, dog) also were the most frequent entries in the lexicons of the children learning to speak. In addition, there was a high degree of similarity across language modalities both in the number of items contained within each of Nelson's semantic categories (e.g. animal names, vehicles, household items) and in the specific lexical items included in these categories. Classification of the young sign-learning children's vocabularies by grammatical category also largely mirrored those reported by Nelson for children learning to speak. Overall, with relatively few exceptions, the resemblance in the lexicons between the children learning to sign and their speaking counterparts was quite striking. Through 18 months of age, the children's lexicons were nearly identical in their content across language modalities.

One of the few exceptions to the general pattern of similarity in vocabulary content across modalities was for those lexical items classified by Nelson as function items. Signs that fit this grammatical category were not present in any of the children's 10-sign vocabularies and accounted for only 1% of all entries in their 50-sign vocabularies. This very low incidence of function items or functors in the signing children's lexicons may largely reflect inherent differences between ASL and English. Functors typically are not specifically signed in ASL. Instead, the structural or relational information that function words provide in English often is incorporated into the gestural production of sign utterances in other ways (e.g. how signs relate to each other in the signing space). It is thus quite possible that the vocabulary content of children learning ASL and their counterparts learning English may diverge as the children get older as a result of structural differences between the languages.

Iconicity

A major difference between signs and words is that a substantial number of signs look like the concepts they denote whereas words rarely do so. That is, certain signs are iconic or pantomimic in that they resemble the actions, objects, or properties for which they stand. With the exception of a few onomatopoeic words, the tie between a word and its concept is essentially an arbitrary one. It might be supposed that young children would find iconic or pantomimic signs particularly easy to learn and that such signs would constitute a large portion of their early vocabularies. Indeed, there is some evidence that deaf parents believe that this may be the case. These parents have commented that they typically used iconic or pantomimic signs more often when interacting with their young children because they felt such signs would be more easily learned. The iconic aspect of certain signs also has been advanced as a possible explanation for young sign-learning children's accelerated early vocabulary growth.

Is there compelling evidence to support this notion that iconic signs are acquired more easily? Not, at least, among very young children. When young children's initial ASL lexicons were examined in two studies (Folven & Bonvillian, 1991; Orlansky & Bonvillian, 1984), it was found that iconic or pantomimic signs accounted for only about one-third of all the children's vocabulary items. Although this proportion probably is higher than the proportion of iconic signs found in ASL overall, it also indicates that the large majority of the children's signs are non-iconic. Moreover, if the parents truly tend to make more iconic signs when interacting with their young children, the level of iconic signs found in the children's lexicons may simply reflect parental input.

Signing after infancy

Language acquisition, of course, does not end with the attainment of a core vocabulary and the onset of sign combinations. Many semantic and grammatical skills remain to be acquired. Over the past two decades, a number of studies have been conducted that have examined young deaf children's sign language development. Comparisons of the results from these studies with those from studies of children's spoken language development have shown that there are many parallels in the language acquisition process across language modalities. For example, at about 2 years of age, ASL-learning children incorporate the use of pointing gestures for pronominal reference into their signing (Pettito, 1987). This age is close to that for equivalent pronoun usage in children learning to speak.

Additional evidence of resemblance in development can be seen in the findings of studies of the emergence of semantic relations (Newport & Ashbrook, 1977), of how negation is expressed (Anderson & Reilly, 1997), of the acquisition of verb agreement (Meier, 1981, 1987), and the addition of inflectional or derivational morphology (Newport & Meier, 1985). Young deaf children, in their two-sign combinations, typically produce the full range of semantic relations (e.g. possession of object, location of object) that have been shown to be present in hearing children's two-word utterances. Moreover, when the order of emergence of different semantic relations was examined within individual children, it was found that semantic relations emerged in about the same order regardless of language modality (Newport & Ashbrook, 1977).

A study of ASL-learning deaf children showed that they typically began to communicate negation when they were about 1 year old (Anderson & Reilly, 1997). This was accomplished, in most instances, by a negative headshake. This gesture was not considered by the investigators to be part of the children's manual signing at this age, but rather to be a form of non-linguistic communication. The children used their headshakes to reject others' requests or suggestions. Hearing children have also been found to begin expressing negation around this same age. Like the deaf children, hearing children begin by conveying negation through non-verbal gestures. The next step in deaf children's emerging ability to express negation was their production of specific negative signs (e.g. NONE, a fingerspelled "n-o"). These negative signs were produced without a co-occurring headshake. This ability to produce specific negative signs typically was manifested by the deaf children by the time they were 18 months old. Their hearing counterparts of about the same age usually have a word to indicate negation among the entries in their initial 50-word vocabularies. Finally, the deaf children learned to accompany their production of negative signs with negative headshakes. This linguistic integration of signs and headshakes typically began when the children were about 20 months old.

Anderson and Reilly (1997) observed that there were similarities in the course of ASL-learning children's acquisition of negation and their mastery of verbs. An early step in deaf children's verb production was found to be their modification of the verb stem so that it agreed in its orientation and direction with the location of its associated noun (Meier, 1981, 1987). In their acquisition of complex verbs of motion, however, ASL-learning children first produced a particular morpheme (for direction or for manner of motion) sequentially, rather than simultaneously as in the adult system (Newport & Meier, 1985). Only later did the children integrate their production to the adult-like simultaneous production. Anderson and Reilly concluded that this pattern of acquisition was quite similar to that reported for spoken language acquisition, in which the acquisition of free morphemes preceded the acquisition of bound morphemes.

Phonological development

Since the study of sign language development emerged as a research domain, most of the investigations have focused primarily on children's acquisition of vocabulary and grammar. Only rarely did investigators carefully examine children's acquisition of sign phonology. This relative dearth of systematic research on sign phonological acquisition is somewhat surprising in light of the advantages sign languages have for research on phonological acquisition. Sign languages, by their very nature as visual and gestural languages, utilise articulators (primarily the hands and face) that are more easily observed than those of spoken languages. Beginning in the early 1990s, various investigators began redirecting their research efforts to collect information on sign phonological acquisition. Today, there are at least a handful of research groups studying the topic. In the past few years, much has been learned about how children acquire sign formational skills; much, however, remains to be learned.

Most of the studies of sign phonological acquisition have relied heavily on Stokoe's model of ASL formational structure. Stokoe identified three formational aspects of ASL that distinguished one ASL sign from another. According to Stokoe (1960; Stokoe et al., 1965), every ASL sign is composed of three aspects: the place where the sign is made, the shape and orientation of the hand or hands making the sign, and the action or movement of the hand or hands forming the sign. Each of these aspects (commonly referred to as location, handshape, and movement) consists of a limited set of formational elements that function largely analogously to phonemes in spoken languages. (Stokoe coined the term "cheremes" to designate these sign phonemes, but this term has never been widely adopted.) In the years since Stokoe first advanced his model of sign structure, additional parameters have been proposed to describe signs more precisely. Most researchers, however, have continued to use the three aspects first identified by Stokoe as their basic classes of phonological units in their studies of lexical signs.

Of the three sign formational aspects, the location aspect is the one most often produced correctly by young ASL-learning children (Conlin, Mirus, Mauk, & Meier, in press; Siedlecki & Bonvillian, 1993). This tendency to accurately produce the location aspect emerges early in development. Beginning with their very first signs, young children typically make them in the correct location. A likely explanation for this high formational accuracy is that location phonemes tend to be relatively broad categories that do not require fine distinctions in their production. To produce many location phonemes correctly may require that the infant only be capable of making relatively gross motor movements.

Although the location aspect of signs as a group often is produced accurately even by young children, certain sign locations are more readily acquired than others. Young children tend to acquire highly contrastive locations (e.g. chin, forehead, on and in front of the trunk) first (Bonvillian & Siedlecki, 1996). Locations that often are acquired later in development are those that may involve smaller areas for contact or require the child's active signing hand to cross the body's midline. Of the relatively few location phoneme errors children make, many are made adjacent to the correct adult location.

Of the three sign formational aspects, handshape initially is produced by children with the lowest accuracy. Unlike the other two aspects, children show a clear development in accuracy of handshape formation between their first and third years. The accuracy of handshape production typically improves both as children's age and vocabulary size increases. In children's early signs, four basic handshapes (5-open hand, G-index finger extended, B-flat hand, and A-fist) predominate. With increasing development, children learn to produce hand configurations that are more and more complex.

Boyes-Braem (1973/1990) attempted to account for children's handshape acquisition by examining the anatomical factors that constrain development. Analyses of children's handshape acquisition provide support for the view that anatomical and physiological factors strongly influence handshape acquisition order. These two factors may also underlie the finding that most young children acquire handshapes in a definite sequence (Siedlecki & Bonvillian, 1997). At the same time, other factors, such as sign input and formational context, also impact on formational accuracy. These additional factors may help explain why some children clearly deviate from the general sequence of handshape acquisition.

Young ASL-learning children often produce the movement aspect of signs with intermediate accuracy. In general, there is little change in production accuracy of sign movements during children's first two years. In contrast, the number of different movement phonemes and the complexity of sign movements increases with age and vocabulary size. Of the different sign movements identified by Stokoe, contacting action is by far the most frequently produced. Contacting action, however, also serves partly as a location specification (Wilbur, 1987). If contacting action were to be reclassified as a location rather than as a movement phoneme, then children's production accuracy of the movement aspect would be much lower.

At a very general level, there are several similarities in phonological acquisition across language modalities. One clear similarity is that phonological development occurs over a period of at least several years in each mode. Children do not become precise signers overnight just as they do not suddenly master the sounds of their spoken language. A second similarity is that there are general sequences of phonological development in each language mode. Certain sign phonemes tend to be acquired before others, much as certain speech phonemes typically are mastered before others. A third similarity is that there are individual differences in phonological acquisition in both modalities. Although there are general patterns or sequences in development, particular individuals may follow different routes to phonological mastery. A fourth similarity is that there are various general processes of perceptual and motor learning that appear to transcend language modalities. For example, examination of children's acquisition of the location aspect of signs revealed a pattern of learning reminiscent of Jakobson's (1941/1968) principle of maximal contrasts. Early-learned locations required only broad distinctions, whereas later-learned locations required finer discriminations. A final similarity in phonological acquisition across modalities is evident in the phenomenon known as child homonymy.

Child homonymy.   Child homonymy occurs when a child makes use of a single phonetic form for two (or more) linguistic targets that are phonetically distinct for adult language-users. It is not clear, however, whether child homonymy is the result of an unintentional action (i.e. the child is not yet able to produce certain adult forms or does not perceive them) or is an active strategy that enables the child to produce new lexical forms without having to learn new phonetic sequences.

Although the phenomenon of child homonymy has long been recognised as a characteristic of young children's speech production (Ervin-Tripp, 1966; Jakobson, 1941/1968), it has only recently been identified as occurring in children's early signing (Siedlecki & Bonvillian, 1998). Each of nine ASL-learning children who were examined were found to produce homonymous forms (i.e. a single manual form is used to represent two or more different adult target signs). Moreover, the incidence of homonymy in these children's early ASL sign formation did not differ significantly from that reported for normally developing children learning to speak (Ingram, 1981). This finding of homonymy in children's early signing is somewhat surprising because homonyms are either extremely rare or nonexistent in the lexicons of adult signers (see Rimor, Kegl, Lane, & Schermer, 1984). Thus, young children acquiring a sign language produce homonymous forms early in their development even though their parents are unlikely to have produced homonyms for them to observe.

Conclusions

Clearly, there are a very large number of similarities in language acquisition across language modalities. These similarities are evident during infancy in babbling, phonological development, referential language onset, and vocabulary content. Additional parallels during early childhood are seen in the acquisition of pronouns, verb agreement, semantic relations, and inflectional morphology. This strong overall resemblance in language development across modalities indicates that the human capacity for language is fully functional for both visual-motor and auditory-vocal languages. The many parallels in acquisition across modalities also lend support to the research approach of studying sign languages as a way to learn more about language phenomena more generally.

But the issue of whether or not development is "virtually identical" across modalities is more difficult to resolve. Aspects of language acquisition that depend more on cognitive development (e.g. onset of referential language) appear to be virtually identical. Aspects of language acquisition that depend more on the development of control of production components (e.g. onset of recognisable words and signs) appear to differ considerably in their emergence across modality. Thus, the timetable of early vocabulary development often favours children learning to sign.

Unfortunately, the debate over how much sign language acquisition resembles speech acquisition has served to obscure a serious flaw in the sign language acquisition research literature. That flaw is that only a few longitudinal studies have been conducted that involved more than several sign-learning children. Until more large-scale studies are completed, it will not be possible to resolve definitively the debate about modality differences in development.

HAND PREFERENCE IN EARLY SIGNING

At first glance, the hand preference of children as they sign would appear to be a research topic that fairly begged to be explored. After all, the notion that hand preference and hemispheric control of language are related has been around for a long time. In 1865, the French physician Paul Broca proclaimed that the cerebral hemisphere controlling speech production was the one opposite an individual's preferred hand. For most individuals, their right hand is their preferred hand and their left hemisphere is dominant for language. Although Broca eventually acknowledged that there were exceptions to this contralateral pattern, and that cerebral control of speech and handedness were not necessarily conjoined (Eling, 1984; Harris, 1991, 1993), he was critically important in establishing the view that language dominance and hand preference are closely interrelated.

The specific suggestion to study hand preference and signing also dates back to the 19th century. In 1895, James Mark Baldwin, a prominent American psychologist, recommended the study of hand preference as it is manifested in signing as a fruitful line of research. Following this approach, one could readily observe how language production and arm and hand movements were intertwined. Baldwin, although an accomplished scholar in the area of children's development of hand preference, knew very little about signing. His suggestion to study hand preference in signing was based on correspondence he had with Garrick Mallery, an American military officer. Mallery had made pioneering observations of the Plains Indians and their sign communication system. The Plains Indians, he wrote to Baldwin, used their right hands most of the time when communicating in their sign system. Despite the apparent ease of studying hand preference in signing, as well as Baldwin's authoritative recommendation to do so, it was not until quite recently that this topic was systematically examined.

Several studies have now probed the emergence of hand preference in young children learning to sign. Although these studies differed widely in their scope and duration, their pattern of findings has been quite consistent. In the first study (Bellugi, Klima, Lillo-Martin, O'Grady, & Vaid, 1986), a deaf child's hand preference was determined for both her production of signs and non-sign actions (e.g. reaches, object manipulation). These signs and non-sign actions had been captured on videotapes that had been made of her development beginning when she was 12 months old and continuing through her 34th month. Of the 284 videotaped signs this child of deaf parents made with a single hand, 282 were made with her right hand. This child also tended to favour her right hand in non-sign actions or movements, but the magnitude of this preference was not nearly as great.

In a second study (Marentette, Girouard, & Petitto, 1990), the hand preferences of four hearing children were examined longitudinally when they were between 6 and 18 months of age. Two of the children had deaf parents who communicated with them in signs; the other two children had hearing parents who communicated with them in speech. Both of the children who were learning to sign showed a very strong right-hand preference in their sign production. This right-hand preference for sign production was considerably greater than that obtained for any of the other manual actions coded for any of the children. Moreover, this right-hand preference was evident beginning with the two signing children's initial sign productions.

In the largest study to date on sign language acquisition and hand preference, 24 young children (3 deaf, 21 hearing) of deaf parents who communicated with them in ASL were followed longitudinally (Bonvillian, Richards, & Dooley, 1997). For most of the children, their preference for their right hand in signing was much stronger than it was for non-sign manual actions. This pattern of a strong right-hand preference for signing emerged early in the development of most of the children and was relatively consistent throughout infancy. Of the four children who were exceptions to this pattern, two eventually became left-handed signers. Although the children in this study also tended to prefer their right hands in their production of non-sign actions, the magnitude of this preference was much less than it was for sign production.

This strong right-hand preference in young children learning to sign stands in marked contrast to findings about the emergence of hand preference in the large majority of children who are learning a spoken language as their first language. During infancy, children learning to speak typically display only small asymmetries in their hand preference. At the midpoint of their first year, most such infants show just a small preference for their right hands in motor actions; this preference, moreover, often is not consistent over time, as there are frequent changes in hand preference (McCormick & Maurer, 1988). At one year of age, a substantial minority of children demonstrate a preference for their left hand. With increasing age, the proportion of children showing a left-hand preference declines considerably (Bishop, 1990). By 3 years of age, hand preference is well-established in most normal children (McManus, Sik, Cole, Mellon, Wong, & Kloss, 1988). In contrast, most of the young children learning to sign had a well-established signing hand preference by the beginning of their second year.

What might account for such a distinct signing hand preference? One possibility is that this preference is the direct outcome of parental modelling or training. The large majority of deaf signers show a distinct right-hand preference in their signing (Bellugi, 1991). Presumably, when these deaf adults have children, their children would grow up in an environment consisting largely of right-handed signers. But there are several problems with this parental-model explanation. First, in some cases, the parents' hand preferences and those of their children are not in accord. A second is that relatively few instances of the parents directly moulding their children's hands into the correct sign formation were captured on videotape. A third difficulty with this explanation is that infants often saw their parents' signing from a range of viewpoints. Sometimes the children would sit on their parents' laps, sometimes the children and their parents would be side-to-side, but, in most instances, the parents and children would face each other while signing. When the children would sign while facing their parents, the children typically would use the hand contralateral to their parents' dominant signing hand. In using their contralateral hand, the children would need to suppress a tendency to respond with the hand on the same side as their parents' signing hand. It is unlikely, then, that parental training or modelling would account for their children's strong right-hand preference for signing.

A more likely explanation than parental training is that the children's strong right-hand preference for signing reflects fundamental hemispheric differences in language and sequential motor processing. Most of the children's strong right-hand preference for signing was evident from the time they began to form their first signs. This asymmetry most likely reflects a built-in or early-activated left cerebral hemispheric specialisation for language skills and complex motor movements. This explanation would be consistent with previous findings of left hemispheric involvement in infants' speech processing (Entus, 1977; Molfese, Freeman, & Palermo, 1975) and in the production of complex motor movements (Heilman, 1979). Because the children's sign production depends on both motor and language abilities, it is not clear which might be contributing more to the establishment of a distinct right-hand preference. Indeed, for signing children, language ability and the production of complex fine motor movements may be so closely intertwined as not to be separable.

THE DEVELOPMENT OF GESTURAL COMMUNICATION IN THE ABSENCE OF A LANGUAGE MODEL

As social creatures, human beings have a fundamental need to communicate with others. Childhood deafness, however, often seriously impedes or precludes children's acquisition of their parents' spoken language. When the only language that parents use in their interaction with their deaf children is a spoken one, these children frequently are left with a need to communicate but they are without a useful language model. How children respond to such a situation has been the primary focus of Goldin-Meadow and her associates' research for more than two decades. This research has been one of the most valuable sources of information about children's capacities, in the absence of effective language input, to construct their own gestural communication system.

To learn about children's language generating capacities, Goldin-Meadow and her colleagues studied the development of 10 young children who were either severely or profoundly deaf. When this study began, these children ranged in age from 16 to 49 months. Their parents, who were hearing, wanted very much for their children to acquire facility in speech. Most of the children participated in programmes to enhance their speech skills. Their parents did not sign with them. Despite the parents' efforts to foster spoken language skills, none of the children made significant progress in acquiring speech. Instead, the children's primary means of communication became a gestural one.

The investigators made periodic visits to the children's homes during which they made videotapes of the children's gestural production. From their analyses of these videotapes, the investigators identified three different types or groups of gestures made by the children (Goldin-Meadow & Feldman, 1977; Goldin-Meadow & Mylander, 1984, 1990). One group, deictic gestures, was used by the children to indicate specific objects, persons, and locations. This was done mostly by pointing. The second group of gestures consisted of stylised pantomimes known as characterising gestures. These gestures resembled the objects or actions to which the children were referring. For example, a child's twisting action was interpreted as representing the action of opening a jar. Similarly, the pounding of a fist in the air was identified as the action of hammering. The third category of gestures, called markers, clearly resembled many of the hand and facial gestures used by most members of American society. In this group were such gestures as nodding or shaking the head to affirm or negate and the extension of a finger to signify "wait". This latter group of gestures appears to have been incorporated by the deaf children into their communication systems through interactions with the larger hearing society.

When the deaf children were first visited in their homes, eight were already combining gestures. The other two children, after a period of using single gestures in isolation, began combining gestures. Many of the children's gestural combinations were of one particular form: a point, to indicate a specific object, was combined with a characterising gesture, to designate an action or attribute. Analysis of the children's gestural combinations revealed that the children used them to express a range of semantic relations. Furthermore, the semantic relations expressed in the children's gestural combinations closely resembled those that typically appear in hearing children's two-word utterances. Systematic examination of each deaf child's gestural sequencing indicated that individual children often combined gestures in a distinct order. This ordering, moreover, appeared to be characteristic of each child, as it did not reflect the order of the gestural input of the child's parents. From these findings, the investigators concluded that young children, without linguistic input, have the capacity to form their own basic lexicons, to express a range of semantic relations, and to generate basic rules for gestural combination.

To a large extent, the young children's success in developing a communication system with various language-like characteristics is a most impressive accomplishment. The gestural systems that the children developed consistently exceeded the level of the gestural input they received. The children, thus, took the lead in making their communicative systems more complex; their parents played a lesser role. The systems that the children developed, moreover, were used effectively to communicate a wide range of meanings.

Although these children's achievements are impressive, it is also important to reflect on what was not accomplished. First, aspects of the children's communication systems, especially the use of deictic gestures, are largely dependent on the immediate context. Full languages, spoken or signed, are not nearly so dependent. Second, the characterising gestures developed by the children were quite pantomimic. The use of iconic or pantomimic gestures may have been necessary for the children to communicate effectively with others. Yet one of the hallmarks of a full language is that the relationship between word (or sign) and concept is an arbitrary one in most instances. With the children's characterising gestures largely resembling the objects, actions, or attributes they wished to indicate, the children's system contrasts markedly with the symbolic relationships evident in full languages. Finally, it should be noted that the children's mothers apparently played a role in their children's development of gestural communication systems. Not only were the mothers responsive to their children's gestures, they used the communicative gestures in roughly the same proportions as their children.

One of the original 10 children, David, has been the focus of continuing investigation. His development has shown that a child's gestural communication system can become more language-like over time. As he got older, David learned to refer to absent objects; he did this by making his gestures either near or directed at perceptually similar objects (Butcher, Mylander, & Goldin-Meadow, 1991). David also altered slightly the form of his characterising gestures to indicate whether the gestures served a noun or verb role (Goldin-Meadow, Butcher, Mylander, & Dodge, 1994). Finally, many of David's gestures began to resemble ASL signs structurally in that they were made in the same locations as ASL signs and often involved very similar movements (Singleton, Morford, & Goldin-Meadow, 1993). Taken together, the changes that David introduced to his communication system made it much more language-like.

In conclusion, most of the children studied by Goldin-Meadow et al. probably should be viewed as creating communication systems that have several properties in common with languages. David, however, with increasing age, created a system that shares many more properties with languages. As we shall see shortly, though, it may take both more time and the presence of a community of others who share a communicative gestural system for the transition to a full language to occur.

THE EMERGENCE OF A NEW SIGN LANGUAGE

Linguists and psycholinguists rarely have the opportunity to witness firsthand a new language emerge. But the strange vicissitudes that often accompany deaf education have provided scholars just such an opportunity in recent years. This emergence of a new language, in sign, also has provided researchers with a window from which to view children's remarkable capacity to transform input with limited linguistic structure into a rule-governed linguistic system.

When the Sandinista government came to power in Nicaragua in 1979, it set about establishing a programme of public education for deaf students. When schools for the deaf opened in 1980, the educational approach adopted was an oral one. In this approach, particular stress was placed on teaching the deaf students how to speechread (lipread) and on their mastering of spoken language. The results of these efforts in most cases proved disappointing.

The schools did succeed, however, in bringing together for the first time a generation of deaf students who previously had not had much contact with each other. When these students were not in their classrooms, they needed to be able to communicate effectively with each other. To accomplish this, many of the deaf students relied on the pantomimic gestures or homesigns that they had used when they were growing up amidst hearing family members. Within a relatively short period, these gestures coalesced into a limited set of signs used by a number of students—these children had created the roots of a new sign language.

When a new generation of young deaf children entered the schools in the late 1980s and early 1990s, they encountered the newly established sign system used by the older students. As the younger children learned the sign system of their elders, they enriched and transformed it (Senghas, 1994). Over time, individual signs became less pantomimic and more arbitrary or stylised. In comparison with the signing of the older students and young deaf adults, the younger students' signing was more fluid and compact. The children also introduced a range of grammatical forms that were not present in the older students' signing. The younger children made clear noun–verb distinctions, used pronominal referents, modulated sign movements, marked verb agreement, and used spatial devices for grammatical contrast (Morford & Kegl, 1996; Senghas, 1996). Furthermore, comparisons of this newly evolved system with other, older sign languages revealed that the new system had a number of structural similarities with more established sign languages. Thus, in just a few years, a fully grammaticised form of Nicaraguan Sign Language seems to have emerged.

What factors might contribute to the tendency of young children to transform the gestural communication input they receive into a full language-like system? Although at present we can only speculate as to what mechanisms are involved, at least several seemed to be operating. One very noticeable change in individual signs over time is that they typically become less pantomimic. When deaf students spend much of their time interacting with non-signing hearing persons or with deaf persons with whom they do not share a sign system, they need to produce signs that are readily identifiable and easily learned. Pantomimic signs fit these needs; their transparent meanings ensure successful communication. But the situation is quite different for young children growing up in an environment already containing such pantomimic signs. First, young children may not recognise the relationship between a pantomimic gesture and its referent. Young children thus may not be motivated to continue using the pantomime. Another reason why young children's signs may become less pantomimic is that their motor skills are still developing. The more complex movements and handshapes in a pantomimic gesture may be assimilated into the children's more basic motor routines. A final reason why signs may become less pantomimic is that with an established signing community it may no longer be necessary to form highly iconic or pantomimic signs. If the child forms a sign in nearly the same location and with a movement that approximates that of the original pantomimic gesture, then that may be sufficient for successful communication.

The reasons behind the other changes that young deaf children often introduce to sign communication systems are even less apparent than those used to explain the modification of pantomimic signs. Perhaps many of the changes are akin to those processes that occur when hearing children grow up exposed to a pidgin as their first language. For young children to communicate a full range of meanings, they need to be able to indicate who performed the action, when it took place, how and where it was performed, etc. The changes that are introduced to a pidgin by children to accomplish their communication needs (e.g. the marking of tense and number) result in the pidgin becoming a creole language. The same or a very similar pidgin-to-creole process may occur when deaf children encounter the more limited sign systems of their elders.

Another possible explanation for why sign systems evolve is that there may be a very strong tendency for children to over-regularise their language. We often see this happen in English when young children apply the regular past-tense endings to irregular verbs. Similarly, deaf children as they learn to sign may note some level of systematicity in the gestural utterances they observe. These children may then over-apply this systematicity to other instances they encounter in their signing (Singleton & Newport, 1995). Unless the children receive specific feedback or correction, the over-regularised forms may persist. This explanation has been advanced to account for the signing success of a 7-year-old deaf boy, Simon (Singleton & Newport, 1995). Both of Simon's parents are deaf and received an oral education; neither began learning ASL until the age of 15. They embraced signing, but like many late-language learners, did not achieve fluency. Simon's signing, however, became more ASL-like than that of his parents despite the fact that his parents were almost his only source of sign input. Both Simon and the young Nicaraguan children may have noted some level of systematicity in the gestures they observed and then applied this systematicity to other instances. By doing this, they may have improved on the regularity of their elders' signing.

Finally, when young children are learning to sign, they may deviate from the ways spoken languages often use to convey meanings partly because they may not have learned these particular mechanisms. For example, whereas word order may be a useful way to convey meaning in spoken languages, taking advantage of spatial relationships may be a much more effective way to convey meaning in a visual and motor language. Regardless, the capacity of young children to transform input with limited linguistic structure into a rule-based language system is a very impressive accomplishment.

IS THERE A CRITICAL PERIOD FOR SIGN LANGUAGE ACQUISITION?

Because deaf children begin learning to sign across a wide range in ages, they constitute a most attractive population to study to help answer questions about the existence of a critical period for language acquisition. The view that a period in development exists during which language must be acquired if it is ever to be fully learned is known as the critical period hypothesis. This hypothesis was advanced most forcefully by Eric Lenneberg. According to Lenneberg (1967), this critical period extends from early childhood to puberty. In Lenneberg's model, as an individual ages, acquiring a first language becomes progressively more difficult and attaining full mastery of that language less likely.

Soon after the critical period for language acquisition was first hypothesised, investigators recognised that it would be very difficult to test in hearing populations. In most instances, those hearing children who were not exposed to language during childhood were reared in families with severe psychopathology.

In such cases, it is not possible to determine whether any abnormalities in language that were observed should be attributed to late exposure to language or to the sub-human conditions in which the children were reared. The use of deaf children to test the critical period hypothesis, however, avoids this pitfall. Deaf children of hearing parents typically are reared in loving and caring families. The parents, however, often have a singular focus on their deaf children's acquisition of speech. Because many deaf children are unsuccessful in acquiring speech skills and their parents refuse to sign, these deaf children often fail to make progress in language acquisition in any mode throughout their childhood. Often these children do not make substantial progress in language learning until they enter a residential school for the deaf where signing is used.

In a series of studies, Mayberry and her associates have examined the relationships between the ages at which deaf individuals began learning to sign and their sign language processing abilities as adults. In an initial study (Mayberry & Fischer, 1989) that involved ASL-using deaf college students, it was found that performance on sign language tasks declined linearly with decreasing sign experience. In other words, the more years of experience a deaf student had with ASL, the fewer signing errors a student typically made. Analyses of the students' error patterns further revealed that there were differences by age of acquisition in the types of errors the students made. Those who were younger when they began acquiring ASL tended to make more semantic (or content) errors than phonological (or formational) errors. For example, students who were young when they learned ASL might incorrectly remember that the topic of a sign sentence was the older brother when the focus of the stimulus sentence actually involved the younger brother. In contrast, those students who were older when they began learning ASL typically made more sign phonological errors than semantic errors. That is, older learners often incorrectly recalled signs that were similar in shape or form to signs that appeared in the stimulus sentences. Older learners tended both to make more errors and different types of errors than those who had learned to sign when they were younger.

Mayberry and Eichen (1991) then asked whether age at which individuals began learning to sign was related to eventual levels of signing skill. To answer this question, the investigators located 49 congenitally deaf persons whose signing experience ranged from 21 to 60 years. While all the participants had lengthy signing backgrounds, the ages at which they began learning ASL varied widely. Some reported that they began learning in infancy (native signers), some that they started between the ages of 5 and 8 years (in childhood), and some between 9 and 13 years of age (early adolescence). In general, with increasing age at acquisition, the participants tended to respond in grammatically acceptable ASL utterances less frequently. Age at acquisition also was strongly negatively correlated (−.62) with the participants' performance on a test of ASL sentence recall. These findings indicate that age at sign acquisition is tied to eventual signing skill even among deaf persons who have had lengthy signing experience.

In observing the performance of those deaf individuals who reported learning to sign during adolescence, Mayberry noticed that differences in language training histories appeared to be highly related to performance on the ASL tasks she used to assess signing ability. These observations were then tested systematically by examining the performance of two groups of deaf persons who were late-learners of sign language. In one group were deaf individuals who had failed to make significant progress in spoken language acquisition early in their development and who had learned ASL as a first language during adolescence. In the second group of late-learners of ASL were deaf individuals who acquired ASL after already mastering a number of English language skills. To a large extent, the members of this second group were learning ASL as their second language. When tested, this latter group made considerably fewer errors on the ASL tasks than those deaf persons who had learned ASL as their first language in adolescence. In general, the better a participant's English skills were, the better his or her sign language skills were. Furthermore, the two groups differed in their patterns of signing errors. Those individuals who had acquired ASL more as a late second language made a higher proportion of semantic errors than sign phonological errors. This error pattern closely resembled that of early ASL learners in previous studies. In contrast, the late-learners of ASL as a first language made as many phonological as semantic errors on the same tasks. Apparently, the experience of acquiring a language in early childhood—even one in a different modality—positively influences the efficiency with which subsequent languages are learned (Mayberry, 1994).

In conclusion, studies of sign language acquisition provide strong support for the existence of a critical period for language acquisition. Moreover, the sign language acquisition data are not constrained by concerns about family psychopathology, a problem that often has plagued studies of hearing children not exposed to language. The sign language acquisition data also indicate that a critical period for language operates independently of language modality. One basis for this claim is the finding that younger sign learners consistently demonstrate greater sign language facility than later learners. A second source of support is the finding that early success in acquiring spoken language skills positively influences later signing skills. Finally, it should be noted, the later sign language learners differed from the younger learners across the whole spectrum of sign language skills. All aspects of language facility thus appear to be affected by later acquisition.

SIGN COMMUNICATION TRAINING FOR MUTE, LOW-FUNCTIONING CHILDREN

Deaf children are not alone in experiencing difficulty in learning to speak. A large number of children with normal or near-normal levels of hearing also fail to make progress in acquiring spoken language. Some of these children have

failed to make progress in speech-training programmes often learned to communicate their basic needs and desires for the first time. Altogether, the results of more than 30 studies have underlined the potential effectiveness of sign training with autistic children (Bonvillian, Nelson, & Rhyne, 1981; Layton, 1987). Moreover, gains in sign communication skills often were retained for long periods by autistic children (Gaines, Leaper, Monahan, & Weickgenant, 1988), in contrast to rather poor word retention frequently evident in vocal language interventions. Concomitant with their enhanced sign communication skills, most of the mute, autistic children manifested improved attention, motivation, and social behaviour. After first acquiring some facility in sign communication, some of the children went on to learn to communicate in speech. Occasionally, there were also reports of substantial gains in IQ scores.

Evidence also has accumulated in recent years of wide individual differences in the outcomes of sign language or manual communication training programmes for mute, low-functioning autistic children (Bonvillian & Blackburn, 1991; Konstantareas, 1985; Layton, 1987). Some of the children made remarkable progress, acquiring a large lexicon of signs and learning to combine signs in sentence-like form to express a range of meanings. Some of these children also made considerable progress in acquiring speech skills. At the other end of the training outcome spectrum have been children who made only minimal progress in acquiring signing skills. Despite receiving essentially the same training as the more successful sign learners, these children often learned many fewer signs and used them only sporadically. The range in individual training outcomes notwithstanding, the introduction of sign communication training provided the first effective means of communication for many thousands of mute, low-functioning children with autistic disorder.

Although it is not possible to predict perfectly beforehand which low-functioning autistic children will make the most progress in manual communication training programmes, certain factors often are associated with greater success. In general, those children with higher scores on intelligence tests and better receptive language abilities, social skills, and fine motor abilities tend to make the greatest progress (Bonvillian & Blackburn, 1991; Gaines et al., 1988). The size of autistic children's sign vocabularies also tends to grow as the length of their participation in manual communication training programmes increases. However, in comparison with the rapid expansion in vocabulary size evident in young normal children learning to speak, or of children of deaf parents learning to sign, vocabulary growth of most autistic children is much more gradual. Often, the children must be trained daily on specific lexical items for periods of weeks before they attain minimal levels of mastery. Even for those children who eventually acquire a substantial sign vocabulary, the learning of initial signs may be quite slow. In many cases, these children apparently need to recognise that objects and actions can have manual or gestural labels before they make more rapid progress (Carr, Binkoff, Kologinsky, & Eddy, 1978).

Along with their advances in communication skills, virtually all of the autistic children who participated in sign training programmes showed improved social and personal behaviour. Typically, investigators reported a marked decrease in temper tantrums, self-injurious behaviours, and soilings in accord with progress in sign communication training. Indeed, for those children who learned only a few signs, just learning the sign "toilet" often made a dramatic difference in their level of daily functioning.

A number of possible explanations have been advanced to explain why autistic children, many of whom failed to make recognisable progress in speech-oriented training programmes, acquired considerable communication facility in sign (Bonvillian & Nelson, 1982). One possible reason is that sign languages depend on an individual's visual, motor, and kinaesthetic systems; these systems may be relatively more intact in autistic children than their auditory-vocal mechanisms. A second explanation focuses on the different teaching or training strategies available to a language in the manual mode. A teacher or parent can readily mould or shape a child's hand into the correct sign formation, whereas an equivalent degree of control would not be possible in a spoken or auditory-vocal language. Another characteristic that differentiates signed from spoken languages is that some signs clearly resemble the objects or events for which they stand. This iconic or pantomimic aspect of certain signs may make it easier for autistic children to grasp the symbol-referent relationship of these signs in the early stages of sign learning. Such signs typically are acquired more quickly than non-iconic signs by autistic children (Konstantareas, Oxman, & Webster, 1978). A final explanation is that by training autistic children to control their motor movements in the process of forming signs, this may indirectly lower the incidence of autistic children's stereotyped movements and gestures. These bizarre motor movements purportedly interfere with autistic children's cognitive processing (Bram, Meier, & Sutherland, 1977); lowering their frequency might enhance the children's ability to learn.

With regard to the question posed at the beginning of this chapter, "Can hearing individuals who fail to acquire a spoken language make progress in learning a sign language?" the answer appears to be a qualified "yes". Clearly, many persons who fail to make even minimal progress in acquiring speech skills may make much greater progress in learning to communicate through sign. (It should be noted, however, that whereas most participants learned signs more readily than spoken words, there were some exceptions to this general trend.)

So why the *qualified* "yes"? The principal reason is that even the most successful participants in the sign communication programmes for children with autistic disorder never approached language fluency. The most successful participants often required years of systematic training to acquire lexicons that never exceeded 1000 different signs and their sign utterances rarely contained more than five or six signs. These utterances, moreover, typically were devoid of any grammatical markers. These children's accomplishments, in

comparison with their earlier levels of communication, are remarkable; however, these achievements probably should be considered important steps in the acquisition of communication skills, not as the attainment of language. The language facility demonstrated by most normal preschoolers easily surpasses these autistic children's hard-earned achievements.

CONCLUDING REMARKS

In most ways, the acquisition of sign language parallels closely the acquisition of spoken language. This is true whether language acquisition takes place in infancy, childhood, or adolescence. Yet there is also evidence that the timetable of the emergence of certain language milestones differs slightly. In the future, these differences in the timetable of development may help elucidate which aspects of language acquisition rest primarily on cognitive abilities and which aspects are more dependent on visual-motor and auditory-vocal skills (Meier & Newport, 1990).

The finding that most aspects of language development transcend the modality of expression probably indicates that signed and spoken languages overlap considerably in their neurological base. This position is given additional support by the finding that most children's initial signs are made with their right hands, strong evidence of left-hemispheric involvement in early sign language production. In light of these findings, several scholars have speculated that, for most of human history, the principal means of communication was primarily a gestural one (Armstrong, Stokoe, & Wilcox, 1995; Kimura, 1993). According to this view, spoken language emerged relatively recently in human evolution and is based on a neurological foundation that initially served sequential gestural production. Finally, the finding that many children with autistic disorder can make progress learning to communicate through signs after failing to do so in speech is consistent with this view that sign language, not speech, may be the more fundamental form of human communication.

REFERENCES

Anderson, D.E., & Reilly, J.S. (1997). The puzzle of negation: How children move from communicative to grammatical negation in ASL. *Applied Psycholinguistics, 18*, 411–429.

Armstrong, D.F., Stokoe, W.C., & Wilcox, S.E. (1995). *Gesture and the nature of language.* Cambridge, UK: Cambridge University Press.

Bailey, A., Le Couteur, A., Gottesman, I., Bolton, P., Simonoff, E., Yuzda, E., & Rutter, M. (1995). Autism as a strongly genetic disorder: Evidence from a British twin study. *Psychological Medicine, 25*, 63–77.

Baldwin, J.M. (1895). *Mental development in the child and the race, methods and processes.* New York: Macmillan.

Bates, E., Benigni, L., Bretherton, I., Camaioni, L., & Volterra, V. (1979). *The emergence of symbols: Cognition and communication in infancy.* New York: Academic Press.

Bates, E., Camaioni, L., & Volterra, V. (1975). The acquisition of performatives prior to speech. *Merrill-Palmer Quarterly, 21*, 205–226.

LIVERPOOL
JOHN MOORES UNIVERSITY
AVRIL ROBARTS LRC
TEL. 0151 231 4022

Bellugi, U. (1991). The link between hand and brain: Implications from a visual language. In D.S. Martin (Ed.), *Advances in cognition, education, and deafness* (pp. 11–35). Washington, DC: Gallaudet University Press.

Bellugi, U., Klima, E.S., Lillo-Martin, D., O'Grady, L., & Vaid, J. (1986, October). *Examining language dominance through hand dominance*. Paper presented at the Boston University Conference on Child Language Development, Boston, MA.

Bishop, D.V.M. (1990). *Handedness and developmental disorder*. London: MacKeith Press.

Bloom, L., Lifter, K., & Broughton, J. (1985). The convergence of early cognition and language in the second year of life: Problems in conceptualization and measurement. In M. Barrett (Ed.), *Children's single-word speech* (pp. 149–180). Chichester, UK: Wiley.

Bonvillian, J.D., & Blackburn, D.W. (1991). Manual communication and autism: Factors relating to sign language acquisition. In P. Siple & S. Fischer (Eds.), *Theoretical issues in sign language research: Vol. 2. Psychology* (pp. 255–277). Chicago: University of Chicago Press.

Bonvillian, J.D., & Miller, A.J. (1995). Everything old is new again: Observations from the nineteenth century about sign communication training with mentally retarded children. *Sign Language Studies, 88*, 245–254.

Bonvillian, J.D., & Nelson, K.E. (1982). Exceptional cases of language acquisition. In K.E. Nelson (Ed.), *Children's language* (Vol. 3, pp. 322–391). Hillsdale, NJ: Lawrence Erlbaum Associates Inc.

Bonvillian, J.D., Nelson, K.E., & Rhyne, J.M. (1981). Sign language and autism. *Journal of Autism and Developmental Disorders, 11*, 125–137.

Bonvillian, J.D., Orlansky, M.D., & Novack, L.L. (1983). Developmental milestones: Sign language acquisition and motor development. *Child Development, 54*, 1435–1445.

Bonvillian, J.D., Orlansky, M.D., Novack, L.L., Folven, R.J., & Holley-Wilcox, P. (1985). Language, cognitive, and cherological development: The first steps in sign language acquisition. In W. Stokoe & V. Volterra (Eds.), *S L R '83: Proceedings of the Third International Symposium on Sign Language Research* (pp. 10–22). Silver Spring, MD: Linstok.

Bonvillian, J.D., Richards, H.C., & Dooley, T.T. (1997). Early sign language acquisition and the development of hand preference in young children. *Brain and Language, 58*, 1–22.

Bonvillian, J.D., Richards, H.C., & Saah, M.I. (1996, July). *Sign language acquisition and motor development in infancy*. Paper presented at the VIIth International Congress for the Study of Child Language, Istanbul.

Bonvillian, J.D., & Siedlecki, T., Jr. (1996). Young children's acquisition of the location aspect of American Sign Language signs: Parental report findings. *Journal of Communication Disorders, 29*, 13–35.

Bowerman, M. (1973). *Early syntactic development: A cross-linguistic study with special reference to Finnish*. Cambridge, UK: Cambridge University Press.

Boyes-Braem, P. (1973/1990). Acquisition of the handshape in American Sign Language: A preliminary analysis. In V. Volterra & C. Erting (Eds.), *From gesture to language in hearing and deaf children* (pp. 107–127). Heidelberg, Germany: Springer-Verlag.

Bram, S., Meier, M., & Sutherland, P.J. (1977). A relationship between motor control and language development in an autistic child. *Journal of Autism and Childhood Schizophrenia, 7*, 57–67.

Broca, P. (1865). Sur le siège de la faculté du langage articulé. *Bulletin de la Société d'Anthropologie de Paris, 6*, 377–393.

Butcher, C., Mylander, C., & Goldin-Meadow, S. (1991). Displaced communication in a self-styled gesture system: Pointing at the nonpresent. *Cognitive Development, 6*, 315–342.

Capute, A.J., Palmer, F.B., Shapiro, B.K., Wachtel, R.C., Schmidt, S., & Ross, A. (1986). Clinical linguistic and auditory milestone scale: Prediction of cognition in infancy. *Developmental Medicine and Child Neurology, 28*, 762–771.

Carr, E.G., Binkoff, J.A., Kologinsky, E., & Eddy, M. (1978). Acquisition of sign language by autistic children: I. Expressive labeling. *Journal of Applied Behavior Analysis, 11*, 489–501.

Carroll, J.J., & Gibson, E.J. (1986). Infant perception of gestural contrasts: Prerequisites for the acquisition of a visually specified language. *Journal of Child Language, 13*, 31–49.

Cattell, P. (1940). *The measurement of intelligence of infants and young children.* New York: Psychological Corporation.

Clark, E.V. (1973). What's in a word? On the child's acquisition of semantics in his first language. In T.E. Moore (Ed.), *Cognitive development and the acquisition of language* (pp. 65–110). New York: Academic Press.

Conlin, K.E., Mirus, G.R., Mauk, C., & Meier, R.P. (in press). Acquisition of first signs: Place, handshape and movement. In C. Chamberlain, J.P. Morford, & R.I. Mayberry (Eds.), *Language acquisition by eye.* Mahwah, NJ: Lawrence Erlbaum Associates Inc.

DeCasper, A., & Fifer, W.P. (1980). On human bonding: Newborns prefer their mothers' voices. *Science, 208*, 1174–1176.

Eimas, P.D., Siqueland, E.R., Jusczyk, P., & Vigorito, J. (1971). Speech perception in infants. *Science, 171*, 303–306.

Eisenberg, L. (1956). The autistic child in adolescence. *American Journal of Psychiatry, 112*, 607–612.

Eling, P. (1984). Broca on the relation between handedness and cerebral speech dominance. *Brain and Language, 22*, 158–159.

Entus, A.K. (1977). Hemispheric asymmetry in processing of dichotically presented speech and nonspeech stimuli by infants. In S.J. Segalowitz & F.A. Gruber (Eds.), *Language development and neurological theory* (pp. 63–73). New York: Academic Press.

Ervin-Tripp, S. (1966). Language development. In L.W. Hoffman & M.L. Hoffman (Eds.), *Review of child development research* (pp. 55–105). New York: Russell Sage Foundation.

Fenson, L., Dale, P.S., Reznick, J.S., Bates, E., Thal, D.J., & Pethick, S.J. (1994). Variability in early communicative development. *Monographs of the Society for Research in Child Development, 59* (5, Serial No. 242).

Folven, R.J., & Bonvillian, J.D. (1991). The transition from nonreferential to referential language in children acquiring American Sign Language. *Developmental Psychology, 27*, 806–816.

Gaines, R., Leaper, C., Monahan, C., & Weickgenant, A. (1988). Language learning and retention in young language-disordered children. *Journal of Autism and Developmental Disorders, 18*, 281–296.

Gesell, A., & Thompson, H., assisted by C.S. Amatruda (1934). *Infant behavior: Its genesis and growth.* New York: McGraw-Hill.

Goldin-Meadow, S., Butcher, C., Mylander, C., & Dodge, M. (1994). Nouns and verbs in a self-styled gesture system: What's in a name? *Cognitive Psychology, 27*, 259–319.

Goldin-Meadow, S., & Feldman, H. (1977). The development of language-like communication without a language model. *Science, 197*, 401–403.

Goldin-Meadow, S., & Mylander, C. (1984). Gestural communication in deaf children: The effects and non-effects of parental input on language development. *Monographs of the Society for Research in Child Development, 49* (3–4, Serial No. 207).

Goldin-Meadow, S., & Mylander, C. (1990). Beyond the input given: The child's role in the acquisition of language. *Language, 66*, 323–355.

Goodwyn, S.W., & Acredolo, L.P. (1998). Encouraging symbolic gestures: A new perspective on the relationship between gesture and speech. In J. Iverson & S. Goldin-Meadow (Eds.), *The nature and functions of gesture in children's communications* (pp. 61–73). San Francisco: Jossey-Bass.

Harris, L.J. (1991). Cerebral control for speech in right-handers and left-handers: An analysis of the views of Paul Broca, his contemporaries, and his successors. *Brain and Language, 40*, 1–50.

Harris, L.J. (1993). Broca on cerebral control for speech in right-handers and left-handers. A note on translation and some further comments. *Brain and Language, 45*, 108–120.

Heilman, K.M. (1979). The neuropsychological basis of skilled movements in man. In M.S. Gazzaniga (Ed.), *Handbook of behavioral neurobiology: Vol. 2. Neuropsychology* (pp. 447–461). New York: Plenum.

Holmes, K.M., & Holmes, D.W. (1980). Signed and spoken language development in a hearing child of hearing parents. *Sign Language Studies, 28,* 239–254.

Ingram, D. (1976). *Phonological disability in children.* New York: Elsevier.

Ingram, D. (1981). *Procedures for the phonological analysis of children's language.* Baltimore: University Park Press.

Jakobson, R. (1941/1968). *Child language, aphasia, and phonological universals.* The Hague, The Netherlands: Mouton.

Kanner, L. (1943). Autistic disturbances of affective contact. *The Nervous Child, 2,* 217–250.

Kimura, D. (1993). *Neuromotor mechanisms in human communication.* New York: Oxford University Press.

Klima, E.S., & Bellugi, U. (1979). *The signs of language.* Cambridge, MA: Harvard University Press.

Konstantareas, M.M. (1985). Review of evidence on the relevance of sign language in the early communication training of autistic children. *Australian Journal of Human Communication Disorders, 13,* 77–97.

Konstantareas, M.M., Oxman, J., & Webster, C.D. (1978). Iconicity: Effects on the acquisition of sign language by autistic and other severely dysfunctional children. In P. Siple (Ed.), *Understanding language through sign language research* (pp. 213–237). New York: Academic Press.

Layton, T.L. (1987). Manual communication. In T.L. Layton (Ed.), *Language and treatment of autistic and developmentally disordered children* (pp. 189–213). Springfield, IL: Charles C. Thomas.

Lenneberg, E.H. (1967). *Biological foundations of language.* New York: Wiley.

Locke, J.L. (1983). *Phonological acquisition and change.* New York: Academic Press.

Locke, J.L. (1993). *The child's path to spoken language.* Cambridge, MA: Harvard University Press.

Lockyer, L., & Rutter, M. (1969). A five to fifteen year follow-up of infantile psychosis: III. Psychological aspects. *British Journal of Psychiatry, 115,* 865–882.

Lotter, V. (1974). Factors related to outcome in autistic children. *Journal of Autism and Childhood Schizophrenia, 4,* 263–277.

Lovaas, O.I. (1977). *The autistic child: Language development through behavior modification.* New York: Irvington.

Lovaas, O.I., Koegel, R., Simmons, J.O., & Long, J.S. (1973). Some generalizations and follow-up measures on autistic children in behavior therapy. *Journal of Applied Behavior Analysis, 6,* 131–166.

Maestas y Moores, J. (1980). Early linguistic environment: Interactions of deaf parents with their infants. *Sign Language Studies, 26,* 1–13.

Marentette, P.I., Girouard, P.C., & Petitto, L.A. (1990, April). *Hand preference as evidence for laterality of language in the early stages of sign language acquisition.* Paper presented at the 7th international conference on Infant Studies, Montreal.

Mayberry, R.I. (1994). The importance of childhood to language acquisition: Evidence from American Sign Language. In J.C. Goodman & H.C. Nusbaum (Eds.), *The development of speech perception* (pp. 57–90). Cambridge, MA: MIT Press.

Mayberry, R.I., & Eichen, E.B. (1991). The long-lasting advantage of learning sign language in childhood: Another look at the critical period for language acquisition. *Journal of Memory and Language, 30,* 486–512.

Mayberry, R.I., & Fischer, S.D. (1989). Looking through phonological shape to sentence meaning: The bottleneck of non-native sign language processing. *Memory and Cognition, 17,* 740–754.

McCarthy, D. (1954). Language development in children. In L. Carmichael (Ed.), *Manual of child psychology* (2nd edn., pp. 492–630). New York: Wiley.

McCormick, C.M., & Maurer, D.M. (1988). Unimanual hand preferences in 6-month-olds: Consistency and relation to familial-handedness. *Infant Behavior and Development, 11*, 21–29.

McIntire, M.L. (1977). The acquisition of American Sign Language hand configurations. *Sign Language Studies, 16*, 247–266.

McManus, I.C., Sik, G., Cole, D.R., Mellon, A.F., Wong, J., & Kloss, J. (1988). The development of handedness in children. *British Journal of Developmental Psychology, 6*, 257–273.

Meadow, K.P. (1980). *Deafness and child development*. Berkeley, CA: University of California Press.

Meier, R.P. (1981). Icons and morphemes: Models of the acquisition of verb agreement in ASL. *Papers and Reports on Child Language Development, 20*, 92–99.

Meier, R.P. (1987). Elicited imitation of verb agreement in American Sign Language: Iconically or morphologically determined? *Journal of Memory and Language, 26*, 362–376.

Meier, R.P. (1991). Language acquisition by deaf children. *American Scientist, 79*, 60–70.

Meier, R.P., & Newport, E.L. (1990). Out of the hands of babes: On a possible sign advantage. *Language, 66*, 1–23.

Meier, R.P., & Willerman, R. (1995). Prelinguistic gesture in deaf and hearing infants. In K. Emmorey & J.S. Reilly (Eds.), *Language, gesture, and space* (pp. 391–409). Hillsdale, NJ: Lawrence Erlbaum Associates Inc.

Molfese, D.L., Freeman, R.B., Jr., & Palermo, D.S. (1975). The ontogeny of brain lateralization for speech and nonspeech sounds. *Brain and Language, 2*, 356–368.

Morford, J.P., & Kegl, J. (1996, September). *Grammaticization in a newly emerging signed language in Nicaragua*. Paper presented at the 5th international conference on Theoretical Issues in Sign Language Research, Montreal.

Nelson, K. (1973). Structure and strategy in learning to talk. *Monographs of the Society for Research in Child Development, 38* (1–2, Serial No. 149).

Newport, E.L., & Ashbrook, E. (1977). The emergence of semantic relations in American Sign Language. *Papers and Reports on Child Language Development, 13*, 16–21.

Newport, E.L., & Meier, R.P. (1985). The acquisition of American Sign Language. In D.I. Slobin (Ed.), *The crosslinguistic study of language acquisition: Vol. 1. The data* (pp. 881–938). Hillsdale, NJ: Lawrence Erlbaum Associates Inc.

Oller, D.K., & Eilers, R.E. (1988). The role of audition in infant babbling. *Child Development, 59*, 441–466.

Orlansky, M.D., & Bonvillian, J.D. (1984). The role of iconicity in early sign language acquisition. *Journal of Speech and Hearing Disorders, 49*, 287–292.

Petitto, L.A. (1987). On the autonomy of language and gesture: Evidence from the acquisition of personal pronouns in American Sign Language. *Cognition, 27*, 1–52.

Petitto, L.A. (1988). "Language" in the pre-linguistic child. In F. Kessel (Ed.), *The development of language and language researchers* (pp. 187–221). Hillsdale, NJ: Lawrence Erlbaum Associates Inc.

Petitto, L.A. (1996). In the beginning: On the genetic and environmental factors that make early language acquisition possible. In M. Gopnik & S. Davis (Eds.), *The biological basis of language* (pp. 46–71). Oxford, UK: Oxford University Press.

Petitto, L.A., & Marentette, P. (1991). Babbling in the manual mode: Evidence for the ontogeny of language. *Science, 251*, 1493–1496.

Prinz, P.M., & Prinz, E.A. (1979). Simultaneous acquisition of ASL and spoken English: Phase I, early lexical development. *Sign Language Studies, 25*, 283–296.

Rimor, M., Kegl, J., Lane, H., & Schermer, T. (1984). Natural phonetic processes underlie historical change and register variation in American Sign Language. *Sign Language Studies, 43*, 97–119.

Rutter, M. (1978). Diagnosis and definition. In M. Rutter & E. Schopler (Eds.), *Autism: A reappraisal of concepts and treatment* (pp. 1–25). New York: Plenum Press.

Rutter, M., Greenfield, D., & Lockyer, L. (1967). A five to fifteen year follow-up study on infantile psychosis: II. Social and behavioural outcome. *British Journal of Psychiatry, 113*, 1183–1199.

Schein, J.D., & Delk, M.T., Jr. (1974). *The deaf population of the United States*. Silver Spring, MD: National Association of the Deaf.

Schein, J.D., & Stewart, D.A. (1995). *Language in motion: Exploring the nature of sign*. Washington, DC: Gallaudet University Press.

Scott, W.R. (1847). *Remarks, theoretical and practical, on the education of idiots, and children of weak intellect*. Exeter, UK: Spreat & Wallis.

Senghas, A. (1994, October). *The development of Nicaraguan Sign Language via the language acquisition process*. Paper presented at the Boston University Conference on Child Language Development, Boston.

Senghas, A. (1996, September). *The creolization of agreement in Nicaraguan Sign Language*. Paper presented at the 5th International Conference on Theoretical Issues in Sign Language Research, Montreal.

Shirley, M.M. (1933). *The first two years*. Minneapolis, MN: University of Minnesota Press.

Siedlecki, T., Jr., & Bonvillian, J.D. (1993). Location, handshape, and movement: Young children's acquisition of the formational aspects of American Sign Language. *Sign Language Studies, 78*, 31–52.

Siedlecki, T., Jr., & Bonvillian, J.D. (1997). Young children's acquisition of the handshape aspect of American Sign Language signs: Parental report findings. *Applied Psycholinguistics, 18*, 17–39.

Siedlecki, T., Jr., & Bonvillian, J.D. (1998). Homonymy in the lexicons of young children acquiring American Sign Language. *Journal of Psycholinguistic Research, 27*, 47–68.

Singleton, J.L., Morford, J.P., & Goldin-Meadow, S. (1993). Once is not enough: Standards of well-formedness in manual communication created over three timespans. *Language, 69*, 638–715.

Singleton, J.L., & Newport, E.L. (1995). *When learners surpass their models: The acquisition of American Sign Language from impoverished input*. Unpublished manuscript, University of Illinois, Champaign, IL.

Stokoe, W.C., Jr. (1960). Sign language structure: An outline of the visual communication system of the American deaf. *Studies in Linguistics, Occasional Papers 8*. Buffalo, NY: University of Buffalo.

Stokoe, W.C., Jr., Casterline, D., & Croneberg, C. (1965). *A dictionary of American Sign Language on linguistic principles*. Washington, DC: Gallaudet College Press.

Volterra, V., & Caselli, M.C.C. (1985). From gestures and vocalizations to signs and words. In W. Stokoe & V. Volterra (Eds.), *S L R '83: Proceedings of the Third International Symposium on Sign Language Research* (pp. 1–9). Silver Spring, MD: Linstok Press.

Volterra, V., & Iverson, J.M. (1995). When do modality factors affect the course of language acquisition? In K. Emmorey & J.S. Reilly (Eds.), *Language, gesture, and space* (pp. 371–390). Hillsdale, NJ: Lawrence Erlbaum Associates Inc.

Whitney, W.D. (1867). *Language and the study of language: Twelve lectures on the principles of linguistic science*. New York: Scribner's.

Wilbur, R.B. (1987). *American Sign Language: Linguistic and applied dimensions* (2nd edn.). Boston: College Hill.

Williams, J.S. (1976). Bilingual experiences of a deaf child. *Sign Language Studies, 10*, 37–41.

CHAPTER TWELVE

Language development in atypical children

Helen Tager-Flusberg
Eunice Kennedy Shriver Center, Waltham, USA

INTRODUCTION

Child language researchers have always been fascinated with the study of language in atypical children. From early discussions about the Wild Boy of Aveyron, to contemporary studies of Genie, we have always believed that these unusual individuals can offer significant insights for our theories of how all children come to acquire this remarkable system called *language*. Perhaps the most intriguing of all cases is Christopher, the linguistic savant whose extraordinary, singular achievements in the domain of language have been so carefully documented by Smith and Tsimpli (1995). Christopher's superb linguistic skills have provided him the means to learn somewhere between 15 and 20 different languages in both oral and written forms, despite the fact that he is mentally retarded with an IQ score in the mild to moderate range. Christopher, like other individuals with neurodevelopmental disorders, provides important clues about the organisational structure and representation of language, as well as the relationship between language and other cognitive abilities. The study of atypical children is important for what can be learned about universal and non-universal aspects of language and the acquisition process. In most retarded individuals the period of language acquisition is delayed and protracted, allowing one to view the stages of development in far greater detail and to investigate what may be variable among different children. In this chapter I explore language acquisition in a few different retardation syndromes, to address the kinds of questions that have been raised about the nature of language.

Model of language acquisition

Studies of children with unique patterns of language acquisition demonstrate the complexity of the language system, which is made up of several distinct components. I have proposed that there are three critical neurocognitive mechanisms, each processing different categories of information (Tager-Flusberg, 1997). The first mechanism is a *computational* system, dedicated to processing hierarchical linguistic information as in phonological and grammatical structures. The second mechanism, called the *theory of mind* system, processes both visual and vocal information about people, and builds conceptual representations of mental constructs, propositional attitudes, and, more broadly, social stimuli. The final mechanism is amodal, and involves *general cognitive systems* that are critical in building conceptual structures that are the foundation for categorisation and the lexical-semantic components of language (Jackendoff, 1983). While these mechanisms are integrated and must interact to allow for normal functioning, there is evidence, particularly from atypical children, to suggest that they represent independent systems, that are based on distinct neurobiological substrates (Baron-Cohen, Ring, Moriarty, Schmitz, Costa, & Ell, 1994; Fletcher, Happé, Frith, Baker, Dolan, Frackowiak, & Frith, 1995; Mazoyer, Tzourio, Frak, Syrota, Murayama, Levrier, Salamon, Dehaene, Cohen, & Mehler, 1993; Wilkins & Wakefield, 1995).

In mental retardation there are broad ranging cognitive impairments so that the delays in conceptual and linguistic development that are characteristic of all groups of retarded children can be attributed to deficits in functioning of the general cognitive systems. Different degrees of retardation will be related to the severity of these deficits, and also to the degree of delay and level of functioning in the domain of language. But in addition to such general deficits, some syndromes are associated with specific additional impairments to either the computational (e.g. Down syndrome) or the theory of mind mechanism (e.g. autism). It is through studies of such groups of children that the contributions each of these systems makes to the overall process of language acquisition can be explored in greater detail. Differential degrees of impairment to any of these critical systems will lead to a picture of developmental asynchrony, which may be how we define deviance in language development that is associated with particular disorders (Tager-Flusberg, 1988). In the remainder of this chapter I provide illustrations of these ideas through the detailed presentation of language acquisition in a number of different neurodevelopmental disorders, including Down syndrome, Williams syndrome, autism, and hydrocephalus.

DOWN SYNDROME

Down syndrome is the most common neurodevelopmental disorder, occurring in about 1 in 800 live births. It was also the first distinct syndrome to be identified about 100 years ago. Down syndrome is associated with the presence of a third chromosome 21. As in all syndromes, despite the relative uniformity of the underlying aetiology, the phenotype varies quite broadly, with IQ scores in the population ranging from near-normal levels to the severely retarded range, though the majority of children with Down syndrome have moderate levels of retardation, in the 45–55 range. Although there are controversies surrounding the ability to identify a unique behavioural phenotype for Down syndrome (Belmont, 1971; Flint, 1996), recent studies suggest that language is relatively more impaired than other cognitive functions, though the sources and nature of this deficit have still not been clearly resolved (Chapman, 1995; Fowler, 1990; Miller, 1988, 1992). Because of the prevalence of the syndrome, the lengthy history of research with this population, and the fact that it is typically diagnosed at birth, one might have expected that most of these controversies would, by now, have been settled. Yet until recently, most of the studies conducted on children with Down syndrome were methodologically flawed in that appropriate control groups were not included, and poor measures of language and related functioning were adopted. Research on language acquisition in Down syndrome has also shifted radically in recent years, following the conceptual and theoretical advances that have been made in the field of psycholinguistics as a whole.

Vocal and phonological development in Down syndrome

During the first year of life infants develop the capacity to produce speech sounds. They proceed through stages of cooing, vocal play, and babbling. In the second half of the first year, canonical babbling begins, marking the most important developmental precursor to meaningful speech (Oller, 1986). Research on babbling in infants with Down syndrome has led to contradictory findings. Although some studies have found no delays in the vocal development of Down syndrome infants (Dodd, 1972; Smith & Oller, 1981), these studies may not have used the most sensitive measures of vocal quality. Recently, Oller and his colleagues have shown that there are, in fact, delays in the onset of canonical babbling in Down syndrome infants (Lynch, Oller, Eilers, & Basinger, 1990; Oller & Siebert, 1988; Steffens, Oller, Lynch, & Urbano, 1992). Comparing infants with Down syndrome to a group of normally developing infants, the age of onset for the infants with Down syndrome was about 2 months behind the normally developing infants, though there was some overlap between the groups. This significant delay in the onset of babbling was not the result of mild hearing loss, which is fairly common among Down syndrome, nor was it correlated with the health status of the infants. Once canonical babbling began in the Down syndrome infants, it was significantly less stable than for the normally developing infants. Studies have also shown that the onset of canonical babbling in infants with Down syndrome emerges at the same time as rhythmic hand banging, as has been found for normally developing infants, suggesting that both milestones reflect underlying rhythmic behaviour (Coco-Lewis, Oller, Lynch, & Levine, 1995; Levine, Fishman, Oller, Lynch, & Basinger, 1991). Lynch et al. (1990) suggest that the delays in canonical babbling in Down syndrome might be related to the motor delays and hypotonicity that are characteristic of this population (Wishart, 1988). Thus, infants with Down syndrome show specific patterns of delay in vocal development, which, in turn, are correlated with later measures of communicative functioning (Lynch et al., 1990). These delays suggest that the biological mechanisms underlying the articulatory system in particular, and motor functioning in general, may be especially vulnerable in Down syndrome.

Problems in expressive aspects of language continue in children with Down syndrome, as they typically have difficulties with the phonological aspects of language, once they begin producing words. Dodd (1976) compared the phonological errors produced by severely retarded children with Down syndrome, children with non-specific retardation, and normally developing children, matched on overall cognitive mental age. The children with Down syndrome produced more errors overall than either of the other groups, more different error types, and their phonological development lagged significantly behind their cognitive level. In a study of spontaneous speech produced by a group of mildly retarded children with Down syndrome, Stoel-Gammon (1980) found that her subjects were capable of producing all the phonemes of English and their error patterns were systematically related to the adult forms of target words. This suggests that there was no evidence for linguistic deviance in this domain of language. Moreover, Stoel-Gammon found that the phonological abilities of children with Down syndrome were comparable to normally developing children at the same language level. However, she had not included her own control group, and, like Dodd (1976), her subjects with Down syndrome were clearly delayed relative to their cognitive mental age levels.

Articulatory difficulties often persist in older children and adolescents with Down syndrome (Chapman, Schwartz, & Kay-Raining Bird, 1989; Rosin, Swift, Bless, & Vetter, 1988). They contribute to the reduced intelligibility of individuals with Down syndrome, but are not simply attributable to anatomical features such as enlarged tongue (Margar-Bacal, Witzel, & Munro, 1987). Interestingly, they are linked to more pronounced delays in syntactic development, as measured by sentence length (Crossley & Dowling, 1989).

Communicative and pragmatic development in Down syndrome

The first year of life is a period rich with parent–child interaction. Social interaction patterns are organised, reciprocal, and finely tuned, involving both vocalisations and eye-gaze coordination (Jaffe, Stern, & Perry, 1973; Trevarthen, 1979). These patterns culminate in the onset of intentional communication at around the age of 9 months, with a move from dyadic to more complex triadic interactions (Adamson & Bakeman, 1982), including joint attention. Joint attention is typically classified as an example of *protodeclarative* communication, defined as a comment or a statement about an object or event (Bates, Camaioni, & Volterra, 1975). Infants at this time also express *protoimperative* meanings, and *social-regulatory* communicative acts, such as greetings.

Infants with Down syndrome show delays in the onset of mutual eye contact (Berger & Cunningham, 1981), they vocalise much less than other infants (Berger & Cunningham, 1983), and early on, their dyadic interactions with their mothers are less well coordinated (Jasnow, Crown, Feldstein, Taylor, Beebe, & Jaffe, 1988). But by the second half of the first year, infants with Down syndrome catch up, and they then show significantly higher levels of mutual eye contact with their caregivers. At this stage they fixate primarily on the eyes rather than exploring other facial features, and they vocalise more than normal infants (Berger & Cunningham, 1981). This increased interest in people in the latter part of the first year, expressed through eye gaze, is accompanied by a lower level of interest in objects and toys. Thus, 1-year-olds with Down syndrome have difficulty interacting with their mothers and playing with objects at the same time (Kasari, Mundy, Yirmiya, & Sigman, 1990; Landry & Chapieski, 1990; Ruskin, Kasari, Mundy, & Sigman, 1994).

These early differences in the social patterns of Down syndrome infants continue to be reflected in play and intentional communication in the second year of life. Across several different studies of toddlers with Down syndrome similar results have been obtained. Following earlier studies (Gunn, Berry & Andrews, 1982; Jones, 1980; Krakow & Kopp, 1983), Mundy and his colleagues conducted a comprehensive study comparing a large group of toddlers with Down syndrome to mental-age matched subjects with non-specific retardation and normally developing children on the Early Social Communication Scales (Mundy, Sigman, Kasari, & Yirmiya, 1988). They found that the children with Down syndrome showed higher frequencies of social interaction behaviours, mirroring the findings of infant studies, but lower frequencies of object request behaviours, or protoimperatives. These findings, which were specific to Down syndrome, were not related to caregivers' skills or responsiveness, but were correlated with expressive language ability in the toddlers with Down syndrome with lower mental ages. Among the children with Down syndrome who had higher mental ages, the relationship to expressive language did not reach significance. Thus we see that children with Down syndrome distribute their attention and communication between people and objects in a unique way, focusing significantly more on people and less on objects. Other studies have found that communicative intents tended to be expressed in the Down syndrome children only through gesture, rather than the more typical pattern of gestures combined with vocalisation or word (Greenwald & Leonard, 1979; Singer, Bellugi, Bates, Jones, & Rossen, 1994), which fits with the vocal and phonological difficulties discussed earlier.

In contrast to their deficits in phonology and expressive language, pragmatic ability appears to be an area of relative strength for children with Down syndrome. In one cross-sectional study, a group of four children with Down syndrome, whose mean lengths of utterance (MLUs) ranged from 1.7 to 2.0, were compared to an MLU-matched group of four normally developing children (Coggins, Carpenter, & Owings, 1983). Conversations were taped as the children interacted with their mothers. Overall, the findings were that the children with Down syndrome expressed the same range of communicative intents, or speech acts, as the normally developing children. Even at early stages of language acquisition, children with Down syndrome are very similar to nonretarded children in their use of different speech acts. Nevertheless, an inspection of the frequency data hints at a potential difference between speech acts involving instrumental functions (mainly requests; e.g. *Want cookie*) and those involving interpersonal functions (e.g. *See this*). Although groups differences did not reach statistical significance, the frequency data suggest that the children with Down syndrome used *relatively* fewer requesting behaviours than the normally developing children, while the frequencies of comments, answers, and protests were essentially equivalent.

This asymmetric pattern was also reported in a larger study of children with Down syndrome who were compared to a group of young MLU-matched and a group of slightly older mental age-matched normally developing children. Beeghly, Weiss-Perry, and Cicchetti (1990) found that the children with Down syndrome, who were at similar early stages of language development as the subjects in Coggins et al.'s (1983) study, produced significantly fewer requests than the mental-age matched normally developing children, but they were more comparable in their requesting behaviour to the language-matched group. These differences provide some interesting parallels with the differences in prelinguistic communicative functions that were discussed earlier. Young children with Down syndrome are relatively more focused on the use of communication to interact and engage socially with other people, than to regulate their environment. But because children with Down syndrome do use language to express some requesting functions, the more limited use of requests may be viewed as related to their lower arousal and passivity (Beeghly et al., 1990).

The major developmental change that takes place in conversational ability is in the capacity to maintain a topic over an increasing number of turns (Bloom, Rocissano, & Hood, 1976; Brown, 1980). Beeghly et al. (1990) found that their subjects with Down syndrome spent significantly more turns on the same topic than language-matched controls. Similarly, Tager-Flusberg and Anderson (1991) found that children with Down syndrome were able to maintain a conversational topic at levels higher than the normally developing children studied by Bloom and her colleagues, suggesting that this aspect of language is a genuine strength for this population.

During the early stages of language development, young normal children are only beginning to demonstrate a sensitivity to their conversational partner. Studies in this area have focused on the capacity to repair or revise an utterance when there has been a communication breakdown (Foster, 1990). Even 2-year-olds tend to repeat utterances or change the form of an utterance if their partner does not respond or they have not been clearly understood. As in other areas of pragmatic ability, children with Down syndrome are surprisingly good at conversational repairs. Coggins and Stoel-Gammon (1982) found that even at early stages, young children with Down syndrome will revise, rather than simply repeat, all requests for clarification from an adult conversational partner. Similar results were obtained by Scherer and Owings (1984). However, lack of intelligibility and limited syntactic knowledge can interfere with pragmatic intent: Older children who used primarily single-word sentences, were fairly limited in the success of their repair strategies, depending more on sign than on speech to accomplish their goals (Bray & Woolnough, 1988).

Older children and adolescents with Down syndrome have been shown able to provide socially appropriate responses in discourse contexts (Loveland & Tunali, 1991) and in more structured referential communication tasks (Jordan & Murdoch, 1987). Adults with Down syndrome also show extended discourse coherence in conversations with their caregivers (Bennett, 1976). However, not surprisingly, on discourse tasks that depend on expressive language ability, such as story-telling, adolescents with Down syndrome perform more poorly than mental-age matched controls. Thus across the life-span, we see that pragmatic aspects of language are relatively spared in Down syndrome, although very young children may distribute their communicative acts in unique ways.

Lexical development in Down syndrome

Theories of semantic development have been concerned with how young children can acquire such a large vocabulary so rapidly and effortlessly. The major emphasis has been on the role of conceptual factors and operating principles which guide and constrain the hypotheses that children entertain about the possible meanings of new words that they encounter (Golinkoff, Mervis, & Hirsh-Pasek, 1994; Markman, 1989). These principles include a set of biases or constraints about the most likely meanings for novel words. Such principles limit the set of possibilities that children must consider when they hear a new word.

Recent research on lexical development in children with Down syndrome has focused on their use of operating principles in acquiring new words (mostly object labels). In normally developing children, early words are used to label objects at the so-called *basic* level (e.g. *car*, *dog*) rather than at the more specific subordinate (e.g. *Volkswagen*, *terrier*) or more general superordinate (e.g. *vehicle*, *animal*) levels. Objects, too, are categorised at the basic level, so that children tend to sort all cars together in a group, all boats, all dogs, and so forth (Mervis & Rosch, 1981; Rosch, Mervis, Gray, Johnson, & Boyes-Braem, 1976). In a longitudinal study of six young children with Down syndrome, Mervis and her colleagues (Cardoso-Martins, Mervis, & Mervis, 1985; Mervis, 1988, 1990) found that all the children's early object labels were at the basic level. Even in older children with Down syndrome who had quite large vocabularies, comprehension of words at the basic level was significantly better than at either the subordinate or superordinate levels (Tager-Flusberg, 1985a). In addition, pictures of objects were almost always named at the basic level (Tager-Flusberg, 1986).

Other lexical operating principles that are known to be important early in normal development have also been found to constrain the word meanings acquired by children with Down syndrome. For example, one important principle in acquiring a new word is knowledge that the word can be *extended* to objects beyond those initially labelled with that word (Golinkoff et al., 1994). A related principle, called the principle of *categorical scope*, states that words can be extended to other objects in the same basic level category. Extension will primarily be based on how close other exemplars are to the *prototype* or central core of the category, demonstrating the organised structure of children's conceptual categories and word meanings (Mervis & Pani, 1980; Rosch et al., 1976). Again, longitudinal observational, and cross-sectional experimental studies by Mervis and her colleagues have confirmed that children with Down syndrome extend the meanings of words according to these principles (Cardoso-Martins et al., 1985; Mervis, 1988, 1990; Mervis & Bertrand, 1997). One cognitive achievement that has been proposed as an important universal link to semantic development is the ability to exhaustively sort objects into categories. This ability demonstrates the child's knowledge that all objects belong to a category or group of similar items, which, it has been argued, should be strongly linked to the naming explosion and the ability to fast map the meanings of novel words (Gopnik & Meltzoff, 1987). Studies have indeed shown that normally developing toddlers (Gopnik & Meltzoff, 1987) and young children with Down syndrome (Mervis & Bertrand, 1997) begin to sort objects at the same point in time as they begin the naming explosion and are able to fast map. In relation to vocabulary growth, some young children with Down syndrome develop vocabularies at a rate that is comparable to their mental age level, while others appear to be significantly delayed, perhaps because of their additional articulatory deficits (Miller, Sedley, Miolo, Murray-Branch, & Rosin, 1992).

Morphological and syntactic development in Down syndrome

We have already noted the significant delays and specific impairments in the expressive language of children with Down syndrome (Chapman et al., 1989, 1991). Studies also suggest that there are comprehension impairments in Down syndrome, particularly when complex sentences have been included in the test stimuli (Chapman, Schwartz, & Kay-Raining Bird, 1991). These deficits have been directly linked to specific deficits in acquiring grammatical aspects of language, though the literature in this field has been primarily descriptive, rather than directly linked to current syntactic theories.

Studies of young children with Down syndrome have found widely varying rates of change in MLU within this population, which are only partially explained by individual differences in chronological age and IQ (Beeghly et al., 1990; Fowler, Gelman, & Gleitman, 1994). For example, Fowler et al. (1994) report on one young girl with Down syndrome, who did not begin combining words productively into two-word utterances until about the age of 4. Yet her rate of development after this point was rapid, and not that different from normal, at least until her MLU reached 3.5 when she was 5.5 years old. Similar relatively rapid rates of development during these early stages of syntactic growth were found by Tager-Flusberg and her colleagues for two out of six young children with Down syndrome, who were followed longitudinally (Tager-Flusberg, Calkins, Nolin, Baumberger, Anderson, & Chadwick-Dias, 1990). Most other children with Down syndrome, particularly those whose IQ scores are below 50 (Fowler, 1988), may not begin combining words until the age of 5 or 6. They then spend a protracted period during which they use relatively few two-word utterances. Their rate of development is very slow and these children may never develop beyond the early stages of grammatical development (Dooley, 1976; Miller, 1988).

These findings confirm other studies reporting significant delays in syntactic development in Down syndrome. Relative to the size of their vocabulary, children with Down syndrome use simpler and shorter sentences compared to both normally developing children and children with Williams syndrome (Singer et al., 1994). Most children with Down syndrome fail to ever acquire knowledge of more complex grammatical constructions such as sentence embedding or correct use of complex questions, and Fowler argues that they generally do not progress much beyond an MLU level of about 3.0 (Fowler, 1990; Fowler et al., 1994). There does not, however, appear to be an absolute ceiling on the levels of language that are achieved by older children with Down syndrome, and development continues through the adolescent years. For example, Chapman and her colleagues have found that MLU continues to increase, and more complex sentences appear in the narratives of older adolescents (Chapman, Schwartz, & Kay-Raining Bird, 1992).

To what extent do the significant delays in grammatical development in Down syndrome mirror the deficits found in children with specific language impairment? Few studies have directly compared these groups. Bol and Kuiken (1990) studied Dutch-speaking children with Down syndrome and with language impairment, and found that both these groups showed significant impairments in morpho-syntax. Another study of English-speaking children investigated whether at similar MLU levels children with Down syndrome and language impairment use a similar range of grammatical constructions as normally developing children, by comparing the groups on the Index of Productive Syntax (IPSyn). Developed by Scarborough (1990), the IPSyn is designed to provide detailed information about the emergence of a wide range of grammatical constructions. Scarborough, Rescorla, Tager-Flusberg, Fowler, and Sudhalter (1991) compared the relationship between MLU and IPSyn for these (and other) groups and found that for both the Down syndrome and language impaired children MLU significantly overestimated IPSyn scores, especially at higher MLU levels. Scarborough et al. argue that for both these groups the lower IPSyn score may reflect specific morpho-syntactic limitations. Chapman et al. (1992) also report significantly lower use of free and bound morphemes in the narratives produced by children and adolescents with Down syndrome.

All these studies are consistent with the view that Down syndrome may involve specific deficits in acquiring *functional categories*, though clearly there are some exceptional cases of individuals with Down syndrome who show no deficits in this domain (Rondal, 1994). It is, nevertheless, unfortunate that research on Down syndrome language remains largely descriptive and has not advanced at the same pace as the research on specific language impairment, which has taken advantage of current theoretical advances in the field of linguistics (Leonard, 1996; Rice & Wexler, 1996).

What might account for the specific deficits that have been identified in the grammatical development of children with Down syndrome, which go beyond what might be predicted on the basis of age or mental age? One hypothesis is that specific weaknesses in auditory working memory or short-term memory might explain the language deficits, and there is some evidence from correlational studies to support this view (Chapman, 1995). This hypothesis would fit with the vocal/phonological impairments discussed earlier, and would provide some support for the widely used intervention approach of teaching sign language skills to children with Down syndrome (though see Woll & Grove, 1995, for evidence that sign language is not more advanced that spoken English in a pair of twins with Down syndrome). Clearly more research is needed to explore the relationship between auditory working memory and grammatical impairment in Down syndrome.

Summary of language acquisition in Down syndrome

Relative to other cognitive domains, the phenotype of Down syndrome typically involves specific delays and deficits in the acquisition of language. While lexical and pragmatic development appear to be closely tied to overall cognitive levels, most children show more profound delays in phonological and grammatical aspects of language acquisition. While some studies suggest that these delays may be specifically related to impairments in auditory working memory, further research is needed that goes beyond correlational and descriptive studies and which begins to incorporate a more explicit theoretical linguistic framework that will provide a deeper understanding of the nature of syntactic impairment in Down syndrome.

WILLIAMS SYNDROME

Williams syndrome is a very rare genetic disorder, occurring in only 1 in 20,000 to 50,000 births. It is characterised by a set of unusual facial characteristics (called "elfin facies"), physical problems, and a unique cognitive profile (Williams, Barratt-Boyes, & Lowe, 1961). This set of characteristics is now known to be causally related to a small deletion on the long arm of chromosome 7, which appears to involve several contiguous genes, two of which have already been identified (Ewart, Morris, Atkinson, Jin, Sternes, Spallone, Stock, Leppert, & Keating, 1993; Frangiskakis, Ewart, Morris, Mervis, Bertrand, Robinson, Klein, Ensing, Everett, Green, Proschel, Gutowski, Noble, Atkinson, Odelberg, & Keating, 1996). This syndrome has captured the interests of developmental psycholinguists because part of the cognitive phenotype appears to involve relatively spared language abilities (Bellugi, Bihrle, Neville, Jernigan, & Doherty, 1992; Bellugi, Marks, Bihrle, & Sabo, 1988; Bellugi, Wang, & Jernigan, 1994; Morris, Thomas, & Greenberg, 1993). Along with good language skills, individuals with Williams syndrome are unusually interested in people, highly sociable or even overly friendly, and have relatively spared face recognition and auditory memory skills (Bellugi et al., 1994; Karmiloff-Smith, Klima, Bellugi, Grant, & Baron-Cohen, 1995; Mervis, Morris, Bertrand, & Robinson, in press). In contrast, they have extremely deficient visual-spatial constructive abilities and are usually retarded in the mild/moderate range (Mervis et al., in press). Studies on children and adults with Williams syndrome have focused on whether their language skills are significantly better than would be predicted from their mental age, suggesting a genuine dissociation of language from other cognitive abilities, and whether, because of their unusual cognitive profile, they acquire language in unique ways.

Vocal and phonological development in Williams syndrome

Because Williams syndrome is usually not diagnosed until children are over the age of 1 year, there has been significantly less opportunity to study early vocal development in this population. Mervis and Bertrand (1997) report on the early development of two infants who were less than 6 months old when they entered their larger longitudinal study. These infants reached the stage of canonical babbling slightly later than normally developing infants: one at 7 months, and one at 8 months of age. Interestingly, for both infants, the onset of canonical babbling was reached at same time as they began rhythmic hand banging, which has been argued by other researchers to be a universal link between a specific linguistic and cognitive achievement (Coco-Lewis et al., 1995). Thus, data from Williams syndrome infants support this view, and are consistent with data from other populations (Coco-Lewis et al., 1995; Levine et al., 1991).

Although there have not been any detailed studies of phonological development in children with Williams syndrome, they do not appear to have particular problems with articulation. One recent study of a relatively large sample of children with Williams syndrome found that their articulation was significantly better than a mental age matched group of children with non-specific retardation, suggesting that this is an area of particular strength for this population (Gosch, Städing, & Pankau, 1994).

Communicative and pragmatic development in Williams syndrome

As noted earlier, young children with Williams syndrome are extremely interested in human faces, and spend extended periods of time looking intently at another person's face (Bellugi et al., 1992). One girl with Williams syndrome was followed for a year beginning when she was about 20 months old (Bertrand, Mervis, Rice, & Adamson, 1993). During this period, she showed intense interest in both familiar and unfamiliar faces, spending significantly more time than normally developing children engaged with other people. This extreme social interest seemed quite inappropriate in both quality and quantity but it is not clear yet how this unusual pattern of social attention influences early communicative development in Williams syndrome. There are some clues from this case study and other work on early gestural development in Williams syndrome to suggest that perhaps pre-linguistic development is quite delayed in this population, despite strong social interest.

The toddler followed by Bertrand et al. (1993) was somewhat delayed in the onset of coordinated joint attention, but there are no data available yet on her prelinguistic communications. A larger study of children with Williams syndrome which used a parent report measure, found that compared to children with Down syndrome at the same developmental level, the children with Williams syndrome appear to be impoverished in their use of gestures (Singer et al., 1994). Another study (Mervis & Bertrand, 1997), which followed longitudinally a group of 10 children with Williams syndrome found that they did not produce a referential pointing gesture until well after the onset of language (see also Goodman, 1995). Not only did these children not produce pointing gestures, it appeared that they did not understand and were unable to respond appropriately to pointing gestures produced by their mothers, at the same time as they were beginning to speak referentially.

Few studies have been designed to focus on aspects of pragmatic functioning in older children with Williams syndrome, and the data seem somewhat

contradictory. Kelley and Tager-Flusberg (1995) explored the discourse characteristics in the spontaneous speech of 20 children with Williams syndrome, who
were between the ages of 3 and 8. They found that the children were relatively
good at providing responses to requests for clarification, and were able to
maintain a topic over several turns, adding more information to the ongoing
discourse. Because there was no control group, these findings are difficult to
interpret. Reilly and her colleagues (Reilly, Harrison, & Klima, 1995; Reilly,
Klima, & Bellugi, 1990) report that older children with Williams syndrome were
relatively good at narrating coherent stories, and showed an unusual ability to
express affective engagement in their narratives, in comparison to both Down
syndrome and mental age matched normal controls.

On the other hand, Volterra and her colleagues report that their larger sample
of children with Williams syndrome showed certain deficits in their narratives,
and they often were not able to directly respond to questions, suggesting other
discourse-level difficulties (Volterra, Sabbadini, Capirci, Pezzini, & Ossella,
1995). And other researchers have described the language of children with
Williams syndrome as "cocktail party" speech, which is filled with stereotypic
social phrases, little content, and is not well tuned to their conversational partner
(Udwin & Yule, 1991).

The studies of pragmatic ability in Williams syndrome have thus far been
largely descriptive and incomplete, often lacking appropriate comparisons to
either other aspects of the children's language profile, or to well matched control
groups. Questions, therefore, remain regarding whether this domain represents
one of relative strength in this population either in relation to their overall
cognitive abilities, or to other aspects of language functioning.

Lexical development in Williams syndrome

In the previous section it was noted that children with Williams syndrome begin
acquiring words before they are able to use or understand a referential point or
other gestures. On average, there was a 6-month delay between the onset of
referential speech and referential pointing in the children with Williams syndrome (Mervis & Bertrand, 1997), a highly unusual pattern of findings. Mervis
and Bertrand suggest that although episodes of joint attention are critical for
acquiring lexical knowledge, especially object labels, children with Williams
syndrome depend on means other than referential pointing for achieving joint
attention. In particular, they suggest that adults direct episodes of joint attention
by using the children's eye gaze to determine what they are looking at or deliberately placing an object in front of the children's eyes before labelling it
for them. Thus, the early stages of lexical development in Williams syndrome
appear to be more dependent on adults determining the contexts in which new
words are acquired than for other groups of children such as normally developing children or children with Down syndrome.

Mervis and her colleagues have also explored whether children with Williams syndrome use operating principles to constrain the meanings of newly acquired words, as they had found in children with Down syndrome. Using both parental report data and direct observations of the children in their longitudinal study, Mervis and Bertrand (1997) found that children with Williams syndrome almost always acquired the *basic level* names for objects before either the subordinate or superordinate label. Furthermore, these labelling patterns paralleled the children's play behaviour in that the children with Williams syndrome sorted and played with objects at the level of basic categories (e.g. playing in similar ways with cars and trucks). Other lexical principles that have been investigated in children with Williams syndrome include the *whole object* constraint (Macnamara, 1982; Markman & Wachtel, 1988) or *object scope* (Golinkoff et al., 1994), which states that words label whole objects rather than parts or attributes of objects. Studies by Mervis and Bertrand (1997) have shown that even though children with Williams syndrome are unusually interested in parts of objects (Bellugi et al., 1992), like other children, they learn words for whole objects, long before they learn any attribute or object part names.

Perhaps the most significant operating principle that has been studied across a wide range of children is the *novel name–nameless category* principle (N3C), which states that when children hear a new word they will assume that it names a category for which they do not currently have a label (Golinkoff et al., 1994; see also Clark, 1983 and Markman, 1989, for a similar kind of principle). The novel name–nameless category principle is very important in accounting for children's rapid word learning abilities, especially their capacity to *fast map* meanings of new words. Once children achieve the insight expressed in the N3C principle, that all objects have a name, hearing a new word in the presence of an object which currently has no label in the child's lexicon will immediately motivate the child to map the new word to this object. Mervis and Bertrand (1997) report that across six children participating in their longitudinal study, all reached the point of being able to fast map new words (operationally defined as tapping the N3C principle) between the ages of about 2 years 6 months, and 3 years 8 months. Furthermore, these children also showed evidence of acquiring the novel name–nameless category principle at about the same time that they are able to sort objects exhaustively, suggesting that both the linguistic (N3C principle) and the cognitive achievement (exhaustive sorting) reflect the same knowledge that all objects have names.

Some researchers have also suggested that these developmental achievements of exhaustive sorting and fast mapping should be closely linked to the vocabulary spurt, which should occur once the naming insight is attained (Gopnik & Meltzoff, 1987). While studies have found that this relationship does hold for normally developing toddlers (Gopnik & Meltzoff, 1987) and young children with Down syndrome (Mervis & Bertrand, 1997), Mervis and Bertrand (1997) did not find this for their children with Williams syndrome. For all but one of the children with Williams syndrome in their longitudinal study, the vocabulary spurt began at least 6 months *before* they could sort objects exhaustively into categories. Mervis and Bertrand (1997) suggest that for children with Williams syndrome, an increase in auditory memory for words or greater attention to verbal input may be more important for the onset of the naming explosion than other factors, suggesting alternative developmental routes to lexical growth.

As children with Williams syndrome get older, they continue to acquire a rich vocabulary as indexed by performance on standardised tests of receptive vocabulary, such as the Peabody Picture Vocabulary Test (PPVT–R). Indeed, lexical knowledge appears to be a genuine strength in this population (Mervis et al., in press). Mervis and her colleagues have given the PPVT–R to a very large sample of children and adults with Williams syndrome, most of whom scored in the retarded range on IQ tests. Yet over 40% of their sample of over 120 subjects with Williams syndrome scored within the normal range on the PPVT–R. These findings confirm other reports in the literature on older individuals with Williams syndrome (Bellugi et al., 1992, 1994) which has also reported PPVT–R scores exceeding mental age levels.

Bellugi and her colleagues have also examined how the semantic system of adolescents with Williams syndrome is organised (Bellugi et al., 1992, 1994). They asked a group of adolescents with either Williams syndrome or Down syndrome to list as many animals as they could think of in one minute. They found that the Williams syndrome subjects produced overall more animal names, and had significantly more unusual, or infrequent exemplars on their lists (e.g. *newt, ibex,* and *yak*). This latter finding was interpreted as evidence for deviant semantic organisation in Williams syndrome, and it fits with anecdotal reports of their use of odd, rather pedantic vocabulary in everyday conversation. Other studies also suggest that individuals with Williams syndrome have trouble defining words that they use, and may have deficits in accessing their lexicons (Bromberg, Ullman, Marcus, Kelley, & Levine, 1995; Pinker, 1994; Rossen, Bihrle, Klima, Bellugi, & Jones, in press).

A more recent study using a larger sample of adolescents with Williams syndrome matched on mental age and chronological age to different normally developing and Down syndrome groups did not, however, replicate Bellugi's findings (Scott, Mervis, Bertrand, Klein, Armstrong, & Ford, 1995). These researchers found no differences between the adolescents with Williams syndrome and Down syndrome, although both groups were more likely to provide infrequent exemplars than the younger mental age matched normal controls, suggesting that knowing unusual animal names might be more related to experience than to mental age. On other measures derived from this task the subjects with Williams syndrome performed the same as the mental age matched controls, suggesting delayed but not deviant semantic organisation in this group (Mervis et al., in press; Scott et al., 1995). Similarly, in on-line semantic priming tasks adolescents and adults with Williams syndrome exhibited the same categorical and functioning priming effects as normal control subjects, suggesting similar patterns of representing lexical-semantic knowledge in both groups (Tyler, Karmiloff-Smith, Voice, Stevens, Grant, Davis, Howlin, & Udwin, in press).

In sum, studies of lexical development in children with Williams syndrome suggest that this domain is an area of genuine strength for this population. Although they are delayed, relative to age-matched normally developing children, they begin acquiring words during the toddler years, according to evidence from Mervis and her colleagues (but see Singer et al., 1994 for a different view). In certain respects, they show similar patterns of development as other groups of young children, but in other ways they seem to follow a unique path, for example beginning to speak before they use pointing gestures, and reaching the vocabulary spurt before they sort objects exhaustively. Despite early evidence of deviant semantic organisation and lexical use, current studies suggest that their lexicons are organised along the same categorical and thematic dimensions as found in normal or other retarded groups.

Morphological and syntactic development in Williams syndrome

Early reports of children and adolescents with Williams syndrome identified grammar as an area of strength in their language profile, and indeed the descriptions of these individuals using fluent complex syntactic constructions despite moderate levels of retardation was taken as evidence for the dissociation between grammar and general cognitive abilities (Bellugi et al., 1988, 1992). More recent studies have questioned these conclusions, but the finding of relatively good syntactic ability has been generally supported.

One study compared parent report data for a relatively large group of young children with Williams syndrome, and children with Down syndrome (Singer et al., 1994), matched on age. The main findings were that the children with Williams syndrome had significantly higher scores on the grammatical complexity measure, and in the mean length of their longest utterances. These differences were not simply attributable to the overall larger vocabularies used by the children with Williams syndrome. Furthermore, Singer et al. (1994) report that many of their subjects with Williams syndrome appeared to progress on measures of grammatical development at a normal rate of development. Another cross-sectional study of 39 children with Williams syndrome ranging widely in age (2 years, 6 months to 12 years) and IQ (40–88), used direct measures of spontaneous speech that were collected in a half-hour standard play session with a researcher (Mervis et al., in press). Mervis and her colleagues found that the children with Williams syndrome were, in fact, delayed on measures of MLU and IPSyn. Nevertheless, the relationship between MLU and IPSyn scores for children with Williams syndrome was the same as in normally developing children, in contrast to all the other retarded groups who were investigated by Scarborough et al. (1991). Thus, Williams syndrome is the first retardation syndrome, according to Mervis et al. (in press), for which there is a normal relation between utterance length and grammatical knowledge.

Using a standardised measure of grammatical comprehension, the Test for Reception of Grammar, or TROG (Bishop, 1989), Mervis and her colleagues (in press) found that a large cross-sectional sample of children and adults with Williams syndrome showed evidence of continued growth in syntactic know-ledge through adolescence. About half the subjects scored within the normal range, though the majority were still unable to correctly understand the most complex embedded sentences. Looking at patterns of ability across measures of grammatical ability, general and specific cognitive abilities, and vocabulary scores, Mervis et al. (in press) report that the measures of grammatical ability (IPSyn and TROG scores) were strongly correlated with measures of auditory working memory (forward and backward digit span), but were lower than expected based on vocabulary level (PPVT–R), or auditory short-term memory. Overall, gram-matical ability in this study was at the same level as general cognitive abilities (composite mental age level), supporting other studies by Gosch et al. (1994), and Udwin and Yule (1991). Karmiloff-Smith, Grant, Berthoud, Davies, Howlin, and Udwin (1997) replicated these findings with 18 English-speaking children and adults with Williams syndrome, using the TROG. In a second study of 14 French-speaking children and adults with Williams syndrome, Karmiloff-Smith et al. found that, compared to young normal French-speaking children, the sub-jects with Williams syndrome—even the adults—showed specific difficulty in correctly assigning grammatical gender on both real and nonce words. Karmiloff-Smith et al. (1997) suggest that the subjects with Williams syndrome have difficulty extracting the underlying system of morpho-phonological cues to gram-matical gender. This may be a result of later language acquisition, or because the Williams syndrome subjects rely too much on their rote memory of exemplars.

Summary of language acquisition in Williams syndrome

Studies of children and adolescents with Williams syndrome have demonstrated that, in general, language ability is an area of relative strength for this popula-tion, especially in contrast to their impaired visual-spatial constructive abilities (Bellugi et al., 1992, 1994; Mervis et al., in press). The onset of language is delayed, though appears to be commensurate with mental age levels. This con-tinues to hold through childhood and adolescence, with grammatical comprehen-sion and production closely tied to mental age level. In contrast, children and adults with Williams syndrome show genuine strength, greater than predicted for their mental age levels, in lexical knowledge, and careful studies by Mervis and her colleagues (Mervis & Bertrand, 1997; Mervis et al., in press) suggest that children with Williams syndrome may follow an unusual pathway in acquiring lexical knowledge, and that their strong language abilities may be closely tied to their unusually intact auditory working memory. Further research is needed to investigate the pragmatic abilities of individuals with Williams syndrome to explore whether they are spared or impaired relative to other aspects of their language profile, or to other retarded populations.

AUTISM

Autism is a complex neurodevelopmental disorder which is still diagnosed exclusively on behavioural criteria (American Psychiatric Association, 1994; Volkmar, 1996), because a unique biological marker has yet to be identified. One of the core impairments in autism is in the domain of language and non-verbal communication, which, together with impairments in reciprocal social interaction and a restricted repertoire of activities and interests, make up the key diagnostic criteria for this syndrome. Over the past several decades there has been a considerable number of descriptive studies on the nature of the language impairment in autism (see Paul, 1987; Tager-Flusberg, 1981, 1989, for reviews). These studies all focus on verbal autistic children, though it is important to note that about half the population never acquire functional language (Bailey, Phillips, & Rutter, 1996). More recently, research in this area has explored language deficits from a more theoretical perspective, in light of work on other aspects of social-cognitive deficit in autism. Specifically, it has been demonstrated that autism involves specific impairments in the acquisition of a theory of mind (Baron-Cohen, 1996; Baron-Cohen, Tager-Flusberg, & Cohen, 1993), and so studies of language and communication in this population have focused on the relationship between these two domains in this population (Happé, 1993; Tager-Flusberg, 1993, 1996, 1997). These current studies have explored the impact of deficits in acquiring a theory of mind on selective components of language acquisition in autism, specifically aspects of pragmatic and communicative development.

Vocal and phonological development in autism

Because autism is never diagnosed during infancy, there are no studies of early vocal development in this population. Nothing is known about the onset of babbling in infants with autism, in contrast to the research that has been done on Down syndrome or Williams syndrome. There have, however, been studies of the phonological development in this population. Controlled studies of children with autism have found that their phonological skills are relatively unimpaired; what errors they do make are similar to those reported in the literature on normal development (Bartolucci & Pierce, 1977). By middle childhood, as in normally developing children, children with autism who develop some functional language generally have mature phonological systems, however their voice quality and intonation patterns are strikingly atypical and these problems appear to

There have also been a number of studies investigating more advanced discourse skills, specifically narrative skills, in higher functioning autistic children. Narratives provide rich information about children's developing linguistic, cognitive, and social knowledge (Bamberg & Damrad-Frye, 1991; Britton & Pellegrini, 1990). Theory of mind knowledge is particularly relevant for the interpretation of characters' intentions, motivations, beliefs, and reactions that must be woven into the depiction of event sequences within an overall story structure (Astington, 1990; Bruner, 1986). Baron-Cohen, Leslie, and Frith (1986) asked subjects with autism to narrate stories using a series of pictures depicting physical causation, behavioural, and false belief stories that they had previously sequenced. Only half the subjects with autism and Down syndrome in this study were in fact able to tell any stories in this context. The stories that were produced were coded only for the presence of mental state language, and not surprisingly, the subjects with autism were significantly worse than the matched Down syndrome and normal subjects in using mental state terms to explain the false belief stories.

A more detailed study was conducted by Loveland and her colleagues, who asked individuals with autism and Down syndrome, matched on chronological and verbal mental age, to retell the story they were shown in the form of a puppet show or video sketch (Loveland, McEvoy, Tunali, & Kelley, 1990). Compared to the controls, the subjects with autism were more likely to exhibit pragmatic violations including bizarre or inappropriate utterances and were less able to take into consideration the listener's needs. Some of the subjects with autism in this study even failed to understand the story as a representation of meaningful events, suggesting that they lacked a cultural perspective underlying narrative (Bruner & Feldman, 1993; Loveland & Tunali, 1993). Loveland et al. (1990) concluded that the discourse problems they had identified in the autistic children's narratives reflected their deficits in theory of mind.

Tager-Flusberg (1995) compared the stories narrated from a wordless picture book by 10 autistic and 10 verbal mental age matched mentally retarded and normal children. Overall, the children with autism produced significantly shorter and more impoverished stories, and, as in Loveland et al.'s study, a small number of children with autism did not interpret the picture book as a narrative sequence of events and therefore failed to produce more than simple independent descriptions of each page in the book. Another significant difference was found in this study: Not one of the subjects with autism included in their narratives any causal explanations for the events in the stories. Not only did the subjects with autism not use mentalistic explanations, they also failed to provide even physical causal explanations, suggesting that they had quite fundamental impairments in viewing behaviour and action within a causal-explanatory framework.

One study has directly investigated the relationship between narrative abilities and performance on a standard theory of mind (false belief) task in subjects with autism (Tager-Flusberg & Sullivan, 1995). A larger group of individuals

with autism was matched on IQ and standardised measures of language production and comprehension to a group of individuals with mental retardation. Again,
a wordless picture book was used to elicit a story. Subjects were later probed
about the emotional states of characters in the story. As in the previous study, the
subjects with autism were significantly worse at providing appropriate explanations for the emotional states of the story characters. In addition, in the autistic
group, all the narrative measures (including length, number of connectives,
emotion and cognition terms) were significantly correlated with performance on
the false belief task.

The findings from this set of studies confirm that theory of mind deficits in
autism are reflected in difficulties found among even high functioning autistic
individuals in narrating a story. Such difficulties vary widely from an inability to
perceive a related sequence of pictures or events as a coherent narrative, to
limitations in producing a rich and complex narrative that places the sequence of
events in the story within a causal explanatory framework.

Lexical development in autism

Several researchers had hypothesised that autism was characterised by a fundamental inability to form concepts and extend word meanings (Menyuk, 1978).
This proposal was used to account for the idiosyncratic use of words and phrases
that had been reported in the early clinical literature, as well as other behavioural
and social features that define autism. However, experimental studies with
children with autism, matched on verbal mental age to children with retardation and normally developing children, found no support for this hypothesis
(Tager-Flusberg, 1985b). The autistic subjects were no different from the matched
control groups in their organisation and representation of basic level and superordinate level concepts. The autistic and mentally retarded subjects recognised
the same kinds of systematic and well-structured relationships among pictures of
objects as do normally developing children at both basic and superordinate
levels of taxonomic hierarchies. For all the subjects, basic level concepts were
psychologically more salient confirming the kinds of universal constraints that
operate on conceptual representation. Furthermore, in looking at word meanings
in both comprehension and production, the autistic children had no difficulty
extending words to a range of different exemplars, and their extensions were
based on a prototype organisation of their semantic concepts (Tager-Flusberg,
1985a, 1986).

These findings suggest that for the autistic children word meaning develops
in a highly systematic and constrained way. The data are consistent with the
view that lexical development in autism, as in normally developing and other
retarded populations, is constrained by a set of operating principles (Golinkoff
et al., 1994), however there have not been the same kinds of systematic studies
of the *process* of lexical development in autism, as has been conducted for other

populations. Data from naturalistic longitudinal data (Tager-Flusberg et al., 1990) and standardised measures such as the PPVT–R suggest that vocabulary development can be an area of relative strength for individuals with autism; some subjects have been found to score well above the mean on the PPVT–R, indicating an unusually rich knowledge of words.

Nevertheless there is wide variation in lexical use among individuals with autism, even those who acquire functional language. For example, individuals with autism often misuse words and phrases producing idiosyncratic terms and neologisms (Volden & Lord, 1991) or *metaphorical language* as Kanner (1946) described it. Rutter (1987) suggests that these abnormal uses of words may be functionally similar to the kinds of early word meaning errors made by young normally developing children. It is their persistence in autistic children which defines them as abnormal and they may reflect the fact that autistic children are not sensitive to the corrective feedback provided by their parents because of their social impairments.

Morphological and syntactic development in autism

Few studies have systematically investigated grammatical aspects of language acquisition in autism. The longitudinal study of six autistic boys conducted by Tager-Flusberg and her colleagues found that these children followed the same developmental path as Down syndrome comparison children who were part of the study, and to normally developing children drawn from the extant literature (Tager-Flusberg et al., 1990). Both the autistic and Down syndrome children showed similar growth curves in the length of their utterances (MLU), which is usually taken as a hallmark measure of grammatical development. Not surprisingly, however, for most of the children the *rate* of growth was slower than in normally developing children. The autistic and Down syndrome children acquired grammatical structures in the same order as normally developing children: The order of acquisition of syntactic and morphological aspects of language is determined by linguistic complexity.

To test whether MLU in the autistic subjects reflects the same level grammatical knowledge as in other groups of children, Scarborough et al. (1991) compared the relationship between MLU and IPSyn scores, using the data from Tager-Flusberg et al.'s (1990) longitudinal study. The main findings were that at higher MLU levels, MLU tended to significantly overestimate IPSyn scores for the subjects with autism. Scarborough et al. (1991) suggest that for the children with autism the limited growth in IPSyn reflects the tendency of these children to make use of a narrower range of constructions and to ask fewer questions, which accounts for a significant portion of the IPSyn score.

Despite the similarity in developmental *patterns* reported by Tager-Flusberg et al. (1990), some researchers have argued that developmental *processes* might be different in autism. Prizant (1983) proposed that children with autism are especially dependent on the gestalt or holistic approach to acquiring language (see Peters, 1983). The primary evidence cited for the use of gestalt processes in the acquisition of grammar is reliance on imitation, repetitions, and formulaic routines. Because children with autism are known to be highly imitative (or *echolalic*), Prizant (1983) and others have argued that imitation is a crucial process in language acquisition, particularly grammatical development, for this population.

Tager-Flusberg and Calkins (1990) investigated whether variations in levels of imitation were tied to differences in the process by which grammar was acquired in autism, when compared to language matched groups of normally developing children and young children with Down syndrome. As predicted, the children with autism at the early stages of language development produced the most echolalic, repetitive, and formulaic speech. For all children, imitation and formulaic speech declined quite rapidly over the course of development. In order to investigate whether the more imitative autistic children were using imitation as a means for acquiring new grammatical knowledge, Tager-Flusberg and Calkins compared imitative and spontaneous speech drawn from the same language sample, for length of utterances using MLU, and for the complexity of grammatical constructions using IPSyn. If imitation is important in the acquisition of grammatical knowledge, then length and grammatical complexity should be more advanced in imitation than in spontaneous speech produced at the same developmental point. This hypothesis was not confirmed for any of the children in this study. On the contrary, across all language samples, spontaneous utterances were significantly longer and included more advanced grammatical constructions suggesting that imitation is not an important process in facilitating grammatical development in autism, though it clearly reflects a different conversational style, and plays an important role in children's communication with others, especially when they have very limited linguistic knowledge.

Studies of grammatical development in autism have found that this domain of language is not specifically impaired in autism. It is still not known whether autistic individuals have subtle impairments in the acquisition of more complex syntactic constructions, since no studies have addressed this issue in older individuals with autism.

Summary of language acquisition in autism

Delays and deficits in acquiring language are among the core features of autism. There is enormous variation in this domain, ranging from no functional language and very limited communicative ability to performance in the high normal range on standardised language measures. Nevertheless, across the spectrum of autism, there are selective deficits in those aspects of communication and language use that entail a theory of mind. In contrast, computational and lexical-semantic

aspects of language are relatively less impaired, at least among h
ing individuals with autism.

OTHER ATYPICAL POPULATIONS

In comparison to Down syndrome, Williams syndrome, and autism, far less is
known about the acquisition of language in other well-defined populations of children with neurodevelopmental disorders. With few exceptions, studies of other
disorders have been limited to cross-sectional studies in which only standardised
measures of language have been used, to descriptive studies of naturalistic language samples, or to case study reports. Here we briefly consider language
acquisition in a few other groups of children who provide interesting comparisons and contrasts to the syndromes covered in detail in previous sections of
this chapter.

Fragile X syndrome

Fragile X syndrome is a genetic disorder that involves mutations in a single gene
located on the X chromosome. Both boys and girls can be affected; however,
there is greater variability in the phenotypic expression among girls. This variability is related to the degree of disruption in the production of the FRM1
protein, which is under the control of the gene involved in fragile X (Hagerman,
in press). The cognitive phenotype of fragile X syndrome does not appear to
involve specific impairments in language ability (Mazzocco & Reiss, in press);
nevertheless descriptive studies, which have looked primarily at boys, suggest that
there may be some selective impairments in aspects of language functioning.

Males with fragile X syndrome are known to have poor eye contact, which is
characterised as primarily gaze aversion. Although little work has been done
with very young fragile X children, Cohen and his colleagues did not find any
age changes in the gaze avoidance of older males with fragile X in the context of
dyadic interactions (Cohen, Fisch, Sudhalter, Wolf-Schein, Hanson, Hagerman,
Jenkins, & Brown, 1988). It is not known which communicative functions are
expressed by children with fragile X in the prelinguistic period, however, given
the parallels with autism we might predict that they would produce fewer
protodeclarative and social-regulatory gestures and vocalisations.

Descriptive and clinical studies of boys with fragile X syndrome have shown
that this population has particular problems both with articulation errors, and
with the rate and fluency of speech production (Dykens, Hodapp, & Leckman,
1994). The persistent speech deficits in this group are sometimes referred to as
cluttering, a form of verbal clumsiness that may be related to higher-level motor
encoding problems (Dykens et al., 1994). Nevertheless, the kinds of errors
that males with fragile X syndrome make in their speech production are similar
to those reported for other populations (Hanson, Jackson, & Hagerman, 1986).
Because these difficulties with speech production are not related to either mental

age or IQ, Dykens et al. (1994) hypothesise that they may be linked to attentional and sequencing deficits that are characteristic of this population. Studies of syntactic ability in fragile X syndrome have mostly included only older male subjects and the few existing studies yield contradictory findings (Marans, Paul, & Leckman, 1987; Newell, Sanborn, & Hagerman, 1983; Sudhalter, Scarborough, & Cohen, 1991).

Finally, according to several descriptive studies, males with fragile X syndrome have difficulties maintaining conversational topic. They tend to perseverate more than other subjects with non-specific retardation, and they use a considerable amount of inappropriate language (Ferrier, Bashir, Meryash, Johnston, & Wolff, 1991). In the area of pragmatic abilities, several researchers have highlighted the broad similarities between autism and fragile X syndrome, whose deficits in conversational competence have been directly linked to the social impairments that are characteristic of both syndromes.

Future research on fragile X syndrome should explore more explicitly the relationship between language, social, and cognitive functioning in this population from a more developmental perspective. Comparisons of boys and girls would also add to our understanding of this interesting and unique group of individuals who may show parallel language profiles to children with autism, with the exception of the specific deficits that have been found in phonological production.

Prader-Willi syndrome

Prader-Willi syndrome is another rare genetic disorder which usually involves a small deletion of a number of genes on the long arm of chromosome 15 (Butler, 1990). The phenotype of Prader-Willi syndrome involves a unique constellation of physical, endocrine, cognitive, and behavioural characteristics (Greenswag & Alexander, 1995), including mental retardation. Unfortunately there have been no studies comparing the language characteristics of children with Prader-Willi syndrome to other groups of retarded children.

In preliminary data based on a sample of 12 children with Prader-Willi syndrome, Tager-Flusberg and her colleagues found that on standardised measures overall levels of language functioning were significantly lower than mental age levels. Receptive vocabulary scores on the PPVT–R, however, were a relative strength, sometimes exceeding mental age levels (Tager-Flusberg, Sullivan, Boshart, & Levine, 1996). Looking within language, there were no significant differences between overall receptive and expressive abilities, though across the majority of children performance was lowest on tests of grammatical morphology. These findings support other work in this area (Downey & Knutson, 1995; Kleppe, Katayama, Shipley, & Foushee, 1990) which suggests that language may be relatively impaired in Prader-Willi syndrome.

The most striking deficits in language functioning in Prader-Willi syndrome are in the domain of phonology, which some have linked to hypotonia in this population (Kleppe et al., 1990). The speech of children with Prader-Willi syndrome may be difficult to understand because of phonological deficits. Some children appear to show normal patterns of development though errors persist over lengthy periods of time (Dyson & Lombardino, 1989), while others may show more atypical patterns suggesting apraxia or phonological disorders. It is not clear whether phonological deficits are associated with the impairments in grammatical morphology mentioned above. Finally, it has also been noted in one review (Downey & Knutson, 1995) that both younger and older children with Prader-Willi syndrome may have mild pragmatic difficulties, including maintaining topic, speaker-listener roles, and turn taking in conversation, however it is unclear whether these difficulties are unique to Prader-Willi syndrome or similar to those found among other retarded individuals.

The profile of language ability in Prader-Willi syndrome suggests some similarity to what has been reported in the literature on children with specific language impairment, or in children with Down syndrome. Direct comparisons of these groups on both standardised measures and in naturalistic speech samples could offer new insights into the language characteristics of Prader-Willi syndrome.

Hydrocephalus

Hydrocephalus is a feature found in a set of neurodevelopmental disorders, in which increased cerebrospinal fluid and enlarged ventricles alter the microstructure of early brain development and function in a number of important ways. It may be the result of either congenital or postnatal causes, the most common of which is spina bifida (Dennis, Barnes, & Hetherington, in press). It is typically associated with mild levels of retardation though not all individuals with hydrocephalus score in the retarded range. Their cognitive profile is especially interesting in that it includes specific deficits in visual-spatial cognition and motor impairment, but relatively spared language. The language of individuals with hydrocephalus has been termed "cocktail-party" speech, because of its fluent chatter that has relatively little content (Hadenius, Hagberg, Hyttnas-Bensch, & Sjogren, 1962; Ingram & Naughton, 1962; Tew, 1979). In fact only about 40% of individuals with hydrocephalus associated with spina bifida fit criteria for cocktail party syndrome, and interestingly, it tends to occur primarily in those with lower IQ scores (Tew, 1979).

The most detailed case study of an individual with cocktail party syndrome associated with hydrocephalus has been described by Cromer (1994). Cromer's subject, called DH, was a teenager when she was studied using a wide range of standardised and experimental tests of language and other cognitive domains. DH had an IQ of 44, on the Wechsler test (WISC–R), but her verbal IQ was significantly higher than her performance IQ. On a range of cognitive tasks she performed at the level of a 4- or 5-year-old, but interestingly she was able to pass a standard theory of mind task (demonstrating her understanding of false belief). On standardised measures of grammatical ability DH did not perform well, scoring at only about a 5-year-old level; however, her spontaneous speech included many examples of complex grammatical constructions that were correctly and appropriately used. Furthermore, she demonstrated on sentence judgement tasks that she could distinguish between grammatical and ungrammatical sentences, and knew how to correct the ungrammatical ones. Her strongest performance on standardised measures was on the British equivalent of the PPVT, measuring receptive vocabulary, on which she scored at the level of a 9- or 10-year-old.

Cromer (1994) argues that all aspects of DH's linguistic knowledge and use were intact and excellent, from phonology, lexical knowledge, to grammar and even pragmatics. She demonstrated intact conversational skills and, like other individuals with cocktail party syndrome, she seemed eager to talk all the time. Cromer concludes that despite the disparaging name for the kind of language produced by individuals with hydrocephalus, like others with this disorder DH appears to have an intact linguistic system, despite severe impairments in other cognitive domains. Cognitive deficits in hydrocephalus do, however, impact language use in complex discourse contexts. Dennis and her colleagues have demonstrated that children and adolescents with hydrocephalus have great difficulty drawing semantic inferences, integrating information, or building mental models from a text they have heard or read (Dennis & Barnes, 1993; Dennis, Jacennik, & Barnes, 1994; Dennis et al., in press). These deficits lead to problems in comprehension of complex linguistic material at a discourse level.

CONCLUSIONS

The general picture of language acquisition across different populations of atypical children provides strong evidence for both important differences as well as similarities among children with various neurodevelopmental disorders. The most striking findings are the contrasting profiles that are found between populations across domains of language. These asynchronies are the hallmark of language acquisition in atypical children (Tager-Flusberg, 1988).

The between-group comparisons suggest a clear dissociation between developments in grammar and in pragmatics. Thus, studies of grammatical development have shown very different developmental profiles in Down syndrome and Prader-Willi syndrome compared to Williams syndrome and (perhaps) autism, relative to other aspects of language development. These differences parallel the findings on phonological development in these populations in that impairments in phonology tend to co-occur with impairments in morphosyntactic aspects of language. Together these findings suggest that the computational aspects of language are impaired in Down syndrome but relatively spared in Williams syndrome and autism. Impairments to the computational aspects of language are also associated with impairments in auditory working memory, while populations who show relative strengths in acquiring phonology and grammar show relatively intact working memory. This relationship between a non-linguistic cognitive skill and a specific component of language suggests that there may be important integral neurobiological connections between the substrates that serve these cognitive functions.

Studies of pragmatic abilities have shown that this is an area of strength in Down syndrome, and perhaps also in Williams syndrome at the early stages. In contrast, from the beginning, pragmatic abilities are significantly impaired in autism. These patterns highlight the central role of social functioning, particularly theory of mind, in the acquisition of the communicative aspects of language. Finally, it is interesting to note that across all the syndromes considered in this chapter one consistent finding was the relative strength in lexical development. On standardised measures children with different neurodevelopmental disorders scored highest on the PPVT, sometime even above general mental age level. Because lexical knowledge is closely tied to general cognitive level, one would expect a fairly close relationship between the lexicon and mental age measures, and indeed, this was a highly consistent finding across studies with different populations.

The asynchronies across different populations that have been documented in this chapter underscore the need for a complex model of language acquisition. This model involves the interaction of several partially independent mechanisms that process different types of information. This chapter has illustrated some of these asynchronies which suggest that in different syndromes different mechanisms may be impaired. Thus in autism impairments are primarily to theory of mind mechanisms that play a role in language and communication (Locke, 1993), whereas in Down syndrome there are specific impairments in the computational mechanisms that underlie the processing of grammatical information.

At the same time, research on atypical children has also highlighted some of the universal constraints that operate on the acquisition of phonology, meaning, and grammar. Within each of these domains there are uniform sequences of development, and certain principles that constrain the process of development. There are not multiple alternative ways of acquiring language, though as each of these components develop over time, they may become integrated in different ways, which lead to syndrome-specific profiles.

As research on language development in neurodevelopmental disorders progresses over the next decades, the overall quality of the work conducted in this field will need to be enhanced. Future studies need to incorporate more detailed, theoretically driven methodologies, comparisons across several populations using appropriate matching variables and control groups, and investigations of both comprehension and production using methods that are specifically adapted for use with a variety of populations. The effort invested in research of this sort will pay off by providing genuine advances in our knowledge and theoretical models of language acquisition in atypical as well as in normally developing children.

ACKNOWLEDGEMENTS

This chapter was written with grant support from the National Institutes of Health (R55 HD/OD-33470), the National Institute of Child Health and Human Development (RO1 HD-33470), and the National Institute on Deafness and Other Communication Disorders (RO1 DC-01234).

REFERENCES

Adamson, L., & Bakeman, R. (1982). Affectivity and reference: Concepts, methods, and techniques in the study of communication development of 6- to 18-month old infants. In T. Field & A. Fogel (Eds.), *Emotion and early interaction* (pp. 213–236). Hillsdale, NJ: Lawrence Erlbaum Associates Inc.

American Psychiatric Association. (1994). *Diagnostic and Statistical Manual of Mental Disorders* (4th edn.) (DSM–IV). Washington, DC: APA.

Astington, J. (1990). Narrative and the child's theory of mind. In B. Britton & A. Pellegrini (Eds.), *Narrative thought and narrative language* (pp. 151–171). Hillsdale, NJ: Lawrence Erlbaum Associates Inc.

Bailey, A., Phillips, W., & Rutter, M. (1996). Autism: Towards an integration of clinical, genetic, neuropsychological, and neurobiological perspectives. *Journal of Child Psychology and Psychiatry, 37*, 89–126.

Ball, J. (1978). *A pragmatic analysis of autistic children's language with respect to aphasic and normal language development.* Unpublished doctoral dissertation, Melbourne University.

Baltaxe, C.A.M. (1977). Pragmatic deficits in the language of autistic adolescents. *Journal of Pediatric Psychology, 2*, 176–180.

Bamberg, M., & Damrad-Frye, R. (1991). On the ability to provide evaluative comments: Further explorations of children's narrative competencies. *Journal of Child Language, 18*, 689–710.

Baron-Cohen, S. (1989). Perceptual role-taking and protodeclarative pointing in autism. *British Journal of Developmental Psychology, 7*, 113–127.

Baron-Cohen, S. (1993). From attention-goal psychology to belief-desire psychology: The development of a theory of mind and its dysfunction. In S. Baron-Cohen, H. Tager-Flusberg, & D.J. Cohen (Eds.), *Understanding other minds: Perspectives from autism* (pp. 59–82). Oxford, UK: Oxford University Press.

Baron-Cohen, S. (1996). *Mindblindness.* Cambridge, MA: MIT Press.

Baron-Cohen, S., Leslie, A.M., & Frith, U. (1986). Mechanical, behavioural and intentional understanding of picture stories in autistic children. *British Journal of Developmental Psychology, 4*, 113–125.

Baron-Cohen, S., Ring, H., Moriarty, J., Schmitz, P., Costa, D., & Ell, P. (1994). Recognition of mental state terms: A clinical study of autism and a functional neuroimaging study of normal adults. *British Journal of Psychiatry, 165*, 640–649.

Baron-Cohen, S., Tager-Flusberg, H., & Cohen, D.J. (Eds.). (1993). *Understanding other minds: Perspectives from autism.* Oxford, UK: Oxford University Press.

Bartolucci, G., & Pierce, S. (1977). A preliminary comparison of phonological development in autistic, normal, and mentally retarded subjects. *British Journal of Disorders of Communication, 12*, 134–147.

Bates, E., Camaioni, L., & Volterra, V. (1975). The acquisition of performatives prior to speech. *Merrill-Palmer Quarterly, 21*, 205–224.

Beeghly, M., Weiss-Perry, B., & Cicchetti, D. (1990). Beyond sensorimotor functioning: Early communicative and play development of children with Down syndrome. In D. Cicchetti & M. Beeghly (Eds.), *Children with Down syndrome: A developmental perspective* (pp. 329–368). New York: Cambridge University Press.

Bellugi, U., Bihrle, A., Neville, H., Jernigan, T., & Doherty, S. (1992). Language, cognition and brain organization in a neurodevelopmental disorder. In M. Gunnar & C. Nelson (Eds.), *Developmental behavioral neuroscience* (pp. 201–232). Hillsdale, NJ: Lawrence Erlbaum Associates Inc.

Bellugi, U., Marks, S., Bihrle, A., & Sabo, H. (1988). Dissociation between language and cognitive functions in Williams syndrome. In D. Bishop & K. Mogford (Eds.), *Language development in exceptional circumstances* (pp. 177–189). London: Churchill Livingstone.

Bellugi, U., Wang, P., & Jernigan, T. (1994). Williams syndrome: An unusual neuropsychological profile. In S. Broman & J. Grafman (Eds.), *Atypical cognitive deficits in developmental disorders: Implications for brain function* (pp. 23–56). Hillsdale, NJ: Lawrence Erlbaum Associates Inc.

Belmont, J. (1971). Medical behavioral research: Retardation. In N.R. Ellis (Ed.), *International review of research in mental retardation* (pp. 1–81). New York: Academic Press.

Bennett, T. (1976). Code-switching in Down's syndrome. *Proceedings of the 2nd annual meeting of the Berkeley Linguistics Society*, Berkeley, CA.

Berger, J., & Cunningham, C. (1981). The development of eye contact between mothers and normal versus Down's syndrome infants. *Developmental Psychology, 17,* 678–689.

Berger, J., & Cunningham, C. (1983). The development of early vocal behaviors and interactions in Down syndrome and non-handicapped infant-mother pairs. *Developmental Psychology, 19,* 322–331.

Bertrand, J., Mervis, C., Rice, C., & Adamson, L. (1993). *Development of joint attention by a toddler with Williams syndrome.* Gatlinburg Conference on Research and Theory in Mental Retardation and Developmental Disabilities, Gatlinburg, TN.

Bishop, D. (1989). *Test for the reception of grammar.* Manchester, UK: Chapel Press.

Bloom, L., Rocissano, L., & Hood., L. (1976). Adult-child discourse: Developmental interaction between information processing and linguistic knowledge. *Cognitive Psychology, 8,* 521–552.

Bol, G., & Kuiken, F. (1990). Grammatical analysis of developmental language disorders: A study of the morphosyntax of children with specific language disorders, with hearing impairment and with Down's syndrome. *Clinical Linguistics and Phonetics, 4,* 77–86.

Bray, M., & Woolnough, L. (1988). The language skills of children with Down's syndrome aged 12 to 16 years. *Child Language Teaching and Therapy, 4,* 311–324.

Britton, B., & Pellegrini, A. (Eds) (1990). *Narrative thought and narrative language.* Hillsdale, NJ: Lawrence Erlbaum Associates Inc.

Bromberg, H., Ullman, M., Marcus, G., Kelley, K., & Levine, K. (1995). A dissociation of lexical memory and grammar in Williams syndrome: Evidence from inflectional morphophonology. *Genetics Counseling, 6,* 166–167.

Brown, R. (1980). The maintenance of conversation. In D. Olson (Ed.), *Social foundations of language and thought* (pp. 86–102). New York: Oxford University Press.

Bruner, J. (1986). *Actual minds, possible worlds.* Cambridge, MA: Harvard University Press.

Bruner, J., & Feldman, C. (1993). Theories of mind and the problem of autism. In S. Baron-Cohen, H. Tager-Flusberg, & D.J. Cohen (Eds.), *Understanding other minds: Perspectives from autism* (pp. 269–291). Oxford, UK: Oxford University Press.

Butler, M. (1990). Prader-Willi syndrome: Current understanding of cause and diagnosis. *American Journal of Genetics, 35,* 319–332.

Cardoso-Martins, C., Mervis, C., & Mervis, C. (1985). Early vocabulary acquisition by children with Down syndrome. *American Journal of Mental Deficiency, 90,* 177–184.

Carr, E., Schreibman, L., & Lovaas, O. (1975). Control of echolalic speech in psychotic children. *Journal of Abnormal Psychology, 3,* 331–351.

Chapman, R. (1995). Language development in children and adolescents with Down syndrome. In P. Fletcher & B. MacWhinney (Eds.), *The handbook of child language* (pp. 641–663). Oxford, UK: Blackwell.

Chapman, R., Schwartz, S., & Kay-Raining Bird, E. (1989). *Are children with Down syndrome language delayed?* Paper presented at the American Speech-Language-Hearing Association Meeting, St. Louis, MO.

Chapman, R., Schwartz, S., & Kay-Raining Bird, E. (1991). Language skills of children and adolescents with Down syndrome: I. Comprehension. *Journal of Speech and Hearing Research, 34*, 1106–1120.

Chapman, R., Schwartz, S., & Kay-Raining Bird, E. (1992). *Language production of children and adolescents with Down syndrome.* 9th World Congress of the International Association for the Scientific Study of Mental Deficiency, Gold Coast, Australia.

Clark, E. (1983). Meanings and concepts. In J. Flavell & E. Markman (Eds.), *Handbook of child psychology: Vol. 3. Cognitive development* (pp. 787–840). New York: Wiley.

Coco-Lewis, A.B., Oller, K., Lynch, M., & Levine, S.L. (1995). *Relationships among motor and vocal milestones in normally developing infants and infants with Down syndrome.* Gatlinburg conference on Research and Theory in Mental Retardation and Developmental Disabilities, Gatlinburg, TN.

Coggins, T., Carpenter, R., & Owings, N. (1983). Examining early intentional communication in Down's syndrome and nonretarded children. *British Journal of Disorders of Communication, 18,* 99–107.

Coggins, T., & Stoel-Gammon, C. (1982). Clarification strategies used by four Down's syndrome children for maintaining normal conversational interaction. *Education and Training of the Mentally Retarded, 16,* 65–67.

Cohen, I.L., Fisch, G., Sudhalter, V., Wolf-Schein, E., Hanson, D., Hagerman, R., Jenkins, J.T., & Brown, W.T. (1988). Social gaze, social avoidance and repetitive behavior in fragile X males in a controlled study. *American Journal of Mental Retardation, 92,* 436–446.

Cromer, R. (1994). A case study of dissociations between language and cognition. In H. Tager-Flusberg (Ed.), *Constraints on language acquisition: Studies of atypical children* (pp. 141–153). Hillsdale, NJ: Lawrence Erlbaum Associates Inc.

Crossley, P., & Dowling, S. (1989). The relationship between cluster and liquid simplification and sentence length, age, and IQ in Down's syndrome children. *Journal of Communication Disorders, 22,* 151–168.

Curcio, F. (1978). Sensorimotor functioning and communication in mute autistic children. *Journal of Autism and Childhood Schizophrenia, 8,* 282–292.

Dennis, M., & Barnes, M. (1993). Oral discourse after early-onset hydrocephalus: Linguistic ambiguity, figurative language, speech acts, and script-based inferences. *Journal of Pediatric Psychology, 18,* 639–652.

Dennis, M., Barnes, M., & Hetherington, C.R. (in press). Congenital hydrocephalus as a model of neurodevelopmental disorder. In H. Tager-Flusberg (Ed.), *Neurodevelopmental disorders.* Cambridge, MA: MIT Press.

Dennis, M., Jacennik, B., & Barnes, M. (1994). The content of narrative discourse in children and adolescents after early-onset hydrocephalus and in normally developing age peers. *Brain and Language, 46,* 129–165.

Dodd, B.J. (1972). Comparison of babbling patterns in normal and Down syndrome infants. *Journal of Mental Deficiency Research, 16,* 35–40.

Dodd, B.J. (1976). A comparison of the phonological systems of mental-age-matched severely subnormal, and Down's syndrome children. *British Journal of Disorders of Communication, 11,* 27–42.

Dooley, J. (1976). *Language acquisition and Down's syndrome: A study of early semantics and syntax.* Unpublished doctoral dissertation, Harvard University, MA.

Downey, D., & Knutson, C.L. (1995). Speech and language issues. In L.R. Greenswag & Alexander, R.C. (Eds.), *Management of Prader-Willi syndrome* (pp. 142–155). New York: Springer Verlag.

Dykens, E., Hodapp, R., & Leckman, J. (1994). *Behavior and development in fragile X syndrome.* Thousand Oaks, CA: Sage.

Dyson, A., & Lombardino, L. (1989). Phonological abilities of a preschool child with Prader-Willi syndrome. *Journal of Speech and Hearing Disorders, 54,* 44–48.

Ewart, A., Morris, C.A., Atkinson, D., Jin, W., Sternes, K., Spallone, P., Stock, A., Leppert, M., & Keating, M. (1993). Hemizygosity at the elastin locus in a developmental disorder, Williams syndrome. *Nature Genetics, 5*, 11–16.

Ferrier, L., Bashir, A., Meryash, D., Johnston, J., & Wolff, P. (1991). Conversational skills of individuals with fragile X syndrome: A comparison with autism and Down syndrome. *Developmental Medicine and Child Neurology, 33*, 776–778.

Fletcher P.C., Happé, F., Frith, U., Baker, S.C., Dolan, R.J., Frackowiak, R.S.J., & Frith, C.D. (1995). *Cognition, 57*, 109–128.

Flint, J. (1996). Annotation: Behavioral phenotypes: A window onto the biology of behavior. *Journal of Child Psychology and Psychiatry, 37*, 355–367.

Foster, S. (1990). *The communicative competence of young children.* New York: Longman.

Fowler, A. (1988). Determinants of rate of language growth in children with Down syndrome. In L. Nadel (Ed.), *The psychobiology of Down syndrome* (pp. 217–245). Cambridge, MA: MIT Press.

Fowler, A. (1990). Language abilities in children with Down syndrome: Evidence for a specific syntactic delay. In D. Cicchetti & M. Beeghly (Eds.), *Children with Down syndrome: A developmental perspective* (pp. 302–328). New York: Cambridge University Press.

Fowler, A., Gelman, R., & Gleitman, L. (1994). The course of language learning in children with Down syndrome: Longitudinal and language level comparisons with young normally developing children. In H. Tager-Flusberg (Ed.), *Constraints on language acquisition: Studies of atypical children* (pp. 91–140). Hillsdale, NJ: Lawrence Erlbaum Associates Inc.

Frangiskakis, J., Ewart, A., Morris, C.A., Mervis, C., Bertrand, J., Robinson, B., Klein, B. Ensing, G., Everett, L., Green, E., Proschel, C., Gutowski, N., Noble, M., Atkinson, D., Odelberg, S., & Keating, M. (1996). LIM-kinase 1 hemizygosity implication in impaired visuospatial constructive cognition. *Cell, 86*, 59–69.

Golinkoff, R., Mervis, C., & Hirsh-Pasek, K. (1994). Early object labels: The case for a developmental lexical principles framework. *Journal of Child Language, 21*, 125–155.

Goodman, J. (1995). Language acquisition in children with Williams syndrome. *Genetics Counseling, 6*, 167–168.

Gopnik, A., & Meltzoff, A. (1987). The development of categorization in the second year of life and its relation to other cognitive and linguistic developments. *Child Development, 58*, 1523–1531.

Gosch, A., Städing, G., & Pankau R. (1994). Linguistic abilities in children with Williams-Beuren syndrome. *American Journal of Medical Genetics, 52*, 291–296.

Greenswag, L.R., & Alexander, R.C. (Eds.) (1995). *Management of Prader-Willi syndrome.* New York: Springer Verlag.

Greenwald, C.A., & Leonard, L. (1979). Communicative and sensorimotor development of Down's syndrome children. *American Journal of Mental Deficiency, 84*, 296–303.

Gunn, P., Berry, P., & Andrews, R. (1982). Looking behavior of Down syndrome infants. *American Journal of Mental Deficiency, 87*, 601–605.

Hadenius, A., Hagberg, B., Hyttnas-Bensch, K., & Sjogren, I. (1962). The natural prognosis of infantile hydrocephalus. *Acta Paediatrica, 51*, 117–118.

Hagerman, R. (in press). Physical and behavioral problems and molecular/clinical correlations in fragile X syndrome. In H. Tager-Flusberg (Ed.), *Neurodevelopmental disorders.* Cambridge, MA: MIT Press.

Hanson, D.M., Jackson, A.W., & Hagerman, R. (1986). Speech disturbances (cluttering) in mildly impaired males with the Martin-Bell/fragile X syndrome. *American Journal of Medical Genetics, 23*, 195–206.

Happé, F. (1993). Communicative competence and theory of mind in autism: A test of relevance theory. *Cognition, 48*, 101–119.

Ingram, T., & Naughton, J. (1962). Pediatric and psychological aspects of cerebral palsy associated with hydrocephalus. *Developmental Medicine and Child Neurology, 4*, 287–292.

Jackendoff, R. (1983). *Semantics and cognition.* Cambridge, MA: MIT Press.

Jaffe, J., Stern, D., & Perry, J. (1973). Conversational coupling of gaze behavior in prelinguistic human development. *Journal of Psycholinguistic Research, 2,* 321–329.

Jasnow, M., Crown, C.L., Feldstein, S., Taylor, L., Beebe, B., & Jaffe, J. (1988). Coordinated interpersonal timing of Down-syndrome and nondelayed infants with their mothers: Evidence for a buffered mechanism of social interaction. *Biological Bulletin, 175,* 355–360.

Jones, O. (1980). Prelinguistic communication skills in Down's syndrome and normal infants. In T. Field, S. Goldberg, D. Stern, & A. Sostek (Eds.), *High-risk infants and children: Adult and peer interactions* (pp. 205–255). New York: Academic Press.

Jordan, F.M., & Murdoch, B.E. (1987). Referential communication skills of children with Down syndrome. *Australian Journal of Human Communication Disorders, 15,* 47–59.

Kanner, L. (1946). Irrelevant and metaphorical language. *American Journal of Psychiatry, 103,* 242–246.

Karmiloff-Smith, A., Bellugi, U., Klima, E., Grant, J., & Baron-Cohen, S. (1995). Is there a social module? Language, face processing, and theory of mind individuals with Williams syndrome. *Journal of Cognitive Neuroscience, 7,* 196–208.

Karmiloff-Smith, A., Grant, J., Berthoud, I., Davies, M., Howlin, P., & Udwin, O. (1997). Language and Williams syndrome: How intact is "intact"? *Child Development, 68,* 246–262.

Kasari, C., Mundy, P., Yirmiya, N., & Sigman, M. (1990). Affect and attention in children with Down syndrome. *American Journal on Mental Retardation, 95,* 55–67.

Kelley, K., & Tager-Flusberg, H. (1995). Discourse characteristics of children with Williams syndrome: Evidence of spared theory of mind abilities. *Genetics Counseling, 6,* 169–170.

Kleppe, S., Katayama, K., Shipley, K., & Foushee, D. (1990). The speech and language characteristics of children with Prader-Willi syndrome. *Journal of Speech and Hearing Disorders, 55,* 300–309.

Klin, A. (1991). Young autistic children's listening preferences in regard to speech: A possible characterization of the symptom of social withdrawal. *Journal of Autism and Developmental Disorders, 21,* 29–42.

Krakow, J.B., & Kopp, C. (1983). The effects of developmental delay on sustained attention in young children. *Child Development, 54,* 1143–1155.

Landry, S., & Chapieski, M.L. (1990). Joint attention of six-month-old Down syndrome and preterm infants: 1. Attention to toys and mother. *American Journal of Mental Retardation, 94,* 488–498.

Leonard, L. (1996). Characterizing specific language impairment: A cross-linguistic perspective. In M. Rice (Ed.), *Toward a genetics of language* (pp. 243–256). Hillsdale, NJ: Lawrence Erlbaum Associates Inc.

Levine, S.L., Fishman, L.M., Oller, K., Lynch, M., & Basinger, D.L. (1991). *The relationship between infant motor development and babbling in normally developing, at risk, and handicapped infants.* Gatlinburg Conference on Research and Theory in Mental Retardation and Developmental Disabilities, Gatlinburg, TN.

Locke, J. (1993). *A child's path to spoken language.* Cambridge, MA: Harvard University Press.

Loveland, K., & Landry, S. (1986). Joint attention and language in autism and developmental language delay. *Journal of Autism and Developmental Disorders, 16,* 335–349.

Loveland, K., Landry, S., Hughes, S., Hall, S., & McEvoy, R. (1988). Speech acts and the pragmatic deficits of autism. *Journal of Speech and Hearing Research, 31,* 593–604.

Loveland, K.A., McEvoy, R.E., Tunali, B., & Kelley, M.L. (1990). Narrative story telling in autism and Down's syndrome. *British Journal of Developmental Psychology, 8,* 9–23.

Loveland, K., & Tunali, B. (1991). Social scripts for conversational interactions in autism and Down syndrome. *Journal of Autism and Developmental Disorders, 21,* 177–186.

Loveland, K., & Tunali, B. (1993). Narrative language in autism and the theory of mind hypothesis: A wider perspective. In S. Baron-Cohen, H. Tager-Flusberg, & D.J. Cohen (Eds.), *Understanding other minds: Perspectives from autism* (pp. 247–266). Oxford, UK: Oxford University Press.

Lynch, M., Oller, K., Eilers, R., & Basinger, D. (1990). *Vocal development of infants with Down's syndrome.* Symposium for Research on Child Language Disorders, Madison, WI.

Macnamara, J. (1982). *Names for things.* Cambridge, MA: MIT Press.

Marans, W., Paul, R., & Leckman, J. (1987). *Speech and language profiles in males with fragile X syndrome.* Paper presented at the annual convention of the American-Speech-Language-Hearing Association.

Margar-Bacal, F., Witzel, M., & Munro, I. (1987). Speech intelligibility after partial glossectomy in children with Down's syndrome. *Plastic and Reconstructive Surgery, 79,* 44–49.

Markman, E. (1989). *Categorization and naming in children.* Cambridge, MA: MIT Press.

Markman, E., & Wachtel, G. (1988). Children's use of mutual exclusivity to constrain the meaning of words. *Cognitive Psychology, 20,* 121–157.

Mazoyer, B.M., Tzourio, N., Frak, V., Syrota, A., Murayama, N., Levrier, O., Salamon, G., Dehaene, S., Cohen, L., & Mehler, J. (1993). The cortical representation of speech. *Journal of Cognitive Neuroscience, 5,* 467–479.

Mazzocco, M., & Reiss, A. (in press). A behavioral neurogenetics approach to understanding the fragile X syndrome. In H. Tager-Flusberg (Ed.), *Neurodevelopmental disorders.* Cambridge, MA: MIT Press.

Menyuk, P. (1978). Language: What's wrong and why. In M. Rutter & E. Schopler (Eds.), *Autism: A reappraisal of concepts and treatment* (pp. 105–116). New York: Plenum.

Mervis, C. (1988). Early lexical development: Theory and application. In L. Nadel (Ed.), *The psychobiology of Down syndrome* (pp. 101–143). Cambridge, MA: MIT Press.

Mervis, C. (1990). *Early conceptual development of children with Down syndrome: A developmental perspective* (pp. 252–301). New York: Cambridge University Press.

Mervis, C., & Bertrand, J. (1997). Relations between cognition and language: A developmental perspective. In L.B. Adamson & M.A. Romski (Eds.), *Research on communication and language disorders: Contributions to theories of language development* (pp. 75–106). New York: Brookes.

Mervis, C., Morris, C., Bertrand, J., & Robinson, B. (in press). Williams syndrome. Findings from an integrated program of research. In H Tager-Flusberg (Ed.), *Neurodevelopmental disorders.* Cambridge, MA: MIT Press.

Mervis, C., & Pani, J. (1980). Acquisition of basic object categories. *Cognitive Psychology, 12,* 496–522.

Mervis, C , & Rosch, E. (1981). Categorization of natural objects. *Annual Review of Psychology, 32,* 89–115.

Miller, J. (1988). The developmental asynchrony of language development in children with Down syndrome. In L. Nadel (Ed.), *The psychobiology of Down syndrome* (pp. 167–198). Cambridge, MA: MIT Press.

Miller, J. (1992). Development of speech and language in children with Down syndrome. In I.T. Lott & E.E. McCoy (Eds.), *Down syndrome: Advances in medical care* (pp. 39–50). New York: Wiley-Liss.

Miller, J., Sedley, A., Miolo, G., Murray-Branch, J., & Rosin, M. (1992). *Longitudinal investigation of vocabulary acquisition in children with Down syndrome.* Symposium on Research in Child Language Disorders, Madison, WI.

Morris, C., Thomas, I., & Greenberg, F. (1993). Williams syndrome: Autosomal dominant inheritance. *American Journal of Medical Genetics, 47,* 478–481.

Mundy, P., & Sigman, M. (1989). The theoretical implications of joint attention deficits in autism. *Development and Psychopathology, 1,* 173–183.

Mundy, P., Sigman, M., & Kasari, C. (1990). A longitudinal study of joint attention and language development in autistic children. *Journal of Autism and Developmental Disorders, 20,* 115–123.

Mundy, P., Sigman, M., & Kasari, C. (1993). The theory of mind and joint-attention deficits in autism. In S. Baron-Cohen, H. Tager-Flusberg, & D.J. Cohen (Eds.), *Understanding other minds: Perspectives from autism* (pp. 181–203). Oxford, UK: Oxford University Press.

Mundy, P., Sigman, M., & Kasari, C. (1994). Joint attention, developmental level and symptom presentation in autism. *Development and Psychopathology, 6,* 389–401.

Mundy, P., Sigman, M., Kasari, C., & Yirmiya, N. (1988). Nonverbal communication skills in Down syndrome children. *Child Development, 59,* 235–249.

Newell, K., Sanborn, B., & Hagerman, R. (1983). Speech and language dysfunction in the fragile X syndrome. In R. Hagerman & P.M. McBogg (Eds.), *The fragile X syndrome: Diagnosis, biochemistry, and intervention* (pp. 75–100). Dillon, CO: Spectra.

Oller, K. (1986). Metaphonology and infant vocalizations. In B. Lindblom & R. Zetterstrom (Eds.), *Precursors of early speech.* Basingstoke, UK: Macmillan.

Oller, K., & Siebert, J.M. (1988). Babbling in prelinguistic retarded children. *American Journal of Mental Retardation, 92,* 369–375.

Ornitz, E., Guthrie, D., & Farley, A.J. (1977). Early development of autistic children. *Journal of Autism and Childhood Schizophrenia, 7,* 207–229.

Paul R. (1987). Communication. In D.J. Cohen & A.M. Donnellan (Eds.), *Handbook of autism and pervasive developmental disorders* (pp. 61–84). New York: Wiley.

Pinker, S. (1994). *The language instinct.* Harmondworth, UK: Penguin Press.

Peters, A. (1983). *The units of language acquisition.* New York: Cambridge University Press.

Prizant, B. (1983). Language acquisition and communication behavior in autism: Toward an understanding of the "whole" of it. *Journal of Speech and Hearing Disorders, 48,* 296–307.

Prizant, B., & Duchan, J. (1981). The functions of immediate echolalia in autistic children. *Journal of Speech and Hearing Disorders, 46,* 241–249.

Pronovost, W., Wakstein, M., & Wakstein, P. (1966). A longitudinal study of the speech behavior and language comprehension of fourteen children diagnosed atypical or autistic. *Exceptional Children, 33,* 19–26.

Reilly, J., Harrison, D., & Klima, E. (1995). Emotional talk and talk about emotion. *Genetics Counseling, 6,* 158–159.

Reilly, J., Klima, E., & Bellugi, U. (1990). Once more with feeling: Affect and language in atypical populations. *Development and Psychopathology, 2,* 367–391.

Rice, M., & Wexler, K. (1996). A phenotype of specific language impairment: Extended optional infinitives. In M. Rice (Ed.), *Toward a genetics of language* (pp. 215–238). Hillsdale, NJ: Lawrence Erlbaum Associates Inc.

Ricks, D., & Wing, L. (1976). Language, communication and the use of symbols. In L. Wing (Ed.), *Early childhood autism: Clinical, educational, and social aspects* (2nd edn, pp. 93–134). New York: Pergamon Press.

Rollins, P. (1994). *A case study of the development of communicative skills for six autistic children.* Unpublished doctoral dissertation, Harvard University, MA.

Rondal, J. (1994). Exceptional cases of language development in mental retardation: The relative autonomy of language as a cognitive system. In H. Tager-Flusberg (Ed.), *Constraints on language acquisition: Studies of atypical children* (pp. 155–174). Hillsdale, NJ: Lawrence Erlbaum Associates Inc.

Rosch, E., Mervis, C., Gray, W.D., Johnson, D.M., & Boyes-Braem, P. (1976). Basic objects in natural categories. *Cognitive Psychology, 8,* 382–439.

Rosin, M., Swift, E., Bless, D., & Vetter, D. (1988). Communication profiles in adolescents with Down syndrome. *Journal of Childhood Communication Disorders, 12,* 49–64.

Rossen, M., Bihrle, A., Klima, E., Bellugi, U., & Jones, W. (in press). Interaction between language and cognition: Evidence from Williams syndrome. In J.H. Beitchman, N. Cohen, M. Konstantareas, & R. Tannock (Eds.), *Language learning and behavior.* New York: Cambridge University Press.

Ruskin, E., Kasari, C., Mundy, P., & Sigman, M. (1994). Attention to people and toys during social and object mastery in children with Down syndrome. *American Journal of Mental Retardation, 99,* 103–111.

Rutter, M. (1987). The "what" and "how" of language development: A note on some outstanding issues and questions. In W. Yule & M. Rutter (Eds.), *Language development and disorders* (pp. 159–170). London: MacKeith Press.

Scarborough, H. (1990). Index of productive syntax. *Applied Psycholinguistics, 11*, 1–22.

Scarborough, H., Rescorla, L., Tager-Flusberg, H., Fowler, A., & Sudhalter, V. (1991). The relation of utterance length to grammatical complexity in normal and language disordered groups. *Applied Psycholinguistics, 12*, 23–45.

Scherer, N., & Owings, N. (1984). Learning to be contingent: Retarded children's responses to their mothers' requests. *Language and Speech, 27*, 255–267.

Scott, P., Mervis, C., Bertrand, J., Klein, B., Armstrong, S., & Ford, A. (1995). Semantic organization and word fluency in older children with Williams syndrome. *Genetics Counseling, 6*, 172–173.

Shapiro, T. (1977). The quest for a linguistic model to study the speech of autistic children. *Journal of the American Academy of Child Psychiatry, 16*, 608–619.

Simmons, J.Q., & Baltaxe, C.A.M. (1975). Language patterns of adolescent autistics. *Journal of Autism and Childhood Schizophrenia, 5*, 333–351.

Singer, N.G., Bellugi, U., Bates, E., Jones, W., & Rossen, M. (1994). *Contrasting profiles of language development in children with Williams and Down syndromes*. Technical Report No. 9403, Project in Cognitive and Neural Development, University of California, San Diego, CA.

Smith, B.L., & Oller, K. (1981). A comparative study of pre-meaningful vocalizations produced by normally developing and Down's syndrome infants. *Journal of Speech and Hearing Disorders, 46*, 46–51.

Smith, N., & Tsimpli, I.-M. (1995). *The mind of a savant: Language learning and modularity*. Oxford, UK: Blackwell.

Steffens, M.L., Oller, K., Lynch, M., & Urbano, R. (1992). Vocal development in infants with Down syndrome and infants who are developing normally. *American Journal of Mental Retardation, 97*, 235–246.

Stoel-Gammon, C. (1980). Phonological analysis of four Down's syndrome children. *Applied Psycholinguistics, 1*, 31–48.

Stoel-Gammon, C., & Otomo, K. (1986). Babbling development of hearing-impaired and normally hearing subjects. *Journal of Speech and Hearing Disorders, 51*, 33–41.

Sudhalter, V., Scarborough, H., & Cohen, I. (1991). Syntactic delay and pragmatic deviance in the language of fragile X males. *American Journal of Medical Genetics, 38*, 493–497.

Tager-Flusberg, H. (1981). On the nature of linguistic functioning in early infantile autism. *Journal of Autism and Developmental Disorders, 11*, 45–56.

Tager-Flusberg, H. (1985a). The conceptual basis for referential word meaning in children with autism. *Child Development, 56*, 1167–1178.

Tager-Flusberg, H. (1985b). Basic level and superordinate level categorization in autistic, mentally retarded and normal children. *Journal of Experimental Child Psychology, 40*, 450–469.

Tager-Flusberg, H. (1986). Constraints on the representation of word meaning: Evidence from autistic and mentally retarded children. In S.A. Kuczaj & M. Barrett (Eds.), *The development of word meaning* (pp. 139–166). New York: Springer-Verlag.

Tager-Flusberg, H. (1988). On the nature of a language acquisition disorder: The example of autism. In F. Kessel (Ed.), *The development of language and language researchers* (pp. 249–267). Hillsdale, NJ: Lawrence Erlbaum Associates Inc.

Tager-Flusberg, H. (1989). A psycholinguistic perspective on language development in the autistic child. In G. Dawson (Ed.), *Autism: New directions in diagnosis, nature and treatment* (pp. 92–115). New York: Guilford Press.

Tager-Flusberg, H. (1993). What language reveals about the understanding of minds in children with autism. In S. Baron-Cohen, H. Tager-Flusberg, & D.J. Cohen (Eds.), *Understanding other minds: Perspectives from autism* (pp. 138–157). Oxford, UK: Oxford University Press.

Tager-Flusberg, H. (1995). "Once upon a ribbit": Stories narrated by autistic children. *British Journal of Developmental Psychology, 13,* 45–59.

Tager-Flusberg, H. (1996). Current theory and research on language and communication in autism. *Journal of Autism and Developmental Disorders, 26,* 169–172.

Tager-Flusberg, H. (1997). Language acquisition and theory of mind: Contributions from the study of autism. In L.B. Adamson & M.A. Romski (Eds.), *Research on communication and language disorders: Contributions to theories of language development* (pp. 135–160). Baltimore: Paul Brookes Publishing.

Tager-Flusberg, H., & Anderson, M. (1991). The development of contingent discourse ability in autistic children. *Journal of Child Psychology and Psychiatry, 32,* 1123–1134.

Tager-Flusberg, H., Calkins, S., Nolin, T., Baumberger, T., Anderson, M., & Chadwick-Dias, A. (1990). A longitudinal study of language acquisition in autistic and Downs syndrome children. *Journal of Autism and Developmental Disorders, 20,* 1–21.

Tager-Flusberg, H., & Calkins, S. (1990). Does imitation facilitate the acquisition of grammar? Evidence from a study of autistic, Down syndrome and normal children. *Journal of Child Language, 17,* 591–606.

Tager-Flusberg, H., & Sullivan, K. (1995). Attributing mental states to story characters: A comparison of narratives produced by autistic and mentally retarded individuals. *Applied Psycholinguistics, 16,* 241–256.

Tager-Flusberg, H., Sullivan, K., Boshart, J., & Levine, K. (1996). *Social relationships and social understanding in children with Prader-Willi Syndrome.* Northeast Regional Conference on the Prader-Willi Association, Albany, NY.

Tew, B. (1979). The "cocktail party syndrome" in children with hydrocephalus and spina bifida. *British Journal of Disorders of Communication, 14,* 89–101.

Trevarthen, C. (1979). Communication and cooperation in early infancy: A description of primary intersubjectivity. In M. Bullowa (Ed.), *Before speech* (pp. 321–349). New York: Cambridge University Press.

Tyler, L., Karmiloff-Smith, A., Voice, J.K., Stevens, T., Grant, J., Davis, M., Howlin, P., Udwin, O. (in press). Do individuals with Williams syndrome have bizarre semantics? Evidence for lexical organization using an on-line task. *Cortex.*

Udwin, O., & Yule, W. (1991). A cognitive and behavioral phenotype in Williams syndrome. *Journal of Clinical and Experimental Neuropsychology, 13,* 232–244.

Volden, J., & Lord, C. (1991). Neologism and idiosyncratic language in autistic speakers. *Journal of Autism and Developmental Disorders, 21,* 109–130.

Volkmar, F. (1996). Brief report: Diagnostic issues in autism: Results of the DSM-IV field trial. *Journal of Autism and Developmental Disorders, 26,* 155–157.

Volterra, V., Sabbadini, L., Capirci, O., Pezzini, G., & Ossella, T. (1995). Language development in Italian children with Williams syndrome. *Genetics Counseling, 6,* 137–138.

Wetherby, A. (1986). Ontogeny of communication functions in autism. *Journal of Autism and Developmental Disorders, 16,* 295–316.

Wetherby, A., & Prutting, C. (1984). Profiles of communicative and cognitive-social abilities in autistic children. *Journal of Speech and Hearing Research, 27,* 364–377.

Wilkins, W.K., & Wakefield, J. (1995). Brain evolution and neurolinguistic preconditions. *Behavioral and Brain Sciences, 18,* 161–226.

Williams, J., Barratt-Boyes, B.G., & Lowe, J.B. (1961). Supravalvular aortic stenosis. *Circulation, 24,* 1311–1318.

Wishart, J.G. (1988). Early learning in infants and young children with Down syndrome. In L. Nadel (Ed.), *The psychobiology of Down syndrome* (pp. 7–50). Cambridge, MA: MIT Press.

Woll, B., & Grove, N. (1995). *On language deficits and modality in children with Down syndrome: A case study.* Boston University Conference on Language Development, Boston.

CHAPTER THIRTEEN

Specific language impairment

Paul Fletcher
University of Hong Kong, China

INTRODUCTION

Many children fail to develop language normally, for a variety of reasons. The most obvious cause, perhaps, is a congenital hearing impairment, where the consequent lack of access to spoken input from the ambient language seriously inhibits the development of linguistic competence. For other children, their inability to acquire their language at the same rate as their peers may be linked to cognitive abilities which are outside normal limits: "language development is an area of specific additional difficulty for many children with Down syndrome" (Chapman, 1995, p. 641; see also Tager-Flusberg, this volume). For other children still, normal conditions for acquisition are interrupted by brain injury, with consequences for their language learning (Eisele & Aram, 1995). And in the behavioural syndrome referred to as autism, as Tager-Flusberg (1988, this volume) points out, atypical language development is one of the core characteristics. In this chapter, in contrast, we consider the children for whose non-normal language acquisition there is no identifiable physical or psychological basis. These individuals have normal hearing, intelligence within normal limits, an apparently intact neurological substrate, and no behavioural or emotional disorder. They nevertheless have persisting linguistic difficulties. The term used to describe this phenomenon is "specific language impairment" (henceforth SLI). This is a puzzling condition, affecting nearly three times as many boys as girls, in a small percentage of the population. We know that unless one or more of these factors (hearing impairment, cognitive deficit, neurological damage) is present, language acquisition is robust in the face of a wide range of circumstances and environments. The vast majority of children learn the phonology and grammar of the language of their community, and a significant proportion of its vocabulary, in their pre-school years. What is it that inhibits similar learning in SLI children? As we shall see, there is as yet no satisfactory answer to this question. Before addressing it we review the subject selection criteria for SLI individuals in more detail, and summarise what is known about the effects of SLI on the grammars of learners of English and of other languages.

SUBJECT DESCRIPTION

Non-linguistic status

In most published studies on SLI (see Fletcher & Ingham, 1995, p. 604 for a review), researchers do not themselves test the hearing status of the subjects in their study, but rely on testing previously performed by audiologists. The SLI subjects included in research studies have usually already been identified by speech and language therapists, and hearing status will have been established. While the existence of permanent hearing impairments among SLI subjects is not therefore an issue, the possibility of intermittent hearing impairment, brought about by recurring middle ear infection, has been investigated as a possible contributory factor. If a child has recurring otitis media in infancy and early childhood, then this could reduce language input at a critical period for development. Even if later testing reveals normal hearing, the earlier less than optimal input could still be affecting the child's language. (The issues are reviewed in Friel-Patti, 1992 and Bishop, 1992.)

The usual requirement for a child to be included in an SLI group in published studies, so far as intellectual ability is concerned, is a non-verbal IQ performance within one standard deviation of the mean (inevitably verbal IQ performance will be depressed). The use of the IQ criterion has recently been questioned from two directions. First, while the potential involvement of hearing impairment or neurological damage or a syndrome such as autism in language learning is clear, since these factors may have a direct causal involvement in language deficit or disorder, the relationship between a relatively mild intellectual deficit as represented by a non-verbal IQ of, say, 75 and any particular feature of specific language impairment is not so apparent (Fey, Long, & Cleave, 1994). Second, experimental work has made it clear that SLI children who do meet the exclusion criterion for IQ nevertheless display cognitive deficits in non-verbal functioning (Johnston, 1992).

An exclusion criterion also operates in relation to neurological status, to allow a child to be considered: In this case a child would only be included as SLI if there was no history or evidence of neurological impairment. This has not however inhibited researchers from using modern brain scanning techniques to investigate children identified as SLI, to attempt to identify previously undetected structural abnormalities (see Bishop, 1992 for a summary of these studies).

Linguistic status

An early attempt at a precise statement of linguistic criteria which children should meet in order to be considered as SLI was attempted by Stark and Tallal (1981). They deemed that language-impaired children should have a language age (LA) at least 12 months lower than their chronological age (CA) or their performance mental age (MA) whichever was the lower. LA was to be arrived at by taking a mean of the child's receptive language age and the child's expressive language age, with these being operationally defined via standardised tests. Not all subsequent studies have used the Stark/Tallal criteria. In particular, while children's comprehension ability has continued to be assessed by standardised tests (albeit tests which may be different to those Stark and Tallal propose), their expressive language has increasingly come to be measured (for research purposes at any rate) via mean length of utterance (MLU) measures derived from spontaneous speech samples. This follows the practice adopted by Brown (1973) in his longitudinal study of three normal children. Rate of acquisition varied among his subjects, and so Brown used MLU as an alternative to chronological age as a comparison measure for investigating grammatical development. Similarly, researchers who wish to investigate grammatical differences between SLI and normal children have used MLU as a way of identifying language-age matched normal subjects. Variations in linguistic inclusion criteria means that caution is needed in generalising about the grammatical effects of SLI, within and across languages. Nevertheless researchers have not been slow to identify some general features of the grammar of SLI individuals, and to attempt to explain them. In what follows we concentrate on recent work on grammatical impairment. (For a review of issues in phonological impairment in children see Leonard, 1995.) Before turning to empirical work on SLI, it would be useful to highlight at the outset a major difference in methodology between studies of SLI and those of normal language acquisition. SLI may usefully be seen as a special case of language acquisition. Its study has however had until recently a somewhat distinct history. While the methodology of choice in studies of normal children has involved case-based longitudinal studies, SLI research has favoured cross-sectional group studies. The major reason for this is variation in rate of development in normal children, which makes the identification of impaired individuals unreliable until late in the pre-school years. In the first part of this chapter we will concentrate on data and explanations arising from the finding that in the cross-sectional studies, it has become apparent that English-speaking SLI individuals, at least, have particular problems with grammatical morphology. There are two explanatory frameworks within which the data has been treated. One is essentially Chomskyan, and assumes a competence deficit. The second, performance deficit, approach relies on processing explanations for the morphological problems in SLI children. These approaches, and their advantages and disadvantages, will be dealt with in turn. We will then consider grammatical impairment in SLI more broadly.

THE LAD DEFICIT HYPOTHESIS

A recent approach to the effects of SLI is to look for evidence of a malfunctioning language acquisition device (LAD) of the Chomskyan variety. Such a device is modular, operates only on positive evidence, and relies on crucial data from input to trigger parameter settings in relation to functional categories such as tense and agreement (Meisel, 1994). Indications that SLI individuals have difficulty acquiring functional categories could be taken as *prima facie* evidence of an impaired language learning device. We can refer to this as the LAD deficit hypothesis. Tense represents one useful testing-ground for a LAD deficit hypothesis; as a functional category it is represented in most languages (though by no means all—Chinese languages represent a major exception). It thus lends itself to cross-linguistic scrutiny. If it is a feature of a particular language, it is obligatorily marked in sentences. In those European languages in which SLI has been widely studied, tense occurs on verbs as an inflection (sometimes accompanied by an auxiliary verb). Similarly agreement, like tense a functional category and seen as closely related to finiteness, is marked on verbs as an inflection. If SLI involves the inefficient acquisition of a grammatical system, then categories such as tense and agreement which are at the heart of that system should be candidates for problems: Learning these categories involves learning rules or morphological paradigms or both. If the language acquisition mechanism is not functioning in SLI children as it does in normal children, then they may have difficulties forming appropriate underlying representations for tense and/or agreement in the language they are attempting to learn.

English-speaking children, in mastering past tense, are faced with a group of about 200 frequently occurring irregular verbs which form past tense in a variety of ways (*sing/sang, think/thought, hit/hit, go/went*). But the vast majority of the verbs children encounter, plus all new verbs added to the language, form past tense in an entirely predictable fashion by adding the phonologically appropriate form of -*ed*. The child's task is to determine what the regular rule for past tense is (essentially, the morphophonemically appropriate form for a particular verb stem), which are the verbs to which it does not apply, and for those (irregular) verbs, how to mark them for past. Studies of normal children have shown correct regular markings for past tense appearing during the third year of life, though it takes some time before past tense is marked in all the contexts in which it should appear. A couple of years may elapse between the first appearance of regular past tense and exceptionless application of the past tense rule. Along the way, children tend to produce overregularisations of those verbs which should be irregular (e.g. *singed, hitted*), though at relatively low frequencies (Marcus, Pinker, Ullman, Rosen, & Xu, 1992). Such overregularisations are usually taken as evidence that the child has determined the conditions under which the appropriate forms of past tense applies. Verb agreement in English is limited to present tense, and in standard dialects of English is only overtly marked on third person singular forms of main verbs: *the boy sings/the boys sing, she sleeps a lot/they sleep a lot.* Aside from forms of *be, have,* and *do* (*is/are/was/were, has, does*), there are no irregular forms of verb agreement in standard English.

Gopnik on tense

One detailed attempt to account for language impairment in terms of a LAD deficit hypothesis in language-impaired individuals comes in the work of Gopnik and her associates. Beginning with a report on a British three-generation family, half of whose 30 members are language-impaired (Gopnik, 1990), this research has now been extended cross-linguistically, and currently focuses on tense deficits in English, Greek, and Japanese (Dalakakis, 1994; Fukuda & Fukuda, 1994; Gopnik, 1994; Ullman & Gopnik, 1994). Gopnik, in addressing the English data, faces squarely the central problem that LAD deficit accounts face, namely the variable use of past tense by affected individuals. There is no question that in English, the provision of tense in obligatory contexts is problematic for SLI individuals. Data are available from a number of sources, which concur: SLI individuals and language-age matched normals are significantly different in their ability to supply past tense in obligatory contexts. Estimates vary: Rice, Wexler, and Cleave (1995) report an average past tense provision in obligatory contexts in spontaneous speech samples of 18%, and of 27% via elicitation. Schelleter, Fletcher, Ingham, King, and Sinka (1996), using a narrative re-tell procedure based on a video cartoon, find an average 28.44% provision, with a range from 6% to 57.1%. Ullman and Gopnik (1994), reporting on data from the K family, indicate a 56.2% success rate, based on elicitation of past tense marking from seven of the affected members of the family.

The figures clearly reveal incompetence with respect to past tense on the part of these subjects, but they also seem to indicate they know *something* about past tense. Is it possible to square variable use of past tense in SLI individuals, with an explanatory stance which sees the problem as a malfunctioning grammar acquisition device? Ullman and Gopnik (1994, p. 111) are quite clear about the source of the problem in the affected members of the family:

> ... the hypothesised genetic dysfunction resulted in the lack of normal development of certain structures necessary for the acquisition of the missing grammatical mechanisms. Thus there might be a dysfunction of neural and linguistic structures necessary for the acquisition of paradigms, or of the structures necessary for the acquisition of feature checking.

The presence of some past tense marking in obligatory contexts in the family members is explained in terms of a compensatory strategy: In the absence of an inflectional grammar, subjects learn to use lexical forms with an -*ed* suffix via a conscious strategy of "explicitly" adding the suffix, relying on forms they have heard. Subjects understand the semantics of pastness, but without the ability to build an inflectional system, or the understanding that tense is obligatory, they rely on past tense forms they have memorised, and hence use the inflection sporadically. Crucial evidence attested for this view is the very poor performance of the affected family members on novel forms in an elicitation task. They are unable to form the past tense of *crive*, for example, which it is argued they should be able to do if they have internalised a rule for past tense formation which operates independently of whether a specific past tense form has previously been heard or memorised.

Extended optional infinitives

This account of variable past tense use in SLI individuals crosses one hurdle, but then faces another. Numerous studies of the normal course of inflectional development in English-speaking children have found that the acquisition of past tense or third person agreement takes time. From the first appearance of a form to criterion (usually set at provision in 90% of obligatory contexts) can take 2 or more years. In the longitudinal study by Brown (1973), criterion for past tense was reached by one of three children at 42 months, and by a second at 4 years. During the period of acquisition, children are inevitably using the form variably. The issue then arises of how to distinguish between variable use of an inflection by a normal child, and variable use by an impaired individual. Why in one case is 30% provision, for example, a waypost on the road to an adult grammar, whereas in the other it is evidence of a deficit?

One possible answer to this question is provided by Rice et al. (1995). They suggest that the data can be explained if we assume that SLI children have what they refer to as "young" grammars for an extended period of time: Indeed some SLI individuals, such as the older members of the family Gopnik has studied, may never emerge from this stage, referred to as a "period of extended optional infinitive". The optional infinitive stage in normal children's development is that period during which they do not mark tense and agreement obligatorily in main clauses, but they nonetheless know the grammatical properties of finiteness. Finiteness is the term traditionally used to refer to verbs in matrix (main) clauses which are "limited" by inflections for number, person, tense, aspect, or mood (Koptjevskaja-Tamm, 1994). While children learning English can use appropriate tense and agreement forms, they appear to alternate correct use of these forms (*he talks*) with what Rice et al. interpret as non-finite forms (*he talk*). Evidence for this interpretation is that the child does not use finite forms in contexts where the adult grammar does not allow them. For instance the form **I goes* is unattested, as is the use of past tense in non-past time contexts. For a certain span of development, then, normal children will accept both finite and non-finite main clauses as grammatical, but they will eventually emerge from this stage and accept that all main clauses have to be finite, selecting the appropriate tense and agreement forms for lexical verbs and also for auxiliaries *be*, *have*, and *do*. The SLI individuals in the Rice et al. sample, who also accept both finite and non-finite main clauses, and do not use ungrammatical tense and agreement forms, differ from their normal counterparts only in maintaining the optional infinitive stage for a longer period of time, perhaps permanently. Because the Rice et al. (1995) study is cross-sectional, it is not possible to determine how long the extended optional infinitive stage (EOI) might persist in the SLI subjects. The evidence for the stage is arrived at by demonstrating that the SLI subjects (mean age 60.17 months), matched for MLU with younger normal children (on average about 2 years younger), had significantly fewer tense and agreement inflections in obligatory contexts than their language-age matches, leading to the conclusion that they were still in an EOI period.

This is a somewhat different account to that of Ullman and Gopnik (1994), in that it appears to acknowledge that children in the EOI stage do have a sub-set of the grammatical knowledge necessary for tense and agreement marking, presumably arrived at via their language acquisition device: They can distinguish between finite and non-finite forms of verbs, they are aware that if a form is finite it has to have tense and agreement inflections, and they use subject-verb agreement. Rice et al.'s account is similar to Ullman and Gopnik however, in that in order to explain why their SLIs lack the knowledge that finiteness marking is obligatory, they need to presume a LAD deficit, though they are not precise about the nature of the deficit. The value of these accounts is that they embed both their descriptions of the phenomena and their explanations within a coherent linguistic framework which motivates an important strand of current theorising about language acquisition. The disadvantage is that responsibility for the observed deficits is transferred to an unobservable language acquisition device which fails to account for important features of the deficit (e.g. why the EOI persists in SLI children) or to hold out much hope for any remediation of the SLI individual's condition (e.g. the presumably genetically based congenital unavailability of a feature-checking device in the affected members of the family reported in Ullman & Gopnik, 1994).

SLI IN OTHER LANGUAGES

Inflection in Greek and Japanese

Cross-linguistic studies of SLI have the potential for advancing our understanding of the problem by allowing us to examine the effect of impairment on languages with different structural characteristics. Such studies do pose two immediate methodological problems, however: The commensurability of the systems being compared, and the comparability of subjects. If we compare the tense systems of English and Greek, there is an immediate parallel in that only the past/non-past contrast is grammaticalised via inflection. English expresses future in a variety of ways, for example by using a present progressive form (*she's arriving at six*), or a periphrastic form (*she's going to leave*). Greek future uses an auxiliary form plus the present tense (*tha khano—I'm going to lose*). But while the *-ed* form for past, and the third person singular form, exhaust the range of regular inflections for tense and agreement that English children have to learn, Greek manifests a complex set of paradigms, with imperfective and perfective stems admitting distinct forms for first, second, and third person singular and plural in various past and non-past conjugations. The finiteness system in Greek appears, on the face of it, dramatically more complex, as a learning problem for the child. The comparison of subjects is also not straightforward: Different societies vary in the degree to which they recognise SLI as a distinct condition; if suitable standardised tests are not available, application of the Stark/Tallal criteria for subject identification may not be possible; and even if such procedures are available for comprehension assessment, the assessment of production level via MLU may not be equally feasible for the languages being compared.

As part of a cross-linguistic investigation of possible impairments of inflection in other languages, and to compare with her familial data on English, associates of Gopnik have studied Greek- and Japanese-speaking SLI individuals. Dalakakis (1994) addresses the hypothesis that SLI affects the underlying grammar, looking in detail at eight non-familial subjects ranging in age from 5 years, 8 months to 17 years, 7 months. It is clear from the report that in spontaneous speech data subjects make errors in verb form selection. Examples are given in which a future particle is missing, an inappropriate verb form is selected for a subjunctive particle, and (singular) noun and (plural) verb do not agree. In an elicitation procedure for tense marking, the SLIs score on average 20%, while their age-matched normal counterparts score on average 87.1%. There were apparently no language-matched controls, so it is not possible to determine if younger Greek children of a similar language level to the SLI group would have had similar grammatical behaviour. Greek, unlike English, does not permit bare verb stems, so the errors of the Greek children with respect to verb forms always involved a substitution of an alternative form for the correct one. The study does not report preferences for particular substitution errors, if indeed any exist.

Data on Japanese SLI are reported by Fukuda and Fukuda (1994), for eight subjects and age-matched normal controls. Again no language-age matched group is reported. The impaired subjects range in age from 8 years, 9 months to 12 years, 1 month. Japanese as an agglutinating language marks verbs for tense, aspect, and addressee status, but does not indicate number on the verb, so subject-verb agreement is not an issue. Adjectives are also tense-marked. As with Greek, in the adult grammar bare stems are unavailable, so verb errors are likely to involve substitutions. The Japanese data indicate that the average performance of the impaired group is just over 40% on a tense form elicitation task, while age-matched normal controls perform at just over 90%.

It is useful to consider what we can and can not conclude from the cross-linguistic data summarised here. We can (subject to the usual caveats with regard to generalisation from small samples) infer that school-age language-impaired individuals learning Greek and Japanese have, like their English counterparts, problems producing appropriate verb forms on demand. But because of structural differences across the verb systems of the three languages, it is not possible for us assert that language-impaired individuals in these three language communities all have problems with tense and agreement, or even just with tense. The (formally very different) Greek and Japanese verb systems require the child learning one of these languages to consider a much wider range of grammatical alternatives than the English child. These paradigmatic choices code a more extensive set of meanings. Describing the precise nature of the impairment in Greek and Japanese would require close attention to a comparison of patterns of substitution and omission by language-impaired children and *language*-age normal controls. Only then would it be possible to say which forms, if any, were consistently omitted, or consistently substituted for by which other forms, and so suggest possible generalisations about SLI verb forms in each language. For example in the Japanese data Fukuda and Fukuda report that when subjects were required to produce the present progressive form, they experienced more difficulty with this form than any of the others, tending to supply a present tense form, which is not grammatical in the temporal adverbial context used for the prompt. If this is a replicable finding, it would indicate that it is aspect, not tense, which is one typical grammatical problem in Japanese SLI. This finding would not find a parallel in English data, where the progressive suffix -*ing* is a very early feature of normal acquisition, and is the verb inflection which affords least difficulty to language-impaired children (Johnston & Schery, 1976). So it seems as if the interaction between an impaired language learning mechanism and a particular language is going to have consequences specific to the structure of that language.

The second reason for caution in making cross-linguistic generalisations about language impairment concerns subjects. The subjects in Ullman and Gopnik (1994) belong to a family in which there is an inherited speech and language disability. As Vargha-Khadem, Watkins, Alcock, Fletcher, and Passingham (1995) and Fletcher (1996) make clear, the problems which affected members of the family have with inflection coexist with severe pronunciation difficulties, and problems with non-verbal voluntary movements of lips, jaw, and tongue, suggesting an underlying neurological problem. The affected family members also have relatively intact syntactic comprehension (at an average 10-year-old level as measured by a standardised test). This profile makes it a matter for debate as to whether the affected family members meet the Stark/Tallal criteria for SLI, and so whether they are strictly comparable with the Greek and Japanese subjects, who are not related, and for whom praxic problems are not reported.

Leonard on Italian

Some earlier cross-linguistic work on SLI, again concentrating on morphology, avoids by its methodology the subject comparability issue, and may via certain restricted comparisons have also circumvented the system commensurability issue. Research by Leonard and his co-workers (Leonard, Bortolini, Caselli, McGregor, & Sabbadini, 1992; Leonard, Sabbadini, Leonard, & Volterra, 1987) has compared English and Italian SLI children, using a methodology that matches SLI children with language age and chronological age controls within each language, before attempting any cross-language comparison. The results demonstrate that for certain forms of verbs, Italian SLI children perform as well as both groups of controls. In a procedure that involved conversation and picture description, each child supplied at least 10 obligatory contexts for each morpheme of interest. For third person singular present verb forms (*canta–s/he sings, vede– s/he sees, dorme–s/he sleeps*), the mean scores for the three groups were: SLI, 92.7%, Language-Age Controls, 93.1%, Age Controls, 93.3%. All groups are performing at the same level. The SLI children did not perform as well as the control groups on all verb forms however. On third person plural present (*cantano–they sing, vedono–they see, dormono–they sleep*), the SLI group provided the correct form in 50% of obligatory contexts on average, most frequently substituting the third person singular form in its place. As in Greek, children do not have the option to provide a bare stem—some verb form must be selected. While it is not possible from these data to say that the ISLI children had no difficulty with verb agreement, the striking discrepancy between their facility with third person singular agreement and the ESLI's problems with English third person singular agreement deserve more detailed scrutiny. The English SLI children (who had a similar MLU range to the Italian children and were similar in age) achieved a third person singular score of only 34%. What could explain the difference? It is at this point that we need to consider explanations for the effects of SLI other than the LAD deficit approach.

Leonard's response to his data has been to consider processing limitations as a possible basis for the grammatical deficits we have so far considered. The "surface" hypothesis suggests that it is the physical properties of the morphemes which code third person singular present agreement in the two languages which may be responsible for the discrepancy in performance between the two groups of SLI. The word-final non-syllabic consonant which in English is added to a stem to signal agreement is relatively non-salient compared to the stressed, syllabic vowel form that signals third person singular agreement in Italian. The learnability problem for the child learning English or Italian is the formation of morphological paradigms for verb forms. As Leonard (1994, p. 100) puts it: ". . . limited processing capacity makes inflections with difficult surface characteristics more vulnerable to loss when combined with the operations of paradigm building". In the procedure described by Pinker (1984), children go from word-specific paradigms based on present and past forms of particular words, to general paradigms in which the morphological material common to a number of words is abstracted. To explain the performance difference in the two SLI groups, it is assumed that the relative phonetic salience of Italian third person agreement forms is more facilitative of paradigm construction than the English form. English children need more frequent exposure to the forms to overcome the limitations of their reduced processing capacity.

This account has some immediate appeal in terms of the differences between English and Italian, and also more generally in its potential for dealing with the thorny problem of partial knowledge of inflection, as reflected by variable but gradually improving use of an inflection over a lengthy period of time. The interaction of an inefficient processing device and a paradigm builder which could produce partial inflectional generalisations over a subset of vocabulary would help to account for the long period of acquisition that we see (for data on changes in SLI children's use of English morphemes over time see Johnston & Schery, 1976, p. 241, reprinted in Kent, 1994, p. 214). However, as Leonard points out, a more detailed account is required, if the processing account is ultimately to have credibility, of what the limited processing capacity hypothesised for the SLI child entails. We await some independent specification of the relative complexity of the various linguistic and non-linguistic operations that a limited processing capacity might affect.

HOW SPECIFIC IS SPECIFIC LANGUAGE IMPAIRMENT?

To professionals who assess and remediate SLI individuals, this concentration on morphology might appear almost perverse, in the light of the sheer diversity of linguistic symptoms displayed by their clients (phonological, grammatical, referential, conversational—see Haynes, 1992; Miller, 1987). It does reflect however a major effort in the research literature over the last decade. Learning grammar, though, is more than the learning of morphological paradigms. Can we find evidence that grammatical impairment extends beyond the functional categories with which we have been dealing up to this point? In their early account of the K family, Gopnik and Crago (1991) emphasise the selectivity of the impact of the feature-related deficit on the family by claiming that verb argument structure is unimpaired. They investigated family members' ability to identify ungrammatical complementation with verbs, as in *The girl eats a cookie to the boy*. Their subjects were no more likely to accept such sentences than were normal controls, and from these responses and others where their impaired subjects correctly accept grammatical sequences, they conclude that verb argument structure is unimpaired. This is a very limited test of language-impaired subjects' knowledge of verb argument structure, which is a topic we will now address in more detail, but only in relation to English. Interest in the learning of verbs in normal children has been considerable in recent years (Pinker, 1989; Tomasello, 1992; Tomasello & Merriman, 1995), but is only now being extended to SLI children (Ingham, Fletcher, Schelletter, & Sinka, in press; King, 1994; Schelleter et al., 1996; Van der Lely, 1994).

In considering whether SLI and normal subjects differ in their verb argument structure performance, an initial question analogous to that asked in relation to morphology concerns the provision of obligatory (internal) arguments. One influential view of how verbs are learned, referred to as semantic bootstrapping, assumes that the child's knowledge of features of verb meaning will enable him to project syntactic arguments from those features. So the semantic knowedge that *giving* entails a benefactor, a beneficiary and a transfer of goods or services will (given further assumptions about the child's innate repertoire of thematic roles and "linking" rules between these roles and the syntax) assist the building of an argument structure for the verb *give* in English which has a direct object NP (for theme) and an oblique PP (for benefactive), in that order—*Joyce gave a brooch to Nora.* (We ignore for the moment the complication of the argument structure alternation for *give* which permits an NP NP sequence, with the first NP realising the benefactive role—*Joyce gave Nora a brooch.*) However, such a strategy would only get the child so far in constructing grammatical argument structures for verbs, as languages make their own idiosyncratic lexico-syntactic choices as to whether particular internal arguments are obligatory or not. For example in English *shave* can be, in traditional terms, transitive, or intransitive: It can either have a direct object NP or not—both *he shaved* and *he shaved his beard* are acceptable. However the translation equivalent of *shave* in Cantonese requires a direct object NP. In English semantically similar verbs such as *eat* and *devour* are different in their argument structure requirements: *eat* permits either zero complementation or a direct object NP, while *devour* requires a direct object: **he devoured greedily* is ungrammatical.

An initial test of SLI children's knowledge of obligatory arguments is reported in King (1994). If grammatical impairment in these individuals extends to verbs argument structure, we might expect this to be reflected in the omission of internal arguments, analogously to their omission of grammatical morphemes. A comparison of omission errors in conversational data from school-age SLI children and matched normal counterparts revealed a very low incidence of error: For the SLIs the proportion was 3% (32/1062), while for the normal children it was 1.9% (19/981). These are very low values. With the proviso that spontaneous speech data might not be the appropriate test bed for investigating children's grasp of obligatory arguments (since any particular verb may occur only once in a sample), it seems that this aspect of SLI children's knowledge of verbs is secure.

A further pass through the same conversational data ensued in which a second issue relevant to children's knowledge of verbs was explored, this time the optionality of arguments/complements, and the extent to which SLI children, compared to normals, are prepared to deploy the full range of arguments available to them with a particular verb. We have already seen that direct objects with certain verbs are optional. It is also the case that with "true" intransitives—using the verb in its traditional sense to refer to verbs such as *smile* in *Lisa smiled hugely*, or *melt* in *the ice melted slowly*—the verb can either occur with no post-verbal complement or it can take a PP. Similarly, transitive verbs—those with direct object NPs—can be supplied with a bare NP or can have an (optional) PP added. On the basis of findings by Johnston and Kamhi (1984) it was predicted that the SLI children's reluctance to exploit the full range of argument structure would result in SLI children using (1) fewer PPs with intransitive verbs; and (2) fewer NPPPs with transitive verbs. Both these predictions were borne out (King, 1994).

The third area of scrutiny was that of argument structure alternations. These have been highlighted in the normal acquisition literature as a particular learnability problem. So for example the alternation between inchoative and causative versions of verbs like *melt*—*he melted the ice/the ice melted* seems to be limited in apparently unpredictable and often language-specific ways: The verb *fall*, for instance, can only occur in an inchoative argument structure: *the doll fell/*she fell the doll*. Children are reported as overgeneralising this alternation to the verb *fall*, and producing ungrammatical causative versions from which they will have to retreat (learnability issues for argument structure alternations are explored in Pinker, 1989, and an attempt there made to account for the apparent unpredictability of the restrictions on alternations in semantic terms). SLI children's knowledge of argument structure alternations can serve as the central test case for Gopnik's LAD deficit hypothesis, limited as it is to functional categories. If Gopnik and Crago (1991) are right to generalise their grammaticality judgement results for a restricted set of argument structures to SLI individuals' knowledge of the syntax of verbs generally, then their characterisation of SLI as a highly selective grammatical deficit holds. An alternative hypothesis is that SLI grammar exhibits a generalised deficit, affecting a range of areas in syntax and morphology. If this is the case then morphological deficit should be accompanied by a deficit in argument structure alternations.

To determine if this association existed, Schelleter et al. (1996) examined morphological ability and the ability to manipulate argument structure alternations in 42 SLI children aged between 5 years, 1 month and 8 years, 9 months. A group of 82 normal children provided chronological age-matched and language-matched normal controls. The procedures used for assessing the childrens' morphological status involved free conversation, and narratives elicited by video cartoon. To assess verb alternations (and other aspects of children's knowledge of the syntax and semantics of verbs) a series of illustrative scenes were filmed and shown to the children, who were required to describe the scene. So for example for the verb *bounce*, which like *melt* allows theme as subject or direct object, a boy is shown bouncing a ball across a patio. For the scene expected to elicit the causative version with the agent *boy* as subject NP, the film clip shows the boy initiating the action. For the scene designed to elicit the inchoative form, with the theme *ball* as the subject NP, the boy was edited out of the scene. In all, three types of alternation were illustrated in this way and tested in the experiment. In addition to the inchoative/causative alternation (which also included *wave*, *move*, and *open*), we illustrated the following types of verb:

LOCATIVE/CONTACT
rub/bump/load/scrape
DATIVE/BENEFACTIVE
give/throw

The scenes for causative/inchoative alternations were varied in terms of presence or absence of agent. For the locative/contact and dative/benefactive alternations, the different alternants were made visually salient by a focusing shot on the theme in one scene, and the goal in the second scene for a particular verb, before the action itself began. So for example in the scene for *scrape* which expected theme as direct object (*he scraped the spade on the fence*), an initial shot held on the spade for several seconds before the activity of a man scraping the spade along the fence was shown. A group of adults ($n = 10$ undergraduates) provided responses to the film clips in addition to the three groups of children.

In assessing inflectional performance, provision of past tense in obligatory contexts (which we have seen is a widely used dependent measure in the research literature) was taken as the index of morphological ability. A sub-set of 11 of the SLI children, with an average past tense success rate of 28%, was identified, using 50% provision as the cut-off performance for inclusion in a –M(orphology) group. They were compared with another subset, average past tense success rate 89%, for whom the criterion for inclusion in a +M(orphology) group was past tense provision above 70%. When the performance of these groups on inchoative/causative alternations was assessed, it turns out that they are significantly different: The average score for the –M group was 1.36 alternations, while for the +M group it was 3.18 alternations. More generally, if we consider just those verbs for which all adults provided alternating argument structures in the task, and ask how the child groups fared against this adult criterion, we find the CA matched group doing best, with 75% of the group achieving adult performance. In the LA matched group, 50% of the children reached the adult criterion, while 58% of the SLI+M group did so. This is in contrast to just 8% of the SLI–M group. It seems reasonable to conclude from these data that a morphological deficit (as measured by past tense provision) will be accompanied by a verb argument structure deficit (as measured via the alternations illustrated in the film clips). It does appear that the impairment of the grammar of at least some SLI children goes beyond the grammatical categories which have been the focus of so much research. (It is also clear from these data that there are school-age SLI children for whom grammar may no longer be a difficulty, though they may well continue to have pragmatic problems. Pursuing this question was not part of this research, but see Craig, 1995).

We began this section by asking about the selectivity of specific language impairment in respect of the grammar. An early and persisting generalisation about SLI in English concerned inflection, and the details of grammatical deficit in relation to morphology have been assiduously pursued by researchers. In part this is because inflectional deficits undoubtedly do exist in these children, in part it is because identifying morphological error is straightforward in easily procurable data, such as free conversation, and in part it is because functional categories, particularly those associated with verb inflection, have had a significant role in recent grammatical theory. However if we design the right tools for exploring other areas of the grammar, it seems that we can identify other deficits which correlate with the inflectional gaps. Even without experimental investigation, additional grammatical features that are symptomatic of language impairment have been isolated. Gavin, Klee, and Membrino (1993), using a discriminant analysis technique on grammatical profiles derived from spontaneous speech, identify the underdevelopment of the noun phrase as one of three variables (the others being errors in the verb phrase and an over-use of one-word utterances) which characterise their SLI group. If SLI has effects on grammar that encompass inflection, verb argument structure, and the noun phrases, then a reasonable conclusion would be that these individuals are exhibiting a generalised set of symptoms reflecting a system that is generally degraded, with no selective deficit that targets any one area of the grammar. As we indicated at the outset, differing ages of subjects, and distinct ways of identifying them, mean that great caution is required in relation to any generalisation about SLI, but at present the "general degradation" view seems more plausible than a selective deficit position.

RESIDUAL ISSUES

This review of some recent empirical work on SLI grammars has concentrated on the linguistic details of particular studies, in the belief that it is these facts that ultimately need to be explained. In the process there are issues that have either been briefly addressed or not raised at all, which the remainder of the chapter will be devoted to.

Delay vs. deficit

One conceptualisation of SLI sees the affected individuals as simply delayed— as passing through the same stages of language development as normal children, but at a slower rate. Some SLI children will quite possibly plateau at some point of the normal course prior to full acquisition, but even for these children their grammar will be recognisably one that is attested at some stage of normal development. In support of this view there are two types of evidence. First of all the data from SLI children show little sign of deviance—linguistic errors (for example of constituent order), that would indicate that these children are constructing "wild" grammars. Second, the errors that are found—in English the omissions of inflections that we have seen, and other non-adult forms that we have not discussed, such as the omission of auxiliaries, the use of accusative pronouns in subject position, lack of agreement in noun phrases—occur both in normal and SLI children. In studies in which a comparison is made only between SLI children and age-matched normals, either by using two groups of subjects or by using norm-referenced procedures on SLIs, or in studies in which no difference is found, on the measures of interest, between SLI and language-matched subjects (but differences are found between these groups and chrono-logical age matches), it is not possible to conclude anything other than delay.

Because of individual differences in rate of language development, it may not always be easy to distinguish between a delay that represents a normal child at the bottom end of the normal distribution, and a child who is genuinely impaired. In a longitudinal study Bishop and Edmundson (1987) identified a group of 87 SLI children at 4 years of age. Eighteen months later, when tested again, about half the cohort could be characterised as within normal limits. Whatever problems they had at 4 years were resolved. For those children who in the school-age years continue to be language-impaired, delay is never simple. The indications are that they never catch up, and that oral language problems are succeeded by educational difficulties, and later social problems (Haynes, 1992). For researchers also, delay constitutes a challenge, if it means that an immature grammatical system fossilises and fails to develop further. As with any other aspect of development, failure to thrive is a cause for concern and requires an explanation. The question is: Why do those children reliably identified as persist-ing language-impaired fail to pass smoothly and effortlessly through the remain-der of the acquisition process with the facility shown by their normal counterparts?

Deficits are identified via the methodology that looks cross-sectionally at SLIs and language-matched controls, and finds significant differences in their performance on measures of interest. An example has already been discussed in the work of Leonard and his associates (Leonard et al., 1987). Carefully matched groups of English SLIs and language controls show differences in performance on third person singular. Similarly, for the comparable Italian groups, there are significant differences in performance on object clitic pronouns. If the language-matching is reliable, and the groups can be considered to be at the same general stage of language development, the difference in performance signals a specific deficit. Notice though that the difference is relative not absolute. It is not that the SLI group simply do not have the relevant form available at all. This is reminis-cent of a very early paper (Morehead & Ingram, 1976). They reported on groups of SLI children at each of the five stages of language development established by Brown (1973) on the basis of MLU. Their conclusion was that the SLI children's grammatical systems were very similar to language-matched normals at each of the stages of development, but that they use the resources available to them less frequently (see also Ingram & Carr, 1994).

Representation and processing

Competence and performance. It is clear from the accounts of SLI that we have looked at that there is a school of thought that sees grammatical performance in SLI as resulting from a "deviant" syntactic competence (see Clahsen, 1991 in addition to the research of Gopnik and associates discussed above). There is another school of thought which holds that the grammatical errors we see are the result of a performance limitation; in the words of Bishop (1994): "slowed processing in a limited capacity system that is handling several operations in parallel may lead to omission of grammatical morphemes". In a test of the Ullman and Gopnik hypothesis that SLI individuals do not have a rule-based representation for past tense (and other grammatical morphemes), Bishop examined speech samples from a group of SLI children between 8 and 12 years of age. She tested a "vulnerable markers" hypothesis, in which the prediction is that grammatical accuracy will decline as the complexity of utterance formulation increases. The perspective here is that of an on-line production processing model (e.g. that elaborated in Bock & Levelt, 1994), involving the real-time assembly of lexical items and inflections into legal syntactic structures to convey the speaker's message. This system is responsible in the normal adult for delivering speech at about three words per second, and it is certainly worth considering the possibility that some of the error data that we see in transcriptions of spontaneous speech from SLI subjects is a consequence of processing limitations under the pressures of real-time language production, rather than representational deficiency. Bishop finds some evidence for the "vulnerable markers" prediction, with some children in her sample showing a positional effect for some grammatical morphemes. She is of the view however that transcriptions of spontaneous speech are not adequate for testing hypotheses concerning processing thoroughly, and that experimental studies are needed.

Auditory temporal processing deficit. Two aspects of SLI children's input processing have also been invoked to try to account for their problems. One strand of research claims that a deficit in processing rapidly changing auditory inputs is responsible for these individuals' phonological and grammatical difficulties. The specific problem is evidenced in their inability to discriminate syllable-initial consonants (e.g. *ba/da*) where the contrast depends on formant transitions that take place in tens of milliseconds. One problem with this hypothesis has been that it is not easy to see how this specific discrimination deficit is linked to the kinds of grammatical problems we have reviewed, and some scepticism has been expressed (see for example Rees, 1973). However, a study by Tallal, Miller, Bedi, Byma, Wang, Nagarajan, Schreiner, Jenkins, and

Merzenich (1996), while it still does not explain what the link might be between the inefficient processing of rapid spectral changes and, for example, lack of awareness of argument structure alternations, does appear to demonstrate via training studies that the remediation of the auditory processing deficit can improve language comprehension. In the first study a small group of children ($n = 7$, with a mean age of 7 years, 3 months—referred to in the study as LLI—language-learning impaired) took part in a six-week study with daily exposure to speech which was acoustically modified to overcome their presumed deficit: The duration of the signal was enhanced by 50% while its natural quality was preserved, and transitional elements (formant transitions from consonants to vowels) were amplified. After the conclusion of the training period the children's speech discrimination scores improved significantly, but so also did their language comprehension scores. Since the improvement in these subjects could have come about through the sheer intensity of their remediation (training occurred daily, for three hours a day in the laboratory and one to two hours a day at home over a four-week period), a second study on different children utilised a control group who received training of the same intensity but using materials which had not been acoustically modified, as well as an experimental group receiving roughly the same remediation as the group in the first study. Both groups showed improvement from pre-training to post-training measures, but the group exposed to acoustically modified materials showed significantly greater gains than the control group.

What is notable about this result is that the effect is achieved in the space of a month with children whose inefficient language learning has been going on for some time, and who would presumably resemble in their grammatical abilities the children in the Bishop (1994) or Schelleter et al. (1996) studies discussed above. What is also notable is that while the training described might be expected to improve subjects' speech discrimination, it also appears to have improved their "language processing" (as measured by the Token Test for Children—DiSimoni, 1978), and their language comprehension (as measured by the CYCLE-R, by Curtiss & Yamada—unpublished, but see Curtiss, 1991). The Token Test maintains a very simple vocabulary throughout (using circles and squares of different colours and shapes, and of two sizes) while manipulating the length and complexity of instructions to the child for arrangements of the tokens. The CYCLE-R (as described in Curtiss, 1991) involves items that are morphological (e.g. plural, past tense) and syntactic (e.g. relative clauses on both subject and object NPs). In attempting to explain the relationship between their hypothesised deficit and the improvements identified in language performance, Tallal et al. (1996, p. 82) suggest the following:

> . . . this basic temporal processing deficit may disrupt the normal sharpening of neurally represented phonetic prototypes for the native language in LLI children, resulting in a cascade of negative effects on subsequent receptive and expressive language development.

This still seems to leave the link between temporal processing and grammatical competence something of a mystery, despite the impressive results of the training study. In this connection it would be interesting to know more about the linguistic nature of the gains reported on the CYCLE-R. If they tended to be concentrated on those items which involve inflectional endings, which as we have already noted tend to be phonetically brief and non-salient in English, then we may be seeing a direct link between trained improvement in temporal processing of rapidly changing acoustic events in the speech signal, and a particular feature of the grammar of English, so far as comprehension is concerned. If the gain in grammatical comprehension extends also to the parsing of syntactic sequences such as relative clauses on the head nouns of subject NPs, then we are looking at a much more general effect of the sharpening up of "phonetic prototypes", and we may need to consider seriously an important new method of remediation.

Phonological short-term memory.   Another line of enquiry which posits a deficit in input processing in language-impaired individuals, this time linked to memory, was set in train by Gathercole and Baddeley (1990). Their finding that SLI children, who as we have seen typically have comprehension and production abilities which are immature for their chronological age, also fail to perform as well as matched normals in being able to repeat "words" of increasing length made up of nonsense syllables, suggests to Gathercole and Baddeley that the memory deficit may be causally linked to the language problems. In their model a phonological loop serves in working memory as a slave system which retains verbal material in sequence long enough for it to be acted upon by a central executive. The loop comprises two separable components: a phonological store and a sub-vocal rehearsal process. Phonological representations of verbal material are held in the store, and will eventually decay unless reactivated by the rehearsal process. The inefficient functioning or premature degrading of temporarily stored verbal material may inhibit learning (for example of new words) or interfere with comprehension. Not all comment on this hypothesis has been favourable. Dollaghan, Biber, and Campbell (1993) have emphasised the importance of careful choice of materials in nonsense syllable tasks: Stimuli which are prosodically word-like, or partly word-like in terms of the syllables they contain, will be treated differently by subjects to non-wordlike stimuli in phonological STM studies. While there is some evidence that phonological STM and sentence comprehension are linked (Gathercole, Willis, Emslie, & Baddeley, 1994; Montgomery, 1995), other indications are that this is not the case (Butterworth, Campbell, & Howard, 1986; Carpenter, Miyake, & Just, 1995, p. 103). And it is clear from a study by Van der Lely and Howard (1993) that not all SLI children have short-term memory problems, a finding which throws doubt on phonological STM as a general causal factor in the various grammatical deficits we have considered. Perhaps the most plausible role for the phonological STM is in the learning of new words, otherwise referred to as "fast mapping" (see for example

Dollaghan, 1987). Children's early vocabulary learning requires the efficient extraction of information about the phonological, semantic, and syntactic characteristics of words, often on the basis of a single hearing (Carey & Bartlett, 1978). Gathercole and Baddeley (1990) have demonstrated experimentally the relationship between phonological working memory and word learning with preschool children. They compared the rate at which 5-year-olds of low and high phonological memory skills learned novel names for novel toys. The children in the high memory group were more effective learners. It seems reasonable to suppose that a phonological STM deficit could get in the way of word learning for SLI children.

CONCLUSION

Lying as it does at an intersect of language acquisition studies and developmental psychology, as well as providing an interest for behavioural genetics (Gilger, 1995), specific language impairment attracts a diversity of methodological approaches, descriptive frameworks, and explanatory accounts. This does not always make it easy to see what the fundamental problem is, or how to deal with it educationally. There are problems with subject description and characterisation, both within and across languages, that make generalisations suspect. Nevertheless after a couple of decades of empirical work, mostly on English, recent cross-linguistic research, and more sophisticated approaches to possible causes of the problem, suggest that we are on the brink of interesting developments in the field.

REFERENCES

Bishop, D. (1992). The biological basis of specific language impairment. In P. Fletcher & D. Hall (Eds.), *Specific speech and language disorders in children* (pp. 2–17). London: Whurr Publishers.

Bishop, D. (1994). Grammatical errors in specific language impairment: Competence or performance limitations? *Applied Psycholinguistics, 15*, 507–550.

Bishop, D., & Edmundson, A. (1987). Language impaired 4-year-olds: Distinguishing transient from persistent impairment. *Journal of Speech and Hearing Disorders, 43*, 227–241.

Bock, K., & Levelt, W. (1994). Language production: Grammatical encoding. In M. Gernsbacher (Ed.), *Handbook of Psycholinguistics* (pp. 945–984). London: Academic Press.

Brown, R. (1973). *A first language: The early stages.* London: George Allen & Unwin.

Butterworth, B., Campbell, R., & Howard, D. (1986). The uses of short-term memory: A case study. *The Quarterly Journal of Experimental Psychology, 38A*, 705–737.

Carey, S., & Bartlett, E. (1978). Acquiring a single new word. *Papers and reports in Child Language Development, 15*, 17–29.

Carpenter, P., Miyake, A., & Just, M. (1995). Language comprehension: Sentence and discourse processing. *Annual Review of Psychology, 46*, 91–120.

Chapman, R.S. (1995). Language development in children and adolescents with Down syndrome. In P. Fletcher & B. MacWhinney (Eds.), *The handbook of child language* (pp. 641–663). Oxford, UK: Blackwell.

Clahsen, H. (1991). *Child language and developmental aphasia: Linguistic studies in the acquisition of German.* Amsterdam: John Benjamins.

Craig, H. (1995). Pragmatic impairments. In P. Fletcher & B. MacWhinney (Eds.), *The handbook of child language* (pp. 623–640). Oxford, UK: Blackwell.

Curtiss, S. (1991). On the nature of language impairment in language-impaired children. In J. Miller (Ed.), *Research on child language disorders: A decade of progress* (pp. 189–210). Austin, TX: Pro-Ed.

Dalakakis, J. (1994). Familial language impairment in Greek. In J. Matthews (Ed.), *Linguistic aspects of familial language impairment* (pp. 216–227). *McGill Working Papers in Linguistics, 10*, 1 & 2.

DiSimoni, F. (1978). *The token test for children.* Boston: Teaching Resources Corporation.

Dollaghan, C. (1987). Fast mapping in normal and language-impaired children. *Journal of Speech and Hearing Disorders, 52*, 218–222.

Dollaghan, C., Biber, M., & Campbell, T. (1993). Constituent syllable effects in a nonsense-word repetition task. *Journal of Speech and Hearing Research, 36*, 1051–1054.

Eisele, J.A., & Aram, D.M. (1995). Lexical and grammatical development in children with early hemisphere damage: A cross-sectional view from birth to adolescence. In P. Fletcher & B. MacWhinney (Eds.), *The handbook of child language* (pp. 664–689). Oxford, UK: Blackwell.

Fey, M., Long, S., & Cleave, P. (1994). Reconsideration of IQ criteria in the definition of specific language impairment. In R. Watkins & M. Rice (Eds.), *Specific language impairments in children* (pp. 161–178). Baltimore: Paul H. Brookes Publishing Co.

Fletcher, P. (1996, April). *Language impairment in a British family: Characteristics and interpretation.* Paper presented at the Evolution of Human Language Conference, Edinburgh, UK.

Fletcher, P., & Ingham, R. (1995). Grammatical impairment. In P. Fletcher & B. MacWhinney (Eds.), *The handbook of child language* (pp. 603–622). Oxford, UK: Blackwell.

Fletcher, P., Ingham, R., King, G., Schelleter, C., & Sinka, I. (1996). *Verb-related impairments in children with specific language impairment.* Final Report, ESRC Project R000234135.

Friel-Patti, S. (1992). Research in child language disorders: What do we know and where are we going. *Folia Phoniatrica, 44*, 126–142.

Fukuda, S.E., & Fukuda, S. (1994). Developmental language impairment in Japanese: A linguistic investigation. In J. Matthews (Ed.), *Linguistic aspects of familial language impairment* (pp. 150–177). *McGill Working Papers in Linguistics, 10*, 1 & 2.

Gathercole, S., & Baddeley, A. (1990). Phonological memory deficits of language disordered children. Is there a causal connection? *Journal of Memory and Language, 29*, 336–369.

Gathercole, S., Willis, C., Emslie, H., & Baddeley, A. (1994). The children's test of non-word repetition: A test of phonological working memory. *Memory, 2*, 103–127.

Gavin, W., Klee, T., & Membrino, I. (1993). Differentiating specific language impairment from normal language development using grammatical analysis. *Clinical Linguistics and Phonetics, 7*, 191–206.

Gilger, J. (1995). Behavioral genetics: Concepts for research and practice in language development and disorders. *Journal of Speech and Hearing Research, 38*, 1126–1142.

Gopnik, M. (1990). Feature-blind grammar and dysphasia. *Nature, 344*, 317.

Gopnik, M. (1994). Impairments of tense in a familial language disorder. *Journal of Neurolinguistics, 8*, 109–133.

Gopnik, M., & Crago, M. (1991). Familial aggregation of a developmental language disorder. *Cognition, 39*, 1–50.

Haynes, C. (1992). A longitudinal study of children from a residential school. In P. Fletcher & D. Hall (Eds.), *Specific speech and language disorders in children* (pp. 166–182). London: Whurr Publishers.

Ingham, R., Fletcher, P., Schelletter, C., & Sinka, I. (in press). Resultative VPs and specific language impairment. *Language Acquisition.*

Ingram, D., & Carr, L. (1994, November). *Why morphological ability exceeds syntactic ability: A case study.* Poster presented at the American Speech-Language-Hearing Association, New Orleans.

LIVERPOOL
JOHN MOORES UNIVERSITY
AVRIL ROBARTS LRC
TEL. 0151 231 4022

Johnston, J. (1992). Cognitive abilities of language impaired children. In P. Fletcher & D. Hall (Eds.), *Specific speech and language disorders in children* (pp. 105–116). London: Whurr Publishers.

Johnston, J., & Kamhi, A. (1984). Syntactic and semantic aspects of the utterances of language-impaired children: The same can be less. *Merrill-Palmer Quarterly, 30,* 65–86.

Johnston, J., & Schery, T. (1976). The use of grammatical morphemes by children with communication disorders. In D. Morehead & A. Morehead (Eds.), *Normal and deficient child language* (pp. 239–258). Baltimore: University Park Press.

Kent, R. (1994). *Reference manual for communicative sciences and disorders: Speech and language.* Austin, TX: Pro-Ed.

King, G. (1994). Verb complementation in language-impaired schoolage children. In M. Aldridge (Ed.), *Child language* (pp. 84–91). Clevedon, UK: Multilingual Matters.

Koptjevskaja-Tamm, M. (1994). Finiteness. In R. Asher & J. Simpson (Eds.), *The encylopedia of language and linguistics* (Vol. 3, pp. 1245–1248). Oxford, UK: Pergamon Press.

Leonard, L. (1994). Some problems facing accouints of morphological deficits in children with specific language impairment. In R. Watkins & M. Rice (Eds.), *Specific language impairments in children* (pp. 91–105). Baltimore: Paul H. Brookes Publishing.

Leonard, L. (1995). Phonological impairment. In P. Fletcher & B. MacWhinney (Eds.), *The handbook of child language* (pp. 573–602). Oxford, UK: Blackwell.

Leonard, L., Bortolini, U., Caselli, M.C., McGregor, K., & Sabbadini, L. (1992). Morphological deficits in children with specific language impairment: The status of features in the underlying grammar. *Language Acquisition, 2,* 151–179.

Leonard, L., Sabbadini, L., Leonard, J., & Volterra, V. (1987). Specific language impairment in children: A cross-linguistic study. *Brain and Language, 32,* 233–252.

Marcus, G., Pinker, S., Ullman, M., Rosen, T., & Xu, F. (1992). Overregularisation in language acquisition. *Monographs of the Society for Research in Child Development, 57,* 4.

Meisel, J. (1994). Getting FAT: Finiteness, agreement and tense in early grammars. In J. Meisel (Ed.), *Bilingual first language acqusition: French and german grammatical development* (pp. 89–129). Amsterdam: John Benjamins.

Miller, J. (1987). A grammatical characterisation of language disorder. In J.A. Martin, P. Fletcher, P. Grunwell, & D. Hall (Eds.), *Proceedings of the 1st international symposium on Specific Speech and Language Disorders in Children* (pp. 100–113). London: AFASIC.

Montgomery, J. (1995). Sentence comprehension in children with specific language impairment: The role of phonological working memory. *Journal of Speech and Hearing Research, 38,* 187–199.

Morehead, D., & Ingram, D. (1976). The development of base syntax in normal and linguistically deviant children. In D. Morehead & A. Morehead (Eds.), *Normal and deficient child language* (pp. 209–238). Baltimore: University Park Press.

Pinker, S. (1984). *Language learnability and language development.* Cambridge, MA: Harvard University Press.

Pinker, S. (1989). *Learnability and cognition: The acqusition of argument structure.* Cambridge, MA: MIT Press.

Rees, N. (1973). Auditory processing factors in language disorders: The view from Procrustes bed. *Journal of Speech and Hearing Disorders, 38,* 304–315.

Rice, M., Wexler, K., & Cleave, P. (1995). Specific language impairment as a period of extended optional infinitive. *Journal of Speech and Hearing Research, 38,* 850–863.

Schelletter, C., Fletcher, P., Ingham, R., King, G., & Sinka, I. (1996, April). *English-speaking SLI children's use of locative/contact and causative alternations.* Paper presented at Child Language Seminar, Reading, UK.

Stark, R., & Tallal, P. (1981). Selection of children with specific language deficits. *Journal of Speech and Hearing Disorders, 46,* 114–122.

Tager-Flugsberg, H. (1988). On the nature of a language acquisition disorder: The example of autism. In Frank S. Kessel (Ed.), *The development of language and language researchers: Essays in honor of Roger Brown* (pp. 249–267). Hillsdale, NJ: Lawrence Erlbaum Associates Inc.

Tallal, P., Miller, S., Bedi, G., Byma, G., Wang, X., Nagarajan, S., Schreiner, C., Jenkins, W., & Merzenich, M. (1996). Language comprehension in language-learning impaired children improved with acoustically-modified speech. *Science, 271,* 81–84.

Tomasello, M. (1992). *First verbs: A case study of grammatical development.* Cambridge, UK: Cambridge University Press.

Tomasello, M., & Merriman, W. (Eds.). (1995). *Beyond names for things: Young children's acquisition of verbs.* Hillsdale, NJ: Lawrence Erlbaum Associates Inc.

Ullman, M., & Gopnik, M. (1994). The production of inflectional morphology in hereditary specific language impairment. In J. Matthews (Ed.), *Linguistic aspects of familial language impairment* (pp. 81–118). *McGill Working Papers in Linguistics, 10,* 1 & 2.

Van der Lely, H. (1994). Canonical linking rules: Forward vs. reverse linking in normally developing and specifically language impaired children. *Cognition, 51,* 29–72.

Van der Lely, H., & Howard, D. (1993). Children with specific language impairment: Linguistic impairment or short-term memory deficit? *Journal of Speech and Hearing Research, 36,* 1193–1207.

Vargha-Khadem, F., Watkins, K., Alcock, K., Fletcher, P., & Passingham, R. (1995). Praxic and non-verbal cognitive deficits in a large family with a genetically transmitted speech and language disorder. *Proceedings of the National Academy of Sciences, USA, 92,* 930–933.

CHAPTER FOURTEEN

Towards a biological science of language development

John L. Locke
University of Sheffield, UK

The capacity for language is part of human biology, not human culture.
Steven Pinker, 1995

Questions which begin with "What?" and "How?" are sufficient for explanation in the physical sciences. In the biological sciences no explanation is complete until a third kind of question has been asked: "Why?"
Ernst Mayr, 1974

INTRODUCTION

For all the scholarly disciplines that are concerned with the development of language, it is remarkable how little interest has been expressed in the actual processes by which linguistic capacity gets cranked up in the young of our species. Each of the relevant disciplines has, appropriately, pursued its own empirical agenda. Linguists have described children's language, and attempted to account for observed trends and individual differences in linguistic terms. Psychologists have explored the social and cognitive processes associated with language learning. Clinical scientists have concerned themselves with the nature and reversibility of obstacles to efficient language learning. And recently, a new breed of neuroscientists has begun to ask about the genetic bases of language, and the brain developments associated with the emergence of linguistic communication.

Language development has benefited from this mix of disciplines, to be sure, but none of the interested parties has done much with frankly biological issues. We know, of course, that linguistic capacity is produced by genes, maturation, and experience, but *all behaviours* depend on these things. We must therefore

373

find out how these factors interact to produce linguistic capacity. If language is a uniquely human ability, as we are so frequently told, ontogenetic theories of language should look rather different from theories of behaviours that cut across mammalian and primate groups.

Few of those endorsing the genes-maturation-experience "explanation" have gone on to ask the obvious follow-up questions: What causes infants to generate and take advantage of experiences that promote language development? If ontogeny operates over a period of several years, as now seems clear, what is "in it for the child"—not at the end, where many of the advantages of knowing a language are obvious—but at each of the many points along the way, when the infant is not yet linguistically communicative? In this chapter, I hope to identify some issues that will have to be considered in a biological approach to language development.

Of organs and instincts

When Noam Chomsky referred to a language "organ", our attention was drawn to the possibility that humans have dedicated brain systems that become operable mainly through maturation, a prospect kept alive by Steven Pinker's (1994) book on the instinct for language. I am largely in sympathy with this tilt toward genetics and modularity, but the organ-instinct hypothesis must be regarded not as an answer but a point of empirical departure. As George Miller (1990, p. 11) has said, "Anyone who takes [linguistic innateness] arguments seriously should also take seriously the search for innate neurological mechanisms corresponding to the unlearned principles."

Unfortunately, those who have taken the term "instinct" literally have drawn the mistaken conclusion that there is no such thing as the *development* of linguistic capacity. For if language is an instinct, they claim, the learning of language is intrinsically rewarding and there is nothing more to be explained. There are at least two problems with this. Whether the concept of instinct ever had any real meaning or not, it tends to be used meaninglessly. Developing behaviours tend to follow a path. One accepts that the reasons for the path, and its particular configurations, are to be found under the multiple layers of our species' evolutionary history. But the young are held on their growth paths by *behavioural* mechanisms (Scarr, 1983). These mechanisms have their own evolutionary histories, and can be studied in their own right, apart from their role in guiding the infant toward language. Some of them are empowered by experience that occurs so early and universally that it escapes detection. Lacking an observable *development*, observers will thus be tempted to invoke "instinct". But guidance mechanisms can be studied and, in principle, understood.

Clinical work encourages this perspective. In clinics, one tries to find *reasons* why a particular infant is *not* acquiring language. Parents of language-delayed children cannot truthfully be told that their progeny are "missing the language instinct", or that some seriously delayed children have half an instinct and those with milder delays have two-thirds of one. Thus, clinicians look for credible reasons and clinical theorists find themselves postulating ontogenetic mechanisms that might be at fault. This makes one wonder why the normally developing child does acquire language uneventfully. But of course it *is* eventful—it is just that when development is normal, the responsible events are hidden from our view.

The other problem with instinct is the concept of intrinsic reward. To say that animals are rewarded intrinsically may be true at some level of consideration, but to say it dismissively is to close down the field of psychobiology. Surely one is entitled to ask what the intrinsic rewards are, how they work, how they came to have their rewarding effects, what other functions they might also serve, and so on.

Chomsky and Pinker have served us well, but they have not offered ontogenetic explanations. Neither has said much about the specific processes or mechanisms by which infants come to possess linguistic capacity. A truly ontogenetic explanation requires us to peel away the various layers and phases of the neurogenetic process. I will begin by proposing here that the child develops linguistic capacity because it has mechanisms that keep it on a developmental growth path that leads to that capacity. I will also suggest that this adhering function is, to some extent, a secondary consequence of the actions of those mechanisms. The primary consequences—perhaps the ones initially selected for in evolution—are unrelated to language.

Guidance mechanisms

There has been remarkably little interest in, or even awareness of, ontogenetic guidance mechanisms for language. This may be because they do their job well, thus inconspicuously. But that would be no reason to ignore them. Our colleagues in biology would not avoid the study of development because it usually takes place "normally".

One mechanism that causes infants to learn a spoken language is their disposition to pay attention to talking people (Locke, 1993b, 1994a; Reddy, this volume). To understand language development, we must ask questions about the processes that are responsible for these attentional biases. Do infants pay more attention to some talkers, or types of talking, than others? How does the preference for talking over non-talking behaviour arise? What components of the *talking display*—the constellation of facial and social cues given off by talking people—most command infants' attention? Is there a correlation between degree of orientation to talking behaviours and rate of lexical learning?

The behaviours that need to be addressed by a biological account of language development begin when the infant is first exposed to relevant stimulation and initially engages in relevant activity. In humans, the period of gestation is relatively shorter than it is in the other primates (Lovejoy, 1981). Therefore, relatively less brain development occurs before birth in the human than in monkeys and apes (Dobbing & Sands, 1979). Human infants are thus more helpless at birth than newly born non-human primates, but where social learning is concerned this gives our young a distinct advantage. They are dependent on other humans for their very lives, therefore on one or more physically intimate human relationships. Human infants are thus consistently exposed to facial and vocal stimulation during a protracted period in which cortical areas of the brain are developing.

Ducklings are dependent, too, and they are quick to form a special relationship with the first animals they see after hatching. Usually, this will be the mother. Ever since Konrad Lorenz first described this "imprinting" process, there have been countless studies of the following response of ducklings (Bolhuis, 1991). Following is not possible in the less motile human infant, but it has access to other evolved behaviours that have an attracting effect. Smiles tend to cause nurturant caregivers to approach and remain nearby. These proximity-promoting behaviours are enabled by brain mechanisms that mature early, and therefore endow infants with some control over ocular, facial, and vocal activity.

The human infant actively seeks stimulation. It preferentially attends to certain types of stimulation that *as it so happens* relate to language. The stimulation includes the things people do while talking. This appetite for social stimulation has developmentally positive consequences because the things infants crave— vocalisation, facial displays, interactions of various sorts—happen to be the same activities infants *should* seek if they wished to prepare their brain for communication and language.

The environment has a role to play, but that role is not fulfilled merely by providing "input" to the child. Research reveals a positive relationship between the quality of maternal attachment and the rate of language development (Van IJzendoorn, Dijkstra, & Bus, 1995). An emotionally secure mother–infant relationship provides a framework for language learning, but may also promote vocal learning by enhancing the infant's orientation to vocal and facial behaviour, vocal turn taking, and various incorporative and accommodative processes.

The helplessness of infants has produced well-developed patterns of nurturance. Crying begets maternal reaction (Barr, 1990). Among indulgent hunter-gatherer communities, the average response time to infant distress signals such as crying and fretting is about six seconds (DeVore & Konner, 1974). In an experiment by Hunziker and Barr (1986), mothers who increased the duration of their non-contingent carrying and holding from 2.7 hours a day to about 4.4 hours experienced a 43% reduction in the total amount of daily crying and fussing.

EXPLAINING LANGUAGE DEVELOPMENT

To explain language development, we need an account of the infant's motivation to engage in the activities that precede and facilitate linguistic operations. This means asking a great many *why* questions. According to the founder of ethology,

Niko Tinbergen (1951), there are four components to the complete why question. The evolutionary component relates to how the capability evolved in the species. The developmental component asks how immature members of the species develop the capability. What happens in the nervous system when the behaviour occurs is the mechanistic component. And finally, from a functional standpoint, one can ask why a particular individual behaves as it does when in a particular circumstance.

Teleological explanations

Biological scientists have long warned each other to avoid teleological explanations for evolutionary phenomena (Mayr, 1992). In teleological explanations, the evolution of behaviour is motivated and guided by an end state. An example would be to say that insects developed wings *in order to* fly. In actuality, insects developed wings and *thereby* were able to fly (Kingsolver & Koehl, 1985). In contemporaneous behaviour, Ernst Mayr (1974) supplied the example of birds migrating to warm climates "in order to escape the low temperatures and food shortages of winter". Their action has this consequence of course, as Mayr pointed out, but presumably the "decision" to migrate is largely made for the birds by mechanical systems that react to changes in ambient conditions.

Teleological explanations are frequently applied to language development. For example, babbling infants are said to be *practising* the movements needed for speech. This is an interesting piece of conjecture. Certainly, a number of developmental scientists would be surprised to know that 7-month-old infants are able to determine which movements are needed for speech, then take steps that will aid them in the future by systematically engaging in appropriate physical exercises.

Behaviours that occur in the early phases of development may *lead to* grammatical language, but that is not to say the infant does them for that reason. One cannot assume infants carry out early behaviours because these will enhance their long-term chances of learning a language. As Halliday (1975, p. 43) once said, the child "cannot seriously be thought to be storing up verbal wealth for future uses he as yet knows nothing about".

It is often said that infants acquire language *in order* to communicate. At first glance this might seem to be indisputable, but there is not a shred of evidence to support the statement, and there are many reasons to consider it preposterous. First, we might ask, to communicate what? Let us assume that the answer can only be: thoughts. Now we have a serious problem, because according to formal models of communication the motivation to convey information springs from the prospective speaker's recognition that he or she knows something that the listener does not. There is a growing body of research to indicate that children acquire this "other minds" concept somewhere between 2 and 4 years of age (Baron-Cohen, Tager-Flusberg, & Cohen, 1993)—long after the typical infant begins to talk. Even if they did have a theory of other minds, it is nothing short of adventurous to suppose that 12- to 18-month-olds are able to figure out for themselves that we talkers are exchanging thoughts with stereotyped patterns of vocalisation. Indeed, much of their own talking is done when alone or while ignoring any people that happen to be present. Whatever factors motivate crib talk and private speech thus belong to the list of *multiple functions* of talking.

It seems more likely that infants begin to talk for contemporaneous reasons that we do not know but should be trying to discover, and that in talking infants gradually become aware that this activity can be used as a tool to communicate thoughts. But we will be unable to consider such possibilities until we adopt a model of development that avoids teleology, that avoids "seeing the end in the beginning" as Michael Studdert-Kennedy (1991) has put it. But what kinds of models do we have to choose from?

Once we avoid teleology, then what?

In the paper in which Mayr (1974) expressed concern about the use of teleological explanations, he also described an alternate model of development that is worth our consideration here. The alternative is teleonomy. First proposed by Pittendrigh (1958), teleonomic processes are goal-directed, but they derive their goal-directedness from the operation of a programme.

Programmes can be either open or closed, in relative terms. The more closed programmes are heavily due to the influence of genes, allowing little in the way of behavioural influence. The relatively more open programmes are better able to admit "new" information by way of experience. These distinctions run parallel to Greenough's experience-expectant and experience-dependent information storage programmes (Greenough, Black, & Wallace, 1987).

Aside from their nonteleological nature, there are two properties of teleonomic programmes that lend them to our consideration. One is that in some cases "the behavior consists of a series of steps, each of which serves as reinforcement for the ensuing steps" (Mayr, 1974, pp. 104–105).[1] The other is that a teleonomic programme "does not induce a simple unfolding of some completely preformed Gestalt, but ... always controls a more or less complex process which must allow for internal and external disturbances. Teleonomic processes during ontogenetic development, for instance, are constantly in danger of being derailed even if only temporarily. There exist innumerable feedback devices to prevent this or to correct it" (Mayr, 1974, pp. 99–100).

In teleonomy, then, programmes both animate the developing infant and channel its forward developmental movement. The infant is kept in the channel by a series of behaviours that are also goal-directed. Although these guiding

---

[1] In a personal conversation, Professor Mayr said he would accept "to facilitate" in place of "as reinforcement for" (2 August, 1995).

behaviours are not strictly or wholly linguistic in and of themselves, we will see later that they cause the infant to reach that end-state by moving step by step toward behaviours that require the operation of a "grammatical module".

Developmental psycholinguists have their own name for the feedback devices to which Mayr referred. Dissociated from their biological function, they think of them, chronologically or statistically, as *precursors to language*. We will inspect a short list of the attested precursors shortly, but first, it may be beneficial if we first prepare ourselves for the explanations they will require.

Primary and secondary explanations

Although mechanisms that facilitate language development were inserted into the species by natural selection, to understand their development we still must deal with the fourth component of Tinbergen's larger "Why" question: What causes the infant to emit particular behaviours at particular times? A theory of language development thus requires an account of the *immediate* functions that are served when an infant does the behaviours that are precursive to language. These precursors include behaviours that favour word production, including joint attention, vocal development, and lexical imitation (Collis, 1977; Snow, 1989; Tomasello & Farrar, 1986; Vihman, 1986).[2]

The sensory and motoric experience associated with these immediate functions is likely to be pleasurable to the infant. At the most proximal level, the pleasurability of experience probably accounts for its long-term developmental effect. As Boyd and Richerson (1995, p. 158) said, "Learning mechanisms embedded in the human psyche have been shaped by natural selection, and, thus, pleasurable, reinforcing events are usually fitness enhancing, and unpleasant, aversive events are usually deleterious."

In taking a proximate view of behaviours that appear to facilitate development of language in the infant, I will speak, as I have elsewhere (Locke, 1996), of immediate or primary (non-linguistic) consequences and long-term or secondary (linguistic) consequences.

ONTOGENETIC PHASES

The full, species-typical capacity for language is realised gradually, in phases— coherent ontogenetic periods during which specific cognitive and neural capabilities associated with some aspect of language, or the path to it, "come on line". Phases in the development of linguistic capacity should not be confused with stages in the development of language. The latter usually refer to "child developments" such as crawling and one-handed grasping; or "language developments" such as babbling and two-word utterances. Stages are superficially descriptive,

---

[2] A more detailed treatment of the causes of language development appears in Locke (1996), from which this section is adapted.

at best, and occasionally misleading. They do not say anything about what the infant experiences when babbling, the cognitive processes by which the words that co-occur in phrases get combined, or how any of the later behaviours are facilitated by earlier ones.

"Language", viewed broadly, depends on two component systems: *a social cognition network* that is responsible for lexical acquisition and a *grammatical system* that carries out utterance analysis (at levels corresponding to linguistic units) and computation. Social cognition is a neural specialisation that comprises individual operations. Before the socially cognitive system acquires utterances, and certainly before grammatical capability is activated, a number of behavioural capabilities develop and a number of different precursive operations are carried out by the infant. Some of these have been functionally linked to lexical development. Others may be so linked in the future, since research in this area has begun only recently.

Socially cognitive operations that may or do facilitate utterance acquisition include vocal learning. In the vocal learning phase of language development, infants learn and respond to properties of the human voice. This learning begins prenatally (DeCasper, Lecanuet, Busnel, Granier-Deferre, & Maugeais, 1994). Newborns typically prefer their mother's voice to the voices of other women (DeCasper & Fifer, 1980) and display a preference for the "language" spoken by the mother during pregnancy (Moon, Cooper, & Fifer, 1993). The infant's initial preference for the mother's "voice" may thus be a preference for her speech—the sound pattern of her language as well as any personally identifying information.

Although the infant's perception of segmental contrasts has been of paramount important to researchers (Plunkett & Schafer, this volume), indexical and affective qualities of the voice are probably more important to the infant (Reddy, this volume). Not only are there biological reasons to suppose that such would be the case, there also is evidence that 9-month-olds retain voice quality information—once thought to be irrelevant because it is "prosodic" and "non-segmental"—for at least 2 weeks (Jusczyk, Hohne, Jusczyk, & Redanz, 1993).

The primary consequence of vocal learning, and the communication that occurs therein, may be of at least two kinds: (1) indexical, involving recognition of caregivers; and (2) affective, involving interpretation of caregivers' behaviours. Of course these broad classes of cues probably interact. It was reported recently that 1-month-olds prefer infant-directed over adult-directed prosody, but only when the voice belongs to a stranger; no similar preference was expressed at that age when the voice was the mother's (Abraham & Cooper, 1994). This is exactly what we should expect if infants learn that their mother is usually nurturant, but strangers vary.

In the second 6 months of life, infants respond to vocal affect and linguistic content independently (Fernald, 1993). During this period, vocal learning continues, even intensifies, as infants' initial sensitivities to phonetic contrasts are realigned and sharpened by active listening experience (Plunkett & Schafer, this volume; Werker & Polka, 1993). This effect occurs during a period in which the immediate benefits to the infant of maternal facial and vocal activity continue to grow. One of the non-linguistic reasons for this includes a need by the increasingly motile infant to monitor the affect of individuals who are capable of judging risk, and the infant's need for reassurance when separated from familiars (Bertenthal & Campos, 1990; Bowlby, 1969).

As Fig. 14.1 suggests, when the infant becomes familiar with the voice of its mother, an obvious primary consequence is that the infant then recognises its mother from her voice, and preferentially responds to her when she is talking. Preferential responding is assumed to increase the mother's responsiveness to the infant, increasing, in turn, the physical proximity and vocal interaction between these parties, thereby abetting language learning. Recognition of the mother's voice also reduces the infant's fear in some circumstances, which would be expected to increase vocal play (Locke, 1993a) and facilitate phonetic learning (Kugiumutsakis, 1993).

It is assumed that maternal voice recognition secondarily enhances infant survival and, with this, the infant's opportunity to learn language. The extreme right side of the figure contains an additional speculation, that in evolutionary history language learning increased the infant's chances of survival into childhood. A complete Tinbergen type of account would thus hold that neonates learn vocal material because the capability of doing so was selected for; serves contemporaneous functions as hypothesised above; and is possible because the infant has vocal learning mechanisms that, with development, become sufficiently

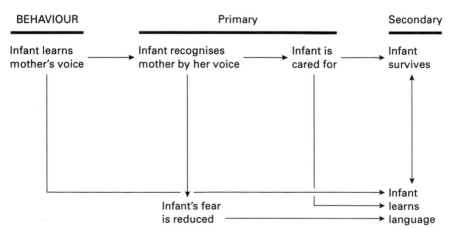

FIG. 14.1.   Primary and secondary consequences of maternal vocal learning, with particular reference to language (adapted from Locke, 1996). Reprinted by permission of Cambridge University Press.

operational for learning to occur in time to be assessed in the first week of postnatal life.

There may be other proximate influences on vocal learning that affect acquisition of language material. For example, avoidance of strangers tends to increase with maternal attachment during the second 6 months of life (Bowlby, 1969). Although this action is primarily defensive, it ensures that the infant's vocal learning capabilities will be applied preferentially to maternal utterances during a period when the infant's perceptual processing system is being tuned by experience. This should have the secondarily linguistic effect of biasing the infant toward its mother's language as well as her vocal qualities. It would be interesting to know how much of the infant's preference for the sound of its native language is due to such a bias.

As they approach the end of their first year, infants reveal a secondary consequence of vocal learning—a preference for ambient language sounds both in listening (Jusczyk, Friederici, Wessels, Svenkerud, & Jusczyk, 1993; Plunkett & Schafer, this volume) and in vocalisation (Boysson-Bardies, Vihman, Roug-Hellichius, Durand, Landberg, & Arao, 1992). Vocal learning thus biases the infant's perceptual system towards specific sources of ambient stimulation, perhaps even *tunes* it to that stimulation, thereby increasing the efficiency of speech processing and storage (Nygaard, Sommers, & Pisoni, 1994).

As infants import information about the vocal characteristics of the ambient language, they also store utterances. We can infer this because comprehension—which, as tested, is an observable act that requires prior storage of utterances and referential information—is demonstrable in the second 6 months of life, when perceptual learning is first apparent. In light of evidence that lexical comprehension is typically underway by 8 months, we may assume that infants begin to store utterances before that age.

Whatever the 6- or 7-month-old infant's initial reasons for storing utterances, they could not include "learning the names of things", as Halliday reminded us. But if infants do not store vocal material in order to comprehend or produce it later, why *do* they do it? One reason might be to predict caregivers' behaviour. As helpless individuals, infants need to know when the adults on whom they usually rely are acting strangely. When infants store utterances, they incorporate information about the speaker along with the individual speech sounds that comprise the words. One primary consequence of utterance storage may be that it permits infants to know when their talking caregivers are behaving as usual or deviating from their usual routines. According to this hypothesis, a primary consequence of storing vocal characteristics and utterances is the achievement of a behavioural prototype for each of its caregivers, thus conferring upon helpless individuals the ability to detect the unexpected.

In the second 6 months of life, vocal learning is not just *about* vocal behaviour, but *of* vocal behaviour. The early utterances stored by infants appear to be well specified prosodically and under-specified at the level of individual sounds

(Echols, 1993; Ingram, this volume; Nelson, 1981; Peters, 1977). These *formulaic* utterances often contain articles and pronouns—words that are otherwise late to develop—and may not occur elsewhere in the speech of the child (Hickey, 1993; Lieven, Pine, & Dresner Barnes, 1992; Tomasello & Brooks, this volume). Since the storage of utterances enables infants to comprehend spoken language, this phase represents an important step towards speech and the development of grammatical capacity. The secondary consequences of utterance storage is lexical development and language comprehension.

Talking

Some talk-like behaviours occur early on (for an extended discussion of this issue, see Reddy, this volume). For example, vocal turn-taking occurs as early as 3 months (Ginsburg & Kilbourne, 1988) and increases in subsequent months (Papousek & Papousek, 1989). Typically developing infants usually begin to babble, an activity that resembles the syllabic and articulatory patterns of speech, some time between 6 and 10 months of age (Oller & Eilers, 1988). Their intonation contours also vary with communicative functions (e.g. requesting, protesting) at several points during this interval (D'Odorico, 1984). Thus, talking behaviours occur during the period in which utterances are first stored.

Suzanne Langer saw long ago that the infant's initial motivation to talk could only be extra-communicative. Although unable to define its primary consequences, she understood that "there must be immediate satisfaction in this strange exercise, as there is in running and kicking" (Langer, 1960, p. 45). And indeed, infants talk whether they could be intending to communicate or not. They talk when alone, and do not necessarily direct their talk to others when in social situations (Fay, 1967; Furrow, 1984). If infants do talk to other individuals, they rarely do so in a propositional way, expressing their thoughts with words. Rather, in the early stages of talk at least, infants appear merely to state the obvious. They say the names of objects while looking at, pointing to, or physically contacting the objects that are named (Dromi, this volume; Nelson, 1985). In these cases, it would be difficult to argue that the infant is appropriating words in order to communicate thoughts. It seems more likely that the infant wants others to recognise that it knows and can say the names of things.

There are several primary consequences of talking. In order to blend in with the individuals with whom they share an emotional relationship—family members who spend most of their time talking—infants may develop the impression that they must also talk. By talking, infants convey an important piece of information: that they wish to become a fully-fledged member of their group. This fits with the belief that talking is a way of achieving "personhood" (Shatz, 1994).

Talking individuals are also likely to be looked at by the listeners in their environment, and infants are increasingly aware of what others are looking at as they approach the age of 8 to 10 months (Scaife & Bruner, 1975), that is, when about to begin talking. Infants probably notice that adults turn towards them when they talk, and it is likely that they receive unusual levels of looking when they first begin to talk. This enhanced level or type of regard by others may be an additional reason why infants begin to talk.

Words are the products of vocal imitation and, as such, may initially manifest a disposition to share social and emotional experience with others. Consider the phenomenon called "speech accommodation", in which speakers reproduce vocal, phonetic, or lexical characteristics of an influential person with whom they are interacting (Giles, 1984). The accommodating individual apparently believes implicitly that he can increase his perceived attractiveness to the listener by increasing similarity of speech and speaking behaviours. The speaker also may accommodate in order to increase his level of interpersonal involvement with the listener.

When the infant's motility increases, so does the range of actions it effects on its physical environment. Perhaps this disposition is what Schaffer (1989) had in mind when he drew from a review of the literature on social factors in lexical development the "very definite impression of a strong endogenous system pushing to emerge in the face of whatever constraints it may encounter". And this endogenous system may be what various developmentalists have had in mind when they attributed a range of early behaviours to *effectance*, the goal of a neuromuscular system that "is otherwise unoccupied or is gently stimulated by the environment" (White, 1959, p. 321), and seeks to attain "an effect upon the environment that is contingent upon the organism's own action" (Bronson, 1971, p. 270). Vocalising and talking are of course excellent ways of exerting an effect on a social environment.

An infant could acquire a moderately proportioned lexicon without knowing much about structure at any level of language and use it appropriately in social situations without the faintest signs of generativity. Once the infant has begun to talk, it is unclear how engaging in this activity affects later linguistic developments. It is of course logical to assume that the act of talking promotes attention to words not yet learned, and to the various uses of words, but we do not know this. It would be interesting to see if motorically impaired infants experience an acceleration in the rate of receptive lexical learning at about the same time that they would normally be adding new words to their expressive vocabulary, were they capable of speech. We will see below that children who begin to talk "on time" typically go on to develop grammatical capacity without delay, and those who are late to talk frequently end up with residual grammatical difficulties.

Grammatical capacity

The grammatical system is less easily reducible to a series of identifiable operations than the socially cognitive network. But there are several operations that can be identified: (1) analysis of utterance material into smaller pieces that correspond to phonemes, syllables, and words; (2) detection of sequences and patterns of these pieces; (3) in development, construction of a mental system that characterises these patterns; and (4) expressive use of that system to generate novel forms at and above the level of the word.

The grammatical system acts upon stored utterances. Since it has no acquisitive capability, these must be supplied by the socially cognitive system, which is acquisitive. The grammatical system has no *linguistic* function to perform without utterances, and may have no *non-linguistic* functions to perform under any circumstance.

Grammatical capability commences with the activation of an analytic system that parses stored utterances into segment-sized pieces of speech, locates recurring segments within and across utterances, and thereby permits the child to discover the rules by which utterances are to be computed (Plunkett & Schafer, this volume; Tomasello & Brooks, this volume). In effect, then, the analytic system makes available to the child the units that will be needed for morphology, phonology, and the lexicon.

The initial, and perhaps most conspicuous, form of internal evidence that an analyser is at work comes from children's regularisation of irregular verbs. When this happens, words like "went" may be temporarily and inconsistently expressed as "goed" (Marcus, Pinker, Ullman, Hollander, Rosen, & Xu, 1992); words such as "feet" may be uttered as "foots" (Marcus, 1995). These forms are *generated*, not merely heard and reproduced, by children. There also may be changes at other levels of language, including phrase regressions, as formulaic phrases begin to come apart (Plunkett, 1993); vocabulary-level alterations, as stored words are altered in accordance with recent phonological gains (Macken, 1980); and phonological regressions, as precocious items stored before a system was in place are restructured under the constraints of a simple phonology (Moskowitz, 1980).

I have proposed elsewhere (Locke, 1997) that the storage and expression of an extensive vocabulary hastens onset of utterance analytical and computational operations that support grammar. Grammatical mechanisms are assumed to be experience-dependent; if the infant has no stored utterances, there will be nothing for its analytical mechanisms to work on, and no stored forms to reconfigure by application of computational rules.[3] The induction of grammatical capability therefore depends upon a certain amount of prior success. Where vocal learning and utterance storage are affected by external factors, including the availability of appropriate stimulation, grammatical functions are influenced primarily by internal factors. That is to say, the development of utterance analysis capability is only indirectly affected by exposure, insofar as environmental stimulation is

---

[3] In using the term "experience-dependent" I am of course referring to the instatement of brain mechanisms that are responsible for linguistic operations, not the learning of particular languages, which obviously depends on experience.

correctly relayed to the structure analyser by the efficient operation of subordinated processing systems.

Now as we saw earlier, the child's first utterances appear to be prosodically organised and held in a prosodic type of memory. As a system that contains no discrete, combinable units like the phoneme, prosodic memory is assumed to have a limited storage capacity. If lexical items continued to accumulate in prosodic form, the system would overload and begin to slow down. The problem is brought to a head by the so-called "lexical spurt", a marked quickening of the pace at which new words are comprehended and/or produced (Benedict, 1979; Dromi, this volume). Expressive lexical spurts tend to occur at about 18 to 20 months, or when children have somewhere between 15 and just over a 100 words in their expressive lexicon (Mervis & Bertrand, 1995). Bates, Bretherton, and Snyder (1988) found that if vocabulary "bursts" at the 50-word stage, then about two-thirds of the children in their sample had experienced their burst by 20 months. At this age, there may be as many as five words comprehended to every word produced (Benedict, 1979). I have proposed that this sharp increase in comprehended words triggers or reinforces the activation of analytical mechanisms. It is evidently not the result of maturation alone, for chronological age is less highly correlated with onset of grammatical operations than prior success in accumulating utterances (Bates et al., 1988).

As members of a highly adaptive, self-organising species (Thelen, 1991; Thelen & Fogel, 1989), our evolutionary ancestors presumably evolved a capability for grammar in response to a rapidly increasing need to store and manipulate vocal forms that, until that point, had been poorly analysed at the level of the phonological segment. Those who were particularly able to detect patterns in their own vocal behaviour—not an altogether remote possibility given the biases and constraints of the human vocal tract (Locke, 1983)—would have been more likely to excel at language. The brain of modern humans thus became specialised to deal with grammar because this capability increased the adaptability of our ancestors (Cosmides & Tooby, 1994) just as it does in the young modern human.

A PROPOSED GOAL-DIRECTED MODEL

Non-human primates, whose ability to learn and express themselves in a grammatical human language is yet to be demonstrated, may nonetheless be capable of some degree of vocal learning, utterance storage, and sentence comprehension. Studies of a bonobo, Kanzi, are evidence enough for that (Savage-Rumbaugh, Murphy, Sevcik, Brakke, Williams, & Rumbaugh, 1993). Although we do not know why a specially handled bonobo would store human utterances (Sugarman, 1983), the fact that they do it tells us something: The individual organism—of any species, including our own—need not be "headed for" language in order to carry out operations that could conceivably prepare it for that eventuality. That is, if these operations do not owe their existence to a grammatical end-state in selected non-human primates, there is little reason to assume that they only arise for that reason in the human infant. But, as we know, the human infant will *do something linguistic* with these capabilities.

Babbling, joint attention, and utterance storage are demonstrably related to vocabulary development and, as we have seen, there are statistical relationships between vocabulary development and grammar. From a biological standpoint, then, these "feedback devices" may be supposed to keep the infant moving along a developmental growth path that leads to grammatical language.

Language is thus massively polygenic, with genes for every sub-development on the path that leads to linguistic competence. There are genes for structures that process faces and voices, seek shared experience, store and process vocal patterns, engage in rhythmic vocal activity, and interpret social displays, and genes for structures that infer, tune, and creatively apply organisational schemas to stored lexical forms. The path to language is paved with non-linguistic stones, stones that are neither uniquely human nor particularly modern. The normally developing infant moves in the direction of grammatical language not because it is pulled there by an impatient parsing or computational mechanism, and not because the infant senses value to itself in getting there. It attains that level of mastery because that is the way this teleonomic system is set up, presumably reflecting a phylogenetic path traversed by evolutionary ancestors who were no more teleological than the modern human infant.

According to this conception, many of the attested precursors to language are not truly precursive. They are just as legitimately a part of language as grammar. It is probably not true that some linguistic unity develops gradually. It is more likely that the multiple components of language develop one-by-one. The "feedback devices" are, themselves, components of language as well as signposts that guide infants to the grammatical and pragmatic endpoint (Locke, 1998).

Of course grammatical mechanisms, like other brain mechanisms, may mature gradually. If so, preferences for the speech of caregivers—as a form of systemic learning—may be revealed earlier in the developmental cycle than would have been the case in our protolinguistic ancestors. That is, some portion of the "native language preference" expressed toward the end of the first year may reveal the low-level functioning of a partially mature grammatical mechanism, one whose responsibilities include, among other things, phonetic pattern recognition (Locke, 1997). This latter effect, if it occurs, would look teleological because an infant would seem to be "struggling to be grammatical" well before the scheduled moment.

If the achievement of full, species-typical levels of linguistic competence requires the operation of free-standing mechanisms that are not, in and of themselves, linguistic, the question remains as to whether the functions of these mechanisms must be coordinated by an overarching mechanism that looks for the linguistic significance of, and integrates the operations of, all cognitive systems. Such a supervisory function would be expected to supplement the construction and organisation of a linguistic system as well as oversee the socially adaptive applications of linguistic knowledge. With supramodal oversight, it would not be surprising for the acquisition of languages using different sensory and motor systems to ultimately come together at some stage. It is interesting in this regard that while the first several words of children reared in signing homes may appear before the words of orally reared children, the larger systems —morphology and syntax—tend to emerge at about the same age (Bonvillian, this volume; Meier & Newport, 1990).

New models of brain development needed

A model of neurolinguistic development must account for all the processes that lead to full competence in communicating with a language. It must identify the neural systems that animate and guide infants along non-linguistic tributaries to a linguistically communicative end-state. The model will, therefore, have to embrace the phylogenetically older mechanisms that regulate the emotions, including fear, mechanisms that attract and control attention to social behaviours (Kalin & Shelton, 1989; Kalin, Shelton, & Takahashi, 1991). It must deal with mechanisms that interpret vocal and facial cues that identify individuals and hint at their intersubjective intentions.

The cognition that supports vocal learning and utterance acquisition is socially "hot" and must be driven by a primary affective system (Norman, 1981). That system comprises, among other things, temporal cortical regions that house face- and voice-sensitive cells; the frontal lobes generally; the hypothalamic-pituitary-adrenal system, including the amygdala; and a great many other areas that have been excluded from neurolinguistic processing models in adults.

The ability to infer dispositions and intentions is a highly evolved social capability. In primates, such socially cognitive acts depend on neural specialisations and modular properties that stand somewhat apart from other forms of cognition (Brothers, 1990; Brothers & Ring, 1992). It has been suggested that social cognition may not be a unitary set of capabilities (Karmiloff-Smith, Bellugi, Klima, Grant, & Baron-Cohen, 1995). Although it is specialised, it is clearly not modular in the way that grammatical operations are (Locke, 1992).

There are many reasons to assume that early vocal learning and utterance acquisition are primarily due to the right hemisphere in young children. That hemisphere is disproportionately responsible for vocal affect and prosody, from which early word-like material emerges (Locke, 1993a). The mature right hemisphere participates heavily in the processing of idiomatic or formulaic utterances of the type that young children typically produce (Van Lancker, 1990). There is evidence of an association between facial affect, a function that is controlled predominantly by the right hemisphere, and early word production (Bloom,

1993). Electrophysiological studies indicate that in order to measure the differ-ence between known and unknown words in pregrammatical infants, brain activity must be recorded from the right as well as the left hemisphere (Mills, Coffey-Corina, & Neville, 1993). Finally, young children with unilateral *right* hemisphere lesions perform significantly worse on lexical comprehension, rel-ative to healthy controls, than do young children with left hemisphere lesions (Aram & Eisele, 1994; Eisele & Aram, 1993; Thal, Marchman, Stiles, Aram, Trauner, Nass, & Bates, 1991).

Thus, prior to the first evidence of morphological creativity, there is little or no evidence of grammatical operations and little evidence of left hemisphere dominance in language processing. The onset of grammatical operations in the child seems to coincide with an increase in activity in the left hemisphere.

A clinical conundrum

Specific language impairment (Fletcher, this volume) first comes to light not when something specifically linguistic does or does not occur—in the sense that the word "linguistic" is usually reserved for phenomena that are grammatical—but when expressive vocabulary fails to develop at the rate that it should (Locke, 1997). Consequently, children frequently are brought into clinics at 18 to 24 months with a lack of *prelinguistic* development that is in danger of becoming a linguistic disorder. As I have argued elsewhere (Locke, 1994b, 1997), the "danger" arises from the fact that grammatical capacity develops within a circumscribed time window; if vocabulary development occurs too slowly, non-optimal patterns of neural resources may be used for grammar, to less than optimal effect.

There is evidence of significant family histories in cases of developmental language disorders, and higher rates of concordance in identical than fraternal twins (Bishop, North, & Donlan, 1995; Lewis & Thompson, 1992; Tomblin, 1989). What phases of language development are affected by abnormal gene action is less clear. Gopnik and Crago (1991) reported on a family that across three generations had the same specific grammatical disorder, and seemingly no other linguistic impairment. By itself, this suggested a grammar-specific genetic disorder, but other investigators later found that this family had a broad range of cognitive, linguistic, and motor-programming deficits (Fletcher, this volume; Vargha-Khadem, Watkins, Alcock, Fletcher, & Passingham, 1995).

Whether some language-disordered children, e.g. those with pervasive developmental disorders or autism, have an "intrinsically" defective grammatical mechanism is currently unknown (Tager-Flusberg, this volume). This is partly because the (endogenous) stimulation needed to activate such a mechanism—utterances and referential information—is insufficient when socially cognitive systems fail to operate efficiently during earlier points in development.

CONCLUDING REMARKS

Language development is a weave of individual strands—strands of face-voice processing, vocal turn-taking, accommodation and mimicry, sound making and signalling, and so on. Actions shift with development. The infant attends to faces and voices for one set of reasons in early infancy and a different set of reasons later on. Just as an infant begins to fall out of the "linguistic canal", new guideposts rise up to keep it on track.

One assumes that developmental degrees of freedom are reduced as the process continues since there are very few children who make significant progress along the path to language and then begin to falter (Locke, 1998). It thus appears that infants are channelled toward spoken language for fundamentally the same reason that our evolutionary ancestors chanced upon vocal and symbolic-referential behaviours that permit exchange of thought. The difference is that infants have experience-expectant mechanisms that contribute to grammatical capacity. If these mechanisms mature gradually, they could subtly regularise experience that has non-linguistic sources of regularity and is still, technically, precursive.

The sequential operation of these mechanisms will make the process appear to be headed somewhere. But ontogeny will also seem to be goal-directed for the reasons mentioned earlier—the behaviours that occur prior to grammatical language are naturally predisposing of that result. This is not just a coincidence, since similar developments may have occurred in our protolinguistic ancestors. Ontogeny thus looks recapitulatory, because the old genetic programmes responsible for social orientation and learning exist today as precursive, linguistically facilitative behaviours.

The infant's interest in, and ability to reproduce, language-like features of vocalisation—that is, its attentional and imitative mechanisms—are assumed to have been elevated by natural selection. Whatever non-linguistic goals these mechanisms now serve, they facilitate, or at least position the infant to take advantage of, activation of a grammatical mechanism. Hence, some infants may not reach the "linguistic end-point" because they lack efficiently functioning mechanisms that typically move infants along a path (emplaced by one or more "programmes") that prepares infants for behaviours and capacities that are considered to be straightforwardly "linguistic".

The infant's development of language is thus produced by a mix of systems. There is a relatively new programme for grammar and a series of older programmes that produce individual behaviours that lead to grammar. Vocal learning and utterance storage act like "feedback devices" for language, but in actuality they, too, are the result of "programmes" that have other functions. Ironically, the older programmes are not necessarily less open than the newer ones. Genes for vocal learning, as a means of kin recognition, developed early in evolutionary history, but they presumably build open behaviour programmes that accept environmental information, that is, are tunable. On the other hand, the range of linguistic grammars that can be hypothesised by the infant mind is presumably fairly limited.

In the journey to spoken language, the human infant is not animated by a single powerful goal—master language in order to convey information. Rather, as I have suggested here, it is sent along its way by a series of non-linguistic and quasi-linguistic behaviours that have fundamentally the same effect.

ACKNOWLEDGEMENTS

I wish to acknowledge helpful comments on the manuscript by Peter Carruthers and Alan Fogel.

REFERENCES

Abraham, J.L., & Cooper, R.P. (1994). Developmental changes in preferences for maternal infant-directed speech. (Abstract.) *Infant Behavior and Development, 17*, 480.

Aram, D.M., & Eisele, J.A. (1994). Limits to a left hemisphere explanation for specific language impairment. *Journal of Speech and Hearing Research, 37*, 824–830.

Baron-Cohen, S., Tager-Flusberg, H., & Cohen, D.J. (Eds.). (1993). *Understanding other minds: Perspectives from autism.* New York: Oxford University Press.

Barr, R.G. (1990). The early crying paradox: A modest proposal. *Human Nature, 1*, 355–389.

Bates, E., Bretherton, I., & Snyder, L. (1988). *From first words to grammar: Individual differences and dissociable mechanisms.* Cambridge, UK: Cambridge University Press.

Benedict, H. (1979). Early lexical development: Comprehension and production. *Journal of Child Language, 6*, 183–200.

Bertenthal, B.I., & Campos, J.J. (1990). A systems approach to the organizing effects of self-produced locomotion during infancy. In C. Rovee-Collier & L.P. Lipsitt (Eds.), *Advances in infant research* (Vol. 6, pp. 1–59). Norwood, NJ: Ablex.

Bishop, D.V.M., North, T., & Donlan, C. (1995). Genetic basis of specific language impairment: Evidence from a twin study. *Developmental Medicine and Child Neurology, 37*, 56–71.

Bloom, L. (1993). Language acquisition and the power of expression. In H.L. Roitblat, L.M. Herman, & P.E. Nachtigall (Eds.), *Language and communication: Comparative perspectives.* Hillsdale, NJ: Lawrence Erlbaum Associates Inc.

Bolhuis, J.J. (1991). Mechanisms of avian imprinting: A review. *Biological Review, 66*, 303–345.

Bowlby, J. (1969). *Attachment.* New York: Basic Books.

Boyd, R., & Richerson, P.J. (1975). Life in the fast lane: Rapid cultural change and the human evolutionary process. In J.-P. Changeux & J. Chavaillon (Eds.), *Origins of the human brain* (pp. 155–163). Oxford, UK: Clarendon Press.

Boysson-Bardies, B. de, Vihman, M.M., Roug-Hellichius, L., Durand, C., Landberg, I. & Arao, F. (1992). Material evidence of infant selection from the target language: A cross-linguistic phonetic study. In C. Ferguson, L. Menn, & C. Stoel-Gammon (Eds.), *Phonological development: Models, research, implications.* Timonium, MD: York Press.

Bronson, W.C. (1971). The growth of competence: Issues of conceptualization and measurement. In H.R. Schaffer (Ed.), *The origins of human social relations* (pp. 269–280). New York: Academic Press.

Brothers, L. (1990). The social brain: A project for integrating primate behavior and neurophysiology in a new domain. *Concepts in Neuroscience, 1*, 27–51.

Brothers, L., & Ring, B.A. (1992). Neuroethological framework for the representation of minds. *Journal of Cognitive Neuroscience, 4*, 107–118.

Collis, G.M. (1977). Visual co-orientation and maternal speech. In H.R. Schaffer (Ed.), *Studies in mother-infant interaction*. New York: Academic Press.

Cosmides, L., & Tooby, J. (1994). Origins of domain specificity: The evolution of functional organization. In L.A. Hirschfeld & S.A. Gelman (Eds.), *Mapping the mind: Domain specificity in cognition and culture*. Cambridge, UK: Cambridge University Press.

DeCasper, A., & Fifer, W.P. (1980). On human bonding: Newborns prefer their mothers' voices. *Science, 208*, 1174–1176.

DeCasper, A., Lecanuet, J.P., Busnel, M.-C., Granier-Deferre, C., & Maugeais, R. (1994). Fetal reactions to recurrent maternal speech. *Infant Behavior and Development, 17*, 159–164.

DeVore, I., & Konner, M.J. (1974). Infancy in hunter-gatherer life: An ethological perspective. In N.F. White (Ed.), *Ethology and psychiatry*. Toronto, Canada: University of Toronto Press.

Dobbing, J., & Sands, J. (1979). Comparative aspects of the brain spurt. *Early Human Development, 3*, 79–83.

D'Odorico, L. (1984). Non-segmental features in prelinguistic communications: An analysis of some types of infant cry and noncry vocalizations. *Journal of Child Language, 11*, 17–27.

Echols, C.H. (1993). A perceptually-based model of children's earliest productions. *Cognition, 46*, 245–296.

Eisele, J.A., & Aram, D.M. (1993). Differential effects of early hemisphere damage on lexical comprehension and production. *Aphasiology, 17*, 513–523.

Fay, W.H. (1967). Marathon monologues of a three-year-old. *Journal of Communication Disorders, 1*, 41–45.

Fernald, A. (1993). Approval and disapproval: Infant responsiveness to vocal affect in familiar and unfamiliar languages. *Child Development, 64*, 657–674.

Fogel, A. (1993). *Developing through relationships: Origins of communication, self, and culture*. New York: Harvester Wheatsheaf.

Furrow, D. (1984). Social and private speech at two years. *Child Development, 55*, 355–362.

Giles, H. (Ed.) (1984). The dynamics of speech accommodation. *International Journal of the Sociology of Language, 46*, 1–155.

Ginsburg, G.P., & Kilbourne, B.K. (1988). Emergence of vocal alternation in mother-infant interchanges. *Journal of Child Language, 15*, 221–235.

Gopnik, M., & Crago, M. (1991). Familial aggregation of a developmental language disorder. *Cognition, 39*, 1–50.

Greenough, W.T., Black, J.F., & Wallace, C.S. (1987). Experience and brain development. *Child Development, 58*, 539–559.

Halliday, M.A.K. (1975). *Learning how to mean: Explorations in the development of language*. London: Edward Arnold.

Hickey, T. (1993). Identifying formulas in first language acquisition. *Journal of Child Language, 20*, 27–41.

Hunziker, U.A., & Barr, R.G. (1986). Increased carrying reduces infant crying: A randomized controlled trial. *Pediatrics, 77*, 641–648.

Jusczyk, P.W., Friederici, A.D., Wessels, J.M.I., Svenkerud, V.Y., & Jusczyk, A.M. (1993). Infants' sensitivity to the sound patterns of native language words. *Journal of Memory and Language, 32*, 402–420.

Jusczyk, P.W., Hohne, E.A., Jusczyk, A.M., & Redanz, N.J. (1993). Do infants remember voices? *Journal of the Acoustical Society of America, 93*, 23–73.

Kalin, N.H., & Shelton, S.E. (1989). Defensive behaviors in infant rhesus monkeys: Environmental cues and neurochemical regulation. *Science, 243*, 1718–1721.

Kalin, N.H., Shelton, S.E., & Takahashi, L.K. (1991). Defensive behaviors in infant rhesus monkeys: Ontogeny and context-dependent selective expression. *Child Development, 62*, 1175–1183.

Karmiloff-Smith, A., Bellugi, U., Klima, E., Grant, J., & Baron-Cohen, S. (1995). Is there a social module? Language, face processing, and theory of mind in individuals with Williams syndrome. *Journal of Cognitive Neuroscience, 7*, 196–208.

Kingsolver, J., & Koehl (1985). Aerodynamics, thermoregulation, and the evolution of insect wings: Differential scaling and evolutionary change. *Evolution, 39*, 488–504.

Kugiumutsakis, G. (1993). Intersubjective vocal imitation in early mother-infant interaction. In J. Nadel & L. Camaioni (Eds.), *New perspectives in early communicative development.* New York: Routledge.

Langer, S.K. (1960). *Philosophy in a new key: A study in the symbolism of reason, rite, and art.* Cambridge, MA: Harvard University Press.

Lewis, B.A., & Thompson, L.A. (1992). A study of developmental speech and language disorders in twins. *Journal of Speech and Hearing Research, 35*, 1086–1094.

Lieven, E.V.M., Pine, J.M., & Dresner Barnes, H. (1992). Individual differences in early vocabulary development: Redefining the referential-expressive distinction. *Journal of Child Language, 19*, 287–310.

Locke, J.L. (1983). *Phonological acquisition and change.* New York: Academic Press.

Locke, J.L. (1992). Neural specializations for language: A developmental perspective. *Seminars in the Neurosciences, 4*, 425–431.

Locke, J.L. (1993a). *The child's path to spoken language.* Cambridge, MA: Harvard University Press.

Locke, J.L. (1993b). The role of the face in vocal learning and the development of spoken language. In B. de Boysson-Bardies, S. de Schonen, P. Jusczyk, P. MacNeilage, & J. Morton, (Eds.), *Developmental neurocognition: Speech and face processing in the first year of life* (pp. 317–328). Dordrecht, The Netherlands: Kluwer Academic.

Locke, J.L. (1994a). Development of the capacity for spoken language. In P. Fletcher & B. MacWhinney (Ed.), *Handbook of child language.* Oxford, UK: Blackwell Publishers.

Locke, J.L. (1994b). Gradual emergence of developmental language disorders. *Journal of Speech and Hearing Research, 37*, 608–616.

Locke, J.L. (1996). Why do infants begin to talk? Language as an unintended consequence. *Journal of Child Language, 23*, 251–268.

Locke, J.L. (1997). A theory of neurolinguistic development. *Brain and Language, 58*, 265–326.

Locke, J.L. (1998). Are developmental language disorders primarily grammatical? Speculations from an evolutionary model. In R. Paul (Ed.), *The speech/language connection.* Baltimore: Paul H. Brookes.

Lovejoy, C.O. (1981). The origin of man. *Science, 211*, 341–350.

Macken, M.A. (1980). The child's lexical representation: The "puzzle-puddle-pickle" evidence. *Journal of Linguistics, 16*, 1–17.

Marcus, G.F. (1995). Children's overregularization of English plurals: A quantitative analysis. *Journal of Child Language, 22*, 447–459.

Marcus, G.F., Pinker, S., Ullman, M., Hollander, M., Rosen, T.J., & Xu, F. (1992). Overregularization in language acquisition. *Monograph of the Society for Research in Child Development 57* (Serial No. 228).

Mayr, E. (1974). Teleological and teleonomic, a new analysis. *Boston Studies in the Philosophy of Science, 14*, 91–117.

Mayr, E. (1992). The idea of teleology. *Journal of the History of Ideas, 53*, 117–135.

Meier, R.P., & Newport, E.L. (1990). Out of the hands of babes: On a possible sign advantage in language acquisition. *Language, 66*, 1–23.

Mervis, C.B., & Bertrand, J. (1995). Early lexical acquisition and the vocabulary spurt: A response to Goldfield and Reznick. *Journal of Child Language, 22*, 461–468.

Miller, G.A. (1990). The place of language in a scientific psychology. *Psychological Science, 1*, 7–14.

Mills, D.L., Coffey-Corina, S.A., & Neville, H.J. (1993). Language acquisition and cerebral specialization in 20-month-old infants. *Journal of Cognitive Neuroscience, 5*, 317–334.

Moon, C., Cooper, R.P., & Fifer, W.P. (1993). Two-day olds prefer their native language. *Infant Behavior and Development, 16*, 495–500.

Moskowitz, B.A. (1980). Idioms in phonology acquisition and phonological change. *Journal of Phonetics, 8,* 69–83.

Nelson, K. (1981). Individual differences in language development: Implications for development and language. *Developmental Psychology, 17,* 170–187.

Nelson, K. (1985). *Making sense: The acquisition of shared meaning.* New York: Academic Press.

Norman, D.A. (1981). Twelve issues for cognitive science. In D.A. Norman (Ed.), *Perspectives on cognitive science* (pp. 265–295). Hillsdale, NJ: Lawrence Erlbaum Associates Inc.

Nygaard, L.C., Sommers, M.S., & Pisoni, D.B. (1994). Speech perception as a talker-contingent process. *Psychological Science, 5,* 42–46.

Oller, D.K., & Eilers, R.E. (1988). The role of audition in infant babbling. *Child Development, 59,* 441–449.

Papousek, M., & Papousek, H. (1989). Forms and functions of vocal matching in interactions between mothers and their precanonical infants. *First Language, 9,* 137–158.

Peters, A.M. (1977). Language learning strategies: Does the whole equal the sum of the parts? *Language, 53,* 560–573.

Pinker, S. (1994). *The language instinct: The new science of language and mind.* London: Penguin Books.

Pinker, S. (1995). Facts about human language relevant to its evolution. In J.-P. Changeux & J. Chavaillon (Eds.), *Origins of the human brain.* Oxford, UK: Clarendon Press.

Pittendrigh, C.S. (1958). Adaptation, natural selection, and behavior. In A. Roe & G.G. Simpson (Eds.), *Behavior and evolution* (pp. 390–416). New Haven, CT: Yale University Press.

Plunkett, K. (1993). Lexical segmentation and vocabulary growth in early language acquisition. *Journal of Child Language, 20,* 43–60.

Savage-Rumbaugh, E.S., Murphy, J., Sevcik, R.A., Brakke, K.E., Williams, S.L., & Rumbaugh, D.M. (1993). Language comprehension in ape and child. *Monographs of the Society for Research on Child Development* (Serial No. 233), 58.

Scaife, M., & Bruner, J.S. (1975). The capacity for joint visual attention in the infant. *Nature, 253,* 265–266.

Scarr, S. (1983). An evolutionary perspective on infant intelligence. In M. Lewis (Ed.), *Origins of intelligence: Infancy and early childhood* (pp. 191–223). New York: Plenum.

Schaffer, H.R. (1989). Language development in context. In S. von Tetzchner, L. Siegel, & L. Smith (Eds.), *The social and cognitive aspects of normal and atypical language development.* New York: Springer.

Shatz, M. (1994). *A toddler's life: Becoming a person.* Oxford, UK: Oxford University Press.

Snow, C.E. (1989). Imitativeness: A trait or a skill? In G.E. Speidel & K.E. Nelson (Eds.), *The many faces of imitation in language learning.* Springer-Verlag.

Studdert-Kennedy, M. (1991). Language development from an evolutionary perspective. In N. Krasnegor, D. Rumbaugh, R. Schiefelbusch, & M. Studdert-Kennedy (Eds.), *Language acquisition: Biological and behavioral determinants.* Hillsdale, NJ: Lawrence Erlbaum Associates Inc.

Sugarman, S. (1983). Why talk? Comment on Savage-Rumbaugh et al. *Journal of Experimental Psychology: General, 112,* 493–497.

Thal, D.J., Marchman, V., Stiles, J., Aram, D., Trauner, D., Nass, R., & Bates, E. (1991). Early lexical development in children with focal brain injury. *Brain and Language, 40,* 591–527.

Thelen, E. (1991). Motor aspects of emergent speech: A dynamic approach. In N. Krasnegor, D. Rumbaugh, M. Studdert-Kennedy, & R. Schiefelbusch (Eds.), *Biological foundations of language development.* Hillsdale, NJ: Lawrence Erlbaum Associates Inc.

Thelen, E., & Fogel, A. (1989). Toward an action-based theory of infant development. In J. Lockman & N. Hazen (Eds.), *Action in a social context: Perspectives on early development.* New York: Plenum.

Tinbergen, N. (1951). *The study of instinct.* Oxford, UK: Clarendon Press.

Tomasello, M., & Farrar, M.J. (1986). Joint attention and early language. *Child Development, 57,* 1454–1463.

Tomblin, J.B. (1989). Familial concentration of developmental language impairment. *Journal of Speech and Hearing Research, 54,* 287–295.

Van IJzendoorn, M.H., Dijkstra, J., & Bus, A.G. (1995). Attachment, intelligence, and language: A meta-analysis. *Social Development, 4,* 115–128.

Vargha-Khadem, F., Watkins, K., Alcock, K., Fletcher, P., & Passingham, R. (1995). Praxic and nonverbal cognitive deficits in a large family with a genetically transmitted speech and language disorder. *Proceedings of the National Academy of Science, USA, 92,* 930–933.

Vihman, M.M. (1986). Individual differences in babbling and early speech: Predicting to age three. In B. Lindblom & R. Zetterstrom (Eds.), *Precursors of early speech.* New York: Stockton Press.

Werker, J.F., & Polka, L. (1993). Developmental changes in speech perception: New challenges and new directions. *Journal of Phonetics, 21,* 83–101.

White, R.W. (1959). Motivation reconsidered: The concept of competence. *Psychological Review, 66,* 297–333.

Author Index

Subject Index